CU01433411

Britain and the Abadan Crisis, 1950-51

For George
with best wishes
Gill

Britain and the Abadan Crisis, 1950-51

Edited by Gill Bennett and Richard Smith

Documents from the British Archives: No. 5

Documents from the British Archives: a thematic series with documents drawn from, or supplementing, volumes of *Documents on British Policy Overseas*, produced by the Foreign, Commonwealth and Development Office Historians.

Series editors: Patrick Salmon & Richard Smith

This publication is available online: www.issuu.com/fcohistorians

Published by the Foreign, Commonwealth and Development Office
King Charles Street, London, SW1A 2AH

© 2022 Crown Copyright

Cover illustration: Abadan, city of oil (Wikimedia Commons)

ISBN: 9798360433323

CONTENTS

Rohan D'Olier Butler (1917–1996)

INTRODUCTION

This publication reproduces in full Rohan Butler's 1962 report on *British Policy in the Relinquishment of Abadan in 1951*.[1] Butler, a Fellow of All Souls College Oxford, joined the Foreign Office in 1945 as an editor of the official documentary history of British foreign policy, *Documents on British Foreign Policy 1919-1939*. He compiled the Abadan report in response to a suggestion made in 1957 by the Cabinet Secretary that Whitehall departments should commission internal histories of significant episodes of policy or administration that would enable the administrator 'to see current problems in perspective'. Submitted in March 1962, the report documents the loss of the Anglo-Iranian Oil Company's key refinery at Abadan, Britain's biggest single overseas investment, following the nationalisation of Iran's oil industry. The episode was a humiliating blow to British prestige and influence in the Middle East brought about by a range of factors: a weakened Labour government, unimaginative and complacent thinking in official circles, an inability to project military power following the loss of India, and a lack of support, as well as adverse interference, from the United States. Butler's critical study of the crisis not only provided a comprehensive narrative of events but also drew out political and administrative conclusions for the future administration of foreign policy. Despite the length of the report, there was general agreement that it was a valuable document not only in substance but for the lessons it drew and it was circulated internally, to certain heads of mission and to other government departments.

The report is published along with several related documents. The first is a commentary by Lord Strang, the Permanent Under-Secretary of the Foreign Office at the time of Abadan. He candidly assessed his own performance, along with that of Ministers, diplomats and the Foreign Office during the crisis, making his commentary an important and interesting addendum to the report itself. Strang concluded by picking up on Butler's call for a 'resolute reappraisal' of British foreign policy as the basis for 'a more compact and positive policy,' and asked whether British diplomacy needed 'a new look' in the post-imperial age, one based more on national self-interest, like that of the French. Sir Harold Caccia, Permanent Under-Secretary when Butler's report was submitted, posed this question in a letter to heads of mission in February 1963. Coming just after the rejection of Britain's first application to join the EEC, the letter prompted plenty of response. Butler was asked to analyse and synthesise the replies, which he submitted in May 1963 as 'A New Perspective for British Diplomacy'—the second additional document. In it Butler made several recommendations: increased public relations at home in mobilising support for British foreign policy, matched by 'sharper thinking and plainer speaking' in its execution; the strengthening and modernisation of representation abroad; and a high-level 'Positive Planning Committee' to review possibilities for imparting 'extra thrust' into diplomatic effort. This latter recommendation was to lead to the formation of the Foreign Office Planning Staff (today called the Strategy Unit). The final additional document is a despatch from the British Ambassador in Tehran from December 1956, reflecting on the state of

---

[1] FO 370/2964, The National Archives (hereafter TNA).

Anglo-American-Iranian relations following the final settlement of the Abadan crisis in 1954. It is a remarkably sanguine 'all's well that ends well' assessment, especially in relation to the actions of the Americans. It illustrates, perhaps, the collective amnesia that had begun to settle over such a painful episode before the publication of Butler's report.

Gill Bennett and Professor Ali Ansari, from St Andrew's University, came up with the idea to publish the report while the latter was working as a Knowledge Exchange Fellow at the Foreign, Commonwealth and Development Office. Both contribute essays placing the Abadan crisis in a longer historical context. Ali Ansari traces the complex history of Britain's involvement in Iran and its oil industry, whilst questioning whether opportunities were missed for avoiding the crisis altogether. Gill Bennett compares the crisis in Abadan to the Suez crisis in a way that Butler was perhaps unable to do at the time, despite his commenting that the episodes were 'contrasting yet largely complementary'.

In the preface to his report Butler admitted it was a source of regret that, given the confidential nature of the topic, his work would 'not see the light of day' in the form of publication. Sixty years on, this has been remedied. The report has been available for many years at The National Archives, Kew. However, given its size, it is unlikely that many scholars have had the time to read it in situ, or the inclination to photograph all 324 pages, or the financial means to get it copied. It is hoped, therefore, that publication will make its contents more accessible to scholars and the public. It also complements discussion of Anglo-Iranian relations found elsewhere in *Documents on British Policy Overseas*.[2] Butler thanked in his preface 'Miss Sturgess' for typing the 'long and complicated manuscript with expert care'. Today we have to thank Gill Bennett for the herculean task of retyping the 250,000 words in Butler's report. Thanks also go to Sue Fleming and Paul Bali for their assistance in the editorial process and Tom Loft for providing the map. References to, and cross-references within, the report have been changed to reflect the page numbering in this volume rather than the original document. However, footnotes in the report, along with spellings and place names, have been left as in the original.

Finally, Butler thought it would be a 'happy outcome' if his study made a 'small but constructive contribution' towards strengthening British foreign policy 'for the great tasks and great opportunities which now lie ahead'.[3] The Report stands, in the words of Gill Bennett, as 'a singular testament to the potential influence, on both policy and administration, of an historical case study'.

Richard Smith

---

[2] Issues relating to Anglo-Iranian relations, oil policy, the Soviet threat and US interests are principally covered in DBPO, Series I, Volume 7, *The United Nations: Iran, Cold War and World Organisation, January 1946-January 1947* (London: The Stationary Office, 1995) and also found in DBPO, Series I, Vol. 1, *The Conference at Potsdam, July-August 1945* (London: TSO, 1984) and Vol. 2, *Conferences and Conversations 1945: London, Washington and Moscow* (London: TSO, 1985).

[3] 'Abadan and After in light of the comments by Lord Strang' by Rohan Butler, 15 February 1963, FO 370/2964, TNA. The Strang commentary is undated.

The Butler Report on the Relinquishment of Abadan:
An Unnecessary Crisis?
A.M. Ansari

Introduction

Few episodes have come to define British-Iranian relations more than the Oil Nationalisation crisis of 1951-53. The febrile political atmosphere which led to the nationalisation of the Anglo-Iranian Oil company in 1951 and to the subsequent overthrow of the Mosaddeq administration in an Anglo-American engineered coup in 1953, has probably generated more literature that any other single event in the relationship, and catapulted its central figure, Dr Mohammad Mosaddeq, to an iconic status in the gallery of modern Iranian political figures. It would not be an exaggeration to say that he has transcended history and become a figure of popular mythology, and as a consequence has cast a very long shadow over contemporary Iranian politics. Championed by dissidents and establishment figures alike, Mosaddeq is, to paraphrase Hegel, an individual who has become identified with a principle.[1] He has come to represent, in the popular imagination, the moment when democracy was derailed, and the autocracy of the Shah re-established under the imperial tutelage of the United States and Great Britain. This is regarded as the pivotal moment in the history of modern Iran to which all other developments— largely negative—can be traced: *the* original sin, for which the West must repent.

Like all good political myths, this narrative is painted in primary colours. There are sinners—Britain and the United States—and those sinned against—the Iranians—with little nuance or subtlety afforded. If debates have raged among Iranians about the level of domestic complicity in the coup, there is little such exploration of the diversity of opinion in Britain, nor the broader context of developments. This is a strictly bilateral exercise in which the wider political terrain remains firmly blurred and marginalised into irrelevance, where the British and American 'States' impose their inevitable imperialist desires on a subjected people largely devoid of any agency. Even where it is acknowledged that internal political forces aligned themselves against Mosaddeq, these are at best deluded and at worst mere lackeys of the West, unthinking, and to paraphrase Franz Fanon— whitewashed.

This debate, as febrile and contentious as it is, at least exists. While few Iranian intellectuals will criticise Mosaddeq's ambitions, there is a lively debate about his methods and barely disguised irritation at some of the imprecision that has come to characterise the more popular histories, most obviously Mosaddeq's status as the 'first democratically elected prime minister' of Iran, a statement so bland it serves to disguise both the reality of politics at this time and the Parliamentary system to which Iran aspired.[2] British attitudes to Mosaddeq were mixed. Negotiators came to

---

[1] G.W.F. Hegel, 'The German Constitution' (1802), in *Hegel's Political Writings,* trans. T. M. Knox, (Oxford: Oxford University Press, 1964), p. 216.

[2] Mosaddeq himself famously protested the elections to the 16th Majlis: see Ervand Abrahamian, 'The Coup', (New York, New Press, 2013), p. 52. It is worth noting that in the ten years following Reza Shah's deposition, Iran had 17 Prime Ministers, the longest serving being that of Qavam in 1946-7 at one year and 324 days, the

admire his civility, but he was also regarded as a romantic wedded to views that were impractical. Given to florid oratory which both attracted and deterred his countrymen depending on their political prejudices British assessments dismissed him as 'a demagogue, a windbag',[3] a view that would be echoed in Butler's report.

Butler's report on the relinquishment of Abadan in 1950-51 provides the reader with a window into the complexity of the British position and perspective. For a crisis in which few if any sources can be considered impartial, he adds important granularity to an otherwise bland and largely over-simplified British position. Here we find the heated debates which existed within Government and crucially between HMG and the Company, as well as the often-fractious relations with the United States whose unsympathetic views on the British position were both seized upon and exploited by nationalists in Iran. Far from oblivious to Iranian demands, British ministers often struggled to reconcile what they viewed as legitimate Iranian concerns with wider British interests. All the while they were contending with a changing international order, cast in the shadow of the Second World War, in which the Cold War loomed large and through which almost all problems were filtered.

Whatever the merits of this position, oil nationalisation in Iran was but one of many problems facing British statesmen and their frame of reference was quite different to that of the Iranians. These perspectives mattered, and they helped shape approaches and one might argue, distinctive mentalities, towards the problem, driving both parties into uncompromising positions. Butler does not directly address the events that led to the coup in August 1953, but coup narratives are present in the text—both pro and anti-communist—while in one passage Foreign Secretary Anthony Eden refers to the possibility of the Shah dismissing Mosaddeq 'which might involve a *coup d'état*'.[4] The crisis which culminated in the coup of 1953 was not inevitable, but it was undoubtedly shaped by the wider historical inheritance and cultural misunderstandings that afflicted both sides.[5]

Oil and Iran

Oil transformed the Iranian state and redefined its relationship with Britain. The concession granted to the British-Australian entrepreneur William Knox-D'Arcy in 1901, was the last in a series of concessions offered to British economic interests in the aftermath of the Anglo-Persian War of 1856-7. The war which had been fought over the status of Afghanistan and settled its borders with Iran—effectively ceding Herat to the new Afghan state–had resulted in the comparatively lenient Treaty of Paris in 1857, an exemplary case of Britain not only winning the war but winning the peace. Iranian statesmen, having expected a repeat of the punitive Treaty of Turkmenchai with Russia in 1828 breathed a collective sigh of relief that the Treaty of Paris required no reparations and no further loss in territory.[6] The consequence

---

shortest, that of Reza Hekmat, lasting 11 days. It did not help matters that each Majlis sat for a two-year period with administrations having little time to settle before the next election was launched.

[3] Report on Leading Personalities in Persia, 5 June 1946, FO 371/52755/E5131, TNA.

[4] Butler, p. 237; it is worth noting that Eden was voicing contingency planning that had been drawn up in the previous administration.

[5] We see coup narratives as a product of the Cold War, but they might better be understood as a legacy of the Second World War.

[6] 'The Sedr-Azem, on listening to the paragraphs of the Treaty . . . exclaimed . . . "Is that all?" and on being told there was nothing more, he uttered a fervent "Alhamdulillah! –Praise be to God', Robert Watson, *A History of Persia from the beginning of the 19th Century to the year 1858* (London: Smith, Elder and Co, 1865), p. 459.

was that they viewed Britain and the application of British political ideas as the route to salvation and sought ways to engender a political transformation through economic change.

A series of economic concessions were offered, some of which were ill considered and most of which reflected the relative economic power of the participants. For Iranian statesmen, it was important to provide an attractive package to prospective entrepreneurs. For many observers (Iranian or otherwise), they came precariously close to selling off the family silver wholesale. Curzon famously described the Reuter's Concession of 1872 as 'the most complete and extraordinary surrender of the entire industrial resources of a kingdom into foreign hands that has probably ever been dreamed of, much less accomplished in history'.[7] International criticism, not least from within the Foreign Office, who were anxious about Russian reactions, resulted in the cancellation of the concession, with Reuter's offered by way of compensation a reduced concession in 1888 involving the establishment of a bank—the British Imperial Bank of Persia—with sole rights over the issue of bank notes.

A few years later another ill-fated concession—that for the monopoly rights over the sale of tobacco—also had to be cancelled at much expense following international disquiet and a boycott of tobacco at home. Ironically, as the Tobacco Protest revealed, British economic penetration was catalysing protest inspired by British political ideas about rights and 'national' self-determination. This was the rejection of British policy through the application of British political ideas,[8] and it revealed the complexity of the British relationship with Iran and the diversity of interests involved. Iranians tended to see the British as homogenous and singular in their approach. Those who engaged with Britain were increasingly aware of the diverse and often conflicting interests that were involved, not least between the governments in India and Britain, and between commercial interests and the government, as well as what we might term 'dissident' opinion within Britain, increasingly vocal in their criticism of British imperial policy.[9] It was this 'dissident' opinion, not always to be found outside government, which helped shape and define the Constitutional revolution of 1906 and saw British political ideas and influence reach their apogee in Iran, only for these gains to be abandoned the following year. The decision by Sir Edward Grey, the Liberal Foreign Secretary, to sacrifice the achievements of 1906 on the altar of a rapprochement with Russia—the Anglo-Russian Convention of 1907—was the cause of considerable consternation in diplomatic circles. Cecil Spring-Rice, British minister in Tehran in 1907, made clear to Grey that 'we are regarded as having betrayed the Persian people'.[10]

Perhaps more surprising was the fact that on pure self-interest, the Anglo-Russian convention made no concession to British commercial interests in Iran. The Convention was intended to settle wider imperial disputes with Russia in the

---

[7] G.N. Curzon, *Persia and the Persian Question* (London: Frank Cass, 1966, first published 1892), p. 480.

[8] For a wider discussion of this see my 'Taqizadeh and European Civilization' *IRAN*; also Jamal al Din al Afghani, 'The Reign of Terror in Persia'.

[9] On this dissent, see M. Bonakdarian, 'Iranian Constitutional Exiles and British Foreign-Policy Dissenters, 1908-9', *International Journal of Middle East Studies*, 27(2), 1995, pp. 175-191.

[10] Quoted in Wright, 'The English amongst the Persians', (London: I.B. Tauris, 1985), p. 30. See also the reference to the questions raised in the House of Commons in Nazem al Islam Kermani, '*Tarikh-e Bidari Iranian* (The History of the Iranian Awakening), Tehran, Farhang, 1349/1970, [first published 1910] p. 22.

interests of a détente in Europe so that the threat posed by Germany might be better contained. As far as Iran was concerned this resulted in quite divergent spheres of influence, where Russia was accorded the lion's share of the north—the most populated areas—while Britain satisfied herself with a buffer zone in Baluchistan, a zone which even the Government of India, in whose interests in was secured, considered meaningless. South-Western Iran, where Knox-D'Arcy had been granted a licence to explore for oil, was ignored, a remarkable omission when one considers the strategic importance Iranian oil was to assume for Britain. It is, nonetheless, a salutary reminder not to read back into the historical record the prejudices and perceptions of the present. For Grey, what mattered was the wider geopolitical situation; commercial contracts were of secondary importance, not least because this was considered a private matter, and oil had yet to be discovered in viable quantities.[11]

Even after oil was struck a year later in 1908, it would take years of investment in infrastructure before the new Anglo-Persian Oil Company (APOC), as the subsidiary of Burmah Oil was christened, would deliver on its substantial promise. It was in these early years, when money was tight, when one Winston Churchill, as First Lord of the Admiralty, took the fateful step of encouraging the government to take a majority stake in the new company, arguing with considerable foresight that 'Persian oil' would soon come to be the mainstay of supply to the Royal Navy, as the ships were converted from coal to oil. The agreement, reached on the eve of the Great War on 20 May 1914 (it is worth remembering that the initial agreement was not reached with the immediate expectation of war—Archduke Franz Ferdinand was not assassinated till 28 June, some five weeks later), doubling the company's capital in return for two *ex officio* directors who held a veto on the company's decisions, was a move that many considered contrary to the principles of 'free enterprise'. Perhaps to deflect any criticism the Treasury issued a letter (which remained confidential for 15 years) that provided assurances on the limited circumstances when a veto may be exercised—essentially restricting it to issues of national security—and it was on this basis that Churchill's plan was approved by act of Parliament in August 1914, some six days after the outbreak of war. Churchill, in displaying such strategic foresight, was considered a latter-day Disraeli by the APOC chairman: '. . . indeed the successful operations of the company, centred upon Abadan, soon demonstrated that by its investment, His Majesty's Government had added to the Suez Canal another great interest in the Middle East.'[12]

Such foresight does not seem to have burdened the negotiators from the Qajar court who viewed the interest in this new resource with some bewilderment, blithely unaware of its economic potential. The terms of agreement were generous to Knox D'Arcy, reflecting in part the risk he was undertaking and the investment that might be required to make any venture profitable, but the fact that the terms were agreed for a period of sixty years suggested little appreciation of the industrial nature of the

---

[11] It is interesting to note that the concession merited a single sentence in the Government of India annual review for 1901/2, reprinted in R. M. Burrell, *Iran: Political Diaries 1881-1965*, Vol. II (London: Archive Editions 1997), p. 95. Similarly, the discovery of oil on 28 May 1908 warranted a modest factual notice in the report for the month of May 1908; there was nothing noted in the annual review, with the greatest space devoted to political developments (Vol. III, p. 172).

[12] Butler, p. 38.

enterprise.[13] The length of the agreement was, to be sure, not much different from others—the concession of the Imperial Bank was likewise for sixty years, to 1948— but this agreement was for the establishment of an industry that, if successful, had the and potential to grow exponentially. That this was not understood was clear from the manner in which the negotiations were approached and the contract sealed, with the sense from the Iranian side that Knox D'Arcy was on a fool's errand. Given the initial difficulties in striking oil they might have been excused this complacency. While Knox D'Arcy had paid £20,000 for the concessionary rights (around £2.3m in today's terms), with a further £20,000 in paid-up shares,[14] he had spent considerably more prospecting for oil (in the process selling most of his rights to Burmah Oil) before finally striking oil at the eleventh hour in 1908.[15]

In retrospect the contract, which envisaged Iran receiving a royalty of 16% on the company's profits, was clearly misconceived, not least because by 1919 with the balance of power between the two parties even more stark Britain decided to delimit more strictly what might constitute the profits of the company.[16] There was some merit in clarification given the diverse and growing nature of the industry, but the clarification went against Iran and while accepted by the Iranian government was nevertheless regarded as a convention and gentleman's agreement rather than a contractual revision. It was accepted for much of the 1920s in part because the turmoil of the post war years meant there was little ability to challenge the decision, but also because the steady rise in royalty payments (they tripled over the decade) meant there was also little appetite to do so.

That said, with the overthrow of the Qajars and the establishment of the Pahlavi dynasty in 1925, there was a renewed attempt by Iranian politicians to have the contract reviewed and revised. Quite apart from the clarity required on the nature of the payments afforded to Iran it was clear to the Iranian government that royalties payable on 'profits' were far too opaque and open to abuse especially as the complexity of company operations grew. But in addition, the new intensely nationalist administration argued that the concession had been agreed by the then Shah prior to the Constitutional Revolution of 1906, and therefore as an arbitrary act of a despot lacking any form of legitimacy. Matters came to head by the end of the 1920s as the Great Depression affected the company's profits and by extension Iran's royalties, so that these were now considerably less than the tax paid to the British exchequer. The Iranian government was certainly not shy in expressing its views, and the Minister of Court, Abdolhossein Teymourtash, pointedly referred to this 'fine asset' when he visited the refinery at Abadan in 1928. A British diplomat noted that the Minister of Court's 'general attitude was one of paternal pride in the

---

[13] See R. Ferrier, *The History of the British Petroleum Company: Vol. 1, The Developing Years 1901-3* (Cambridge: CUP, 1982), p. 42. Ferrier notes that the concession was not unusual by the standards of the day and the risk involved (p. 43).

[14] The additional shares noted in Ferrier, p. 42, are omitted from Butler's account. The total of £40,000 is the same as that offered for the Reuter's Concession in 1872 and suggests little imaginative thinking on the part of the Iranians.

[15] Ferrier, *The History of the British Petroleum Company*, p. 60, notes that by 1903, D'Arcy had spent £160,000 on prospecting and was seeking another £120,000, much to the chagrin of Curzon who was sceptical of finding any workable deposits of oil in Persia. See also J. Bamberg, *The History of the British Petroleum Company: Volume II, The Anglo-Iranian Years 1928-1954* (Cambridge: CUP, 1994), p. 3.

[16] Ferrier described Article 10, 'a sum equal to 16% of the annual profits of any company or companies', as 'vague' (p. 42).

Oil Company, as though it was a Persian institution'. To which a Whitehall official minuted in the margins: 'One hopes that the pride of the MoC in the oilfields will not become too paternal.'[17]

It was clear to the company that to satisfy the change in mood that permeated an Iranian government now more comfortable and confident in its own position, some sort of renegotiation of the original concession would have to take place. Although overshadowed by the crisis of 1951-53, this was the first time that Iran moved to abrogate the concession unilaterally. It came as a result of a not-unexpected impasse in the negotiations following an initial offer by the APOC to clarify the calculation of profits which did not yield the sort of revenue the Iranian government expected, especially when viewed in the context of the global downturn of the economy. Teymourtash for his part had been pushing for a 25% share of the company, pointedly noting that if the Agreement had been reached anew now, Iran might have easily expected a 50-50 partnership. In the absence of progress Reza Shah decided to raise the stakes by abrogating the concession, forcing the parties to seek legal redress at the League of Nations (with the Iranian delegation now led by the noted constitutionalist and nationalist ideologue, Hasan Taqizadeh). By this stage (1932) it was clear that the negotiations would have to take place between the respective governments, and the British Government decided to take a direct hand in an exercise that was to provide more drama than substance. Faced with the collapse of the talks and the threatened withdrawal of the British, Reza Shah suddenly compromised:

> At a farewell audience, Sir John Cadman so prevailed upon the Shah, that he attended a meeting whereat he scrapped the proposals of his bewildered Ministers and enjoined their acceptance of the essentials of the company's draft. If the personal intervention of the arbitrary Reza Shah had been decisive for the cancellation of the concession of the Anglo-Persian Oil Company on November 27, 1932, it was no less so for the conclusion of the agreement of April 29, 1933, between the company and the Persian Government. A month later this agreement was ratified by the Majlis.'[18]

The disappointment of some ministers and officials was palpable, and it is difficult not to see the impact of this encounter on the later crisis. For Iranian nationalists, Reza Shah had shamelessly conceded ground to the British. For the British, on the other hand, the somewhat theatrical Iranian bark appeared a good deal worse than its bite. For Reza Shah, however, the reasoning was simple. He had tested the boundaries of the envelope and decided that discretion was the better part of valour. It was not a popular decision, but in the context of the time, not difficult to understand. The new concession offered a new means of calculating the royalty— no longer based on profits but 'physical volumes of oil and the financial distribution which the Company made to its shareholders'—with additional safeguards that ensured a minimum income for the Iranian government of £750,000 per year.[19]

---

[17] See 'Modernisation,' 17 December 1928, FO 371/13071/E5964, TNA.
[18] Butler, p. 41.
[19] Bamberg, *The History of the British Petroleum Company,* Vol II, p. 50. Bamberg is more generous to the skills of the Iranian negotiators than Butler and notes that Cadman had noted in his diary, albeit with a flourish, that he felt he 'had been well and truly plucked', p. 48. Others such as G Brew, 'In search of "Equitability": Sir John Cadman, Reza Shah and the cancellation of the D'Arcy Concession, 1928-33', *Iranian Studies* Vol. 50 (1), p. 139, stress that the agreement remained more favourable to the Company.

Moreover, an additional royalty would be paid in lieu of internal taxation for the next thirty years, and the Company agreed to pay a further £1m in settlement of all outstanding claims. It is nonetheless worth recognising that under this new procedure British tax receipts from the Company—a persistent refrain and complaint from Iranian nationalists—only exceeded the monies paid to the Iranian government from 1942 when the British Government increased corporate taxation. For all the irritation it justifiably caused, it was not a direct consequence of the agreement reached in 1933.[20]

A commitment was made to train up more Iranians with a view to reducing the number of non-Iranians employed by the company, while it was agreed that by 1938 the company's (renamed the Anglo-Iranian Oil Company in 1935)[21] concession would be restricted to 100,000 square miles, a reduction of some 80% from the original agreement. In return the Company secured a number of assurances of its own. In the first place the concession was extended by 32 years to 1993, after which the Company's assets in Iran would pass to the Iranian government; it was protected from any attempt at nationalisation; and any disagreements would be settled by arbitration. The Company could voluntarily divest itself its concession or be deprived of it if arbitration had concluded that it had defaulted on the Agreement.

It was this agreement that would ultimately be disputed in 1950, as further changes geopolitically and economically placed increasing strains on the relationship between the Company and the Iranian government, but perhaps more surprisingly, between the AIOC and the British Government itself, who found the Company's excessive legalism to be politically difficult to manage. The Company's view was that it operated in Iran under a legal agreement, and it saw no reason to change the terms of that agreement going forward. The British Government's view was that legal agreements, especially between states, could only operate realistically within an understood political framework. If it grew to sympathise with the Iranians on that particular point, it did not share the dramatic re-evaluation of political realities that some Iranian nationalists espoused.

The 1930s and 1940s witnessed dramatic changes in the politics and economics of the AIOC. With the rapid adoption of the motor car, the company's business grew dramatically as world oil production leapt from 20 million tons in 1900 to 278 million tons in 1939.[22] Abadan was soon transformed into the world's largest oil refinery employing some 15,245 people in 1929, doubling to 27,180 the following year and reaching 55,000 employees by 1949, including, much to the chagrin of local Iranians, labour imported from India.[23] Conditions were difficult and worker's rights, especially for local employees, limited. If the company catered generously for its British employees, welfare provisions were less evident for its Iranian workers, who were increasingly agitating for their rights. Indeed, one of the

---

[20] Bamberg, Vol. II, p. 324-5. These were from 1943 substantially higher than the revenues received by Iran and of course did not account for the benefits accrued to the British state from being able to buy oil at preferential rates for the Navy and in Pound Sterling. See Ervand Abrahamian, *The Coup*, (New York: New Press, 2013), p. 11. Butler notes that tax revenues 'far exceeded' payments to the Iranian government from 1939.

[21] In 1934, the Government of Iran requested that all foreigners use the indigenous name for the country as opposed to 'Persia'. This came into effect in 1935, hence the change in the Company's name.

[22] Butler, p. 42.

[23] S. Cronin, 'Popular Politics, the new state and the birth of the Iranian working class: the 1929 Abadan Oil Refinery Strike', in *Middle Eastern Studies*, September 2010, 46: 5, p. 705.

interesting aspects of the growth of the AIOC was that it was in effect Iran's first major industrial development, complete with the emergence of a distinct industrial working class. As Cronin notes by way of comparison, 'In 1925 Iran had fewer than 20 modern industrial plants', of which 'only five had more than 50 workers.'[24] Even the semantics began to change and for the first time, the term 'worker' (*kargar*), a term previously used for non-Asian labour, began to be applied to the Iranian workforce,[25] as workers petitioned for better rights. By 1929, these workers went on strike for better conditions, and a shorter working day, and while the strike was crushed, it signified a new sense of cohesion among workers in Abadan.[26]

What was perhaps most striking about these developments was the juxtaposition of a modern industrial power with a traditional workforce and the frictions this was bound to engender. The Anglo-Iranian Oil Company was a behemoth even by the standards of the industrial West. Its development and expansion in a country with no prior experience of industrial work practices was bound to be a shock to the system. As Atabaki argues, 'Although national culture was directly affected by modernisation, the rhythms of modern urbanized life nevertheless could not prevail. Persia was a society composed essentially of an upper class of literati, and a large mass of peasants who counted their time in "days and months, not in minutes and hours", where "the clock had little chance to play the role of a useful practical contrivance".'[27] The consequence of all this was that the impending clash was not simply one between two states and enterprises disagreeing on the terms of their relationship, but a far deeper clash of mentalities. If each side decried the incomprehensibility—and obstinacy—of the other, there was some justification for it. As more Iranians were trained and gained work experience—as the 1933 concession demanded—so the distinction diluted, but cultural differences in approach were reinforced by deeper prejudices that proved difficult to shift.

How some of these relationships worked out might best be seen in the experience of the other great British corporate interest in Iran, the British Imperial Bank of Persia. The establishment of the Bank predated that of the AIOC by some thirty years and as the AIOC grew in importance that of the bank declined, though many of its officials were seemingly unwilling to countenance such an eventuality and strenuously failed to adapt the changing circumstances, despite the occasional urging of HMG. Its fate should have really served as a warning light to the AIOC. Granted a monopoly over the issue of banknotes in Iran, a situation which effectively made it the de facto central bank of Iran, this privileged position was systematically to be eroded by the government of Reza Shah. Reza Shah achieved this by hiring one of the Imperial Bank's own rising stars, Abolhasan Ebtehaj, and getting him to found a new National Bank—Bank Melli—which would henceforth act as the country's Central Bank. Ebtehaj drew on his experiences and training at the Imperial Bank to turn on his former masters with great effect, not least because his former masters refused to take the challenge seriously and refused to adapt to changing

[24] Cronin, 'Popular Politics', p. 705.
[25] T. Atabaki, 'Amaleh (Labor) to Kargar (worker): recruitment, work discipline and making of the working class in the Persian/Iranian Oil Industry', in *International Labor and Working Class History*, Fall 2013, 84, p. 172.
[26] For the details of the strike itself and the juxtaposition of traditional and modern means of protest see Cronin, 'Popular Politics', pp. 699-732.
[27] Atabaki, 'Amaleh', p. 170.

circumstances.

Matters were to come to head during the Second World War and the Allied Occupation of Iran, which lasted from 1941-46. The Occupation was to have several profound consequences for the socio-economic and political life of the country. Quite apart from releasing the straitjacket of Reza Shah's authoritarian rule and breathing new life—including a measure of histrionics—into the politics of the country, it also marked the first time that most Iranians had regular contact with Britons, Americans and Soviet Russians who were neither diplomats nor enjoyed any form of cultural acclimatisation. The culture-shock which resulted was matched by the disruption to the economy caused by the Occupation, with currency manipulation, liquidity and inflation. But more intriguing for our purposes were the frictions that were apparent between the Allies, not only between the Anglo-Americans and the Soviets as might have been expected, but between the Americans the British.

Surveys conducted at the time indicate that the British were caught between the mutual animosity of the Soviet and American soldiers, and that American soldiers frequently rated their Soviet counterparts more highly.[28] Ebtehaj was able to exploit this distrust by ensuring that the Americans banked with the National Bank rather than the Imperial Bank, a choice which clearly surprised and rattled the managers of the latter who had simply assumed they would be the natural choice. Ebtehaj, who had mastered his craft at the Imperial Bank, would prove in time to be the Imperial Bank's nemesis, in large part because despite repeated urgings from Foreign Office observers it grew complacent and refused to adapt. In 1948, when the concession ran out, the Imperial Bank quietly closed its doors, and left with little fuss or fanfare.

The quiet departure of the Imperial Bank should have been a salutary lesson for all seeking a redefinition of the Anglo-Iranian relationship. But there were more warning signs—studiouslyignored by the management of the company—that should have been heeded. Under the terms of the Occupation, allied troops were honour bound to withdraw from Iran no more than six months after the end of hostilities. While both the British and Americans adhered to the terms of the agreement the Russians proved less than enthusiastic, remaining instead to foster separatist movements among the Kurds and in Iranian Azerbaijan. The crisis, in Azerbaijan in particular, proved to be the opening salvo of the emerging Cold War. It was eventually resolved when the 'wily' Qavam al Saltaneh, Iran's 'elastic' Prime Minister, suggested to Stalin that in return for a Russian withdrawal Iran would grant the Russians an oil concession in the north to match that of the British in the south (although the agreement envisaged would be for a 50-50 joint company), subject he said to the ratification of the Majlis, which he assured Stalin would be a formality. The Russians duly withdrew, the separatist movements collapsed, and Qavam, never sincere about the ratification, delayed presenting it until it was finally rejected in 1947. This political sleight of hand, which saw Stalin effectively out-manoeuvred, excited possibilities among Iranian nationalists who, blind to the Cold War context and Truman's support of the Iranian position, turned their eyes onto the prize in the south. American support against Russia, they concluded, would be replicated in any contest against the AIOC.

They were not, as the British were to discover, altogether wrong even if American

---

[28] A. Jackson, *Persian Gulf Command* (London: Yale University Press, 2018), p. 327.

support was always predicated on and conditional to their own national interests. This made the ongoing dynamic much more complex and nuanced than many narratives, lacking the granularity of Butler's history, allow. This was not simply a contest between Britain and Iran, but a contest between Britain and America, diverse elements and opinions within the respective countries, frictions between the Company and the British Government, as well as differing understandings of the emerging Cold War order in its critical formative period. If the British and Americans tended towards global perspectives, having emerged victorious against Germany and Japan (though with hugely divergent economic consequences), Iranian interlocutors were squarely focused on the particulars of their own problem, seeing that writ large on the global stage, rather than as a part of a much larger whole as the Western allies would have understood it.

Thus, the British interpreted a huge strike (the workforce now stood at around 70,000) at the refinery in 1946 entirely through the lens of the Cold War and Russian attempts to undermine British interests (through the communist Tudeh party) in light of the difficulties they faced in securing their own concession, while the Iranians viewed it as first and foremost a struggle for labour rights against a company whose approach remained stubbornly archaic.[29] As Butler noted only too accurately, while the British government supported the Company, Labour ministers were less than enamoured with its strategy and management practices. Ernest Bevin, the Foreign Secretary, found the government's room for manoeuvre limited, complaining that 'It is virtually a private company with State capital and anything it does reacts upon the relationships between the British Government and Persia. As Foreign Secretary I have no power or influence, in spite of this great holding by the government to do anything at all.'[30] Following the strike, a parliamentary delegation noted with dismay the prevailing working conditions, reporting that, 'Here were to be seen Persian labour living in squalid conditions under tents, etc., and without doubt this was the worst place we visited from the point of view of social amenities.'[31] Bevin was explicit about the need for change:

> Although we have a Socialist government in this country there is
> no reflection of that fact in the social conditions in connexion with
> this great oil production in Persia. On the other hand, what
> argument can I advance against anyone claiming the right to
> nationalise the resources of their country? We are doing the same
> thing here with our power in the shape of coal, electricity, railways,
> transport and steel. The Russians have overcome this difficulty by
> the Russian Government and the Persian government entering into
> a 50-50 company . . . The more I have studied the question the more
> I have come to the conclusion that instead of anything on the basis
> of royalties it would be preferable to examine the question whether

---

[29] On the strike of 1946 see T. Atabaki, 'Chronicle of a bloody strike foretold: Abadan July 1946', in K. H. Roth (ed), *On the road to global labour history* (Leiden-Boston: Brill, 2017), pp. 93-128. Atabaki notes that the Company encouraged ethnic conflict between Arabs and Iranians to suppress the strike. Remarkably even the local consul at Khorramshahr seemed to toy with the idea of Arab separatism, a move that was likely to inculcate the fiercest nationalist reaction: see p. 17 and 25.

[30] Butler, pp. 46.

[31] BP Archive, ArcRef. 43762. Report on Delegation to Persia, June 1946, quoted in Atabaki, 'Chronicle', p. 13.

> Great Britain and Persia should not now enter into an arrangement
> for a joint company on similar lines [to the Russian-Persian], and
> so establish the relationship between the Abadan Oilfield and the
> Persian government on a basis which is mutually advantageous . . .
> a more secure basis for our oil supplies by virtue of the fact that the
> Persian Government will be protecting its own property instead of
> that of a private company.[32]

This remarkably prescient analysis by Bevin puts the Company's culpability for the events that were to follow in stark relief. As Bevin rightly pointed out, the idiosyncratic relationship between the Company and the Government, a relationship that was lost to Iranian public opinion, effectively ensured that the Government bore the responsibility for the Company's actions, but worse, that the Company, realising it could depend on the government to take the blame and ultimately come to its assistance, had become dangerously complacent. Unlike the British Imperial Bank, the AIOC and Abadan in particular was an overseas asset of particular value to an economically depleted post-War Britain: a country that had won a war and had global responsibilities it could ill afford. Abadan provided Britain with a reliable source of oil priced in sterling, which for a new Labour Government keen to stabilise and restructure the national economy was an economic asset of immense importance, further reinforced by the imminent independence of India. Putting the relationship on a stable footing in recognition of new realities, as Bevin argued, might have stemmed the nationalist momentum.

As it was, the Company dithered, regarding developments principally through the lens of the Great Game/Cold War, in which Iranians themselves had little or no agency. This was not only dogmatic and ideological but quite deliberately so. There were no shortage of political assessments going back decades recognising the growth of nationalist ideology in Iran and the emotive power it exerted. One might not agree with it, but to ignore it was reckless.[33] But the Board of Anglo-Iranian was in the government's assessment wholly inadequate to the task at hand. It had already recognised the dictatorial bent of its Chairmen, but Cadman, who stepped down in 1941, had, they concluded, at least been competent, surrounded himself with sound managers and crucially had some appreciation of the political and social climate within which AIOC was operating.[34] William Fraser's appointment meanwhile had been opposed by HMG, as he suffered from the same authoritarian tendencies but with less capacity to listen and much less political awareness. Fraser, one FO official noted, 'is a complete totalitarian and does very little in the way of general consultation with colleagues'.[35] Another noted, 'The judgement of some other people who have seen more of him than I, is that he is not quite of the quality necessary for this immensely important British institution.'[36] Worryingly, given the political environment in which he had to operate, Fraser seemed to have a very thin skin, and was prone to taking offence at the slightest perceived insult, including it

---

[32] Butler, p. 46; this remarkable minute is dated 20 July 1946. See also in this respect Bevin's analysis of the situation dated 23 July.

[33] See for example, Butler, pp. 103-4.

[34] See G. Brew, 'In search of "Equitability": Sir John Cadman, Reza Shah and the cancellation of the D'Arcy Concession, 1928-33', *Iranian Studies*, Vol. 50 (1) p. 130.

[35] Quoted in Bamberg, p. 327.

[36] *Ibid.*

would appear if it emanated from his own side, as when a FO official had treated Fraser a 'little brusquely and had not gone out of his way to . . . treat Fraser as the great man whom he feels himself to be.'[37]

As a result, the Company, much to HMG's irritation, decided to plough on with business as usual, decrying any problem as communist sedition, secure in their rigorous legalism and complacent in the knowledge that the Government would, if push came to shove, come to their assistance. This was reinforced, not without some justification, by a sense of comfort about Britain's place in a world order that her victory in the Second World War had seemingly assured, along with a robust alliance with the United States. The robustness of this alliance was perhaps the second great calculation, as anyone in the Attlee administration might have warned. As the 'brutal' ending of Lend Lease had indicated, wartime alliances were unlikely to transfer unconditionally to peace time and it became increasingly clear that American interests were not synonymous with those of Britain.[38] Roosevelt had famously clashed with Churchill on the future of the British Empire, and if the Labour administration did not aspire to the muscular imperialism of Churchill, it still retained an idea of the 'global Britain' world which sat uneasily with US 'anti-colonialism'.[39]

Indeed, HMG's suspicions of American motives were soon confirmed by their bullish activities in Iran, part of a wider information war against Soviet infiltration but increasingly seen as an attempt to oust Britain from its position of political and economic dominance. If this 'open competition' was not lost on the British, it was certainly not lost on the Iranians who saw in the United States the ally they needed in their struggle against the traditional imperial powers.[40] Sympathies towards the United States as the one nation able to break the power of the imperial powers of Britain and Russia stretched back to the Constitutional Revolution, and the belief in America as a new broom to sweep away colonial cobwebs was strong among the Iranian elite and nationalist intelligentsia. It was an image of course the Americans themselves endorsed and encouraged, much to the consternation of the British who regarded American posturing as somewhat contradictory: at once seeking a strong ally in the Cold War, drawn into sharp relief by the Berlin Airlift (1948) and the onset of the Korean War in 1950, while at the same time working to undermine that ally's prestige and economic position. At the same time, had the American position been more supportive and targeted it may have helped shift the Company towards the sort of position Bevin had been calling for.

Instead, the Company inched towards compromise as the domestic situation in Iran worsened and the international commercial environment became distinctly unsympathetic. Eschewing any movement towards a redrafting of the concession towards a 50-50 agreement, the Company instead offered a Supplemental Agreement that fell well short of other contracts being offered around the world, despite the fact that British assessments suggested that for all the bluster in the Majlis some form of 50-50 arrangement might prove acceptable, and would certainly serve to take the wind out of the sails of the more hard-line Majlis deputies, now gathering round the

---

[37] Bamberg, p. 328.
[38] Peter Hennessy, *Never Again: Britain 1945-51* (London: Penguin, 2006), p. 94.
[39] On this trend, see W. Roger Louis, 'American anti-colonialism and the dissolution of the British Empire', in *International Affairs* (Summer 1985), pp. 395-420.
[40] Butler, p. 74.

figure of Mohammad Mosaddeq and his newly formed National Front.

Mosaddeq, as noted above, was not unknown to the British, but as the poster child of Iranian nationalism he symbolised the gulf in understanding that was emerging between the British and Iranians, a polarisation of opinion which would lead to the marginalisation of the very moderate voices required for compromise. Mosaddeq emoted nationalist sentiment, much to the satisfaction of his supporters, but his romantic allusions elicited the derision of British interlocutors, who whatever their sympathies could not take seriously the febrile state of Iranian politics, with its frequent change in governments, occasional assassinations and dubious voting practices. It lent weight to the Company position and hindered sober analysis of the developing situation. In reinforcing the prejudices outlined above it ensured that any progress in negotiations was both slow and proceeded with some apparent reluctance.

This became increasingly clear in the protracted and fateful negotiations with General Razmara, who had been appointed Prime Minister in 1950. Razmara, who had masterminded the reoccupation of Iranian Azerbaijan after the Soviet withdrawal, became Prime Minister with a view to finally solving the impasse. Eschewing his military rank in strict conformity with the Constitution, Razmara concluded that while nationalisation of the AIOC might be justified, it was not practical, both politically and materially. Iran simply did not have the economic wherewithal to run an entire industry, and despite encouraging signs from the Americans, the politics of the process, for all its romantic attractions, would be painful.[41] The Supplemental Agreement suggested by the Company was simply not going to satisfy the Majlis, but a 50-50 agreement which was increasingly the norm in oil contracts being signed around the world, seemed to offer a solution that would ultimately satisfy all. By the beginning of 1951 the Company had come round to the idea, albeit with some reluctance, when they were suddenly—and by their account, unhelpfully—trumped by revelations of the impending Aramco agreement in Saudi Arabia on the basis of a 50-50 profit sharing agreement.[42]

With this revelation the Company's position was becoming untenable. Meanwhile calls for wholesale nationalisation were becoming more vocal, much to the irritation of the British negotiators who protested that it was impossible to proceed under such 'unrealistic' threats. As Butler noted, a reluctance to face worsening political realities resulted in a lack of preparation: 'While there is always much to be said for not crossing one's bridges before one comes to them, and for hoping for the best, yet there might have been a valuable gain in time and in clarity if, in preparation against the worst, rather earlier consideration had been given to the possible implications of Sir Francis Shepherd's increasing warnings as to the rising tide of Persian nationalism . . .'.[43]

Ultimately Razmara would fall victim to the procrastination of the Company and the growing zealotry of the deputies. Keeping the prospect of a 50-50 agreement, which the Company had reluctantly coming to terms with, firmly under wraps, he

---

[41] See M. R. Ghods, 'The Rise and Fall of General Razmara', *Middle Eastern Studies*, Jan 1993, Vol 29, pp. 32-33.

[42] The AIOC argued that the Supplemental Agreement guaranteed income irrespective of the market, while in bad years the 50-50 arrangement might yield nothing. But irrespective of the financial realities, perspective mattered.

[43] Butler, p. 118.

had pushed back against the practicalities of nationalisation in a speech to the Majlis on 3 March 1951 (12th *Esfand* 1329).[44] Four days later (7 March), he was dramatically assassinated, as he attended a memorial service in a Mosque in Tehran, by a member of the Fedayin-e Islam, who had in Butler's words, 'penetrated the cordon of police with surprising ease'.[45] The British suspicion, adduced from later assessments, was that Razmara had been assassinated to prevent an Agreement— which he was inching towards—from being successfully concluded. In one of the more controversial parts of the report, Butler noted: 'It was only months later, in October, that Mr Pyman of His Majesty's Embassy received an account, from what he believed to be a reliable source, of a meeting three days before the murder whereat, it was reported, 15 members of the Fidayan-i-Islam had conferred with Dr Musaddiq and M. Kashani. Both were reported to have stated categorically that the welfare of Persia depended upon the disappearance of General Razmara.'[46]

Although the insinuation of complicity reflects little more than rumour—and Mosaddeq was himself to express fears for his own security—the response to Razmara's assassination was decidedly mixed. The Tehran bazaar reportedly rejoiced, while mullahs refused to perform the oration at Razmara's funeral. Some condemned the assassination, but few regretted it, and a number celebrated,[47] while the President of the Senate merely referred to the assassination as an 'unexpected event'.[48] The Majlis was eventually moved to give the assassin a parliamentary pardon (granted in 1952), while it moved with haste that can best be described as indecent to propose the bill nationalising the AIOC the day after Razmara's demise. The movement to nationalise the AIOC, a political act, had by virtue of the assassination acquired a sacral quality. Above all it reflected the intensely febrile, emotive and at times paranoid political culture of the time which an impartial observer might have difficulty in calling 'democratic'.[49]

None of this was calculated to reassure the British negotiators, and Mosaddeq's move towards the premiership over the next few weeks as he manoeuvred to secure the passage of the nationalisation bill through the Majlis was regarded as theatrical as it was 'unscrupulous'.[50] Stung by the assassination of Razmara and the enthusiasm with which his death had apparently been greeted, to say nothing of the brief tenure

---

[44] Azimi suggests that Razmara had made members of the National Front aware of the possibility of a 50-50 agreement: see F. Azimi, *Iran: The Crisis of Democracy* (London: I.B. Tauris, 2009), p. 239.

[45] Butler, p. 122. The offer to discuss a 50-50 arrangement was noted a letter from the British ambassador Shepherd to Razmara, reproduced in Persian translation in Mostafa Fateh, *Panjah sal-e naft-e Iran* (Tehran: Payam, 1335/1956).

[46] Butler, p. 122. The suggestion that members of the National Front had conspired with the Fedayin to rid themselves of their troublesome Prime Minister is recounted in both Ibrahim Safai, *Eshtebah-ye Bozorg: Melli shodan Naft* (Tehran: Ketab-e Saara, 1371/1992), pp. 136-39, and Ali Rahnema's *Nirohayeh mazhabi bar bastar-e nezhat-e melli* (Tehran, Gam-e No, 1384), pp, 193-200. The title of Safai's book translates as 'The great mistake: the nationalisation of oil. See also Christopher de Bellaigue, *Patriot of Persia*, (London: Bodley Head, 2012), pp. 151-2. None of this confirms anything more than that the rumour of complicity was widespread (there have also been suggestions for example that both the Shah and the Americans wanted Razmara out of the way because of his apparent links to Tudeh Officers in the army), but the reaction and later exoneration of the assassin speak for themselves. Mosaddeq does not cover this period in his memoirs.

[47] F. Mokhbari, 'Iran's 1953 Coup: revisiting Mosaddeq', *Bustan: The Middle East Book Review*, Vol 7, 2 (2016), p. 118.

[48] 'Internal Situation', 11 March 1951, FO 248/1514/10101/78/51, TNA. The muted reaction extended far beyond the borders of Iran to the pages of Elwell-Sutton's *Persian Oil* (London: Lawrence and Wishart, 1955), p. 55.

[49] Mokhbari, 'Iran's 1953 Coup', p. 126. Mosaddeq himself famously protested the elections to the 16th Majlis.

[50] Butler, p. 160.

of his subsequent nominee, Hussein Ala, the Shah refused to nominate a new prime minister (his preference being the noted Anglophone Seyyed Zia), urging the Speaker instead to first sound out the Majlis. The Majlis decided that since the National Front (dominant on the oil commission but a small minority—with 11 deputies—of the overall Majlis) had proposed nationalisation, they should be given the opportunity to see it through. Having persistently demurred on account of ill health, Mosaddeq much to everyone's surprise 'promptly consented to become Prime Minister of Persia'.[51]

Six months later Mosaddeq ruefully reflected on the impasse that had now cemented itself between Britain and Iran. Effusive about the support of the Americans, who he argued had been prevented from constructive mediation by the intransigence of the British, he pointedly noted that had the 50-50 Agreement been proposed several years earlier, it was unlikely any of these problems would have emerged. It was a remarkable statement to make, but one that echoed the frustration of Ernest Bevin some five years earlier.[52] It begs the question whether, had wiser counsel prevailed as Bevin had suggested, and the nature of the problem better appreciated by the Company in particular, this tragic episode in Anglo-Iranian relations might have been avoided altogether.

---

[51] *Ibid.*
[52] Fateh, '*Panjah sal-e naft-e Iran*', p. 582. Speech at the Majlis, on 20th Azar 1330/12th December 1951. Mosaddeq was especially effusive about George McGhee.

Erbil
Kirkuk
Sanandaj
Tikrit
Hamadan
Kermanshah
I R A N
(PERSIA)
Ramadi
Baghdad
Isfahan
Tigris
Najaf
I R A Q
Yezd
Euphrates
Ahwaz
An Nasiriyah
Abadan
Shiraz
Basra
Kuwait
Neutral Zone
KUWAIT
Persian Gulf
S A U D I
Charak
Buraida
A R A B I A
BAHRAIN
Manama
FCDO GIS72 Persian Gulf 1960s
QATAR
Hufuf
Doha

Tehran

BRITISH POLICY IN THE RELINQUISHMENT OF ABADAN IN 1951

by Rohan Butler

PREFACE

This history of British policy in the relinquishment of Abadan in 1951 has been written in accordance with a decision taken by the Permanent Under-Secretary of State in 1959. This decision followed from a letter addressed to him and to other Heads of Government Departments on September 5, 1957, by Sir Norman Brook.[1]

Sir Norman Brook suggested that, as the work on the Civil Series of the Official Histories of the Second World War was drawing to a close, it might be possible to continue to 'fund experience for Government use' in a more modest way by preparing 'departmental histories' of particularly significant episodes of policy or administration. He believed that such histories, which would provide a consecutive narrative of administrative experience over a specified period, might enable the administrator to see current problems in perspective as regards both policy and administrative practice. It was a feature of our administrative system, wrote Sir Norman Brook, that we made many forecasts but few retrospects. More postmortems would, he thought, be salutary for an analysis of how initial judgments and forecasts had stood the test of time.

The suggestion of Sir Norman Brook was followed up in the Foreign Office by the then Librarian, Mr C.C. Parrott, and by the Steering Committee under the chairmanship of the Permanent Under-Secretary of State.[2] After consideration of various possibilities it was decided that I should undertake the present study. In selecting the Abadan crisis of 1951 it was hoped that it would provide a particularly instructive case-history. It was an outstanding episode of lasting significance in British foreign policy of recent years; it represented a complex concentration and critical balance of factors, political, economic, juridical and military.

The expectations entertained of the subject have, I think, proved justified. By the same token, however, it has also proved to be a rather more than usually difficult history to write. In accordance with my understanding of the purpose of Sir Norman Brook and Lord Inchyra, the narrative of events often endeavours to explain not only what happened but why one thing was done rather than another, why in a particular way at a particular time, and what were the frequently conflicting considerations which underlay critical decisions. This inevitably renders the study more confidential—and long. As it is, the narrative is much concentrated from thousands upon thousands of original papers, often of rather an elaborate kind. To compress it further would have run serious risk of over-simplification and unfairness both to policies and to individuals.

A long study, though, has obvious drawbacks for busy readers. In order to meet this so far as may be, two main devices have been employed. First, all the chapters

---

[1] The footnotes in this preface are editorial. Cabinet Secretary from 1957 until late 1962.
[2] Sir F. Hoyer Millar (later Lord Inchya), PUS at the Foreign Office from 1957-62.

are divided into titled sections and these sections, together with a further summary of the main contents of each, are listed in the Table of Contents on pp. 22-35. Secondly, the political and administrative conclusions emerging from the narrative are here presented in front of it in Chapter XVI, placed immediately after the Table of Contents. This chapter, is, however, paged consecutively to the others and, if the study is printed, should follow them.[3] The political conclusions are highly condensed. To facilitate their further elucidation and justification, the conclusions include page references to some of the main passages in the narrative to which they relate.

Mention of conclusions raises considerations of which the writer has been particularly conscious. Attempts to draw lessons from history can be of practical value since, as has been observed by my predecessor, Sir Llewellyn Woodward, while history does not repeat itself, historical situations do recur. The deduction of such lessons, though, always calls for caution. Because historical wisdom is always wise after the event. The historian most often, and inevitably, enjoys the two large if dubious advantages of hindsight and of residual authority, in so far as the subjects of his study are not alive to answer back. The present writer has been keenly aware of the rather salutary absence of the second, at least, of these doubtful privileges. Many people are still active who, unlike myself, had first-hand experience of the Abadan crisis.

A first thought was naturally to consult and learn from those who were concerned with the crisis. But after careful consideration, and in consultation with Mr Parrott, it appeared that in the present case such a course would be liable to raise considerable difficulties, besides rendering the work slower than it has in any case had to be. To mention but two of the difficulties, it seemed questionable how far it would be just to consult only members of the Foreign Service; and it would in any case have been difficult, indeed impossible, to consult all those who had been concerned; thus the personal testimonies would inevitably have been to some extent partial and incomplete, with obvious dangers for the historian. On balance it seemed preferable to forgo the advantages which personal interviews would have procured, in the interests of trying to prepare a case-history strictly from such archival and other written evidence as a historian could only use in examining a remoter period.

In these circumstances it is especially desirable that the narrative of events should be allowed to speak for itself, and this I have endeavoured to do throughout. It would have been evidently prudent, and easy, to leave it at that. In view of the expressed intentions of Sir Norman Brook, however, it seemed desirable to try to make the critical study constructive. I have on occasions ventured to 'break the drowsy spell of narrative' in order to assess a situation, suggest a question or pose a possibility. I have also sought to draw political and administrative conclusions, if not always quite so directly as might be strictly required by Sir Norman Brook's proposed checks on the validity of initial assumptions. Such checks would indeed appear to be largely inherent in the history, and in a number of cases to be more or less clearly deducible, as I have tried to indicate. But to attempt to reduce this to too rigid an exercise would, I fear, be unduly mechanistic and unrealistic in view of the complexity of ever-shifting diplomatic problems, of their particularly high political content by comparison with the work of most other Government departments, and of the

---

[3] Chapter XVI was placed at the end of the Report in the printed copy, as it is in the present publication.

tiresome fact that diplomacy deals with foreigners not subject to the authority of the Secretary of State.

The conclusions in Chapter XVI are also limited in another respect. They are historical conclusions. The direct relation of those regarding administration, for instance, is necessarily to the practice of about 1950. It may well be that the most valuable and practical conclusions remain to be drawn by those who, unlike the present writer, have a close knowledge of current political and administrative problems, enabling them to draw analogies and comparisons.

A further necessary limitation is that, as the title indicates, this is a history of British official policy in the relinquishment of Abadan in 1951. It is primarily based upon the archives of the Foreign Office (all file references are to files of the year in question unless the contrary is indicated); occasional use has also been made, as necessary, of the archives of the Cabinet Office. It would of course be possible to write histories of the crisis from other perspectives and other archives, for instance those of the then Anglo-Iranian Oil Company or of the Persian Government.

It is a natural regret to me, as an author, that my work should not see the light of day in the form of publication. I have fully accepted, however, that this is scarcely a current possibility, and this history, which had to be frank in order to be useful, was primarily written with a view, not to present publication, but to confidential official use. In these circumstances I must reluctantly conclude that for obvious reasons it would be best all round that the existence of this study should also not be publicised at the present time.

These recognised considerations against publication and publicity render it the more unfortunate that, as I have already represented elsewhere, my understanding of the basis upon which I undertook this large historical task has not proved wholly correct, in so far as I have not been permitted to see all relevant papers in the Foreign Office.[4] A certain number of relevant telegrams and papers have been withheld from me. Apart from obvious personal considerations, I need not emphasise the gravity of this from a historical point of view. It compels me, as a matter of historical principle, to disclaim in advance all responsibility for all errors or omissions of fact or inference due to this cause.

I am specially sorry to be obliged to make this reservation in view of all the personal kindness and help which I have received in the Foreign Office from Lord Inchyra, Mr C.C. Parrott, Mr R.W. Mason[5] and the staff of the Library and Reference Room. I further owe a deep and special debt to Miss M.E. Lambert, Assistant Editor of *Documents on British Foreign Policy*, who has been my sole and indefatigable assistant throughout the heavy labour of research, preparation and checking required for this history. It owes more than I can briefly indicate to her zealous accuracy and good judgment. Last but not least I would thank Miss F.L.J. Sturgess, who has typed and retyped the particularly long and complicated manuscript with expert care.

February 20, 1962   ROHAN BUTLER

---

[4] Butler was not specific about the documentation he was not permitted to see, but it is likely that he was referring to the papers of the Permanent Under-Secretary's Department, the liaison department between the Foreign Office and the UK's intelligence agencies.

[5] Librarian and Director of Research in the Foreign Office, in succession to Mr Parrott.

TABLE OF CONTENTS

Foreign Office urges an imaginative approach in the light of the
Aramco agreement—the company fighting for its life—Mr Bevin's
concern regarding the prevailing system—the Treasury, unwilling to
press the company—the company's attitude towards a 50-50
agreement—Sir Francis Shepherd to represent British concern to
General Razmara—reduction of impetus in London—internal criticism
of AIOC.

Secretary—Earl Mountbatten's proposal for prompt visit by a British minister to Tehran is held over.

ministerial decisions of August 22 on issues of British staff at Abadan
and use of force—Chiefs of Staff's views on Operation Buccaneer—
Mr Stokes suspends negotiations after Dr Musaddiq's further offer on
management—criticism of Mr Stokes' negotiations—Shah's views on
Persian political developments—President Truman's statement of
August 23 and Mr Attlee's appeal for his support—British reversion to
The Hague ruling—withdrawal of Fields staff—effects on British
position of Harriman Formula and Stokes Mission.

evacuation of Canal zone (July 1954)—analyses of Mr Julian Amery and Mr Eden—British reverses and opportunities in an era of transition.

CHAPTER I

THE BACKGROUND OF BRITISH ENTERPRISE IN PERSIA, 1901-47

By the middle of the 20th century Great Britain had forged a special link with Persia. The most modern oil refinery in the world, the outstanding achievement of the Anglo-Iranian Oil Company upon the sweltering mud-flats of Abadan, nourished by the oilfields of South Persia, had become the greatest single British investment overseas. Yet the summer and autumn of 1951 brought a British decision, under Persian pressure, to relinquish Abadan by closing down the huge enterprise and withdrawing every Englishman. This was one of the heaviest decisions taken by any British Government since the close of the Second World War. Nor has its political importance diminished in the perspective of after-years. This decision was embedded in an especially close complex of considerations, political, economic, juridical and military. The grave task of relating and resolving these considerations for the United Kingdom fell primarily, subject to the authority of Cabinet and Parliament, upon the Secretary of State for Foreign Affairs and his advisers in the Foreign Office. In order to understand how this task was undertaken and accomplished it is first necessary to gauge the many operative, and often conflicting, forces and factors for decision.

1. The Persian Setting and the D'Arcy Concession

In 1950 Persia comprised about 15 million inhabitants and 630,000 square miles, approximately the area of Great Britain, France, Germany and Italy put together. The Iranian plateau between the valleys of the Indus and the Tigris, the Caspian Sea and the Persian Gulf of the Arabian Sea, has retained its strategic importance since the days of the Median and Achaemenid empires. Persia largely commands the approaches to the Middle Eastern land bridge, across the Straits of the Bosphorus into Europe, and across the Gulf of Suez into Africa. Already in the first half of the 18th century Persia focused the attention of the two emergent empires of Great Britain and of Russia.

The entry of Russia upon the European scene under Peter the Great significantly coincided with her advance against Persia. Russian forces captured Baku and Russian engineers in disguise operated at times in the armies of the conquering Nadir Shah who rose to power in Persia shortly after the death of the Czar Peter. At that period British interest in Persia was primarily commercial. The East India Company maintained factories there and Persian commandeering of the company's ships for service in the new navy of Nadir Shah was only one of the exactions and dangers which often compelled the East India Company, there as elsewhere in Asia, to pursue a flexible and diplomatic policy in order to preserve its position before the advent of the more massive imperialism of the 19th century.

Persia became strategically important to Great Britain in the interests of covering her Indian Empire against Russian expansionism. In the Persian Gulf British influence often became, in the 19th century, a more immediate reality than that of the weak and impecunious Persian governments of the Qajar dynasty. In 1906 His Majesty's Government won much popularity in Persia by supporting, against Russian interests, a movement of constitutional reform which instituted a Parliament, the Majlis, as an important new factor for good and ill in Persian affairs.

This British popularity was, however, largely eclipsed in the following year by the Anglo-Russian convention of August 31, 1907, which reconciled, on paper at least, the rivalry of the two Powers in Central Asia, notably in the buffer States of Persia, Afghanistan and Tibet. For Persia this convention delimited a Russian sphere of influence in the north, stretching down through Isfahan to Yezd, and a British sphere in the south-east behind the line Bandar Abbas Kerman-Birjand. A neutral zone separated the two spheres.

At the end of 1907 the Government of India strengthened the guard at the British Consulate at Ahwaz in the neutral zone by a small detachment of Bengal lancers under the command of Lieutenant (later Sir) Arnold Wilson because of attack by Bakhtiari tribesmen against British oil prospectors who were operating in the region. This drilling was in accordance with the 60-year concession which the Persian Government had granted on May 28, 1901, to Mr William Knox D'Arcy, a gold millionaire who never visited Persia. This concession was for the discovery, exploitation and export of petroleum throughout Persia, except the five northern provinces, under Russian influence. At Masjid-i-Sulaiman in the early morning of May 26, 1908, oil was struck at a depth of 1,180 feet and a gusher shot 50 feet or more above the top of the rig. British working of Persian oil had begun.

In April 1909 the Anglo-Persian Oil Company was formed with an initial capital of £2 million, of which nearly half was held by the Burmah Oil company. Assistance was received from the Foreign Office and the Admiralty, keenly pursuing the conversion of the Royal Navy to oil fuel. Mr Winston Churchill, as First Lord of the Admiralty, was the driving force within the Government which encouraged it to conclude the agreement of May 1914 with the company, then in need of financial assistance. By this arrangement the company's capital was doubled and the new shares were taken up by His Majesty's Government, which would have 52-55 per cent of the voting interest. Two directors *ex officio* were to be appointed by the Treasury one of them as a direct representative of the Admiralty, and each of them with a power of veto on the board of directors; the other directors could appeal against such a veto to His Majesty's Government, with whom the final decision would rest (Article 91(A) of the 1914 Articles of Association of APOC). A contract with the Anglo-Persian Oil Company for the supply of oil to the Royal Navy at preferential and secret rates was concluded on May 20, 1914.

Also on May 20, 1914, Sir John Bradbury, Joint Permanent Secretary to the Treasury, addressed to the board of the company a letter of lasting importance for the definition of the relationship between His Majesty's Government and the company. Sir John Bradbury stated that, while 'it would not be prudent, or indeed practicable to qualify the generality of the right of veto' of the Government directors, it would in practice only be exercised in regard to 'matters of general policy such as: (1) the supervision of the activities of the company as they may affect questions of foreign, naval or military policy, (2) any proposed sale of the company's undertaking or proposed change of the company's status . . . and interference (if any) in the ordinary administration of the company as a commercial concern will be strictly limited to the minimum necessary to secure these objects'. This, it was explained, was not a binding agreement but 'an assurance as to the general lines'[1] upon which His Majesty's Government would act.

---

[1] Parliamentary Debates, 5th Series, H. of C., Vol. 226, col. 2263.

The arrangements of May 1914 aroused considerable contemporary criticism from liberal supporters of free enterprise, including even Admiral Lord Fisher, a keen advocate of naval conversion to oil fuel. Sir John Bradbury's letter was not published for 15 years but it was upon an understanding in general conformity with its terms that Parliament approved the arrangements in an act which received the Royal Assent six days after the outbreak of war in August 1914. The venture was a calculated risk and it was only in 1915 that the company balanced its account and was able to pay a modest dividend. The chairman of the Anglo-Persian Oil Company had compared Mr Winston Churchill to Lord Beaconsfield. And indeed the successful operations of the company, centred upon Abadan, soon demonstrated that by its investment His Majesty's Government had added to the Suez Canal another great imperial interest in the Middle East.

During the First World War the Anglo-Persian Oil Company largely contributed towards ensuring that, in the phrase of Lord Curzon, the Allied cause floated to victory upon a wave of oil. After the war and the Russian Revolution, with its temporary relaxation of the Russian grip on Northern Persia, it was Lord Curzon at the Foreign Office who, with strategic imagination and proconsular relish, pursued a forward policy in Persia, leading to the Anglo-Persian Agreement of August 9, 1919. This political agreement, which established British influence as paramount in Persia and was accompanied by a British loan, aroused sharp criticism in France and the United States: Lord Curzon did not favour a suggestion from Lord (formerly Sir Edward) Grey that the American Government be associated with the agreement.

One of the British advisers to the Persian Government appointed in accordance with the agreement of 1919 was Mr S.A. Armitage-Smith of the Treasury as Financial Adviser. On December 22, 1920, Mr Armitage-Smith on behalf of the Persian Government, signed with the Anglo-Persian Oil Company two related agreements, the first for the settlement of reciprocal claims arising out of the First World War, whereby the company made a lump payment of £1 million to the Persian Government; the second agreement settled the method of calculating the royalty of 16 per cent of the company's net profits, which had been assigned to the Persian Government on very favourable conditions by the original D'Arcy Concession of 1901. It was not stipulated that the Persian royalty should be calculated on profits from the winning, refining and marketing of Persian oil, whether refined and marketed within Persia or abroad. The company was not, however, to pay royalty to Persia on profits from transporting oil by its tankers (the British Tanker Company had been formed in 1915).

The Armitage-Smith Agreement was an interpretative agreement in respect of the D'Arcy Concession and was not regarded either by the company or Mr Armitage-Smith as requiring ratification by the Majlis. In 1928, after a sharp and temporary dip in royalties, the Persian Government first claimed that the unratified Armitage-Smith Agreement was invalid. In practice, however, it was accepted as the basis of relations between the Anglo-Persian Oil Company and the Persian Government throughout the 1920s when Persian royalties roughly trebled, from £469,000 for the year ending March 31, 1920, to £1,437,000 for that ending December 31, 1929.

Ratification by the Majlis was certainly required for the political Anglo-Persian Agreement of 1919, but the Persian Government omitted to submit it for parliamentary approval. Persian opposition to the agreement increased against a background of renewed Russian menace. British influence in the ephemerally independent republics of the Caucasus melted away. Soviet troops, emulating the advances of Peter the Great just on two centuries before, captured Baku in April 1920 and went on to land at Enzeli. The weak British forces there withdrew, leaving most of the province of Gilan under Soviet occupation. The stringent economy prescribed by His Majesty's Government in the aftermath of the First World War entailed the withdrawal from Persia of both British subsidies and British forces. At midnight on February 21, 1921, General Reza Khan with Cossack detachments, the self-designated protectors against the Soviets, entered Tehran and overthrew the Persian Government as the first stage towards the subsequent eviction of the Qajar dynasty and proclamation of the general as Reza Shah Pahlevi in December 1925. Five days after his initial *coup,* on February 26, 1921, a Soviet-Persian treaty of friendship was signed. It may be that future historians, commanding a longer perspective, may see in these events an early index to the decline of the British Empire against the ascendant vigour of the Soviet Union.

The Soviet-Persian treaty of 1921 liquidated Russian claims in Persia upon terms generous to the latter. Of lasting importance for the future was Article VI of this treaty: 'If a third party should attempt to carry out a policy of usurpation by means of armed intervention in Persia, or if such Power should desire to use Persian territory as a base of operations against Russia, or if a foreign Power should threaten the frontiers of Federal Russia or those of its allies, and if the Persian Government should not be able to put a stop to such menace after having been once called upon to do so by Russia, Russia shall have the right to advance her troops into the Persian interior for the purpose of carrying out the military operations necessary for its defence. Russia undertakes, however, to withdraw her troops from Persian territory as soon as the danger has been removed.'[2]

The interpretation of Article VI was laid down in the so-called Rotstein Note of December 12, 1921, to the Persian Government. In this note the Soviet representative at Tehran confirmed 'that Articles V and VI are intended to apply only in cases in which preparations have been made for a considerable armed attack upon Russia or the Soviet Republics allied to her, by the partisans of the régime which has been overthrown or by its supporters among those foreign Powers which are in a position to assist the enemies of the Workers' and Peasants' Republics and at the same time to possess themselves, by force or by underhand methods, of part of the Persian territory, thereby establishing a base of operations for any attacks—made either directly or through the counter-revolutionary forces—which they might meditate against Russia or the Soviet Republics allied to her'.[3] The Rotstein Note was subsequently registered, as part of the Soviet-Persian Treaty with the League of Nations by the Persian Government.

2. Cancellation of D'Arcy Concession and negotiation of the Concession of 1933

By the later 1920s Persian pressure for a larger cut was again building up against the Anglo-Persian Oil Company, which entered into discussions for the consolidation of its position, possibly by a new form of concession to admit shareholding participation by the Persian Government in the company's operations and profits. These discussions produced an agreement concerning the calculation of

---

[2] British and Foreign State Papers, Vol. 114, pp. 902-3.
[3] *Ibid,* p. 908.

profits, which was sent in May 1932 to Tehran for ratification. This was not forthcoming since publication of the company's accounts for 1931 showed that owing to the world-wide slump the royalty to the Persian Government, which had been £1,288,000 for 1930, would be reduced for 1931 to £307,000 on almost the same quantity of oil produced. Further negotiations with Persian ministers were abruptly interrupted by a personal intervention by Reza Shah which caused the Anglo-Persian Oil Company to be notified on November 27, 1932, that the D'Arcy Concession was unilaterally cancelled by the Persian Government.

His Majesty's Government quickly decided that the company could not be left to conduct the dispute alone, and on November 30, 1932, Mr R.H. Hoare, His Majesty's Minister at Tehran, was instructed to present to M. Feroughi, the Persian Foreign Minister, a note demanding immediate withdrawal of the cancellation and reserving the right to 'take all legitimate measures' to protect British interests. On the previous day Mr Hoare had already spoken strongly to the Persian foreign minister and had observed, so he reported, that 'the action of the Persian Government made it impossible for me to advise His Majesty's Government to be conciliatory'.[4] Almost immediately afterwards Mr Hoare received a report, which subsequently proved somewhat exaggerated, that Persian police were removing or defacing the company's signboards. His Majesty's Minister immediately rang up the Persian Foreign Minister 'and demanded that immediate action be taken to put a stop to this'.[5] It was taken within two hours.

A week later a second British note gave the Persian Government one week within which to notify its intention of withdrawing the cancellation, failing which his Majesty's Government would refer the question as an urgent issue to the Permanent Court of International Justice at The Hague under the Optional Clause and would request the Court to indicate provisional measures to preserve British rights. The Persian reply of December 12 denied the jurisdiction of the Permanent Court: the Persian declaration of acceptance of its compulsory jurisdiction made on October 2, 1930, and recently ratified on September 19, 1932, had specifically confined it to subsequent disputes 'with regard to situations or facts relating directly or indirectly to the application of treaties or conventions accepted by Persia and subsequent to the ratification of this declaration, with the exception of . . . disputes with regard to questions which, by international law, fall exclusively within the jurisdiction of Persia'.[6] According to the Persian Government this proviso excluded its dispute with the Anglo-Persian Oil Company in respect both of the contractual date and of domestic jurisdiction. The Persian note of December 12 further indicated that Persia might complain to the Council of the League of Nations concerning British threats and pressure.

In view of the Persian attitude and reservations with regard to the Optional Clause His Majesty's Government foresaw a possibility that proceedings might in any case be removed from The Hague to Geneva. In order to avoid the danger of appearing before the League of Nations as defendant, His Majesty's Government on December 14, 1932, requested the Secretary-General of the League to bring the Persian dispute before the Council under Article 15 of the Covenant. This move relieved Persian

---

[4] E 6746/3880/34.
[5] *Ibid.*
[6] League of Nations Treaty Series, Vol. 104, pp. 492-3.

fears of more forcible British action, and the Persian Press, which had been recently moderated, 'began soon afterwards to surpass its earlier efforts in vituperation'.[7]

On January 26 1933, the legally skilled Secretary of State for Foreign Affairs, Sir John Simon, opened the British case before the Council of the League of Nations with notable effect. On February 3 it approved a formula whereby the two parties agreed that the Anglo-Persian Oil Company should immediately enter into negotiations with the Persian Government, which should meanwhile continue its previous practice *de facto* of allowing the company's operations to proceed as before. These negotiations in Tehran were conducted for the company primarily by its vice-chairman Mr William Fraser; they resulted on April 23 in a decision of the two parties to announce their failure. At a farewell audience, however, the chairman of the company, Sir John Cadman, so prevailed upon the Shah that he attended a meeting whereat he scrapped the proposals of his bewildered Ministers and enjoined their acceptance of the essentials of the company's draft. If the personal intervention of the arbitrary Reza Shah had been decisive for the cancellation of the concession of the Anglo-Persian Oil Company on November 27, 1932, it was no less so for the conclusion of the agreement of April 29, 1933, between the company and the Persian Government. A month later this agreement was ratified by the Majlis.

The new concession, in replacement of the original D'Arcy Concession, sought to obviate the recently demonstrated risk to Persia from fluctuation of profits by substituting for the previous Persian royalty of 16 per cent on profits on Persian oil a royalty of 4s per ton of oil sold in Persia or exported, with safeguards against depreciation of sterling. Tonnage royalty was, however, combined with a share in the company's world-wide profits by providing that the Persian Government should also receive a sum equal to 20 per cent of any distribution made to the company's ordinary stockholders in excess of £671,250 in any year. Under these two heads a minimum annual payment of £750,000 was guaranteed. In addition, the Persian Government was to receive further royalty of 6d to 1s per ton in commutation of internal taxation for 30 years, with a guaranteed annual minimum of £225,000 rising after 15 years to £300,000. On the expiry of the concession the Persian Government would receive 20 per cent of the difference between the company's general reserve then and on December 31, 1932. With regard to the present, Persian royalties for 1931 and 1932 were to be calculated on a new basis yielding £1,339,000 and £1,525,000 respectively. An additional sum of £1 million would be paid by the company in settlement of all outstanding claims. Other concessions by the company notably included agreement to the preparation of 'a general plan of yearly and progressive reduction of the non-Persian employees with a view to replacing them in the shortest possible time, and progressively by Persian nationals' (Article 16). Furthermore the company's concession was, by the end of 1938, to be restricted to 100,000 square miles, less than a quarter of the original D'Arcy grant.

In return for all these advantages to the Persian Government under the agreement of 1933 the Anglo-Persian Oil Company received three main safeguards: first, the term of its concession was extended by 32 years, from 1961 as under the D'Arcy Concession, to December 31, 1993, when all the company's property in Persia would pass to the Persian Government; secondly, Article 21 stipulated that 'this Concession shall not be annulled by the [Persian] Government, and the terms therein shall not

---

[7] E 2439/2439/34 of 1933: Persia; Annual Report for 1932, para. 267.

be altered either by general or special legislation in the future, or by administrative measures or any other acts whatever of the executive authorities'; thirdly, under Article 22, 'any differences between the parties of any nature whatever and in particular any differences arising out of the interpretation of this Agreement . . . shall be settled by arbitration'; to which Article 26 added: 'Before the date of December 31, 1993, this Concession can only come to an end in the case that the Company should surrender the Concession (Article 25) or in the case that the Arbitration Court should declare the Concession annulled in consequence of default of the Company in the performance of the present Agreement.'

Thereafter, throughout the 1930s and 1940s, the concession of 1933 governed relations between the Persian Government and the Anglo-Iranian Oil Company, as its title became in 1935. By then these relations were excellent and in 1936 agreement was reached on a 'general plan' for the 'Persianisation' of the company's staff. The Anglo-Iranian Oil Company was forging ahead and the Government of Reza Shah, intent upon his autocratic and headlong modernisation of Persia, drew royalties which increased from £1,812,000 in 1933 to £5,545,000 in 1937, though dipping next year to £3,307,000. The new industrial revolution of the petrol engine had arrived, with world oil-production standing in 1939 at 278 million tons as against 20 million tons in 1900.

Within the Middle East as a whole, however, the Anglo-Iranian Oil Company had had to accommodate itself to that American intrusion which had begun after the First World War, during which the United States had not declared war upon the Turkish Empire. American pressure had produced the Red Line Agreement of 1928, and an international cartel which became known as the Iraq Petroleum Company. The Anglo-Persian Oil Company had sacrificed half its share in order to facilitate the entry into the cartel of the Near East Development Corporation comprising Standard Oil of New Jersey and other American companies, already concerned at the depletion of their domestic oil reserves. An accommodation between British and American interests was also reached both at Bahrein (Bapco) and at Kuwait. In 1939 oil production in the whole of the Middle East still only accounted for something like 5.5 per cent of world production. But the spectacular development of the Arabian oilfields, wherein American interests were to become prominent, lay just over the horizon when the Second World War came to alter all perspectives.

3. Allied occupation of Persia in the Second World War and the aftermath

In the Second World War, as in the first, Persian oil was of critical importance for the British war effort, and despite commercial difficulties, the Anglo-Iranian Oil Company in August 1940 guaranteed the Persian Government a minimum oil revenue of £4 million per annum. The importance of Persia not only for oil but also for strategy was obvious in relation to the campaigns in the Middle East and was reinforced when Russia was jerked into the war against Germany in June 1941. Failure by the Persian Government to give satisfaction to reiterated Anglo-Russian demands for the expulsion of the influential German colony, numbering some 2,000, provoked a joint Anglo-Soviet invasion of Persia on August 25, 1941, in order to secure what Mr Winston Churchill called 'the Levant-Caspian front' against German penetration of the Caucasus.

The Soviet Government adduced the Soviet-Persian Treaty of 1921 in support of the advance of its forces into northern Persia. In the south the British landing at

Abadan overcame slight Persian opposition, and two Persian sloops were sunk. Soviet terms were accepted by Reza Shah, who had vainly appealed to President Roosevelt to intervene in order to 'put an end to the acts of aggression'. Sir Reader Bullard, His Majesty's Minister in Tehran, reported that Reza Shah had previously been 'on the point of abdicating or running away'[8] from growing Persian resentment against his arbitrary misdeeds, responsibility for which was widely attributed, like so much else in Persia, to British influence. Sir Reader Bullard was concerned lest the British intervention be construed as support for the weakening Reza Shah, and suggested that the Persian Service of the BBC should make clear the British attitude by stressing the need for reform in Persia. This was done with notable effect. His Majesty's Minister reported on September 11 that the Persian Prime Minister, M. Feroughi, was 'convinced that the Shah must go if any reform is to be effected'.[9]

Mr Churchill had suggested on September 3, 1941, that Sir Reader Bullard should use 'the leverage of a possible Russian occupation of Tehran'[10] to secure Persian compliance with further British requirements. Six days later the Foreign Secretary, Mr Eden, observed to the Soviet Ambassador in London that 'perhaps the best solution of all would be if the Persian politicians were to invite us into Tehran in order to carry through a *coup d'état* to get rid of the Shah'.[11] On September 12 Mr Eden and M Maisky agreed that Sir Reader Bullard should be instructed 'to approach the Persian Government both on the suggestion of a successor to the Shah and on the subject of a Russian-Persian Alliance'.[12] Four days later the Shah abdicated in favour of his eldest son, Mohammed Reza Pahlevi, recognised without enthusiasm by His Majesty's Government. On September 17 British and Russian forces occupied Tehran.

By the time that the Anglo-Soviet-Persian treaty of alliance was concluded on January 29, 1942,[13] the United States had entered the war; but Persian endeavours to secure American adhesion to the treaty were unsuccessful. The Persian authorities remained largely uncooperative and inefficient, and Persian opinion, more fearful of Russia than of Britain, tended to blame the latter especially for food shortages and rampant inflation. Great Britain suffered severely in Persian estimation from her renewed association with Russia, in zones of occupation somewhat reminiscent of the spheres of influence of the Anglo-Russian agreement of 1907.

British unpopularity in Persia was liable to be not displeasing to the Russians, nor even perhaps to the Americans, who assumed a large and increasing share in the economic supply of Persia and in that military supply to Russia across Persia which became the chief strategic object of the allied occupation. Sir Reader Bullard encountered some unfriendliness from the American Minister in Tehran, and there were renewed indications of the traditional hostility of the State Department towards the alleged imperialism of British policy in Persia. American oil advisers, one of whom was Mr Herbert Hoover, Junior, are said to have drawn the attention of the Persian Government to a recent Venezuelan concession signed by a subsidiary of Standard Oil of New Jersey, which stipulated a 50-50 division of profits between the

---

[8] E 5372/3326/34.
[9] E 5578/3326/34.
[10] E 5396/3326/34G.
[11] E 5519/3326/34.
[12] E 5481/3326/34.
[13] British and Foreign State Papers, Vol. 144, pp. 1017ff.

company and the Venezuelan Government. Two American oil groups had by then applied for concessions in Eastern Persia. In September 1944 a Soviet Deputy Commissar for Foreign Affairs, M. Kavtaradze, arrived in Tehran to press, in revival of earlier Russian claims, for an exploratory oil concession for the five northern provinces of Persia. The Persian Government decided that it would grant no new oil concessions whatever till after the war.

After the rejection of the Soviet claim Persia was subjected to a war of nerves which included a show of force by Russian troops in Tehran in October 1944, and subsequent demonstrations by the Tudeh Party, the Soviet political instrument in Persia forged two years previously. Nevertheless on December 2 Dr Mohammad Musaddiq, an elderly Deputy for Tehran who had been imprisoned by Reza Shah, introduced into the Majlis a Bill prohibiting the Persian Government, under heavy penalties, from all further negotiations concerning oil concessions, unless by specific consent of the Majlis. That body promptly passed the Bill under its procedure of 'double urgency'. A week later M. Kavtaradze returned to Russia. In a speech on December 19 Dr Musaddiq defended his policy of 'passive balance' whereby no concessions harmful to Persian interests should be granted to any foreign Government. He rejected the 'positive balance' of granting an oil concession to Russia because the British already held one. At the same time Dr Musaddiq defended his refusal to back a Bill for the cancellation of the Anglo-Iranian Oil Company's concession by arguing that existing agreements should not be unilaterally cancelled; otherwise there would next be a Bill for the cancellation of the Soviet-Persian treaty of 1921.

By the end of 1944 the Foreign Office had abandoned hope of real co-operation in Persia with the Russians, and expected that they would seek to revenge their failure with regard to oil by seeking to undermine the position of the Anglo-Iranian Oil Company. British policy aimed at the restoration of Persia as an independent buffer-State through the implementation of the Anglo-Soviet-Persian treaty of 1942: it had notably provided that Great Britain and the Soviet Union would withdraw their forces from Persia not later than six months after the end of the war. Early in 1945 the Foreign Office considered the possibility, which was not ultimately pursued, of requiring M. Stalin to agree to stop putting pressure on Persia before His Majesty's Government would agree to his demand for a veto in the Security Council of the future organisation of the United Nations.

A week after the signature of the armistice with Japan on September 2, 1945, the Persian Government addressed a note to the occupying Powers requesting the total evacuation of their forces by March 2, 1946. British and American forces were duly evacuated during this six-month term. In December 1945 Soviet influence in northern Persia stimulated an Azerbaijani *coup* which established a Communist regime in the province and proclaimed a republic. Russian refusal to evacuate Persia until 'the situation was clarified' provoked a Persian complaint to the United Nations. The inadequately effective support given by that organisation to the Persian Government encouraged it to enter into negotiations with the Soviet Government. On March 6, 1946, an American note informed the Soviet Government that the United States could not remain indifferent to retention of Russian troops in Persia.[14]

---

[14] E 2568/5/34.

President Truman followed this up with 'a blunt message to Premier Stalin'[15] which appears to have produced such notable effect as to constitute, perhaps, one of the major successes of American post-war diplomacy.

By April 4, 1946, the new Persian Premier, M. Qavam-as-Sultaneh, the stormy petrel of Persian politics, was able to conclude an agreement with Russia whereby the Persian complaint to the United Nations would be withdrawn and a Soviet-Persian oil company formed to exploit a 50-year concession in north Persia. In June 1946 Soviet forces were withdrawn from Persia. The province of Azerbaijan was thereafter reintegrated under Persian administration, and local Communism reduced.

During this phase the shrewd and subtle M. Qavam was in no hurry to submit the proposed Soviet-Persian oil agreement for the required ratification by the Majlis. The agreement was so submitted in August 1947 and on October 22 the Majlis rejected it by 102 votes to two. The Persian gambit of refusal of ratification by the Majlis, which had nullified the Anglo-Persian agreement of 1919, had now been employed with equal success against the Soviet Union. This rejection had been encouraged by American advices, whereas British counsels having regard to the stake at Abadan, had favoured caution. This attitude probably did not enhance British standing in Persia. And in fact the law enacted by the Majlis on October 22, 1947, declaring the proposed Soviet-Persian agreement to be null under Dr Musaddiq's law of December 1944, threatened a back-hander against British interests by providing: 'The Government are charged in all instances where the rights of the people of Persia in the sources of the country's wealth, whether below or above the ground, have been impaired, especially regarding the oil in the south, to undertake the necessary negotiations and measures with a view to redeeming the rights of the nation, and they shall inform the Majlis of the results.'[16]

In 1946 the Anglo-Iranian Oil Company had made a series of concessions to Persian labour at Abadan concerning terms of employment, but the Tudeh Party of Persian sympathisers with Communism fomented local unrest which culminated in July in a general strike and riots at Abadan. His Majesty's Ambassador in Tehran, Mr J. Le Rougetel, informed the Persian Government that it was held responsible for the maintenance of order, British warships anchored off Abadan in Iraqi waters of the Shatt-el-Arab, and a brigade group (Force 401) was sent from India to Basra, in Iraq adjacent to Persia, with the announced purpose of protecting, if necessary, Indian and British lives and interests in Southern Persia. These measures had been agreed by the British Cabinet on July 15 on the recommendation of the Foreign Secretary, who also advocated a 'more sympathetic treatment' of Persian labour by the Anglo-Iranian Oil Company. Mr Ernest Bevin told the Cabinet that 'he fully realised the implications of employing British forces on Persian soil and that as one of the consequences Russian forces would probably enter Northern Persia; but he felt that we must be ready to take action to save British lives and to safeguard our vital Middle East supplies of oil.'[17]

The bold British policy was swiftly justified. Intervention at Abadan proved unnecessary since the Persian Government, while protecting strongly against the British military movements, itself quickly restored order. This successful show of

---

[15] Harry S. Truman, *The Memoirs of Harry S. Truman* (London, 1955-56), Vol. 2, p. 101.
[16] Translation as in EP 1531/529 of 1951.
[17] E 6622/401G.

strength was the last such use of troops from an undivided India under British rule.

4. The post-war position of the Anglo-Iranian Oil Company in Persia

The threat to the Anglo-Iranian Oil Company at Abadan in July 1946 had evoked a strong response from the Foreign Secretary, but he was by no means uncritical of the relationship between the company and His Majesty's Government, as laid down in 1914. Mr Bevin on July 20, 1946, sent an important minute to Mr Emanuel Shinwell, the Minister of Fuel and Power, and Mr Hugh (later Lord) Dalton, Chancellor of the Exchequer, wherein the Foreign Secretary recapitulated that relationship, with the governmental majority-holding and representation by two directors with power of veto. Mr Bevin commented: 'As far as I can judge, this power of veto would only be used in the case of the services being affected in any way . . . It is virtually a private company with State capital and anything it does reacts upon the relationships between the British Government and Persia. As Foreign Secretary I have no power of influence, in spite of this great holding by the Government, to do anything at all. As far as I know, no other Department has. Although we have a Socialist government in this country there is no reflection of that fact in the social conditions in connexion with this great oil production in Persia. On the other hand, what argument can I advance against anyone claiming the right to nationalise the resources of their country? We are doing the same thing here with our power in the shape of coal, electricity, railways, transport and steel. The Russians have overcome this difficulty by the Russian Government and the Persian Government entering into a 50-50 company.'[18]

The Foreign Secretary continued in his minute of July 20, 1946: 'The more I have studied the question the more I have come to the conclusion that instead of anything on a basis of royalties it would be preferable to examine the question whether Great Britain and Persia should not now enter into an arrangement for a joint company on similar lines [to the Russian-Persian], and so establish the relationship between the Abadan Oilfield and the Persian Government on a basis which is mutually advantageous . . . a more secure basis for our oil supplies by virtue of the fact that the Persian Government will be protecting its own property instead of that of a private company.'[19] Within five years, at the next crisis at Abadan, the relevance of Mr Bevin's preoccupations, and even of his tentative prescriptions, was to be demonstrated. They were, however, of so radical an order that it is scarcely surprising that arguments were then adduced against them, not least by the Minister of Fuel and Power.

No comment from the Treasury on the Foreign Secretary's minute has been traced in Foreign Office archives. Mr Shinwell replied to Mr Bevin on July 31, 1946: 'We must be very careful.' Among other arguments Mr Shinwell represented: 'If British oil companies have to go into partnership with foreign Governments, it is clear to me that we shall not have the degree of freedom which is so important, commercially and economically, and which is vital from a strategic point of view. Even if we were to enter into arrangements on, say, a 50-50 basis, how long would it be before the country granting the concession desired to have a larger say, and we

---

[18] E 7357/583/34.
[19] *Ibid.*

would have to accept a 60-40 or 70-30 basis, or perhaps to drop out altogether?'[20] Mr Shinwell enclosed to Mr Bevin a memorandum wherein he 'emphasised the need to safeguard our Middle East supplies of oil at all costs for our vital strategic needs and our equally vital economic and industrial needs.'[21]

Some months later the Foreign Secretary, in a letter to the Prime Minister, remarked that Mr Shinwell had earlier taken 'a most chauvinistic attitude regarding our oil supplies in Persia'.[22] Mr Bevin's suggestion concerning the transformation of the Anglo-Iranian Oil Company had not borne fruit. Nor had His Majesty's Embassy in Tehran been among the posts which had received from the Foreign Secretary a circular despatch of May 11, 1946, enclosing a statement agreed by the then Ministerial Committee on External Economic Policy and entitled 'The General Policy of His Majesty's Government towards Measures of Nationalisation in Foreign Countries.'[23]

The above statement of general policy laid down that His Majesty's Government 'naturally do not question the right of foreign Governments to . . . place local industries under Government ownership or control. We reserve the right to claim full and appropriate compensation in respect of British industries which might be involved . . . We do not regard payment in foreign currency for local use, or shares in a State enterprise, as adequate compensation to British interests when they hold all or a substantial proportion of the shares in a foreign company . . . We should, therefore, insist on the right of payment across the exchanges in sterling.'

By 1947 British negotiations regarding nationalisations in Czechoslovakia and Poland had led the Board of Trade and the Treasury to favour a more opportunistic approach, especially in respect of exchange control; on their view by then, as summarised in the Foreign Office, 'we should, in each individual case, try to get the maximum for ourselves while conceding the least possible to other countries.'[24] The Foreign Office accordingly proposed to the Board of Trade on August 1, 1947, that it should revise the policy statement of the preceding year regarding foreign nationalisation of British interests.

The end of that same month of August 1947 incidentally marked the conclusion at long last of the negotiations with the Mexican Government which had been dragging on since it had in 1938 expropriated the Mexican Eagle Oil Company, an associate of Royal Dutch Shell, together with the smaller holdings of American oil companies in Mexico. On the behalf of the latter the United States Government had confined itself to demanding 'adequate, effective and prompt compensation', and an American-Mexican settlement had been reached in 1942, somewhat to the detriment of the Mexican Eagle Company. Now in 1947 the latter reached an agreement with the Mexican Government whereby the expropriated company would receive over a period of 15 years compensation of the order of US$ 130 million.

After nearly a year the Board of Trade on July 5, 1948, replied to the letter of August 1, 1947 from the Foreign Office and produced proposals for a revision of the policy statement of 1946. This draft notably substituted 'adequate and effective' for 'full and appropriate' compensation, and included the following: 'We have always

---

[20] E 7877/401G.
[21] *Ibid.*
[22] Francis Williams, *A Prime Minister Remembers* (London, 1961), p. 180.
[23] UE 1838/499/53.
[24] UE 4216/343/53.

recognised that we had to rest our case largely on the principle of equity. It has never been definitely established in international law that foreign countries are bound to give adequate compensation to foreign nationals whose property they have expropriated . . . though there is good material on which to found a case for assuming such a right as a basic principle, and we would always strive to maintain this principle.'[25]

For some reason the revised policy statement was apparently not issued to British representatives abroad. The somewhat outdated statement of 1946 regarding foreign nationalisation of British interests continued to hold the field so far as anything did. Yet this statement stood in evident contrast to the concern of Mr Bevin and Mr Shinwell for the safeguarding of British oil supplies. The potential contradiction in British policy was to emerge as a critical weakness when serious trouble next threatened Abadan.

In contrast to the prescient preoccupations of the Foreign Secretary regarding the future of the Anglo-Iranian Oil Company, it was then, in the aftermath of the Second World War, economically stronger and more prosperous than ever before. Between 1940 and 1949 the number of its employees at Abadan and the outlying wells collectively known as Fields more than doubled, from about 26,000 to 55,000. In the same period, wherein such additional factors as wage increases and inflation operated, the company's bill for wages and local expenditure rose from £650,000 to £20,610,000. Persian staff were trained in courses, agreed with the Persian authorities, at the company's excellent Technical Institute at Abadan.

Mr Bevin had indeed written to Mr Shinwell: 'I am not convinced that the policy of the company is sufficiently progressive. Here we have a company in a country where the standard of life is low and it is not saying much for us that we are a little above the average.'[26] The company, however, forged ahead with taking up the wartime slack in material welfare. In 1948 it spent £4,500,000 upon its manifold welfare services. These came to include three hospitals and 35 dispensaries. In 1950 the company was to spend £2 million on its medical services alone and almost as much again on education. 30 schools were built by the company. Since this great enterprise was situated in the remote and scorching wastes of southern Persia, the Anglo-Iranian Oil Company felt it specially incumbent to provide for its employees comprehensive facilities and amenities, which were, however, by the same token, but little known or appreciated in the rest of Persia.

Conditions of geography and technology isolated the oilfields and refineries of Abadan as a somewhat closed community, and it is perhaps understandable that its atmosphere should to some extent have approximated to that of a British colonial settlement of a slightly old-fashioned pattern. While Abadan was technologically in the van, with the largest and most modern oil refinery in the world, it was socially somewhat hierarchic and paternalistic, remote from the main stream of Persian life and the rising aspirations of Persian nationalism. Mr Attlee subsequently remarked of the outlook of the Anglo-Iranian Oil Company at this period: 'Ernie Bevin tried hard to get them to change and they did make some improvements, but they never made an attempt . . . really to adjust themselves to new conditions . . . It was quite the opposite in Burma. Burmese independence created a difficult position for our

---

[25] UE 5731/1065/53.
[26] E 7357/583/34.

people, but the Burma Oil people went right in and got the Burmese into their show and made it not just a British enterprise but one in which local people were interested.'[27] The failure by contrast of the Anglo-Iranian Oil Company in Persia was more psychological than material.

The stipulation of 1933 for the progressive persianisation of skilled staff had, under the General Plan of 1936 and subsequent working arrangements to meet rapid expansion, become a question of reducing the proportion, rather than the number, of employees who were not Persian. In 1950 this proportion was about 7.3 per cent, some 4,500 men of whom about 2,725 were British and the rest Indian. By 1951 there were indeed to be 68 Persians studying at British universities and technical colleges at the company's expense. Yet it remained true that in Abadan British still heavily outnumbered Persians at the highest level of the best jobs, the best clubs and amenities, including the largest allowances of precious water and ice.

All unskilled labour at Abadan was Persian. It had some grievances of its own, notably the company's employment through contractors of a considerable number of casual labourers (16,410 in 1949) who were not included in the company's wage structure or scheme of facilities. The blackest spot, however, was housing, of which there was an acute shortage at Abadan as throughout most of the world after the Second World War. Large numbers of Persian workers lived in more or less squalid conditions. The company, though, was seeking to remedy them by a vigorous policy of housebuilding in the face of particular difficulties. Tribute was paid to this effort in a report on the company's activities published by the International Labour Office in 1950. This report was on the whole notably favourable to the management of the Anglo-Iranian Oil Company, which was undoubtedly the best, as well as the largest, employer of labour in Persia. Persian trades unions were still in their infancy but the report of the International Labour Office showed that in 1949 only 1,167 out of 42,614 workers on daily wage rates were being paid as little as the Persian legal minimum for the Khuzistan region of 40 rials a day, nominally equivalent to about £2 a week. The company further calculated that this pay was effectively doubled by the value of its subsidised supplies to workers.

In the later 1940s the Anglo-Iranian Oil Company spent capital on an almost unprecedented scale and oil production in the fields based on Abadan nearly doubled between 1945 and 1950, rising from 16.8 to 31.75 million tons a year. The output of the refinery at Abadan had doubled between 1939 and 146, and the figure of 17.8 million tons for the latter year had risen by 1950 to more than 24 million tons.

Such economic prosperity within an otherwise poor country increased political risks for the company inside Persia, enhancing as it did the company's failure to integrate itself sufficiently in the life of the nation. That in turn emphasised the dependence of the Anglo-Iranian Oil Company for its dominant position, in the last resort, upon the political support of His Majesty's Government, as during the crisis in 1932-33, and even perhaps in 1946. The international position of the United Kingdom had, however, weakened rapidly in the aftermath of that Second World War wherein, it is almost true to say, she had by a supreme effort saved the free world at the cost to herself of dire impoverishment.

---

[27] Francis Williams, *op. cit.*, pp. 178-9.

5. The post-war position of Great Britain in the Middle East

Great Britain had emerged from the Second World War as France had done from the first, great in prestige but materially exhausted, almost a marginal victor. By the end of the war Britain's external indebtedness had shot up to £3,355 million, and it was conservatively estimated that during the war her total capital loss of wealth overseas amounted to £4,198 million.[28] Central here was the drain of gold and dollar reserves as one index to the decline of Great Britain as a world Power in relation to the new super-power of the United States, standing over against the hard-stretched Soviet Union.

The United States, after her ruthlessly abrupt termination of Lend-Lease in August 1945, reverted to generous policies of enlightened self-interest at the inception of the Cold War and largely underwrote British and other European post-war reconstruction in terms of the Marshall Aid of the European Recovery Programme. Under this programme Great Britain had by the end of 1950 received $2,694 million. It was against a background in Britain of continued austerity, shortages and rationing that the Labour Government after 1945 devoted much enthusiasm and money to internal policies for channelling the ferment of post-war aspirations into the British social revolution of the Welfare State.

In the military sphere the strength of the armed forces of the United Kingdom was reduced from over 5 million men in 1945 to 787,000 in 1948. In that year the comparable American strength was nearer to double the British figure. The Russians in 1948 had a strength of about 4 million. Furthermore in August 1946 the adoption by the United States of the MacMahon Bill against disclosure of atomic information had put paid to legitimate British claims for Anglo-American atomic co-operation. Great Britain did not explode an atomic bomb until 1952. It was perhaps more than coincidence that in the early aftermath of the Second World war it was Great Britain, more than the much stronger United States, which bore the brunt of Soviet hostility.

Directly after the end of the Second World War Mr Ernest Bevin had decided that, as regards the Middle East, 'His Majesty's Government would continue to assert their political predominance in that area and their overriding responsibility for its defence'. In the same memorandum of September 17, 1945,[29] the Foreign Secretary observed that 'the Americans are commercially on the offensive in the Middle East . . . and we should not make any concession that would assist American commercial penetration into a region which for generations has been an established British market'. It was under British aegis that Mr Bevin hoped to encourage economic expansion in the Middle East in accordance with his policies both of 'peasants not pashas' and of developing the region as a producing area in replacement of India to assist the economy of Great Britain.

Yet in the case of Persia, for instance, the Foreign Secretary was already to be found in April 1946, in connexion with the Russian military withdrawal and northern oil concession, expressing the feeling that as regards untapped oil in south-eastern Persia 'there would be great local political advantage in bringing the Americans into this field and that on general grounds it would be undesirable to seek to exclude them'.[30] This reflected the dilemma of British post-war policy in the Middle East,

---

[28] Cmd 6707 of 1945, *Statistical Material presented during the Washington Negotiations*, pp. 10-12.
[29] E 7151/175G.
[30] E 3479/2806G.

wishing to contain American economic penetration while yet seeking American political support to balance the British decline. In the face of this and of the Soviet menace, a radically new policy in the Middle East was proposed by the Prime Minister, who had already caused the Chief of the Imperial General Staff, Field-Marshal Lord Alanbrooke, to write on September 3, 1945: 'We were shaken by Attlee's new Cabinet paper in which apparently the security of the Middle East must rest on the power of the United Nations.'[31]

The Chancellor of the Exchequer recorded on March. 9 1946: 'Attlee is pressing on the Chiefs of Staff and the Defence Committee a large view of his own, aiming at considerable disengagement from areas where there is a risk of clashing with the Russians. We should pull out, he thinks, from all the Middle East, including Egypt and Greece, make a line of defence across Africa from Lagos to Kenya, and concentrate a large part of our forces in the latter . . . We should put a wide glacis of desert and Arabs between ourselves and the Russians. This is a very fresh and interesting approach, which appeals to me.'[32] It appealed much less to the Chiefs of Staff and the Imperial Defence College. They subsequently advised that the only preventive to attack on the United Kingdom was an effective threat of counter-attack and that the only bases from which Russia could then be attacked were situated in the Near East; the maintenance there of British influence and British forces was therefore essential to the safety of Great Britain; as a corollary it was necessary to secure British oil supplies in the Near East and, if at all possible, communications through the Mediterranean.

After recapitulating this in a minute of January 5, 1947 to Mr Ernest Bevin, the Prime Minister observed that for several reasons, notably the military and economic cost of supporting there 'vested interests and reaction against reform and revolution in the interests of the poor', he considered 'the strategy outlined above as a strategy of despair. I have the gravest doubts as to its efficacy. The deterrent does not seem to me to be sufficiently strong. I apprehend that the pursuit of this policy so far from preventing may precipitate hostilities. Unless we are persuaded that the USSR is irrevocably committed to a policy of world domination and there is no possibility of her alteration, I think that before being committed to this strategy we should seek to come to an agreement with the USSR after consideration with Stalin of all our points of conflict . . . Could we not get an agreement as to oil rights in Persia?'[33]

The Prime Minister's minute was discussed in the Foreign Office and Mr Bevin replied in a minute of January 9, 1947, that he was not convinced that the Prime Minister had really met the strategic case of the Chiefs of Staff. Even apart from that, wrote the Foreign Secretary, 'the political arguments against your proposals seem to me overwhelming . . . a reversal of the whole policy I have been pursuing in the Middle East . . . Your main argument is that our position in the Middle East, even though it is defensive, will seem to the USSR the preparation for an offensive . . . The argument that we must drop any policy that might seem to the Russians a preparation for an offensive is a dangerous one . . . I think we must accept the fact that the present rulers of Russia are committed to the belief that there is a natural conflict between the capitalist and the Communist world . . . It would be as idle to

---

[31] Sir Arthur Bryant, *Triumph in the West* (London, 1959), p. 491.
[32] Lord Dalton, *High Tide and After* (London, 1962, p. 105).
[33] Prime Minister's minute M 15/47 to Foreign Secretary.

place reliance on gaining our own security by large-scale one-sided concessions to Russia as it was with Hitler . . . It would be Munich over again, only on a world scale.'[34]

The Foreign Secretary further argued that 'after our abandonment of India and Burma, a retreat from the Middle East would appear to the world as the abdication of our position as a world Power and encourage India to gravitate towards Russia . . The effect would be felt throughout Africa, and our projects for a base in East Africa and any prospect of holding North Africa would be threatened . . . It would lead the United States to write us off.' As regards specific agreements with the Russians, 'we can probably', wrote Mr Bevin, 'get an agreement about oil rights in Persia, but there is no need to abandon our whole Middle Eastern position to this end.'[35]

The proposals of the Prime Minister for British abandonment of the Middle East as a whole were not put into effect. The British position there was, however, greatly weakened by the end of the British Empire in India on August 15, 1947. Field-Marshal Viscount Alanbrooke subsequently commented: 'With the loss of India and Burma, the keystone of the arch of our Commonwealth Defence was lost, and our Imperial Defence crashed. Without the central strategic reserve of Indian troops ready to operate either east or west we were left impotent and even the smallest of nations were at liberty to twist the lion's tail.' Lord Alanbrooke added: 'And yet I do not see how we could have remained in India and I think we were right in withdrawing when we did; but few realised what the strategic loss would amount to.'[36]

Despite such heavy handicaps and setbacks Great Britain continued, in relation to much of the Middle East, to provide a central core of strength with her special positions and interests in Egypt, Suez and the Sudan, in Libya and Cyprus, East Africa and Aden, around the Arabian shores and the Trucial Coast to the Persian Gulf, Bahrain and Kuwait. The latter States were, together with Transjordan and Iraq, included in the Sterling Area. In Transjordan the Arab Legion received British subsidy and leadership. In Iraq the British presence was manifest in oil interests, in use by the Royal Air Force of bases at Habbaniya and Shaiba, and by the Royal Navy of Iraqi territorial waters in the estuary of the Shatt-al-Arab opposite to Abadan, as in 1946. These military rights had been conferred by the 25-year Anglo-Iraqi Treaty of Alliance of 1930, and were substantially retained by its revision in the Anglo-Iraqi Treaty of Portsmouth of January 15, 1948. Britain, however, thereby surrendered, notably, her facilities in the post and base of Basra. In the event these were nevertheless retained and the treaty of 1930 continued in force owing to the fact that the Treaty of Portsmouth was promptly nullified by violent nationalist opposition in Iraq, symptomatic of the rising tide throughout the Middle East in the face of the decline of Western influence.

Despite immediate gains with Arab opinion, it was perhaps with questionable wisdom in the long run that Great Britain—certainly in French eyes—had helped to edge France out from Syria and the Lebanon at the close of the Second World War. In this connexion the French Foreign Minister, M. Bidault, in June 1945 warned

---

[34] Foreign Secretary's minute PM/47/8 to Prime Minister.
[35] *Ibid.*
[36] Sir Arthur Bryant, *op. cit.,* p. 533.

Great Britain: *Hodie mihi, cras tibi.*[37] By October 1947 Sir Oliver Harvey, then Deputy Under-Secretary of State, was explaining to a meeting in the Foreign Office, held 'to discuss Anglo-French economic relations and the possibility of a Western European Economic Group', that the Foreign Secretary 'now wanted closer integration with France, the joint utilisation of our African resources, and finally the building up of a stable group between the United States and Soviet Russia. Subsequently, Mr Bevin wanted Belgium, the Netherlands, Portugal, Italy and Eire brought in.'[38]

Some days before this meeting of October 8 the French Ambassador in London, in conversation with Sir Oliver Harvey, had alluded to the Anglo-French community of interest in that 'both our countries were becoming increasingly dependent on Middle East oil with its vast resources'.[39] The idea of an Anglo-French exchange of views on the subject was mooted, but was not then pursued, partly, apparently, because M. Massigli himself did not press it and partly because it became overlaid by Anglo-American conversations in Washington on the Middle East.

An early exemplification of M. Bidault's warning was American pressure towards edging Great Britain out of her unhappy mandate for Palestine. At the beginning of 1947 the British Chiefs of Staff had advised that 'any defence plan for the Middle East must centre on the defence of Egypt . . . [which] can only be conducted effectively against attacks from the north by holding Palestine.'[40] Nine months later, in the month after the end of the British Empire in India, His Majesty's Government announced its decisions to transfer its main stores-depot in the Canal Zone to Kenya, and also to relinquish its mandate for Palestine.

The Jewish terrorism and Zionist propaganda which precipitated the inglorious relinquishment of the mandate on May 15, 1948, had so strained Anglo-Jewish relations that there could be no question now of British bases in Israel to buttress those in Egypt, already compromised by increasing Egyptian pressure for revision and whittling down of the Anglo-Egyptian Treaty of 1936. Great Britain got the worst of both worlds. For encouragement of the Jewish National Home since the Balfour Declaration, and now abdication mainly in favour, in practice, of the successfully militant Israel, gravely impaired British influence with that Arab League which British policy had actively supported since 1945, not least in the interests of a friendly cohesion against Soviet expansion in the Middle Eastern theatre of the Cold War.

At the inception of the Cold War the United States, under the Truman Doctrine of March 1947, largely took over the military and economic support of Greece and Turkey which Great Britain was relinquishing. The American Government soon extended this support to Persia, with an American military mission to train and supply the Persian Army and American economic advisers on a Seven-Year Plan. The United States, however, remained remote and relatively inexperienced in relation to Persia which was still closely linked financially with Great Britain, to mutual advantage, through Persia's large sterling revenue from oil. By virtue of the so-called Memorandum of Understanding concluded in October 1947 and annually

---

[37] Editorial note: Today to me, tomorrow to you.
[38] Z 9053/25G.
[39] Z 9053/25G.
[40] E 301/46G.

renewable, Great Britain agreed that Persian sterling might be transferred to American account or to other hard-currency countries in payment, primarily, for essential goods not obtainable on equivalent terms for sterling. This involved a heavy commitment in dollars, and in itself suggested the potential extent to which the United States now stood behind that northern tier of States which formed the Outer Ring against Soviet penetration of the Middle East. Within this ring American influence was also ascendant now in Saudi Arabia.

American oil interests had secured a large concession in Saudi Arabia in 1933, and in 1944 took the title of the Arabian American Oil Company (Aramco). During the Second World War these interests had encouraged American diplomacy in a rather crude policy of supplanting British influence in this kingdom of Ibn Saud, the most effective friend of Britain among the Arabs. Sensitivity regarding oil reached such a pitch that on February 20, 1944, Mr Churchill was telegraphing to President Roosevelt: 'There is apprehension in some quarters here that the United States has a desire to deprive us of our oil assets in the Middle East on which, among other things, the whole supply of our Navy depends.'[41] Two days later President Roosevelt replied that he was 'disturbed about the rumour that the British wish to horn in on Saudi Arabian oil reserves.'[42]

Protracted negotiations between Great Britain and the United States produced the Shinwell-Ickes Agreement on Petroleum of September 24, 1945. Its general purpose was 'to facilitate the orderly development of the international petroleum trade,'[43] to which end the two Governments agreed to establish an international Petroleum Commission. American oil interests, however, frustrated the ratification of this agreement for some governmental supervision of their commercial enterprises.

American oil companies in the Middle East may have retained certain feelings of jealousy, in particular towards the Anglo-Iranian Oil Company and its attitude, as they tended to think, of somewhat aloof superiority. Nevertheless potential rivalries were considerably reduced by a 20-year agreement concluded in 1947 for the supply by the Anglo-Iranian Oil Company of large quantities of crude oil for the refineries of Standard Oil of New Jersey and the Socony-Vacuum Oil company. This was one illustration of the extent to which the operations of British and American oil companies tended to be coordinated. And on November 7, 1947, the previously noticed Anglo-American conversations between diplomatic representatives in Washington resulted in a secret understanding concerning the overall co-ordination of policies in the Middle East. The British and American representatives agreed to recommend to their respective Governments the adoption of a policy 'based on the general principles set forth below . . .

1. The security of the Eastern Mediterranean and of the Middle East is vital to the security of the United States and of the United Kingdom and to world peace.
2. This policy can be implemented only if the British maintain their strong strategic, political and economic position in the Eastern Mediterranean and the Middle East, including the sea approaches to the area through the Straits of Gibraltar and the Red Sea, and if the British and American Governments pursue parallel policies in that area.

---

[41] W 2642/34G.
[42] W 2968/34G.
[43] Cmd 6683, p. 4.

3. It follows from the above that both Governments should endeavour to prevent either foreign countries, commercial interests, British or American or other, or any other influences from making capital for themselves by playing off one of the two countries against the other in the Eastern Mediterranean or the Middle East. It should be the parallel and respective policies of the two Governments to adopt the general principle that they will endeavour to strengthen each other's position in the area on the basis of mutual respect and co-operation. It should be contrary to the policy of either Government to make efforts to increase its country's influence at the expense of the other. Likewise, the policy of the two countries should be to strengthen and improve each other's position by lending each other all possible and proper support. This support should also apply to the retention or development of strategic facilities, including civil air development.'[44]

These impressive principles were accepted, and were confirmed in further Anglo-American conversations in 1949.[45] The degree of Anglo-American co-operation attained in the Middle East in the aftermath of the Second World War was a striking, if somewhat delicate, achievement. It was to be severely tested, not least, nor last, in Persia.

---

[44] AN 3997/3997G.
[45] E 15374/1026/65.

CHAPTER II

THE NEGOTIATION AND NON-RATIFICATION OF THE SUPPLEMENTAL OIL AGREEMENT, OCTOBER 1947-JUNE 1950

1. The Supplemental Oil Agreement of 1949

The Anglo-Iranian Oil Company was not unduly perturbed by the Persian law of October 22, 1947, with its back-handed threat against the company's interests (cf. p. 45). The Persian Government raised several specific questions for discussion and a particular problem was created by the company's finances for 1947. In that year its gross profit more than doubled from about £19 million to £40 million, on about the same quantity of oil produced. If, however, the company were to limit its dividends in accordance with the general policy of the British Labour Government, that would spell a considerable loss of immediate revenue to the Persian Government, whose receipts other than royalty were, under the concession of 1933, directly related to the dividends paid, rather than to the profits made by the company.

The Anglo-Iranian Oil Company represented the position to His Majesty's Government but on May 27, 1948, Sir Stafford Cripps, who had succeeded Mr Dalton as Chancellor of the Exchequer, informed the chairman of the company, Sir William Fraser (later Lord Strathalmond): 'While appreciating your company's wish to safeguard the position of the Imperial Iranian Government, I nevertheless consider it desirable that your company should conform to the policy of dividend stabilisation.'[1] Sir Stafford Cripps had replied in the same sense to a similar representation from Mr Eden on his return from a visit to Persia. In September 1948 Mr Ernest Bevin represented to the Chancellor of the Exchequer that the Persian Government might have 'some legitimate grievance'[2] over the British policy of dividend limitation. That policy was, however, maintained and the Anglo-Iranian Oil Company complied with it.

The resultant position was that from the gross profit of about £40 million in 1947, the Persian Government received only the same amount, about £7 million, as in 1946; whereas His Majesty's Government drew about £15 million in taxation alone. This prolonged the pattern of the years 1939 to 1946 when 'on tax alone His Majesty's Government was receiving more than twice Persian's total oil income'.[3] Furthermore the British exchequer gained to a considerable extent from the Persian Government's loss, since those profits which might have been distributed as dividends were liable to taxation on transfer to the company's general reserve. On the other hand the Persian share of distributed profits was appreciably reduced by the company's preferential sales to the Admiralty at the secret price of 20s to 30s per ton of oil.[4]

In order to remedy the prejudicial situation which had arisen for the Persian Government, its representatives and those of the Anglo-Iranian Oil Company began conversations in 1948, as had been suggested by Sir Stafford Cripps and Sir William Fraser. These conversations related, in effect, to modifications of the 15-year-old

---

[1] E 12132/1223/34.
[2] E 11662/1223/34.
[3] EP1531/105 of 1950.
[4] This Persian loss for 1950 was estimated in the Foreign Office as being 'up to £600,000' when the market price was 70s per ton: cf. EP 1538/1.

concession, and included discussion of an arrangement for a 50-50 division of profits. Nothing came of this proposal since the Persian Government claimed half the profits from the company's operations not only within Persia, which the company was disposed to consider, but throughout the world. The company, urged from the Foreign Office to reach agreement with the Persian Government, ultimately did so along other lines. A Supplemental Agreement to the company's concession agreement of 1933 was signed in Tehran on July 17, 1949, by Mr N.A. Gass, a managing director of the Anglo-Iranian Oil Company, and M. Gulshayan, Minister of Finance in the Government of the somewhat ineffectively agreeable M. Saed.

The Supplemental Oil agreement increased the tonnage royalty of the Persian Government from 4s to 6s gold and the tax composition to 1s, together equivalent to 14s 5d sterling per ton after the devaluation of 1949. In addition to the 20 per cent of the gross sum distributed to the company's ordinary stockholders, as paid under the terms of the main agreement of 1933, the Persian Government was now to receive 20 per cent also of any amount placed to the company's general reserve, before deduction of British income tax, instead of receiving 20 per cent of the company's reserves on the expiry of the concession in 1993, as had been provided in 1933. The sum of these two annual payments was guaranteed at a minimum of £4 million. In addition the special discount on sales of oil products within Persia was increased from 10 to 25 per cent.

The Supplemental Agreement was retroactive and on its coming into force the company would make an additional payment to the Persian Government of £14.5 million. A further £9.4 million was to accrue in respect of 1949. In general the new agreement would probably yield the Persian Government less revenue than under the formula of 'half the profits of operation within the country' in a year of high profits, but more in a bad year. And in fact no concession on such a 50-50 basis was yet operative in the Middle East: nor any concession on terms so favourable to the local Government as those of the Supplemental Agreement.

The Supplemental Agreement largely increased the financial profit of the Persian Government without altering the main structure of the concession of 1933. The new agreement, though comparatively simple in essentials, was couched in terms of considerable complexity, partly owing to its supplemental character. This defect rather points the question whether it might not have been preferable to try to negotiate a fresh agreement altogether to take account of a position which had changed radically since the concession of 1933 was concluded at a time of low profits from an oil production concentrated in Persia; whereas by 1947 profits were high and, while Persian oil remained much the largest interest of the Anglo-Iranian Oil Company, it was in 1949 deriving 5.6 million tons from Kuwait and 1.4 millions from Iraq, with Qatar coming into the picture; also, the company's tanker fleet of 134 vessels was more than half as large again as that of 1934.

While a 50-50 share of the company's world-wide profits, which the Persian Government had sought, would evidently have been unreasonable in current terms, some lower percentage on that overall basis might perhaps have possessed the attractive merits of simplicity and of broadly exemplifying that Anglo-Persian partnership which Mr Bevin was anxious to encourage. Such an arrangement would among other things have met Persian suspicions that profits on Persian operations were pegged down in favour of the company's interests outside Persia.

An alternative might possibly have been some hiving off of the strictly Persian operations of the Anglo-Iranian Oil Company into a separate company. Persian directors might have sat on upon this local board, if not upon that of the parent company: its articles of association laid down that all directors must be British subjects, though they co-operated with a Persian delegate in London. A possible accompaniment or variation might have been some arrangement for direct shareholding by the Persian Government, as under the original terms of the D'Arcy Concession and as had been mooted again before the concession of 1933. This might have provided some match to the plan which the Burmah Oil Company, at the request of the Burmese Government, had put forward in 1948; this proposed that the Government should hold a third share in the Burmese oil industry and eventually produced the joint Venture of 1954. In 1948 the Burmah Oil Company, of which Sir William Fraser was also a director, was indeed still in difficulties over restoring production after wartime destruction and insurrection: a very different situation from that of the Anglo-Iranian.

The Anglo-Iranian Oil Company could, furthermore, adduce strong arguments regarding sanctity of contract in the 60-year concession of 1933 and the dangers of unnecessarily radical departures when the fresh claims of the Persian Government could be equitably and even generously met by the Supplemental Agreement. But if this was financially true, it was less so politically. The basic grievance of the Persians subsisted: a great industrial monopoly under wholly British ownership wielded preponderant power over the weak economy of their native country.

The last article of the Supplemental Agreement read: 'This agreement shall come into force after ratification by the Majlis, and on the date of its promulgation by Decree of His Imperial Majesty the Shah. The Government undertakes to submit this agreement as soon as possible for ratification by the Majlis.' The Persian Government duly submitted the agreement to the Majlis two days after signature, on July 19, 1949, and on the next day it was published in the Persian Press. The Supplemental Agreement was debated on July 23-26 in the Majlis, where it was weakly defended by the Government of M. Saed—His Majesty's Ambassador thought that many Ministers had always been against it. Whereas the Opposition was strongly led, largely to factional ends, by adherents of Dr Musaddiq, described by Sir John Le Rougetel as 'a whole-hearted but hysterical jingo'.[5] They claimed that the terms were inadequate, and did not meet a number of points advanced earlier by the Persian Government, notably as regards prejudice to its share of profits caused by the company's preferential sales of oil to the British Admiralty, provision for Persian participation in the direction of the company and acceleration of Persianisation of the higher staff.

A filibuster against the agreement was staged by one of Dr Musaddiq's sympathisers, M. Husein Makki, the ambitious and notoriously 'die-hard Deputy' for Abadan (Foreign Office minute of August 1949).[6] M. Makki had earlier that year supported an unpassed bill for the cancellation of the concession of the Anglo-Iranian Oil Company and now, it is reported, asked M. Gulshayan the loaded question: 'Now that the legality of the 1933 Concession is in question, why are you so insistent that it should be confirmed by the ratification of this supplemental

[5] EP 1011/1 of 1950.
[6] E 9639/1531/34.

agreement?'[7]

M. Makki talked out the debate on the Supplemental Agreement and no decision on it was reached before the 15th Majlis was dissolved on July 28, 1949. Sir John Le Rougetel believed that 'with a little more cohesion and determination on the part of the Government and the President of the Majlis' the agreement could have been passed by a substantial majority. Sir John Le Rougetel was, however, convinced that if His Majesty's Embassy had listened to suggestions that it should stimulate the adoption of the Supplemental Agreement in the Majlis by according 'moral support' to friendly Deputies, it would, even if it had not defeated its purpose, have been 'undesirable and, in the long run, prejudicial to our interests'.[6] In the event British interests were anyway to be gravely prejudiced.

The latter part of the year was taken up with protracted procedures and pressures of a Persian election, for the 16th Majlis. Tension was heightened in November 1949 when M. Hazhir, the unpopular Minister of Court, was assassinated by a member of the fanatical religious sect of the Ridayan-i-Islam, the Sacrificial Warriors of Islam, controlled by M. Kashani. In the Tehran elections governmental gerrymandering did not ultimately prevent a majority of seats from being won by Dr Musaddiq and members of his newly-formed National Front.

The year 1950 opened with the Supplemental Oil Agreement still unratified.

2. British objection to modifying the Supplemental Agreement early in 1950

At the opening of 1950 the Shah of Persia, who was on close terms with His Majesty's Ambassador and anxious for ratification of the Supplemental Oil Agreement, told Sir John Le Rougetel that in order to secure this the Anglo-Iranian Oil Company must make some additional concession: especially since under the agreement His Majesty's Government would still be deriving more from the company in taxation than the Persian Government would receive. This proposal provoked the comment in the Eastern Department of the Foreign Office on January 11, 1950, that Persian opposition to the agreed terms of the Supplemental Agreement was due to 'emotion and prejudice', and that 'the Persian appetite for concessions "grows with what it feeds on" and any weakening of our present attitude [of adhering to the agreed terms] at this stage would instantly wreck whatever chances we may have of getting ratification.'[8]

Two days earlier, on January 9, Sir John Le Rougetel had further reported that Mr Wiley, the American Ambassador in Tehran, had told him that he 'did not believe we should reach agreement [with Persia concerning oil] if we adopt a "take it or leave it" attitude. I told him that as far as I was aware that is precisely what we intended to do and that whatever the company's attitude might be His Majesty's Government would not press the company to make further concessions.'[9] This expectation was substantially confirmed by the Foreign Office at the end of January in reply to an unofficial expression of concern from the United States Embassy in London. The opening of 1950 already revealed an Anglo-American difference of appreciation concerning the ratification of the Supplemental Agreement, which was to persist, more or less, throughout the year.

---

[7] L.P. Elwell-Sutton, *Persian Oil* (London, 1955), pp. 180-1.
[8] EP 1531/1.
[9] EP 1531/2.

Early in 1950 Mr George McGhee, a former oil executive who was Assistant Secretary of State for Near Eastern Affairs in the State Department, was also urging concessions to the Persians upon the representative in New York of the Anglo-Iranian Oil Company, which Mr McGhee considered 'too conservative'.[10] The Assistant Secretary 'emphasised the general importance of early ratification in that agreements in other countries were contingent' upon it. On February 2 the British Embassy in Washington was proposing to inform Mr McGhee 'that the one certain way of dragging out negotiations indefinitely is if the Persian Government should be given any grounds for believing that the United States was pressing the company to modify further the terms of the Supplemental Agreement'.[11] Such a warning was timely. On February 7 the Persian Ambassador in Washington, M. Husein Ala, asked the United States Government to intervene with His Majesty's Government in favour of more favourable terms, but was refused. In this connexion it was reported that Mr McGhee recognised that on an output of 25 million tons the Supplementary Agreement would yield Persia a higher rate per ton than under the agreement which Aramco had with Saudi Arabia.[12] On March 9 M. Saed, the Persian Prime Minister, suggested to Mr V.G. Lawford, Counsellor in His Majesty's Embassy, that discreet publicity might be done on such lines. The Shah too suggested publicity by the Anglo-Iranian Oil Company.

During his conversation of March 9 with Mr Lawford, the Persian Premier had expressed grave anxiety regarding the effect just then of the company's recent dismissal of some 500 Persian workers at Abadan. At the Foreign Office Mr Michael Wright, Assistant Under-Secretary of State superintending the Eastern Department, thereafter suggested to Mr Gass that this action 'from the company's point of view could not have been worse timed'.[13] Sir William Strang, Permanent under-Secretary of State for Foreign Affairs, also referred to the timing, in relation to the Supplemental Agreement, in a letter of March 16, 1950, to Sir William Fraser. But the Anglo-Iranian Oil Company assured the Persian authorities that for the time being it would phase further reductions of staff so as to cause the least upset.

On March 19, 1950, M. Saed resigned and was succeeded by the astute, if mercenary, M. Ali Mansur. On the following day, Sir Francis Shepherd presented to the Shah his credentials as His Majesty's Ambassador in succession to Sir John Le Rougetel. The Shah discussed the Supplemental Agreement with the new Ambassador and 'mentioned that he had heard that the Americans were negotiating a new agreement with Saudi Arabia which might result in a higher rate of royalty. I said', reported Sir Francis, 'that I had heard nothing of such a new agreement.'[14] Nor had the Foreign Office according to a minute of early April in Eastern Department. There is no evidence that this report was reviewed there in relation to Mr McGhee's earlier linking of ratification of the Supplemental Agreement with 'agreements in other countries'; nor of any attempt to check the Shah's information through His Majesty's Ambassadors at Washington and Jedda, the Anglo-Iranian Oil Company, the Ministry of Fuel and Power or the representatives of the State Department who visited London in the following month.

---

[10] EP 1531/4.
[11] *Ibid.*
[12] EP 1531/7.
[13] EP 1532/7.
[14] EP 1891/2.

3. The Anglo-American Conversations of May 1950

In May 1950 the American Secretary of State, Mr Dean Acheson, visited London and participated in general conversations with Mr Bevin concerning the Middle East; complementary Anglo-American discussions on the official level were held at the Foreign Office. These conversations produced declarations on May 19 and 25. The latter was the Anglo-Franco-American Tripartite Declaration directed towards the pacification of the Middle East, notably as between Israel and the Arab States. The declaration of May 19 concerning Persia took the form of separate but parallel British and American statements on agreed lines. Mr Bevin referred to his speech of May 18, 1949, after the signature of the North Atlantic Treaty, and now reaffirmed 'that His Majesty's Government remain vitally concerned in the independence, integrity and security of Greece, Turkey and Persia'.[15]

In the preceding Anglo-American conversations it had been agreed that of the three countries forming the outer bastion of the Middle East against the Soviet Union, Persia was the weakest and was 'an important and critical sore spot'.[16] Conditions were deteriorating in Persia, where an economic depression coincided with one in morale comparable, in the view of the State Department, to that which had earlier beset Nationalist China. Persian hopes of the International Bank for Reconstruction and Development may have been rather disappointed and a visit by the Shah to the United States had not produced the results looked for. The State Department now proposed that Persia should be offered an American loan by the Export-Import Bank, and Mr Hare, the leading American official at the talks at the Foreign Office, had also suggested on May 5 that His Majesty's Government 'might do something to expedite the ratification of the Anglo-Iranian Supplemental Oil Agreement. Such a step might in itself settle the whole problem'[17] through the additional royalties which it would secure to the Persian Government.

In reply Mr G.W. Furlonge, Head of the Eastern Department of the Foreign Office, said at the Anglo-American meeting on May 5 that this ratification 'was our first important objective', but pointed out that no specific application for modification of the Supplemental Agreement had been received from the Persian Government; he did not think that in the meantime His Majesty's Government would feel justified in asking the Anglo-Iranian Oil Company to take the initiative in that direction. Mr Hare mentioned a report that the company favoured some delay in ratification. Sir Francis Shepherd subsequently suggested that this inaccurate impression 'may have been created by its policy of not appearing anxious about ratification'.[18]

On May 10, 1950, Mr Wright felt able to assure Mr Dean Acheson that as regards Persia, 'the United States and the United Kingdom were in close accord and our representatives in Tehran were pursuing a common line of persuasion and explanation with the Persians to the effect that it was really in their best interests to ratify the Supplemental Oil Agreement'.[19] This assessment was perhaps somewhat optimistic in the subsequent light of a further meeting of British and American officials on May 16. Mr Hare then returned to the charge, observing that the State

---

[15] R 1074/1: *The Times*, May 20, 1950.
[16] E 1023/42G.
[17] E 1023/43G.
[18] EP 1022/3.
[19] ZP 2/161G.

Department 'felt that oil companies in the Middle East had to carry responsibilities over and above those of an ordinary commercial enterprise. They had wondered whether the United Kingdom Government were satisfied that sufficient account had been taken of political considerations in the negotiation of the [Supplemental] Agreement. Mr Wright said that he could give a full assurance on this point . . . He would not ask the State Department to express any opinion on the terms of the Agreement but he hoped that they might be willing to point out to the Persians that whatever the faults of the Agreement it did offer them very solid benefits and that after talking with the Foreign Office, they were convinced that there was no hope of the Persians obtaining any further concession.'[20] When, later in the meeting, Mr Furlonge 'wondered whether the Americans might be prepared to instruct the United States Ambassador to approach the Shah immediately' in this sense, Mr Hare replied that 'they had not taken up the matter with the Persians hitherto because of the doubts about the Agreement which he had mentioned. They would, however, consider Mr Furlonge's suggestion in the light of the discussion.'[21] This appears to have been the furthest that the Americans then went. They also avoided any commitment that they would, as Sir Francis Shepherd strongly urged, postpone the Export-Import Bank Loan till after ratification of the Supplemental Agreement.

On May 23, 1950, the Foreign Office sent the American Embassy in London an explanatory memorandum on the Supplemental Agreement, further defending the policy, commercially agreeable to the Anglo-Iranian Oil Company, of no concessions to sweeten ratification. Two days later Mr Furlonge was informed that the State Department held that 'any pressure by the United States on the Persian Government to ratify the Supplemental Oil Agreement would be most undesirable since this was entirely a business arrangement between the United Kingdom and Persia',[22] where it was unpopular and ratification might be delayed for several months: which Mr Furlonge thought unduly pessimistic. In reply to further representations the State Department told His Majesty's Embassy in Washington on June 6, 1950, 'that Mr Wiley had all along been impressing on the Persians the importance and advantages of ratification, but they are not prepared to place him in the position of having to express to the Persians an opinion on the terms . . . and on the possibility of obtaining or advisability of pressing for concessions.'[23] Mr (later Sir) Eric Berthoud, Assistant under-Secretary superintending economic departments of the Foreign Office, minuted that he could understand this American reluctance to come out openly in favour of this agreement.

4. The low level of British publicity in Persia in 1950

During the Anglo-Persian conversations of May 1950 [*sic* ?Anglo-American] the Foreign Office had not concealed from the Americans a certain difference of opinion with the Anglo-Iranian Oil Company concerning publicity in Persia for the agreement. On February 6 Sir John Le Rougetel had written to Mr Wright: 'Much—indeed everything—will depend upon the degree to which [Sir William] Fraser is prepared to allow his local representatives some degree of freedom in explaining the

---

[20] E 1023/72G.
[21] *Ibid.*
[22] EP 11345/10.
[23] EP 11345/6.

value of the agreement before it is discussed by the Majlis. Unless some action is taken in this respect, and so far complete silence has been imposed, I am afraid I see little chance of the agreement going through.'[24] On April 21 Sir Francis Shepherd likewise 'most strongly' urged local propaganda by the company to counter the 'profound ignorance of benefits'[25] of the agreement. After each of these representations the Foreign Office took the matter up with the company only to receive negative replies since the company, and evidently its chairman in particular, felt that if it indulged in direct publicity in Persia it would incur the odium of 'foreign propaganda', whereas the supine Persian Government could and should publicise the case for the agreement.

On May 9 Mr R.A. Beaumont of the Information Policy Department of the Foreign Office suggested that as regards publicity for the Supplemental Agreement the Foreign Office might establish contact, apparently for the first time in this connexion, with Mr A.H.T. Chisholm, the company's Public Relations Officer in London, with a view to relay by official information services of material which he might have published in England. Nearly a month later, on June 7, Mr Leavett, dealing with Persian affairs in the Eastern Department of the Foreign Office, approved this proposal but did not dissent from the following rider which Mr Beaumont had added: 'We should not however undertake, in my view, to do direct publicity on behalf of the company, particularly since they are very "weak-kneed" about doing it themselves.'[26] The fallible logic of this argument scarcely matched the urgent warnings of the Ambassadors in Tehran.

Mr Beaumont's observations were minuted on the regular report from the British Embassy in Tehran on information activities in Persia for the first quarter of 1950. The report stated: 'The Persians have carefully watched Americans reports on the Persian oil question and have taken every opportunity to allege that the oil royalties paid by American companies to other Governments are much more generous . . . the general increased resentment against the oil concession has caused a widespread anti-British feeling among all classes . . . It is extremely difficult for us to combat this.'[27] In these circumstances it was perhaps particularly unfortunate that the post of Information Officer at the Embassy in Tehran was left unfilled throughout 1950; though very good work was done by the comparatively junior Acting Information Office, Miss F.M. Young.

The Assistant Under-Secretary of State superintending the Information Departments of the Foreign Office, Mr C.F.A. Warner, had a conversation on May 1, 1950, with M. Bahram Shahrukh, Persian Director-General of Press and Propaganda, then visiting London. M. Shahrukh was an intelligent and agile propagandist who, having been a broadcaster in favour of Germany during the Second World War, now professed his desire to collaborate in the Cold War against Russia and in improving Anglo-Persian relations. To this end, Mr Warner recorded, 'M. Shahrukh wished to undertake publicity in favour of the Anglo-Iranian Oil Company's Supplemental Oil Agreement . . . He had seen the Anglo-Iranian Oil Company in London and, he hoped, persuaded them to canvass the benefits of the

---

[24] EP 1531/11.
[25] EP 1531/4.
[26] PG 13416/2.
[27] *Ibid.*

agreement in Persia. He would attempt discreetly to do likewise.'[28]

M. Shahrukh appears to have taken the main initiative in urging closer Anglo-Persian co-operation in publicity, representing that the Soviet Union was broadcasting to Persia for 15 hours a day. At that period the Persian service of the BBC amounted to three-quarters of an hour a day. Within these limits it continued to be very successful (cf. p. 43), and Mr Shahrukh arranged to relay a quarter of an hour of the BBC programmes daily from Radio Tehran. These influential BBC programmes, however, did not in general venture upon such delicate themes as the merits of the Supplemental Agreement.

5. The reintroduction of the Supplemental Agreement in the Majlis and the advent of General Razmara in June 1950

Towards the end of May 1950 the Shah told Sir Francis Shepherd that he had informed M. Ali Mansur of his desire that the Oil Agreement should be ratified as soon as possible and had instructed him to begin preparing for its passage through the Majlis within the next few days. Sir Francis Shepherd handed the Shah a copy of a 'Child's Guide' to the Supplemental Agreement, which had been communicated to M. Mansur. The Shah referred once more to the possibility of 'some form of lubrication for the agreement'.[29] On June 4 it was announced that the Anglo-Iranian Oil Company had advanced a further £6 million to the impecunious Persian Government.

The Persian Ministers, however, still sought some improvement of the Supplemental Agreement itself, which they claimed was necessary in order to secure ratification by the Majlis. Sir Francis Shepherd had earlier suggested that their aim here was not so much economic, with reference to the actual terms of the agreement, as political, so that they could claim to have secured an improvement on the agreement signed by their predecessors.[30] Indeed His Majesty's Ambassador had quickly formed the personal view that the Supplemental Agreement was politically obsolescent, and he judiciously warned the Anglo-Iranian Oil Company as to the probability that some Persian direction of the industry within Persia must lie in the not distant future. For the present, on June 7, 1950, the Persian Ambassador in London officially asked Mr Kenneth Younger, the Minister of State in the Foreign Office, who was then acting for Mr Bevin, to press the company to improve its terms; this was refused. On the same day a similar conversation took place in Tehran between His Majesty's Ambassador and M. Husein Ala, who had returned from his Embassy in Washington to become Foreign Minister.

While still in Washington, on May 2 M. Ala had had a conversation with Mr B.A.B. Burrows, Counsellor in the British Embassy there and formerly head of Eastern Department; on this occasion reference was made to a suggestion in 1948 (cf. p. 57) that Persia might receive 50 per cent of the Anglo-Iranian Oil Company's profits on its operations in Persia, on the Venezuelan model.[31] M. Ala reverted to this suggestion in his conversation of June 7 with Sir Francis Shepherd and put it forward as one of three points upon which he and M. Mansur considered that the

---

[28] PG 1342/3.
[29] EP 1052/3.
[30] EP 1022/3.
[31] EP 1531/16.

Supplemental Agreement would require modification in order to ensure ratification. The other two points were Persian inspection of the books of the Anglo-Iranian Oil Company (M. Ala admitted that this related to Persian concern over possible loss from the secret terms of the contract with the Admiralty), and acceleration of persianisation of staff.[32] His Majesty's Ambassador referred to these three proposals next day in a conversation with the Shah and repeated to him, in particular, that 'an agreement on the Venezuelan 50-50 analogy would not, in fact, bring the Iranian Government any advantages'.[33] Sir Francis Shepherd told the Shah, however, that M. Ala's three proposals 'indicated that the area of difference was being narrowed', as compared with a memorandum which M. Mansur had left with His Majesty's Ambassador on May 30. The latter had described this memorandum in general terms only, in a letter of June 5 to Mr Furlonge, as an unhelpful 're-hash of a number of points which had originally been brought forward at the beginning of the negotiations between the Government and the company'.[34] The Eastern Department of the Foreign Office was, however, less optimistic that M. Ala's points meant that the Persian Government was now satisfied on others regarding the Supplemental Agreement.[33]

His Majesty's Ambassador in Tehran recorded M. Ala's three proposals of June 7 incidentally in his despatch of June 12, but not in his telegram of June 10, reporting his conversation of June 8 with the Shah. This despatch was received in the Foreign Office on June 16 and was first minuted, in Eastern Department as indicated above, on June 24. No separate record of the important conversation of June 7 between Sir Francis Shepherd and M. Ala was sent to the Foreign Office at that time. Nor was it mentioned in a telegram of June 15 wherein His Majesty's Ambassador enquired regarding particulars of the Venezuelan formula, as compared with the Supplemental Agreement. A telegram from the Foreign Office replied on June 21 that it was impossible to draw any firm conclusion concerning the comparative advantages of the two kinds of agreement.[35]

After his first arrival in Tehran Sir Francis Shepherd had confessed to 'some bewilderment'[36] at the state of Persian politics. But at the same time, on April 28, 1950, he had advanced as one of his first impressions that danger from Communist action by the Tudeh Party was limited. 'I rather think', he presciently wrote, 'that the more immediate danger lies in the existence of a political vacuum. The National Front is at present the only political party, but it is a negative body with little internal cohesion. It is none the less a party of sorts and the political vacuum elsewhere is only too likely to drive politicians into its arms.'[37]

The Persian political vacuum in 1950 was still, largely, that left by the disappearance of Reza Shah. If the breakdown of his centralised Government had been masked by Allied control during the war, M. Qavam had thereafter not succeeded in matching his recovery of Azerbaijan by a political reconstruction of Persia through his Democrat Party. Nor had the assumption of larger powers (rights of dissolving the Majlis and nominating half the newly constituted Senate) in 1949

---

[32] EP 1531/179 of 1951.
[33] EP 1016/53.
[34] EP 1016/46.
[35] EP 1531/22.
[36] EP 1022/2.
[37] *Ibid.*

by the intelligent but weak young Shah produced the hoped-for improvement. Persia remained subject to a feeble central Government, a corrupt and inefficient bureaucracy and an inchoate Parliament, all primarily recruited at the top from the small and traditional class of rich, cultured, absentee landlords. This reflected the enduring feudal pattern of Islam wherein the other elements remained the conservative bazaar merchants and Muslim clergy, a generally illiterate and wretched peasantry, and still powerful tribes such as the Bakhtiari and the Qashqai. This pattern was only beginning to be modified by such newer elements as industrialists, an industrial proletariat and a professional and semi-intellectual middle class reflected in the venal, sensationalist but not uninfluential Press.

In these conditions the aggressive National Front in 1950 commanded an influence in the Majlis quite disproportionate to its muster there of some 10 votes out of 120. The fact that Dr Musaddiq was himself a wealthy landowner and related to the Qajar dynasty symbolised the conservative, rather than radical, affiliations of his party in social policies. The radicalism of the National Front, and such cohesion as it possessed, were to be found rather in the xenophobic propaganda wherewith it played upon Persian susceptibilities by ascribing the ills of the country not to national shortcomings but to the Anglo-Iranian Oil Company, the milch cow now cast as the great scapegoat. Between April and June that year, reported the British Embassy in Tehran, 'we have had to face a growing barrage of abuse in Parliament and Press'.[38]

In the Foreign Office Mr Leavett minuted on June 15: 'It is clear that the Mansur Government has proved even more spineless than its predecessor—to the serious detriment of British interests.'[39] Two days later M. Mansur dismissed M. Shahrukh, who was heavily under fire since it had been revealed, apparently in a broadcast by the BBC, that he had had discussions in London with the Anglo-Iranian Oil Company. This dismissal displeased the Shah, who told Sir Francis Shepherd that he regarded M. Shahrukh 'as the only capable propaganda expert in the country'.[40] The Shah had already lost confidence in M. Mansur, and proposed to replace him by the energetic Chief of the Persian General Staff, General Razmara, who, as Sir Francis Shepherd subsequently observed, 'enjoyed the somewhat outspoken support of the American Embassy'[41] in the hope that he would co-operate in the American programme of economic assistance to Persia. In conversation with the Shah on June 8 Sir Francis Shepherd had mentioned, as a possible alternative to General Razmara, the generally pro-British and anti-Soviet M. Sayyid Zia-ud-Din who, after supporting the Anglo-Persian agreement of 1919, had briefly been Prime Minister after Reza Khan's *coup* in 1921 until his honest zeal for radical reform forced him into exile for over 20 years, during which he achieved practical success as a farmer in Palestine. Now, however, the Shah brushed aside Sir Francis Shepherd's suggestion of M. Sayyid Zia with the remark that 'he was something of a long-haired eccentric and had not proved his capacity for organisation'.[42]

Ten days later, on June 18, His Majesty's Ambassador informed the Persian Monarch that, if he appointed General Razmara Prime Minister, 'the appointment

---

[38] PG 13416/3.
[39] EP 1016/49.
[40] EP 1016/54.
[41] EP 1531/340 of 1951.
[42] EP 1016/53.

would please His Majesty's Government'.[43] In this connexion, however, British and American representations were made to the Shah as to the need for action on constitutional lines, though there would be no objection to the dissolution of the obstructive Majlis provided that fresh elections were duly held. Time, though, was running short and the existing Majlis was active.

On June 13 the tottering M. Ali Mansur had asked the Majlis to take up the Supplemental Agreement again and to appoint a Special Oil Commission. He did not, however, prevent this commission from including Dr Musaddiq as Chairman, M. Makki and a disproportionate strength of their National Front: six deputies in all out of 18 members. This heavy step with regard to the agreement had thus already been taken when General Razmara assumed office as Persian Prime Minister on June 26, 1950, the day after war broke out in Korea. Such was the scale of events in the middle of the 20th century that this development in the Far East swiftly influenced Anglo-American thinking about the Middle East and Persia in particular, as a broader background of preoccupation in relation to the unresolved fate of the Supplemental Oil Agreement.

---

[43] EP 1016/54.

CHAPTER III

THE GOVERNMENT OF GENERAL RAZMARA AND THE WITHDRAWAL OF THE SUPPLEMENTAL OIL AGREEMENT, JUNE-DECEMBER 1950

1. War in Korea and Anglo-American military consultations regarding Persia

The eruption of the cold war into active hostilities in Korea promoted, at the suggestion of Mr Attlee to President Truman, exploratory Anglo-American defence conversations, held in Washington in strict secrecy on July 20-24, 1950. The chief British representatives, His Majesty's Ambassador, Sir Oliver Franks, and Lord Tedder, Chairman of the British Joint Services Mission in Washington, had fruitful meetings with General Omar Bradley, Chairman of the American Joint Chief of Staff, and Dr Philip Jessup of the State Department. With regard to Korea the British representatives agreed to reconsider the question of supplying a British contingent in the light of American representations to that end; a Commonwealth contingent of about 22,000 men subsequently participated with the predominantly American forces of the United Nations in Korea. The Washington talks further gave summary consideration to the possibilities of having to counter Communist aggression throughout the world, notably in the Middle East.

At these defence talks in Washington 'the British representative pointed out the difficulties . . . of their assisting, other than to a certain extent with air forces, in the defence of the outer ring of the Middle East, that is primarily Iran and Turkey . . . The United Kingdom would be obliged, in case of general war, to concentrate on the defence of the inner core which is centred in and about Egypt.'[1] This statement reflected some degree of divergence in the strategic approach to the Middle East adopted by the Americans, usually starting from the outer ring as part of the global containment of Communism, and by the British, thinking outwards from the inner core of their traditional interests in the Middle East; even though there was no British underestimate of 'the vital importance' of Persia, generally regarded as a likely successor to Korea. It was agreed that an overt Soviet attack against the Persian stopline would raise an immediate question of general war.

In the Anglo-American conversations, 'while the United States pointed out that the defence of Iran must be primarily a British responsibility, it was agreed that the United Kingdom and United States should consult together in regard to a means of meeting this problem', recognised as including 'the question of demolition of Iranian oil wells in case of Soviet attack'.[2] Mr Attlee telegraphed on July 30 to Commonwealth Prime ministers concerning the Washington talks: 'The Persian oilfields being of vital concern to world economy, the seriousness was recognised of any situation which might result in Persia being overrun by the Russians.'[3]

Two days later, on August 1, 1950, the Defence Committee of the Cabinet considered a memorandum from the Ministry of Fuel and Power proposing that the highest priority be given to military arrangements for the protection of Persian oil

---

[1] ZP 6/12G.
[2] *Ibid.*
[3] ZP 6/14G.

supplies 'against covert attack in the shape of a local incident'.[4] The committee recognised that 'the effect upon our economy of the loss of Persian oil, and possibly also the oil in Iraq and Kuwait would be so crippling that measures of reinsurance ought to be pursued',[5] notably by asking the United States to provide a strategic stockpile of American oil in Great Britain. This recommendation in practice looked towards the acceleration of a world oil survey which Great Britain and the United States had agreed in the preceding May to undertake jointly. The Minister of State in the Foreign Office was now also to arrange for further discussions with the Americans concerning aid for the Persian Seven-Year Plan; and labour conditions at Abadan were to be studied with a view to minimising the possibility of unrest.

The Defence Committee recognised that in case of trouble around Abadan there were no British troops available for prompt despatch, as had been done from India in 1946 with 'most satisfactory results'. The committee noted, however that the British Chiefs of Staff were already examining 'what military action could be taken to protect the Persian oilfields against both external and internal threats'.[5] This study arose from a request made by the Defence Transition Committee on July 17, before the Washington talks, for an examination of measures to protect British oil supplies throughout the world.[6] This examination of British interests naturally, though perhaps not wholly fortunately, tended thereafter to be subordinated, as regards Persia, to Anglo-American planning.

Throughout August the British Chiefs of Staff, acting through the Joint Planning Staff in collaboration with the Foreign Office, were following up the defence talks at Washington by preparing a study of military possibilities in Persia, issued as COS(50)343 on September 4. This plan estimated that 'the Russians are not yet prepared to risk global war which would result from a direct clash between Russian and Allied forces. Small United Kingdom or United States forces may therefore by their mere presence be sufficient in present circumstances to halt the advance of the Russian troops.'[7] In the light of this and of the estimate, in paper JIC(49)80, that it would take two Russian divisions and two air-regiments 45 days to cross Persia to the southern oilfields, the Chiefs of Staff recommended that if Russia invaded Persia, or a Communist régime was established regionally in Azerbaijan or in all Persia, His Majesty's Government should, rather than declare war, forthwith send one brigade with air-support from the Middle East garrison to Abadan and deploy forces in Iraq, with Persian and Iraqi consent. This operation, designated Course C, was a calculated risk since for fully effective protection a division would be required in South Persia; but for that the necessary reinforcements were not then available to the United Kingdom or her allies. In a fourth eventuality, particularly feared by the Ministry of Fuel and Power, the Chiefs of Staff similarly recommended that Russian fomenting of large-scale disorders in the oil-areas of South Persia should be countered by the despatch to Abadan of a brigade, covered by simultaneous diplomatic action.

On August 12, 1950, the Permanent Under-Secretary of State for Foreign Affairs had minuted on a draft of paper COS(50)343) that in case of Russian invasion of

---

[4] EP 1531/39G.
[5] EP 1531/39G.
[6] ZS 31/11G.
[7] EP 1023/3G.

Persia Course C seemed to him 'the least that we ought to aim at'.[8] In the other three cases he agreed, in particular that Persian consent would be required. The final plan of September 4 proposed immediate consideration of political action to ensure that Iraq would afford the necessary facilities and that Persia would appeal for allied support in the event of a Russian move against her.

Paper COS(50)343 did not go so far as a general review of strategy in the Middle East—COS(50)363 of September 13[9]—where it was suggested that it might be possible to provide an earnest of British intention to uphold her commitments by currently advancing elements of the force earmarked for Persia to forward positions in Iraq, Kuwait or Bahrein. It was, however, pointed out in the plan of September 4 that, with only one brigade actually available instead of the required division, 'the United Kingdom could not ensure fully effective military measures to conserve British oil interests in Persia, if these were threatened now'.[10] This again demonstrated the desirability of securing reinforcement from the Commonwealth and the United States, as was pointed out[11] by Mr Furlonge on September 13, 1950, in recommending the plan of September 4 for the approval of Mr Bevin, subsequently given, as a basis for discussion with the Americans.

Sir William Strang, in his minute of August 12, had correspondingly doubted the wisdom of entering into 'any specific obligation to Persia to go to war' against Soviet aggression by way of a statement more definite than that of the preceding May, or of a treaty similar to those with Turkey and Iraq, or of admitting Persia to the North Atlantic Treaty. 'This', he continued, 'is a matter which we should have to consider carefully with the Americans. It is not prudent to enter into obligations which we are not in a position to fulfil: we have assumed quite enough of these already.'[12]

Three days later, on August 15, 1950, the Shah of Persia had asked Mr Lawford, with whom he was on specially intimate terms, whether there was any chance of discussion between the British and Persian General Staffs concerning the possible defence of Khuzistan and the oil installations in that province. The Shah was 'very keen'[13] on reaching an advance understanding with the United Kingdom and the United States: a hopeful opening which was welcomed in the Foreign Office.

On the same day a Soviet trade delegation arrived in Tehran for negotiations. Thereafter, reported the British Embassy there, 'as a result of the general apprehension and desire to placate the Soviet Government, the general tone of the [Persian] Press changed in the Russians' favour'.[14] They adroitly followed up this advantage by launching a campaign in Persia for 'partisans of peace', which secured the verbal support of Dr Musaddiq among others. Mr Lawford reported on an informal conversation with the Shah about the end of August that 'though he saw no alternative to negotiating a Trade Agreement with the Russians the Shah was worried by the propaganda advantage that would accrue therefrom to the Soviet Union as against the Western Powers.'[15]

---

[8] EP 1023/2G.
[9] E 1193/19G.
[10] EP 1023/3G.
[11] EP 1023/8G.
[12] EP 1023/2G.
[13] EP 1016/72.
[14] PG 13416/4.
[15] EP 1016/76.

A fortnight later, on September 14, 1950, the Shah spoke to Sir Francis Shepherd about possibilities of defending the oilfields and about the need, as he felt, for a more definite pronouncement by the Western Powers to the effect that a Russian attack on Persia would mean general war. A somewhat similar question concerning a further pronouncement had been raised by the State Department[16] before the overture from the Shah was reported by Sir Francis Shepherd in a telegram of September 22.[17] Some days later the Shah went further in a final audience with Mr Lawford, who was unfortunately resigning from the Foreign Service and leaving Persia. A telegram sent on October 6 to Washington by the Foreign Office with the concurrence of the Ministry of Defence reported, for the confidential information of the State Department, that the Shah had told Mr Lawford that he was anxious to be assured that in the event of a Soviet attack 'British forces would be made available forthwith in order to defend the Province of Khuzistan'.[18] The Foreign Office telegram commented that the Shah 'evidently fears that in the eventuality we should merely demolish the [oil] installations without attempting to defend them. This message is clearly of great importance for the purpose of the forthcoming discussions with the Americans on COS(50)343 of September 4,'[19] which was largely along the lines desired by the Shah, although the Chiefs of Staff considered it impracticable to hold Persia in case of war. The Foreign Office suggested for consideration whether the Shah should be told of this measure of agreement, and impressed with the necessity of Persia's appealing at the earliest for Western assistance in the eventualities discussed in the staff study.

Mr Lawford on his return from Tehran had, at Sir Francis Shepherd's request, personally conveyed to Mr Furlonge the message which produced this telegram, with its cogent sense of opportunity towards securing the political precondition of Persian assent to landing British troops in feared eventualities. Though Sir Francis Shepherd reported that Persian Ministers and politicians were 'not anxious to be identified at present with anything that might be provocative to Russia',[20] and he doubted whether the Shah's remarks to Mr Lawford constituted anything so precise as 'a definite *démarche* contained in a special message,'[21] His Majesty's Ambassador advised against a proposed visit to Persia, for general discussions on defence, by General Sir Brian Robertson, Commander-in-Chief, Middle East Land Forces; such a visit, Sir Francis Shepherd considered, would be locally unwelcome as tending to hamper amicable development of Russo-Persian relations. Sir Francis Shepherd nevertheless opined in the same despatch of October 14: 'If it were possible for us to give the Persians some kind of assurance of prompt physical help in an emergency it would greatly assist in the strengthening of morale, and technical advice from us, together with the formulation of some general plan, would undoubtedly be greatly appreciated here.'[22] He therefore considered that there would be considerable advantage in making the intimation to Persia proposed in the Foreign Office telegram of October 6 to Washington.

---

[16] EP 1023/5.
[17] EP 1023/6.
[18] EP 1192/10G.
[19] *Ibid.*
[20] EP 1023/9.
[21] EP 1192/13G.
[22] *Ibid.*

Consultations with the State Department concerning the Shah's message tended, however, to dribble away, notably in respect of American fear that the adoption of Course C in the case of a Communist revolution in Azerbaijan might afford the Soviet Union a pretext to enter northern Persia under cover of the Soviet-Persian treaty of 1921. His Majesty's Embassy at Washington also suggested doubts, in somewhat similar vein to Sir William Strang's minute of August 12, as to the desirability of undertaking too specific commitments with insufficient force to back them in practice.[23] The question further came to be connected with that of the desirability of giving Persia a reassurance that she was not being left out by the association of Greece and Turkey with the North Atlantic Treaty Organisation. It was eventually decided that such reassurance was not called for.

In a letter of October 20, 1950, from Mr Furlonge, Mr Burrows was informed that the Foreign Office nevertheless felt that a reassuring reply must be made to the Shah, and would be glad if its terms could be discussed at the forthcoming meetings with the Americans.[24] The message of October 20 was not telegraphed and only reached Washington after the British and American Chiefs of Staff had held their second series of conversations there, though before the Anglo-American politico-military meeting which was to round off these consultations of October 23-26, 1950, in Washington. The British Chiefs of Staff in Washington formulated some prudential reservations regarding the terms proposed by the Foreign Office for a reply to the Shah, and felt that it would now be inappropriate to consult the Americans at a meeting 'concerned with general principles and not with individual pieces of business, however important'.[25] The British Chiefs of Staff and His Majesty's Embassy in Washington agreed that the matter should subsequently be pursued through ordinary channels.

The scope of the Anglo-American conversations of October 23-26, 1950, had, however, particularly included Persia. The American representatives agreed in general with the British plan COS(50)343 but refused any commitment to an early contribution of forces, especially land forces: this despite the admission by General Omar Bradley that 'we should need all the oil that we could get from the Middle East',[26] and the observation by Lord Tedder that 'although it was agreed that Korea was of little strategic importance the United States had accepted a full commitment there. Iraq and Iran were of great strategic importance.'[27]

In general the Americans considered that British defensive planning for the Middle East was over-cautious,[28] more particularly with regard to holding the Outer Ring in the medium term. As regards Persia, on the other hand, the Americans presented their objection to going so far as to adopt Course C in the Azerbaijan eventuality. Admiral Sherman, American Chief of Naval Operations, 'suggested that there was all the difference between sending forces into Persia and to the borders of Persia',[27] Course B in the British staff study. The American objection probably applied *a fortiori* to the despatch of British forces to Abadan in the event of Communist disorders there, though this was not then recorded. Sir Oliver Franks did

---

[23] EP 1192/14G.
[24] EP 1192/11G.
[25] EP 1192/14G.
[26] UES 1534/66G.
[27] EP 1192/15G.
[28] E 1195/4G.

not concur in the recorded American objection, which remained, significantly, the one specific measure of disagreement concerning Persia in the Anglo-American military conversations of 1950. Looming up behind was the menacing possibility of provoking Soviet entry into Persia, possibly under cover of the treaty of 1921, though the State Department in July had regarded the use of this pretext as unlikely.[29] Russian intervention was nevertheless a lasting bugbear to the Americans, as to the Persians themselves.

On October 26, the day that the military conversations in Washington ended, Mr L.A.C. Fry, Assistant Head of the Eastern Department of the Foreign Office, indicated in a minute[30] on Sir Francis Shepherd's despatch of October 14 that co-ordinated planning with the Persians might be considered in the light of the outcome of those conversations. The prospect of such planning, however, evidently receded behind British planning for the general defence of the Middle East in the light of the Washington conversations. Till that was completed it was not thought possible to say anything very substantial to the Shah. Mr Furlonge wrote to Sir Francis Shepherd on December 3, 1950: 'It has taken us a long time to decide it is better to say nothing at all.'[31] His Majesty's Ambassador evidently did think so, although, as Mr Furlonge explained in a minute of December 12 for Mr Bevin on Soviet-Persian relations, 'the Shah, in conversation with Sir Francis Shepherd, has constantly reverted to the theme of defending Persia against a Russian attack'.[32] In that event he intended to remove himself, his Government and available forces to the mountainous areas of South-West Persia, and hoped that the Western Powers would introduce forces to occupy and defend the oilfields. Meanwhile the Foreign Office, in further study of the disagreement with the Americans regarding the adoption of Course C to counter a Communist *coup* in Azerbaijan, was moving towards acceptance of the American objection.[33]

In his letter of December 3 to Sir Francis Shepherd, Mr Furlonge had also suggested that he should telegraph his further views regarding a visit to Persia by Sir Brian Robertson, who favoured it, as the Foreign Office was inclined to do. It was, however, on December 31 that Sir Francis Shepherd answered by letter that General Razmara saw no objection to the visit and the Shah 'would welcome it and indicated that he hoped Robertson would be able to give him some answer about the defence of Abadan, which . . . he raised with me on December 30',[31] notably regarding possible British supply of anti-aircraft guns and tanks since American supplies of these, which Sir Francis Shepherd suggested, would not stretch to Abadan. His Majesty's Ambassador, while referring to rearmament shortages, agreed to enquire into the question which, he presumed, was one for the joint Anglo-American Chiefs of Staff.[34] This enquiry has not been traced.

His Majesty's Ambassador in Tehran did not, however, exploit the opening conveniently provided by the Shah to follow up a suggestion in Mr Furlonge's letter of December 3 and link the question of defending Abadan with the political precondition of Persian assent to landing British troops in feared eventualities. What

---

[29] EP 11345/18.
[30] EP 1192/13G.
[31] EP 1192/17G.
[32] EP 10338/45G.
[33] EP 1023/14G.
[34] EP 1071/1G of 1951.

had been regarded as a good, and was perhaps a golden, opportunity of securing this essential was neglected against a background of Anglo-American disagreement concerning some, but not all, applications of that course, and American unwillingness to underwrite British military weakness in the Middle East. On November 4, 1950, a new Soviet-Persian trade agreement was signed in Tehran.

2. Anglo-American co-operation and divergences in Persia regarding propaganda and economic aid

Both the Foreign Office and the State Department had long been fully aware that Anglo-American support of Persia in her exposed position in the cold war called not only for military measures but also for economic ones backed by propaganda. As a result of conversations in London in June 1950 between Mr Warner and Mr E.W. Barrett, Assistant Secretary of State for Public Affairs in the State Department, complementary British and American instructions had been issued early in July to respective diplomatic missions throughout the world, and notably in the Middle East, to ensure that as between the two services 'in the field of overseas information, there should be the maximum consultation and co-operation possible in the common interest of the West'.[35] These instructions stood in unhappy contrast to the reports on information activities in Tehran for the second and third quarters of the year. On both these reports members of the Foreign Office recorded that they were disturbed by their evidence of 'open competition' (Mr P.L. Carter, September 19)[36] and a 'note of rivalry with the Americans' (Mr C.F.R. Barclay, November 7).[37] This disquiet in the Foreign Office was conveyed, not to His Majesty's Embassy, but to Mr E.J.F. Scott, who was about to fill the long vacant post of information officer at Tehran, where he arrived just after Christmas 1950.

The expanding United States Information Services in Tehran went beyond the policy pursued by His Majesty's Embassy at Tehran of not issuing material concerning Persian internal affairs: a policy also applied to its news bulletin in accordance with a Persian regulation, infringement of which might provoke suppression. The Information Policy Department of the Foreign Office recognised that American material for Persian consumption was 'a great deal more suitable than our own', largely supplied, apparently, by 'dishing out COI-tailored feature articles'.[36] This, however, did not subsequently prevent a 'notable decline in American popularity',[37] perhaps partly due to the brashness of American technique, but largely reflecting those overriding circumstances which remind a publicist that most often his contribution can be but marginal, important though that margin may be. In this case the Americans suffered in Persian estimation from their reverses in Korea and from what was regarded as the inadequacy of their supplies to Persia, both military (compare the Shah's approach to Great Britain) and economic.

One of the measures adopted by the Defence Committee of the Cabinet at its meeting on Persia on August 1, 1950, had been to enjoin the Foreign Office to arrange for discussions with the Americans concerning the possibilities of financial aid to Persia for her precarious Seven-year Plan.[38] Unfortunately this led towards

---

[35] Foreign Office circular No. 079 Secret of July 7, 1950: P 1013/33G: cf also PR 58/37G.
[36] PG 13416/3.
[37] PG 13416/4.
[38] EP 1531/39G.

another source of Anglo-American disagreement in relation to Persia. The new American Ambassador there, Dr Henry Grady, had formerly been Ambassador in Greece where he had made a reputation as an administrator of American economic aid. It came to be supposed that it was largely under his influential impulsion that the American Government now maintained that Great Britain ought to guarantee dollars under the Memorandum of Understanding for the Persian service of the proposed Export-Import Bank $25 million loan, or rather line of credit.[39] As Sir Oliver Franks observed to Mr George Perkins, Assistant Secretary of State for European Affairs, this seemed 'a paradoxical situation'.[40] It certainly seemed so to the British Treasury. It was only a representation on September 25 from the Foreign Office to the Prime Minister, as to the urgent political necessity of financial aid to Persia,[41] which secured an offer from the Treasury to guarantee the service of the loan for one year, while the Americans made other arrangements. When the latter replied that this was insufficient to enable the loan to go through, the Foreign Office did not feel justified in pressing the Treasury further. Such was the unresolved position when on October 10, with no prior warning from the United States Government to His Majesty's Government, General Razmara, on the strength of assurances from Dr Grady, announced the grant of the $25 million line of credit.

Meanwhile the Bank of England in concert with the Treasury had been negotiating with the Persian national bank, the Bank Melli, and governmental representatives for the annual renewal of the Memorandum of Understanding. On September 14 a brief for these negotiations, embodying the views of the Overseas Negotiations Committee of the Cabinet, had been prepared by the Treasury for Mr Gaitskell, Minister of State for Economic Affairs. This brief notably declared: 'The dominating factor in the whole situation is that we are in no position to bargain. It is more important than ever that Persian oil should not be put at risk . . . At present our relations with Persia are most friendly, and it is of the greatest political, economic and strategic importance that they should continue. There can, therefore, be no question of setting "breaking points" and we must in the end be content with the best terms we can secure by friendly discussions.'[42]

It is sufficiently obvious that, in purely financial terms, His Majesty's Government had been in a position in these negotiations to exert stiff pressure upon the economically feeble Persian Government. That broader considerations, notably concerning oil, should have been held to cancel this advantage completely and preclude any breaking point, renders it somewhat remarkable that the same considerations had not already been brought drastically to bear upon the persistent refusal, still, of the Anglo-Iranian Oil Company to improve its offer in the question of Persian oil. This incipient and dangerous dichotomy in British economic policy towards Persia does not appear to have engaged the immediate attention of the Foreign Office.

The Foreign Office and the Treasury, stimulated by American concern, had become increasingly exercised during the late summer of 1950 with ways of implementing the decision of the Cabinet Defence Committee on August 1 towards

---

[39] Cf EP 1119/16.
[40] EP 1119/31.
[41] EP 1119/39 and 41.
[42] EP 1119/16.

co-operation with the Americans in rendering economic assistance to support the friendly Government of General Razmara. The Foreign Office secured Treasury assent to a proposal for a loan of £2-£3 million by His Majesty's Government to Persia for internal expenditure on projects under the Seven-year Plan. At an early departmental discussion of this proposal on August 28 the Treasury suggested that a large, though not a small, loan might make the Persian Government less inclined to proceed to ratify the Supplemental Oil Agreement. In reply 'Mr Furlonge said that one should not insist too much on the political risks of a loan to Persia because it was precisely to reduce political risks that the loan was required . . . Mr Furlonge stressed that the British loan should be used as an incentive to ratification of the Supplemental Agreement.'[43] Whereas as recently as August 11 Mr Furlonge had still advised that British financial assistance to Persia should be conditional upon ratification of the agreement.[44] Now, however, the Foreign Office was urging to the Treasury considerations similar to those which the State Department had advanced to the Foreign Office in May in favour of making the Export-Import Bank Loan before ratification of the Supplemental Agreement. Such was the economic slide whereby the urgency of that ratification came to compete with the urgency of assisting Persia. In the economic field, as noticed earlier in the strategic, the hostilities in Korea had sharpened concern for Persia in ways liable to promote the protection of British oil interests there but also liable, unless carefully watched, to overlay that vital interest with considerations of broader but more hypothetical relevance to the cold war in general.

Another suggestion was that the Anglo-Iranian Oil Company might, in addition to its previously agreed advances, make a loan to Persia of £5-£10 million, to be guaranteed by His Majesty's Government under the system of Export Credit Guarantee. This ran into difficulty, however, since the company rejected the Treasury's suggestion that the loan should be repayable in seven to ten years. Writing to Mr Wright from Washington on September 14, 1950, Mr Burrows had observed: 'I sometimes seem to detect surprise on the part of the State Department that, in spite of our enormous interests there, we do not appear more interested in supporting Persia both economically and strategically.'[45]

On the economic side a factor here was doubtless the justified reluctance of His Majesty's Government to guarantee dollars for Persian service of the Export-Import Bank loan. While endorsing the British stand in this respect, Mr Ernest Bevin, at a meeting which he held in the Foreign Office on October 10 to discuss economic policy towards Persia, emphasised the importance of such aid, even at a possible cost in dollars. Mr Bevin favoured the proposed £2-£3 million loan by His Majesty's Government, while preferring to hold in reserve the idea of a loan by the Anglo-Iranian Oil Company. It was felt that it would be unwise at that stage to make any mention to the Persians of such a loan, which would be unnecessary if the Supplemental Agreement were ratified.[46]

---

[43] EP 1119/3.
[44] EP 1531/38.
[45] E 1195/3G.
[46] EP 1119/43.

3. The prospects of the Supplemental Agreement and the Foreign Secretary's conversation of August 12 with Mr Lewis Douglas

On July 10, 1950, a fortnight after General Razmara had taken office, Sir Francis Shepherd had rather ominously drawn attention to an indication which the General had given, before that event, to Mr Pyman, Oriental Counsellor in His Majesty's Embassy, that his plans were likely to delay ratification of the Supplemental Agreement for another six months. Before reintroducing it in the Majlis General Razmara, who was anxious to dissipate fears of a military dictatorship, proposed to consolidate his Parliamentary position and initiate some decentralising reform of the Persian Administration. Sir Francis Shepherd suggested in his letter of July 10 that if the Anglo-Iranian Oil Company would offer the Persian Government a local directorship in their activities in Persia, General Razmara might be induced to secure ratification, thus rendering interim financial support for the Persian Government unnecessary.[47] Three days later His Majesty's Ambassador asked that action on this letter be suspended, but he telegraphed on July 29[48] that he thought the time had now come to act on it. It appears, however, that his significant suggestion for a Persian directorship was not followed up until September 19 when Mr Furlonge mentioned it to the Vice-Chairman of the company, Mr Basil Jackson, who remarked that they had indeed thought of it.

The proposal of a Persian director of a subsidiary for Persian activities had in the meantime been overlaid by other proposals which General Razmara made to the Anglo-Iranian Oil Company at the end of July. He asked for an increased advance, namely of £25 million in five monthly instalments, and three additions to the terms of the Supplemental Agreement: Persianisation of staff within 10 years, Persian auditing of the company's accounts in London, and reduction in the local price of petroleum products in Persia. In his telegram of July 29 Sir Francis Shepherd again warned that there was no chance of early and unmodified ratification, and urged that about £15 million should be made available to the Persians.

General Razmara's proposals were considered at a meeting on August 2, 1950, by representatives of the Foreign Office, the Treasury, Ministry of Fuel and Power, and the company. Mr Michael Wright then pointed out 'that owing to a dearth of strong politicians in the Middle East, it has proved impossible in many cases to get good agreements ratified by Middle Eastern Parliaments'.[49] He considered that in this case ratification was now unlikely without further concessions, and suggested that the company should implement the financial provisions of the Supplemental Agreement at once, prior to ratification: it was stated at the meeting that by the end of the year £35 million would stand to the credit of Persia under the agreement. Sir William Fraser, however, 'maintained that these proposals have been put forward merely to delay the ratification', and adopted a generally negative attitude towards them: the company's leading Persian officials advised standing firm on the agreement, and its chief representative in Tehran, Mr E.G.D. Northcroft, considered, even, that if the Persians were given an advance of £5 million a month, they would not be able to spend it. Sir William Fraser's only concession was that, once the Supplemental Agreement was ratified, it might then perhaps be modified. The

---

[47] EP 1531/32.
[48] EP 1531/36.
[49] EP 1531/40.

Foreign Office accepted this position and a week later, on August 9, telegraphed to Tehran that the company might later drop the Persians a hint of the suggested concession.

'We have been consistently unresponsive',[50] Mr Leavett had noted on June 20, to the State Department's suggestions for the early ratification of the Supplemental Agreement, if necessary by advancing its terms and, in particular, accelerating the persianisation of staff. This pressure built up to a conversation on August 12, 1950, between the Foreign Secretary and the American Ambassador in London, who was soon to retire. Mr Ernest Bevin told Mr Lewis Douglas that he had taken a personal interest in the agreement, which had been before the Cabinet; that 'every effort had been made to meet the Persian Government; but that Razmara would never, nor would any other person, tell us exactly what was wanted in order to reach a settlement. It was the bazaar method of negotiating.'[51] This statement was, perhaps, unintentionally somewhat misleading. And here Mr Furlonge's brief for this conversation had stated that 'no specific modification was ever suggested'[52] by M. Mansur in his representations regarding the Supplemental Agreement. Mr Furlonge in turn may have been partly misled by the somewhat incomplete reporting by His Majesty's Ambassador in Tehran of the modifications proposed to him on May 30 by M. Mansur and of June 7 by his Foreign Minister (see [pp. 64-5]): an example, possibly, of how insufficient reporting can snowball into a misapprehension at a high level. As regards General Razmara, the Foreign Secretary's statement above was strictly true if, following Mr Furlonge's brief, 'us' referred to His Majesty's Government in distinction from the Anglo-Iranian Oil Company. At the interdepartmental discussion with the company 10 days earlier the decision not to meet General Razmara's requests to the latter had been taken, however, in accordance with the views of the company but scarcely with those of Mr Wright.

In the conversation of August 12, 1950, Mr Bevin further told Mr Douglas: 'We had already made a good offer to Persia, and I felt we should stick by it . . . The Persians must really make up their minds whether or not they were going to do business.'[53] The Foreign Secretary 'put it to the Ambassador very strongly that there should be agreement between us and the Americans' in regard to economic aid to Persia. Here Mr Bevin, as proposed in Mr Furlonge's brief, suggested that there should be consultations concerning loans; 'something might then emerge', said Mr Bevin, 'which would allow us to make satisfactory proposals to the Persians without increasing the cost to ourselves of the Supplemental and other agreements.' This suggestion was the first of two statements which, Mr Furlonge had proposed in his brief, the Secretary of State might care to make to the American Ambassador if he urged that His Majesty's Government should apply pressure to the Anglo-Iranian Oil Company. Mr Furlonge's second recommendation under this head included an intimation by Mr Bevin 'that the Americans could help us considerably by instructing Mr Grady to disabuse the Persians of any idea that they can obtain further concessions':[54] that is, that the Americans should in effect reverse their previous refusal to do just this (see pp. 62). It might perhaps have been advantageous if the

---

[50] EP 1531/26.
[51] EP 1531/37.
[52] EP 1531/38.
[53] EP 1531/37.
[54] EP 1531/38.

above recommendation had been phrased with more pointed precision to this end, and in favour of a specific request to the Government of the United States for full diplomatic support in Tehran for the Supplemental Agreement or, in the event of refusal, for a clear statement of their reasons: these might have constituted an important consideration for His Majesty's Government in determining whether, after all, the time had come to put pressure on the Anglo-Iranian Oil Company for concessions. As it was, however, it is not recorded that Mr Bevin even went so far as the contingent recommendation which Mr Furlonge had made.

4. The bearing on the Supplemental Agreement of activities of the Iraq Petroleum Company and of Aramco

The Shah, in his conversation of August 15, 1950, with Mr Lawford (cf p. 70), said that 'he very much hoped that the Anglo-Iranian Oil Company would respond favourably as regards the three conditions which he [*sic*] had submitted as being essential if the Supplemental Oil Agreement was to be ratified.'[55] The prospect of securing ratification of the agreement as it stood had just been further prejudiced by the action, largely, of the Anglo-Iranian Oil Company itself in its capacity as a participant in the Iraq Petroleum Company, international but British registered. No information about current negotiations by that company had been reported to His Majesty's Embassy at Tehran so that it received 'a shock'[56] to learn from a Foreign Office telegram of August 14, 1950, that a new oil agreement had been concluded with the Iraqi Government upon improved terms. The swiftness of this agreement, apparently due to a personal initiative by Sir William Fraser, had also surprised the Foreign Office. The Iraqi terms might seem, and at first did seem to Sir Francis Shepherd, to be more favourable than those of the Supplemental Agreement, though this was denied by oil experts.

In reply to a vigorous representation of August 21 from Sir Francis Shepherd, Mr Furlonge wrote five days later, after a meeting with representatives of the Anglo-Iranian Oil Company: 'We fully appreciate the probability that Persian critics of the Supplemental Agreement will represent the new Iraqi agreement as being more favourable than the former, and that Razmara may consequently become more reluctant than ever to put it to the Majlis. On the other hand, it appears to us that the Supplemental Agreement is in fact defensible.'[57]

Sir Francis Shepherd had remarked in his letter of August 21 that the new Iraqi oil agreement came 'at a singularly unfortunate time, since the [Persian] Prime Minister has just decided to proceed to obtain ratification of the Supplemental Agreement. He told Northcroft on August 17 that he was going to have the agreement studied forthwith by a small committee consisting of himself and the Finance and Foreign Ministers, and that he proposed to submit it to the Majlis on September 11,'[58] estimating that it would take two months to pass it through the two chambers. Already in July General Razmara had informed His Majesty's Ambassador that he proposed to withdraw the agreement from the Majlis Oil Commission dominated by the National Front, and submit it to 'a technical

---

[55] EP 1016/72.
[56] EP 1531/44.
[57] EP 1531/44.
[58] *Ibid.*

committee'.[59] It does not appear that Sir Francis Shepherd put any pressure upon General Razmara to adhere to some such procedure, potentially of considerable importance for British interests; nor that the Foreign Office issued any instructions in such a sense. In September 1950 the previously appointed Majlis Oil Commission in fact began to consider documents concerning the Supplemental Agreement which were submitted to it by the Persian Government.

Sir Francis Shepherd had written on August 21 that he did not now see how General Razmara could submit the Supplemental Agreement as it stood to the Majlis; if he did so he would almost certainly be defeated. On September 9 General Razmara said much the same to Sir Francis Shepherd, who telegraphed on the following day that the Persian Premier 'had been disappointed with the attitude of the company as shown by Mr Northcroft and concluded that they did not wish to help the country . . . Opposition has in the meantime launched a petition to cancel the oil concessions altogether. The importance of this is symptomatic rather than practical.'[60] Sir Francis Shepherd cogently commented: 'Although there have been, I think, occasions during the past year when the Persian Government might well have secured ratification by proper preparation and support it is now clear that Razmara's views [in favour of additional concessions] cannot be disputed . . . I consider therefore that there is nothing to be gained by remaining intransigent and that the risk accompanying a changed attitude must be accepted . . . the question is no longer purely commercial or financial but involves fate of the most promising Government Persia has had since the war. Developments of the present situation may also affect the future of the company in Persia.'[61]

This important recommendation for a revision at long last of British policy concerning the Supplemental Agreement prompted the Foreign Office to call another meeting on September 14 of the same agencies as on August 2, but at a somewhat lower level. At this meeting the chief representative of the Anglo-Iranian Oil Company, Mr Jackson, reiterated objections to all three of the previously Persian proposals, explaining, for instance, that the company was 'already 97 per cent Iranianised',[62] and that the Persians could not yet provide the men for the white-collar job which they now wanted. Another representative of the company, Mr L.C. Rice, even maintained that the Persians had never told the company what modifications they desired, and held that General Razmara could get the Supplemental Agreement ratified if he so wished. Mr Furlonge, the chief representative of the Foreign Office, replied that 'although Sir Francis Shepherd disagreed, it might be the case. In any event, Razmara did not intent to put the agreement through', as it stood. The record of the meeting concluded on this bleakly inconclusive note, and neither the Foreign Office nor the Treasury appear to have taken any prompt step to press the company to agree to the more conciliatory policy favoured by Sir Francis Shepherd for strong reasons which were endorsed by the Foreign Office: although the meeting had been held on the same day that the Treasury had prepared its brief concerning the Memorandum of Understanding wherein it envisaged almost unlimited financial concessions to the Persians in the

---

[59] EP 1531/32.
[60] EP 1119/9.
[61] *Ibid.*
[62] EP 1119/28.

interests, not least, of safeguarding Persian oil.

The minute of the meeting on September 14, 1950, did not record that any observations were then addressed to the representatives of the Anglo-Iranian Oil Company with regard either to the new agreement in Iraq, or to certain preliminary indications received in the Foreign Office of the possibility of another new oil agreement which was, in the event, to affect the issue of the Supplemental Agreement still more seriously. On July 15, 1950, Mr T.F. Brenchley of the Economic Relations Department of the Foreign Office had recorded in another connexion that the Ministry of Fuel and Power had received information 'that Aramco are involved in delicate negotiations with Ibn Saud on matters other than the acceptance of sterling [in part payment of royalties] . . . They are not prepared to disclose the nature of these other negotiations.'[63] Four days later Mr A.C. Trott, His Majesty's Ambassador to Saudi Arabia, had reported that the Arabian Minister of Finance, M. Najib Salha, had informed him that he was securing an American expert to advise on income tax, previously non existent there. M. Najib had learnt that the Government of the United States was considering exempting certain firms operating abroad, including Aramco, from some American taxation as part of the programme under Point Four; this might save Aramco $100,000 a year and he did not see why the money should not be diverted to the Arabian Government. Both Mr Trott and the Foreign Office anticipated that 'so dubious an expedient . . . will come to nothing';[64] but Mr P.E. Ramsbotham, just appointed to supervise questions of oil in succession to Mr Brenchley, prudently requested the Treasury about August 12 to institute enquiries in Washington concerning possible exemptions from American income tax (cf. pp. 131).

Less than a fortnight later His Majesty's Embassy at Jedda reported in a letter of August 22 (filed in Foreign Office on September 9) the arrival of an American tax expert; and that it was 'already common knowledge in Jedda that some income tax scheme is in the wind . . . One thing is certain . . . the foreign companies would pay but the Saudi companies would not.'[65] On the same day of August 22 Mr E.W. Noonan, the well-informed representative of the Ministry of Fuel and Power in the British Middle East Office at Cairo, transmitted to his Ministry information received from the American Petroleum Attaché there, Mr Lager, who had visited Tehran in May and June. Mr Lager said that the American Embassy there was doing its best to promote ratification of the Supplemental Agreement provided that it could avoid the impression of ganging up with the British Government. He himself had kept in touch with Mr Northcroft and Mr A.E.C. Drake, the general manager of the Anglo-Iranian Oil Company at Abadan, and had with their knowledge talked to leading Persians taking particular pains, reported Mr Noonan, 'to pour cold water on their fondness for the Venezuelan profit-sharing basis which he judged (rightly I imagine) to be the main distraction.'[66] The helpful Mr Lager had further told the Persians that the Supplemental Agreement gave them better terms than Saudi Arabia had secured from Aramco; but he now told Mr Noonan that if ratification were delayed this might not remain true 'for he believes that an increase in Aramco royalty is in the offing'.

---

[63] UES 1531/34.
[64] ES 1172/1.
[65] ES 1172/2.
[66] EP 1531/45.

In fact, as only became known subsequently, it was two days earlier, on August 20, that the Arabian Government formally requested Aramco to negotiate new terms of agreement: a request which that Government followed up on September 5 by presenting 13 far-reaching demands for revision.

A copy of Mr Noonan's letter of August 22, 1950, to the Ministry of Fuel and Power, was received in the Foreign Office on August 29. Eastern Department had earlier received two letters of August 6 from Jedda Chancery referring to 'the general Aramco feeling of antagonism towards British interests',[67] and to that company's standing policy towards the Arabian Government of ingratiation and 'conciliation at almost any cost'.[68] It was reported that Aramco's 'large public relations branch has carried out such an effective propaganda campaign amongst Aramco's American employees that many a hardened oilman will recoil visibly in the face of a critical remark about the Saudis'. This picture of political and personal relations contrasted strikingly and somewhat ominously with that in the case of the Anglo-Iranian Oil Company in Persia.

The intelligence from the Ministry of Fuel and Power and from Jedda, hardened by Mr Noonan's report from Cairo, following upon the Shah's earlier allusion to Aramco to Sir Francis Shepherd, did not prompt the Foreign Office or, apparently, the Ministry of Fuel and Power itself to make further enquiry or assessment concerning a possible new agreement by Aramco and its bearing upon the Supplemental Agreement. On August 28, however, Mr Furlonge had written to Mr Burrows in Washington that it was 'felt in some quarters that the Americans have been rather overdoing their pressure on us in regard to the IPC and the AIOC'.[69] The reference to the Iraq Petroleum Company may have related more particularly to initial support in the State Department for the highly critical findings on the company recently presented in the so-called Kaukonen Report by an official of the American Department of Labor, who attributed to the company's management 'a primitive approach to labour relations';[70] whereas the Foreign Office and the British Middle East Office were in agreement that in general the Iraq Petroleum Company 'do not deserve the serious, almost vicious indictment made by Kaukonen, nor the odious comparison with Aramco at Dhahran'.[71] Mr Furlonge now further enquired of Mr Burrows regarding a suggestion, to which Mr Furlonge himself did not subscribe, that the State Department, and in particular Mr McGhee, as a former oilman, had been overmuch influenced by American oil companies wishing to see their British competitors 'driven into an uncompetitive position by constant pressure to raise their royalties and labour conditions'.

Mr Burrows replied in a telegram of September 18, 1950, that he had no evidence at all that the attitude of the State Department in regard to the oil companies was other than 'genuinely well-intentioned'.[72] He explained that the State Department reasoned in particular that the companies 'are potentially a great focus point for xenophobia in the Middle East and a big target for Russian propaganda. The conduct of the companies towards the local Governments and peoples must therefore be

---

[67] ES 1532/11.
[68] ES 1532/12.
[69] E 10213/5.
[70] EQ 1531/48.
[71] EQ 1531/90.
[72] EP 1531/51.

beyond reproach. Once the companies have become a subject of criticism, it is extremely difficult for us to recover the initiative. The companies must in their view therefore at least keep up with local opinion and if possible be ahead of it. If the companies have to be goaded into making inch by inch concessions it is only a matter of time before they become a political liability and not an asset to the Atlantic Powers.' This progressive and statesmanlike analysis reinforced Sir Francis Shepherd's recommendation a week earlier for a revision of British policy concerning the Supplemental Agreement. Further impetus in this direction was supplied by conversations in London on September 21-22 whereat representatives of the Foreign Office (Mr Wright and Mr Furlonge), the Treasury and the Ministry of Fuel and Power (Mr V.S. Butler) conferred with Mr McGhee and representatives of the American Treasury concerning general questions of economic assistance to the Middle East and to Persia in particular.

At a meeting on September 21 Mr McGhee said that 'the United States had no quarrel with the [Supplemental] Agreement from the financial viewpoint; it was a fair agreement which gave Persia a royalty rate equal to any in the Middle East.'[73] The trouble was to secure its ratification. 'The United Kingdom did not seem to have felt the same sense of urgency about the position as the United States. American oil executives . . . had said that in AIOC's place they would agree to practically any modification of the agreement, except a Persian majority on the Board of Directors.' Mr McGhee further observed that Persia had several legitimate grievances, such as special sales to the Admiralty. Whereas, Mr McGhee maintained, 'the advantage in negotiations today lay with the country where the oil properties were located and about the best the companies could do was to fight a graceful rearguard action.' Mr V.S. Butler defended the Anglo-Iranian Oil Company, generally in accordance with the arguments advanced by Mr Jackson at the meeting held a week earlier. Mr Butler, however, alluded to the possibility, mentioned by Mr Furlonge to Mr Jackson two days earlier,[74] that it might improve matters if the purely Persian operations of the Anglo-Iranian Oil Company were hived off in a separate concern.

Mr McGhee further informed the British representatives that Saudi Arabia had just put forward demands to Aramco that were 'astounding and extremely sweeping, covering both financial and other concessions.'[75] He could not disclose details, but 'this factor threw an alarming new note of urgency into the need of getting immediate ratification of the Supplemental Agreement' (American record of the meeting) since the demands were 'so far-reaching that when the Persians heard of them the Supplemental Oil Agreement would never go through' (agreed Anglo-American record). The Foreign Office communicated this information forthwith to the Anglo-Iranian Oil Company and informed Sir Francis Shepherd by telegram[76] on September 23 that it had done so. Mr McGhee himself apparently also warned Sir William Fraser and on September 22 the information was corroborated by Mr Paul Parker, United States Financial Attaché at Cairo, who participated in the conversations in London. He estimated that if the demands of Saudi Arabia were conceded her royalty income would be increased from $60 million to $100 million;

---

[73] E 10213/16.
[74] See p. [38]
[75] E 10213/16.
[76] EP 1531/52.

and he promised to keep the Foreign Office informed of developments.

5. The question of sweetening the Supplemental Agreement

The Anglo-American conversations of September 1950 scarcely represented any concrete advance, as regards American support for British policy in relation to the Supplemental Agreement, from Mr Bevin's conversation with Mr Douglas in August: unless one counts the agreed and impeccable resolution that 'the United States and the United Kingdom regard it as essential that the Supplemental Agreement should be ratified with the least possible delay. It was agreed that further discussion should be postponed . . .'.[77]

Postponement on the Persian side was concerning the Shah, who sent for General Razmara on September 30, 1950, and, in Sir Francis Shepherd's words, evidently told him 'to cut the cackle and get on with the Oil Agreement'.[78] On the following day the Persian Prime Minister informed His Majesty's Ambassador that he proposed to announce to the Majlis next week his Government's approval of the Supplemental Agreement. It would be examined by the Majlis Oil Committee which would recommend modifications 'more or less dictated'[79] by him. He now proposed five modifications, in particular: first—to which he attached special importance—royalties should be equated with those of Iraq so that the latter should never exceed the rate of Persian royalties; secondly, the Persian Government should receive free an amount of oil equal to that consumed in Persia by the Anglo-Iranian Oil Company; thirdly, some form of Persian check on exports of oil; fourthly, complete persianisation of the company's staff within 10 years, except for certain high or technical posts; fifthly, gas by-products now destroyed locally to be available free to the Persian Government when they could use them.

A Foreign Office telegram[80] of October 3, despatched on the authority of Mr Wright, replied to Sir Francis Shepherd that the initial reaction of the Anglo-Iranian Oil Company to the proposed modifications was 'decidedly unfavourable', especially as regards the first of them, which it considered 'wholly unacceptable since it appears to envisage a two-way option'. Two days later a further Foreign Office telegram[81] to Tehran, issued on the same authority, confirmed this, while reporting that the company did not wish to close the door to General Razmara. It considered, though, that he should discuss his proposed modifications with the company rather than with His Majesty's Government. This telegram from the Foreign Office continued: 'Our own views, as we have informed the company, are that while the agreement as it stands is wholly fair they would be well advised in their own and the general interest to clinch matters if this is possible even if this involves them in making some further offer which they may dislike always provided that it is not of an excessively injurious character. But it is not for us to recommend the precise nature of any such offer.' On the basis of this modest interpretation of Sir Francis Shepherd's strong recommendation of September 10 in favour of concessions, the latter was now instructed to inform General Razmara, who should get into touch with Mr Northcroft, that His Majesty's Government welcomed his

---

[77] E 10213/20.
[78] EP 1016/84.
[79] EP 1119/33.
[80] *Ibid.*
[81] *Ibid.*

proposed initiative in informing the Majlis of his approval of the Supplemental Agreement, but maintained the view that it was fair and even generous, and could not hold out hope that the company would agree to fundamental modifications, such as some of his proposals involved.

On October 9, 1950, Sir Francis Shepherd wrote to Mr Furlonge that he considered that the Supplemental Agreement was 'likely to be scrambled through somehow, though pretty certainly with a bad grace'.[82] Next day, at the departmental meeting concerning financial relations with Persia held by Mr Bevin,[83] 'the Secretary of State expressed the opinion that, although hitherto he had been unwilling to press the Anglo-Iranian Oil Company to modify the terms of the Supplemental Oil Agreement, he felt that the time had come for the company to be as forthcoming as possible in an attempt to make the agreement acceptable'.[84] This important, and scarcely premature, decision reversed previous policy exactly a month after Sir Francis Shepherd had recommended this. The decision was communicated forthwith by the Foreign Office to the Ministry of Fuel and Power.

On October 13, 1950, General Razmara told Mr Northcroft that since his proposed five modifications to the Supplemental Agreement were apparently either unacceptable or unimportant he wished the Anglo-Iranian Oil Company to suggest additional concessions, which might possibly be embodied in an exchange of letters so as not to alter the text of the agreement. On October 18 Mr L. Barnett, who had in July succeeded Mr Leavett in charge of Persian affairs in the Eastern Department of the Foreign Office, minuted on the telegram from Sir Francis Shepherd reporting this development: 'It is a great pity that the company have not tried to build up what little they feel able to offer the Persians into something that might look impressive.'[85] On the same day of October 18 General Razmara informed the Persian Senate that he favoured the Supplemental Agreement. His Majesty's Embassy in Tehran subsequently reported that the Persian Premier had at last instructed the Persian department for propaganda to make known to the public the facts about the agreement. This was 'a definite step forward'.[86]

Another fresh step was the conversation which Sir William Strang and Mr Michael Wright had on October 20 with Sir William Fraser. He was told of the Secretary of State's view that in order to secure the ratification now of the Supplemental Agreement by the Majlis 'something more was required, and Mr Bevin hoped the company would be able to find something to offer, even if it were somewhat painful, provided always it was not disastrous'. Mr Wright's minute continued: 'Sir William Fraser, who responded in the most friendly possible manner, said that he agreed with our judgment of the position . . . He himself would not hesitate at finding further sums of even several million pounds if the right method could be devised, but he was at a loss to find the right answer.'[87] It would be unwise to offer a higher rate of royalty, which would only upset the position again in Iraq since 'the royalty rate under the Supplemental Agreement would, it was now calculated, work out at something slightly more advantageous than the terms' of the

---

[82] EP 1016/84.
[83] See p. [38]
[84] EP 1531/61: cf EP 1531/57.
[85] EP 1531/63.
[86] EP 1531/74.
[87] EP 1531/70.

recent Iraqi Agreement.

Sir William Strang and Mr Wright suggested to Sir William Fraser the possibility of agreeing 'to one or two of General Razmara's suggestions which the company had so far been inclined to argue against on the grounds that they would not benefit Persia. Would it not be wise to make a virtue of them?'[88] They put forward as additional alternative possibilities that the Anglo-Iranian Oil Company might make some particular contribution, such as free or cheap oil, to the Seven-Year Plan, or 'some exceptional contribution to Persia' in view of the fact that 'it could be argued that the company had enjoyed one or two exceptionally good years, to a degree which no other company had enjoyed in any other country'. Sir William Fraser said he would consider these suggestions. Sir William Strang and Mr Wright told him that they felt that his personal intervention now would be as valuable as it had been recently in securing the new agreement for the Iraq Petroleum Company.

'If Sir William Fraser is prepared to set aside a few million pounds for Persia on a non-recurring basis—which seems to me the right way—it is surely possible to devise a means of doing so. It might even be wise to fix the sum and ask Razmara for suggestions.'[89] This minute of October 23 on Mr Wright's record of the meeting with Sir William Fraser three days earlier, was written by Mr E.A. Berthoud—before becoming the Assistant Under-Secretary of State superintending the economic departments of the Foreign Office, Mr Berthoud had served in the Ministry of Fuel and Power, and, for 13 years before the war, in the Anglo-Iranian Oil Company. His minute was initialled by Mr Wright and Sir William Strang on October 24, after a second meeting with Sir William Fraser and Mr Gass on the previous day. At this meeting on October 23 Sir William Fraser said that he proposed to instruct Mr Northcroft that the company could not agree to any alteration of the Supplemental Agreement itself, which was more advantageous to Persia than estimated when signed: under it Persia would receive for 1950 about £30 million, nearly twice as much as under the agreement of 1933, plus arrears totalling £24 million. Mr Northcroft could, however, inform General Razmara at his discretion that the Anglo-Iranian Oil Company would agree to four additional concessions: first, an increase in the quarterly payments making up the minimum annual royalty of £750,000 stipulated in the 1933 agreement; secondly, an arrangement for Persian checking of measurements of oil (compare General Razmara's third proposed modification of October 1); fourthly, a reduction in the price to Persia of certain products, notably lubricating oil and bitumen. The company was also considering making a special contribution for Persian education, perhaps once more at Tehran University. Sir William Fraser further told Sir William Strang and Mr Wright what he did not then propose to tell Mr Northcroft: that if the latter failed to get the agreement through on these terms, the company would consider some further, non-recurrent offer. Sir William Fraser, however, wished to keep this 'up his sleeve'.

The representatives of the Foreign Office at the meeting of October 23 did not suggest to Sir William Fraser any advance, either in substance or in speed, on his proposed terms; and they agreed to his request that Sir Francis Shepherd should not be informed of the ultimate, unspecified offer which he envisaged. On October 24 Sir Francis Shepherd was instructed to convey to General Razmara from the

---

[88] EP 1531/70.
[89] *Ibid.*

Secretary of State a personal message which went no further as regards the agreement than to hope that the General would secure ratification without attempting to obtain modifications of substance which the company would not feel able to accept. Mr Bevin's message, however emphasised the interest of His Majesty's Government in Persian welfare and in the Seven-Year Plan in particular and stated that he was prepared to negotiate immediately a sterling loan of £2-3 million to the Persian Government to provide for additional currency to meet local expenditure under the plan.

At the same time Sir Oliver Franks was instructed to communicate to Mr Acheson a message from Mr Bevin that, while His Majesty's Government could not advance its position concerning the servicing of the Export-Import Bank loan, it would be prepared over the next two years, while the Americans were devising appropriate arrangements for assisting Persia, to furnish her with up to $6 million for purchasing in the United States agricultural and other machinery which was unobtainable from non-dollar sources, but needed for the Seven-Year Plan.[90] This latter offer was not conveyed to General Razmara. And when Sir Francis Shepherd was informed by telegram on October 17 of Sir William Fraser's instructions to Mr Northcroft it was explained that the latter was still to emphasise the benefits which the Supplemental Agreement would bring rather than the concessions which the company would now make 'since these might prove on analysis by the Majlis to bring relatively trivial benefits'.[91] It may be thought that the concessions to sweeten the agreement which the company was at last prepared to offer still approximated more to the 'inch by inch' variety against which Washington had earlier warned, than to a bold and imaginative initiative to swing the agreement through quickly on more generous lines to match the growing concern of His Majesty's Government for the economic support of Persia.

On November 12, 1950, General Razmara handed Sir Francis Shepherd a reply to Mr Bevin's message. The British offer of a £2-3 million loan was politely refused. In the Eastern Department of the Foreign Office Mr Barnett ascribed this mainly to 'Persian pride'[92] and doubted whether General Razmara would ever accept so small a sum. His Majesty's Ambassador at Tehran commented, in a letter of November 24 to the Secretary of State, upon this 'rather cool reception' of his offer, explaining that if General Razmara had publicised it his Government 'would immediately be accused of being helplessly under pressure from the British Government',[93] and prospect of securing ratification of the Supplemental Agreement would be much worsened. With regard to the Supplemental Agreement Sir Francis Shepherd now commented: 'I find it rather Gilbertian to have spent eight months imploring the Persian Government to be good enough to pocket an immense sum of money that anyone else would have jumped at, and a rather wry aspect of this affair is that numbers of Persian politicians insist on telling me that British influence is irresistible in Persia.'

---

[90] EP 1119/29.
[91] EP 1119/33.
[92] EP 1119/59.
[93] EP 1119/62.

6. The Supplemental Agreement surpassed by the Aramco Agreement of December 1950

It is when empires are in decline that they are especially liable to be accused of oppression. On November 25, 1950, the day after Sir Francis Shepherd wrote his letter to Mr Bevin, His Majesty's Embassy at Tehran reported that the opposition Press there was loudly proclaiming that there was now no need for Persia to be afraid of Great Britain. India and Pakistan were independent, and Egypt was showing the way by insisting on the withdrawal of British troops.[94]

Already on November 16 the Persian Government had suspended indefinitely the relay by Tehran radio of Persian broadcasts by 'Voice of America' and by the BBC. The immediate occasion of this ban was, somewhat significantly, said to have been a broadcast by 'Voice of America' wherein the Soviet Ambassador in Tehran was characterised as 'the butcher of Azerbaijan'. As not infrequently in such cases, the consequences of American shortcomings were visited also upon British interests, and indeed came to be primarily directed against them. Arising out of this, Mr Barnett minuted on November 23 that 'Eastern Department had made it abundantly clear to I[nformation] P[olicy] Department that they wanted no publicity given to the [Supplemental] Agreement at this stage'.[95] The BBC subsequently informed the Foreign Office that, apart from factual news items, only one comment on the agreement had been broadcast, on November 18 after the Persian banning of relays. On November 20 Sir Francis Shepherd telegraphed that propaganda by the Persian Government in favour of the agreement had so far been 'very weak and hesitating'.[96]

The significance of the Persian ban on relays from the BBC was enhanced by the fact that it was imposed shortly after M. Shahrukh had been reinstated as Persian Director of Propaganda. He told the British Acting Information Office at Tehran that if he had not extended the ban to the BBC as well as to the 'Voice of America' he would have been labelled as a British spy: he now had to be 'more nationalist than the patriots of the National Front'[97] although, as he stated, he was under instructions that his main task was to swing public opinion in favour of the Supplemental Agreement. Miss Young suspected that M. Shahrukh bore malice because of the BBC news item concerning his negotiations with the Anglo-Iranian Oil Company, which had occasioned his fall in the summer. The loss of so valuable, if volatile, a friend as M. Shahrukh was liable to be clearly detrimental to British interests at that difficult juncture, suggesting as it did that if, as Sir Francis Shepherd perhaps rather hopefully reported, there was a tendency in Persia to turn again to Great Britain, it might perhaps not be the dominant one. Neither the Foreign Office nor Sir Francis Shepherd, however, apparently advocated any special attempt to woo back M. Shahrukh; nor any firm pressure upon the other hand towards ensuring, for instance, that if the Persian Government would not resume its relay of the BBC, it would at least conduct its own propaganda for the Supplemental Agreement with real vigour. Sir Francis Shepherd proposed to ask for resumption of the relay only after the question of the agreement was settled, and then, if possible, to offer reciprocity for British relay of Persian broadcasts, to enable the Persians to counter Soviet

---

[94] PG 1346/7.
[95] P 10167/57.
[96] EP 1531/80.
[97] P 10167/57.

complaints of discrimination. Such reciprocity was found, however, to present difficulties, and on November 26, 1950, Sir Francis Shepherd was instructed not to press for resumption of the Persian relay of the BBC.[98] The deterioration of the position as regards British interests was accepted without official protest.

At the same time as the Persian ban on relays from the BBC, the Foreign Office received from a different quarter another serious warning concerning the chances of the Supplemental Agreement. On November 16, 1950, the British Middle East Office at Cairo transmitted and endorsed a cogent minute on the agreement, written on the previous day by Mr Noonan, whose views were said to be shared by Mr L. Waight, the Treasury's representative in the Middle East. Mr Noonan argued that after the long delay in the ratification of the Supplemental Agreement it now 'stands virtually no chance at all. I think this must be plain to all open-minded observers and that AIOC are probably alone in stubbornly refusing to face up to things as they are, and make the most of the opportunity presented by the advent to power of Mr Razmara.'[99]

Mr Noonan proceeded to develop two main arguments: first, along familiar American lines, he wondered 'whether the driving of hard bargains put over by hard-boiled business brains is anyhow quite the proper basis of relationship between a country in which Britain has so much at stake, transcending the raking off of the lion's share of commercial profit, and a company in which His Majesty's Government holds the controlling interest'; secondly, Mr Noonan considered that the company should reach the best agreement possible with General Razmara before the situation deteriorated, instead of still trying to extract terms which he regarded as excessive, especially by comparison with the Venezuelan 50-50 agreement and with American reports of possible new terms between Saudi Arabia and Aramco. These reports looked towards additional annual payment by Aramco of $42 million. This sum, which tallied with Mr Parker's estimate in September, was, in Mr Noonan's words, 'reckoned to mean a total payment of around 27s per ton—still a long way from the Venezuelan figure—or 50 per cent of the profits to be inferred for Aramco, but practically half as much again as the AIOC offer to Persia.' Some inconclusive reports about forthcoming negotiations by Aramco were reaching the Foreign Office from Jedda and Washington, and on November 17 Mr Burrows wrote (received on November 23)[100] that the Aramco negotiators were leaving America on November 22. On receipt of this letter Mr Furlonge wrote to Mr Butler of the Ministry of Fuel and Power: 'this makes clearer than ever the imminent danger of the AIOC's difficulties in Persia being increased by developments in Saudi Arabia.'[101] The Foreign Office did not, however, communicate at that time with Sir Francis Shepherd regarding these reports.

Mr Noonan's appreciation reached the Foreign Office on November 20, and on the following day Mr Fry minuted that even if further consultation 'were to show that Mr Noonan is right and we have been wrong, we could hardly alter our attitude at this juncture',[102] but only after a breakdown of the current negotiations. On November 22, however, Mr Ramsbotham of Economic Relations Department

[98] *Ibid.*
[99] *Ibid.*
[100] ES 1532/34.
[101] EP 1531/85.
[102] *Ibid.*

advised that Mr Noonan's paper should be seriously considered and suggested that the Anglo-Iranian Oil Company should be 'a little more forthcoming . . . I would recommend that the Foreign Office should advise AIOC that, if they have additional concessions up their sleeve, these should be offered immediately as there is just a chance that there is time for Razmara to sway the verdict of the Parliamentary Commission.'[103]

It is not clear whether Mr Ramsbotham's minute (which also noticed that Great Britain depended upon her oil industry 'to an alarming extent to maintain our favourable overall balance of payments') was received in Eastern Department before Mr Bowker (who had recently succeeded Mr Wright as Assistant Under-Secretary), Mr Furlonge and Mr Barnett held a meeting with Messrs Gass and Rice of the Anglo-Iranian Oil Company on the same day of November 22. Mr Gass reported that on November 17 General Razmara had presented some further demands (cement factories and gas piping) and, especially, had ventilated the idea of a 50-50 division of profits on Persian operations, including calculation of the oil supplied to the Admiralty as though it were sold on the free market. The company's representatives explained that this would entail separating off Persian operations, and complicated discussions; but the company would in fact be prepared to negotiate on such a basis if the Supplemental Agreement were rejected. Mr Gass said in conclusion that the 'company had now come to the end of their tether as regards concessions to Persia and asked whether Mr Furlonge did not agree. Mr Furlonge made no reply.'[104] No proposal by the representatives of the Foreign Office to those of the company in favour of larger or swifter concessions was recorded.

Three days later, on November 25, the Majlis Oil Commission unanimously resolved that the Supplemental Agreement 'was not sufficient to restore the rights of Iran'. The National Front headed by the Commission's chairman, Dr Musaddiq, had further been trying to get a Bill for oil nationalisation on to the agenda. On November 29, 1950, the spokesmen of the National Front on the Majlis Oil Commission introduced there a resolution which had, substantially, been issued by the National Front as a manifesto on November 6, and which read: 'For the sake of the prosperity of the Iranian nation and with a view to ensuring world peace, the undersigned propose that the oil industry should be entirely nationalised, i.e. the entire operations for exploration, exploitation and extraction be controlled by the Government.'[105] This resolution was not adopted and in its concluding report of December 10 the Oil Commission confined itself, by a majority vote, to its unanimous resolution of November 25 against the Supplemental Agreement.

Initially Sir Francis Shepherd commented somewhat blankly that the resolution of November 25 was satisfactory in that it did not refer to the concession of 1933, whereas the National Front had been pressing for a resolution calling for its cancellation.[106] On November 27, however, he wrote to Mr Furlonge that the moderate members of the commission took its unanimous resolution 'to mean that the agreement can still be passed with a few modifications, while the extremists consider that it involves its complete rejection . . . I do not think Razmara has used

---

[103] EP 1531/88.
[104] EP 1531/84.
[105] EP 1531/910 of 1951: Proceedings of Majlis Oil Commission, p. 145.
[106] EP 1531/83.

his forces very cleverly over this and the resolution puts him into a difficult position
. . . Although there is likely to be a certain amount of anti-oil company and anti-
British hysteria for a short period it is too early to admit defeat, although the
Government has obviously lost the first skirmish.'[107] If it was the first skirmish, it
had been fought and lost dangerously late.

Two days later, on November 29, 1950, His Majesty's Ambassador at Tehran
telegraphed to the Foreign Office, repeating to Jedda, a request for urgent
information concerning a report which had reached the Persian Government to the
effect that the Arabian Government had forced Aramco to sign an agreement on
much advanced terms.[108] This report was premature. On the same day of November
29, however, Sir Oliver Franks sent by Saving telegram (received on December 4) a
message from Mr Dean Acheson wherein he replied to that of October 24 from the
Secretary of State concerning economic aid for Persia, and concluded with a warning
that, as British officials had been informed, Aramco might have to make
considerable concessions which would render the position of the Anglo-Iranian Oil
Company in relation to the Supplemental Agreement 'far more difficult'.[109] In this
connexion Sir Francis Shepherd telegraphed on December 7 to propose that the
Secretary of State might suggest to Mr Acheson that he advise Aramco to delay
making any such definite agreement with Saudi Arabia 'in order to help us in solving
the Persian problem'.[110]

The Foreign Office apparently did not reply to Sir Francis Shepherd's suggestion
of December 7, which was considered in Eastern Department to be unlikely to
commend itself either to Mr Bevin, who however called for a paper on it, or to the
State Department. Minutes on this argued that the harm had already been done by
Aramco and cited the reluctance of the American Government, largely for domestic
reasons, to intervene in American oil undertakings, and the failure of the Shinwell-
Ickes agreement. This failure was now making itself felt. Mr Bowker minuted on
December 22 that he was not convinced that nothing could be done and that 'this
cut-throat competition between the oil companies threatens to land us in ever-
increasing political complications'.[111] On December 27 Mr Berthoud agreed that
'too much is at stake for a policy of complete inaction'.[112] Some days later Mr Butler
of the Ministry of Fuel and Power expressed the view that the Aramco negotiations
would be protracted. He was wrong. It was already too late. It was soon, but not
immediately, known that on Boxing Day Aramco and the Saudi Arabian
Government had signed a new agreement which set a new standard of liberality for
oil companies in the Middle East and notably accorded to Saudi Arabia a 50-50 share
in profits on the Venezuelan model already familiar to American oil companies.

7. The Attlee-Truman conversations of December 1950 and British military planning for Persia

In the absence that December of Anglo-American consultations concerning the
Aramco negotiations in relation to British interests in Persia, other Anglo-American

---

[107] EP 1531/89.
[108] ES 1532/35.
[109] EP 1119/61.
[110] EP 1531/95.
[111] EP 1531/13 of 1951.
[112] *Ibid.*

conversations, partly economic, were being held at the highest level in the strategic setting of the contest with the Communist Powers. The visit of Mr Attlee to Washington on December 4-8, 1950, was mainly prompted by anxiety regarding the critical military position in Korea and the dangerous propensities of General MacArthur. Whereas the restricted size and speed of British support in the Korean War had provoked criticism in America.

On December 5, 1950, Mr Attlee gave President Truman an assurance of continued British support in the critical bridgehead around Seoul and Inchon, and told the National Press Club in Washington on the following day: 'You may be certain that, in fair or foul weather, where the Stars and Stripes fly in Korea, the British flag will fly beside them. We stand by our duty. We stand by our friends.'[113] In the same speech the Prime Minister alluded incidentally to Britain's 'very close relation with the peoples of the Middle East'. Some American reciprocity there might have been most welcome. If the Government of the United States insisted upon British military participation in the Far East as well as insisting, as it had in the conversations in October, that the Middle East was above all a British military responsibility, then it might well have been worth trying, at least, to extract in return firm American undertakings to give at any rate full moral and diplomatic support to British policies in the Middle East including Persia with its oil potential. This, however, was not attempted.

On the economic side Mr Attlee and President Truman urgently discussed mutual difficulties regarding supplies of scarce raw materials such as cotton, zinc and sulphur from American resources, and, from British, tin and rubber. This category did not include oil, though a Foreign Office telegram of December 6 to Washington, providing a brief for Mr Attlee, had included the statement: 'We are also anxious to see more rapid progress made in the Anglo-American discussions on oil requirements and supply in war.'[114] This reflected a letter of November 30 from Mr Kelf-Cohen of the Ministry of Fuel and Power to Mr Berthoud wherein the writer had dwelt upon American delays in concerting the world oil survey, and had emphasised its importance in relation to a decision of the British Chiefs of Staff, just notified to the Ministry, that no further decision could be taken concerning the defence of Middle Eastern oil supplies until the world oil survey had gone further and until further examination had been given to a general defence policy in the Middle East.[115] Meanwhile, however, limited military planning for the protection if necessary of British interests in Abadan Island in peacetime had in November produced what became Plan Accleton. This plan, on the assumption of Persian co-operation, provided for the move by air of two British battalions to Abadan with the object of safeguarding British lives and property in the Abadan area and assuring the export of oil.[116]

On December 12, 1950, Mr Furlonge, in his minute for Mr Bevin on Soviet-Persian relations (see p. 73) had concluded with regard to the Anglo-Persian staff talks suggested by the Shah that 'pending completion of our plans for Middle East defence, it is not possible to give him more than a very general reassurance as to our

---

[113] ZP 3/3G.
[114] UR 1030/13G.
[115] UES 1534/68G.
[116] EP 1015/177G of 1951.

intentions'.[117] Although the opening from the Shah related to defence of the Persian oilfields against Russian attack, once military conversations with the Persians had been initiated it might have been an appropriate British objective to secure, though adroit and purposeful diplomacy, a certain extension in their coverage to include, perhaps as a *quid pro quo*, marginal cases wherein more strictly British interests at Abadan might require military protection, as in 1946, preferably without too specific connexion with a hypothetical Communist menace. As it was, in relation to the conversations in Washington, it came to be understood in the Foreign Office that the desideratum concerning oil advanced in its telegram of December 6 'was not taken up by the Prime Minister: indeed, in his statement on the establishment of a central authority for Raw Material allocations, he expressly excluded food and oil from his proposals' (minute of December 18 by Mr Ramsbotham).[118]

Plan Accleton for the protection of British oil interests, limited to the Abadan area, supposed Persian co-operation, for which early consultations might have proved beneficial. But for the defence of the oilfields in South Persia, British consultations with eager Persian authorities had become dependent upon broader and more complicated planning for the defence of the Middle East as a whole, and also to some extent, apparently, upon the still broader and more rarified world oil survey. It would seem that planning for defence of Persian oil was approximating dangerously to a vicious circle. While any particular plan clearly needs to be set correctly within general policy, the evident danger, as here, is of allowing planning for specific objects to bog down in a proliferation of contingent studies and calculations. No doubt, though, that is only one way of indicating the old difficulty of aiming at ideal results through the cluttered imperfections of everyday existence.

Any critical estimate of British diplomacy in regard to military planning to cover Persia towards the close of 1950 needs to pay the same attention that the Chiefs of Staff and the Foreign Office naturally did at the time to the hard fact of British military weakness, and the dangers of entering into unrealisable commitments. To some extent, however, it may be that the background of British power and prestige, as in the Second World War and in the Indian Empire, was as yet too close to permit a full psychological adjustment to changed circumstances wherein Great Britain might well need to reinforce her position of strength, still, in relation to lesser powers such as Persia by exploiting the techniques of bargaining from weakness in negotiating with great Powers like the United States. Hence, perhaps, the impression sometimes that British policy regarding Persia was at once too rigid and too weak.

8. Withdrawal of the Supplemental Agreement in December 1950

On December 9, 1950, His Majesty's Embassy in Tehran reported in its weekly summary of the Persian Press (initialled in Foreign Office on December 19): 'Most newspapers regard the approval by the Majlis of the Oil Commission's rejection of the Supplemental Oil Agreement as a foregone conclusion. It is widely thought that the Majlis will charge the Government with the reopening of negotiations but the National Front appear to think they can prevent this by tabling a Bill for the nationalisation of the oil industry.'[119] On the same day the Embassy telegraphed that

---

[117] EP 10338/45G.
[118] UES 1534/68G.
[119] PG 1346/7.

the Anglo-Iranian Oil Company had been advised by Mr Max Thornburg, the head for Persia of the American firm of Overseas Consultants Incorporated advising on the Seven-year Plan, to save the financial situation of the Persian Government by paying it at least part of the funds they would have received under the Supplemental Agreement, even if it were rejected by the Majlis. The company had rejected this suggestion with 'a flat *non possumus*'.[120]

On December 15 the Secretary of State sent a letter to Sir Francis Shepherd in reply to his of November 24 concerning the Persian refusal of the offered British loan. Mr Bevin wrote: 'For the present . . . there does not seem to be anything which I can do to help Razmara until the Majlis has finally pronounced one way or another . . . I agree on the matter of offering advice to the Persians. We must certainly avoid errors, into which others have fallen, of appearing to dictate to these tiresome and headstrong people.'[121] The Foreign Office, however, so far from adopting any dictatorial or repressive line with the Persians, was seemingly content to await the fate of the Supplemental Agreement in the Majlis with a considerable degree of detachment. It was not until December 21 that any instructions or enquiries in this connexion were addressed to Sir Francis Shepherd, who had reported, but not emphasised, Persian tendencies towards nationalisation.

Meanwhile, in the later words of the British Labour Attaché at Tehran, 'nearly all sections of the [Persian] community joined in the clatter and clamour for the nationalisation of oil'.[122] Even Persian editors friendly to Britain were constrained to attack her,[123] though the non-communist trades unions were notable exceptions from the stampede whipped up by the National Front and the fanatical religious leader, M. Ayatullah Kashani. With few exceptions, Persians did not even dare to discuss the actual terms of the Supplemental Agreement.[124] In the debate on oil in the Majlis on December 17 M. Makki, in the absence of Dr Musaddiq owing to illness, presented a proposal, signed by 11 deputies, for nationalisation. Four days later General Razmara, who had endeavoured without much success to curb the nationalist Press, suggested to His Majesty's Ambassador that a new agreement, simpler than the Supplemental Agreement, be submitted to the Majlis. In the same conversation Sir Francis Shepherd expressed regret that General Razmara had not given a strong lead to the Majlis, and protested against the wide and vituperative accusations against Great Britain made by speakers there. General Razmara avoided any promise that he would rebuke them. In the Foreign Office Mr Barnett considered this 'most unsatisfactory' but 'of course understandable'.[125]

On December 20 Mr Drake had telegraphed from Abadan to Mr Gass that the Shah was not entirely satisfied with General Razmara's handling of the Supplemental Agreement and wished to intervene personally. This information came from M. Perron, a Swiss secretary and confidant of the Shah, who had sent him to ask Mr Drake to see the Shah since that monarch considered that Mr Northcroft was too inflexible and unsuitable to handle the situation. Mr Drake replied that Mr Northcroft had the full confidence of the company, but M. Perron urged the former

---

[120] EP 1531/94.
[121] EP 1119/62.
[122] EP 2181/3 of 1951.
[123] PG 1344/1 of 1951.
[124] EP 1531/7 of 1951.
[125] EP 1531/108: also EP 1531/98.

to meet the Shah secretly, saying that a desperate situation called for desperate measures.[126] The company consulted the Foreign Office, who consulted His Majesty's Ambassador. Sir Francis Shepherd replied on December 23 in a sense personally favourable to Mr Northcroft and unfavourable to M. Perron, with the comment: 'It looks as if the Shah is clutching at straw in order to avoid the rejection of the supplemental agreement. But the Government has allowed the question to reach an emotional state in which I cannot imagine any practicable concessions which the companies [*sic*] could make would be effective at this particular moment.'[127] This was presumably sound advice at that stage; and the Shah was scarcely the man to emulate his father's feat in 1933, when he had browbeaten his Government into accepting the terms which he had himself agreed with the company. It is nevertheless permissible to wonder, perhaps, whether the Supplemental Agreement might have fared better if at a rather earlier stage the Foreign Office, or His Majesty's Ambassador, or the Anglo-Iranian Oil Company had preceded the Shah in considering the possibility of trying exceptional and urgent procedures which the evident goodwill of the monarch might have facilitated.

On December 18 representatives of the Foreign Office (Messrs Bowker, Furlonge, Ramsbotham and Barnett) had held a meeting with those of the Treasury (Messrs Flett, Young and Waight) to discuss economic aid for Persia. This question, as the resultant telegram of December 21 to Sir Francis Shepherd observed, depended upon the fate of the Supplemental Agreement, and it was assumed that 'ratification without amendment is now most unlikely'.[128] Further envisaged was the possibility of its outright rejection, in which case His Majesty's Government should make to the United States Government early and 'concrete proposals for a co-operative effort to assist Persia'. Such proposals, arising from Mr Bevin's exchanges with Mr Acheson, were now to receive inter-departmental study; so too was the Supplemental Agreement in the light, in particular, of the Venezuelan agreement and of the Aramco negotiations.

The comparative study of the Supplemental Agreement was incorporated by the Foreign Office in a memorandum of December 21 which explained that it was being undertaken in order to counter any 'American criticism that our failure to make further concessions led to the rejection of the [Supplemental] Agreement and any consequent economic crisis which may arise in Persia'.[129] That aspect, even more than the possible consequences to British oil interests, was then the main preoccupation of the Foreign Office in regard to the possibility, now nearly accepted in advance, of the failure of the Supplemental Agreement as it then stood. In the light of the comparative study, however, His Majesty's Government would need to consider 'to what extent we should be justified in pressing the company to make concessions':[130] in other words, to what extent really effective force should be given to the decision of principle which the Secretary of State had taken so long ago as October 10.[131] It was thought that this might involve a redefinition of the attitude of His Majesty's Government towards the Anglo-Iranian Oil Company since, as Mr

---

[126] EP 1531/100.
[127] EP 1531/101.
[128] EP 1119/61.
[129] EP 1531/105.
[130] EP 1119/61.
[131] See p. [46].

Furlonge wrote in a letter of December 27 to Mr Butler of the Ministry of Fuel and Power, 'we have hitherto been most scrupulous in avoiding any suggestions that His Majesty's Government, although a major shareholder, interfere with the policy of the company'.[132]

The Anglo-Iranian Oil Company had indeed received no more than representations from Whitehall, though the policy of His Majesty's Government was liable, through high taxation and dividend limitation (cf p. 56), to intensify the company's difficulties with the Persian Government. The comparative study estimated that in 1950, under the terms of the Supplemental Oil agreement, the Persian Government would receive £30 million, while the company retained £29 million, a division roughly corresponding in itself to the Venezuelan 50-50 arrangement, if no regard were had to His Majesty's Government's large receipts of £37.5 million in taxation and dividends. These figures, without their implications, were transmitted to Mr Furlonge to Mr Butler on December 27, with a copy to Mr M.T. Flett, an Under-Secretary in the Treasury.

Also on December 27, 1950, Mr Barnett in the Eastern Department of the Foreign Office minuted on a telegram from Sir Francis Shepherd, commenting on his conversation of December 21 with the Persian Premier, that he, Mr Barnett, considered that General Razmara had done well, more particularly in refusing to make promises to the deputies in the Majlis. His Majesty's Ambassador had reported, for the first time 'in so many words', that the majority of them would like to see the Supplemental Agreement passed; Mr Barnett commented: 'The National Front represents nothing except a noisy minority of malcontents in Tehran, and it is high time its bluff were called.'[133]

Three days earlier, on Christmas Eve, the Persian Minister of Finance, M. Furuhar, had made a bold speech in the Majlis wherein he was the first member of the Government to defend the Supplemental Agreement in detail and to reject nationalisation of oil. In accordance with a decision of General Razmara, however, this was only the covering prelude to an announcement by M. Furuhar that since the Oil Commission of the Majlis considered that the agreement did not safeguard Persian interests, the Government was withdrawing the Bill for its ratification. Sir Francis Shepherd reported that when lunching with the Shah on December 30 he had said to the latter 'that it would be particularly unfortunate if M. Furuhar were to be allowed to resign. His was the only speech made since the agreement was signed in which some attempt was made to explain it. (On this, the Shah said, "Don't you think that speech would have been more effective if it had been made three months ago?") If Ministers were to be forced to resign merely for explaining the contents of an agreement signed by the Government, this would remove all basis for further negotiations. The Shah agreed.'[134]

His Majesty's Ambassador's representation to the Shah in favour of M. Furuhar appears to have been the furthest that he went, with either the Persian monarch or Prime Minister, in the direction of a minatory communication in the face of the stinging rebuff to British interests represented by the withdrawal of the Supplemental Agreement. Sir Francis Shepherd reported no protest by himself in reply to General

---

[132] EP 1531/105.
[133] EP 1531/99.
[134] EP 1015/1 of 1951.

Razmara's explanation, in a conversation of December 27 on the withdrawal that 'he had been unable to conduct a propaganda campaign or take any measures to explain the contents of the agreement because the matter had been with the Majlis and the Government was not therefore entitled to intervene in this manner. He thought however than when the excitement had died down it was necessary for the question to be explained to the people.'[135]

In the same conversation of December 27 the Persian Premier asked His Majesty's Ambassador for his views concerning a dissolution of the Majlis, which he proposed to recommend to the Shah, and 'on the possibilities of getting something done about the oil question'. On the latter score, Sir Francis Shepherd said he could not give any opinion at present and pointed out that 'the Supplemental Agreement had never been discussed under any of the last three Governments'. He supposed that constitutional dissolution was probably the correct course and if, as General Razmara expected, a new Majlis would be better than the existing one then 'there would be an advantage in dissolution over the other alternatives. I asked, however, whether he did not think that dissolution might lead to a violent Press campaign and disturbances. He said that there was a possibility of this and that probably martial law would be imposed for one or two months until the situation was quite calm.'[136]

Sir Francis Shepherd's balancing attitude with regard to a dissolution of the Majlis was reproduced in the Foreign Office, though with somewhat more emphasis, perhaps, upon its desirability under certain conditions. Mr Bevin stated in a telegram of December 29 to Tehran, approved by himself and by Sir William Strang, that only the Shah and General Razmara could judge the best course, and it was neither possible nor desirable to advise them about it. For Sir Francis Shepherd's own information, 'I agree however that dissolution is probably necessary if general improvement is to be hoped for'.[137] If General Razmara were to proceed with the dissolution, Sir Francis Shepherd was to persuade him if possible that any announcement in that connexion should be couched in general terms and should not particularise the difficulties over the oil Bill, in order to minimise the evident danger that the dissolution of the Majlis might 'be ascribed to British influence and any resulting disturbances exploited by the Russians'.

Such prudential considerations were of evident importance; but it might perhaps have been worth while for the Foreign Office or His Majesty's Ambassador to have sought to balance them up against some prompt consideration of whether, after such long and fruitless attempts to have the Supplemental Agreement piloted through the Majlis, the time might not have come to encourage the Shah and General Razmara to hoist things out of the rut by striking out on a new and firm line such as might perhaps have developed from the general's suggestive linking of his questions to His Majesty's Ambassador concerning the dissolution of the Majlis and doing something about the question of oil. In the absence of such consideration, and in the light of instructions, it was natural that Sir Francis Shepherd did not comment when the Shah told him at their luncheon on December 30 that he was not 'in a hurry to dissolve the Majlis and would await events in the immediate future to see whether some

---

[135] EP 1531/6 of 1951.
[136] *Ibid.*
[137] EP 1531/106.

further effort could not be made to induce them to work'.[138]

On the following day, at the close of the year, Sir Francis Shepherd addressed to the Secretary of State a long despatch reviewing the fate of the Supplemental Agreement, the withdrawal of which from the Majlis 'marks a crisis in the conduct of the Anglo-Persian oil question'.[139] Sir Francis Shepherd wrote: 'I cannot recall any point at which any reasonable concession could usefully have been made, other than those worked out during the last month or two for Razmara's benefit. He was, for a soldier, surprisingly hesitant in coming to a decision . . . I conclude, therefore, that in spite of the accusations of undue rigidity that have been levelled at the oil company, particularly by our American friends, there was never an opening where a concession by them could have been combined with a real determination on the part of the Government to secure ratification. Nothing would have had the desired effect short of the scrapping of the Supplemental Agreement and the initiation of further negotiations on an entirely new basis. This would have led to considerable delay and would not have been justified in the circumstances.' This consoling verdict was not perhaps in strict contradiction with Sir Francis Shepherd's recommendation of September 10 (cf p. 80) in favour of a 'changed attitude' towards additional concessions. But it is not entirely clear what relation his retrospective view may have borne to his suggestion as early as July 10 (cf p. 77) that the Persian Government should be offered a Persian director of a Persian subsidiary company: a suggestion made at the time when General Razmara was proposing to withdraw the Supplemental Agreement from the Majlis Oil Commission, and five weeks before his reported decision 'to proceed to obtain ratification'.

Sir Francis Shepherd added in his despatch of December 31, 1950: 'So far as finance is concerned, I am prepared to accept the company's contention that they have gone to a reasonable limit in the Supplemental Agreement.' His Majesty's Ambassador had not then heard that five days earlier Aramco had signed its 50-50 agreement with Saudi Arabia. It was to nail up the coffin of the defunct Supplemental Agreement. For the security of Great Britain's very important oil interests in Persia the year 1951 opened with much unaccomplished, much threatened.

9. The perspective of British policy regarding Persian oil in 1950

The defence by Sir Francis Shepherd of the somewhat unyielding policy concerning the Supplemental Agreement pursued during 1950 by the Anglo-Iranian Oil Company and, in support of it, by His Majesty's Government must evidently carry considerable weight. That policy was not in fact successful and it is easy to be wise after the event. But an attempt to secure the firm ratification of a fair agreement already signed by the Persian Government, rather than to plunge down the slippery slope of revisions and concessions to such sharp customers as the Persians, possessed very evident advantages during the first half of the year and perhaps for some time even after Sir Francis Shepherd's suggestions for additional concessions on July 10 and again on September 10. It is true that at that period, with some inversion of traditional roles, the Americans consistently urged that British dealings with Persia should be less hard-headedly businesslike and more generously statesmanlike. It is also true that it is easier to indulge in generous statesmanship when somebody else

---

[138] EP 1015/1 of 1951.
[139] EP 1531/7 of 1951.

is going to foot the financial bill for it. It would appear that this honourable scruple rightly weighed with the Foreign Office in its highly considerate dealings with the Anglo-Iranian Oil Company. Nevertheless the Americans did practise what they preached, and with conspicuous success, in the case of Aramco in Arabia: it came to be reported that the idea of a 50-50 arrangement originated unofficially with the American Treasury.[140] And a similar policy in Persia came to be advocated by the British Middle East Office.

The decision taken by the Secretary of State on October 10, 1950, towards exerting pressure upon the Anglo-Iranian Oil Company to be more forthcoming, stands out as timely, if not indeed overdue. For the subsequent period to the end of the year it is difficult to resist the impression that the Foreign Office implemented this decision with excessive mildness and caution, in contrast with the keener sense of urgency consistently voiced by the State Department. The reluctance of the Foreign Office to press the company to make substantial concessions quickly to the Persians was the more striking in the light of the Treasury brief of September 14 advocating virtually unlimited concessions to them in other financial negotiations in the paramount interest of safeguarding the oil resources. It would be more striking still, if, as one might infer from subsequent evidence, it was the Treasury itself which notably advocated a policy of forbearance and absence of pressure upon the company. The Treasury was in any case the department responsible for the interests of His Majesty's Government in the Anglo-Iranian Oil Company; and the company expected to conduct its own negotiations with the Persian Government. In dealings with that Government concerning oil interests the Foreign Office therefore tended to be notably handicapped by having to conduct them, so to speak, at one remove, if not two.

While considerable allowance needs to be made for the delicate relationship between the Foreign Office and the Anglo-Iranian Oil Company, somewhat later evidence suggests that in 1950 those mainly concerned in the Foreign Office may have been rather insufficiently aware of the constitutional basis of this relationship and the extent of the powers which it secured to His Majesty's Government. This applied, in particular, to the terms of Sir John Bradbury's letter of 1914, which remained the operative instrument, and to the functions, as indeed the names, of the two government-appointed directors of the company. In 1950 these were in fact Field-Marshal Lord Alanbrooke and Sir Thomas Gardiner, formerly Director-General of the General Post Office; neither of them, perhaps, possessed quite the experience of Sir George Barstow, who had been a governmental director from 1927 to 1946. Any lack of clarity in the Foreign Office concerning such arrangements perhaps suggests some neglect—comprehensible in a very busy department—of the historical background and the research facilities for supplying it.

If His Majesty's Government had felt able to press the Anglo-Iranian Oil Company harder towards meeting General Razmara with generous concessions which might have been presented as an imaginative programme, it might have been necessary, in order to swing it through, to back it by more effective publicity and by a policy of firmness, made sufficiently clear but held in reserve. Such a policy needed to take particular account of the circumstances that while Great Britain was the great Power of the West with a special stake in Persia, any British measures to defend that

---

[140] ES 1531/19 of 1951.

vital interest must be concerted with special regard to the policies and interests of the two stronger Powers, America and Russia. This consideration was of course almost taken for granted at the time in the Foreign Office. But its implications for the broad conduct of British policy towards Persia might possibly have repaid close examination in a special memorandum. Such a political appreciation, which was not in fact undertaken, might to some extent have complemented the staff studies on the military side.

As regards America, possibilities have already been mentioned for British bargaining for her firm support in Persia in consideration of reciprocity in Korea and of the importance of the Middle East for the Western alliance as a whole in terms both of economics—precisely oil—and of strategy. That involved the Russian angle on Persia. It was an acute one in view, more particularly, of the Soviet-Persian Treaty of 1921 which, whatever the precise legal significance of the terms, could be invoked by Russia as at any rate a specious cover for intervention in the event of any British military action in South Persia in defence of oil interests. No British policy could, or did, fail to take account of this dangerous possibility, which conspicuously frightened the Americans and, still, more immediately, the Persians themselves. It does not appear, however, that any early or thorough consideration was given to the possibility that, instead of only stringing along with the Americans and acquiescing in this fear, British policy might seek to exploit it to its own advantage.

It is at any rate not inconceivable that the balance of advantage might have lain in the early adoption of an adroit and resolute policy designed to put a bold front on the Russian danger. The moment to deploy it might possibly have been when the Persian clamour for nationalisation of oil assumed serious proportions, in December 1950 if not earlier. No doubt the issue of nationalisation was a particularly awkward one for the British Labour Government, but so great was the economic stake in Persia that if the issue had been faced in 1950, rather than early in 1951 as in fact occurred, the result might well have been the same: recognition by His Majesty's Government that, more particularly in view of the categorical terms of the concession of 1933, nationalisation of the Persian assets and interests of the Anglo-Iranian Oil Company could not and should not be conceded. In that event there might have been great advantage in using such a resolve as a peg upon which to hang an entirely friendly but serious warning to the Shah and General Razmara as to the urgency of ratifying the Supplemental Agreement and conjuring the threat of nationalisation with its incalculable consequences, not even excluding, it might have been hinted, British dispositions for the use of force, as in 1946. It might have been possible, for example, to introduce such a warning deftly into any negotiations with the Persian Government, had they been pursued as the Shah wanted, for joint defence of Southern Persia against Russian aggression; in that case it might even have contributed towards an agreement in advance upon the modalities of the all-important Persian request for British intervention: the critical factor for world opinion and the United Nations. If the Persians had made any representation that the introduction of British forces to protect threatened British interests at Abadan would be liable to provoke Russian intervention, it might have been feasible to reply with equanimity that that was precisely why His Majesty's Government was so anxious that the Persian Government should do everything to allay any threat to vital British interests since otherwise the consequences might be so evidently dangerous and disagreeable for the Persians themselves (compare the leverage suggested by Mr

Churchill in 1941: cf p. 43).

Such a policy of pressure could only be justified by the magnitude of the British interests at stake. It would, like most firm policies, and indeed like many weak ones, have entailed evident risk. It would clearly have required Cabinet consideration. This might in any event have been to the good at a time when in point of fact Persian issues were seldom raised in the Cabinet by the Foreign Secretary. And a policy of warning pressure upon the Persian Government would have been designed precisely to prevent the growth of such a threat to British interests that their preservation might ultimately have required military action even at the risk of going to the brink of war against the Soviet Union in Persia. Though even in that extreme case the considered opinion of the British Chiefs of Staff, as already noticed and as they were to reiterate in 1951, was that the Russians were not in fact ready to risk a global war arising from a direct clash in Persia.

The most immediate difficulty, and a very serious one, for His Majesty's Government in adopting any such firm policy towards Persia would doubtless have been strenuous American opposition. That in itself might well have seemed to rule it out when Great Britain, at a time of economic and military weakness, was heavily committed to the United States in the North Atlantic Treaty Organisation and in other ways, partly psychologically. His Majesty's Government had become accustomed to making sacrifices in the interests of American co-operation, and it was the sincere inclination of the Government, and of Mr Ernest Bevin in particular, not to make trouble with friends and allies. Such benevolent considerations, however, needed to be balanced against others such as the magnitude of the Persian interests for Great Britain both economically and politically in relation to her whole position in the Middle East. Great Britain remained America's chief ally and, as noticed, was far from possessing no cards even if some of them represented a lead from material weakness. That was a diplomatic art which Great Britain had largely been able to neglect during the 19th and early 20th centuries whereas now conditions called for some revival, perhaps, of techniques familiar enough in the 18th century.

If His Majesty's Government had faced up to the United States Government in all candour, in advance, concerning the absolute necessity, if occasion arose, of protecting British oil installations in Persia, it is conceivable that it might have been possible, in part at any rate, to draw the sting of American disapproval before any acute crisis occurred, or at least to have extracted firm pledges of American diplomatic support in a concerted policy so long as there was no British resort to force. It would have been of inestimable benefit for British interests in Persia if resolute British diplomacy could have set the Americans calculating that, in order to conjure their bugbear of Russian intervention there, it was above all desirable to appease, not the Persian Government, but the British. As it was, the absence of such an American calculation affords the key to much of the whole development of the Persian crisis in 1951.

On so important an issue it would not, one may think, have called for any impossible measure of foresight to have begun in 1950 to concert some such British policy, or some appropriate and closely reasoned alternative. But it would have demanded forward-looking discrimination and resolution at a high level. Whereas the immediate issue of the ratification of the Supplemental Agreement was to a considerable extent a technical and economic one which only occasionally in 1950 reached the level of the Secretary of State for Foreign Affairs. Nor was it of predominant importance even for the hard-worked Eastern Department, which was then responsible, perhaps rather too widely, for all the Arab countries of the Middle East together with Israel and Persia.

The handling of Persian questions by the Foreign Service during 1950 probably suffered also to some extent from its having been a somewhat unlucky years [*sic*] as regards personnel owing to illness and transfers. During the first nine months of the year Mr Bevin only worked in the Foreign Office for a few weeks in all. He was repeatedly absent owing either to illness or to official visits abroad, to Ceylon, Egypt, Italy, Strasbourg, Paris, The Hague and New York. At the end of the year he was within four months of his death. An especially heavy burden was thrown upon Sir William Strang. One can readily understand, as well as regret, the rarity of his substantive minutes like that of August 12 (cf pp. 69-70) on Persian affairs. In November Mr Bowker succeeded Mr Michael Wright as the Assistant Under-Secretary superintending Eastern Department. Both, however, had previous experience of the Middle East, as also had Mr Furlonge in chiefly consular capacities. The same was true of Mr Barnett. Mr Fry came from the Indian Political Service. Mr Warner, the Assistant Under-Secretary superintending information departments, was absent for several months owing to illness late in 1950 and early in 1951.

At Tehran Sir John Le Rougetel had been succeeded as Ambassador early in 1950 by Sir Francis Shepherd, whose successful consular career had not embraced previous experience of the Middle East but had included several posts in time of crisis, at Barcelona during the Spanish Civil War, at Dresden during the Sudeten crisis, at Danzig in 1939, at Reykjavik early in the Second World War, and thereafter in the emergent nationalism of Indonesia. Sir Francis Shepherd, unlike his predecessor, apparently did not enjoy personal relations with Sir William Fraser. The new ambassador soon succeeded Sir John Le Rougetel in the personal confidence of the Shah, though perhaps not with quite the same degree of intimacy as that enjoyed by the Counsellor in His Majesty's Embassy, Mr Lawford. The latter had represented Sir Francis Shepherd at times when he was indisposed in July-August 1950. In the following month, however, Mr Lawford left Tehran and was succeeded by Mr G.H. Middleton. Both His Majesty's Ambassador and his Counsellor were thus new to Persian affairs. The Oriental Counsellor was the experienced Mr L.F.L. Pyman but, as noticed, the post of Information Officer was throughout the year only filled by a lady in an acting capacity.

All personal factors, however, were doubtless subsidiary to the main trend of economic and political developments. Looking back over the fortunes of British oil-interests in Persia in 1950 it is possible to understand why it largely appears in retrospect as a year of drift and deterioration in the direction of worse to follow in 1951.

CHAPTER IV

THE THREAT OF PERSIAN OIL NATIONALISATION AND THE ASSASSINATION OF GENERAL RAZMARA, JANUARY 1-MARCH 7, 1951

1. Reactivation of the Majlis Oil Commission and resignation of M. Furuhar, January 1-14

The New Year opened out for British interests in Persia, from the economic setback of the withdrawal of the Supplemental Agreement, into a political deterioration. On January 4, 1951, the Majlis passed a unanimous resolution disapproving the whole of the speech made by the Persian Minister of Finance on December 26. His Majesty's Ambassador, however, did not think it 'necessary to analyse too closely the implications of the resolution because it was passed under stress of emotion and in consequence of the ascendancy which the extremists of the National Front have managed to attain by their assumption of a monopoly of patriotism'.[1] This observation, possibly reflecting some underestimate of the rising tide of Persian nationalism, occurred in a despatch of January 6, received on January 11, but not minuted in Eastern Department until January 20. Two days later Mr Fry commented on Sir Francis Shepherd's allusion to Persian emotionalism 'that emotion, as it seems to me, is by far the biggest factor with which AIOC—and we— have to deal. As for the vociferousness of a minority with patriotic slogans on its lips, Indian history in 1940-47 provides an excellent example of the power that can thus be exerted.'[2] Air Commodore K.C. Buss, Assistant Head of the Research Department and an expert on Middle Eastern affairs, agreed and observed that Persia was not the only country in the Middle East where the friends of Britain dare not profess their friendship. He suggested that the fact that Ireland was mentioned in the Majlis debate 'shows clearly that the feeling that Great Britain can be defied with impunity has a good deal to do with the attitude taken up by the Opposition'. The Air Commodore held that Sir Francis Shepherd should have included this factor in his analysis, in his despatch of December 31 1950, of the basic reasons for Persian opposition to the Supplemental Agreement.

The withdrawal of the Supplemental Agreement intensified the financial straits of the Persian Government, which accordingly terminated as from January 1, 1951, its contract with Overseas Consultants incorporated on behalf of the Seven-Year Plan. This provoked Mr Thornburg some days later into making a statement to the Press wherein he criticised Persian administration but also opined 'that the oil company was not paying a just royalty and that company was responsible for most of economic ills of Persia'.[3] This squirt of oil upon the flames of Persian hostility to the Anglo-Iranian Oil Company afforded another illustration, after that of the cancellation of Persian relays of British broadcasts, of the way in which Persian-American differences were apt to be visited upon the British scapegoat.

As regards the financial position of Great Britain in relation to the United States at the opening of the year, Mr Gaitskell, now Chancellor of the Exchequer, informed

---

[1] EP 1015/5.
[2] *Ibid.*
[3] EP 1102/1.

the Commonwealth Ministers of Finance that 'the sterling area position is certainly much stronger now tha[n] it has been at any time since the end of the war'.[4] This, however, largely reflected special circumstances, notably the temporary economic boom resulting from the Korean war. The Treasury, as it is right to recall in relation to Persian preoccupations, was already estimating that in the coming year the United Kingdom balance with the dollar area would gravely decline. Mr Gaitskell told his Commonwealth colleagues, 'it appears certain that during 1951 the quarterly surpluses will diminish and may vanish altogether', and referred to 'this darkening picture'.

Against the darkening background in Persia Mr Barnett in the Eastern Department of the Foreign Office correctly inferred from a telegram of January 10 from Tehran that 'the prospect of an early dissolution of the Majlis seems to have receded . . . I hope Ramara is not getting cold feet . . . It seems as if bulldozing action by His Majesty's Government will be required. At the same time it would be a pity if the impression got about that we had been frightened into action by the nationalisation campaign.'[5] This understandable argument perhaps approached rather perilously the vicious circle of postponing action because action had been previously postponed. In the same telegram Sir Francis Shepherd had reported that discussion continued concerning the possible alternatives of the appointment by the Persian Government of a new consultative committee on the oil question and of continuing the former Majlis Oil Commission. As in the preceding summer, General Razmara again did not prevent the second and, for British interests, less favourable alternative.

On January 11, 1951, the Majlis passed a unanimous resolution, calling for a further report from its Oil Commission within two months. Sir Francis Shepherd considered that the dominant motive of the Deputies in voting for this course was that of 'avoiding opposing anything desired by the National Front',[6] and that they reckoned that if the oil question remained before the Majlis, its dissolution was less likely. He nevertheless thought that the delay of two months should reduce 'political misgivings' in Tehran. This was not the effect in the Foreign Office. And on January 13 M. Furuhar bowed to the storm and resigned. On the following day Sir Francis Shepherd, in some contrast to his pointed representation of December 30 to the Shah against such a course, only told the latter that 'it was a pity that the Minister of Finance had had to resign.'[7]

In his long conversation of January 14 with the Shah, Sir Francis Shepherd found him distressed by recent developments. The Shah said that he and General Razmara planned that there should now be introduced in the Majlis a programme of fiscal reform, to include income and luxury taxes and land reforms. If the Majlis, which 'represented too strongly the moneyed interests of the country',[8] did not co-operate it would be dissolved; and since free elections were impossible in prevailing conditions the election of public-spirited people would have to be arranged. It might appear that judicious support of this policy by Sir Francis Shepherd would have been a valuable step towards implementing the views communicated to him by the

---

[4] UEE 7/3.
[5] EP 1531/17.
[6] EP 1531/22.
[7] EP 1015/9.
[8] *Ibid.*

Secretary of State on December 29 in favour of a dissolution of the Majlis, but not in connexion with the question of oil: especially since Sir Francis Shepherd himself now considered that the best hope for that question was to hold it in abeyance until a dissolution.[9] It would appear however that in this conversation His Majesty's Ambassador mainly contented himself with offering 'a number of more or less obvious platitudes regarding the transitory nature of the present political muddle', and negativing the Shah's rather striking enquiry 'whether it was British policy to encourage a National Front Government or the inclusion of National Front members in the present Government'.[10]

In the same conversation the Shah recorded his disagreement with the recent dismissal, once more, of the unsteady M. Shahrukh, and said that he had insisted that his Government should submit to him a programme for properly co-ordinated propaganda. In this connexion it might perhaps have been worth exploring the possibility of providing the Persian Government in some way with a British adviser on propaganda, comparable to the already functioning British adviser on security. The Foreign Office, however, gave the Shah's potentially important initiative concerning propaganda a somewhat platonic welcome, estimating that it probably would not be in time to produce any early effect. And when a few days later Mr C.F.R. Barclay, of Information Policy Department, suggested publicity for Anglo-American measures for economic assistance to Persia, as with the Export-Import Bank Loan, Mr Barnett minuted on January 19: 'While there might be advantage in publicising these schemes at the present moment of crisis in Anglo-Persian affairs, the publicity would certainly lead to renewed attacks on us by our enemies in Tehran.'[11] This prudent, if somewhat defensive, argument against action was approved in the Eastern Department and Economic Relations Department of the Foreign Office.

Sir Francis Shepherd's report of his conversation of January 14, 1951, with the Shah did not cause the Foreign Office to despatch any instructions for the adoption of a more vigorous political line. On the economic side His Majesty's Ambassador was already urging upon the Foreign Office the need for immediate action to promote a settlement between the nearly bankrupt Persian Government and the endangered Anglo-Iranian Oil Company. Sir Francis Shepherd had telegraphed on December 31, 1950, that 'Dr Musaddeq [*sic*]. . . appears to think that ratification of the Supplemental Agreement would lead the Russians to demand oil concessions in the north [cf p. 44]. This explains the apparently senseless demand for nationalisation.'[12] On the same day His Majesty's Ambassador had further written in his long and important despatch No. 376: 'The heart of the matter is the Persian feeling that they have no control over their main source of revenue, once it is sold to the oil company. I confess that I sympathise with the Persians here . . . At the present time it is too easy for accusations to be made that the company is exercising an authority approaching that detestable thing 'colonisation' in monopolising the southern oil resources without considering national rights. This is a feeling which it will be best to take into consideration. It is not unique to Persia, and the examples of

---

[9] EP 1531/25.
[10] EP 1015/9.
[11] EP 1119/42 of 1950.
[12] EP 1531/1 of 1951.

Mexican oil and Argentine railways spring to mind.'[13]

Sir Francis Shepherd accordingly made three proposals: first, hiving off the purely Persian operations of the company, with one or more directorships for Persians in the Persian subsidiary; secondly, an accompanying financial arrangement, which need not cost the company more than the Supplemental Agreement but which 'could perhaps be clothed in similar garments to that of the Venezuelan agreement and so satisfy the cry for equal shares';[14] thirdly, the company should, as the Shah and General Razmara had suggested to Sir Francis Shepherd, meanwhile pay forthwith and *ex gratia* the increased royalty provided for by the Supplemental Agreement. For, argued His Majesty's Ambassador, 'it is fundamentally absurd . . . that large sums of money should be available in the company's possession and by consent due, after the completion of formalities, to the Persian Government, at a time when the money is badly needed to rescue the country's finances and to improve the position of her people: at a period, moreover, of international strain, when the dangers of Communism require to be continuously fought. It is abundantly evident that every possible effort should be made to remedy this bizarre and potentially disastrous situation.'

This important despatch of December 31 was received in the Foreign Office on January 4, 1951, and was remitted on the following day to Eastern Department. There it remained for just over a fortnight till it was first minuted on January 20 by Mr Barnett and sent up to Mr Fry and Mr Furlonge, who both saw it for the first time on January 24, nearly three weeks after its initial receipt. Mr Fry minuted his regret at this delay, considering that it would have been better if the Department had known that its views were in fact shared by Sir Francis Shepherd before entering upon the important conversations which the Foreign Office had meantime been holding with the Treasury and the Anglo-Iranian Oil Company (see pp. 107-10). It is imaginable that in the days, say, of Lord Curzon and Sir Eyre Crowe, more serious notice would have been recorded on a file displaying such a grave weakness in office procedure. The file also illustrates the kind of dangers for diplomatic correspondence produced by the modern press of work and proliferation of paper, wherein important material sent from posts abroad by despatch, instead of expensively by telegram, can all too easily become overlaid.

2. Consultations in London between the Foreign Office and the Anglo-Iranian Oil Company, January-February 7

The proposals which Sir Francis Shepherd had advanced were in fact closely matched by those which were emerging in the Foreign Office in the New Year and tending to overtake the original object of the interdepartmental studies initiated on December 18. This object had been to provide a convincing assessment of the Supplemental Agreement in relation to the 50-50 principle; the Foreign Office was evidently anxious to present this British case through our Embassies in Washington and in the Middle East, and to avoid the delay likely to result from referring the brief to the Anglo-Iranian Oil Company. The Foreign Office, however, left a decision on this to the Ministry of Fuel and Power, where Mr V.S. Butler insisted upon bringing

---

[13] EP 1531/7 of 1951.
[14] *Ibid.*

the company in.[15]

The Foreign Office joined the Ministry of Fuel and Power in a meeting with representatives of the company on January 3, 1951, the day on which news of the latest Aramco agreement with Arabia reached London. The Foreign Office reacted swiftly to this intelligence and put to the company 'the very tentative opinion that the Supplemental Oil Agreement could possibly now be regarded as outmoded'.[16] For the company Mr Gass, while rather naturally inclined to defend the Supplemental Agreement with somewhat negative arguments, stated that the company 'had never closed the door on the "50-50" suggestion' now advanced by the Foreign Office. Mr Bowker and Mr Berthoud, minuting on the record of this meeting, both advocated an imaginative approach on a partnership basis, which would remove 'the perpetual complaint in Persia and elsewhere . . . that one of the main national reserves is in foreign hands'.[17]

At the meeting the Foreign Office also emphasised, as Sir Francis Shepherd had done, Persia's urgent need of the royalties assigned to her by the Supplemental Agreement, and revived the idea of a government-backed loan by the Anglo-Iranian Oil Company. Mr Gass agreed there was scope for compromise here but thought it might be illegal to touch the arrears of royalties under the unratified agreement. The company was awaiting a personal report from Mr Northcroft who, with the encouragement of the Shah, was to visit London.

The Foreign Office proposed to follow up these consultations with a programme of further investigation and consultation, indicative of its appreciation of the seriousness of the situation, if also liable to involve further delay. Mr Bowker minuted on January 9 that reports from Mr Furlonge and from Mr Waight of the Treasury, who were both to visit Tehran in February, would need to be considered before holding further discussions, for which the Americans were anxious, concerning economic assistance to Persia. Mr Bowker remarked however: 'We do not want to give the impression to the Americans that we are being too dilatory.'[18] He therefore proposed that Mr Rountree, Head of the Office of Greek, Turkish and Iranian Affairs in the State Department, might visit London for preliminary conversations in the first half of February. On January 9 Sir William Strang minuted on this: 'I think these arrangements will do very well.' To which Mr Bevin added the following undated minute: 'The present system will not work.'[19] There is no record of any immediate follow-up or elucidation in the Foreign Office of this broadly important if somewhat cryptic minute, possibly reflecting the Foreign Secretary's earlier concern regarding the relationship between His Majesty's Government and the Anglo-Iranian Oil Company.

In a further minute of January 10 Mr Furlonge emphasised the need for short-term aid to Persia since 'it will take months to negotiate a firm [oil] agreement with the Persians, however forthcoming the company may be (and so far there has been little evidence of any such inclination). Meanwhile we must expect the situation in Persia to deteriorate.'[20] On the same day Mr Furlonge wrote a letter to Mr Burrows

---

[15] EP 1531/105 of 1950 and EP 1531/28 of 1951.
[16] EP 1531/19.
[17] *Ibid.*
[18] EP 1112/6.
[19] *Ibid.*
[20] EP 1102/1.

at Washington, copied to Sir Francis Shepherd and the British Middle East Office, wherein he explained the tentative thinking about Persia in the Department pending the visits to Tehran of himself and Mr Waight. Mr Furlonge concluded: 'When dealing with Persia, in fact, we seem always to be waiting for something.'[21]

On the same day of January 10 Sir Francis Shepherd telegraphed from Tehran that it rather looked 'as if the idea of nationalisation is gaining ground and this makes it all the more desirable to take immediate and imaginative action.'[22] Three days later his Majesty's Ambassador, following up on his third recommendation of December 31, specified that in his view the Anglo-Iranian Oil Company should before the end of January announce its willingness to pay the Persian Government royalties on the scale of the Supplemental Agreement, or at least comply with General Razmara's request for the immediate payment of the £6¾ million which the Persian Government would have received but for British dividend-limitation.[23] Three days later again, on January 16, Sir Francis Shepherd telegraphed that 'very strong pressure should be brought on the company, if necessary at the highest level',[24] in order to secure these payments. 'I do not think', he continued, 'any measure less than this will now save the situation. It is no use expecting that financial pressure will bring the Persians to reason: it is having the opposite effect.' Action should not be postponed till after Mr Furlonge's visit: 'The time for waiting for something has passed. Nor does the solution lie in palliatives; what is needed is fairly long term and imaginative action.'

In writing to Mr Furlonge on January 14 Sir Francis Shepherd had expressed the view that, what with the trend towards nationalisation, the time had come to sober the Persians with some sign that His Majesty's Government was not indifferent to their vilification of the Anglo-Iranian Oil Company and the British generally. His Majesty's Ambassador believed that 'many Persians would welcome some official indication that the antics of the extremists are being followed with distaste by His Majesty's Government.'[25] Sir Francis Shepherd transmitted a draft note to the Persian Government to this effect. The draft was considered admirable in the Foreign Office but in the event Sir Francis Shepherd's forceful suggestion was reduced to the Parliamentary answer of February 21 (see p. 117).

Already on January 13 representatives of the Foreign Office, supported by Dr Nuttall of the Ministry of Fuel and Power, had been arguing that Persia must be helped quickly and that things could not be allowed to drift. This was at an important meeting held with representatives of the Treasury in preparation for further discussion with the Anglo-Iranian Oil Company after the arrival of Mr Northcroft. The representatives of the Foreign Office explained that they were 'worried by the increasing demand in Persia for the "nationalisation" of the oil industry; it appeared that the company had now not only to get a new agreement, but to fight for its life'.[26] The Foreign Office proposed that the company should make immediate and substantial advances to the Persian Government although it was appreciated that

---

[21] EP 1531/16.
[22] EP 1531/17.
[23] EP 1531/22.
[24] EP 1531/23.
[25] EP 1531/25.
[26] EP 1531/31.

such a large payment had hitherto 'been anathema to the company'.[27] The Foreign Office further advocated, as Sir Francis Shepherd had done earlier, a Persian subsidiary company, possibly operating on a 50-50 basis. For the Treasury, Mr Flett replied, without referring to Sir John Bradbury's letter of 1914, that 'this was something we could not dictate to the company'[28] (cf pp. 135 and 314).

According to the record of this meeting, 'the Treasury representatives were of the opinion that there was no case to put up to Ministers yet, because (*a*) we had no assessment of Persia's needs; (*b*) we did not know what the company's thinking was. While we could be fairly certain that the company's view was that the Persians must speak first, it was necessary to make sure . . . The Foreign Office representatives pointed out that if we succeeded in getting the Persians to say what they wanted, they would probably ask for "nationalisation"; it was therefore unsafe to wait for them to speak first.'[29] The Treasury does not appear to have entertained a comparable sense of urgency. It is understandable enough that it did not now favour a government-guaranteed British loan to Persia, which would require the assent of the Majlis. But, since the Supplemental Agreement remained unratified, the Treasury was also unwilling to do more than press the company to advance royalties at the old rate of 1933: to go beyond that 'would require high-level intervention'.

The record ended on a bleakly inconclusive note: 'It was decided that in talking to the company next week it would not be possible to produce agreed views as between the departments who would accordingly put forward their own views as departmental ones.' It does not appear that any immediate attempt was made to resolve, by reference to Ministers before the meeting with the company, this serious inter-departmental disagreement concerning the greatest single British investment overseas at a time when it was, in the view of the Foreign Office, fighting for its life.

The arguments for recasting the structure of the Anglo-Iranian Oil Company, as advanced by the Foreign Office, were substantially those put to Mr Berthoud three days later, on January 16, by M. Imami, the Persian representative with the company in London. M. Imami said that he had, however, been unable to convince Sir William Fraser and Mr Gass, whom he characterised as 'stubborn and unimaginative'.[30] In this connexion Mr Berthoud subsequently advised that the Secretary of State should urge Sir William Fraser to adopt a more imaginative approach. This recommendation was caught up with those issuing from the meeting which representatives of the Foreign Office (Messrs Bowker, Furlonge, Fry, Ramsbotham and Barnett), the Treasury and the Ministry of Fuel and Power held on the same day of January 16 with the company's representatives, Mr Gass, Mr Rice and Mr Northcroft from Tehran.

Mr Northcroft reported that the Shah and General Razmara were angry with the Majlis and disposed 'to alter things "within the framework of democracy"'.[31] Mr Northcroft did not attach much importance to the Persian cry for nationalisation; whereas Mr Gass said that at the moment it overshadowed the demand for the introduction into Persia of the 50-50 principle. Its adoption by Aramco had increased the oil-royalty of the Arabian Government from about 18s to about 24s a ton. This

---

[27] EP 1112/4.
[28] EP 1531/31.
[29] *Ibid.*
[30] EP 1531/26.
[31] EP 1531/112.

figure, however included an exchange-differential whereas under the Supplemental Agreement a differential of about 5s a ton was additional to the basic royalty to Persia, which would have been 18s in 1949. Indeed Mr Gass represented that Persia would receive more from the Supplemental Agreement than under the 50-50 principle. If Mr Gass thus incidentally confirmed earlier evaluation of the two financial bases of agreement, he proceeded to argue by contrast that the 50-50 principle was nevertheless 'a disastrous one for the Middle East' because the countries there wanted equality of treatment, which was measured by the rate per ton, and because it involved among other things much more Persian intervention in the company's affairs. Mr Gass further touched on a real and persistent difficulty in representing that the separating off of the company's Persian operations, which a profit-sharing arrangement would necessitate, was unlikely to be acceptable to the Persian Government as involving the surrender of its existing rights in profits made by the company outside Persia. For the company had already refused (cf p. 56) to pay Persia half the profits on all its operations.

The latter difficulty was stressed in telegrams of January 19, 1951, to Tehran expressing inter-departmental views in the light of the meeting three days earlier. The important conclusion was drawn that a 'regularisation' of the company's operations in Persia was unlikely at least during 1951 except in the improbable event of a dissolution of the Majlis and the election of a better one. It was, however recognised that, unless Razmara's unwillingness to take a strong line with the Majlis could be modified, it seemed likely that matters would drag on for two months or more, after which the company would be faced with 'wholly unacceptable demands'.[32] Despite his disappointing performance General Razmara was still the person to assist with prompt financial aid, in order to prevent a dangerous deterioration, but—the Treasury's point—there was inadequate information for assessing how much assistance Persia really required. The Anglo-Iranian Oil Company, Sir Francis Shepherd was further informed, would at Persia's request deposit £10 million in the Bank Melli to back the Persian currency, and was thinking of making an advance to the Persian Government 'against future royalty payments' on an unspecified basis.

Mr Furlonge, in recommending that Sir William Strang should have an early discussion with Sir William Fraser, had recorded in a minute of January 19, copied to the Treasury at its request, that the Treasury was anxious for Sir William Strang to have a meeting first with Sir Henry Wilson Smith, a Second Secretary in that department, in order to agree the views of the Foreign Office and the Treasury, especially as to how far to press the Anglo-Iranian Oil Company to make further advances. Mr Bevin minuted on this: 'I agree. There is so much dynamite in all this the Cabinet should have a paper setting out all the facts and recommendations.' The submission of separate memoranda, under the two heads indicated, had in fact already been decided at a meeting held in the Secretary of State's room on January 12, and on January 22 there was circulated to the Cabinet the factual memorandum CP(51)28,[33] explaining recent developments and expressing views in accordance with the telegrams of January 19 to Tehran.

The Foreign Office memorandum noticed 'an unrealistic suggestion by the

---

[32] EP 1531/23.
[33] EP 1015/11G.

National Front minority that the Persian oil industry should be "nationalised"', and described the Supplemental Agreement, in the old formula, as 'fair and even generous'. Its withdrawal from the Majlis was not mentioned in so many words, but only that the agreement, 'after various political manoeuvres, is still before the Majlis Commission, which is unlikely to report for some two months'.[34] This perhaps conveyed something less than the recent keen concern of the Foreign Office, despite the ensuing warning, particularly in the light of the Aramco agreement, that a settlement between the company and the Persian Government was unlikely for many months or 'on any terms comparable with those of the Supplemental Agreement'.

At a meeting held on the following day, January 23, with Sir Henry Wilson Smith, Sir William Fraser and Mr Gass, the Permanent Under-Secretary of State for Foreign Affairs opened by emphasising the politico-strategic importance of Persia, standing 'on the front line' but apparently subject to 'multiple crises'; the Majlis Oil Commission would probably report at best in favour of a 50-50 arrangement, 'at worst plumping for nationalisation'.[35] Sir William Fraser, while refusing to make payments to the Persian Government under the unratified Supplemental Agreement, said that he was sending Mr Northcroft back to Tehran with discretion to agree to further substantial advances. The company hoped that this would tide over the situation for the next few months so that General Razmara might make some move. Mr Northcroft was not to refuse to discuss a 50-50 basis, if the Persian Government raised it. It is not recorded that Sir William Strang questioned this possibly important proviso, or pressed Sir William Fraser, who had indeed moved some way, to proceed further or faster. A telegram of the following day informed Sir Francis Shepherd that the Foreign Office considered that in the circumstances the instructions to Mr Northcroft were satisfactory.

On January 24, 1951, a second telegram, approved by Mr Bevin and Sir William Strang, was sent to Sir Francis Shepherd, instructing him to speak to General Razmara and, at his discretion, to the Shah, concerning Anglo-Persian relations. His Majesty's Government did not wish to comment on the suggestion for a dissolution of the Majlis, but reiterated its concern for Persian economic stability and in particular referred, perhaps rather belatedly, to the impression, created by the Persian stoppage of British and American wireless relays, that the Persian Government desired 'to placate Russia and . . . co-operate less closely with the Western powers'.[36] His Majesty's Government could not be indifferent to the affairs of the 'important British interest' of the Anglo-Iranian Oil Company and felt that they could only be solved if the Persian Government as a whole agreed on a solution and took 'resolute action to push it through the Majlis', where the main opposing elements were understood to be 'a small if vociferous minority'. Meantime 'we do not consider that the company can justifiably be expected to pay monies to the Persian Government except on the basis of a duly ratified agreement'.[37]

Nevertheless a week later, on January 31, Mr Northcroft gratified General Razmara by promising, as an offer from his company, that, in addition to the £10 million deposit in the Bank Melli, it would advance the Persian Government £25

---

[34] *Ibid.*
[35] EP 1531/35.
[36] EP 1531/35.
[37] *Ibid.*

million, of which £5 million at once and the rest in 10 monthly instalments of £2 million. In the light of this development Sir Francis Shepherd did not at once execute the instructions in what apparently became known in Foreign Office circles as the 'Dutch Uncle' telegram of January 24. He subsequently reported,[38] however, that he had previously spoken in that sense many times to General Razmara, and had not expected the message to stir him to vigorous action.

The Anglo-Iranian Oil Company was indeed now proving forthcoming in promising a large advance and was willing to consider, at any rate, a 50-50 principle. On that main issue, however, of the Supplemental Agreement or an alternative, Mr Ramsbotham on February 1 recorded his regret that the inter-departmental study of it had been held up, as he considered, by its earlier reference to the company against the opinion of the Foreign Office. 'The result', he wrote', 'is a long delay while we dispute with the company on points of detail. Meanwhile our case goes by default and will soon be only of historic interest.'[39] The broad impression is indeed that, through January 1951, the initial urgency of the need felt by the Foreign Office and by Sir Francis Shepherd for pursuing imaginative solutions of the problem as a whole was somewhat drained away in discussions with the company and, it might appear, under some influence from the Treasury. While the new Aramco agreement may have spurred initial concern for a settlement in Persia, it may subsequently have actually tended to retard action towards that end by emphasising the magnitude of the problem.

It is difficult not to see a run-down and postponement of the main problem in the acceptance by the Foreign Office, in its exposition of January 19 to Sir Francis Shepherd, of a likely delay of yet another year in determining relations between the company and the Persian Government. And that at a time when, as the Foreign Office had represented less than a week earlier, the company was already fighting for its life; and when it was already reckoned in the Foreign Office that there might possibly be only two months, say till the Majlis Oil Commission reported again, before the company was faced with wholly unacceptable demands. In fact Sir Francis Shepherd reported on February 4 that the commission had asked the Persian Government for information as to the practicability of nationalising the oil industry.

At about this time the Foreign Office was receiving several representations from individual employees of the Anglo-Iranian Oil Company as to the seriousness of the situation and the need for drastic action. Mr Geoffrey Keating, who was on the company's staff in Tehran, had recently been doing a good deal of lobbying, apparently without much success, among Deputies in the Majlis, especially members of the Oil Commission. These contacts lent significance to his proposal now, towards the end of January 1951, that British policy should aim at friendly relations with the National Front. Mr Fry, however, minuted on January 30: 'It is often wise to make friends with one's adversaries and attempt to educate them, but I have no hope that we could accomplish that (apart of course from using substantial bribes) with Musaddiq and his friends.'[40] That argument, and the accompanying decision to continue to support General Razmara despite his evident shortcomings, was on balance probably correct. It seems possible, however, that our Embassy in Tehran

---

[38] EP 1015/15.
[39] EP 1531/28.
[40] EP 1015/13.

may have been somewhat lacking in informally non-committal but useful contacts even with extremist circles in Persian politics. The difficulties here are evident enough. It would appear, though, that, as it was, His Majesty's Embassy was seldom if ever in a position to give advance advice of any very specific kind concerning the manoeuvres and intentions of the National Front; and the Embassy's telegraphic reports of proceedings in the Majlis sometimes seem somewhat less than fully informative than those, for instance, reaching the Anglo-Iranian Oil Company.

Mr Fry's mention of bribery dismissed it by implication; and indeed his suggestion that it might have been effective with the fanatics of the National Front may in any case have been excessive. Bribery is always a dangerous and distasteful expedient, but its time-honoured role in Persian politics and the magnitude of British interests now involved perhaps precluded its automatic rejection. There was also British reluctance to pursue what might have been an alternative policy as regards the Majlis, towards the promotion of its dissolution. His Majesty's Embassy in Tehran did some 'discreet lobbying'[41] of Deputies but a prudent yet firm lead to the Shah in favour of dissolution might conceivably have produced greater results. In the event the Majlis, holding one of the keys to the whole problem, continued to range itself in increasing opposition to British interests.

If the Foreign Office understandably disagreed with Mr Keating's prescription it did largely agree with that of another servant of the Anglo-Iranian Oil Company, its Labour Adviser, Sir Frederick Leggett, formerly Deputy Secretary in the Ministry of Labour. On February 6 Sir Frederick stressed to Mr Fry the urgent need for the company in Persia to make 'a fresh start, on the basis of equal partnership.' Whereas Sir Frederick Leggett characterised the board of the company, in his own adjectives, as 'helpless, niggling, without an idea between them, confused, hide-bound, small-minded, blind'.[42] He advocated 'firm direction from His Majesty's Government. It seemed to him to be for Whitehall to take a strong line with the company and infuse realism and sense into their "helpless and hopeless" consultations.' Mr Bowker minuted on this on February 7 that Mr Berthoud was going 'to make discreet enquiries in order to ascertain the functions of the two Government directors of the company, of whom I understand Lord Alanbrooke is one'. It would thus appear that some measure of uncertainty still prevailed in the Foreign Office concerning the fundamental issue of the constitutional relations between the company and His Majesty's Government: and that the Office was unaware of any consultations with the governmental directors. On the same day of February 7 Sir William Fraser thanked Sir William Strang for recent support from the Foreign Office against criticism by the State Department of the company's negotiations.[43]

3. General Razmara's 50-50 proposal and first British reactions to threat of Persian oil nationalisation, February 7-24, 1951

Also on February 7, 1951, Mr Fry and Mr Ramsbotham held a conversation with Mr Rountree of the State Department, who was paying his projected visit to London. Mr Fry alluded, notably, to the 'abysmal ignorance'[44] of the Supplemental

---

[41] EP 1015/15.
[42] EP 1531/47.
[43] EP 1531/49.
[44] EP 1022/2.

Agreement in Tehran and elsewhere, and observed that His Majesty's Government had been unaware of the course of the recent Aramco negotiations with Saudi Arabia and were a little surprised that they had not at least been informed that a 50-50 profit-sharing agreement was under consideration. The State Department had certainly not been uniformly helpful in the past and had scarcely kept the Foreign Office fully informed of the Aramco negotiations. It nevertheless seems fair to recall the particularly urgent warning concerning Saudi demands on Aramco which Mr McGhee had given the Foreign Office as early as September 1950 (p. 83). The damage was done now, but the Foreign Office would have liked to have tried to prevent a recurrence by reaching some informal agreement with the Americans along the general lines of the abortive Shinwell-Ickes Agreement of 1945 for reducing harmful rivalry among oil interests. Mr Rountree, however, at once said that the 'United States anti-trust laws would prevent what he termed any "ganging-up" of oil companies'.[45]

The discussion in the Foreign Office with Mr Rountree also covered the general situation in Persia, as to which the Foreign Office took 'a serious but not over-pessimistic view', and Anglo-American arrangements for economic assistance to her along the lines previously discussed. This general economic concern was, however, becoming increasingly subordinated to the search for agreement between the Anglo-Iranian Oil Company and the Persian Government even though the Foreign Office still included this among 'long-term measures'.[46] Here Mr Rountree did not advance beyond the distinctly restricted measure of support previously given by the Americans. He intimated that 'while it would not be proper for them to express an opinion on the merits of any particular agreement, they would certainly speak [in Tehran] in favour of concluding an early agreement'.[44]

In his minute of February 7 on Sir Frederick Leggett's representation Mr Bowker doubted whether the Foreign Office could or should do any more with the Anglo-Iranian Oil Company for the moment, pending the outcome of Mr Northcroft's negotiations and, possibly, the return of Mr Furlonge, who was arriving in Tehran that day. Three days later, and three days after Sir Francis Shepherd had delivered the homily in the Dutch Uncle telegram (cf p. 112), on February 10, 1951, General Razmara proposed a 50-50 arrangement to Mr Northcroft, who said that his company was willing to examine it and that it would take a year to form the new subsidiary company which would be necessary. General Razmara's proposal, not unhopeful in itself, was made against an unhopeful background. In accordance with his earlier treatment of the Supplemental Agreement, he had also refused to publicise the agreement of the Anglo-Iranian Oil Company to advance £25 million to the Persian Government so that, as the Treasury had pointed out in a letter of February 6 to Mr Fry, the company got no credit for its helpfulness and its case went by default in Persia.

Mr C.F.R. Barclay of the Information Policy Department of the Foreign Office had not seen the letter of February 6 from the Treasury when he wrote a minute on February 9 questioning the earlier policy of silence which had stifled the Supplemental Agreement under the general ignorance in Persia of its merits. 'I cannot help feeling', wrote Mr Barclay, 'that we should have used our propaganda

---

[45] UES 1536/5.
[46] EP 1015/17G.

machine in some way, and particularly for getting something out to the Persians over the BBC daily Persian broadcast'.[47] Mr Barclay noticed that the Anglo-Iranian Oil Company had now agreed to make large advances *ex gratia* to the Persian Government, and that the Shah himself had on January 14 advocated strong propaganda in such a case. Mr Barclay proposed action in this sense: propaganda on behalf of the company should be concerted in Tehran between the Information Officer at the British Embassy and the Persian Government; in London the Foreign Office should take parallel action with the BBC and Central Office of Information.

Mr Barclay, who was conspicuous in his anxiety to promote effective action, was here pointing the way towards a potentially important consolidation of the British propagandist effort which, in the Persian field at any rate, would appear to have suffered somewhat as one might expect from its perhaps inevitable diffusion through the separate organs of the Foreign Office, the Central Office of Information and the BBC. By March 1951, if not earlier, fortnightly meetings, usually chaired by Mr Furlonge, were held with the BBC, in particular, to indicate appropriate lines for the Persian service.

Mr Barclay's minute of February 9 was discussed orally but not, apparently, circulated at once. The timeliness of his proposal was further suggested, however, by a report which Sir William Strang received four days later, through Sir William Fraser, from M. Fuad Rouhani, the legal adviser in Tehran of the Anglo-Iranian Oil Company. This respected Persian commented, in a thoughtful and sombre survey of Anglo-Persian relations, upon 'the existing deplorable situation in which any Iranian who displayed friendly feelings towards the British in general would be accused of wanting in patriotism . . . The wisdom of [British] passivity and silence is extremely doubtful.'[48]

Against this background Sir Francis Shepherd was telegraphing on February 10-11 that support for the extremists of the National Front had grown considerably in recent weeks: 'there is a definite danger that the [Oil] Commission might be stampeded by the National Front with [*sic*] voting for nationalisation . . . I propose to try to influence those members of the Commission who are amenable to press for a 50-50 arrangement on Aramco lines as against nationalisation.'[49] Mr A.C.E. Malcolm, Head of the Information Policy Department, minuted on this on February 13: 'This looks dangerous. Would Eastern Department agree to our taking such a line . . . in broadcasts in Persian'[47] as that proposed by His Majesty's Ambassador. It was considered in Eastern Department, however that such broadcasts 'would only exacerbate Persian feelings'.[50] These feelings had risen hitherto in the absence of effective presentation of the British case; now, by a depressingly circular argument, such presentation was still to be eschewed for fear, precisely, of exacerbating those feelings. Nevertheless the viewpoint of the Eastern Department was fully shared, if indeed it was not partly inspired, by Mr Chisholm of the Anglo-Iranian Oil Company. Mr Barclay recorded on February 26 that he had discussed his proposals of February 9 with Mr Chisholm who considered that any publicity from known British official sources would do more harm than good and 'would cause added

---

[47] PG 13437/1.
[48] EP 1051/7.
[49] EP 1531/42.
[50] *Ibid.*

hostility'.[51]

'We have never wished to appear to intervene in the company's affairs . . . the line which ordinarily commends itself to the Treasury. To try to gain public kudos now from the company's action [in making advances to the Persian Government] might associate us indissolubly in Persian minds with the company.'[52] This defensive argument was adduced by Mr Fry in his reply of February 13 to the Treasury letter of a week earlier. Primarily, however, he endorsed an argument which General Razmara had used to Sir Francis Shepherd to the effect that he had good reason to keep secret for the present an arrangement which might be dangerously exploited against him by his political opponents.

His Majesty's Ambassador in Tehran had been unenthusiastic about delivering the homily in the Dutch Uncle telegram since, as he explained in a telegram of February 15, he considered that such criticism 'should not be directed against the Shah and Razmara who are . . . doing their best to help in difficult circumstances. It is the obstinate attitude of the Majlis that is most to blame.'[53] In the latter connexion, however, Sir Francis Shepherd had evidently learnt with some regret from Mr Furlonge, on his visit to Tehran, that there might be objection to delivering to the Persian Government the stiffish note which he had proposed in his letter of January 14. On February 10 Sir Francis Shepherd telegraphed that he still felt strongly 'that some action by His Majesty's Government is called for'[54] to warn the Persians against the nationalisation of oil. He now proposed that a parliamentary question, which could be answered in this sense, should be arranged in the House of Commons, preferably for between February 14 and 17.

On February 13 Mr Fry minuted that Sir Francis Shepherd's proposal meant 'that we should, in effect, pronounce against a policy of nationalisation. I do not think that the Department can recommend this line, when nationalisation is so much an issue in the United Kingdom.'[55] Mr Bowker agreed that 'it would be difficult for any reference of this kind to be made which would not be regarded as inconsistent with the nationalisation policy of His Majesty's Government.'[56] Mr Fry further considered, with the agreement of Mr Bowker, that the timing desired by His Majesty's Ambassador was 'ruled out' by the fact that Mr Thomas Reid, Labour Member of Parliament for the Swindon Division, already had down for February 21 a relevant question to which an appropriate reply would be prepared; it was not thought that 'in any event . . . a delay of a few days will make much difference'.[55]

On February 15, 1951, the Shah himself indicated to Sir Francis Shepherd 'that to have any effect, the [proposed parliamentary] answer should indicate that an attempt to nationalise oil would lead to a delicate situation and have a bad effect on Anglo-Persian relations'.[57] But Mr Bowker and Sir William Strang approved a submission of February 17 that Eastern Department 'still feel unable to endorse'[56] such a firm line. Mr Ernest Davies, Parliamentary Under-Secretary of State for Foreign Affairs, accordingly stated in the House of Commons on February 21: 'His

---

[51] PG 13437/1.
[52] EP 1531/39.
[53] EP 1531/51.
[54] EP 1531/43.
[55] EP 1531/52.
[56] EP 1531/63.
[57] EP 1531/53.

Majesty's Government cannot be indifferent to the affairs of this important British interest [the AIOC]. The company's present concession is valid until 1993, and His Majesty's Government are confident that Persia will honour her agreement. As to the supplemental oil agreement, His Majesty's Government regard it as fair and reasonable. But, as the matter is under review in Persia, I cannot say more at present except to express the hope that a satisfactory conclusion will soon be reached.'[58]

Although it is questionable, as the Shah had indicated, how far a statement in this form would in any event have produced an effect upon the Majlis and its Oil Commission, yet Eastern Department may have been somewhat over-optimistic in supposing that to delay it for a few days would not make much difference. For in fact two days earlier, on February 19, Dr Musaddiq, perhaps reflecting the extent to which rich nationalists drew their revenues from land rather than from oil, had criticised the Shah's recent proposals for agrarian reform and had tabled a motion in the Oil Commission for the nationalisation of oil in the whole of Persia. And on February 21 Sir Francis Shepherd telegraphed that General Razmara now informed him that if a 50-50 proposal was to get through the Oil Commission lip-service must be paid to nationalisation.[59] The Persian Premier communicated to Sir Francis alternative formulae for resolutions to this effect. This ominous communication of February 21, 1951, marked the next downward step for British interests after the withdrawal of the Supplemental Agreement from the Majlis on December 26, 1950.

In his telegram of February 21, 1951, Sir Francis Shepherd commented, in some contrast to his defence of General Razmara less than a week before: 'The movement for nationalisation has arisen because of the Persian Government's failure to explain the situation to the public. I do not think that Razmara should be allowed to reap the benefit from his unhelpful conduct by means of any endorsement by us of the principle of nationalisation.'[60] In the light of this telegram an inter-departmental meeting was held on February 22 between representatives of the Foreign Office, the Treasury, the Ministry of Fuel and Power, and also of the Bank of England, and the Anglo-Iranian Oil Company. Mr Fry recorded 'the unanimous opinion of the meeting that a clear distinction required to be drawn between nationalisation, as such and in principle, and the nationalisation of an industry which, on the security of a regularly negotiated Concession, valid until 1993, had operated in Persia in all good faith and spent enormous sums of money in developing that industry. Under Articles 21 and 26 [cf pp. 41-2] of the company's Concession, the company's operations cannot legally be terminated by such an act as nationalisation, a consideration which was implied in the answer given on February 21 to a Parliamentary Question.'[61] The above distinction, if it did not go so far as Sir Francis Shepherd advocated, yet represented an advance upon the previous unwillingness in the Foreign Office to adopt any specific position against nationalisation of the British oil industry in Persia; and the legal argument in defence of the concession of 1933 was to become central for the British case.

---

[58] Parliamentary Debates, 5th Series, H. of C., Vol. 484, cols. 1261-2.
[59] EP 1531/60.
[60] *Ibid.*
[61] EP 1531/62.

4. From the British note verbale of February 24 to the assassination of General Razmara, February 24-March 7

The British legal argument was duly advanced in the *note verbale* communicated by Sir Francis Shepherd to the Persian Premier on February 24, 1951, in accordance with the terms of a telegram of the preceding day, which had been agreed at the inter-departmental meeting on February 22 and approved by Mr Kenneth Younger, Minister of State for Foreign Affairs. The *note verbale* explained that the statement of February 21 in the House of Commons expressed the considered view of His Majesty's Government. It was represented that the Anglo-Iranian Oil Company obviously could not be expected to discuss an agreement on a basis of equal profit-sharing 'except on the clear understanding that the term[62] of the existing concession would be unaltered. They could not enter into any such arrangement under threat of nationalisation.' It was further represented that the financial advances by the company should now be made public.

In conclusion the British *note verbale* of February 24, 1951, stated that 'His Majesty's Government cannot be expected to comment on any proposed resolution referring to nationalisation'.[63] This rather lame ending underlined a comment by Mr Bowker on February 23 on the 'dilemma' which the Persian demand for nationalisation presented for His Majesty's Government; and which was largely to compel it to fight the issue, so to speak, with one hand tied behind its back. Mr Bowker thought that 'it may be necessary soon to get our ideas on this subject absolutely clear and explain them to Sir Francis Shepherd'.[64] It would look as though the effective sifting of such ideas had largely begun at the inter-departmental meeting of the previous day, after the Persian Prime Minister had himself desiderated lip-service to Persian nationalisation of the British oil industry. It was on March 1, in the course of further deliberation in the Foreign Office, that Mr Ramsbotham referred to the British statement of 1946 on policy towards foreign nationalisation (cf p. 47).

While there is always much to be said for not crossing one's bridges before one comes to them, and for hoping for the best, yet there might have been a valuable gain in time and in clarity if, in preparation against the worst, rather earlier consideration had been given to the possible implications of Sir Francis Shepherd's increasing warnings as to the rising tide of Persian nationalism in favour of that nationalisation of oil which the Foreign Office memorandum for the Cabinet of a month before had described as an unrealistic suggestion. Studies of this kind at a further series of inter-departmental meetings might most usefully, perhaps, have filled in the interval in London during February, when the focus of activity had shifted to Mr Northcroft's negotiations in Tehran.

In Tehran His Majesty's Ambassador decided on his own responsibility to remit the *note verbale* to General Razmara under cover of a letter from himself which was something of an adaptation of the note which he had proposed in January. In this letter Sir Francis Shepherd represented to General Razmara, in terms of impressive cogency and vigour, that the growth of Persian propaganda towards Great Britain

---

[62] This word is as in the instructing telegram of February 23, 1951, to Sir Francis Shepherd, on EP 1531/62. In the copy of the *note verbale* filed on EP 1531/72 this word reads 'terms' but the 's' is bracketed in pencil. In the text in Cmd 8425, p. 23, the word is printed wrongly, and misleadingly, as 'terms'.
[63] EP 1531/72.
[64] EP 1531/62.

and the demand for nationalisation of oil, 'the propaganda of which is founded upon misrepresentation and ignorance',[65] had been promoted by the failure of the Persian Government to give a lead and to publicise the goodwill of the Anglo-Iranian Oil Company as regards financial advances and willingness to consider a 50-50 arrangement.

The letter from Sir Francis Shepherd to General Razmara valuably reinforced the *note verbale* in reply to his communication of February 21. This 'difficult and pressing development' (Mr Bowker) had been primarily handled in the Foreign Office by Mr Fry as acting Head of Eastern Department in the absence of Mr Furlonge, who had returned from his tour of the Middle East so unwell that he had to take to bed for a time. Mr Fry was held to have met the test very well, by charting a course described by Sir William Strang as 'both prudent and skilful'.[66]

Prudent skill and devoted work in the Foreign Office and in His Majesty's Embassy at Tehran could minimise but not wholly redeem the unlucky circumstance that British foreign policy then lacked strong ministerial direction at the highest level. Mr Ernest Bevin was so incapacitated that he was shortly to be replaced as Foreign Secretary. And in general, *The Times*, in a leading article of February 23, 1951, on 'a year of government with a small majority', emphasised the strain which this imposed upon Ministers. It remarked that 'constant attendance at the House does not make the efficient conduct of a department's business easy and, even more serious, it leaves Ministers with little time to think . . . The result is, inevitably, inflexibility—with always the possibility of a creeping paralysis of decision at the highest level.' The article referred to greater bitterness in party conflict since the New Year owing to the nationalisation of steel, to a Conservative belief that the Government had lost the confidence of the electorate, and to a strong feeling that it had also 'lost control of events'.

On February 26, 1951, His Majesty's Embassy in Tehran reported a growing feeling in the Majlis that for Persia the correct foreign policy was one of neutrality between the Western and the Communist *blocs*, as instanced in a recent speech by M. Hairizadeh. This Deputy of the National Front and supporter of the Partisans of Peace had, in particular, gloated over the new weakness of the British Empire and its reluctant tendency to retreat in Egypt.[67] The British *note verbale* of February 24 to the Persian Government was attacked in the Persian Press as being 'violent' and 'unfriendly',[68] but Sir Francis Shepherd significantly reported: 'Military circles appear not dissatisfied with this show of British strength. Military Attaché's relations with the General Staff [are] unaffected or if anything improved.'[69] The Military Attaché subsequently reported that General Garzan, the Chief of the Persian General Staff, 'definitely welcomed'[70] Mr Davies' statement of February 21 regarding the interest of His Majesty's Government in the affairs of the Anglo-Iranian Oil Company.

Sir Francis Shepherd does not appear to have protested when General Razmara, whose position was becoming weaker, still refused on February 26 to do as His

---

[65] Cmd 8425, p. 24.
[66] EP 1531/62.
[67] EP 1022/5.
[68] EP 1531/70.
[69] EP 1991/1.
[70] *Ibid.*

Majesty's Government desired and publicise the exchange of letters arranging the financial advances of the Anglo-Iranian Oil Company; though he would read the rest of the *note verbale* to the Oil Commission and his remarks to it would be published. On the same day the Shah in his turn sought to persuade His Majesty's Ambassador to acquiesce in some reference to nationalisation in a resolution by the Majlis Oil Commission. Sir Francis Shepherd, proceeding along the lines of the conclusion of the *note verbale*, answered that 'if the Persian Government were convinced that nothing could be done without such a formula that was their affair—they could scarcely expect the representative of His Majesty's Government to endorse it.'[71] This rather mild reply also reflected His Majesty's Ambassador's own view that in fact 'the Shah is right in thinking that the idea of nationalisation has come to stay and that the best way to shelve it is some suitable formula. I will telegraph further on this point.'[72]

In a telegram of March 1, 1951, to the Foreign Office Sir Francis Shepherd actually proposed a formula, drafted by himself, wherein the Oil Commission would be described as 'having examined the possibility of the nationalisation of the oil industry in Southern Iran'[73] and having been assured that it was impracticable since there were insufficient trained Persians to carry on the industry, and the financial burden of acquiring it would be excessive. This proposal was considered in London on the following day at an inter-departmental meeting on the official level, and the Anglo-Iranian Oil Company was called in. As a result there was despatched to Tehran on that evening of March 2 a Foreign Office telegram which took a stronger line than that of the recent *note verbale*. Sir Francis Shepherd was now informed that 'any resolution which does not refer to the illegality of nationalisation must be unacceptable to His Majesty's Government . . . You should leave Razmara and the Shah in no doubt about the feeling of His Majesty's Government in this matter.'[74] An alternative form of resolution which would be acceptable in this respect was, however, now proposed for use if Sir Francis Shepherd did suggest one.

Already, however, on the afternoon of March 2, His Majesty's Ambassador in Tehran had communicated his originally proposed formula to General Razmara. In reply to the latter Sir Francis Shepherd had further said that he 'did not see any objection to the endorsement of the principle of nationalisation so long as it was rejected in practice as in the draft resolution'.[75] This contradiction of the line which His Majesty's Ambassador had himself advocated on February 21, when the Persian Premier had first called for come acknowledgement of nationalisation, passed without recorded comment in the Foreign Office, despite the fact that policy there was tending to stiffen at the same time as Sir Francis Shepherd's views were apparently evolving in an opposite sense. On March 4, however, His Majesty's Ambassador followed his latest instructions and added a sentence about the illegality of nationalisation to the formula which he had given General Razmara.[76]

The instructing telegram of March 2, 1951, from the Foreign Office to Sir Francis Shepherd had urged that General Razmara should now publicise the position of the

---

[71] EP 1531/69.
[72] EP 1531/69.
[73] EP 1531/74.
[74] *Ibid.*
[75] EP 1531/77.
[76] EP 1531/79.

Anglo-Iranian Oil Company, at least to the extent indicated by him on February 26 if not also with regard to the company's advances. Persian clamour for nationalisation of the oil industry had at long last induced the company to adopt a more positive attitude concerning propaganda. In particular the company now put out two carefully reasoned memoranda against nationalisation, starting from the technically correct premise that 'the oil is in the ownership of the [Persian] State, and to this extent the industry is already nationalised'.[77] But as Mr Rothnie of Eastern Department commented in a minute, these memoranda were 'appeals to reason and, in so far, can have in Persia only very limited effect and that very long term'.

Sir Francis Shepherd had proposed in a telegram of February 26 that the BBC should broadcast a talk to Persia based on the answer of February 21 in the House of Commons and on points in the *note verbale* of February 24, with particular reference to Articles 21 and 26 of the concession of 1933. The Foreign Office accordingly prepared a brief, which however did not mention the two articles, for the general guidance of the BBC. The draft brief, in which Mr Chisholm concurred, was submitted to Mr D.R. Serpell of the Treasury and Mr V.S. Butler of the Ministry of Fuel and Power. They both objected to a passage stating that 'no one can dispute the ultimate right of a nation to adopt such measures as it chooses within its own borders'.[78] This might indeed seem a somewhat remarkable statement to make 15 years after the German reoccupation of the Rhineland and five years after the Nuremberg Trials, to cite only two obvious examples. The offending sentence was omitted from the final text of the brief.

The broadcast was delivered on March 4, 1951, on the Persian service of the BBC by its diplomatic correspondent. 'In the first place', he said, 'the Persian emotion in favour of nationalisation, the instinct that Persia should have all the benefits of her principal form of national wealth is fully understood.' The Anglo-Iranian Oil Company had, however, developed its vast enterprise in Persia on the faith of the concession of 1933, and its repudiation would injure Persia's international reputation, 'especially . . . if proper compensation were not paid'.[79] Nor were these the only points in this blundering broadcast which aroused the consternation of the Anglo-Iranian Oil Company, as expressed in a letter of March 9 from Mr Gass to Mr Furlonge, enclosing a lamentation from Mr Northcroft in Tehran. Mr Gass understandably feared a very harmful effect from this broadcast, with its 'note of apologetic regret that a British concern should be standing in the way of Persian aspiration'.[80] Such was the outcome of the first major attempt by British propaganda to present the case against Persian nationalisation in the light of what Mr Berthoud had referred to on March 8 as 'the vital necessity for us to keep this, by far our largest remaining overseas asset'.[81]

On March 3 General Razmara faced the Majlis Oil Commission and expounded to it the reports of the commissions of the main Persian Ministries which he had constituted to prepare replies to the Oil Commission's earlier request for information concerning nationalisation. These replies in general gave a clear lead against nationalisation; it was in broad accordance with the judicial report that the political

---

[77] EP 1531/83.
[78] EP 1531/68.
[79] *Ibid.*
[80] EP 1531/439.
[81] EP 1531/151.

report argued that 'the nationalisation of oil necessitates dispossessing the company and will violate the oil concession'[82] of 1933. On March 5 the Persian Prime Minister further recommended these reports at a Press conference as providing a better basis to work on than merely 'patriotic sentiments'.[83] Nevertheless, as the Foreign Office pointed out in a telegram of March 6 to Tehran, he has still said nothing concerning the willingness of the company to consider a new agreement,[84] as on a 50-50 basis. On the same day Sir Francis Shepherd reported that he was seeking an audience of the Shah in an endeavour to overcome what looked like continued delay by the Persian Premier. But next day set a different and a sudden term to his procrastination.

On the morning of March 7, 1951, General Razmara was attending a memorial service at the Mosque Masjid-i-Shah in Tehran when he was shot dead by an assassin who had penetrated the cordon of police with surprising ease. The murderer was a member of the fanatical religious sect of Fidayan-i-Islam, the Sacrificial Warriors of Islam, controlled by M. Kashani, who was also a supporter of the National Front. It was only months later, in October, that Mr Pyman of His Majesty's Embassy received an account, from what he believed to be a reliable source, of a meeting three days before the murder whereat, it was reported, 15 members of the Fidayan-i-Islam had conferred with Dr Musaddiq and M. Kashani. Both were reported to have stated categorically that the welfare of Persia depended upon the disappearance of General Razmara. This account suggested to His Majesty's Embassy in the after-event that General Razmara may have been coming very near to forming a majority in the Majlis Oil Commission for a 50-50 arrangement.[85]

The assassination of General Razmara was certainly advantageous to the National Front, as also to the Communist Tudeh organisation. They did not, however, at once celebrate the crime with the same open relish as the organs of the Fidayan-i-Islam, which linked it with the assassination in November 1949 of M. Hazhir (cf p. 59). The prospects of an Anglo-Persian settlement regarding oil had received a brutal setback.

---

[82] EP 1531/94.
[83] EP 1531/85.
[84] EP 1531/81.
[85] EP 1015/372.

CHAPTER V

DETERIORATION FOR BRITISH OIL INTERESTS IN PERSIA DURING THE GOVERNMENT OF M. HUSEIN ALA AND THE FAILURE OF ANGLO-AMERICAN CONVERSATIONS IN WASHINGTON, MARCH 8-APRIL 28, 1951

1. The Government of M. Ala and approval by the Majlis of proposed oil nationalisation, March 8-15

A few days after the assassination of General Razmara, His Majesty's Ambassador in Tehran significantly reported on the development of the Tudeh Party. Although it was thought to number only about 2,500 members in Persia, of whom some 2,000 were in Tehran, and although its direction was still clandestine, yet Sir Francis Shepherd estimated that it was more strongly organised than a year previously, and had considerably increased its propaganda. This had coincided with a weakening in the attitude of General Razmara's Government towards the Tudeh, which had in February 1951 followed up its Partisans of Peace of the preceding year with a new organisation called the National Association for the Struggle against the Southern Oil Company. This association had been able to stage a mass demonstration in the Majlis Square on February 16, although the National Front apparently regarded as an unwelcome rival.[1] Opposed Persian political parties were thus ominously finding common ground in attacking the Anglo-Iranian Oil Company as the current target of their xenophobia.

In an analysis of the advance of the National Front Sir Francis Shepherd at that period referred to its great success in playing upon the fact that 'even Persians who think that it is for the good of the country to co-operate with foreigners cannot escape a feeling of guilt'.[2] His Majesty's Ambassador also drew attention to the 'tenacity of purpose' of the National Front in exploiting the question of oil in order, as he considered, to bring into power a Government acceptable to it. The National Front lost little time in exploiting the confused alarm after the murder of General Razmara.

On March 8, 1951, the Majlis Oil Commission, presided over by Dr Musaddiq, passed a unanimous resolution adopting the proposal 'to nationalise oil throughout the country'[3] (compare the proposal of the National Front on November 29, 1950: cf p. 91). In view of this and 'since the time left for studying the execution of this proposal is not enough', the resolution continued, 'the Special Oil Commission requests the Majlis to grant an extension of two months for this purpose'.[4] This resolution was reported by Sir Francis Shepherd in a telegram on which Mr Herbert Morrison on March 10, his first day in the Foreign Office as Secretary of State, minuted to Sir William Strang: 'We shall have to talk. Dangerous.'[5] The danger had been underlined the day before in Tehran by a triumphantly anti-British and anti-American demonstration which M. Kashani had promptly organised. In this connexion Mr Bevin, by one of his last acts as Secretary of State, had supported the

---

[1] EP 1016/12.
[2] EP 1015/51.
[3] EP 1531/97 (revised text).
[4] Cmd 8425, p. 25. (In this text the earlier part of the resolution is as amended by the Majlis on March 13, 1951: see below.)
[5] EP 1015/38.

line taken by Sir Francis Shepherd, who had already had conveyed to the Shah representations in favour of a declaration of martial law and the appointment of a strong Prime Minister.

It does not appear that His Majesty's Ambassador, in his representations to the Shah, had specifically proposed a dissolution of the Majlis, which would automatically have terminated its oil commission. And Mr Bevin, in his telegram of March 8, had been unable to judge whether this course 'would be justifiable or desirable', though he had for some time had the impression that 'the Majlis is making it impossible for any Persian Government to govern'.[6] In his reply next day Sir Francis Shepherd, however, represented the difficulties attendant upon a dissolution of the Majlis, even advancing as an objection thereto the necessity of securing an early settlement of 'the oil question and the note-issuing question'.[7] He remarked in a letter of March 12 to Mr Bowker that the activities of M. Kashani 'presented an excellent opportunity for the Shah to take action in the direction of proclaiming martial law and dissolving the Majlis. Unfortunately there was nobody available who could second the Shah in such action.'[8] Doubtless His Majesty's Ambassador himself could not play such a part, but it was perhaps unfortunate that his instructions from the Foreign Office were appreciably less firm and urgent in tenor than a minute of March 13 wherein Mr Rothnie observed that 'the National Front are almost certain to try to rush the resolution [of the Commission in favour of oil nationalisation] through and the only safe assurance that this will not happen is that the Majlis be dissolved.'[9]

The two strongest and most likely candidates to succeed to the Persian Premiership were M. Qavam (cf p. 45) and M. Sayyid Zia (cf p. 66). Both these politicians enjoyed considerable support in the Majlis, which they were unlikely to dissolve, but appreciably less from the Shah. In his telegram of March 8 Mr Bevin had authorised Sir Francis Shepherd to indicate to the Shah, if he were asked, the preference of His Majesty's Government for M. Sayyid Zia. It was subsequently ascertained, however, that neither he nor M. Qavam enjoyed the support of the Government of the United States, which favoured the former Persian Ambassador in Washington and Foreign Minister of the preceding year, M. Husein Ala. The Shah also preferred this intelligent but weak politician, who was said to cherish some anti-British sentiments from having been bullied at Westminster School. (He was, however, reported to have criticised the cancellation of the D'Arcy Concession in 1932.) The representations of His Majesty's Ambassador in favour of a strong Prime Minister were set aside and M. Husein Ala was nominated on March 11, 1951.

Sir Francis Shepherd commented on the following day: 'I imagine that as soon as a Government is formed it will declare martial law.'[8] He further reported that he had received assurances, from an unspecified source, that the resolution of the Oil Commission would not be put to the Majlis, at any rate in its then form. Both the supposition of Sir Francis Shepherd and the assurance were quickly proved, again, to be over-optimistic. The next day, on March 13, he was reporting the anxiety of M. Husein Ala to avoid proclaiming martial law as it 'would only raise [the] political

---

[6] EP 1015/24.
[7] EP 1015/30.
[8] EP 1015/46.
[9] EP 1531/96.

temperature'[10] whereas, the following day again, the Premier considered 'that all that is needed is appeasement and a period of tranquillity'.[11] This was not exactly the view of Dr Musaddiq and the National Front. On March 13 it cowed the Majlis into voting in favour not only of considering under its procedure of double urgency the resolution of the Oil Commission, but that in a text revised so that the original reference to nationalisation of oil in Persia now related to the nationalisation of 'the oil industry'. This ominous amendment was forced through by M. Makki.

On the same day Mr Herbert Morrison minuted with reference to developments in Persia: 'We must keep on top of this. It's not good.'[12] In the Foreign Office a note to the Persian Government was being drafted at speed. This note in the main followed the line of the British *note verbale* and covering letter of February 24, while it now represented that His Majesty's Government had learnt 'with much concern'[13] of the recent attitude of the Majlis Oil Commission. The British note drew a specific distinction 'between the principle of nationalisation and the expropriation of an industry which has been operating in Iran on the security of a regularly negotiated agreement valid until 1993'. The Persian Government was reminded of the terms of Article 22 of that agreement, stipulating the procedure through the Permanent Court of International Justice at The Hague for arbitration in the event of disagreement with the Anglo-Iranian Oil Company.

On March 14, 1951, Sir William Strang handed this note to M. Soheily, the Persian Ambassador in London; Sir Francis Shepherd, who thought the Majlis should know the terms of the note before voting on the resolution of the Oil Commission, remitted another copy to M. Husein Ala, with the request that he would communicate it to the President of the Majlis. The Persian Prime Minister agreed to do this, and to the publication of the note. On the same day Lord Henderson, Parliamentary Under-Secretary of State for Foreign Affairs, spoke in the House of Lords on the lines of the lines of the note in reply to a question from Lord Vansittart, the erstwhile Permanent Under-Secretary of State for Foreign Affairs. He had agreed beforehand the form of a supplementary question in reply to which Lord Henderson sought, with perhaps doubtful effect, to discredit M. Kashani as an irresponsible, 'convicted of helping the German agents in the last war',[14] who had also been expelled from Persia for alleged connexion with the attempted assassination of the Shah in 1949.

Lord Vansittart had further suggested a public reference to Persian unilateral denunciation of treaties. Mr Furlonge, however, had pointed out that the Anglo-Iranian Oil Company's concession of 1933 from the Persian Government was not an intergovernmental treaty but a contractual agreement.[15] This legal weakness in the British case was later to assume critical significance in relation to the jurisdiction of the International Court at The Hague.

Sir Francis Shepherd telegraphed on March 14: 'We are doing all we can to arrange that there shall not be a quorum'[16] at the session of the Majlis on the

---

[10] EP 1015/34.
[11] EP 1531/105.
[12] EP 1015/38.
[13] Cmd 8425, p. 26.
[14] Parliamentary Debates, 5th Series, H. of L, Vol. 170, col. 1905.
[15] EP 1531/102.
[16] EP 1531/105.

following day to vote on the resolution of the Oil Commission. To this end the British Embassy in Tehran worked, in particular, through the Shah and through his friend, the former Minister of Labour, M. Asadullar Alam. The latter, however, doubted 'if sufficient Deputies would have the courage to stay away'.[17] For instance Dr Alavi, court physician to the Shah and a pro-British member of the Oil Commission, felt that he must vote for the resolution, which he had signed, because of the 'atmosphere of terror created by the minority'.[18] Such was the atmosphere after the murder of General Razmara and the failure of his successor to declare martial law. Subsequently the British Military Attaché reported of even the Chief of the Persian General Staff, who had welcomed the more vigorous British attitude towards the end of February: 'His reaction to the assassination of General Razmara was not however what I had expected. Instead of being angry and wishing martial law to be imposed he appeared frightened of further assassinations and unwilling to take any strong action.'[19]

On March 15 the Majlis, which was apparently not in fact informed of the British note of the previous day, hysterically adopted the revised resolution of its Oil Commission, in favour of the proposal to nationalise the oil industry and of a delay of two months to study its execution, by the unanimous vote of 95 Deputies. This marked the third critical stage in the increasingly hostile trend in Persia against Britain's vital oil interests, progressively manifested first by the withdrawal of the Supplemental Agreement at the end of December 1950 and then two months later by General Razmara's request for recognition of the principle of nationalisation. The slope downhill was steepening at an alarming rate.

Sir Francis Shepherd estimated that the President of the Majlis had probably been afraid to communicate to it the British note of March 14. The debate in the Majlis had, however, generated much indignation at Lord Henderson's corresponding statement. After the vote His Majesty's Ambassador expected 'that there may be jubilations and a short anti-British Press campaign but this should die down during the Persian New Year holidays [beginning on March 21]. I do not think we should do anything in the meantime that could exacerbate the situation. Ala has our note to be going on with.'[20] The representatives in Tehran of the Anglo-Iranian Oil Company agreed, as did the Foreign Office. But the British note had already failed to achieve its primary object of restraining the Majlis.

The resolute optimism wherewith Sir Francis Shepherd reacted to each successive reverse was backed in this case by his understanding that, as he telegraphed on March 15, the Shah's plan was to replace M. Husein Ala by M. Sayyid Zia about mid-April and then dissolve the Majlis. The Oil Commission would thus disappear before it had time to fulfil its mandate. His Majesty's Ambassador further reported on the following evening: 'It is thought that the Commission's two months extra will probably begin about the middle of April when Parliament reassembles.'[21] Mr Younger had made a statement to this effect in the House of Commons on the same day of March 16.[22]

---

[17] EP 1531/136.
[18] *Ibid.*
[19] EP 1991/1.
[20] EP 1531/108.
[21] EP 1015/36.
[22] Parliamentary Debates, 5th Series, H. of C., Vol. 485, col. 1966.

2. British and American reactions to the opening of the crisis over Persian oil, March 15-25

Whatever might be the precise duration of the respite before the next phase of the Persian attack on British interests, the crisis with regard to nationalisation of the Anglo-Iranian Oil Company had now begun. This crisis was emphasised at its outset by a deterioration in the already weak American support of British interests. Mr C.E. Steel, the Minister in charge of the British Embassy in Washington in the absence of Sir Oliver Franks, reported on March 16 that the State Department was 'clearly still somewhat unhappy'[23] about the delivery of the latest British note to the Persian Government. It 'urged that from now on there should be consultation between us before either we or they take any important steps in regard to the whole Persian situation.' The background to this was the development of considerable support in the State Department for the idea that Great Britain should 'meet nationalisation half-way rather than be dragged into it reluctantly after a prolonged rearguard action'.[24]

The State Department told the British Embassy on March 15 that it expected that Mr Acheson would be closely questioned at his Press conference on the following day on the latest resolution of the Majlis: 'it would be most difficult for him to say anything which implied disapproval of Persian action in this matter. He would of course equally not say anything implying approval of nationalisation.' Mr Steel commented that the State Department 'are clearly much impressed by the theory that if the Western world and the United Kingdom in particular is too "tough" to the Persians about nationalisation, we shall risk driving them into the arms of the Russians, whose radio propaganda is strongly supporting the National Front agitation for nationalisation.'[25] This American theory was to bedevil the whole of the Abadan crisis.

On the evening of March 17, 1951, Mr McGhee of the State Department, who was on a tour of the Middle East and India, arrived in Tehran. He immediately saw Sir Francis Shepherd and launched 'a spirited attack' on the slow rigidity of the Anglo-Iranian Oil Company. According to Mr McGhee the 'Foreign Office allowed the chairman of the company to dictate its policy about oil in Persia. Although the Americans had expressed a stronger respect than we had for the independence of private companies they did not hesitate to guide their oil companies.' Sir Francis Shepherd continued in his report of this conversation: 'When I said that the Aramco agreement had thrown a monkey wrench into Persian oil machinery he retorted that he warned Sir William Fraser last September of what was likely to happen. He accused the Anglo-Iranian Oil Company of being unwilling to co-operate with Aramco.' Mr McGhee evaded any expression of view about the future 'except to say that they were anxious to help to combat the idea of nationalisation. He considered that the history of oil concessions did not encourage reliance on the sanctity of contracts and that it would probably be necessary to fight a rearguard action as gracefully as possible on the legal aspects of the case. He asked if I thought some form of token nationalisation was becoming inevitable to which I replied I did not

---

[23] EP 1531/114.
[24] EP 1023/1.
[25] EP 1531/110.

think it was inevitable but that the principle had evidently come to stay.'[26]

The visit of Mr McGhee to Tehran may not have been helpful to British oil-interests, especially in view of the fact that the Persian prime minister was liable to be somewhat susceptible to American influence. Even if Mr McGhee did not repeat to Persians his criticisms of the Foreign Office and the Anglo-Iranian Oil Company, as one report at first suggested, yet M. Husein Ala was certainly aware of the existence of such American criticism of British policy. He described to Mr Chisholm, who was also visiting Tehran, how on March 17, Saint Patrick's Day, he had at the American Embassy drunk the health of two Irish Americans, Dr Grady and Mr McGhee; M. Ala added the reflexion that 'there are many Irishmen in the United States who are critical of Britain.'[27]

In reply to the warning from the State Department regarding Mr Acheson's attitude at his Press conference, the Foreign Office had mildly stated on March 16, 1951, in a telegram approved by Sir William Strang, that it hoped 'that Mr Acheson will find it possible to be entirely non-committal if he cannot support our point of view'.[28] This Mr Acheson did do. Subsequent information, however, caused the Foreign Office, in a telegram of March 19 to Washington, to express surprise at the adverse reaction of the State Department to the British note of March 14. The telegram explained that His Majesty's Government had had to show the uneasy British public that 'they had promptly taken a firm line'[29] to defend the threatened British interest, and that there had been no time to consult the State Department in advance.

The same telegram from the Foreign Office aptly recalled the American refusal in May 1950 to assist with the Supplemental Agreement on the grounds that it was entirely an Anglo-Persian business arrangement (cf p. 62); and also 'the State Department's consistent criticisms of both the company and His Majesty's Government over the oil question', as most recently by Mr McGhee to Sir Francis Shepherd. The hope was expressed that 'this divergence of views with the State Department over Persian oil, which we regret', could be dealt with frankly in forthcoming Anglo-American conversations which were then being arranged. Meanwhile the Foreign Office was both ready and anxious to exchange views most fully with the State Department concerning the political situation in Persia. One can readily appreciate the grounds for this rather firmer British tone towards the State Department, now first employed a few days after Mr Morrison had succeeded Mr Bevin at the Foreign Office.

Already on March 15, 1951, the new Secretary of State had minuted as regards the Persian crisis: 'Continue to *consider* possible courses of action if necessary, not excluding military and naval protective movements, though that would need careful thought and Cabinet authority.'[30] Mr Morrison may possibly not have been aware that immediately after the murder of General Razmara, on March 7, Vice-Admiral G.N. Oliver, British Commander-in-Chief, East Indies, had telegraphed to Commodore A.H. Wallis, Senior British Naval Officer, Persian Gulf, granting him discretion to station frigates as necessary to protect British interests, subject to advice

---

[26] EP 1531/116.
[27] EP 1531/171.
[28] EP 1531/110.
[29] EP 1531/114.
[30] EP 1531/120G.

from the British authorities in Persia, with whom he would be keeping in the closest touch. On March 15, however, Rear-Admiral Sir Anthony Buzzard, Director of Naval Intelligence, complained to Mr D.P. Reilly, Assistant Under-Secretary of State supervising military liaison, that His Majesty's Embassy at Tehran was not repeating telegrams about the Persian situation to Vice-Admiral Oliver, who was most interested in case naval action was required.[31] A similar complaint was being voiced by the Senior Naval Officer in the Persian Gulf on March 26.[32] Arrangements were made to remedy this, but action was also to be necessary to meet corresponding complaints from Sir John Troutbeck, His Majesty's Ambassador at Baghdad, on April 19[33] and, so late as May 2, from General Robertson in his command of Middle East Land Forces.[34] That day Sir John Troutbeck complained that he had not seen any of the replies from the Foreign Office to the telegrams from Tehran which he was now receiving.[35] Next day Sir Gladwyn Jebb, permanent United Kingdom representative at the United Nations in New York, explained that general information regarding British policy on Persian oil would be useful to him,[36] and on May 5 His Majesty's Embassy in Washington requested quicker repetition thither of telegrams from Tehran.[37] The danger of wasteful copying of messages evidently calls in time of crisis for especially careful balance against that of leaving the interested diplomatic and military authorities with inadequate information.

On March 19, 1951, Commodore Wallis reported that Mr Drake at Abadan considered that the Persian security forces should be strong enough to maintain order there and in the Fields area, and as the weak British forces probably available would be insufficient to restore order against the certain opposition of the local population and security forces, such British forces should not be sent unless the situation were desperate.

Meanwhile, however, the Foreign Office was following up the instruction of the Secretary of State, and on March 20 Mr Furlonge addressed a long letter to Captain E. Butler-Bowden, RN of the Ministry of Defence. Mr Furlonge referred to the military planning for Persia in 1950, but pointed out that 'the use of force to prevent the Persian Government from seizing the oil installations does not seem to be covered by any plans at present':[38] whereas in the last resort this might have to be considered. The Chiefs of Staff were requested to arrange for the necessary studies to be undertaken urgently. On the political side the Foreign Office now doubted how far even the Iraqi Government would be prepared to facilitate such British troop-movements. In this context it would seem regrettable that, after the Shah and General Razmara had by the beginning of the year agreed to the proposed visit of General Sir Brian Robertson, it had been further postponed, latterly at his suggestion in the aftermath of the assassination: although the Foreign Office learnt on March 19 that the Shah and General Garzan were still anxious for the visit.[39]

In another direction, however, the Foreign Office took a further initiative on

---

[32] EP 1991/2.
[33] EP 1015/131.
[34] EP 1991/1.
[35] EP 1531/251.
[36] EP 1531/347.
[37] EP 1531/251A.
[38] EP 1531/120G.
[39] E 1201/67G.

March 20, 1951. Sir William Strang presided at what he termed an extraordinary meeting at a high level between representatives concerned with Persian affairs in the Foreign Office, Treasury, Bank of England, Ministry of Defence, Admiralty and Ministry of Fuel and Power. Sir William Strang briefly told the meeting of a conversation which he had had on the previous day with Sir William Fraser, to whom he had in fact communicated the criticisms of Mr McGhee. Sir William Fraser had fully endorsed the British note of March 14 and had notably said, now, that he was not afraid of the word 'nationalisation' but would consider any solution which left the management of the Persian oil-industry to his company. Subsequently, on March 21, he was to inform Sir William Strang that he proposed to act in accordance with counsel's opinion that the legal position of the company would not be weakened if it made no representation to the Persian Government against the Majlis resolution on oil-nationalisation. Sir William Strang did not dissent from this forbearing course.[40]

In considering the possible promotion of negotiations with the Persian Government, the meeting of March 20 noted that the Anglo-Iranian Oil Company had not engaged in bribery, though it had made 'certain arrangements with the Bakhtiari chieftains for protection'. Mr Berthoud thought that if the company adopted bribery in Persia, where Governments and officials were constantly changing, it would set in motion forces which it could not control. The meeting agreed, once again (cf p. 63), that publicity had been a weak point with the company and that the possibility of official assistance here should be studied.

Mr Furlonge expressed the view at this meeting that 'although there had been reticence on the part of AIOC in the past about discussing matters with Whitehall, the company now seemed more forthcoming'.[41] Lord Henderson held that 'the whole AIOC problem had become a matter for the Government', which would be held responsible if things went wrong. The meeting agreed that henceforth there must be constant consultation between His Majesty's Government and the Anglo-Iranian Oil Company, more particularly with regard to the alternative proposals which, it was further decided, the company should have ready to advance within two months at the maximum, preferably in anticipation of the final report of the Majlis Oil Commission.

At the special interdepartmental meeting of March 20, 1951, the representatives of the Ministry of Fuel and Power said that if, at the worst, no more oil were obtained from Persia 'it would mean a loss to the United Kingdom of 22 million tons of oil products plus 7 million tons of crude oil per annum. The United Kingdom would therefore have to buy oil elsewhere, for dollars and other currency amounting perhaps to $200 million and the equivalent of $50 million in other currencies a year ... The Admiralty representatives said that the Royal Navy at present obtained about 2 million tons per annum of a particular kind of oil from AIOC, representing something like 85 percent of their needs. Unless another company could supply that special kind of oil, the Admiralty would have to draw on their war stocks, a source sufficient for only two years.' When Sir Roger Makins, Deputy Under-Secretary of State supervising relations with the United States, suggested that it should be impressed upon the Americans that the threat to Middle Eastern oil supplies

---

[40] EP 1531/129.
[41] EP 1531/149G.

concerned them as much as it did Great Britain, Sir Donald Fergusson, Permanent Secretary of the Ministry of Fuel and Power, 'pointed out that for the Americans their overseas oil companies were a sideline; for the United Kingdom, theirs were vital.'[42] Even so, as Mr McGhee was subsequently to point out, the State Department during 1950 had if anything shown itself more anxiously concerned than the Foreign Office over the fate of the Supplemental Agreement.

Sir William Strang informed the meeting that the Secretary of State had told him that 'he wanted a paper for the Cabinet, but first needed to formulate his policy; he was prepared to take a strong line, and certainly not to retreat'. He had enquired whether a British warship of suitable tonnage was in the Persian Gulf and also concerning the possible use of troops which the Chiefs of Staff had just been asked to study. It was agreed that their views might form an appendix in the comprehensive paper which was now to be produced by an interdepartmental Working Party on Persia. This should be convened at once by Mr Bowker and Mr Furlonge, and prepare a brief for the Anglo-American conversations concerning Persia which were shortly to be held in Washington.

On the following day, March 21, 1951, the Foreign Office despatched to all major posts abroad an intelligence telegram, Intel No. 58 Saving,[43] with a view to promoting a wide realisation of the adverse implications of the nationalisation of the Anglo-Iranian Oil Company. Seventeen more or less familiar arguments against it were listed, beginning with the fact that 'it is a misuse of the term to refer to nationalisation of the Persian oil industry . . . as the oil is in the ownership of the State, and to this extent the industry is already nationalised'. And the Persians certainly would not have the skill or resources to run efficiently a highly technical industry which required an annual expenditure of some £40-50 million in Persia alone to keep it at concert pitch, and which was dependent as to 95 percent or more upon export markets. Complete Persian nationalisation of the Anglo-Iranian Oil Company would swiftly produce Persian unemployment and economic dislocation. Next day the Treasury wrote to the Chairman of the Board of Inland Revenue suggesting that it should examine the position of oil companies under the current Finance Act in the light of criticism in the Middle East that His Majesty's Government benefited more than local Governments from oil profits, and of the suggestion of a 50-50 arrangement in Persia more or less on the Arabian model of Aramco, which had, however, fiscally, passed the pinch on to the United States Government.[44] Such a device in relation to His Majesty's Government was not, however, apt to be favoured by its financial advisers; the general question of tax remission for oil companies in the Middle East was to subsist as a vexed one in regard to American practice.[45]

By about March 20, 1951, the Foreign Office and, now, other Departments, had recaptured the urgency of early January and were getting a firm grip upon the problem of concerting measures in the interests of an acceptable settlement over Persian oil. This was in response to the impulsion of sternly adverse developments in Persia and of a British public opinion which was, as Lord Vansittart advised Lord

---

[42] *Ibid.*
[43] B 11/12G.
[44] EP 1531/182.
[45] Confidential/General/415.

Henderson in Parliament on March 21, tending to become 'not only uneasy but angry'.[46] The new Secretary of State for Foreign Affairs was, however, vigorously responsive to the situation.

On March 20, 1951, the Persian Senate, though more moderate in composition than the Majlis, unanimously approved its resolution favouring the nationalisation of the oil industry. On the same day an attempt to murder the Minister of Education in General Razmara's Government at last stirred M. Husein Ala into imposing martial law in Tehran and giving it a strong Military Governor in the person of General Hijazi. An attempt to murder the latter four days later in turn induced the Persian Government to heed the urging of Sir Francis Shepherd and to arrest some members of the Fidayan-i-Islam, though not such leaders as M. Kashani. Thereafter disturbance in Tehran subsided and His Majesty's Ambassador reported on March 27 that if M. Ala's Government succeeded in restoring tranquillity, it might not after all be quickly replaced; this 'introduces a new element into the situation'.[47] For the time being the likelihood of an early accession to office of M. Sayyid Zia receded.

3. Strikes at Abadan and consultations in London, March 26–April 9

It was at Abadan that the bubbling cauldron of Persian oil was next stoked up by the Tudeh and its Association for the Struggle against the Southern Oil Company. They inspired and exploited strikes which broke out on March 26 at the Bandar Mashur and Agha Jari workings in the Fields area around Abadan. These strikes were illegal owing to disregard of machinery for conciliation, as were the others which promptly followed. In Abadan itself Persian apprentices struck on the ground that the passmark of 50 percent required by the Persian Ministry of Education in the technical examinations conducted by the Anglo-Iranian Oil Company should be reduced to 30 percent: a ridiculous commentary upon claims for Persianisation of the industry. Another strike followed at the Masjid-i-Suleiman workings on behalf of an 80 percent increase in wages 'because the industry had been nationalised': a demand related to the campaign of the Association for the Struggle against the Southern Oil Company.

These frivolous strikes had, however, been triggered off at Bandar Mashur and Agha Jari by the company's stoppage there, owing to improved conditions, of hardlying allowances, and that just at the Persian holiday of the New Year. The company had given six months' notice of these cuts and had, so it stated, secured assent to them from the Persian Ministry of Labour.[48] Nevertheless, as the Foreign Office more or less had to admit to the critical Americans, the local imposition of the cuts at that particular juncture evidenced, not for the first time (cf p. 60), some political ineptitude on the part of a concern which still appeared to be thinking here primarily in terms of economics. The Persian Government appointed a Conciliation Commission, with which the company co-operated closely, and also declared martial law in the province of Khuzistan. Sir Francis Shepherd subsequently reported, however, that the Persian Government 'seemed reluctant to arrest the agitators who attempted, without much success, to turn the strike into a political demonstration in

---

[46] Parliamentary Debates, 5th Series, H. of L., Vol. 170, col. 1248.
[47] EP 1015/56.
[48] EP 1915/146.

favour of nationalisation'.[49]

Against this background His Majesty's Government decided at the end of March that in the Persian Gulf the three British frigates, HMSS *Wild Goose, Flamingo* and *Wren* should be held within two days' call of Abadan but should otherwise continue their normal programme.[50] It proved necessary to reassure the American Government concerning exaggerated reports of these movements. On April 4 the Foreign Office telegraphed to Sir Francis Shepherd[51] that the kind of action envisaged by Mr Morrison, namely a projected visit to the Persian Gulf by a cruiser, HMS *Gambia*, would not now take place because the Admiralty had represented that it could hardly be described as normal, and could only be undertaken at the direct request of the Foreign Office,[52] which was not made as yet. On the broader issue Sir Francis Shepherd had opined to Mr Furlonge, more sombrely than usual, in a letter of March 26 received on March 30: 'There seems no reason to expect any [Persian] politicians to take a courageous stand in the future. This means that we may have to show a little of the mailed fist, though if we choose our time right it may need to be only a distant glimpse.'[53]

In these circumstances did the British Chiefs of Staff prepare the study requested by Mr Morrison on the 'Implications of Military Action in Persia', COS(51)173 of March 27, 1951.[54] This memorandum considered three possible courses. First, a show of force without entering Persian territory, roughly on the model of 1946; the provision of forces for this presented no particular military problem and a naval force could be despatched at comparatively short notice. Secondly, Plan Accleton had, on the assumption of Persian co-operation, provided for the move by air of two British battalions to Abadan with an object now described as the protection of the main oil-installations on Abadan island and the evacuation of British nationals. (There appear, however, to have been slight doubts about the precise object of Accleton. The Ministry of Defence referred later to the evacuation of 'AIOC personnel from the oilfield area'. In reply GHQ, MELF on May 3 drew attention to the object of Accleton as given in the original instruction of November 1950: cf p. 92).[55] Persian hostility, the Chiefs of Staff considered, would render the force for Accleton insufficient to maintain order and protect the installations for any length of time. The execution of the plan would entail serious military and political risks, notably of exacerbating Persian nationalist feeling and—in contrast to the assessment of the Chiefs of Staff in the preceding autumn—of provoking Russian intervention under the Treaty of 1921, with 'grave risk of contact between British and Russian forces and of a situation that might develop into global war' or, at least, of one 'of which the Russians are unlikely to be slow to take advantage in the United Nations'. These dangers applied *a fortiori* to the third course of a British defence of Abadan and the south-west Persian oilfields against action by the Persian Government or mob violence. Such an expedition would involve the equivalent of at least the whole British Middle East Garrison, which would need to be replaced from elsewhere. This

---

[49] EP 1013/19.
[50] EP 1212/11.
[51] EP 1212/12.
[52] EP 1192/11G.
[53] EP 1015/74.
[54] EP 1192/9G.
[55] EP 1015/177G.

could only be done by partial mobilisation and 'at the most serious cost to our global strategy in peace and war', especially since the strategic reserve in the United Kingdom was as yet only in process of formation.

On the perhaps cautionary date of April 1 Sir Oliver Franks reported that 'even so anti-imperialist a paper as the *Washington Post* contemplated with calm'[56] a possible British show of military force towards Persia. Although in the United States 'the feeling that we have been slow in meeting the situation tends to neutralise proper recognition of the benefits conferred on Persia by the workings of the AIOC', yet on the whole Americans reactions were 'much better than might have been expected'. At a meeting of the Defence Committee of the Cabinet on the following day the Chiefs of Staff, recalling the military conversations of the preceding October in Washington, even considered that the Americans might possibly agree to send an aircraft carrier into the Persian Gulf; though it was observed that 'any direct intervention by the Americans in Persia was likely to be regarded in Moscow as a serious provocation'.[57]

On April 4, 1951, the Foreign Office informed His Majesty's Ambassador in Tehran not only of the decision against the cruise of HMS *Gambia* but also, in the longer term, that 'plans have been prepared for moving troops to the vicinity of Abadan at short notice should it become necessary to protect refinery area in the event of serious disturbances or a threat of Persian governmental action. It is, however, recognised that any premature move of this kind might increase hostility to ourselves not only in Persia but throughout the Middle East and might not command the support of other Commonwealth countries.'[58]

The memorandum of the Chiefs of Staff, COS(51)73, which informed these decisions and considerations, had, as previously proposed, been annexed to the Foreign Secretary's general paper on Persia, DO(51)38 of March 29, 1951, drafted by the recently appointed Persian Working Party, agreed with the Chancellor of the Exchequer, the Minister of Defence, Mr Shinwell, and the First Lord of the Admiralty, Lord Hall, and considered by the Defence Committee of the Cabinet on April 2. This memorandum still held that the two-months' term for the work of the Majlis Oil Commission was 'apparently to run from April 14', though it was now recognised that the commission would probably report in favour of nationalisation 'perhaps before the expiry of the two months'.[59] Such nationalisation would, it was agreed, have an 'extremely grave' effect upon the British economy, especially as regards balance of payments; for Great Britain 'the consequences to the national standard of living, and to the rearmament programme . . . could not fail to be considerable . . . Politically the effect would be scarcely less serious . . . the loss of prestige resulting from the eviction of the AIOC, or its replacement by another foreign concern, would be most harmful to our standing throughout the Middle East, and indeed over a wider field; Persian nationalist success would encourage extreme nationalist demands elsewhere, to the certain detriment of our interests.'

Mr Morrison's memorandum of March 29 accordingly reached the agreed conclusions that 'our first objective must clearly be to prevent the Persian

---

[56] PG 14582/19.
[57] EP 1192/14G.
[58] EP 1023/5.
[59] EP 1192/9G.

Government from implementing the resolution to "nationalise'" the oil industry . . . To negotiate at all with the Persians a prerequisite would be the emergence of a Prime Minister and a Government sufficiently strong to be able to discuss matters reasonably.' The dissolution of the Majlis, with its Oil Commission, 'might also be found necessary'. It seemed likely that all this could only be obtained if the 'well-intentioned but weak' Shah took resolute action. Pressure on him might be necessary and the co-operation in this of the American Government was being sought. Finally, His Majesty's Government should, as previously proposed, exercise a close control now over the actions of the Anglo-Iranian Oil Company since 'this is not a commercial affair, but a vital national interest'. It had taken months to get that quite clear and to confront the consequences.

In connexion with the preparation of this memorandum, and of an accompanying draft letter to the Anglo-Iranian Oil Company for the revision of its relations with His Majesty's Government, Mr Berthoud had minuted on March 27, 1951: 'I am struck by the extent to which the letter [from Sir John Bradbury] of May 20, 1914, does entitle His Majesty's Government to be consulted and if necessary to oppose the policies of AIOC over a wide field. In fact the Treasury attitude of caution about interference does not seem to be justified by what has been laid down between His Majesty's Government and the Company.'[60] (Compare, however, p. 314.) If this observation illustrates the extent to which primary responsibility for official relations with the company had hitherto lain outside the Foreign Office, it may also suggest the importance of ensuring that the busy departments of the Foreign Office, usually dealing with impressive precision with a very heavy burden of current work, should yet receive full and early briefing on historical issues of current or likely importance.

The letter to the Anglo-Iranian Oil Company, in revision of that of May 20, 1914, was communicated as a draft to Sir William Fraser by Sir Edward Bridges, Permanent Secretary to the Treasury, at a meeting on April 3, 1951. Sir William Fraser considered that his company had hitherto kept in close touch with Whitehall and that the proposed change in favour of more intensive consultation would be welcome and not fundamental.[61] The minute of this conversation made by Sir William Strang, also present, does not record that Sir Edward Bridges followed his brief from the Treasury so far as to raise specifically with Sir William Fraser 'the question of the part to be played in the future by the Government Directors who appear to be allowed to play a very limited role in return for their annual emoluments of £2,950 per annum'.[62] Sir Edward Bridges and Sir William Fraser arranged for immediate consultations between the company and Government Departments in a phase of rethinking about arrangements for Persian oil which also included meetings on April 2-3 with Mr McGhee, on his way back through London from the Middle East to Washington.

In a telegram of March 28, 1951, Sir Francis Shepherd had argued among other things that in any event His Majesty's Government should not relinquish to Persia control over such a strategic interest as the southern oilfields and refineries unless the Russian right, whether legal or specious, to send troops into Persia under the treaty of 1921 were balanced by securing a British right to use military forces to

[60] EP 1192/9G.
[61] EP 1537/2.
[62] EP 1537/4.

protect the oilfields: to which the words 'against foreign interference' were added in the Foreign Office.[63] This was one of the practical considerations which, Sir Francis Shepherd felt, should be safeguarded by His Majesty's Government while making play with the admission virtually made by him to Mr McGhee on March 17, that the 'general principle of nationalisation of the industry may be conceded'. This proposition was significantly amended in the Foreign Office to read that the 'general principle of the right of nationalisation may be conceded, but has been legally alienated in the short-term by the concession agreement'.

The Secretary of State's memorandum of March 29 did not even go so far as to admit the principle of the Persian right to nationalise the oil industry; though at the Defence Committee of the Cabinet on April 2 the Minister of Labour, Mr Aneurin Bevan, argued that this would be perfectly satisfactory provided that the Anglo-Iranian Oil Company were able to secure from the Persian Government a lease to exploit the oil resources:[64] a view which was subsequently disputed within the Foreign Office. Between February and April 1951 opinion in the Foreign Office had evidently hardened against admitting Persian nationalisation of the oil industry to any considerable extent. It seems uncertain, however, how far this was reflected in any observations made to Mr McGhee by Mr Bowker next day with the American Assistant Secretary of State.

Mr McGhee broadly reiterated the criticisms of past British policy which he had previously made to Sir Francis Shepherd. But he now proposed, at the meeting on April 2, that in order to create a favourable atmosphere for negotiations between the Persian Government and the Anglo-Iranian Oil Company it might be useful for the Governments of the United Kingdom and of the United States to issue a joint statement in 'support of oil concessions throughout the Middle East based on some profit-sharing arrangement'.[65] This important proposal was considered at a British interdepartmental meeting held at the instigation of the Treasury on the following day at the Ministry of Fuel and Power. No minute of this meeting has been traced but the main impression derived by Mr Ramsbotham, who attended for the Foreign Office, was of the Treasury's misgivings concerning the proposed declaration: for instance it seemed questionable what would be a fair formula for profit-sharing, how it could be applied uniformly under varying conditions, what the attitude of the oil companies would be. Against this Mr Ramsbotham thought that such difficulties should not prove insuperable: the profit-sharing principle had come to stay and the Anglo-Iranian Oil Company was actually working on a plan for a 50-50 arrangement; such a joint declaration as Mr McGhee proposed should notably help to meet Persian and other nationalist susceptibilities about 'colonial exploitation of the national heritage'.[66] Mr Ramsbotham accordingly recommended agreement to the issue of such an Anglo-American declaration; the question of the participation of France, a partner in the Iraq Petroleum Company and sensitive regarding the Middle East, was for consideration; the British and American Governments should hold early consultations with their oil companies. In agreeing with Mr Ramsbotham, Mr Berthoud observed in a minute of April 4 that if the Americans, with their respect

[63] EP 1531/137.
[64] EP 1192/14G.
[65] EP 1023/10G.
[66] E 1531/11.

for private enterprise, were prepared to issue a joint statement it would be rather absurd for His Majesty's Government, with its controlling interest in the Anglo-Iranian Oil Company, to object for fear of interfering with it.

On April 4, 1951, Mr McGhee's proposal was further discussed at an interdepartmental meeting held by Sir Edward Bridges, evidently at a higher level than that of the preceding day. No minute of this seemingly critical meeting has been traced in Foreign Office archives. Mr Bowker briefly recorded on April 5 that at Sir Edward Bridges' meeting 'opinion generally was against' the proposed Anglo-American declaration. Mr Bowker's minute, together with those of the previous day by Mr Ramsbotham and Mr Berthoud, was seen on that day of April 5 by Sir William Strang, who did not comment upon this reversal of their recommendation, which had been initialed on April 4 by Sir Roger Makins.[67]

Also on April 5 Mr Berthoud minuted that the Treasury was probably concerned lest by issuing such a declaration 'we may be undermining our position for things other than oil in or outside the Middle East',[68] such as Malayan tin, potash in Israel, timber in Siam and base metals in Burma. Another fact may perhaps have been that, for the present at any rate, Mr McGhee's proposal was his own, not an official one from the American Government; and just at that time there was an increasing amount of personal criticism of Mr McGhee in British quarters (cf pp. 141-2). This may have tended to reinforce any doubts as to how far, for instance, the Americans would stand firmly on the declaration if it were challenged, as was only too likely to happen in Persia where, as Mr Gass had presciently pointed out as early as the middle of January (cf p. 110), the demand for nationalisation was overshadowing that for the introduction of the 50-50 principle which he had further strongly opposed.

Despite the possible dangers and drawbacks of the proposed Anglo-American declaration, as of most imaginative acts of policy, the initial reaction of the Foreign Office in its favour could be supported by strong arguments. Here was a chance at last of breaking through the frustrations of Anglo-American friction over Persian oil, of making amends for earlier British neglect of cogent American warnings concerning the Supplemental Agreement by accepting an American proposal which might at the same time allow British policy to catch up gracefully on the accomplished fact of the Aramco Agreement with Arabia. More than that, the joint declaration would set Persian oil in its true perspective as one important part of the whole economic and strategic stake of the Western Powers in the Middle East where, as Mr McGhee himself had observed on April 2, 'United States and United Kingdom oil was really in one pool'.[69] One might be able to take the opportunity to resume where the Shinwell-Ickes Agreement had left off and perhaps to secure precisely that informal Anglo-American coordination of interests in the Middle East which the Foreign Office had vainly broached with Mr Rountree two months earlier (cf p. 114). The association of France in this could perhaps have been valuably developed towards overcoming something, at any rate, of the lamentable and otiose legacy of Anglo-French friction in the Middle East. Finally, in Persia itself, adroit British diplomacy might perhaps have been able to work up the joint declaration into a strong obstacle against outright nationalisation, especially in view of the particular

---

[67] E 1531/11.
[68] E 1531/8.
[69] EP 1023/10G.

American influence upon M. Husein Ala. In order to bind the Americans firmly to the declaration it might by now perhaps have been worth considering concessions to them in some broad and imaginative arrangement for collaboration in the Middle East, perhaps not even excluding some American connexion with, or holding in, the Anglo-Iranian Oil Company. Some such background might, perhaps, have offered good hopes for the forthcoming Anglo-American conversations in Washington.

It is not recorded that these large considerations were advanced by the Foreign Office at the time. But even in the light of those that were the decision taken at interdepartmental level on April 4, 1951, to reject Mr McGhee's proposal was apparently a heavy one, although no record has been traced of its having received Ministerial approval. On the previous day, however, the Economic Policy Committee of the Cabinet had taken note of an expression by Mr Shinwell of his great concern about the oil situation in the Middle East, with special reference to Persia. The Minister of Defence had referred to the possible relevance of the unratified Shinwell-Ickes Agreement (cf p. 54). In discussion it was suggested in the Committee that 'it might possibly be found to our advantage for the United States to increase her economic commitments in the area provided that she were prepared to concert her policy with ours. The economic aspects of the situation could not be considered in isolation from the strategic and political aspects.'[70] It was on the same day of April 3 that the Foreign Secretary, in his conversation with Mr McGhee, had, apparently without referring directly to his proposed declaration, remarked that 'it was profoundly important that United States officials should not adumbrate policies in regard to the Middle East until we had time to consult together. I hoped', recorded Mr Morrison, 'that the United States Government would take special case to ensure that there was not crossing of wires.'[71]

Some of Mr McGhee's more detailed suggestions evoked a response in the Foreign Office. In this connexion Mr Berthoud minuted on April 4 that in his view the Anglo-Iranian Oil Company should offer not only Persian directorships but also 'much lower' prices to the Persians for their own oil for internal consumption: 'the fetish of charging the locals a price based on Gulf of Mexico prices must really be broken once and for all, and the Persians must feel that they are getting their oil at a cheaper price than the Admiralty.'[72] On April 5 the Foreign Office telegraphed to Sir Francis Shepherd that one idea then being discussed with the company was the transfer of its concession of 1933 and its Persian assets and activities to a new British company with some Persian directors and equal profit-sharing with the Persian Government.[73] On the previous day, however, Mr Elkington, a Director of the Anglo-Iranian Oil Company, had emphasised the pride felt by Persians at participating in a worldwide organisation:[74] which was just what the suggested new arrangement would terminate.

Mr Elkington had made his point at a meeting held on April 4 between representatives of the Foreign Office, the BBC and the Anglo-Iranian Oil Company. Mr Elkington supplied much valuable data concerning the activities of the company, for use in the intensified publicity which both Mr Herbert Morrison and Mr Noel-

---

[70] E 1531/7.
[71] E 1024/13G.
[72] E 1531/11.
[73] EP 1531/147.
[74] PG 13437/7.

Baker, Minister of Fuel and Power, were now seeking to stimulate. On April 3 the Foreign Secretary had minuted: 'Keep in mind publicity at home and the United States so that our people understand. Partly depends on His Majesty's Government having a clear mind.'[75] It is uncertain whether this may, partly at least, have been an allusion to the circumstances that on the preceding day Mr Morrison had informed the Cabinet that he had persuaded the Secretaries of State for the Colonies and for Commonwealth Relations to agree to the proposal of the Chancellor of the Exchequer that, in the budget, expenditure on the British Overseas Information Services should be cut from £11,700,000 to £10,150,000.[76]

It was at this time that the Minister of Labour was objecting because in the new budget, contemplating a total expenditure of over £4,000 million, the cost of the National Health Service was to be held at £400 million, whereas the estimates for defence were increased to about £1,500 million. The resignation of Mr Aneurin Bevan on April 21, following the death of Mr Ernest Bevin a week earlier, was to weaken the Government and throw further burdens on the new Foreign Secretary in his capacity as Deputy Prime Minister during Mr Attlee's illness from March 21 to April 31. On April 9 Mr Watson, First Secretary for Information in His Majesty's Embassy at Washington, reported American assurances that collaboration in information activities would not be affected by reduced British expenditure; he added his impression, however, that it was felt in Washington that the British were now less keen on 'political warfare, or at any rate on collaborating with the Americans . . . This is part of the feeling that the British Government is in rather a weary state altogether.'[77]

A Persian prospect of 'a period of comparative tranquillity while the next step in the oil situation was being considered'[78] was envisaged by Sir Francis Shepherd on April 4, 1951, if M. Husein Ala could come to terms with the opposition of the National Front, and if the strikes in the oilfields could be settled. On the following day the Foreign Office indeed agreed to a suggestion from Sir Francis Shepherd that, in order to give him time to work upon M. Ala regarding oil, he should inform him that there was no hurry for a reply to the British note of March 14. Also on April 5 Sir William Strang told the French Ambassador in London that 'we very much hoped that, in time, the present agitation would calm down. The Persian Government were behaving quite reasonably.'[79]

A rather different note was sounded in a letter written on the same day of April 5, 1951, to the First Lord of the Admiralty by Vice-Admiral Earl Mountbatten, Fourth Sea Lord with responsibility for the oil supplies of the Royal Navy. Lord Mountbatten referred to the nature of nationalist movements in the east, and presciently wrote: 'I feel certain that if the Persians, in their present emotional frame of mind, have proclaimed the slogan of nationalisation of the oilfields, they will not be deterred from carrying it through by the fact that their economy may suffer disastrously as a result.'[80] There was little doubt, he felt, that 'nationalisation is now inevitable. The use of force, on our part, to prevent this from happening would, in

---

[75] PG 1341/1G.
[76] CM(51)23.
[77] P 10122/27.
[78] EP 1015/73.
[79] EP 1531/175.
[80] EP 1537/5.

my opinion, be disastrous—if only because any form of fighting around Abadan would imperil the refinery.' This heavy discount of protection for a great British asset was further related in the view of Lord Mountbatten to the evident risk that, were it attempted, Russia might arraign His Majesty's Government as an aggressor before the United Nations where 'it would be a very difficult case indeed to argue on our behalf'.

Lord Mountbatten considered, however, that with regard to Persian nationalisation of the oil industry 'there is surely no reason why we should not try, and try at once, to divert it along lines which would enable co-operation between the Persians and ourselves to continue'. He suggested that a British Minister and a director of the oil company should go to Tehran to negotiate; and 'unless they get there well before mid-April they may be too late to save the situation'. They should seek to secure the co-operation of the Majlis Oil Commission by pointing out that nationalisation of the industry would involve full compensation of a very large order. But if the British delegation were too late the Oil Commission might interpret nationalisation as expropriation without compensation, and 'I fear that we are gravely risking immobilising a large part of our fleet'.[81]

On the same day of April 5 the Foreign Office telegraphed for Sir Francis Shepherd's observations on the similar views which Lord Mountbatten had put to the Foreign Secretary at a meeting three days earlier. This telegram further reported that in Lord Mountbatten's opinion 'His Majesty's Government should take over the direction of the Anglo-Iranian Oil Company. The question of Persian oil could then be dealt with between Governments, perhaps through an intergovernmental board.'[82] Lord Mountbatten further advocated the constitution in London of a standing committee of senior officials to keep in touch with the oil situation. In conveying to Sir Francis Shepherd these views the Foreign Office commented that 'at first sight this approach to the problem looks too drastic'.

His Majesty's Ambassador in Tehran replied on April 7 that he considered that, provided that some face-saving formula concerning nationalisation was included, some such arrangement as that which the Foreign Office was then discussing with the company might be accepted by the Persians, though they would probably fight hard for something better than a 50-50 split.[83] Sir Francis Shepherd held that 'the time has come for us to give a strong lead to the Persians'.[84] Following up Lord Mountbatten's proposal, he suggested telling M. Husein Ala that a junior British Minister would come to Tehran for discussions and to meet the Oil Commission when, as the Persian Premier was now envisaging, it was enlarged so as to be properly representative of the Persian Senate as well as of the lower house of the Majlis. Sir Francis Shepherd estimated that it would be useless for a British Minister to try to influence the existing Oil Commission, or to arrive without 'something more to offer than a mere explanation of the British case'. If, however, the procedure which he advocated were adopted, he thought there was 'a good chance that the Persians in their present perplexity might be prepared to come to a fairly rapid agreement', especially in intergovernmental negotiations. These should preferably

---

[81] EP 1537/5.
[82] EP 1531/168G.
[83] EP 1531/163.
[84] EP 1531/174G.

produce an agreement on principle before the details were discussed with the Anglo-Iranian Oil Company. 'It would lead to difficulties', thought Sir Francis Shepherd, 'if we were to take over the Anglo-Iranian Oil Company'.[85] In any Anglo-Persian governmental negotiations, it would be undesirable to bring in the American Government except as a last resort since 'their idea of a neutral attitude in this question in the past has had damaging results'.[83]

The views of Sir Francis Shepherd were considered together with Lord Mountbatten's letter of April 5 at an interdepartmental meeting which was attended on April 9 by Sir Edward Bridges, Sir William Strang and Sir Donald Fergusson. They recommended that the proposed British mission should proceed to Tehran 'before the end of the month',[81] thus moderating the urgent timetable put forward by Lord Mountbatten. Nor was it felt that any recommendations of policy for this mission could be made till after the Anglo-American conversations concerning the Middle East which were opening that same day in Washington.

4. Failure of the Anglo-American conversations on Persia in Washington, April 9-19

The immediate prelude to the Washington conversations of April 1951 had been inauspicious. It was evidently desirable that these consultations should be held in the same secrecy as the Anglo-American military conversations concerning the Middle East in the preceding year. By March 30, 1951, however, official sources in Washington had leaked information[86] regarding the forthcoming 'secret Anglo-American talks'.[87] The Foreign Office, in its first reaction to the leak, had been particularly concerned to spare French susceptibilities at being left out of any conversations concerning the Middle East. It was therefore given out that the Anglo-American talks would specifically relate to Persia, as certainly was true, although the brief for the British delegation prescribed that they 'should also explore the possibilities of securing an agreed Anglo-American policy on oil in the Middle East'.[88] The public emphasis on Persia, however, had the disadvantages of focusing expectation and ruffling Persian feelings. And the French were still left out, although in the Foreign Office it was already appreciated, for instance, that if the Persians succeeded in nationalising the Anglo-Iranian Oil Company it might encourage the Egyptians to attempt as much with the French-controlled Suez Canal Company.

Another adverse development for the Anglo-American conversations in Washington was the mounting criticism which Mr McGhee, who was to lead the Americans, had aroused both in the Middle East and on his return through London. On March 29 Sir William Houston-Boswell had reported the generally unfavourable impressions which his Legation at Beirut had formed of 'that infant prodigy Mr McGhee, who is only 39' and was said to have amassed already a large fortune from oil.[89] Sir William Houstoun-Boswell mentioned that Mr McGhee's 'opening gambit was to ask, "Well, who's going to get the Mediterranean now?"—and so it went on from there'. On April 3 Sir Thomas Rapp of the British Middle East Office telegraphed that the friendly Mr Lockett of Standard Oil in Cairo had disputed Mr

---

[85] *Ibid.*
[86] EP 1023/8.
[87] *The Financial Times*, April 3, 1951.
[88] EP 1023/11.
[89] E 1024/15G.

McGhee's application to Persia of the Mexican precedent for nationalisation of oil. Mr Lockett had described Mr McGhee as 'a young enthusiast desiring to bring about a rapid increase in the standard of living of the Middle East peoples'.[90] He did not appreciate that in Persia and elsewhere this depended more upon the action of local government than upon the amount of oil royalties.

In retrospect it was perhaps unfortunate that Mr McGhee's proposal for an Anglo-American declaration on profit-sharing in Middle Eastern oil should have been made by Mr McGhee. On April 6 the Secretary of State telegraphed to His Majesty's Ambassador in Washington that at the conversations in the Foreign Office Mr McGhee had been so critical of British policy in Persia and in Egypt that His Majesty's Government were 'not altogether convinced by his assurances that he had "not given anything away" in his conversations with the Persians and the Egyptians'.[91] Mr Morrison suggested that Mr Acheson might be told tactfully that 'Mr McGhee's approach to some of our Middle East problems struck us as being a little light-hearted'. And the Secretary of State recalled the pointed admonition which he had given on April 3 to the lively American official.

Whether or not he may have felt somewhat snubbed in London, Mr McGhee, back in Washington, gave a background briefing to the American Press on April 6, 1951. Already on the following day His Majesty's Embassy in Washington was 'pretty certain' that it was this briefing by Mr McGhee which had inspired a spate of articles in the leading American Press on April 7, 'and that they accurately reflect the views he expressed to them',[92] views such as: 'The United States is now convinced that the decision by the Parliament in Tehran to nationalise the Iranian oil fields cannot be reversed and British interests in Iran must adjust to an accomplished fact' (*New York Times*). 'High British and American officials, sharply at odds in their views, begin a series of discussions here on Monday . . . The stiff-necked policies followed for so many years by . . . Sir William Fraser. Although warned by American diplomats for a long period . . .' (*Washington Post*). 'Secretary of State Dean Acheson is going to twist the British lion's tail. His aim: To get reluctant Britain to give in to tiny Iran . . . "The British gave in too little too late and talked too tough", says one United States expert' (*Wall Street Journal*).

The reverberations in Persia were imaginable. His Majesty's Embassy in Washington at once, on April 7, protested strongly concerning the articles to the State Department, where Mr Rountree said that it had no idea how they came to be written. He undertook, however, to telephone to Mr McGhee, who was weekending in the country, the feelings of His Majesty's Embassy and to inform it of his comments. No record of those has been traced. But on April 9 the *New York Times* published a report of the previous day stating: 'George C. McGhee, Assistant Secretary of State, declared today that that nationalist spirit that had led the Iranian Parliament to approve Government possession of the country's oil fields would serve also to defeat Communist aggression in that area . . . Mr McGhee . . . is expected to tell Sir Oliver tomorrow that this country is convinced that the Iranian Parliament's vote to nationalise Iranian oil resources is irrevocable.'[93] It was apparently only after

---

[90] EP 1531/156.
[91] EP 1023/10G.
[92] EP 1023/29.
[93] EP 1531/216.

Sir Francis Shepherd had enquired on April 17 regarding Persian reports of this statement that His Majesty's Embassy in Washington on April 19 transmitted a copy of the Press report.

In view of Mr McGhee's published indiscretion and of Mr Morrison's preceding message concerning him, it is not wholly easy to resist the impression that now that the milk was spilt, His Majesty's Ambassador might perhaps have taken stiffer and more personal action at a high level. Even if it would have been going too far to insist upon some explanation or investigation, His Majesty's Ambassador might possibly, for example, have marked his grave displeasure by postponing the forthcoming conversations for a day or two upon some appropriate pretext. This might have had the tactical advantage, now that things had gone so far, of tending to reverse the pressure from the American Press by creating an atmosphere wherein disclosures and speculation clearly rendered it all the more essential that any conversations should produce complete unanimity, and that His Majesty's Government now had good reason to hope that the American Government would make a special effort to make amends and to work towards an accommodation with British views in order to procure the necessary outcome.

In fact, however, it was not till three weeks later, in another immediate connexion, that His Majesty's Ambassador made any representation concerning Mr McGhee in the sense of the message of April 6 from the Secretary of State. While the responsibilities were certainly far from resting wholly, or even perhaps mainly, with the British side, one may yet retain the impression that the preliminaries to the Anglo-American conversations in Washington of April 1951 were a striking example for future avoidance in the common interest.

On April 9, 1951, the conversations in Washington opened between Sir Oliver Franks, with advisers from London including Mr Furlonge, and, leading the Americans, Mr McGhee, a former Rhodes scholar who was said to have been a pupil of Sir Oliver Franks at Oxford.[94] At the outset Mr McGhee brought out the American view that the availability of Persian oil, while important, was secondary to the general position of Persia in the cold war against the Soviet Union. Whereas His Majesty's Ambassador argued that for the United Kingdom 'it was a very large thing to start to think in terms of £100 million so to speak on the wrong side of our balance of payments ledger'.[95] To which Mr D.K. Serpell of the British Treasury cogently added that even this 'was in itself of secondary significance. The trouble was to say where the loss of oil on present terms would end. It was like dropping a pebble into a pool of water—the ripples kept on going out.' Mr McGhee recognised that 'this difference of approach was, he thought, the core of the divergence between us'.

Sir Oliver Franks advanced two desiderata as essential in the British interest: first, the period of the Anglo-Iranian concession of 1933 should remain unaltered; secondly, effective control of this asset must remain in British hands. This need not preclude new arrangements concerning profits and partnership but 'we did not consider that the present storm in Persia was of so climactic a nature or of such immediate significance in the cold war as to render our acceptance of the nationalisation principle necessary'.[96] Mr Furlonge took up the metaphor: 'The

---

[94] Parliamentary Debates, 5th Series, H. of C., Vol. 489, col. 799.
[95] EP 1023/36.
[96] EP 1023/16.

present pressure behind nationalisation was, in short, more of a gust than a prevailing wind.'[95] This assessment, in accordance with the usually hopeful reporting of Sir Francis Shepherd, was to be proved correct to a considerable extent on the long view of years to come. In a crisis, however, long views can prove an expensive luxury. And sometimes a gust can strike with fiercer impact than a prevailing wind.

Mr Furlonge suggested that the existing situation in Persia might be turned 'if the findings of the Oil Commission were delayed beyond the two-month period, which might well happen'.[97] Mr McGhee pointed out that hitherto 'time had worked against the United Kingdom'.[95]

This exchange reflected the 'much more pessimistic'[98] assessment of the Persian position by the Americans. They did not consider that the two main British conditions could now be secured. 'Did the United Kingdom', Mr McGhee subsequently enquired, 'really think that they could arrive at any arrangement which would now remain valid for 42 years?'[99] Nor did any solution which did not at least, in Sir Oliver Franks' phrase, make a 'bow to nationalisation' seem to Mr McGhee to stand a chance. And he somewhat ominously remarked that '"nationalisation without compensation" seemed to him a slogan which might command allegiance'.[100] Furthermore Mr Rountree explained that 'the State Department's own estimate was that the National Front were thinking more in terms of kicking the British out of Persia than of achieving "nationalisation" *per se*.'[101] This remark might appear to have offered an admirable, but seemingly unused, opening for His Majesty's Ambassador to lift the discussion to a high and grave level by representing strongly that this precisely illustrated the way in which the present crisis far transcended the formulae of oil management in Persia and was a trial of strength which called in question the whole Anglo-American position in the Middle East in that cold war which was the primary preoccupation of the United States.

Somewhat intricate discussions in fact ensued concerning possible formulae for oil management in Persia. Both Sir Oliver Franks and the Foreign Office appreciated, though seemingly not as a potentially valuable bargaining counter, the fact that the Americans, having successfully outbid the Supplemental Agreement in the Aramco Agreement, were evidently anxious that the latter should not in turn be overtrumped by any agreement which would simply give the Persian Government more than the 50 per cent of profits which Mr McGhee had earlier proposed to consecrate in a joint announcement. Instead, the Americans now urged that the Persians should be accorded not only half the profits but also half the shareholding and ownership, a proposal which, in various forms, tended to shade off into Persian ownership of the assets with the Anglo-Iranian Oil Company operating on a management contract which should give it half the profits and sufficient practical control of the operations. In London, however, there was general agreement with Sir Francis Shepherd, who telegraphed on April 12 that in his view the Persians would be rather contemptuous of a British offer of a management contract and would interpret it as a complete capitulation. Sir Francis Shepherd did not believe that they really expected much more than 50-50 profit-sharing, and commented: 'Even the

---

[97] *Ibid.*
[98] *Ibid.*
[99] EP 1023/37
[100] EP 1023/17.
[101] EP 1023/36.

National Front is showing signs of a calmer mood. I now hear occasional expressions of surprise that we did not react more strongly to the nationalisation resolution and there does not seem much conviction in political circles that any practical form of nationalisation can be achieved.'[102]

On the same day of April 12, 1951, Mr Berthoud mentioned[103] his surprise at being told that the Anglo-Iranian Oil Company had already offered to the Persian Government a nationalised organisation for internal oil distribution, which had however been refused. Also on April 12 Sir Donald Fergusson wrote to Sir Edward Bridges concerning 'the need to have someone who is expert at designing company structures . . . I doubt whether Fraser is really willing or able to address his mind to devising some new structure which would satisfy Persian nationalisation while preserving the vital interests of this country and the company. I fear he still thinks he can get away without conceding anything like what we may find the situation demands. I think too, if I may say so, that the Treasury must reconcile itself to the fact that the happy days when it could get a large tax revenue as well as large dividends out of Persian oil are gone. As Strang has pointed out, the situation cannot be allowed to drift.'[104]

On the afternoon of April 12 Sir Oliver Franks telephoned to the Foreign Office to ask for 'imaginative latitude' in his instructions for the conversations on Persian oil. He felt that Mr Furlonge and his colleagues had come from London without a 'sufficiently constructive case and that they had been rather trying to make bricks without straw'.[105] His Majesty's Ambassador considered it very important to make a bow to Persian nationalisation if that could be done without serious harm. On the same day, however, Sir William Strang minuted that he was disturbed by a telegram of April 10 from Baghdad, drawing attention to the likely adverse effects in Iraq of spreading reports of American pressure on His Majesty's Government to agree to nationalisation of the Persian oil industry. Sir William Strang reflected that 'we must not get into a position' wherein the loquacious Americans 'can wreck our negotiations by indiscretions. After all, it is our negotiation, not theirs, and though their support would be useful, we may pay too heavy a price for it if we are not careful.'[106] Perhaps, however, it was to some extent a question of how far His Majesty's Government had already got into such an awkward position, as was suggested in a somewhat countervailing minute which the alert Mr Berthoud wrote on the following day of April 13: 'I think Sir Edward Bridges is not concerned enough about our getting positive United States support (though not necessarily detailed support). There has been enough leakage about the United States attitude to nationalisation to damage our negotiating position with the Persians unless the United States give us adequate open support now.'[107]

On April 16 the Foreign Secretary telegraphed to Sir Oliver Franks his general agreement, subject to some amendments, with a draft scheme for a solution of the question of Persian oil, which His Majesty's Ambassador had submitted by telegram on the day after he had telephoned to the Foreign Office. This scheme contained two

---

[102] EP 1023/22.
[103] EP 1023/33.
[104] EP 1531/186.
[105] EP 1023/23.
[106] EP 1023/16.
[107] EP 1531/193.

main proposals: first, the concession and assets in Persia of the Anglo-Iranian Oil Company should be transferred to a new company registered in the United Kingdom, with all shares held by the Anglo-Iranian Oil Company but Persian representation on the board and a half share of profits; secondly—the bow to nationalisation—the distribution of oil in Persia should be transferred to a Persian national company. These proposals represented an advance on the earlier British desiderata but evidently remained closer to them than to American ideas; and even so the new scheme only carried the provisional assent of Mr Herbert Morrison since it had not been considered by other Ministers, whose approval could not be assumed; nothing was to be given to the Americans in writing since, as he explained, 'I do not want to run the risk of their holding us to a firm text'.[108] In these circumstances the Foreign Office appreciated the difficulty, represented by Sir Oliver Franks, of reaching a firm agreement with the American Government and agreed with him that the conversations should be terminated as soon as possible. Another inducement here was Persian resentment at the conversations, as emphasised to the Press by the Persian Ambassador in London on April 16.

At a concluding meeting in Washington on April 18 Mr McGhee admitted that the Anglo-American differences had been narrowed by the new British proposals, but insufficiently: if His Majesty's Government put them to the Persian Government 'the Americans would not stand in the way but they could not support us [in] the way which they would have wished'.[109] Although Sir Oliver Franks reacted to this 'with some vigour', yet he concluded in general that 'as a result of these talks the Americans had moved very considerably from their original disapproval and are now anxious to help out. They will at least be benevolent.' No later than the following day, however, His Majesty's Ambassador was reporting that while the State Department had 'admitted somewhat reluctantly that if we made this approach their attitude would be one of "benevolence", they insisted that there had not been agreement on the oil question and that it would seriously endanger their position in Persia if this impression was given.'[110] It was not given. After some American cavilling over the text of the final communiqué, it informed the world on April 19, 1951: 'Among other matters the Persian oil question was discussed in general terms only since it was fully recognised that the problem must be worked out elsewhere by the parties directly concerned.' So much for that 'adequate open support' from the United States which Mr Berthoud had considered that British interests demanded. And already on the same day of April 19 the State Department was requesting British comments on a programme for further American economic aid, with suggested British assistance, to the Persian Government.

On the day the communiqué was issued Mr Herbert Morrison sent to Sir Oliver Franks a telegram of congratulation upon his conduct of the Washington talks, of which the results were, he considered, as satisfactory as could be expected in view of the 'basic difference of opinion'.[111] There was much in this, and on the technical level Sir Oliver Franks had skilfully handled a difficult and disagreeable assignment. The conversations, however, had perhaps not reached a very broad political plane.

---

[108] EP 1023/27.
[109] EP 1023/39.
[110] EP 1023/43.
[111] *Ibid.*

There had apparently been no British initiatives either towards an agreed Anglo-American oil policy in the Middle East (cf pp. 141-2), or towards invoking firm American support under the principles for Anglo-American collaboration in the Middle East adopted in 1947 and confirmed in 1949 (cf p. 54). As things were, it might perhaps have been preferable for the clear conduct of British policy if there had been greater evidence of frank and robust British recognition of the serious failure of the Washington conversations. For not only had they not achieved any appreciable advantage for British policy, but they had actually made things worse.

The Anglo-American conversations of April 1951 on Persia had been initiated, as noticed, under unpropitious auspices; and their outcome illustrates that danger of getting the worst of both worlds which can beset British consultations with the United States on foreign affairs unless considerable precautions are taken. The conversations had been compromised from the start by American indiscretions, and in the event they injured the British case in Persia still further without achieving any compensating advantage in the way of solid and public American support. Irritation in the Foreign Office against the Americans at this period is only too comprehensible, but since British policy was inescapably committed once the conversations were known to have begun there was much to be said for making every possible endeavour to clinch real American support. Such an endeavour might perhaps have inspired both greater flexibility on the one hand, even by making a deeper bow in good time to Persian nationalisation and, especially, by securing prompt ministerial decisions; and, on the other hand, greater firmness in insisting upon the grave impairment of the whole Anglo-American partnership which was liable to result from an American refusal to give loyal support in a case of vital interest to Great Britain.

In the event, however, perhaps the most serious loss from the Anglo-American conversations that April was that of time in despatching to Persia the British mission originally proposed by Lord Mountbatten but delayed pending an agreement upon policy in Washington which was not in fact achieved. The gravity of this aspect was being underlined by developments in Persia.

5. Further deterioration in Persia and deliberation in London, April 8-25

On April 8, 1951, M. Husein Ala had replied to the British note of March 14 in one which pointedly stated that as regards oil 'the Iranian Government's business is with the AIOC';[112] though there was also a reference to his conversation of June 7, 1950, with Sir Francis Shepherd, who, as now came to notice, had not at the time reported it very fully (cf p. 65). In conclusion the brief Persian note merely stated that 'the present position is that both Houses of the Majlis have unanimously accepted the principle of nationalisation of the oil industry and the Special Oil Commission is now studying how to put that principle into practice . . . the Government's only obligation is to await the result of the Commission's deliberations.' It was subsequently reported that the draft of this note had been submitted to the eye of Dr Musaddiq. For the present, however, it seemed in the Foreign Office to be 'positively mild':[113] an illustration, perhaps, of the kind of conditioning which can result from protracted negotiation against stubborn

---

[112] Cmd 8425, p. 27.
[113] EP 1531/165.

opposition. If one is hit over the head often enough, a blow across the back may come as a positive relief.

On the same day as he despatched his note M. Husein Ala lifted martial law in Tehran. For this the Persian Premier was warmly thanked and praised by Dr Musaddiq, who acclaimed him as 'his friend for 30 years'.[114] Martial law was, however, retained in Khuzistan pending the report of the Conciliation Commission. On April 10 it announced agreement by the Anglo-Iranian Oil Company to accommodating conditions which promised an early end to the dwindling strikes. Significantly soon, however, after this improvement there was a serious deterioration inspired, apparently, not by the National Front but by the Tudeh.

On the afternoon of April 12, 1951, there was trouble again at Bandar Mashur, and in Abadan itself savage rioting against British men and women. Among those lynched by the Persian mob were three British subjects; eight others, including children, were injured. At 9.41 a.m. on April 13 Major C.F. Capper, His Majesty's Consul-General at Ahwaz, but temporarily resident at Khorramshahr, telegraphed from the latter locality: 'The situation is worsening this morning at Abadan . . . The Persian security forces are proving totally inadequate to the task.'[115] The Senior British Naval Officer, Persian Gulf, had been informed, and Major Capper suggested that the responsible authorities might be warned to be in readiness to execute Operation Accleton.

When Sir Francis Shepherd discussed the situation on the morning of April 14 with M. Ala, the Persian Premier actually enquired whether it was true that British Marines had landed at Abadan; His Majesty's Ambassador did not report this significant enquiry by telegraph but in a despatch received in the Foreign Office on April 20.[116] Sir Francis Shepherd did telegraph, though, that in this conversation M. Ala evidently wished to be assured that British military intervention would not occur, and in this connexion had suggested that the Russians might perhaps be trying to provoke it so as to provide an excuse for a raid into northern Persia by Kurdish tribes. Neither the Foreign Office nor Sir Francis Shepherd took this alleged threat very seriously, but the latter does not appear to have sought to turn this transparent manoeuvre to advantage by impressing upon M. Ala the danger for Persia of precisely such a Russian chain-reaction unless the Persian authorities took drastic measures to protect British lives and property at Abadan and so obviate the regrettable necessity of British intervention.

M. Husein Ala told Sir Francis Shepherd that the Persian authorities would, he was confident, swiftly restore the situation in the southern oilfields where, M. Ala emphasised, 'Communists were the moving spirit in these strikes'. Twenty thousand troops, including tanks, would soon be there and General Shahbakhti had been specially despatched to take charge of the civil and military authorities in the area. His Majesty's Ambassador considered that this prompt Persian action should have a quicker effect than any military precautions which might be taken by His Majesty's Government. This was most likely true, but so also was the circumstance that the lamentable loss of British lives at Persian hands at Abadan afforded an opportunity, which might well not recur, for British military intervention on the strongest

---

[114] PG 13444/5.
[115] EP 1015/87.
[116] EP 1015/124.

grounds. It does not appear that Sir Francis Shepherd then evaluated the broad political possibilities of this opportunity or that he, or indeed any British military authorities at that time, drew attention to the possible military implications of relying for security at Abadan upon the introduction of strong Persian forces into precisely that area where it might well yet prove necessary to introduce British forces against possible Persian opposition. At the same time, however, General Garzan, Chief of the Persian General Staff, apparently had no thought then 'of opposing us militarily in that area',[117] according to a later report of Colonel H.G.F. Dunn, British Military Attaché at Tehran.

On the afternoon of April 13, 1951, in the House of Commons, Mr Morrison informed Mr Eden, the spokesman of the Opposition on foreign affairs, that if necessary at Abadan 'we should not hesitate to take appropriate action'. The Foreign Secretary further told Mr Emrys Hughes, Labour Member for South Ayrshire: 'It is no good evading the issue that, if British lives are in peril, we have got to do something about it.'[118]

It was more particularly at the instance of the Foreign Secretary that the Chiefs of Staff decided on that day of April 13 that a cruiser, HMS *Gambia,* should now steam at once to Bahrein and two frigates of the Persian Gulf Division to within short call of Abadan at Kuwait. Plans were to be prepared to act on an alternative to Operation Accleton should Iraqi facilities not be available, and the Foreign Office now approached the Iraqi Government for its agreement to British use of base and transit facilities at, especially, Shaiba. The reply of the Iraqi Government, while naturally hoping that any such British movement would carry Persian assent, was broadly satisfactory—an important gain for British policy. At the meeting of the Chiefs of Staff on April 13, however, Lieutenant-General K.G. McLean, Military Secretary to the Secretary of State for War, had reported that 'the Minister of Defence was insistent that British troops must not become involved until the incapacity of Persian security forces to deal with the situation had become absolutely manifest'.[119]

The Persian military at Abadan 'are still virtually ineffective'[120] reported His Majesty's Consul-General at Khorramshahr on April 14. The situation had deteriorated. Intimidation was preventing a return to work, and the Persian soldiers were not under control. The British Military Attaché at Tehran, who visited Abadan that day, reported on April 15 that in his view the new Persian military governor there, General Baghai, 'intends to try and prevent bloodshed but to do as little else as possible to further the company's interest. Shahbakhti's inaction appears to bear this out.'[121] Sir Francis Shepherd commented on the same day: 'We cannot expect Persian troops to act with the efficiency and determination of British troops. It must also be remembered that the Persians not unnaturally feel somewhat reluctant to act against their own countrymen in what they feel to be the interests of a foreign concern.'[122] (Colonel Dunn later reported that in his view, even at the height of the trouble in Abadan, one efficiently-led British battalion could very quickly have got

---

[117] EP 1202/4.
[118] Parliamentary Debates, 5th Series, H. of C., Vol. 486, col. 1334.
[119] EP 1192/19G.
[120] EP 1015/95.
[121] EP 1991/1.
[122] EP 1015/97.

it under control.)[123] Also on April 15 the British Naval Commander-in-Chief, East Indies, telegraphed to the Admiralty, repeating to the Senior Naval Officer, Persian Gulf: 'I consider a very early statement most necessary of the compelling reasons of high policy which require His Majesty's Ships repetition His Majesty's Ships to remain at Kuwait while British lives are endangered at Abadan.' Vice-Admiral Oliver thought it desirable 'to inform Commanding Officers of His Majesty's Ships concerned of the reasons for this departure from their traditional role.'[124]

On April 16 the Admiralty replied to Vice-Admiral Oliver, referring to the conversations which were being held with the Americans as a preliminary, it was hoped, to talks with the Persians. So long as the Persian authorities could control the situation at Abadan a premature British move 'might well increase hostility towards us and talks cannot take place in atmosphere of intimidation'. The danger that British intervention in Persia might provoke Russia was represented; nevertheless plans for Operation Accleton would be held in readiness. On April 18 the Chiefs of Staff, in the absence of a Foreign Office representative, agreed that HMS *Wild Goose*, one of the three British frigates in the Persian Gulf, should leave for Gibraltar on a normal tour of relief. The Foreign Office promptly questioned this decision, concerning which the Admiralty explained that a third frigate was in any case unnecessary for emergency action at Abadan and that 'to maintain three frigates and a cruiser in the Gulf is certainly abnormal'[125]—like the situation itself in the cogent view of the Foreign Office, which asked to be consulted in such cases, but agreed to the recall of *Wild Goose*, signalled on April 20.

Another of the frigates, HMS *Flamingo*, was due, under a longstanding programme, to visit Abadan from April 21 to 27. On April 19 Sir Oliver Franks telegraphed that a somewhat garbled report of this proposed cruise had caused the State Department to express concern lest it might further inflame the situation. The Foreign Secretary minuted on this telegram: 'We have to react sharply against United States interference? They've lost no lives, have they?'[126] This was not the only occasion, however, upon which Mr Morrison's tentative inclination towards a strong line was not projected into executive action. On April 20 Sir Oliver Franks was informed that in view of the situation the Admiralty and the Foreign Office had already decided (in fact on April 18, before receiving a similar recommendation from Sir Francis Shepherd) that HMS *Flamingo*'s visit to Abadan should be cancelled.

Also on April 20 Sir Oliver Franks reported that Mr Rountree had represented the concern of Dr Grady and others in Tehran at the situation arising from the strike at Abadan, which 'might spread dangerously, perhaps even to North Persia'[127]— another pointer towards the overriding American concern with Russia. The State Department considered that the strike must be settled immediately even if the Anglo-Iranian Oil Company had 'to take unusual and extraordinary steps to do so'. (Mr Morrison noted against this: 'Uncle Sam is jittery?') The British Embassy had retorted that this made it wonder how far the State Department 'intended to go in the direction of conciliation or appeasement', first of extreme nationalist groups in Persia and now of Communist strike-leaders. Would not a new attempt to suppress

---

[123] EP 1202/4.
[124] EP 1015/120G.
[125] EP 1015/133G.
[126] EP 1212/16.
[127] EP 1015/146.

the Tudeh be likely to have a favourable effect? Mr Rountree had replied that the Americans did favour this, but felt that most of the strikers were non-communists who would be weaned away from Communist leaders by conciliation. Such was American pressure in favour of a soft line by Britain immediately after the Washington conversations.

'I am much concerned at the apparent failure of the Persian security forces [at Abadan] to act with vigour and to restore complete order quickly.'[128] Thus opened a telegram to Tehran, designated 'Immediate', which had been approved by the Foreign Secretary on April 19 but was not despatched till 5.58 pm on the following day. Sir Francis Shepherd was instructed to speak again to M. Ala on this score and to make it clear that he did so on the personal instructions of the Secretary of State. His Majesty's Ambassador had in fact already, on April 19, been urging prompt and effective Persian action at Abadan upon the Persian Premier, who had recently given what Mr Morrison termed a 'rather impudent'[129] Press interview wherein he warned His Majesty's Government against military intervention. And the Persian Government was now ominously tending to blame the disorders upon the Anglo-Iranian Oil Company in contradiction of M. Ala's earlier indictment of the Communists to Sir Francis Shepherd. On April 20 Mr Bowker informed the Persian Ambassador in London that His Majesty's Government was concerned at this 'extremely unfair'[130] imputation, and also pointed out that General Shahbakhti had not yet even visited Abadan. The Secretary of State minuted: 'Persian Government being weak and going off the rails. We may have to stiffen. ?Ship move^{nts}.'[129]

The Foreign Office was by this time actively considering the political implications of possible British military intervention at Abadan to protect British lives. In this connexion, on April 13, there had been sent to Washington a legal opinion of the Foreign Office regarding the effect of Article VI of the Soviet-Persian Treaty of 1921, which had been under debate with the State Department. The latter had held that the unchallenged invocation of this treaty by the Russians in support of their occupation of Persia in 1941 (cf p. 42) compromised a restrictive interpretation of its terms; though the treaty, in the American view, was now circumscribed by the Charter of the United Nations. The Legal Adviser to the Foreign Office, Sir Eric Beckett, did not agree with this last; while also holding that the correct interpretation of the treaty continued to be restricted, under the terms of the Rotstein note (cf p. 39), to the obsolete case of Czarist activity in Persia. The British opinion, however, suggested that this difference of view with the State Department 'is perhaps not likely to be important in practice'[131] (cf p. 182).

The issues regarding possible British intervention were set out in a memorandum[132] of April 21, 1951, prepared by Eastern Department in collaboration with other Departments of the Foreign Office and the Legal Adviser. He drew what he termed the 'rather unsatisfactory deduction' that a case could be made that such intervention was legitimate under international law and that the Charter of the United Nations did not affect it, but legal opinion was not unanimous. Moreover, in the absence of Persian consent to British action, majority opinion in the United Nations

---

[128] EP 1015/117.
[129] EP 1531/242.
[130] EP 1531/232.
[131] EP 10338/8.
[132] EP 1015/167G.

would be opposed to it as constituting a fundamental infringement of the Charter, which stipulated that all members will refrain from threat or use of force against the territorial integrity or political independence of any State—Article 2(4). This, emphasised the Legal Adviser and the United Nations (Political) Department, would constitute a 'very bad position' for Great Britain at the United Nations. Technically the correct action would be for His Majesty's Government to raise the issue in the Security Council or the General Assembly, though it was recognised that in an emergency resultant action by the United Nations, if any, would be too late; whereas British public opinion would demand prompt and effective measures, if necessary by force. Mr Furlonge added that 'the Americans in Washington seemed sympathetic to this consideration', and that 'the argument that the use of force, or a show of force, would provide a pretext for Russian intervention in Northern Persia seems to me somewhat doubtful'[133] in view of the evident risk that it might unleash a global war, especially in the light of the statements by Mr Bevin and Mr Acheson concerning Persian territorial integrity. Here, too, Persian consent to any British action would lessen the risk of Soviet intervention.

The Foreign Office memorandum of April 21, 1951, accordingly made three main recommendations: first, that the Persian Government be approached with a request, as contained in a draft telegram, that if necessary they should ask for the assistance of His Majesty's Government in the humanitarian duty of protecting British nationals—their evacuation should not be mentioned to the Persian Government since once the Anglo-Iranian Oil Company left Abadan they would almost certainly never get back; secondly, if the Persian Government then or later refused to invoke British assistance, His Majesty's Government, which could cite this rejection, should inform the United Nations when a decision to protect its nationals was likely to be taken, and should then itself implement that decision; thirdly, the Americans should be kept informed, and secrecy enjoined upon them.

Sir Pierson Dixon, a Deputy Under-Secretary of State for Foreign Affairs and United Nations Adviser, minuted on April 21 that in his view the proposed approach to the Persian Government 'would be regarded as a well-known old-fashioned form of pressure. It is outside my province to predict how the Persian Prime Minister would react . . . but I should have thought that the consequences might be unpredictable. I have a feeling that it is easier to do these things under the stress of an emergency. It seems difficult to go to the Persians with such a proposal in, so to speak, cold blood. Would there not be a better prospect of extracting an invitation from the Persians if we had made our mind up to land troops as a result of incidents involving British subjects after the Persian Government had shown itself incapable of protecting them? The timing would obviously be difficult, but this is perhaps not insuperable.'[134] Only perhaps it was irretrievable in relation to the Persian murder of three British subjects nine days earlier. Even if the Foreign Office had ten days sooner thrashed out the implications of military intervention at Abadan, strong arguments would have remained against such sudden and radical action. But firm and adroit diplomacy might perhaps have exploited, or at least tried to exploit, that critical occasion to extract from the then alarmed M. Ala an undertaking to invoke British assistance in restoring the situation in the event of any further serious

---

[133] EP 1014/168G.
[134] EP 1015/167G.

deterioration at Abadan. This might have constituted an important gain for British diplomacy, redressing the failure to secure such an arrangement, with its highly important implications for the United Nations, during military consultations with Persia which the Shah had desired in the autumn of 1950.

As things now were, however, Sir Pierson Dixon's cogent argument helped to postpone any such attempt to retrieve the omission of the preceding year. Mr Bowker and Mr Furlonge agreed with him in the sense of suspending action, especially in view of the reports of improving conditions in the Persian oilfields which now began to come in. The draft telegram to Tehran was not sent. Mr Bowker summed up on April 25: 'The consideration already given to this question will have served to clear our minds, and make it easier for us to reach a quick decision in the event of further difficulties in the oilfields.'[135] This minute was initialled by Sir William Strang and Mr Younger but not by the Secretary of State.

On April 21 Mr Warner had sought to clear his mind in a minute on a telegram wherein Sir Francis Shepherd had reported two days earlier that the true causes of the disorders at Abadan were unknown in Tehran and that he was urging the Anglo-Iranian Oil Company to give the widest publicity to them in order to counter the allegations against itself which were now being made by the Persian authorities. Mr Warner enquired: 'Are the Embassy debarred from giving this publicity, if the company fail to do so properly? What is the position about this kind of thing?'[136] The answer, supplied by Mrs L. O'Malley of Information Policy Department, referred to the meeting of April 4 with the Anglo-Iranian Oil Company but explained that it was still official policy to leave the company to do its own publicity through its comprehensive and expensive machinery since it was thought that intervention by His Majesty's Government might further exacerbate Persian susceptibilities.

It was not Persian susceptibilities which had been mainly exacerbated by the broadcast of a symposium on Persian oil in the Home Service of the BBC on April 17, 1951. The Anglo-Iranian Oil Company had been invited to supply a spokesman to participate in the discussion but had decided not to do so, though it gave the BBC some information and assistance. In the event the Persian case was effectively broadcast by the Persian Press Counsellor in London, whereas 'the company's record was hardly mentioned'.[137] Though another of the participants, Dr A.S.K. Lambton, Reader in Persian in London University, remarked that although the company might be a good employer by local standards it had displayed 'blindness' to the recent growth of Persian national feeling, whereas 'no one in their senses, who was in touch with the Persian people, would have ignored it'. The Anglo-Iranian Oil Company, having apparently 'voluntarily let its case go by default' (minute of May 1 by Mr A.C.E. Malcolm),[138] complained of it to Sir William Strang on April 23 and two days later, in a letter to Sir William Haley, Director-General of the BBC. Mr Warner explained that, so far as the Foreign Office was concerned, the BBC was especially sensitive concerning its independence in respect of home broadcasting, as compared with that overseas.

While the Foreign Office clearly did not bear any primary responsibility in

---

[135] EP 1015/168G.
[136] PG 13437/7.
[137] PG 13437/3.
[138] *Ibid.*

respect of the unfortunate broadcast, yet the recently agreed increase in the supervision of the policy being pursued by the Anglo-Iranian Oil Company was apparently being applied in the field of publicity with considerable looseness, if at all. It was lamentable that the BBC broadcast of April 17 on Persian oil, coming after that of March 4, should also have been bungled from the point of view of British policy. It may have been in the light, more particularly, of Sir William Fraser's letter to Sir William Haley that Sir William Strang apparently did not follow up a suggestion that he should himself make a representation to the Director-General of the BBC. The episode illustrated the delicacy and difficulty for the Foreign Office of coordinating policy through autonomous but governmentally implicated bodies such as the BBC and the AIOC. Nor was it an isolated instance at that time.

In his conversation of April 23 with Sir William Strang, Sir William Fraser told him that he had followed up a representation from the former and had spoken to his Chief Public Relations Officer about the bad impression which he had created some days previously by apparently dissociating the company from the firm line being pursued by His Majesty's Government: Mr Chisholm was reported to have said, in particular, to foreign correspondents that the company 'would very much deprecate any British show of force as it carried with it the serious threat of Russian intervention with its worse evils'.[139] This had bewildered an American correspondent, and it was considered in the Foreign Office that American journalists, especially, derived the wrong impression from Mr Chisholm, who 'with his monocle and indolent air . . . lends colour to suspicions that AIOC is still following a 19th century line'. It was stated that he had kept, and agreed he should keep, in touch with the Foreign Office. There, on April 25, Mr Furlonge recorded that since his return from Washington he had been looking into British publicity in relation to the Persian crisis and was 'not entirely happy about it'.[140] Publicity in the United States was particularly important in view of the stream of tendentious articles in the American Press, 'some of them apparently on State Department inspiration'. Suitable Intels were, however, going out, and it had been suggested to Mr Basil Jackson, the able Vice-Chairman of the Anglo-Iranian Oil Company, that it should engage a publicity agent in New York for a special effort in the United States.

An effort of this kind had been urged by Sir Oliver Franks in a letter of April 21 to Sir William Strang wherein he drew attention to the unpopularity with the American Administration and oil companies of the Anglo-Iranian Oil Company, which had 'not got far enough past the stage of Victorian paternalism'.[141] Sir William Strang showed this letter to Sir William Fraser who 'took it quite well', admitted the unpopularity of his company with the American Administration but not with the oil companies, and defended the propaganda of AIOC, though prepared to consider a new approach. Sir William Strang commented to Sir Oliver Franks on April 25: 'There is certainly a case to be made against the company, and there are those in Whitehall who will state it quite forcibly; but I have a feeling that it has perhaps been a shade overdone':[142] the crisis was due to the character of the Persians rather than to the actions of the company.

---

[139] EP 1531/204.
[140] PG 13437/7.
[141] EP 1531/241.
[142] *Ibid.*

On April 20, the day after the final communiqué on the Washington conversations, the labours in London of the interdepartmental working party on Persia produced a Foreign Office memorandum on Persian oil—CP(51)114[143]— which was considered three days later by the Cabinet. This memorandum suggested six possible technical arrangements for recasting relations between the Anglo-Iranian Oil Company and the Persian Government. Of these the first and preferable one was that provisionally agreed for proposal by Sir Oliver Franks in the latter part of the Washington talks (cf pp. 145-6). It was now explained that this did not go so far as American desiderata, which corresponded to the fourth of the six possibilities, whereby the Anglo-Iranian Oil Company's assets in Persia would pass, without payment, to the nationalising Persian Government, which would in compensation lease them free, for 42 years (the remainder of the company's present tenure), to a United Kingdom incorporated company entirely owned by AIOC; profits would be shared equally. This more radical solution, which would involve the abrogation of the 1933 concession, was in fact preferred by the Ministry of Fuel and Power which, like the Americans, considered such a degree of Persian nationalisation to be inevitable.

The Foreign Office, however, was understandably reluctant to abandon in advance the cardinal position resting upon the validity of the existing concession. The memorandum for the Cabinet cited the views telegraphed by Sir Francis Shepherd, as on April 12 (cf p. 144), against conceding more than a profit-sharing arrangement to the Persians, who were having second thoughts, with even the National Front becoming aware of the risks of full nationalisation. On this point, however, Mr Kenneth Younger observed in a minute of April 21 to the Secretary of State: 'I do not think he [Sir Francis Shepherd] has as yet indicated to us, even in the most general terms, what the evidence is. Frankly I have no real picture in my mind as a result of reading the telegrams from Tehran of the state of effective Persian opinion.'[144] The memorandum for the Cabinet recognised, indeed, that the first proposed solution might not satisfy the Persians since only something like the more radical alternative would provide for nationalisation in the sense of an outright transfer of ownership of the company's assets in Persia. In this connexion Mr Younger commented: 'I do not much like having to give way in the course of negotiations on the principle of nationalisation.'

On April 23, 1951, the Cabinet decided that the first proposed solution, as advanced by Sir Oliver Franks in Washington, should form the basis for opening negotiations with the Persian Government. Sir Francis Shepherd should take soundings and if appropriate there would be sent to Tehran a special mission headed by a suitable person, who should not, however, be a member of the Government: a proviso which reflected Mr Attlee's view that a junior Minister should not be sent since it was not clear that agreement would be reached. Instructions in the above sense for the opening of negotiations with the Persian Government were delayed for two days in the course of clearance with the Treasury and the Ministry of Fuel and Power before they were sent to Sir Francis Shepherd by Foreign Office telegram[145] at 4.40 pm on April 25, 1951.

---

[143] EP 1531/215G.
[144] EP 1531/536.
[145] EP 1531/213.

It was unfortunate that two days before the Cabinet decision of April 23 *The Economist* should have published an article on Persian oil which, while describing the Anglo-Iranian Oil Company as 'a truly monumental scapegoat' for the Persian nationalists, suggested a solution considerably more radical than that which His Majesty's Government was now to propose. *The Economist* suggested the formation of a Persian company to own and operate the oil wells, pumping-stations and pipelines in Persia of the Anglo-Iranian Oil Company, whose role should be reduced to that of refining and marketing the oil. It quickly came to be supposed in Persia that this proposal had been inspired by His Majesty's Government. On May 4 Mr Furlonge spoke to journalists in an endeavour to prevent a recurrence of such an episode. But by that time much had happened in Persia.

By April 25, after belated Persian action against known agitators at Abadan, labour unrest there had subsided and normal working was being resumed under the encouragement from the Anglo-Iranian Oil Company of handsome bonuses to those who resumed their duties. It seemed, however, as though the Persian cauldron was to be kept constantly on the boil, this time by political developments in Tehran where, it came to be supposed, the National Front went into action in order to catch up on the popular activities of the Communists at Abadan.

The Government of M. Husein Ala had received a vote of confidence from the Majlis on April 17, the day after its Oil Commission resumed its meetings to consider the implementation of the approved policy of nationalisation. In this Dr Musaddiq and his followers lost little time. The commission had constituted a sub-commission to consider the enlargement of the commission by senators and representatives of the Government in accordance with the design of M. Husein Ala which Sir Francis Shepherd had regarded as a prerequisite for fruitful work towards a solution of the question of Persian oil. On April 23, however, the sub-commission went beyond its terms of reference in publishing alternative drafts for a law for the liquidation of the Anglo-Iranian Oil Company under the supervision of a committee representing the Majlis, the Senate and the Government.

Sir Francis Shepherd reported that the sub-commission had produced its proposals as a counterblast to the Anglo-American conversations in Washington. Their adverse effect on British interests was further suggested when His Majesty's Ambassador lunched on April 23 with the Shah, who enquired about Anglo-American relations in regard to Persian oil. 'He seemed', reported Sir Francis Shepherd, 'to have retreated somewhat from his previous definite opposition to nationalisation and I fear that the attitude of the Americans may be at least partially responsible for this.'[146] At the same time both the American Embassy in Tehran and the State Department were highly suspicious that Sir Francis Shepherd was 'plotting with Sayyid Zia',[147] who did consider that he could valuably replace M. Husein Ala, with a majority in the Majlis, provided that he enjoyed the support of the Shah, as he now evidently did. Nevertheless it was not M. Sayyid Zia who was within a few days to replace the evidently inadequate Government of M. Husein Ala.

On April 25, 1951, Admiral Lord Mountbatten observed in a letter to Lord Hall, who had been in hospital, that in view of the latest developments in Persia 'it seems that my forecast that unless the representative of His Majesty's Government could

---

[146] EP 1531/209.
[147] EP 1015/139.

reach Tehran by the middle of April we would have lost the initiative has proved to be only too correct'.[148] Lord Mountbatten noticed that Sir Oliver Franks had been expressing views similar to those which he himself had advanced in his previous letter of April 5; but he doubted whether the current British proposals for Persian oil went far enough, and 'it seems to me a thousand pities that we did not seize the initiative in the first instance'. Despite the three weeks' delay since he had last written, Lord Mountbatten felt that 'immediate action by His majesty's Government might still retrieve the situation', but only by sending a junior Minister to Tehran.

A copy of Lord Mountbatten's letter was received in the Foreign Office on April 27 and was discussed by Sir William Strang with Sir Edward Bridges and Sir Donald Fergusson. They noted that the Cabinet had decided not to send a junior Minister to Tehran, and none of them felt that Lord Mountbatten's appreciation 'is sufficiently based upon a knowledge of the facts of the situation'. One may, indeed, be inclined to doubt whether the despatch of a junior Minister to Tehran would any longer have been appropriate to the rapidly evolving situation there. But by that very token one might argue that British diplomacy had failed to seize the initiative, with grave results which were now to appear when it did take a step forward.

6. The British aide-mémoire of April 26 and resignation of M. Ala, April 26-28

On April 26 Sir Francis Shepherd handed to the Persian Prime Minister an *aide-mémoire*[149] embodying the proposals approved by the Cabinet three days earlier. In this connexion Dr Grady had been instructed by the State Department, in a sad echo from the days of the Supplemental Agreement (cf p. 62), to adopt an attitude of 'benevolent neutrality' and, if approached, to inform M. Ala that 'there were some useful features in the British proposals'[150] which he could not discuss in detail, while feeling that a formula should be found quickly: a meagre result indeed from all the effort of the Washington conversations. It was thus scarcely surprising, perhaps, that M. Ala should have told His Majesty's Ambassador that the British proposals fell 'far short' of what the National Front demanded and *The Economist* had suggested. The Premier represented that His Majesty's Government should acknowledge the adoption of the principles of nationalisation. A meeting of the Oil Commission of the Majlis was suddenly called for the afternoon of the same day of April 26. This meeting passed a resolution providing for the practical application of the nationalisation of the oil industry in Persia and the immediate dispossession of the Anglo-Iranian Oil Company.

On April 27 Sir William Fraser telegraphed to Tehran, for transmission to the Persian Prime Minister, a message from the company which had been agreed at a meeting called that day by Sir Edward Bridges. This message referred to the resolution of the Oil Commission and formally protested against the possibility of such a breach of the concession agreement of 1933 and in particular of its Article 21 against subsequent annulment, 'that solemn promise, which was approved by the Majlis, and which became a part of the law of Iran'.[151] At noon the same day Sir Francis Shepherd on his own initiative issued to the Press a long and vigorous

---

[148] EP 1531/273.
[149] Cmd 8425, pp. 28-9.
[150] EP 1531/217.
[151] Cmd 8425, p. 31.

statement explaining and defending British relations with Persia as a whole, beginning with the abortive Anglo-Persian treaty of 1919, which 'was in the nature of a Seven-Year Plan on a smaller scale though perhaps it was 30 years too early'.[152] After reciting the virtues of the concession of 1933, which Persia could not unilaterally denounce, and of the scrupulous withdrawal of British forces after the Second World War, Sir Francis Shepherd explained how Persia would have benefited from the Supplemental Agreement and also the amount of assistance given to Persia by His Majesty's Government and by the Anglo-Iranian Oil Company in practical evidence of British friendship. The excellence of Sir Francis Shepherd's exposition rather sharpens regret that it should have been made only after the prompt dispossession of the company had already been proposed rather than in the preceding months when vigorous and concerted propaganda to Persia along such lines might have contributed towards averting such a proposal.

On that day of April 27, 1951, Sir Francis Shepherd again saw M. Husein Ala who told him that he strongly disapproved of the resolution of the Oil Commission and spontaneously expressed his approval of His Majesty's Ambassador's statement to the Press. It was not so, however, with the State Department. While Mr Dean Acheson expressed to Sir Oliver Franks the hope that His Majesty's Government would be flexible, Mr McGhee went much further in disputing, in particular, Sir Francis Shepherd's statement that the concession of 1933 could not be unilaterally denounced. In any case Mr McGhee thought it unwise to say so publicly now, and he regarded the statement as unwise and a serious departure from the proposals made during the Washington conversations, so that the United States Government might now have to reconsider its attitude. Mr McGhee felt very strongly. So too, however, did Mr Herbert Morrison, who was 'particularly incensed'[153] by Mr McGhee's 'somewhat hectoring attitude'[154] towards British diplomacy in its time of trial. A telegram sent on April 28 from the Foreign Office to Sir Oliver Franks represented: 'it is not on this kind of basis that our relations ought to be conducted.' It was further explained from the Foreign Office that the policy of the National Front, which had by intimidation silenced 'all voices of reason' in Persia, risked jeopardising all oil interests in the Middle East including those of Aramco, and might have incalculable effects in other parts of the world: 'We are in fact faced with a situation in which appeasement such as Mr McGhee seems to favour must in our view be wholly unjustifiable.'[155] Sir Oliver Franks was instructed to speak in this sense to Mr Acheson.

A reply was also sent from the Foreign Office on the same day of April 28 to the previous American request for views on a further programme for economic assistance to Persia. Sir Oliver Franks was informed that an offer of such assistance at that juncture 'would in our view scarcely be compatible with the United States Government's promised attitude of benevolent neutrality'.[156] His Majesty's Ambassador, however, avoided delivering this reply by appositely enquiring whether the supervening change of Persian Government had not caused the State Department to revise its ideas of economic assistance: which received a generally

[152] EP 1531/222.
[153] EP 1531/291.
[154] EP 1531/223.
[155] *Ibid.*
[156] EP 11345/7.

affirmative reply.

It was only now that Sir Oliver Franks reported that he had 'found opportunity to convey . . . the sense'[157] of the Secretary of State's representation of April 6 concerning Mr McGhee to Mr Acheson, who had made no comment. In his immediately following telegram of April 28 His Majesty's Ambassador said that he thought it best not to complain again about Mr McGhee, but that a member of the Embassy had spoken to the latter on the general lines indicated. Mr Christopher Steel further explained in a letter of April 30 to Mr Bowker that Mr McGhee was 'one of the less vulnerable of the State Department hierarchy' and that 'to sneak about him to Acheson'[153] was likely to achieve little except to sour the Embassy's very good personal relations with the culprit. One suggestion advanced by Mr Steel, however, was that the Secretary of State might himself speak about Mr McGhee to Mr Gifford, the new American Ambassador in London, whose view of Mr McGhee incidentally appears to have approximated to that of the Foreign Office. This may have been one occasion, and not the only one, wherein greater and rather earlier use might perhaps have been made of the channel through the American Embassy in London in contrast to that through the British Embassy in Washington.

Mr McGhee suspected that the nature of the British proposals of April 26, 1951, contributed to the resignation of M. Husein Ala, the American protégé, from being Prime Minister after his interview with Sir Francis Shepherd on April 27, and in the face of the resolution of the Oil Commission. The Shah wished to replace M. Ala by M. Sayyid Zia but did not directly appoint him, as he had done General Razmara, since that procedure had been strongly opposed by the Majlis. Instead, the Shah instructed its Speaker on the morning of April 28 to obtain from the Majlis a vote of inclination for M. Sayyid Zia as Premier. But in the Majlis that day it was proposed that since the National Front had sponsored the resolution of the Oil Commission in favour of nationalisation, it should have the responsibility of giving effect to it by forming a Government under Dr Musaddiq. This may have slipped through as a rather empty manoeuvre since it was not believed that Dr Musaddiq would accept the burden of the Premiership. But to the concerned surprise of those involved, including the Shah and M. Sayyid Zia, Dr Musaddiq promptly consented to become Prime Minister of Persia.

[157] EP 1023/10G.

CHAPTER VI

PERSIAN NATIONALISATION OF THE OIL INDUSTRY AND BRITISH APPEAL TO THE INTERNATIONAL COURT OF JUSTICE, APRIL 28-MAY 26, 1951

1. The advent of Dr Musaddiq and the Persian Nine-Point Law nationalising the oil industry, April 28-May 2

Since Dr Musaddiq-us-Sultaneh had sponsored the Oil Law of December 1944 (cf p. 44), the nationalisation of the oil industry in Persia had become a fixed idea for this elderly xenophobe who was now Prime Minister of Persia. Anything but a statesman, Dr Musaddiq had proved himself a clever political manipulator and unscrupulous demagogue. He promptly proclaimed that his health was unequal to his patriotism in assuming office, and indulged in fainting fits described by Sir Francis Shepherd as being 'on more than one occasion completely bogus'. His Majesty's Ambassador reported of the new Persian Premier: 'He struck me as being a pretty tough proposition . . . He is rather tall but has short and rather bandy legs so that he shambles like a bear . . . He looks rather like a cab horse and is slightly deaf . . . He conducts the conversation at a distance of about six inches at which range he diffuses a slight reek of opium. His remarks tend to prolixity and he gives the impression of being impervious to argument.'[1]

Dr Musaddiq assumed office on April 28, 1951, on condition that the resolution from the Oil Commission was enacted as a law by the Majlis that day. This was done. The Senate meekly followed suit and the so-called Nine-Point Law on oil nationalisation was promulgated by the Shah on May 2. Under this law the Persian Government was 'bound to dispossess at once the former Anglo-Iranian Oil Company'[2] under the supervision of a Mixed Committee constituted 'with a view to arranging the enforcement' of the general law of March 20 for the nationalisation of the industry. The Mixed Committee, comprising five Senators, five Deputies and the Minister of Finance or his representative, was to draw up the statute of a new National Oil Company and provide for the gradual replacement of foreign experts by Persians. If the Anglo-Iranian Oil Company 'refuses to hand over at once on the grounds of existing claims on the [Persian] Government, the Government can, by mutual agreement, deposit . . . up to 25 percent of current revenue from the oil after deduction of exploitation expenses in order to meet the probable claims of the company'. Continuity of purchases 'at a reasonable international price' was provided for former customers of the company. The Mixed Committee was to finish its work in three months but could apply to Parliament for an extension.

'Thus', Sir Francis Shepherd briskly summed up on May 5, 1951, 'in little over three months the Grand Nationalisation Stakes had been run at a smart pace from the start to what many Persians see as the finishing post. The main reason for this has been the ascendancy established by the minority National Front group.' Contributing factors, in his view, were Persian feeling against the Anglo-Iranian Oil Company engendered by ignorance of the facts, 'United States "neutrality"', with many

---

[1] EP 1015/201
[2] Cmd 8425, p. 30.

Persians believing that America actively favoured nationalisation, and 'not least the fatal inclination of the Shah to let things slide and avoid drastic decisions'.[3]

Any development in Persia was traditionally apt to be ascribed there to British influence. It was singularly unfortunate, however, that Persians should have obtained the 'curiously strong idea' (Sir Francis Shepherd) that His Majesty's Government had actually engineered the law for oil nationalisation; and that His Majesty's Ambassador himself might unwittingly have contributed to such an idea, which came to be believed by 'many influential and otherwise sensible persons'[4] and may even have spread to some extent to the Persian court. In reply to an enquiry from the Foreign Office concerning a report in the *Financial Times* of April 28, 1951, Sir Francis Shepherd reported that at a Press interview he had 'said that His Majesty's Government had itself carried out the nationalisation of 1947 and had never denied the principle of nationalisation. I added that in my own view nationalisation could not be genuine unless the owners could themselves conduct the industry. In this case there was a valid agreement of international character and expropriation was not an acceptable expedient.'[5] This tendency of His Majesty's Ambassador, in the atmosphere of Tehran, to precede the line from London on the issue of nationalisation was perhaps liable to impair the effect of the excellent terms of his main statement to the Press on April 27. Nor, apparently, was this the only possible confusion in Tehran.

It was only in a letter of May 6, 1951, to Mr Furlonge that Sir Francis Shepherd first gave a circumstantial account of an earlier and important development which, he appreciated, might have stimulated Persian misapprehensions: 'In the middle of April in a very circuitous manner Musaddiq made it known to us that he was thinking on the lines which later became embodied in the recent resolution. He was evidently seeking for our views. I discussed this roundabout approach with Northcroft and Seddon[6] and we thought it was worth while to keep the channel open. In doing so we were careful to make it clear that the proposals were unacceptable but in view of the number of intermediaries concerned in this tortuous approach it seems not impossible that Musaddiq may have got the idea that we were at least interested in his propositions. If so he is quite capable of having used this intrigue as a basis for a carefully nurtured rumour.'[7] This admission evoked no recorded comment in the Foreign Office, which had lately received from a responsible British quarter an appreciation of the calm and most competent manner in which Sir Francis Shepherd was handling a very difficult situation. This tribute had gratified Sir William Strang, who noted on May 1 that a crisis such as the present one had been foreseen when Sir Francis Shepherd had been recommended for appointment to Tehran.

2. British and American reactions to Persian nationalisation of the oil industry, April 30-May 7

In the face of the advent of Dr Musaddiq and his nationalisation of the Anglo-Iranian Oil Company, Mr Herbert Morrison on April 30, 1951, presented to the

---

[3] EP 1013/21.
[4] EP 1015/164.
[5] EP 1531/234.
[6] Mr Richard Seddon was taking over from Mr Northcroft as the chief representative in Tehran of the Anglo-Iranian Oil Company.
[7] EP 1015/201.

Cabinet a draft parliamentary statement and advised that a firm protest against high-handed action was called for. In discussion in the Cabinet, however, it was represented, in particular, that the statement should avoid phrases which would give offence to the Persian Parliament and people and that it should be made clearer that His Majesty's Government were 'not opposed in principle to Persia's nationalisation of her oil resources'.[8] On May 1 the Foreign Secretary sent the Prime Minister a letter discussing possible courses of action and concluding: 'I am not too happy about the "line" which results from the Cabinet discussion. It may involve us in being pushed out with serious consequences to British interests and prestige in the Middle East and generally. We open ourselves to sharp attack for weakness which it will not be easy to repel. If we grumble but do not adequately act, we shall be open to criticism. Indeed Eden made this clear to me yesterday. We are in danger of submitting to ruthless confiscation; contenting ourselves with evacuating (if possible) our nationals and the Anglo-Iranian Oil Company staff, leaving the undertaking to the Persian reactionaries.[9]

It may or may not have been coincidence that on the same day of May 1 Sir Norman Brook, Secretary to the Cabinet, addressed a minute to the Prime Minister, with a copy to Sir William Strang, wherein he pointed out that while there was an interdepartmental Working Party on Persian Oil, and while Sir Edward Bridges held meetings as necessary with Permanent Secretaries and the Anglo-Iranian Oil Company, there was no ready means by which officials could secure from Ministers direction in policy. The Persian situation was developing so rapidly that such direction could not be effectively secured by formal reference to the Cabinet. Sir Norman Brook therefore proposed the formation of a group of Ministers, under the chairmanship of the Prime Minister, who should keep the situation under review and give general guidance on policy. Mr Attlee approved this 'useful suggestion'[10] and the first meeting of this group was in fact held at No. 10 Downing Street at 12.15 pm on May 1. The Ministers included were Mr Attlee, Mr Morrison, Mr Shinwell, Mr Gaitskell and Mr Noel-Baker.

The meeting of Ministers on May 1, 1951, approved a revised draft of Mr Morrison's statement, which he delivered in the House of Commons that day. This statement was a brief survey of the general problem of Persian oil. In particular, one passage which had in earlier drafting stated that His Majesty's Government was not afraid of the word 'nationalisation', was amended to read, as delivered: 'We do not, of course, dispute the right of a Government to acquire property in their own country, but we cannot accept that the company's whole position in Persia should be radically altered by unilateral action.' The Foreign Secretary made it clear, however, that 'the things we are after at the moment are friendly discussion and free negotiation'.[11]

Mr Morrison's statement was welcomed by the American State Department, which did not, however, agree, at any rate in full, with the view of the Legal Advisers of the Foreign Office that a State could, by an agreement such as the concession of 1933 to the Anglo-Iranian Oil Company, limit its sovereign right to nationalise an industry. In Tehran Dr Grady apparently did not fulfil a request by Sir Francis

---

[8] EP 1531/545G.
[9] EP 1531/263.
[10] Cabinet file 14/41/8.
[11] Parliamentary Debates, 5th Series, H. of C., Vol. 487, col. 1012.

Shepherd for public support of his statement to the Press; but in conversation on May 2 Dr Grady did tell Dr Musaddiq that the nationalisation law 'was unilateral action and intolerable. Musaddiq said he appreciated American "non-opposition" in the oil question, which he considered "protection for Persia".'[12] The State Department was made aware of British dissatisfaction in this general connexion and on May 4 Mr Morrison had an informal conversation with Mr Gifford. The Foreign Secretary referred to the attitude of Mr McGhee and told the American Ambassador that he 'failed to understand how the public in the United States who in general did not seem to favour nationalisation were yet supporting it in Persia. It was almost as if American opinion did not approve of nationalisation excepting when it damaged British interests.'[13] From about this time some improvement in American consideration for British interests was noticeable.

Dr Grady was in agreement with Sir Francis Shepherd at the beginning of May that it was not the moment for a dissolution of the Majlis by the incensed Shah, who was talking of replacing Dr Musaddiq by M. Sayyid Zia. His Majesty's Ambassador telegraphed on May 1 that such action 'might well endanger the throne and make a martyr of Musaddiq. It would be likely to cause disturbances in Abadan and the oilfields and the Shah is apparently even thinking of inviting us to land troops to protect the oilfields and installations . . . I think it essential to try to prevent either Musaddiq or the Shah from taking precipitate action.'[14] It would seem that on this occasion at least it would have been scarcely fair to criticise 'the fatal inclination of the Shah to let things slide and avoid drastic decisions' (cf pp. 160-1). Here was another opening, after those earlier neglected (cf pp. 70-4, 93]), for some British exploration of the possibility of securing, if only in case of future need, the all-important Persian request for military protection by Great Britain of the great Anglo-Persian oil interests at Abadan, now directly menaced. Sir Francis Shepherd's rather deprecatory report, however, does not appear to have aroused particular attention in the Foreign Office or, so far as one can tell, in the Ministry of Defence. This last is perhaps somewhat surprising in view of the statement of Mr Shinwell's views concerning Persian oil which was conveyed to the Chiefs of Staff on that same day of May 1, 1951.

Lieutenant-General McLean, by then Chief Staff Officer to the Minister of Defence and Military Deputy Secretary of the Cabinet, was now informed in a minute that the Minister of Defence 'has always maintained that our position in the Middle East, and in particular the assured output of the Persian oilfields, are vital to our national existence. We can, therefore, on no account permit the Persian oilfields to pass out of our control . . . If the Persians should attempt to seize the oilfields we should show ourselves ready and willing to prevent them by force if necessary, and should fly in whatever number of troops was required for that purpose even though they had to be found from outside the Middle East. This might provoke the Russians into occupying parts of Northern Persia, but even so it would be worthwhile to take this risk in order to safeguard our oil supplies.'[15] The Chiefs of Staff on May 1 accordingly telegraphed a request to the Commanders-in-Chief, Middle East, for an

---

[12] EP 1015/181G.
[13] EP 1531/294.
[14] EP 1015/166.
[15] Cabinet file 14/41/8.

estimate of forces required to secure Abadan and the oilfields in South-West Persia in the face of Persian hostility.

The answer of May 2 from the Middle East prefaced discussion of particular considerations for planning with the observation: 'It appears to us that the attitude of the present Nationalist Persian Government now precludes the possibility of obtaining prior agreement to the despatch of a force to Abadan and that if we send the force without such approval it would be opposed by Persian forces.'[16] It is not clear what bearing, if any, Sir Francis Shepherd's telegram of May 1 concerning the inclination of the Shah may have had upon the conclusion of the Chiefs of Staff on May 4 that the above assumption was 'rather too definite and pessimistic',[17] so that the Commanders-in-Chief, Middle East, were informed that the possibility of Persian cooperation was not yet precluded.

In a telegram of May 3, 1951, the Commanders-in-Chief had further drawn attention, apparently for the first time, to the serious consideration that, since the date of previous British military planning with regard to Abadan (cf pp. 148-9), Persian forces had, with British encouragement, arrived there to restore security after the disorders in April, and that in such numbers that it would now be impossible for the allocated British forces to seize and secure the island of Abadan.[18] At the meeting of the Chiefs of Staff in London on the following day it was specified that the two British infantry battalions then designated to execute Operation Accleton in case of need would be liable to encounter on Abadan island a Persian force of four infantry battalions, plus a naval and marine garrison of some 1,200 men, plus a dozen or so modern American tanks and some armoured cars. General McLean was asked to suggest to Mr Shinwell that the Defence Committee should be fully alive to the limitations of previous planning 'and to the important implications of resistance by the Persian armed forces'[19] (cf however, p. 185).

In relation to the preceding strategic discussion the Commanders in Chief, Middle East, informed the Chiefs of Staff four days later, on May 8, that they had issued new operational instructions superseding Plan Accleton. This plan now became, in effect, Plan Jagged. In addition there was now evolved a second operation, Plan Midget. This plan, unlike Jagged, presupposed Persian opposition, and its aim was restricted to covering the evacuation of British staff from Abadan.[20] Plan Midget was henceforth to occupy a central place in the heavy deliberations regarding possible use of force in Persia. On May 4 the *New York Herald Tribune* had published an article by Mr Anthony Eden on the Persian situation wherein he observed, in particular: 'In present circumstances, merely to despatch British forces would provide no solution. It might even so inflame Persian feeling as to damage the prospects of negotiation. And this is the only way finally to settle the business.'

The Foreign Secretary had explained to Sir Francis Shepherd in a telegram of May 1 that while his statement that day in the House of Commons was deliberately moderate and aimed at negotiation, he wished Dr Musaddiq to be left in no doubt that His Majesty's Government was not prepared to submit passively to Persian seizure of a major British asset. Sir Francis Shepherd was instructed to speak to Dr

---

[16] EP 1015/177G.
[17] EP 1015/190G.
[18] EP 1015/177G.
[19] EP 1015/190G.
[20] EP 1015/177G, 219G.

Musaddiq as soon as possible and also to the Shah.[21] Before receiving those instructions, however, Sir Francis had had inconclusive conversations with both of them on May 2. On the same day Mr Morrison matched his instructions to Sir Francis Shepherd in a conversation with the Persian Ambassador in London. M. Soheily, recorded Mr Morrison, 'expressed appreciation of the friendly attitude which I had shown on this question. The principle of nationalisation had been passed by both Houses of the Majlis and the Persian Government was therefore faced with a *fait accompli*. Will His Majesty's Government recognise this? I replied that we did not. His Majesty's Government had nationalised a number of industries, but always after proper discussion with all the interested parties. I had never heard of an act of nationalisation based on little more than a resolution hurriedly passed by a Parliament, except in Communist countries. If Persia took over the Anglo-Iranian Oil Company's assets arbitrarily, she would have no reply to the Russians if they later attempted to take over Persian assets without agreement.'[22]

On the same day of May 2, 1951, however, a Foreign Office telegram authorised His Majesty's Embassy in Washington, at its discretion, to inform the State Department that the Anglo-Iranian Oil Company had instructed Mr Peter Cox, its Fields Manager in Persia, that if the Persian Government should try to exercise control over the company's installations he had discretion to accede if the demand were made on grounds of security against mob violence; if on other grounds, he should submit under written protest; in any case his aim should be to keep the installations running smoothly.[23] On May 3 Mr Morrison minuted with regard to general policy towards Persia: 'We want a plan, a sort of "war book", about this or we shall drift into I know not what . . . It is urgent that His Majesty's Government should have a clear line.'[24]

On the same day of May 3 Sir Francis Shepherd telegraphed that in view of the remarks which he had made to Dr Musaddiq the previous day and of the Foreign Secretary's conversation with M. Soheily, he 'would not propose attacking Musaddiq again immediately'[25] on the lines of his instructions of May 1. On May 5 Mr Morrison, in reply, cogently represented 'the risks of letting the situation draft in the hopes that it will evolve favourably'[26] and requested Sir Francis Shepherd, unless he saw strong objection, to speak to Dr Musaddiq as previously instructed.

Sir Francis Shepherd accordingly saw Dr Musaddiq on May 7, 1951, and, in the light of the natural desire of the Anglo-Iranian Oil Company to safeguard its position by demanding arbitration in accordance with article 22 of its concession of 1933, told him that the company would be transmitting such a request to the Persian Government, as was done next day. His Majesty's Ambassador explained that this need not impede negotiations. His Majesty's Government wished to negotiate as soon as possible but could not do so under duress; which caused Dr Musaddiq to ask: 'How could a small nation like Persia employ duress *vis-à-vis* a great country like Great Britain?'[27] His Majesty's Ambassador further represented that so long as

---

[21] EP 1531/263.
[22] Cmd 8425, p. 32.
[23] EP 1531/280.
[24] EP 1531/260.
[25] EP 1531/262.
[26] *Ibid.*
[27] EP 1531/339.

the 1933 concession remained valid there was no excuse for the Russians to intervene in Persia; the Persian Premier disagreed and held that nationalisation contributed towards strengthening his country in this respect. Dr Musaddiq told His Majesty's Ambassador that he would later discuss with him a message which the Persian Ambassador in London would be conveying to the Foreign Secretary. In the conversation of May 7 Dr Musaddiq was very affable and led Sir Francis Shepherd to conclude that he 'has decided' to take a very conciliatory line at any rate to begin with'.

3. Correspondence between the British and Persian Governments, and American stimulation of British recognition of the principle of Persian oil nationalisation, May 8-19

The message from the Persian Prime Minister which the Persian Ambassador remitted to the Secretary of State on the following day of May 8 was of an uncompromising character. While rebutting Mr Morrison's Communist analogy by a reference to the readiness of the Persian Government 'to consider the claims of the former Oil Company', Dr Musaddiq stood pat upon 'the sovereign right of every nation to nationalise its industries'. His message concluded with a notification that when, in a few days, the Persian mixed committee had been constituted in accordance with the law of May 2, 'the former Oil Company will be invited for arranging matters and implementation of the law'.[28] This *aide-mémoire,* which Mr Morrison thought 'impertinently phrased',[29] was promptly published in Tehran.

On the same day of May 8, 1951, Mr Berthoud received a letter of the previous day from Sir Reginald Hoare, who had been His Majesty's Minister at Tehran from 1931 to 1934 (cf p. 40). Sir Reginald considered it 'essential in certain circumstances to convey an impression of toughness. To suggest that you may become tough if he refuses to be reasonable is futility.' Sir Reginald Hoare translated this pregnant advice into proposals that the staff of the British Embassy in Tehran should forthwith be reduced to a skeleton, that 'vulgar publicity' should be given to the availability in the Persian Gulf of sufficient naval and air forces to protect the evacuation of British personnel from the oilfields and Abadan, and that 'as a foretaste and warning' all women and children should be evacuated without delay. 'I have always believed', added Sir Reginald, 'that the line I adopted when the Shah "cancelled" the agreement [in 1932] was quite a solid contribution to a settlement. I told poor dear Ferroughi that his Government had created a situation so serious that I could not seek to discuss it until I had received instructions; and I then went on to say with all the brutality at my control how poor an opinion I had of the Persian Government. Times may have changed but principles endure.'[30] This letter commanded attention in the Foreign Office, if also the comment: 'Dear old Rex is as belligerent as ever.'

On the day before Sir Reginald Hoare wrote, Sir Francis Shepherd had written to Mr Furlonge, in a letter which was circulated to the recently constituted Cabinet Committee of Ministers: 'We cannot afford I think to beat an ignominious retreat and we shall probably have to show considerable firmness at an appropriate

---

[28] Cmd 8425, p. 33.
[29] Cabinet file: General 363/3rd Meeting.
[30] EP 1051/16.

moment.'[31] On this Mr Furlonge recorded on May 9: 'In the Department's view that moment is now, though the difficulty is to decide exactly on what lines to be firm.' This difficulty was also felt by Mr Berthoud and, apparently, by Sir Francis Shepherd, who further telegraphed on May 9 that the situation was still 'shapeless' and that he thought 'the time has come for us to take a firmer line . . . I believe that a great majority of Persians would now welcome from us not only definite proposals for settlement of oil question but other actions to guide them towards better organisation of the country. I am aware that this last phrase is vague and action required is at present not clear. I think however something could be worked out as situation develops.'[32] In this connexion His Majesty's Ambassador proposed that he should visit London, partly in order to discuss future aid to Persia in combination with the Americans; this proposal was, however, shelved.

In London the interdepartmental Working Party on Persian Oil was at that time further examining possible alternative structures for the oil industry in Persia in the light of the Persian rejection of that proposed in the British *aide-mémoire* of April 26. In contrast, however, to any further consideration of a broad programme of Anglo-American economic aid to Persia, the Treasury on May 8, 1951, produced a paper on 'Economic Sanctions against Persia'.[33] The possible sanctions were listed as: by the Anglo-Iranian Oil Company—refusal to pay over to Persia any royalties, advances or receipts on Persian oil; refusal to allow tankers to load oil at Abadan; legal processes to prevent any other company loading such oil from disposing of it; withdrawal of all British oil technicians; by His Majesty's Government—blocking Persia's sterling balances; suspending or denouncing the Memorandum of Understanding; cutting off Persian supplies of essential materials from the United Kingdom; denying Persia future credit facilities; refusing import licences for Persian goods other than oil.

The Anglo-Iranian Oil Company had in fact suspended, as from May 1, 1951, monthly payments of the £2 million advance on royalties agreed with General Razmara. Beyond that, however, the Treasury argued that 'the introduction of even the less important sanctions might precipitate a situation in which the more lethal sanctions become inevitable . . . The resultant economic chaos in Persia would inevitably be exploited by the Communists and the Tudeh Party, and might even furnish the Russians with a pretext for intervening.' It was the threat, as distinct from the imposition, of sanctions which considerably strengthened the British negotiating position, but 'that position would be greatly weakened if the Persians could call our bluff by obtaining assurances of help from the Americans', to whom British approaches on this were being made. The memorandum accordingly concluded on a somewhat contingent and muffled note. The Foreign Secretary minuted on it: 'It's badly duplicated and I'm not sure it has any conclusions. "What's the good of anythink? Why nothink!"'[34] It was represented, however, at the second meeting of the Cabinet Committee of Ministers on May 8 that, while it might prove necessary to adopt the sanctions specified by the Treasury, they would involve 'very serious

[31] EP 1015/201.
[32] EP 1531/297.
[33] Cabinet file: General 363/2.
[34] EP 1156/11. [Editorial note:'What's the good of Anyfink? Nuffink!' was the title of a song written in 1883 and recorded by Alfred Chevalier in 1911.]

political risks'.[35]

Possible military measures were also under consideration and at the third meeting of the Cabinet Committee on the following day of May 9 it was anticipated that any British military intervention in Persia would probably need to be on a large scale. But the committee was informed that 'in view of the grave threat to our whole strategic position in the Middle East the Chiefs of Staff favoured large-scale operations if these were the only alternative to surrendering the oilfields'.[36] At a full meeting of the Cabinet on May 10 it was further specified that 'our strategic position in the Middle East was dependent upon our ability to maintain our position in Persia. If we were forced by the Persian Government to withdraw from the oilfields the attitude towards us of Iraq, and Israel and particularly Egypt, would be radically changed.'[37] It was recognised that intervention to protect British lives in South Persia would not be difficult militarily or politically whereas protection of British property would require more troops and might have serious political repercussions. 'If such intervention were challenged few countries were likely to support us', and India would probably lead an Asiatic opposition. It was considered 'essential that we should secure the support of the United States Government for any decision to send any military forces into Persia. Some Ministers felt, however, that circumstances might arise in which, for the sake of preserving our prestige in the Middle East, we might have to risk serious opposition in the Security Council'.

The Cabinet decided on May 10 that the old members of the Commonwealth should be informed of the situation and that the Pakistani Government should be invited to try to influence the Persian Government in favour of a settlement by negotiation. The Government of the United States should be immediately consulted concerning the situation and, in particular, the British draft reply to the Persian *aide-mémoire*, which the Cabinet approved that day. This draft had been revised in the light of views expressed in the Cabinet Committee of the preceding day: that the Persians should be told that the issue was now one between the two Governments; and that while His Majesty's Government need not expressly acquiesce in the Persian Nationalisation Law of May 2, it need not insist on any method of negotiation entirely inconsistent with it.

The proposed British reply along these lines fully restated the British case, more particularly with respect to the restrictive validity of the concession of 1933 as regards nationalisation. If the Persian Government were to refuse the arbitration requested by the Anglo-Iranian Oil Company, then 'His Majesty's Government would have an unanswerable right under international law to take up the case' and, if deemed expedient, to bring their complaint against the Persian Government before the International Court of Justice at The Hague. (Mr Furlonge had recorded on May 9: 'Sir Eric Beckett is doubtful whether eventually The Hague Court will accept jurisdiction but feels that to seek it would at least gain time.')[38] His Majesty's Government, however, still looked to negotiations and were prepared to send a mission forthwith to Tehran. The last sentence read: 'I should, however, be less than frank if I did not say that a refusal on the part of the Iranian Government to negotiate,

---

[35] Cabinet file: General 363/2nd meeting.
[36] Cabinet file: General 363/3rd meeting.
[37] EP 1531/2379G.
[38] EP 1531/315.

or any attempt on their part to proceed by unilateral action to the implementation of the recent legislation, could not fail gravely to impair those friendly relations which we both wish to exist, and to have the most serious consequences.'[39]

A draft covering telegram to this draft *aide-mémoire* informed Sir Francis Shepherd that he should leave Dr Musaddiq in no doubt that his message, with its apparent intention of proceeding by unilateral action, had created a deplorable impression: 'We are not prepared with folded arms to watch him embark on a course from which only the Communists can profit. We are convinced of the strength of the company's legal position, and of our own right to intervene to protect its interests if the Persian Government refuse its demand for arbitration and our invitation to negotiate.'

The two drafts were sent on May 11 to Sir Oliver Franks for communication to the American Government, under cover of a telegram which explained: 'In view . . . . of the fact that our proposed reply hints at the possible use of force, we wish before it is sent to Musaddiq to assure ourselves that the United States Government agree with the line we are taking . . . If the Persian Government proceed . . . to take physical possession of the company's installations we should have to consider very seriously even the use of military force if only to protect the lives of British nationals . . . There is a very real danger of the [Persian] Government . . . losing control of the situation and opening the door to something in the nature of a revolutionary *coup* by the Tudeh Party . . . Naturally the use of force would require most careful consideration in view of its probable repercussions in many fields, and we should not wish to proceed with such measures without the closest consultation with the United States Government. We believe, however, that provided the Americans and ourselves speak with the same voice, Musaddiq will realise the necessity of abandoning his present attitude.'[40]

This timely and important message further added: 'The crucial point is that the Americans should make it clear to Musaddiq that he must not under any circumstances take forcible action to seize the company's property and that if he were to do so, thus rejecting a negotiated solution, the Americans would give us their full support in any consequential developments. If the Americans sought to make their support conditional on subsequent British agreement to negotiate on lines approved by them, Sir Oliver Franks was to say that His Majesty's Government were prepared, if necessary, to go substantially further than the scheme which it had put forward the month before in Washington; but that His Majesty's Government did not wish for the moment to get involved in details of possible lines of negotiation in view of the urgency of a firm reply to Dr Musaddiq in order to prevent his taking an irrevocable step, and to induce him to negotiate at all.

On the same day of May 11, 1951, Mr Anthony Eden saw the American Ambassador in London and asked him to let Mr Acheson know of the importance which he attached to American support in the Middle East generally, where the British and American positions were completely interlocked.[41] Also on May 11 Sir Roger Makins, who was visiting America, had a conversation with Mr McGhee, who said that 'he still did not understand what our policy was'[42] in Persia. Mr McGhee

---

[39] EP 1531/326: the final text of this *aide-mémoire* is printed in Cmd 8425, pp. 34-6.
[40] EP 1531/326.
[41] E 1024/22G.
[42] EP 1531/365.

vouchsafed the opinion that the expropriation of the Anglo-Iranian Oil Company and loss of its refinery at Abadan would be extremely serious but not disastrous; the total result would be less serious than the loss of Persia to the West in the cold war. Sir Roger Makins replied that 'those were dangerous thoughts' and that there would be grave consequences were it known 'that the Americans thought the British interest to be ultimately expendable'. The thing now was to close the ranks and secure agreement with Persia. Mr McGhee assented.

In reply to the telegrams of May 11 to Washington Sir Oliver Franks reported on the following day that the American Government would give full and firm support to British resistance to the attitude of Dr Musaddiq in refusing to negotiate. But as regards possible British use of force the Americans substantially followed up the line that they had adopted in the Anglo-American military conversations of the preceding October, which, however, had not been based on the supposition of non-communist Persian opposition. The United States would support British use of force if the Persian Government were losing control of the situation, with a chance of a Communist *coup* (note by Mr Morrison: 'I don't like waiting for this to occur'); but Mr Acheson said plainly that their preliminary reaction was that they would find it very difficult to support British use of force 'if the existing Persian Government tries by unilateral action to take physical possession of the installations of the oil company', not least owing to apprehensions of Russian reactions (note by Mr Morrison: 'Pretty poor: can we tolerate unilateral seizure by Persian "govt."? Possible USSR intervention shd. frighten Persians'). Another reason for American restraint here was that 'their international lawyers would find it difficult to go beyond the view that breach of contract involved payment of damages or compensation and did not justify the use of force' (note by Mr Morrison: 'Quibble? Persian Govt. would be unilaterally seizing first without settling or even adequate admitting other things?')[43]

In the same conversation in Washington Mr Acheson and Mr McGhee told Sir Oliver Franks that they thought that His Majesty's Government should inform Dr Musaddiq that it was prepared to negotiate on the basis of recognising the principle of nationalisation, and should not hold it as a bargaining point. The two Americans attached importance to this, and it would make it much easier for them to give full support to the British case. In reporting this to the Foreign Secretary, His Majesty's Ambassador commented: 'It seems to me that at last we have a real opportunity to get American and British attitudes to these problems harmonised in strong cooperation after they have been divergent in some measure for so long . . . If, as I believe, you are in fact ready in some form or other to give recognition to the principle of nationalisation, your willingness to say so to the Persians now, whether or not it is quite how you would choose to play the hand, has the powerful advantage of swinging the Americans without hesitation into detailed support of our case. From then we should be able to preserve a united front.'[44]

This telegram was received in the Foreign Office at 1.46 am on Whit Sunday, May 13, 1951. Despite the holiday a full reply was drafted with admirable celerity by the Eastern Department of the Foreign Office, was cleared with the Treasury at the official level and sent on the same evening to the Prime Minister, Mr Gaitskell

---

[43] EP 1531/321.
[44] EP 1531/321.

and Mr Morrison. The Foreign Secretary stiffened the draft in several respects (he noted at one point on the original: 'So what? Do we let things drift?'). The amended reply began by describing the American response as being in general encouraging. Mr Morrison agreed with Sir Oliver Franks 'that we should if at all possible take this opportunity to harmonise our attitude; but I attach great importance to stiffening the United States' attitude in support of the line that we are taking.'[45]

Mr Morrison's reply suggested that Persian dispossession of the Anglo-Iranian Oil Company would cause such economic dislocation as might well produce a slide towards Communism in the shape of a Tudeh *coup* or perhaps a Persian appeal for Russian technical assistance. Sir Oliver Franks was instructed: 'While we can leave on one side for the moment the question of any precise understanding with the Americans about our reaction to the seizure by the Persian Government of the company's property, you should emphasise to them the grave consequences of a step of this kind in the light of the above possibilities. You should seek an understanding with them that, between us and if necessary by the use of force, we will prevent the Communists getting control of all Persia—by whatever devious ways they attempt this.'

The Foreign Secretary indicated that, subject to Sir Francis Shepherd's views, he disagreed with another American softening suggestion that a conversation between Sir Francis Shepherd and Dr Musaddiq would be preferable to the delivery of a British note as being 'less likely to evoke a rigid negative'. Mr Morrison held that 'open firmness' would among other things 'help in Iraq . . . and indeed throughout the Middle East, whose reactions we have to keep constantly in mind.'[46] He suggested that Sir Oliver Franks should give the Americans the gist of a Baghdad telegram of May 11 wherein Sir John Troutbeck had reported that the friends of Britain such as the Prime Minister, Nuri Pasha, did not conceal their anxiety over developments in Persia; whereas 'the irresponsible are doubtless waiting to see how far it is possible to twist the lion's tail with impunity. These latter would be greatly encouraged if they saw that by murdering their Prime Minister and flagrantly tearing up their international obligations the Persians . . . had a great part of their demands quickly granted.'[47]

With regard to the question of Persian nationalisation Mr Morrison cited to Sir Oliver Franks his statement of May 1 in the House of Commons as already going 'a very long way towards meeting Persian national aspirations . . . To subscribe to the principle of nationalisation without qualification at this stage would almost certainly be taken by Musaddiq to mean that we accepted in broad outline the terms of the Nationalisation Law. Before we accepted the principle of oil nationalisation in this way we must at least have some idea of what Musaddiq and his party would take our statement to mean.' In view, however, of Mr Acheson's attitude, and subject to Sir Francis Shepherd's view, it was now proposed that the latter, in remitting the British *aide-mémoire* to Dr Musaddiq, should inform him orally that, in particular, His Majesty's Government recognised and—in what might perhaps seem a somewhat excessive phrase—'sympathise with Persian national aspirations in regard to their oil industry'. These could best be met, however, in cooperation with His Majesty's

---

[45] EP 1531/308.
[46] *Ibid.*
[47] EP 1531/306.

Government and[48] the Anglo-Iranian Oil Company. 'His Majesty's Government realise also the implications of recent Persian legislation in regard to Dr Musaddiq's own position: he would surely not wish that the "nationalisation", on a demand for which he came into office, should be frustrated by the economic consequences that would ensure if he rendered it impossible for the company to continue to operate efficiently.'

On the morning of Whit Monday, May 14, 1951, the Prime Minister rang up the Resident Clerk at the Foreign Office and informed him: 'He considered that we must, in view of the present highly charged atmosphere in Persia and in particular of the emotional state of the Persian Prime Minister (who appeared to be on the lunatic fringe), agree to accept the principle of nationalisation. It was no use making this a sticking point. Working out the details of any agreement on this basis was of course another matter and it might well prove that there would be a number of points which we could not accept but we could see about that later. Let us therefore proceed on this basis and see if it proved possible to work out something. It was, the Prime Minister continued, rather like trying to meet the term "Dominion Status" in granting a country independence. In such a case it was the title and all that was implicit in it that was of overriding importance. It might well be that in negotiating an agreement in such a context a number of modifications would be introduced and that the resulting agreement would confer something that was in fact a good deal less than dominion status. He thought the draft reply as it stood was too ambiguous on the nationalisation point. The great thing was to give Musaddiq an opportunity of saving face.'[49]

Mr Gaitskell was then consulted by telephone and thereafter a formula was evolved which was accepted by him and Mr Attlee. This formula read: 'While His Majesty's Government cannot accept the right of the Persian Government to repudiate contracts and while they object strongly to the wording of the Majlis resolutions, they are prepared to negotiate a settlement which, provided it were satisfactory in other respects, involves some form of nationalisation.' While this formula was being drafted in the Eastern Department of the Foreign Office the Resident Clerk, Mr M.R. Starkey, rang up the Secretary of State, who said he 'had some misgivings about the line the Prime Minister was proposing to take. The situation was very tricky and we must proceed with great caution.' In negotiating on any such basis as that proposed it would be essential to make the necessary reservations and to consider Parliamentary and public reactions; 'criticism might be severe and he would have to answer it'. The Resident Clerk 'told the Secretary of State that the Department shared his doubts as to the possibility of proceeding as the Prime Minister suggested without seriously endangering our interests.'[50]

Later that Whit Monday Mr Fry, who was primarily concerned with drafting the telegram to Washington, rang up the Secretary of State. Mr Morrison proposed the insertion in the new formula, after the words 'in other respects', of a parenthesis reading: '(a qualification to which His Majesty's Government attach importance)'. The Foreign Secretary, however, reiterated his misgivings about the formula and expressed apprehension 'about what Musaddiq might say as a result of being told

---

[48] The words 'His Majesty's Government and' were a subsequent addition, included in the final text.
[49] EP 1531/321.
[50] *Ibid.*

that His Majesty's Government were prepared to negotiate a settlement involving nationalisation'.[51] Mr Morrison instructed that his views should be communicated to Mr Attlee, to whom, however, the decision should be left. The Prime Minister replied through his private secretary that the new formula, including Mr Morrison's insertion, should stand: pretty well as much had already been said publicly and the consequences of saying it to Dr Musaddiq must be risked. The formula was accordingly added to the end of the verbal communication, otherwise unchanged, which it was proposed that Sir Francis Shepherd should make to Dr Musaddiq. This was embodied in the reply made by Mr Morrison to Sir Oliver Franks for Mr Acheson, as given above and telegraphed at 8pm on May 14.

On the following day Sir Francis Shepherd represented that the proposed statement on nationalisation for oral communication to Dr Musaddiq was too complex and that he would prefer to make a simpler one. A Foreign Office telegram of May 16 replied regarding the proposed formula that it was realised that Dr Musaddiq might 'not comprehend it fully or interpret our attitude altogether correctly',[52] but that this risk should be taken, partly in order to secure American support. The formula should stand unaltered since it had been approved at the highest level and, now, by the Americans. Such was the heavy responsibility assumed, largely under American pressure, for negotiation upon a critical issue in possibly unclear and misleading terms.

Mr McGhee had informed Mr Steel on May 16 that the United States Government was willing to support the proposed British *démarche* to the Persian Government, which would include the formula on nationalisation. This consent was given only after there had been further argument wherein, in particular, Mr Morrison refused to admit the American contention with regard to the concession of 1933 that a State cannot bind itself to forgo its sovereignty, as expressed in nationalisation: the Legal Adviser of the Foreign Office was unaware of any such general rule, and Persian repudiation of the terms of the concession would be 'a clear wrong under international law'.[53] Nor was British acquiescence given to the tendency now shown by Mr McGhee to try to separate the question of possible intervention in Persia to prevent Communist control from the present issue of Persian expropriation of the oil industry. The American attitude towards use of force in Persia was, however, to be given sharper definition in the light of an intensification of the Anglo-Persian crisis since the latest exchanges with Washington had begun on May 11.

On May 11 Sir Francis Shepherd had a further conversation with Dr Musaddiq. Although he had been advocating greater firmness, His Majesty's Ambassador does not appear to have expressed any disappointment or displeasure at the intransigent tone of the Persian *aide-mémoire* of May 8. Indeed Sir Francis Shepherd would seem to have gone some way towards tacitly accepting that accomplished fact of the Nationalisation Law which Mr Morrison had specifically rejected in his conversation of May 2 with the Persian Ambassador in London: Sir Francis Shepherd now reported that he expressed to Dr Musaddiq his hope that the Mixed Committee constituted under the Nationalisation Law 'would begin their labour by visiting the oilfields and studying their problems on the spot . . . Musaddiq agreed this would be

---

[51] EP 1531/337.
[52] EP 1531/323.
[53] EP 1531/311.

a sensible move'.[54] On the following day His Majesty's Ambassador reported that the constitution, now, of the Mixed Committee revealed a notable preponderance of ardent supporters of the National Front, so that any chance of using the committee to bring about hopeful negotiations had receded. Its members included Dr Ahmad Matin-Daftari, a former Persian Premier who was the nephew and son-in-law of Dr Musaddiq; and its rapporteur, M. Makki, was described by Sir Francis Shepherd as 'a vociferous and bullying nationalist . . . of almost no formal education.'[55]

On May 13, 1951, Dr Musaddiq made a speech in the Majlis wherein, reported Sir Francis Shepherd, he 'ranted like a third-rate "lead" in an old melodrama'.[56] On the following day His Majesty's Ambassador valuably analysed the ideas of the Persian Prime Minister, who was reported to fear Communist infiltration and to wish to counter it by raising living standards. This, he imagined, could be achieved simply by nationalising oil and ridding Persia of what he regarded as the maleficent influence of the Anglo-Iranian Oil Company: he 'probably quite honestly believes that this result can still be achieved without a major row with His Majesty's Government provided the principle of compensation is observed.'[57] Dr Musaddiq, favouring neutralism between East and West in foreign policy, regarded the concession of 1933 as having been concluded only under duress: though in fact the direct pressure on the Persian Government to agree had come from the Shah rather than from His Majesty's Government. The Anglo-Iranian Oil Company was further accused of having utterly failed to fulfil the terms of the concession. This accusation was largely based upon a misinterpretation of Article 10 concerning gold payments, and upon Article 16 regarding Persianisation of staff, admitted by Sir Francis Shepherd to be 'a difficulty' since the agreement apparently contemplated an absolute reduction of non-Persian employees rather than the proportionate one which, in spite of an increase in the number of Europeans, had in fact occurred (cf pp. [41 and 49]). Some days earlier, too, Mr Furlonge had considered that Dr Musaddiq was 'on to something'[58] concerning the high profits apparently made by the company on the sale of crude oil. Points such as these afforded obvious scope for negotiation, if that were attainable.

In his speech of May 13 Dr Musaddiq had emotionally announced that until the oil question was settled he was taking up residence in the Majlis building as a refuge from threats to his life. He was reported to have 'told Makki that the Oil Company had vowed to eliminate him':[56] a slanderous assumption which did not pass without British protest. Sir Francis Shepherd reported at this time that Dr Musaddiq's daughter was in a mental home in Switzerland 'and it really seems as though the Prime Minister himself is not quite normal . . . a fanatic and eccentric at the head of affairs. It augurs ill for any negotiations on a reasonable basis.' Mr Rothnie minuted on this on May 21: 'The despatch makes painful reading. It must be hopeless to do business with such an unbalanced person—and not the first time in history that one of His Majesty's Ambassadors has had to do so. There is little we can do to point out to the Persians that their Prime Minister is abnormal—yesterday's 'Profile' in

---

[54] EP 1531/305.
[55] EP 1531/344.
[56] EP 1015/197.
[57] EP 1531/356.
[58] EP 1531/303.

the *Observer* is about the most we can say.'[59]

Dr Musaddiq had as Foreign Minister M. Baqir Kazimi, said to be a nominee of M. Kazimi's close friend, the fanatical M. Kashani. On May 15 Sir Francis Shepherd had a conversation with M. Kazimi, who suggested that there was only 'a small nuance' between the viewpoint of the Persian Government in being prepared to negotiate on the basis of the Nationalisation Law and that of His Majesty's Government, which took as the basis the concession of 1933.[60] On the same day the Persian Government decreed that the Anglo-Iranian Oil Company should be officially designated 'the former oil company'. And an organ of Persian Press urged that Persia must act quickly on nationalisation before the 'tottering Labour Government gives place to a Conservative Government' in England, a possibility which Dr Musaddiq had envisaged in his speech of May 13.

By the middle of May 1951 there were uncontradicted reports that the British 16th Independent Parachute Brigade was being made ready for possible despatch to Abadan. On May 16 the correspondent of *The Times* in Tehran commented on this that, despite ringing phrases and references to possible Soviet intervention, 'possibly the most interesting fact about the [Persian] Press comment is that no newspaper appears to suggest that the Persian Army would resist British forces were they to take such a step'. On the same day of May 16 the State Department informed Mr Steel that 'the United States is strongly opposed . . . to the use of force or the threat of the use of force on the part of the British Government as a means of solving the oil controversy'.[61] This intimation thus accompanied the other one made that day to Mr Steel, as previously noticed, that the American Government would support the British in its proposed diplomatic approach to Persia, with the deliberate bow to nationalisation in accordance with American wishes. Yet on that same day of May 16 Mr Dean Acheson intimated to a Press conference that the Government of the United States neither approved nor disapproved of the policies of either the British or the Persian Governments, but was urging moderation on both. So much for that American 'strong cooperation', unhesitatingly 'detailed support' and 'united front' which Sir Oliver Franks had foretold only four days earlier as being the consequences of British recognition, now accorded, of the principle of nationalisation of Persian oil.

The American Secretary of State told Sir Oliver Franks on May 17 that 'he was sorry to have had to make lukewarm statements about the Persian situation at his Press conference yesterday. He had no option because of the reports emanating from London the previous day about alerting paratroops and statements by a [British] Government spokesman which were taken to indicate a general identity of view between the British and the Americans. Acheson had to be lukewarm to avoid any impression that he might be associating himself with the use of force.'[62] He had felt that issue to be so serious that he had taken it to the American Security Council and to the President, who felt great concern over possible British use of force in Persia. Sir Oliver Franks said that His Majesty's Government was not proposing to use force against the existing Persian Administration, which was what the Americans feared.

---

[59] *Ibid.*
[60] EP 1531/322.
[61] EP 1531/334G.
[62] EP 1531/354.

If circumstances changed so that that became a possibility, His Majesty's Government had already undertaken to have the closest consultation with the Americans. It might be a little different in the case of protecting 'the 8000 British nationals'. Mr Acheson pressed Sir Oliver Franks very hard as to just what such protection might involve and asked him to ascertain what Mr Herbert Morrison might have in mind. His Majesty's Ambassador commented: 'The Americans are obviously very anxious about what in certain circumstances we might do. They are also now most anxious to help us begin and carry through a satisfactory negotiation.'

Mr Morrison replied in two telegrams of May 18, approved by the Prime Minister, and sought to remove any possible impression in the State Department that His Majesty's Government, in its anxiety to preserve control of Persian oil, was prepared to set aside all other considerations and take unjustifiable risks. The first of the two telegrams recapitulated previous arguments in assessing possible contingencies which might call in question the use of British forces at Abadan, and the measure of Anglo-American agreement, and differences, in this respect. If forces were used to protect British installations, 'our experience of the Persian character does not suggest that any violent reaction from the Persians need be expected but rather that they would be only too anxious to come to terms provided that it was made clear to them that our troops would go as soon as this had been done'. The line taken by Mr Acheson at his Press conference had created a bad impression in London, and 'if the Americans wish us to refrain from the use of force, their best course is surely to exert the maximum pressure on Musaddiq to this end'.[63] It might perhaps have been worth while to try, at all events, to use this argument directly with the Americans, rather earlier in the conversations, in order to lever out of them more binding assurances of effective support, perhaps on terms more favourable to the British case than those which were in fact accepted.

Mr Dean Acheson had earlier, in speaking to Sir Oliver Franks on May 11, drawn a parallel between possible use of force, with the risk of Russian intervention, in Persia and, in connexion with the Korean War, in China, by bombing Manchurian airfields: the course, advocated by the recently recalled General MacArthur, from which His Majesty's Government had been seeking to restrain that of the United States (cf p. 92). The Foreign Secretary now alluded to this analogy but argued that as regards bombing China His Majesty's Government had now 'agreed in principle but wish to be consulted before action. In Persia, the Americans resist the principle of force in what would be justifiable circumstances. I am really rather annoyed at the American attitude of relative indifference to a situation which may be most grave to us all.'[64]

In the second telegram of May 18, however, Mr Morrison suggested that it might be best for His Majesty's Ambassador to take the line with the Americans that 'the only circumstances in which we might have to use force without the fullest possible prior consultation with the Americans would be the urgent need to protect British lives . . . It therefore seems unprofitable for the moment to pursue the question of the hypothetical circumstances in which consultation on the use of force might arise . . . The urgent thing is to show a united front in bringing Musaddiq to the table.'

On the same day of May 18, 1951, the State Department issued a statement urging

---

[63] EP 1531/354.
[64] *Ibid.*

the Persian Government to negotiate with the British for a settlement of the oil dispute, though it added that the United States Government had neither approved nor disapproved any particular British proposal for a settlement. The statement did, however, include the grave warning that if the Persians unilaterally expelled the Anglo-Iranian Oil Company, American technicians would not be available to replace it. This valuable assurance was the most important gain for Britain from the Anglo-American exchanges that May and from the consultations between the State Department and the American oil companies which had been accompanying them. Though how far the declaration represented a real American sacrifice to British interests is perhaps somewhat doubtful. Whatever the attitude towards the Anglo-Iranian Oil Company of its American competitors, they were apparently becoming increasingly apprehensive of possible repercussions elsewhere of the Persian crisis, and it might scarcely suit their broader interests to stab another concessionaire in the back at the behest of a leasing Government. In any case Mr McGhee had been expressing the view that even Standard Oil would be incapable of assembling personnel for the 'immense team required' to replace the Anglo-Iranian Oil Company in Persia.[65]

On May 19, 1951, Sir Francis Shepherd handed the British *aide-mémoire*, in the terms previously agreed,[66] to the Persian Foreign Minister since Dr Musaddiq stated that owing to illness he was unable to receive him. His Majesty's Ambassador reported that since the accompanying oral communication, with the important passage recognising the principle of nationalisation, could only be effective with Dr Musaddiq and the Mixed Committee, he had sent a French text of it to M. Kazimi, who said he would communicate it, along with the *aide-mémoire*, to the Prime Minister and to the Mixed Committee. Some days later, however, Sir Francis Shepherd ascertained that neither M. Matin-Daftari of the committee nor Dr Musaddiq himself had in fact seen the text of the oral communication: omissions which His Majesty's Ambassador proceeded to rectify in conversations with them. It was unfortunate, however, that this initial uncertainty should have arisen concerning the British acceptance of the principle of nationalisation; for this important step had only been taken as a disagreeable means to an end, namely the promotion of those negotiations between the British and Persian Governments which were essential in order to forestall grave developments. For the sake of a determined endeavour to this end it might perhaps have been preferable in the event if His Majesty's Government, having decided to go so far to meet American views, had gone one step further by agreeing to a representation made by the State Department on May 18 in favour of incorporating the formula of the oral communication in the main text of the *aide-mémoire*. The State Department felt that this might make the whole difference to the Persian reception of the *aide-mémoire* as a basis of negotiation. This proposal, however, was not pressed or adopted, the State Department observing that from their own point of view it would do nearly as well if the oral formula were known publicly.[67]

In any attempt at negotiations in Tehran a key figure would be the American Ambassador, whose advice continued to carry great weight with the State

---

[65] EP 1531/296.
[66] Final text printed in Cmd 8425, pp. 34-6.
[67] EP 1531/357.

Department. Sir Francis Shepherd, in a letter of May 14 to Mr Furlonge, described Dr Grady as intelligent and by no means unfriendly but 'a vain man . . . desperately anxious to be the saviour of Persia in the way he believes himself to have been the saviour of Greece and, to a lesser extent, India. He is plagued with an inflated and rather mediocre staff', some of them anti-British, credulous of bazaar rumours and temperamentally unsuited to dealing with Persians, whose deviousness reduced Dr Grady to '110 percent frustration'.[68]

Dr Grady was apparently not instructed specifically to make a *démarche* in support of the British *aide-mémoire* of May 19, but he was already making helpful representations to the Persian Government in that general sense. The *aide-mémoire* plus the American announcement of the preceding day almost for the first time created an impression of real Anglo-American solidarity in Tehran, and produced a sobering effect upon the Persians. To this extent the Anglo-American exchanges of May 1951 had been notably more successful from the British point of view than those of the preceding month. This, however, was a relative success since meantime the position in Persia had gravely deteriorated while His Majesty's Government had been pressed by the United States Government further down the path towards acceptance of it: both acknowledgement of the principle of nationalisation and, on the other hand, by the statement of British unwillingness to intervene militarily for the protection of British property and interests at Abadan without prior consultation with the American Government which had, however, already strongly emphasised its opposition to such intervention. Neither the Foreign Office nor the British Embassy in Washington appears to have contemplated a determined effort to trade British acceptance of the heavy failure to secure any American promise of support for military measures against the extraction of much more binding American assurance of full and loyal support for British diplomacy in Persia, such as Sir Oliver Franks had hopefully envisaged on May 12 as being likely to result in any case from British acceptance of the principle of nationalisation. Whereas in fact the continued lack of loyal American support was becoming disagreeably manifest again within a few days.

By May 25 Mr McGhee was telling Mr Steel that he was under attack for not having exerted greater pressure on His Majesty's Government and that Dr Grady had complained because the United States Government had supported the British *aide-mémoire* of May 19 without having forced His Majesty's Government to go further as regards recognition of nationalisation.[69] Mr McGhee strongly urged a 'forthright statement' of British acceptance of this principle. The Foreign Office, on the other hand, was reckoning on May 24 with the risk that if this were publicised in the British Press, as had not previously been done, 'opinion here would suppose that we had knuckled under':[70] a supposition which would, perhaps, have been not entirely devoid of some element of truth. On the same day, however, Reuter carried a report, presumably from Washington, indicating the step taken by his Majesty's Government.

The Foreign Secretary returned to London from a visit to Germany on May 24. It was Mr Gaitskell, the Minister especially in charge of relations with the Anglo-

---

[68] EP 1531/356.
[69] EP 1531/410.
[70] EP 1531/433G.

Iranian Oil Company, who, in view of the Reuter reports, ordered that the principal newspapers should be told that although His Majesty's Government did not rule out nationalisation of the Persian oil industry within the context of a general settlement, it was inconceivable that the Government would accept the action of nationalisation apparently envisaged by the Majlis in passing the law of May 2. This appeared in the British Press on May 25, 1951. On the same day Mr Furlonge advised that on so important a matter Mr Herbert Morrison should make a statement in the House of Commons when it reassembled after the Whitsun recess.[71] This he did on May 29, informing Parliament of the measures of British recognition of the principle of nationalisation which Sir Francis Shepherd had communicated to the Persian Government when remitting the *aide-mémoire* of May 19.

At the time of the presentation of the *aide-mémoire* to the Persian Government, His Majesty's Government had made approaches to secure diplomatic support from the Governments of Pakistan, India, Turkey, Iraq and France. This useful initiative would not appear to have been premature. In the case of Turkey the British communication, authorised on May 18, opened with regrets for delay in replying to a friendly Turkish memorandum of April 11 concerning Persia.[72]

As regards France, it does not appear that His Majesty's Government had hitherto taken any direct soundings of French feeling concerning the Persian crisis; although its possible effects upon the Iraq Petroleum Company had been alluded to in Anglo-French conversations on the Middle East generally, which had been held on the official level at the Quai d'Orsay on May 10-11. In these conversations the British representatives, led by Mr Bowker, accepted a French proposal that their respective authorities in the Middle East and North Africa should be reminded that in accordance with previous policy (cf p. 60), they should maintain close cooperation.[73] Thus the French Government were at that juncture apparently in a generally cooperative mood regarding the Middle East.

The instructions of May 21 for an approach to the French Government regarding Persia now significantly suggested that 'the French will not have failed to notice the talk in Egypt of "nationalising" the Suez Canal'.[74] In the event the British communication to the French Government, and more particularly a request for official discouragement of French technicians who might be thinking of meeting Persian needs, was couched by the British Embassy in Paris in somewhat blunt phraseology which ruffled French susceptibilities. Generally satisfactory replies were, however, received from all the Governments approached. But in the absence of purposeful coordination in Tehran it is doubtful how much was achieved by their several counsels of reason and moderation upon the Persian Government. His Majesty's Government was conscious, perhaps even to a fault, that any decisive support must come from America. That remained the difficulty.

On May 22, 1951, Mr Berthoud had a conversation with Mr Walter Levy, a Jewish-American oil consultant who was 'in and out of McGhee's room the whole time',[75] but was also friendly to British interests. Mr Levy, who thought it impossible to negotiate with Dr Musaddiq, explained that the State Department was reluctant to

---

[71] EP 1531/428.
[72] EP 1023/25.
[73] E 1027/1.
[74] EP 1531/360.
[75] EP 1531/426.

align itself with His Majesty's Government partly because it wished to retain American influence in Persia in reserve, though 'probably in the event they had fallen between two stools'.[76] On the same day the Foreign Office received a telegram from Washington reporting that the American administration was that week submitting to Congress proposals for foreign aid for 1951-52 which would include economic aid to Persia, possibly for $25 million, the amount of the still unratified Export-Import Bank loan. It was only now that British representations against such aid were made to Mr Rountree in the sense of Mr Herbert Morrison's original instructions of April 28. If they had been made at that time, instead of being sidestepped (cf p. 158), they might at least have given the Americans some pause for thought. Now Mr Rountree was not to be deflected but referred to 'the strong pressure' of American public opinion for economic aid to Persia, which seemed to the British Embassy in Washington a somewhat exaggerated excuse;[77] though it would appear, more generally, that the reserves of the State Department as regards British interests in Persia probably corresponded fairly accurately with such public opinion on the subject as existed in the United States.

The Foreign Secretary now asked whether the Americans should not be asked to hold up their economic aid to Persia. He was advised in the Foreign Office that it was understood from the American Embassy that this would not be possible now that the proposals were before Congress, where their passage would in any case take months. It was further hopefully suggested by Sir Roger Makins that 'if the Persians turned nasty Congress could and probably would cut out the item'.[78] Mr Morrison did not insist. Once again a British interest had been elbowed out in a scrum in which cautiously considerate British policy had been overtaken by the clearer and stronger impulsion of another Government.

4. Further British consideration of, and American objection to, military intervention at Abadan, May 18-25

The British and American attitudes towards Persia now admittedly differed, in emphasis at any rate, in the economic as well as in the military sphere. As regards the latter Sir Oliver Franks, in view of what he described as the 'satisfactory American statement'[79] of May 18, did not think it necessary to speak further to the American Government at the highest level. On May 21 the substance of the second of Mr Morrison's two telegrams of May 18 concerning possible military action in Persia was, however, communicated for record to Mr Rountree, to whom considerations in the first telegram were also briefly mentioned. Mr Rountree once more emphasised that 'the State Department continued to attach particular importance to the question of an invitation being received from the Shah or the Persian Government before British troops were sent in for whatever purpose . . . We said on this point that with the present Persian Government it could hardly be expected that an invitation could come from them. Rountree suggested that in the event of serious trouble the Shah might very likely sack Musaddiq and appoint a new Prime Minister and at the same time invite us to take action.' In the American view,

---

[76] EP 1531/691.
[77] EP 11345/11.
[78] EP 11345/12.
[79] EP 1531/395.

reported His Majesty's Ambassador, some such invitation or consent 'would alter the international situation very much to our advantage'.[80]

On the same day of May 21, 1951, General Omar Bradley, in the course of hearings before Senate Committees on the recall of General Douglas MacArthur from the Far East, went out of his way to make it clear that the United States had 'no commitment of going into Iran with the British; the Joint Chiefs of Staff certainly have not made any such decision'.[81] Public notice of American reluctance as regards military intervention in Persia had been served in advance, without British protest, upon the Russians and the Persians themselves. This was just at the time when British planning in this quarter was especially active.

At a meeting of the Chiefs of Staff on May 18, 1951, Marshal of the RAF Sir John Slessor, Chief of the Air Staff, expressed the view that current preparations in London and, especially, British Headquarters in the Middle East for possible military intervention in Persia were insufficiently urgent. In view of the political situation in Persia and the low value of Persian troops, he thought 'it was possible that sudden action by a comparatively small force would achieve quite disproportionate success; it might be well worth accepting a considerable risk in these circumstances'.[82] Agreement with this view was expressed and a telegram was sent that day to the Commanders-in-Chief, Middle East, indicating that 'bold and quick action might be the only way of saving our whole position in the Middle East from being gravely prejudiced'.[83] They were instructed 'as a matter of great urgency' to submit plans for seizing and securing Abadan Island and protecting the refinery and other installations so that the export of oil could be resumed so soon as it was received from the outlying oilfields: an operation subsequently dubbed Plan X. This plan approximated to an expansion of Plan Jagged (cf p. 164), but on the assumption of Persian opposition. In this connexion the meeting of the Chiefs of Staff on May 18 considered certain practical measures: notably the provision of 24 Hastings aircraft for an initial lift of troops at short notice, and the early despatch to the Middle East of the 16th Parachute Brigade; the Chiefs of Staff, however, warned the Commanders-in-Chief that 'the great majority of the Parachute Brigade is not at present fit to carry out an airborne operation or to be employed in Persia; it must be regarded solely as a replacement for troops taken from elsewhere except that you may like to consider the possibility of employing approximately one or two companies who are trained to drop to ensure that the airfield is clear for the main landing'.

Three days later, on May 21, the agreed views of Eastern, Northern, Southern, African and United Nations (Political) Departments of the Foreign Office were embodied by Mr Fry in a memorandum entitled 'The possible reactions to armed British intervention in the Persian Oil Dispute'.[84] This memorandum argued that such intervention in order to protect British lives could be defended on humanitarian grounds and would be unlikely to arouse serious criticism if taken in agreement with the Persian Government. The other two cases for possible intervention were in order to protect the British oil-installations from Persian seizure, or to forestall a

---

[80] *Ibid.*
[81] EP 1531/382.
[82] Cabinet file: C 14/41/8.
[83] EP 1015/195G.
[84] EP 1192/28.

Communist *coup*. In contrast to the sharp American differentiation of these cases, the Foreign Office thought that the distinction between them was slight: if a Tudeh *coup* was not to be precipitated the Anglo-Iranian Oil Company must continue to function and 'in the interests of Persia no less than in those of the Western Powers it might be desirable to use force to maintain the company'. This argument, it was pointed out, was unacceptable to the Americans; and while British use of force would almost certainly be supported by the countries of the Old Commonwealth (this was somewhat over-optimistic as regards Canada), it would be criticised in India, Pakistan and the United States as well as in the United Nations. Here the memorandum generally agreed with Sir Gladwyn Jebb, who telegraphed from New York on the same day that, except in circumstances involving an obvious collapse of the Persian State, he did not see how military intervention in Persia could be legally harmonised with British obligations under the Charter.[85]

The Foreign Office memorandum of May 21, 1951, argued that British military intervention in Persia would produce in Tehran either an intensification of extremist feeling against Britain and a reduced chance of negotiations, or else 'a turn to moderation, impressed by the show of force and apprehensive of the counter-action by Russia. The latter seems more probable, having regard to the Persian character.'[86] Somewhat similar considerations were liable to apply to reactions in Egypt, whose general attitude 'would also be reflected in her attitude towards the nationalisation of the Suez Canal'.

As regards Russian reactions, the memorandum of May 21 followed conclusions reached five days earlier by the Russia Committee in the Foreign Office. At that meeting Mr Fry had said that 'events in Persia were going favourably for Russia who therefore had no need to intervene'.[87] It was considered, however, that in the event of British military intervention in Southern Persia the legality of countervailing Russian intervention in Northern Persia, though decidedly doubtful, would not be a cardinal issue. For it would not be one for the Russians themselves, and in the circumstances it would be difficult for His Majesty's Government to complain against such action on their part. Even if Soviet forces did intervene, however, it was by no means certain that global war would result. It might well be that the British and Russian detachments would each remain in its own area with a no-man's-land in between, rather than on the pattern of the Anglo-Russian agreement of 1907.

The Foreign Office memorandum of May 21 concluded: 'If Persia suffered a Communist *coup* subsequent Western intervention . . . would not only be more difficult than anticipatory action but might be more likely to provoke a major war: it might be, for example, that the Soviet might feel compelled to support a Persian Communist régime against Western intervention . . . Our conclusion therefore is that to protect the oil installations from seizure would be to forestall a Communist *coup* in Persia and that, in the result, we might well lessen thereby the risk of global war.'[88] In relation to these arguments the Foreign Secretary minuted on May 24: 'This is better!'[89] They certainly tended, among other considerations, to emphasize the cogency of Mr Morrison's earlier suggestion that the danger of Russian intervention

---

[85] EP 1531/373.
[86] EP 1192/28.
[87] NS 1053/26G.
[88] EP 1192/28.
[89] EP 1015/208G.

in Persia to counter British intervention might have a positive application in frightening the Persians, at one remove, as to the consequences of provoking Great Britain. At a meeting with the Chiefs of Staff on May 23 Sir William Fraser expressed the view that in the face of such a threat 'the Persians would probably climb down provided that they were convinced that we were in earnest'.[90] Already, however, in the counsels of His Majesty's Government and its advisers, the pendulum, largely impelled by military advice, was beginning to swing back from its brief inclination towards strong action in Persia.

At a meeting on May 21 the Chiefs of Staff considered a report by the Directors of Administrative Plans on the administrative implications of the evolving Plan X (cf p. 181). Sir John Slessor commented on this report that it was disappointing 'that so few troops could arrive in the first flight. He had sincerely hoped that a plan on the lines indicated might produce a really bold and powerful stroke sufficient by its suddenness to quell any resistance.' In reply Field-Marshal Sir William Slim, Chief of the Imperial General Staff, who had not been present at the meeting of the Chiefs of Staff on May 18, said that 'personally he was in favour of taking a strong line with the Persians. Certain Ministers were also very strongly of this opinion, but he thought that they might well not yet be entirely clear as to the practical possibility of military action to back up a "tough" attitude to the Persians. It was the duty of the Chiefs of Staff to inform the Cabinet what was possible and the cost of such action (this would probably include both the declaration of a state of emergency and partial mobilisation) and also to advise whether military action was a worth-while proposition.' This should be done as soon as possible in order to minimise the very real risk of a disastrous situation where 'a "tough" attitude had been taken both officially and in the Press which we should be unable to back up militarily if necessary to the required degree'. At the meeting there was agreement with the views of Field Marshal Slim. One of the points made in discussion was that 'the military difficulty of mounting an operation in South-West Persia nowadays was almost entirely due to our having been deprived of the use of the Indian Army'.[91]

On the following day, May 22, Mr Furlonge wrote in a covering minute to the Foreign Office memorandum of May 21: 'In general there is much to be said for the contention that if our position in the Middle East is to be preserved we shall sooner or later have to take strong and dramatic action to show that we still have the will and the strength to resist threats to our interests. Whether our resources and our world position are such as to allow this is a different matter. It is virtually certain, in any event, that our success would depend on the weight and speed of our initial blow.' Mr Furlonge cogently stressed the difference between flying a strong force into Abadan in the matter of a day or two and mounting a laborious operation with naval transport, spread over two or three weeks and affording time for opposition to gather in Persia, in the Security Council or from Russia. 'Unfortunately', continued Mr Furlonge, 'the present trend of military opinion suggests that only the latter course will be found practicable.'[92]

Next day, May 23, 1951, the Chiefs of Staff listened to a statement by Sir William Fraser. It seemed to him that the best policy was to keep the production of oil going

---

[90] EP 1531/413G.
[91] EP 1015/202G.
[92] EP 1192/28.

so that any subsequent shutdown would be the fault of the Persians. Thus Persian assumption of control of the installations should probably be accepted under protest, in accordance with the instructions sent to their Field Manager about the beginning of the month (cf p. 165), and the British staff of the company should 'continue working as long as they were decently treated'.[93] It was the marketing factor which would constitute 'the most certain stranglehold on the Persians, who were unlikely to be able to export much oil in the face of the solidarity of the oil companies and probably Russian lack of interest in view of her own vast resources'. Before economic or, especially, military action were taken against Persia British oilmen should be withdrawn from the fields, and preferably from Abadan itself. Otherwise the lives of these 2,500 persons, of whom a third were in the fields, would be jeopardised. This might also occur if any military operation against Abadan were only on a small scale. Sir William Fraser thought, however, that British troop-movements to the Middle East could only do good as a token of determination.

The Cabinet had decided on May 22 that the 16th Parachute Brigade should be sent to the Middle East and two days later the Prime Minister ruled, and secured agreement from the War Office, that its destination should be Cyprus in view of political objections, represented by the Foreign Office, to the use of the Canal Zone, militarily the best solution, and also Tripoli.[94] Twelve Hastings aircraft were also ordered to the Middle East. This was the requirement for Operation Midget, the small operation confined to covering the evacuation from Abadan of British staff in case of Persian threat. For these military movements to the Middle East in fact coincided with a retreat in British military planning.

After Sir William Fraser had withdrawn from the meeting of the Chiefs of Staff on May 23, 'Sir William Slim said he understood that they all now agreed that an operation in Persia quickly mounted and on a small scale was not a sound military proposition'[95] with a view to holding Abadan Island. Sir John Slessor agreed, while observing that 'something of this sort had however been the only chance of bringing the Persian Government to its senses by military action without our being faced with the need for full-scale recapture operations'. If, in retrospect, this observation commands a considerable measure of assent, it also may suggest that the best and psychological moment, both militarily and politically, for any swift stroke would probably have been a month earlier, after the Persian murder of British subjects and before the arrival at Abadan of those Persian reinforcements which still imposed, now, upon British planning. Indeed Sir John Slessor was followed in the discussion by Admiral Sir George Creasy, Vice-Chief of the Naval Staff, who even opined that the whole situation would have been calmed down by sending a cruiser to Abadan two months ago, whereas now planning for a recapture of Abadan was necessary. Lieutenant-General McLean argued that such a full-scale operation would entail even greater political difficulties than a quick stroke to hold Abadan; whereas economic measures would presumably not lead to this sort of trouble; and he rather looked to a small operation like Midget, if necessary. Mr Furlonge, representing the Foreign Office, entirely agreed with General McLean and said that present policy was to get the Persian Government to negotiate or to get into power a Persian

---

[93] EP 1531/413G.
[94] E 1202/2G and 6G.
[95] EP 1015/231G.

Government which would.

Mr Emanuel Shinwell thereafter entered this meeting of the Chiefs of Staff and expressed personal doubt of success in persuading a Persian Government to negotiate, in which case plans should be ready. The Minister of Defence reiterated his conviction, which went further than that of some other Ministers, that His Majesty's Government must be prepared 'to take a really strong line' if necessary. In his view, 'if Persia was allowed to get away with it, Egypt and other Middle East countries would be encouraged to think they could try things on: the next thing might be an attempt to nationalise the Suez Canal. The situation seemed to be rapidly developing where nobody 'cared a damn' about this country; this was quite intolerable; we must be prepared to show that our tail could not be twisted interminably and that there was a limit to our willingness to have advantage taken of our good nature.'[96]

After the meeting of Chiefs of Staff on May 23 a telegram, proposed at that meeting before the entry of Mr Shinwell, was sent to inform General Headquarters, Middle East, that the plan which they had submitted on May 21 for the seizure of Abadan Island was being dropped as too risky: especially, it was subsequently explained, in view of the considerable Persian force, including armour, now concentrated at Abadan.[97] This acceptance of the factor which Middle Eastern Headquarters had represented as early as May 9 (cf p. 164) was not prevented by the circumstances that, in the words of an appreciation of the Persian Armed Forces annexed to a report of May 31 by the Joint Intelligence Committee—JIC(51)44 Final[98] (cf p. 197)—in the Persian Army 'morale is low and it lacks an incentive to resist . . . The Persian Air Force is incapable of offering more than token resistance', and the largest warship in the Persian Navy was one frigate.

The rejection of Plan X left two British plans in the field, the minimal Operation Midget and a Plan Y for a full-scale recapture of Abadan and reoccupation of the oilfields to ensure the resumption of oil production and export. On May 24 Mr Furlonge represented in a minute, which was seen by Sir William Strang and the Foreign Secretary, that Plan Y, with its laborious military build-up and politically dangerous delay, was likely to be 'quite unacceptable' to the Foreign Office; and since Plan X was impracticable, 'this means that the use of force except to secure the evacuation of the AIOC personnel must be ruled out'.[99] On the following day the Chiefs of Staff were informed that while the Foreign Office felt that it might be necessary to mount Operation Midget very quickly and suddenly, they also felt that 'in practice Plan Y was largely academic since they could not envisage circumstances in which, however much provoked, we could carry out what amounted to a deliberate aggression against Persia'.[100] The rejection of Plan X had gone with a swing, away from that military intervention at Abadan advocated in the Foreign Office so recently as May 21 (cf pp. 182-3).

---

[96] EP 1015/231G.
[97] EP 1015/199G.
[98] EP 1192/30G.
[99] EP 1015/231G.
[100] Cabinet file 14/41/8.

5. British appeal to the International Court of Justice against Persian oil nationalisation, May 20-26

All this military planning was but one aspect of consideration within the counsels of His Majesty's Government of what might need to be done if, as was expected, the reply of Dr Musaddiq to the British *aide-mémoire* of May 19 should be uncompromising. That was certainly the nature of the letter which the Persian Minister of Finance, M. Varasteh, sent on May 20 to Mr Seddon in reply to the Anglo-Iranian Oil Company's communication of May 8 (cf p. 165). M. Varasteh summarily rejected its demand for arbitration under the concession of 1933 and invited the company to nominate representatives with a view to making arrangements for carrying out the Oil Nationalisation Law of May 2 and, in particular, concerning any claims by the company to such strictly limited compensation as was envisaged by that law. On May 24 the Persian Minister of Finance addressed a second letter to Mr Seddon warning him that if the company had not nominated its representatives by May 30 the Persian Government 'will have no choice but to act according to its legal duties' under the nationalisation laws.[101]

Consultations in London between the Anglo-Iranian Oil Company, the Foreign Office and other interested Government departments resulted in a correct reply, in the form of a notification from Sir William Fraser, which Mr Seddon sent to M. Varasteh on May 27, 1951. Sir William Fraser stated in answer to M. Varasteh's invitation that Mr Seddon would attend a meeting 'as a measure of respect to the Imperial Government and the Iranian Parliament' but that, in view of the purpose of the discussions, he was only authorised to listen and report. The company could not accept the Persian rejection of arbitration and was accordingly making to the President of the International Court of Justice at The Hague the necessary application for the appointment of a sole arbitrator in accordance with Article 22(D) of the Concession Agreement of 1933.[102]

The proposal that the Anglo-Iranian Oil Company should thus apply to the President of the International Court of Justice had been discussed on May 22 at an interdepartmental meeting at the Foreign Office whereat Sir Eric Beckett stated, in particular, that 'it had been felt that action alone was not strong enough to meet public and parliamentary opinion in this country'.[103]

Coincidental action by His Majesty's Government was under consideration: notably whether it would be preferable for it in the first instance to initiate proceedings against the Persian Government before the International Court of Justice or in the Security Council of the United Nations. In the preceding Anglo-Persian dispute of 1932, concerning cancellation of the D'Arcy concession, His Majesty's Government had taken its case to the League of Nations largely because of doubts concerning the effective jurisdiction of the International Court in respect of the reservations of the Persian Government to its acceptance of the Optional Clause (cf p. 40). The juridical position was now liable to be improved from the British point of view to the extent that the concession agreement of 1933 was concluded after Persian ratification on September 19, 1932, of its acceptance of the Optional Clause; and there was an Anglo-Persian exchange of letters of August-October 1933 with

---

[101] Cmd 8425, p. 37.
[102] *Ibid,* p. 38.
[103] EP 1531/405.

the International Court regarding its acceptance of arbitration under Article 22.[104]
Yet the Persian reservation as regards domestic jurisdiction was still liable to be a
bar since the concession agreement of 1933 between the Persian Government and
the Anglo-Persian Oil Company was not an international treaty such as would of
itself bring into play the Optional Clause in respect of a treaty obligation of the
Persian Government (cf p. 125). That Government did, however, have a general
treaty obligation, under an Anglo-Persian exchange of notes of May 10, 1928, that
henceforth British nationals in Persia would be treated 'in conformity with the rules
and practice of international law'.[105]

In a brief of May 25, 1951, the Attorney-General, Sir Frank Soskice, gave his
opinion that, despite technical difficulties, there was an arguable case for the
contention that the International Court did possess jurisdiction in the matter:[106]
compare, however, Sir Eric Beckett's earlier opinion (pp. 168-9).

The Foreign Office also consulted Sir Gladwyn Jebb, noticing in this connexion
that His Majesty's Government's reference to the League of Nations in 1932 had
produced good results. But, as Sir Gladwyn Jebb replied on May 21, 'the whole
distribution of power in the world has after all changed materially since 1932'[107] so
that any reference now to the United Nations was liable to produce substantially less
satisfactory results. And, as the Foreign Office had already pointed out, Article 36(3)
of the Charter of the United Nations laid down the general rule that legal disputes
should be referred to the International Court. Furthermore, if His Majesty's
Government appealed to the Security Council before applying to the International
Court, the Persian Government might be able to prevent a subsequent application to
the court by denouncing the Optional Clause and thereby withdrawing themselves
from the court's jurisdiction with immediate effect. Both Sir Gladwyn Jebb and Sir
Frank Soskice agreed with the Foreign Office that application should first be made
to the International Court of Justice, and a note to inform the Persian Government of
this action was proposed.

Application to international authority on the one hand and the possibility of
military action on the other did not exhaust the notably comprehensive exploration
of expedients by the Foreign Office in that phase of the Persian crisis. On May 19,
1951, a Foreign Office telegram had informed Sir Francis Shepherd that
consideration was being given to 'whether, if Dr Musaddiq remained intransigent,
the immediate next step, before invoking International Court Procedure, should not
be a formal approach to the Shah' as to his giving 'a positive lead' and replacing the
Government of Dr Musaddiq with one prepared for reasonable negotiations on oil
with His Majesty's Government, who would do everything possible for their success.
The message continued: 'Should the Shah . . . indicate that the degree of United
Kingdom support which he would regard as necessary might include intervention by
British troops, he could be told that this would be a very serious step which might
provoke Russian intervention, and that we should not therefore wish to take it except
in the last resort.'[108]

---

[104] Cf *International Court of Justice Pleadings. Anglo-Iranian Oil Co. Case (United Kingdom v. Iran)*, pp. 270-2.
[105] Cf *ibid*, pp. 179-83.
[106] EP 1531/434G.
[107] EP 1531/373.
[108] EP 1531/354.

His Majesty's Ambassador at Tehran replied on May 23 that both he and the American Ambassador, whom he had consulted, agreed with the proposed action by the Shah despite the evident risk. And on May 22 Mr Levy, the intimate of Mr McGhee, had expressed similar views in his conversation in London with Mr Berthoud. The telegram from Sir Francis Shepherd concluded: 'The Shah is predisposed towards positive action and would only need convincing that the right moment had arrived.'[109] His Majesty's Ambassador, however, did not there allude to what could perhaps have been a somewhat important and contrary factor, mentioned by him two days earlier; in a despatch of May 21, also received in the Foreign Office on May 23, Sir Francis Shepherd had reported that in view of the previous success of Dr Musaddiq in imposing his policy against the wishes of his sovereign, 'it is widely felt that the Shah is no longer, or at least not for the moment, a force in politics'.[110]

It would also appear that views in the Foreign Office concerning the military aspect of an approach to the Shah fluctuated at the same time as those, already noticed, regarding the military possibilities of intervention. In some apparent contrast to the reserved attitude of the Foreign Office proposal of May 19 with reference to any military commitment in connexion with such an approach, Mr Furlonge observed on May 22, in relation to the Foreign Office memorandum of May 21 on armed intervention, that the British position in regard to Persia and to the rest of the world [would] be greatly strengthened if the Shah could dismiss his Government and invite British intervention: 'it might be possible to pursue this aspect if and when we make the formal approach to the Shah'.[111] On the following day of May 23, however, Mr Furlonge was minuting: 'Now that it is becoming clear that military intervention is impractical, even if desirable, it seems likely that our best line may be to press the Shah to bring about a change of Government'.[112] The latter development was indeed becoming an important objective but it is not altogether easy to resist the impression that now as earlier insufficient, or insufficiently consistent, attention was given to the cardinal importance of securing an invitation, or a promise of one, from the Shah for British intervention in southern Persia in case of need. Such an invitation would, most valuably, justify such action in international law and, in particular, according to Mr Rountree as recently as May 21 (cf p. 180), in the eyes of the State Department, which attached especial importance to it.

On May 24, 1951, despite slight uneasiness in the Treasury as to the propriety of communicating to the Americans departmental ideas before ministerial decision, the Foreign Office telegraphed to Sir Oliver Franks, for the information of the State Department, the proposed applications to the international court by the Anglo-Iranian Oil Company and also by His Majesty's Government. In view of the represented urgency of getting in with the latter before the Persians could denounce the Optional Clause it was now proposed that this should precede, rather than follow, the approach to the Shah. The State Department were to be asked how far they would support such an approach and whether it could be linked with the offer of economic

---

[109] EP 1531/384.
[110] EP 1015/207.
[111] EP 1192/28,
[112] EP 1531/691.

aid to Persia which the Americans were proposing to make despite the views of His Majesty's Government.

On May 25 Mr Steel made this communication to Mr McGhee, who was 'in a rather emotional condition', uttering complaints, 'mainly of a retrospective nature', against the personnel of the Anglo-Iranian Oil Company and against the lack or lateness of response by His Majesty's Government to American advice. The American Assistant Secretary of State wrangled along 'the single track which his mind follows in this case, ie the principle of nationalisation' which His Majesty's Government should proclaim as accepted.[113] Mr McGhee felt, as regards applications to the International Court, that the reply from the company to the Persian Government should be more forthcoming and that His Majesty's Government were being too legalistic to the prejudice of possible negotiations with the Persians which he, unlike Mr Levy, still strongly advocated on the basis of optimistic reports from Dr Grady: the Persian Premier and his entourage were represented as anxious for a settlement 'if Musaddiq could have something of a victory'—what Dr Musaddiq had already had, in Mr McGhee's view, was not explained. While Mr McGhee was nevertheless not unwilling to contemplate the probable necessity of another Persian Government, he reacted strongly against the proposed approach to the Shah, which, he felt, should be only made as a last attempt if negotiations failed. The Shah had not felt strong enough to dissolve the Majlis earlier and was not in a position to flout Persian opinion, while his reliance upon outside force 'seemed out of the question': a view which would appear to be in marked contrast to that which Mr Rountree had expressed only four days earlier. It is not recorded that the British Embassy in Washington pointed out such contrasts, and His Majesty's Ambassador suggested to Mr Morrison that every formal endeavour should be made to get started talks with the Persians.[114]

The Foreign Office understandably did not agree with the State Department that the Anglo-Iranian Oil Company should now adopt a more yielding attitude and 'in any case public opinion in this country would never stand for it'. The American disapproval of an approach to the Shah was disappointing since, Sir Oliver Franks was informed, 'we had been coming to the conclusion that this seemed to represent almost the only means remaining for us to arrest the course of events in Persia if the Persian Government themselves could not be brought to face reality'.[113] There was doubtless some force in Mr McGhee's contention that the Shah could not easily afford to flout Persian opinion, and his view might have called for careful correlation with those, for instance, of Sir Francis Shepherd. Yet it was evidently a grave decision to abandon further thought of an approach then to the Shah, in deference to what almost amounted to an American veto: on May 28 the Foreign Secretary reported the American objections to the Cabinet and did not propose any action to counter them.[115]

On May 25 Sir Roger Makins had reported of his recent visit to Washington: 'Anglo-American relations did not seem to be as bad as they looked from London. Relations with the administration are very close and friendly but the administration is weak and is under heavy Congressional attack . . . One line of attack on the

[113] EP 1531/410.
[114] EP 1531/421.
[115] EP 1531/487G.

administration is that it is too much under British influence . . . After China, Iran is now the most delicate and difficult specific problem in the Anglo-American relationship.' Referring to the 'staggering' productive effort of America, Sir Roger forecast that she 'will forge ahead of ourselves and her other allies in terms of power and will make the Anglo-American partnership still more difficult to manage . . . We must strive in every way to avoid again becoming dependent on direct United States economic support.'[116] For the week ending May 17 the gold and dollar balance of the sterling area had, for the first time that year, dipped into a heavy gross deficit of $57.5 million.[117] This adverse trend, even exceeding the forecast by the Treasury (cf pp. 103-4), was to be gravely accentuated in subsequent months.

It was doubtless scarcely to be expected that His Majesty's Government should then have enjoyed relations with the United States Government of such cordial intimacy as those which had subsisted between the wartime Governments of Mr Churchill and President Roosevelt. But this was perhaps one occasion upon which it might have been fruitful to consider, at any rate, some attempt to lift the whole Persian issue on to a higher, graver and at the same time easier level by some such means as a frank and personal correspondence between Mr Herbert Morrison and Mr Dean Acheson, if not between Mr Attlee and President Truman. On the official level, however, Anglo-American relations were just then generally impaired, though probably without special relevance to Persian affairs, by the defection to the Continent on May 25, 1951, of Mr D.D. Maclean, head of the American Department of the Foreign Office, and Mr Guy Burgess, recently a Second Secretary at His Majesty's Embassy at Washington. Both were subsequently stated to have been spies for the Soviet Union, whither they fled.[118]

On May 25 at a meeting of the Cabinet Committee of Ministers on Persia, whereat propaganda was discussed, the extent to which His Majesty's Government still cherished hopes of a change of Persian Government, whether or not by the Shah's intervention, had been evidenced. The Foreign Secretary advanced the desirability of publicising to Persia the conditional British acceptance of the principle of nationalisation, if the Persian reply to the proposed British note regards application to the International Court should be, as expected, uncompromising. The general feeling of the meeting, however, was that a decision on this should be deferred till the prospects of a change of Persian Government were clearer. A new Persian Government might be strengthened if such publicity were withheld till it were established.[119] Meantime Mr Morrison was invited to consider an intensification of propaganda to Persia, where, it was pointed out, 'during the war we had been able to exercise a strong influence through various channels, and it might be possible to work on similar lines again'.

No time was lost, now, in accordingly holding a meeting on the following day at the Foreign Office whereat it was decided to intensify propaganda on the theme that Dr Musaddiq was leading Persia into economic chaos, with its Communist dangers; something must be done urgently to bring his Government to its senses, and the Shah was the only hope.[120] Instructions to stimulate such comment, which could be

---

[116] AU 1054/21.
[117] UEE 7/7G.
[118] Cmd 9577 of 1955.
[119] EP 1531/435G.
[120] EP 1681/1G.

relayed to Persia, were sent that evening to posts in Europe and the Middle East,[121] and the Commonwealth Relations Office telegraphed similarly to New Delhi and Karachi. Broadcasts to Persia were to receive particular attention and the Information Policy Department of the Foreign Office was once more to consult with the BBC. It was thought, however, that it would be difficult to get material directly into the Tehran Press, short of bribery. The Foreign Secretary minuted: 'Why not a bit of bribery?'[120] At all events a strong British propaganda drive against Dr Musaddiq was now under way, though without the political concomitant of an approach to the Shah.

On the same day that Mr Seddon replied to the Persian Minister of Finance, May 27, Sir Francis Shepherd addressed to the Persian Foreign Minister a note expressing the regret of His Majesty's Government that no reply had been received to its *aide-mémoire* of May 19, but that instead M. Varasteh had seen fit to address to the Anglo-Iranian Oil Company his letter of May 20 followed by that of May 24 'in terms which appear to amount to an ultimatum'. His Majesty's Government had accordingly taken the action foreshadowed in the *aide-mémoire* and had on May 26 filed an application with the International Court of Justice, asking it 'to decide that the Imperial Government are under a legal obligation . . . to arbitrate, and additionally or alternatively to decide that the Imperial Government are not entitled to alter the Concession, even by legislation, except by agreement with the company' or as otherwise specifically provided in the concession of 1933.[122] It was emphasised, however, that these legal proceedings could be arrested before judgment was given if, as His Majesty's Government would prefer, the Persian Government indicated its willingness to negotiate and the negotiations were successful.

The British application of May 26 to the International Court had concluded by reserving the right to request the court, in accordance with Article 41 of its statute, to indicate any provisional measures, comparable to an interim injunction, which ought to be taken to protect the rights of His Majesty's Government and the Anglo-Iranian Oil Company pending a substantive decision by the court. In his telegram five days earlier (cf p. 187) Sir Gladwyn Jebb had drawn attention to the possibility of making this request for a provisional ruling that 'Persia should refrain from taking physical possession of the oilfields'.[123] Such an application was not, however, made at that time. The Foreign Secretary had conveyed to the Cabinet on May 24 that he was advised 'that it is probable that the Court would decline to make any such order of interim protection unless the question of its jurisdiction to deal with the dispute had been decided affirmatively'.[124] This was the view of the Attorney-General,[125] and subsequently, on June 7, Sir Eric Beckett added: 'Indeed, I do not see myself how any other attitude could be justified.'[126] It was further considered questionable whether an indication of provisional measures by The Hague Court would be a 'legally binding order'.[127]

The application by His Majesty's Government to the International Court of

[121] P 10151/23.
[122] Cmd 8425, pp. 38-9.
[123] EP 1531/373.
[124] EP 1531/433G.
[125] EP 1531/434G.
[126] EP 1531/616.
[127] *Ibid.*

Justice had been appositely coordinated with that of the Anglo-Iranian Oil Company and an important step had been taken towards staking out the claim of His Majesty's Government to be a party to an international dispute which the Persian Government sought to represent as a domestic one with the company alone. His Majesty's Government still hoped to negotiate with the Persian Government and had only a week earlier recognised the principle of oil nationalisation in some contrast to the application to the International Court on the basis of the concession of 1933; resort to the court represented an expedient rather than a policy in itself. The reasons for adopting this expedient were sufficiently evident, although it also presented, in changed conditions, a contrast to British avoidance in 1932 of recourse to The Hague (cf p. 40). Even if the International Court were ultimately to decide that it now possessed jurisdiction in the case and did give judgment against Persia— considerable conditionals—the Attorney-General admitted in his brief of May 25 that 'the only provision for the enforcement of such an award is by the Security Council under Article 94(2) of the United Nations Charter. In fact, owing to the veto, the prospects of such enforcement are next to valueless': there followed a wry reference to the unenforced judgment of the International Court in favour of Great Britain against Albania in the Corfu Channel Case of 1947-49.[128]

Application to the International Court necessarily subtended a new angle on to any British use of force in Persia. In this connexion the Attorney-General wrote: 'I would conclude that, in my opinion, the United Kingdom has no right at all in international law independently of any United Nations recommendation to intervene by force in Persia to prevent a wrong being committed against one of its nationals or indeed to prevent the implementation of the Persian proposals [for oil nationalisation] even if they constitute a wrong in international law.'[129] Mr G.G. Fitzmaurice, Second Legal Adviser to the Foreign Office, subsequently expressed some reservations with regard to some of the arguments in this memorandum.

In view of the advanced stage which British military planning and preparations had already reached by then, examination of the legal aspects of military intervention in Persia (cf pp. 151-2), and its possible legal justification, had become increasingly urgent. It was also increasingly important now, as compared with rather earlier times, in respect of a more critical public opinion throughout much of the world, the rising tide of Asiatic nationalism, the institution of the United Nations and the declining power of the United Kingdom, the ascendant power of the United States and the Soviet Union. New conditions were priming a swing back from the relative simplicities of the 19th century to something more nearly resembling the older complexity of the legalistic logomachy which had characterised many aspects of international relations in the 18th century.

While His Majesty's Government were embarking upon the long legalities of the International Court, unbacked now by any formal approach to the Shah, there remained the urgent possibility that the Persian Government might attempt to secure physical control of British property and installations at Abadan. The supple instructions on this score which the Anglo-Iranian Oil Company had sent to their local representative at the beginning of May (cf p. 165) were endorsed in a Foreign Office memorandum of May 24, which thought it difficult to perceive any

[128] EP 1531/434G
[129] *Ibid.*

alternative.[130] This conclusion was approved on the following day by the Ministerial Committee on Persia which was also attended by the Attorney-General, Mr Kenneth Younger and Sir Eric Beckett.[131] This heavy decision, which was to have major implications for the whole of the rest of the crisis, corresponded both to Foreign Office concentration now in the military sphere upon Operation Midget alone, and in the economic sphere to the policy of the company, described as being 'to continue to maintain the supply of oil, ignoring or suffering under protest, all insults and injuries as long as possible'.

The above quotation is from a Treasury memorandum[132] of May 26 reconsidering that of May 8 (cf p. 167) on possible economic sanctions against Persia. These might still be called for since the Anglo-Iranian Oil Company envisaged limits to its toleration, notably in regard to Persian interference in operations to the extent of endangering the lives of employees or assuming functions of too great importance to be accepted without undermining the whole position of the company: for instance Persian sale of oil at Abadan. Such circumstances might impel measures of grave economic injury to the Persians, such as the withdrawal of British technicians and of British tankers.

On the same day of May 26 a letter was written from Washington to Mr Furlonge by Mr Burrows, who gave as the joint view of Sir Oliver Franks and himself: 'There is no doubt that the first American reaction to any proposal by us to apply economic pressure [to Persia] would be one of violent disapproval.' And they assumed that His Majesty's Government 'would feel it impossible to achieve our objectives in the face of American opposition'.[133] That, very largely, remained the crux of the Abadan crisis for British policy. It now had to reckon that the United States Government would, for most practical purposes, disapprove of measures to defend British interests against Persian expropriation by means of economic sanctions, military intervention or political approach to the Shah. Any estimate of His Majesty's Government's handling of the crisis needs to take particular account not only of the earlier degree of negativism evinced by the Anglo-Iranian Oil Company, but also of the restriction now of room for manoeuvre between the negative obduracies of Dr Musaddiq and of the State Department.

Traditional British interests in the Middle East generally were also liable to be affected both for good (cf pp. 137-8) and ill by the increasing interest in that area displayed by the American Government. As early as April 3, Mr McGhee had told Mr Morrison that his Government proposed to adopt a new policy towards the Middle East by offering military aid to countries behind those of the Outer Ring, in order to provide stability in depth against Communism. This forward intention marked some departure from the previous American tendency (cf pp. 68-74) to leave the leadership of affairs in that area to Great Britain: Mr McGhee referred to the critical situation, especially in Persia, and perhaps rather brashly remarked that so long as Britain's difficulties there and in Egypt remained unresolved 'they would hinder the implementation of the United States policy in the Middle East'.[134] Mr Burrows commented on May 22 that the Americans were conceiving such a policy

[130] EP 1531/433G.
[131] EP 1531/435G.
[132] EP 1156/5.
[133] EP 1156/9.
[134] E 1024/13G.

of military and economic aid of about $150 million 'in terms of a grand psychological gesture to impress people in the Middle East'.[135] The American policy had been explained to British representatives at a politico-military meeting on May 17 at the Pentagon in Washington. Sir Oliver Franks had there welcomed this development and, in reporting it, stressed that the Americans, in framing their new proposals 'which project them fairly and squarely into the Middle East',[136] had given consideration to the traditional British position there—they had, for instance, suggested joint Anglo-American missions where appropriate in the Middle East in order to prevent the two countries being played off against each other. Sir Oliver Franks, however, warned the Foreign Secretary that, unless Britain made an increased contribution to local economic development, the common front 'successfully kept with the Americans in the Middle East' since the Washington talks in 1947 (cf p. 54) could scarcely be maintained, as there were indications that the Americans considered that British responsibilities had not been adequately discharged. There was a feeling, perhaps mainly subconscious, among many Americans 'that it may be time to draw away from us and "go it alone" in the Middle East'. Present events in Persia were but one focus for American criticism of British policy, increasingly subject to that pressure.

On May 29, 1951, the Foreign Secretary was asked by Mr Emrys Hughes in the House of Commons about consultations concerning Persia with the United States Government and whether, in particular, it had advised against a policy of military intervention. Mr Morrison replied: 'Suitable conversations have taken place with the United States Government and, on the whole, we are acting in cooperation.'[137]

---

[135] E 1024/24G.
[136] *Ibid.*
[137] Parliamentary Debates, 5th series, H. of C., Vol. 488, col. 43.

CHAPTER VII

FAILURE OF THE MISSION TO TEHRAN OF THE ANGLO-IRANIAN OIL COMPANY, MAY 26-JUNE 19, 1951

1. Persian aggravations of May 28-30 and President Truman's message to the Prime Minister

On May 28, 1951, the Persian Government notified the International Court of Justice that it rejected its jurisdiction in the dispute with the Anglo-Iranian Oil Company. On the same day the President of the Court informed the company that he would not proceed with its application of May 25 since it had points in common with that of His Majesty's Government. This decision, accepted by both the British applicants, was scarcely congenial to Dr Musaddiq, who had intimated to His Majesty's Ambassador on May 25 that the dispute was not the concern of His Majesty's Government. Four days later the Persian Premier emerged from his parliamentary lair to lunch with Dr Grady and Sir Francis Shepherd. The latter broached a general formula for negotiation but the American minute of the conversation recorded: 'The Prime Minister completely rejected this opportunity to commence discussions with the British Government.'[1] Sir Francis Shepherd failed to convince the 'completely intransigent' Dr Musaddiq of the great practical difficulties Persia would encounter in trying to market oil or replace British technicians. 'Musaddiq', he reported, 'talked airily about neutral experts and enquired whether the British were gods that others could not do what they could do.'[2]

On the following day of May 30, 1951, the Persian Minister of Finance addressed to Mr Seddon an *aide-mémoire* which, after emphasising Persian wishes to avoid any loss to former buyers and to compensate the company, gave notice of new regulations for the enforcement of the nationalisation laws. Under these Persian regulations the Government was to nominate a Temporary Board of three directors to administer the National Iranian Oil Company under the supervision of the Parliamentary Mixed Committee. This board was empowered to manage the company's affairs with regard to prospecting for, producing, refining, distributing, selling and exploiting Persian oil. Pending approval of the constitution of the new company, the Board would apply the regulations of the Anglo-Iranian Oil Company except where they were at variance with the nationalisation law. Employees of the Anglo-Iranian Oil Company would be regarded as employed by the National Iranian Oil Company. On its arrival in Khuzistan the Temporary Board would notify former oil purchasers that they might continue for one month to receive supplies under existing arrangements and against receipts to the new company; they must apply to the Temporary Board in order to arrange payment.[3]

'This extraordinary document', as Sir Francis Shepherd described the Persian *aide-mémoire*, concluded, however, by expressing the Government's willingness to consider any proposals regarding the regulations which the Anglo-Iranian Oil Company might make within five days, and which did not conflict with the principle

---

[1] EP 1531/556.
[2] EP 1531/445.
[3] Cmd 8425, pp. 39-41.

of nationalisation. This, commented Sir Francis Shepherd on May 31, might at least allow the company to try to explain to their would-be despoilers 'the difference between Anglo-Iranian Oil Company and a small garage. This opening, however, strait, should not be missed.' He observed that the regulations were apparently a draft: 'it is obviously essential to try and prevent Persians from attempting to apply them in anything like their present form.'[4]

The State Department was, despite Dr Grady's report of the abortive luncheon, anxious as usual that any opportunity of beginning British conversations with the Persians should be seized without waiting to secure satisfactory terms of reference.[5] This anxiety was expressed in more diplomatic terms in a personal and secret message which Mr Attlee received on May 31 from Mr Truman. The President wrote: 'Recent information which has reached me has led me to believe that the Iranian Government is willing and even anxious to work out an arrangement with His Majesty's Government'; while the Persian invitation for discussions had been addressed to the Anglo-Iranian Oil Company, 'the Iranian Government has indicated that it would have no objections if such company negotiators were also officials of his Majesty's Government'. And Mr Truman referred to Mr Morrison's indication to the House of Commons, two days earlier, of British acceptance of the principle of nationalisation.[6]

On June 1 the Foreign Secretary told the American Ambassador that it seemed to him that British thinking was not at variance with Mr Truman's, but that he hoped that, in case of need, the United States Government would support British economic measures against Persia, such as the withdrawal of tankers, and also an appeal to the Shah. As regards possible use of force, Mr Morrison knew that there would be American support for it for protection of British lives, but he 'felt the United States Government were drawing an unreal distinction when they said they would support us in any such action against a Communist *coup* in Persia, but not while there was any other form of Persian Government'.[7] With regard to these three cardinal points of actual or potential disagreement with the American Government, Mr Morrison did not, however, record that Mr Gifford made any reply.

The chequered course of Anglo-American consultations was now further prejudiced in Tehran by Dr Grady, to whom a copy of Mr Truman's secret and personal message to Mr Attlee had actually been sent for information without any intimation thereof to Mr Attlee. Dr Grady proceeded to deliver this message as from Mr Truman to Dr Musaddiq. In order to cover up this 'crass error'[8] to some slight extent, at any rate, the Americans then did send an exhortatory message to the Persian Premier, thereby reducing Mr Truman's personal message to Mr Attlee to the level of an American admonition addressed equally to both parties.

2. Further British consideration of military intervention in South Persia and consultation with the United States

At the beginning of June 1951 His Majesty's Government once more needed to consider the courses open to it in order to secure a favourable solution of the

---

[4] EP 1531/472.
[5] EP 1531/496.
[6] EP 1531/571.
[7] EP 1531/484.
[8] EP 1531/481.

depressing crisis concerning Persian oil. The first possibility remained the use of force when appropriate: it was noticeable that His Majesty's Government's despatch of the Parachute Brigade had caused an alarm in Persia (cf p. 175) which contrasted with the calm reception of the news of the British application to The Hague. A report of May 31 by the Joint Intelligence Committee—JIC(51)44 Final (cf p. 185)[9]— approximately recapitulated the assessment in the Foreign Office memorandum of May 21 (cf pp. 181-2) of the reactions which British armed intervention in Persia would be likely to provoke in other countries and in the United Nations. On the military side it was observed that the Persians had available in South Persia three divisions with supporting arms, a few aircraft and small naval patrol vessels: enough to block the sea approaches and airfield at Abadan and, as was initially likely, to oppose a British landing. In view, however, of the poor quality of the Persian forces no long and effective resistance to strong and determined British action was foreseen.

On the same day of May 31, 1951, the Chiefs of Staff circulated a cautious memorandum—DO(51)61[10]—wherein they nevertheless maintained their rejection of a quick operation on the lines of Plan X and emphasised that Plan Y would be liable to entail serious consequences, both political and military. Militarily it would involve, in the conditions of that time, the total replacement from Great Britain of the British garrison in the Middle East, partial mobilisation on a very considerable scale and the impressment of vehicles and shipping. On the other hand Operation Midget could now be mounted quickly, though even that would mean 'serious hazard'—the assumption for all these operations was active Persian opposition. The Foreign Secretary now noted regarding Operation Midget: 'The surrender op[eration]. But I've assured Parlt. and we have a duty. ?Consult Opp[osition]. United States aid?' And he requested Mr Furlonge: 'Please see me with maps. ?Minister/Def[ence] to be present?'[11]

Memorandum DO(51)61 was considered on June 4 at a meeting of the Defence Committee whereat the Chiefs of Staff went rather further as regards Plan Y, expressing 'the opinion that Plans X and Y were militarily unsound and politically exceptionable and [they] would like authority to abandon them'.[12] To this 'the Foreign Secretary said that he was very disappointed in view of the large expenditure on the rearmament programme to learn that so little could be done to support our foreign policy with political action'. Neither he nor the Minister of Defence considered that Plan Y should be abandoned. Another view, however, was that 'in existing circumstances economic action was undoubtedly more effective than military and much more likely to win the support of the United States'. It was generally agreed that Operation Midget should be held in readiness. Summing up the discussion, the Prime Minister said: 'We must at all costs avoid getting into the position where we could be represented as a capitalist Power attacking a nationalist Persia. Rather we should endeavour to arrange things so that our apparent position was one of supporting a legitimate Persian Government against either Russian invasion or Communist insurrection and incidentally to safeguard our oil interests.

---

[9] EP 1192/30G.
[10] EP 1015/226G.
[11] *Ibid.*
[12] *Ibid.*

It might be as well to discuss further with the United States the assistance they could afford to operations of this kind, in particular by the provision of transport aircraft.'

On June 8, 1951, the Foreign Secretary accordingly telegraphed to Mr Steel in Washington the conclusions of the Defence Committee, and invited him to obtain American reactions. As regards Operation Midget, Mr Morrison explained that while Persian agreement beforehand would certainly be sought, 'if this was not forthcoming we might feel obliged to act without it'.[13] As regards the previous American agreement to support British intervention against a Communist *coup* in Persia, Mr Morrison stated: 'We take this to mean that if we should require active assistance (eg the despatch of a carrier to the Persian gulf or the loan of transport aircraft) which they were in a position to supply, they would not hesitate to afford it.' Mr Steel replied that day that the Americans 'understand quite well that we should intervene to protect British lives though they will expect to be consulted or at least informed in advance and would be unlikely to give us support except on a cast-iron case. As regards a Russian invasion or a Communist *coup* they will also theoretically support us but I am convinced that they will not give us any kind of firm commitment on a hypothetical basis . . . In general, I would respectfully deprecate any further raising of this question of force until the political position has developed a good deal further. The Americans are already suspicious and apprehensive and unless we are really on the brink of some new situation, I think their reactions might be most unfortunate.'[14] Mr Steel later added that these opinions had been exactly confirmed by Mr McGhee. On June 12 a Foreign Office telegram informed Mr Steel that the matter might be left as it was for the time being. The Foreign Secretary had minuted: 'We may have to stand on our own judgment.' On this somewhat bleak and inconclusive note ended the main phase of consultation or proposed consultation with the Americans concerning possible British military intervention in Southern Persia.

3. The decision to send to Tehran a mission of the Anglo-Iranian Oil Company

At the other end of the scale from the extreme possibility for His Majesty's Government of taking military action stood that of taking no action at all for the time, leaving the Persians to stew in their own oil. Since diplomacy need not always be obviously active, there were arguments for adopting at some stage a negative policy to counter the negativism of Dr Musaddiq. His by no means impregnable position in Persia was liable to be impaired by a stiff refusal to treat with him. Such policies of abstention, however, probably need to be especially carefully and strongly conceived, in this case, for instance, by advance calculation of how to meet likely Persian aggravations and, in particular, how far recourse to the Shah or economic sanctions might profitably be brought to bear. It may be doubted, however, whether such a policy would in any case have been best suited to that particular juncture, when the initiative remained with the Persians. Indeed, some reflexion of previous Anglo-American divergence regarding the urgency of the question of Persian oil might still perhaps be seen in the Foreign Secretary's somewhat sanguine suggestion to the American Ambassador on June 1 that 'time might be on our side and Mr Gifford would understand if I said that I thought that the State Department

---

[13] EP 1015/211G.
[14] EP 1015/223G.

were inclined to take too alarmist a view of the situation'[15] (cf pp. 143-4).

Some such optimism would appear to have conditioned what was in itself, in all probability, the correct British decision to seize the most immediately constructive opportunity and, in accordance with the view of both Sir Francis Shepherd and the Americans, exploit the opening offered by the Persians for the Anglo-Iranian Oil Company to conduct discussions on however unsatisfactory an initial basis. Such a decision was recommended by Mr Furlonge in a brief of May 31 in the hope that the discussions in Tehran would gain time during which Dr Musaddiq, who appeared to be weakening, might fall.[16] On the following day this recommendation was approved by the ministerial committee on Persia, where it was likewise suggested that the general aim should be to spin matters out in the hope that the Persians might become more amenable as they were brought to realise the practical difficulties inherent in their present policy; though it was appreciated that the situation might deteriorate before it improved.[17]

On June 3, 1951, Mr Seddon accordingly informed M. Varasteh, in reply to his communication of May 30, that his company and, he was authorised to add, His Majesty's Government were entirely ready, as always to negotiate. 'It is not possible', concluded Mr Seddon, 'to formulate proposals on a matter of such complexity within five days'[18] but the company, while reserving its full legal rights, would as soon as possible send representatives to Tehran for discussions. In accordance with another proposal by Mr Furlonge, the remission of Mr Seddon's *aide-mémoire* on June 3 was aptly coordinated with a representation by Sir Francis Shepherd to Dr Musaddiq, 'wearing on this occasion blue pyjamas beneath his khaki ones'.[19] His Majesty's Government could not accept the view which Dr Musaddiq had reiterated on May 25 that the oil question was solely one between the Persian Government and the Anglo-Iranian Oil Company. In reply Dr Musaddiq did not dispute the right of His Majesty's Government to protect the interests of its subjects but maintained, as previously, that there was no ground for governmental intervention since, on his rather special reading of events, no harm had hitherto been done to the company. He would not allow His Majesty's Ambassador to read him a copy of Mr Seddon's *aide-mémoire*, but raised no objection to the company's proposal to send a delegation to Tehran.

On the following day of June 4 in the House of Commons Mr Anthony Eden for the Opposition particularly welcomed Mr Morrison's announcement that Dr Musaddiq had thus been informed that 'His Majesty's Government had every right to intervene in defence of this great British interest in Persia'.[20] Nevertheless the British mission which was to proceed to Tehran was to represent the Anglo-Iranian Oil Company. This was hailed by the nationalist Persian Press as a victory for Dr Musaddiq.

The Persian Premier yet told the Shah on June 3, 1951, that it would help to save his face if the Persian Temporary Board of three directors proceeded at once to Khuzistan in accordance with an announcement in that sense already made by M.

[15] EP 1531/484
[16] EP 1531/520.
[17] EP 1531/546G.
[18] Cmd 8425, p. 41.
[19] EP 1531/609.
[20] Parliamentary Debates, 5th Series, H. of C., Vol. 488, col. 687.

Makki. The Shah was asked to secure His Majesty's Ambassador's agreement to this. When approached accordingly on the following day, Sir Francis Shepherd 'told Alam that I should greatly prefer the commission not to go at this juncture'[21] when the Anglo-Iranian Oil Company had agreed to hold discussions and it seemed that the deadlock was about to be broken. The fact that Dr Musaddiq had seen fit to have Sir Francis Shepherd sounded carries some suggestion, perhaps, that he may possibly have had some slight apprehension concerning the latter's reaction to the grave step proposed. While His Majesty's Ambassador had told M. Alam that the Temporary Board would aggravate the situation, it is not clear that he specifically underlined to him, or to the Foreign Office, the ominous fact that the despatch of the Board would point towards Persian implementation of the first of those regulations which had appeared to Sir Francis Shepherd only four days earlier to be a draft, the application of which it was it was essential to try to prevent. He did not now specifically refuse, for his part, to countenance the despatch to Khuzistan of the Temporary Board, but suggested to M. Alam that the Persian Government could surely wait at least a few days. The Foreign Office did not question the adequacy of this plea as an attempt to stem the swift and adverse current of developments in Persia.

In Whitehall the composition of the Anglo-Iranian Oil Company's mission to Tehran was being discussed in not wholly reassuring terms. With regard to the evidently attractive proposal that the mission should include one of the two governmental directors of the company, Sir Edward Bridges, Sir William Strang and Sir Donald Fergusson 'all agreed, however, that neither of them had the necessary qualifications or was otherwise suitable'.[22] Nevertheless, Sir Thomas Gardiner was appointed a member of the mission to assist its head, Mr Basil Jackson. Despite his ability, the appointment of Mr Jackson himself did not apparently reflect any very enthusiastic estimate of him in either Whitehall or Washington. Mr Jackson in turn insisted that his mission should include Mr Gass although Sir Francis Shepherd had strongly advised against this since it would 'greatly prejudice'[23] chances of success owing to Mr Gass' association with the rejected Gass-Gulshayan Supplemental Agreement. The fourth representative of the company on the mission was Mr E.H.O. Elkington; he had been General Manager at Abadan during the crisis of 1932 but was described in the Foreign Office as 'a typical ex-Indian Army officer. He is ultra-hearty and has for years got away with treating the Persians somewhat roughly.'[24] Despite misgivings in the Foreign Office it was agreed there that Sir William Fraser's choice of personnel should not be over-criticised since otherwise His Majesty's Government would be blamed for any failure of the negotiation. It may be a matter of opinion whether this prudential calculation need have weighed quite so heavily in determining the composition of a critical mission at a period when it had been specifically agreed that the company must keep closely in step with His Majesty's Government.

The weakness of the Anglo-Iranian Oil Company's mission to Tehran unhappily set off that of its permanent representation there, which seemed in Whitehall—and not only there—to be inadequate for such a time. In Tehran Mr Northcroft and Mr

---

[21] EP 1531/489.
[22] EP 1531/504.
[23] EP 1531/485.
[24] EP 1531/523.

Seddon were certainly well informed and, although Sir Francis Shepherd admitted on June 5 that neither was an 'intellectual giant'[25] (but Mr Furlonge was later impressed by Mr Seddon),[26] their main weakness was probably lack of influence with their centralised management in London. On June 6, the day on which the composition of the company's mission was announced, Sir Francis Shepherd telegraphed that his Embassy still favoured the despatch to Tehran at the first opportunity of a British governmental delegation even if this involved the suspension of technical discussions with the company. Something spectacular was still needed to reverse the feeling aroused by the Persian Government and Press against the Anglo-Iranian Oil Company and against Great Britain. His Majesty's Ambassador, however, did not see how to find an opening so long as the National Front was in the ascendant.[27]

On the same day of June 6 Mr Berthoud recorded thoughts which had come to him 'very early' that morning.[28] Mr Berthoud doubted whether in the circumstances the 'cautious and lumbering AIOC delegation' would make progress against Persian *amour propre*—a somewhat similar doubt had already been voiced by the Foreign Secretary to the American Ambassador on June 1. Mr Berthoud felt that the Secretary of State should not lose the initiative, and that the frigid atmosphere called for a little warmth and a return to secret diplomacy, more attuned to the Persian mentality. Mr Berthoud suggested that Mr Morrison should send to Dr Musaddiq a secret envoy, either himself or another, accompanied by the expert Miss Lambton and charged with imaginative proposals which might steer the talks with the company. The possibility of calling in Mr Levy as an honest broker was also raised. Mr Berthoud concluded that 'if Mr Musaddiq is as mad as he seems' such an effort might be entirely wasted, but it could not do much harm, and conceivably some good.

Mr Berthoud's constructive proposal was seen by Sir William Strang, and a departmental meeting to discuss it was arranged for June 12. No recorded upshot from such a meeting has, however, been traced and no such mission as proposed by Mr Berthoud was undertaken. On June 23 Mr Furlonge wrote it off with the annotation, depressingly familiar on papers dealing with the Abadan crisis: 'This has now been overtaken.'[29] Mr Berthoud's proposal was very likely discarded for excellent reasons, which can indeed usually be found for not doing anything. Since they are, apparently, not recorded, however, it is perhaps permissible to regret that this imaginative initiative from Mr Berthoud, like that earlier from Lord Mountbatten, did not materialise. It was arranged, however, that the company's mission to Tehran should be flanked on the technical level by two members of the official Working Party on Persian Oil, Mr Flett of the Treasury and Mr Butler of the Ministry of Fuel and Power. A suggestion that Mr Ramsbotham might also proceed from the Foreign Office was not pursued. Nor does there appear to have been an enthusiastic response to a suggestion from Mr Herbert Morrison that 'one or more of our socialistic expert civil servants' should be sent to Tehran when appropriate.[30]

---

[25] EP 1531/603.
[26] EP 1015/374.
[27] EP 1531/532.
[28] EP 1531/733.
[29] EP 1531/733.
[30] EP 1531/538.

In recent weeks the Working Party on Persian Oil had, as previously noticed, been investigating alternative technical arrangements which might possibly reconcile Persian with British desiderata for the management of the oil industry in Southern Persia. This had produced five suggested solutions which became known in Whitehall as the Five Red Herrings, and were put on ice for use as might be judged expedient by the mission of the Anglo-Iranian Oil Company; and before it left for Tehran the Working Party on Persian Oil produced a report. The suggested solutions were criticised on June 11, 1951, by Mr A. Johnston, a Deputy Secretary of the Cabinet, as not being very profound. He suggested the need for more detailed and informed investigation by a working party of people with practical experience of public corporations and holding companies. Mr Johnston concluded: 'There is a great deal of work to be done, and one does not want to have to do it at short notice in response to some frantic message from Tehran for detailed advice.' On the following day Sir Norman Brook minuted on this to Sir Edward Bridges: 'Is there not something in this? Ministers have a passion now for telling people just to 'spin out the talks' (cf Egypt) in the hope that something will turn up. Do we not rather want to have some *constructive* ideas to put forward?'[31] Sir Edward Bridges thought that the real starting point should be 'the essential points which will have to be conceded . . . It is not a question so much of preparing a sensible scheme on sensible lines as of constructing something which will look like nationalisation but will leave as much as possible of central control in British hands.'[32]

The five technical solutions suggested by the Working Party had been worked out in relation to the general principle of the 50-50 division of profits previously offered to the Persians. A note of June 11 by the Ministry of Fuel and Power estimated that such a 50-50 division would increase payments made to Persia by £15 million. If Britain went so far as a 60-40 division in favour of Persia, and assuming that other concessionary countries demanded similar treatment, the adverse effect on the United Kingdom's balance of payments would be a further £34 million, as compared with about £85 million on a 75-25 division or indeed if Persian oil were completely lost. The Ministry of Fuel and Power concluded from these figures that 'it might be worth considering going to 60-40 but no further'.[33] This conclusion was especially significant in relation to American insistence upon 50-50 as the unsurpassable optimum for oil agreements.

The Working Party on Persian Oil had recognised that the announcement of the despatch of a mission by the Anglo-Iranian Oil Company would have strengthened the position of Dr Musaddiq but advised: 'We should be prepared to pay a reasonable price to safeguard the company's machine, even if this should temporarily strengthen the Musaddiq régime.'[34] A meeting of the Ministerial Committee on Persia held on the night of June 7 approved the brief for the company's mission. The Chancellor of the Exchequer, however, observed that it should not make so many concessions as to prejudice the prospects of the replacement of Dr Musaddiq by someone less intransigent.[35] Substantially the same point was made four days later by Mr Levy to

---

[31] Cabinet file 14/41/8.
[32] *Ibid.*
[33] EP 1531/591.
[34] EP 1531/844G.
[35] EP 1531/587.

Mr Berthoud.[36]

Mr Levy's assessment contrasted sharply with that of Dr Grady, who had on June 5 given a Press conference wherein he had urged the Anglo-Iranian Oil Company to make a prompt financial advance to the Persian Government and had criticised its delay in sending negotiators.[37] This latest instance of what Sir Francis Shepherd termed 'the evident intention of Grady to set himself up as the arch mediator in the oil dispute'[38] induced His Majesty's Ambassador, reluctantly, to make a representation on June 7 against his giving such public advice. Dr Grady, reported Sir Francis Shepherd, did not take this very well, but he thought 'that Grady is so genuinely convinced of the need for a reasonable settlement which will not by implication damage American interests that he will continue to give us support'. Although the State Department in Washington was inclined to support its vain Ambassador it would yet appear that it enjoined upon him greater reticence.

On June 6, the day after Dr Grady had urged financial concessions to the Persian Government, M. Husein Ala, the former Premier and still Minister of Court, came 'warily' to inform His Majesty's Ambassador that Dr Musaddiq had shown the Shah the draft of his reply to the British note of May 19. In the draft Dr Musaddiq agreed to negotiate with the Anglo-Iranian Oil Company under Articles 2 and 3 of the Nationalisation Law of May 2, that is, only concerning claims by the company to limited compensation for dispossession, and under Article 7 with His Majesty's Government, thus only concerning arrangements with it as a purchaser of oil. The draft note accused the company of having put Reza Shah into power; the allegations against his father had angered the Shah but he did not insist on their omission for fear that his Prime Minister would make political capital of it. Sir Francis Shepherd firmly told M. Ala that it sounded as if this communication was deliberately provocative and that 'in spite of his protestations Musaddiq appeared bent on preventing negotiations on a reasonable basis'.[39] His Majesty's Ambassador might find it difficult to transmit such a note and he agreed with M. Ala that its presentation should be delayed pending the arrival of the company's mission. On June 9 Dr Musaddiq agreed with a suggestion from Sir Francis Shepherd in this sense and in the subsequent event this Persian note was never remitted to His Majesty's Government.

Such was the inauspicious prelude to the mission to Tehran of the Anglo-Iranian Oil Company. And although at the beginning of the month Sir Francis Shepherd had reported that the expectation of life for Dr Musaddiq's Government was probably 'inconsiderable',[40] a fortnight later, on June 15, he considered that, despite the fact that the Persian Premier had recently been losing ground, 'the prospects of a strong successor Government are so problematical that it would be unwise to concentrate on unseating Musaddiq in the hope that his successor would be either more reasonable or more capable of securing ratification of an agreement'.[41]

---

[36] EP 1531/696.
[37] EP 1531/526.
[38] EP 1531/602.
[39] EP 1531/543.
[40] EP 1051/19.
[41] EP 1015/236.

4. The darkening scene at Abadan and the appointment of the British Oil Supply Advisory Committee, June 6-14

On the same day that M. Husein Ala visited him, Sir Francis Shepherd had telegraphed that the three-man Temporary Board of Directors of the National Iranian Oil Company was shortly leaving for Khuzistan and proceeding to Abadan. The plea made two days earlier to M. Alam by His Majesty's Ambassador, for delay at least, had proved unavailing. He now reported: 'I am assured that this is a politically necessary gesture but that the [three-man] commission will do no more than show itself in order to diminish criticism that Musaddiq has [?done] nothing since he came into power to implement the nationalisation law.'[42] This, however, was not all. Next day, June 7, *The Times* carried an announcement by Dr Musaddiq's Parliamentary Under-Secretary, M. Fatimi, that in addition a second three-man commission, this time of political members of the Parliamentary Mixed Committee, was also to proceed to Khuzistan (compare Sir Francis Shepherd's suggestion of May 11: cf p. 173).

Growing criticism of Dr Musaddiq in the Persian Press had coincided with a spate of anti-British vituperation. His Majesty's Embassy at Tehran, as it reported on June 4, 1951, had previously imagined that the anti-British agitation 'was mainly confined to large towns and particularly Tehran',[40] but, as was noticed in the Foreign Office, it had 'evidently been an eye-opener' for the Embassy to receive a report of May 26 from Shiraz on the hostile reception of a touring British cinema-van in that traditionally friendly district. Against a background of hostile broadcasts by Tehran Radio the Persian authorities indulged in a series of pinpricks against British interests, though Dr Musaddiq did not then implement with his signature the most serious of them, a decree of May 21 imposing customs dues on the Anglo-Iranian Oil Company in contravention of the concession of 1933. But the grant of Persian residence permits to British subjects was delayed, no action was taken against the editors of Persian newspapers which slandered Sir Francis Shepherd and his staff, and despite representations by His Majesty's Ambassador two prominent British correspondents, the representatives of Reuters and Mr Sefton Delmer of the *Daily Express*, had recently been expelled from Persia. On June 5 Mr Bowker presented these complaints to the Persian Ambassador in London[43] but did not mention the suspended decree of May 21 against the company.

On June 7, 1951, Sir Francis Shepherd transmitted unconfirmed reports that the Temporary Board of the National Iranian Oil Company had secret instructions to encourage Persian workers at Abadan to strike in favour of nationalisation, and that Dr Musaddiq hoped to dispossess the Anglo-Iranian Oil Company without the use of force.[44] The three members of the Temporary Board were officials, M. Bazargan, Deputy Minister of Education and Director of the Tehran Technical Institute, and MM. Bayat and Aliabadi. They would work under the guidance of the three-man Parliamentary Mixed Commission, which comprised MM. Matin Daftari, Makki and Ardalan. On June 8 His Majesty's Ambassador reported that M. Makki had stated that the object of their journey was to introduce the provisional directors to Persian members of the Anglo-Iranian Oil Company. The comparatively moderate M.

---

[42] EP 1531/529.
[43] EP 1051/17 and 20.
[44] EP 1531/552.

Daftari said that the mission was face-saving and fact-finding, to study administrative machinery without interfering with the running of the company or giving instructions; he would restrain the fiery oratory of M. Makki. M. Daftari, regarded as the most authoritative of the three, forecast that they would stay a week in Khuzistan. He wished to be back in Tehran for discussions with the mission of the Anglo-Iranian Oil Company. Sir Francis Shepherd suggested that if the Persians behaved as foretold, the company's employees should be helpful to them. The Foreign Office understood that instructions in that sense had already been issued.[45]

Already on June 7 His Majesty's Consul-General at Khorramshahr had reported that the situation in the oilfields at Agha Jari was causing considerable uneasiness. Persian labour was going slow and showing increasing signs of truculence. This was supported by the notoriously anti-British military Governor, General Majlessi. At Abadan Persian officials had begun to interfere, ordering the Anglo-Iranian Oil Company to re-engage three known Tudeh agitators, demanding houses and cars, and proposing to send accountants to inspect the company's books. On the telegram conveying this intelligence the Secretary of State minuted to Sir William Strang: 'Significant?'[46] The Permanent Under-Secretary initialled underneath on June 11.

On June 8 Mr Drake travelled from Abadan to Tehran in order to emphasise more alarmingly to His Majesty's Ambassador the trends reported by Major Capper on the previous day. Mr Drake also rather matched the recent report from Shiraz and intimated that sustained propaganda against the Anglo-Iranian Oil Company by Tehran Radio was producing an unexpectedly quick and strong effect so that he feared that if it continued for another week 'there was every likelihood of disturbances'.[47] On the following day Sir Francis Shepherd called on Dr Musaddiq and made representations against this propaganda, though without much effect. His Majesty's Ambassador considered that Dr Musaddiq evidently intended to exploit the situation in order to exert pressure on the Anglo-Iranian Oil Company. Sir Francis Shepherd warned the Persian Premier that 'we should hold the Persian Government responsible for damage to British lives and property'.[48] His Majesty's Ambassador said that the nationalisation law was unworkable but it does not appear that he made any representation concerning the serious step towards its attempted implementation represented by the despatch to Abadan of the Persian Temporary Board, plus the Parliamentary Commission; or that he sought at all events to secure a firm assurance that their role would in fact be so strictly limited as it had been reassuringly made out; or indeed that he was instructed to make any such representations.

On the same day of June 9, 1951, the three-man Parliamentary Mixed Commission followed the Temporary Board and set out for Khuzistan. At Abadan the evacuation of British dependants on a voluntary basis was being hastened at the rate of 300 a week.[49] Whereas less than two months earlier Sir William Fraser had said, Sir William Strang had recorded, that 'if this ever happened . . . the company would be on its way out of Persia'.[50] A new and grave phase had opened in the

---

[45] EP 1531/562.
[46] EP 1531/628.
[47] EP 1531/566.
[48] *Ibid.*
[49] EP 1611/18G.
[50] EP 1531/199.

Abadan crisis.

The darkening scene at Abadan was matched by an adverse climate in important parts of the international field. On June 10 Mr Nehru told a Press conference that India was 'positively sympathetic' to Persian nationalisation of the oil industry, and made remarks which Mr Herbert Morrison considered 'most unhelpful and uncalled for'.[51] General Sir Archibald Nye, United Kingdom High Commissioner in India, lodged a very vigorous protest with the more friendly but less representative Indian Ministry of External Affairs. In the other great republic among the liberal democracies Mr Gore-Booth, head of the British Information Service, had written on June 3 to the Foreign Office from Washington: 'I remain a little unhappy about the way Persia has gone in this country. There is too much of the good United States mediating between the stupidly backward British and the naughty Persians. The unanimity with which criticism has concentrated on Anglo-Iranian and personalised itself in its application to Sir William Fraser would startle you. He has just become public villain number one, even if not many people . . . say so publicly . . . Anglo-Iranian don't do anything for themselves here either.'[52]

In some countries, notably Syria, British agencies were, however, particularly successful in inspiring favourable publicity with regard to Persian oil. Although Syrian opinion was generally sympathetic to Persia in the dispute, His Majesty's Embassy at Damascus did conspicuously good work in ensuring that articles favourable to the British case were written up and published in the Syrian Press, which could then be quoted back to Persia.

On June 11 Sir Francis Shepherd telegraphed a recommendation for increased British broadcasts in Persian. It was only thereafter that it was ascertained in the Foreign Office that an earlier decision to add a quarter of an hour to the existing three-quarters of an hour each evening on the Persian service of the BBC had been cancelled owing to the general policy of economy recently imposed upon the BBC: apparently an illustration of the difficulty of ensuring full coordination between the Foreign Office and the BBC even in regard to what was undoubtedly the most tellingly important British instrument of publicity in Persia in that period of crisis. In the Foreign Office Mr C.F.R. Barclay now pursued the question urgently and effectively. An additional morning broadcast of a quarter of an hour on the Persian service began on June 20 and a week later a further quarter of an hour was added at dawn (cf p. 265).

The Foreign Office, working as necessary through British Embassies, was also highly successful in general in ensuring that Western nations would not, except in agreed cases, supply oil experts to the Persian Government. The French Government was in friendly cooperation with His Majesty's Government, notably concerning the recent agreement of the French jurist, Professor G. Gidel, to act as legal adviser to the Persian Government, as he had done earlier, during the negotiation of the Supplemental Agreement. If, in a Press interview published on June 1, Professor Gidel had shown greater sympathy with the Persian case than had been expected,[53] the Anglo-Iranian Oil company a fortnight later welcomed the appointment of Count Carafa, the deputy head of the Azienda Generale Italiana dei Petroli, the Italian

---

[51] EP 1531/644.
[52] PG 14537/10.
[53] EP 1531/482 and 508.

government-owned concern, as an adviser to the Persian Government on oil nationalisation.[54] Dr Musaddiq had expressly requested such an expert of the Italian Government, which nominated Count Carafa in courteous concert with His Majesty's Government and the Anglo-Iranian Oil Company. They preferred him to another and hoped that he might perhaps get the Persian Government to appreciate the practical problems of nationalisation.

Meantime, on the British side, it was announced on June 8, 1951, that at the request of the Minister of Fuel and Power, the three main British oil companies trading internationally, the Shell Petroleum Company, the Anglo-Iranian Oil Company and Trinidad Leaseholds Limited had formed an Oil Supply Advisory Committee to advise His Majesty's Government in that field with particular reference to defence. Although it was denied that the constitution of this industrial committee was related to the situation in Persia, there was promptly referred to it a joint memorandum of May 22 by Shell and Anglo-Iranian estimating the oil position if Abadan shut down (cf pp. 130-1). A related question here, which Mr L.F. Murphy of the Ministry of Fuel and Power mentioned to Mr A.K. Potter of the Treasury in a letter of May 28 concerning this memorandum, was the unlikely possibility of restoring the Anglo-Dutch refinery at Haifa to full capacity.[55] Since the Arab-Israeli war the pipeline from Iraq had been closed and British tankers bound for Haifa had come under an Egyptian embargo on shipping passing through the Suez Canal to Israel.

On June 15 the Ministry of Fuel and Power instructed its representative in Washington, in the light of the slow consideration of the British companies' memorandum by American oil companies, to inform the Petroleum Administration for Defence, an agency of the Department of the Interior, that His Majesty's Government considered that Anglo-American planning for an emergency, such as an interruption in Persian oil supplies, should be undertaken 'with utmost dispatch'.[56] This inaugurated what was probably the most fruitful aspect of Anglo-American collaboration during the Abadan crisis. Planning to meet a cessation of all oilflow from Persia nevertheless formed a bleak background to the arrival in Tehran on June 11, 1951, of the negotiating mission of the Anglo-Iranian Oil Company.

By an ominous conjunction it was on the same day of June 11 that the Persian three-man Parliamentary Mixed Commission, having arrived in the area of Abadan, had the Persian flag hoisted over the General Management Office of the Anglo-Iranian Oil Company at Khorramshahr, in which building the company had allotted rooms to the commission. It also erected a noticeboard announcing that the company was under the temporary management of the National Oil Company of Iran. The general manager there of the Anglo-Iranian Oil company, Mr Drake, apparently did not at once protest in writing, in accordance with the terms of his standing instructions since May 2 (cf p. 165), against this blatant try-on. He did, however, protest vigorously in person at 'a very stormy meeting' which he had on the following day of June 12 with the Parliamentary Mixed Commission and the Temporary Board of Directors. The Persians asked Mr Drake to hand over organisational charts of the industry, a statement of recent sales and 75 percent of

---

[54] EP 1531/625.
[55] UES 15327/7.
[56] UES 15320/19.

monies thenceforth accruing therefrom. The general manager asked for written texts of these demands, which he must refer to his directors in London. When the Persians threatened that he must comply with their demands, Mr Drake, who became very angry, stated that 'he could not and would not obey them'. Subsequently the Foreign Secretary telegraphed the following message for Mr Drake: 'I admire his spirit and respect his firm stand.'[57] This firm stand was not, however, supported by a minatory official communication made to the Persian Government, comparable to that which Mr Hoare had made in the face of a similar try-on in 1932 (cf p. 40). This was one example of a certain neglect, perhaps, of precedents form the previous occasion upon which the Persian Government had arbitrarily overridden the concession of the Anglo-Iranian Oil Company.

In Tehran Sir Francis Shepherd was becoming increasingly apprehensive that local conditions at Abadan might deteriorate more seriously than in the preceding April. On June 14 he instructed Major Capper at Khorramshahr to express to the head of the Persian commissioners the surprise of His Majesty's Ambassador at their having issued a communiqué stating that the employees of the Anglo-Iranian Oil Company were now considered to be employees of the National Iranian Oil Company; whereas in fact British employees could not have their contracts cancelled without their consent.[58] Already on the previous day Mr Jackson had telegraphed to Mr Drake from Tehran that he and Sir Francis Shepherd were making the strongest representations and that 'it will be clearly indicated to the Iranian Government that discussions cannot take place here while our management is being harassed in the south with consequent unsettling effect on British staff'.[59] On the following day of June 14 Mr Herbert Morrison in the House of Commons made a similar statement, which concluded: 'It is obvious that the discussions in Tehran cannot proceed properly if the atmosphere is vitiated by precipitate Persian action in the oilfields.'[60]

5. Failure of the Anglo-Iranian Oil Company's Mission to Tehran (Jackson Proposals), June 14-19

The precise application of the above statements remained somewhat uncertain in view of the fact that on the same day of June 14, 1951, conversations opened in Tehran between the delegation of the Anglo-Iranian Oil Company, headed by Mr Jackson, and a Persian delegation led by M. Varasteh, the Minister of Finance; and that at this meeting representations from the company as to the necessity for a 'minimum of interference' with its operations while the talks proceeded were answered by the Persians with nothing more than a vague assurance.[61] On the same day Sir Francis Shepherd reported on 'the taunting tone of the Tehran Press and jubilations over the Company at Abadan'.[62] The British reasons for not suspending negotiations in Tehran were evidently strong, especially in view of His Majesty's Ambassador's assessment (cf p. 203) that it would be unwise to play for the downfall of Dr Musaddiq. Nevertheless the conversations in Tehran that June, following upon those at Washington in April, perhaps suggest that British diplomacy then, too

[57] EP 1531/607.
[58] EP 1531/605.
[59] EP 1531/895.
[60] Parliamentary Debates, 5th Series, H. of C., Vol. 488, col. 2517.
[61] EP 1531/611.
[62] EP 1531/612.

acutely conscious if anything of its relatively weak position, was in some danger of neglecting the delicate art of not rupturing contacts while yet gravely impressing others with the seriousness of infringing British interests and the heavy consequences which such action was liable to incur. As it was, the absence of strong British reaction first to the despatch to Abadan of the Persian nationalising commissions and then to their initial and symbolic try-on of hoisting the Persian flag over British property at Khorramshahr was to usher in a sweltering summer of British humiliation in Southern Persia.

At the first meeting in Tehran with [the] Anglo-Iranian Oil Company on June 14 M. Varasteh promptly declared that discussion of practical arrangements for settling the oil dispute must be preceded by acceptance by the company of three preconditions matching the demands made locally of Mr Drake two days earlier: Persian dealings of the company to be made only in conjunction with the Persian provisional board of directors, submission of accounts of all sales since the nationalisation law of March 20, and remission of their proceeds to the Persian Government, which would deposit a quarter of them in a bank against the company's claim for compensation. It was concluded on the British side that the Persians wanted to lay their hands on the cash, were unwilling to depart from the strict letter of the nationalisation law, and had, by their insistence upon the preconditions, deliberately frustrated the British hope of gaining a week's grace 'for "sapping and mining"' by initial arguments to demonstrate the impracticability of the law.[63]

On the same day of June 14 in London Mr Bowker ascertained the views of Miss Lambton, who repeated her criticism of the Anglo-Iranian Oil Company while recognising that it was the scapegoat for the complete failure of Persian social policies. She considered that His Majesty's Government should, a month ago, have strengthened its organisation for public relations in Tehran in order covertly to undermine the position of Dr Musaddiq. Miss Lambton suggested the despatch from Oxford to Tehran of Mr R.C. Zaehner, who was said to have been very successful in comparable work there during the Second World War. Mr Bowker thought this suggestion worth considering 'in spite of the well-known views of the Americans on matters of this kind, when it comes to other countries and not themselves'.[64]

The suggestion in question came to be associated with contacts which were then being pursued by the Foreign Office with Colonel G.E. Wheeler who had wide experience in intelligence in the east and had served as Counsellor in His Majesty's Embassy in Tehran until 1950. He was to return thither in July 1951 with the title of Information Counsellor. Mr Zaehner also proceeded to Tehran. In the absence of further evidence it is impossible to say whether or not these keen initiatives were related to, or even substitutes for, the shelved proposal from Mr Berthoud for a secret diplomatic sounding in the Persian capital. It would in any case seem likely that they were more or less related to a decision which was evidently taken shortly afterwards, in contradiction of Sir Francis Shepherd's advice of June 15, for affording British support to a potential Persian successor to Dr Musaddiq: as will subsequently appear.

Meantime sapping and mining operations were being conducted, in no secret fashion, by the Persians at Abadan. Despite a promise to the contrary M. Makki, in particular, indulged in provocative speeches against the Anglo-Iranian Oil

---

[63] EP 1531/623.
[64] EP 1531/674.

Company. On June 15 Mr Drake conducted the Persian Governor-General, M. Amir Alai, the Provisional Board and the Mixed Commission on a three-hour tour of the installations at Abadan. Despite the efforts of M. Makki and rather to the surprise of Mr Drake, the Persian party was unable to elicit any complaints from Persian employees: M. Makki 'laughingly agreed that from that point of view things were better than he had supposed'. Persian authorities appeared shaken by Mr Drake's firm refusal to hand over installations and he recommended adherence to that attitude even if it should temporarily impede negotiations as Tehran. The British general manager noticed that 'the party became visibly gloomier as they realised the vastness of [the] enterprise and one asked anxiously if we had any news of [the] Tehran negotiations'.[65]

The demands which the Persian negotiators in Tehran had made on June 14 were considered in the Foreign Office, in Whitehall generally, by the Anglo-Iranian Oil Company and also, it was reported, by the State Department in Washington, to be wholly unreasonable and unacceptable. A Foreign Office telegram of June 16 to Sir Francis Shepherd described the Persian demands as apparently 'designed to remove all hope of negotiations except on terms of complete capitulation'.[66] This reading corresponded only too well to the character of the second meeting which the company's delegation in Tehran, on the following day, held with the Persians, led this time not by the Minister of Finance but by Dr Shayegan, a member of the Mixed Oil Committee. He presented a demand, virtually an ultimatum, that the company's reply to the Persian desiderata should be received by noon on June 19, subsequently extended by Dr Musaddiq to that evening: failing which the Persian Government would be compelled to take action on June 20. In Abadan MM. Matin Daftari and Makki subsequently underlined this threat, with its local implications, to Mr Drake. He, however, telegraphed to Tehran that he hoped that Mr Jackson would not be influenced by this transparent attempt to influence the company's reply.[67]

On June 17, 1951, the same day that Dr Shayegan imposed the Persian time-limit, Sir Francis Shepherd delivered orally a message from the Secretary of State to the Persian Premier, who was in bed having American blood-transfusions. This message stressed the need that the negotiations in Tehran should be conducted in a friendly atmosphere and made representations concerning provocative Persian actions, more particularly with regard to anti-British publicity and to interference at Abadan. Dr Musaddiq said that the announcement that employees of the Anglo-Iranian Oil Company were regarded as employed by the National Iranian Oil Company had been made without the knowledge of the Persian Government. He was, however, unyielding, in substance, in his insistence on the Persian nationalisation law and consequent demand that the Anglo-Iranian Oil Company should knuckle under.

As regards His Majesty's Ambassador's representation, on behalf of Mr Morrison, concerning hostile Persian publicity, it was an unhappy coincidence that on that same day a Persian newspaper, *Hameh*, published a scurrilously insulting attack against Sir Francis Shepherd in person, characterising him as 'this fool who is void of all moral principles' and who 'should either be expelled from Iran or shut

---

[65] EP 1531/895.
[66] EP 1531/623.
[67] EP 1531/723.

up in a lunatic asylum'.[68] His Majesty's Embassy subsequently proposed that the editor responsible should be punished in accordance with Persian law and that the Persian Government should tender a written expression of regret. It does not appear, however, that this British representation produced any greater effect than other similar ones, for instance concerning the abusive language of M. Makki. The difficulties confronting Sir Francis Shepherd were appreciated by Mr Morrison who had telegraphed to him on June 15 to convey his 'approval of the manner in which you have handled our relations with the Persian Government since the dispute . . . arose. Your defence of British interests has been both judicious and robust.'[69]

On the day after the barren conversation of June 17 between Sir Francis Shepherd and Dr Musaddiq, the latter emphasised to M. Mustafa Fateh, the senior Persian employee of the Anglo-Iranian Oil Company, that the Persian Government was 'determined to get rid of''[70] the company and was only prepared to regard it as a trustee for the Government during a strictly limited interim: Persian public feeling against the company was so strong that in future no Government would dare to be associated with it. The Persian Premier went further than ever before against the company in his categorical insistence now that it must accept dispossession under Article 2 of the law of May 2. Next day, June 19, Dr Musaddiq particularly informed M. Fateh that the remarks which included this intimation could be considered as an official message to Mr Jackson. On the same day His Majesty's Ambassador told the Shah in conversation that Dr Musaddiq had now made it clear that unless his full demands were accepted he would stop the flow of oil at Abadan. The Shah appreciated the danger of this but was not hopeful of securing the resignation of his Prime Minister, who, he felt, must resign on grounds of the demonstrable failure of his policy. This view was shared by Dr Grady, to whom Dr Musaddiq had spoken as to M. Fateh.

Meanwhile in London there was general agreement with the view telegraphed by the Anglo-Iranian Oil Company's mission in Tehran, in accordance with His Majesty's Ambassador: namely that the only practicable proposal to put to the Persians was a combination of the two suggested arrangements which were most favourable to them, out of the five alternatives elaborated by the Working Party on Oil. This meant that the Anglo-Iranian Oil Company should envisage future relations with the National Iranian Oil Company in terms of a combination of leasing and management agreements. The significant advance in favour of Persia from the British proposals of April 26 was that now the Persian assets of the Anglo-Iranian Oil Company would be vested, not in a new British company, but in the National Iranian Oil Company. And the Anglo-Iranian Oil Company would offer prompt financial sweetening.

On June 18 the British ministerial committee on Persia accordingly approved the terms of the *aide-mémoire* which Mr Jackson handed to the Persian delegation at their third meeting at eight o'clock on the evening of June 19. The *aide-mémoire,* which was warmly welcomed by Dr Grady, began with the 'constructive interim proposal' that the Anglo-Iranian Oil Company should make the Persian Government an advance of £10 million against any sum which might become due to it under an

---

[68] EP 1051/23.
[69] EP 1531/646.
[70] EP 1531/659.

eventual agreement, 'on the understanding that the Government undertakes not to interfere with the company's operations while discussions are proceeding'.[71] The Persian Government was further offered a monthly payment of £3 million from July onwards till an arrangement was reached.

The main proposal of the Anglo-Iranian Oil Company's *aide-mémoire* of June 19 was that a possible basis for an arrangement might be found along the lines of a scheme whereby the company's Persian assets would be vested in a Persian National Oil Company which, in consideration of this, would grant the use of the assets to a new company to be established by the Anglo-Iranian Oil Company. The new company would have a number of Persian directors and would operate on behalf of the Persian National Oil Company. Oil distribution in Persia would be transferred on favourable terms to another company entirely under Persian ownership and operation. The *aide-mémoire* ended by refusing the Persian demand that the company should hand over the total proceeds, less expenses, from sales of Persian oil as from March 20, from which 25 percent would be allocated for compensation to the company: 'The delegation has come out for discussions and regards it as unjustifiable that the Persian Government should put forward a demand of this kind before discussions have even started.'

On receiving this *aide-mémoire* the Persian delegation, again led by Dr Shayegan, withdrew to consider it. Half an hour later the Persian spokesman told the delegation of the Anglo-Iranian Oil Company that its *aide-mémoire* conflicted with the Persian oil nationalisation law of May 2. Discussions must depend upon prior compliance with the Persian demands made on the basis of article 2 of the law, providing for the prompt dispossession of the company. Dr Shayegan expressed surprise that there should have been a postponement in the negotiations to allow for the formulation of proposals such as those advanced by the Anglo-Iranian Oil Company. Mr Jackson said that the company accepted the principle of Persian oil nationalisation, but not the letter of the law, whereof Article 2 was quite unacceptable in principle. He asked, what next, 'to which Shayegan replied that we must close the discussions'.[72] On June 20 the delegation of the Anglo-Iranian Oil Company was instructed to leave Tehran. The first special mission sent in 1951 to negotiate with the Persian Government concerning oil nationalisation had failed.

On the day on which the negotiations in Tehran were to break down Mr Drake and the two Persian commissions in Abadan had a meeting which, in contrast to that of June 12, was 'most amicable'.[73] The British general manager agreed to study the cases of certain Persian agitators dismissed from the staff of the company and now proposed by the Persians for re-engagement; but he held out no hope of this. Mr Drake also refused to allot a superior bungalow to each Persian commissioner, except on payment of rent. The Persians then dropped this demand for fear of compromising their legal position. Mr Drake went as far as he judged proper towards meeting a series of other Persian requests for copies of receipts of oil exported by his company, for statistics of staff and organisational charts and for permission to copy accounts. Under the last head Mr Drake agreed to supply what was already available to the auditors of the Persian Government, namely accounts of royalties.

---

[71] Cmd 8425, p. 42.
[72] EP 1531/663.
[73] EP 1531/723.

Next day, June 20, Mr Jackson telegraphed from Tehran to Mr Drake that if he could maintain this limitation so much the better, but that if he were pressed by the Persians he should make available to them such other books as they demanded.[74] This important concession suggested the extent to which the Anglo-Iranian Oil Company was prepared to go in letting the Persian oil authorities in to their affairs at Abadan.

On June 19 in London there had been a Parliamentary exchange in the House of Commons concerning the Persian crisis, before the breakdown of negotiations in Tehran was certain. The Conservative Member for South Paddington, Mr Somerset de Chair, asked the Foreign Secretary whether His Majesty's Government would if necessary take steps to protect the installations at Abadan from Persian seizure. In reply Mr Herbert Morrison reiterated the pledge to protect British lives, but added: 'The other point does raise wider considerations, and I have not given specific answers about it, and do not think I should.' Mr Somerset de Chair reminded Mr Morrison of his Parliamentary statement of June 4 that His Majesty's Government had every right to intervene in defence of this great British interest in Persia (cf p. 199). The Foreign Secretary, however, declined to add to this statement.

On this same occasion in the House of Commons Mr Herbert Morrison also had an exchange with Mr Anthony Eden, who asked him to bear in mind 'that both Abadan and Haifa, the two largest British-owned refineries in the world, are not operating at full capacity'. The Egyptian Government had for two years past been unmoved by British representations that it should raise its embargo on shipping passing through the Suez Canal to Israel, and notably Haifa (cf p. 207). Mr Eden had earlier estimated the resultant loss of petroleum products to Great Britain at not less than £20 million a year. He now observed that in this matter of transit through the canal 'we are absolutely within our international rights, and, if the Egyptian Government are not willing to accord us those rights, there are measures that lie in our power to take with our Allies to ensure the observation of our rights'. When the Foreign Secretary expressed willingness to consider any suggestions from Mr Eden on this point, the latter made the interesting suggestion that, if necessary, it might be 'worthy of consideration to send one of our tankers to the Suez Canal under, if possible, allied, but at any rate effective escort'.[75]

It appears that Mr Eden had in fact put this suggestion privately to the Foreign Secretary something like a month earlier.[76] The Foreign Office had accordingly, in a letter of May 25, 1951,[77] requested the Chiefs of Staff to consider the military possibility of such an operation. On June 6 they advised that it was liable to have serious implications. The Foreign Office agreed and considered that, in general, the disadvantages would outweigh the advantages. On the same day of June 19 on which Mr Morrison had his Parliamentary exchange with Mr Eden concerning the possible escorted passage of a British tanker through the Suez Canal, Mr R.E. Barclay, Principal Private Secretary to the Secretary of State, recorded: 'The Secretary of State had a word about this with Mr Eden who was not altogether convinced by the Department's arguments.'[76] It would rather appear that these arguments may not yet have included, specifically at any rate, those supplied from Washington by Mr

---

[74] EP 1531/677.
[75] Parliamentary Debates, 5th Series, H. of C., Vol. 489, cols. 241-2.
[76] JE 1261/94G.
[77] JE 1261/82G.

Burrows in a letter of June 14 (received on June 17) to Mr Roger Allen, Head of African Department.

Mr Burrows reported that the State Department had mentioned that in London 'certain leading members of the Opposition' had put the suggestion under discussion to the American Ambassador. The State Department, continued Mr Burrows, 'views with horror the possibility that an attempt should be made to force the passage of a tanker in this manner. They consider that it would have the most damaging results on the Western position in the Middle East and might at the same time give a new lease of life to the question of the nationalisation of the canal.'[78] Mr Allen inscribed this letter with an exclamation mark. The Secretary of State saw this letter, probably on June 21. Two days later the Foreign Office was informed that the Prime Minister had commented on the suggestion under review: 'I agree with the Chiefs of Staff.'[76]

Meantime, on the more immediate level, the Foreign Secretary on June 20 reported to Parliament on the failure of the mission to Tehran of the Anglo-Iranian Oil Company, and said of its rejected offer to the Persian Government: 'Money for present needs is there, acceptance of the principle of nationalisation is there, and an obvious foundation for fruitful partnership is there: His Majesty's Government are convinced that all fair-minded opinion will regard the company's proposals as eminently reasonable.'[79] This conviction was certainly justified with regard to informed opinion in both England and America. Criticism there was directed not against the content of the proposals but against their tardiness. Mr Anthony Eden suggested in Parliament on June 21 that they 'might with advantage have been made rather earlier'.[80] In the same debate the Labour Member for Coventry East, Mr Richard Crossman, said that if the latest British offer 'had been made immediately after Razmara's death and accompanied by a top-rank mission to Tehran, [it] might well have saved the position at that time. I think it was a grave error that that was not done, and we shall pay very heavily for failing to do it.'[81] The background there was the lack of negotiating progress throughout 1950, the accepted lull even in February 1951 (cf p. 119), the lateness, perhaps, of full appreciation in the Foreign Office of the constitutional powers of His Majesty's Government in relation to the resistant Anglo-Iranian Oil Company, and the overlaying of the proposal lately made by Lord Mountbatten (cf pp. 139-40 and 157) for a new and urgently imaginative approach through a special mission to Tehran. The *Washington Post* commented on the rejected British offer to Persia that it was reasonable, but made a couple of months too late.

---

[78] JE 1261/107G.
[79] Parliamentary Debates, 5th Series, H. of C., Vol. 489, cols. 520-1.
[80] Parliamentary Debates, 5th Series, H. of C., Vol. 489, col. 751.
[81] *Ibid*, col. 780.

CHAPTER VIII

FROM THE PERSIAN ANTI-SABOTAGE BILL TO THE INTERIM INJUNCTION OF THE INTERNATIONAL COURT OF JUSTICE, JUNE 20-JULY 5, 1951

1. The Persian Anti-Sabotage Bill and the departure from Abadan of the British General Manager, June 20-25

His Majesty's Embassy at Tehran reported that the Persian Press struck 'a note of jubilation' at the breakdown of negotiations with the Anglo-Iranian Oil Company: 'the brusque rejection of the AIOC proposals . . . revived, to a certain extent, the fast waning prestige of Dr Musaddiq and his followers.'[1] He quickly exploited this advantage and, in a broadcast on June 20, 1951, paid a significant tribute to the support received from the Shah. On the same day the Persian Council of Ministers issued decrees providing that: no operational instructions issued by the Anglo-Iranian Oil Company should be valid unless countersigned by the Persian Temporary Board; Persian officials should take over the installation of the company's subsidiary, the Kermanshah Petroleum Company, at Kermanshah and Naft-i-Shah in West Persia; Persian officials were to assume direction of other departments of the Anglo-Iranian Oil Company including its office in Tehran and sales organisation in Persia, while its information departments in Persia should be dissolved; on all the company's nameboards in Persia its name should be replaced by that of the National Iranian Oil Company; revenues from all sales of oil should be deposited to the account of the National Iranian Oil Company.

On June 21 the General Manager at Abadan of the Anglo-Iranian Oil Company received instructions from the Temporary Board of the National Iranian Oil Company for the execution of the decrees of the previous day. Mr Drake was also ordered to stop all leave to his staff. On the same day the Persian police removed the Anglo-Iranian Oil Company's nameboard from its general office at Khorramshahr. At its office in Tehran this function was performed by a large crowd which forced its way into the building, and similar demonstrations against the company occurred elsewhere in the capital. Against this background on June 21 Dr Musaddiq informed the Majlis, which had failed to produce a quorum that morning, that his Government would not be responsible for security after 4 pm unless the Majlis met to give him a vote of confidence. The Shah and M. Sayyid Zia had been trying to persuade the Deputies to absent themselves, and over 40 still did so that afternoon. In the face, however, of Dr Musaddiq's renewed skill in intimidation there was only one abstention when the 91 other Deputies present in the Majlis gave him a unanimous vote of confidence. Even in the more responsible but now cowed Senate, the same vote was carried by 41, with three abstentions.

Also on that crowded day of June 21 in the Persian capital the Majlis was presented, under procedure of 'double urgency', with an anti-sabotage bill. This provided for penalties up to that of death, to be imposed by military courts, against 'any persons engaging treacherously or with ill intent in activities in connexion with the operation of the Persian National Oil Industry'. And on that night the printing works of the Anglo-Iranian Oil Company at Abadan were forcibly seized by the

---

[1] PG 13444/7.

Persian authorities, and the printers were compelled by threats to print forms of receipt whereby the masters of oil tankers would acknowledge that oil received on board at Abadan was received from the National Iranian Oil Company, to whom payment was due. This form of receipt would be the trump-card for Dr Musaddiq to play in implementation of his threat to stop the flow of oil from Abadan unless the British company capitulated. Though indeed his lieutenant on the spot, M. Makki, was more crudely indulging in wild threats to shut the valves on the pipelines, which might produce explosions and conflagration.

Such was the black news reaching Whitehall as it debated and decided the next steps after the failure of the delegation to Tehran from the Anglo-Iranian Oil Company: though, in the press of events, the important tabling of the Persian anti-sabotage bill appears to have been only briefly noted in the British Press and it was not reported by His Majesty's Ambassador till June 24, after it had produced serious consequences.

On June 20, 1951, the Foreign Office produced an admirably clear memorandum, so far as it went, which, on the assumption of Persian prohibition of oil export from Abadan, recommended the following immediate steps in particular: all the European staff of the Anglo-Iranian Oil Company in South Persia should be concentrated in Abadan, where they could if necessary be protected by Operation Midget, whereas 'scattered in the fields, they are hostages to fortune';[2] the Foreign Secretary should advise the House of Commons of the economic consequences of such a stoppage imposed by the Persians, and his statement should also seek to restore the morale of the company's staff, which should be prevented from dispersing; His Majesty's Government should immediately take the action from which it had hitherto refrained in relation to the International Court of Justice, by applying to it for an interim injunction to restrain the Persian Government. If forced, the company should acquiesce in a Persian stoppage of export from Abadan or any other action against its operations. Meanwhile the company should try to ensure that as few tankers as possible came to Abadan to buy from the Persians. These measures taken, His Majesty's Government should ride out the storm till wiser counsels prevailed in Persia. Meanwhile it should exert maximum diplomatic pressure and if possible organise opposition to Dr Musaddiq, beaming intensive publicity at the Persian people. In reserve were the possibilities of economic sanctions and of military action in the form of Operation Midget for safeguarding and evacuating British staff at Abadan.

The Foreign Office memorandum of June 20 was considered that day at a meeting of the Ministerial Committee on Persia, attended by Mr Morrison, Mr Gaitskell, Mr Shinwell and Mr Noel-Baker; others present included Lord Jowitt as Lord Chancellor, the Chief of the Imperial General Staff, Sir William Fraser, Sir William Strang, Sir Donald Fergusson, Mr Bowker and Mr Furlonge. Sir William Fraser said that if tankers were prevented from loading at Abadan, the storage tanks there would be filled. This would take a fortnight, during which the staff could be withdrawn from the outlying fields; or they could be withdrawn forthwith. In either case there would be danger of fires resulting. Only the month before the company had in fact experienced a terrible fire at Rig 20 in the Naft Safid field, with flames 400ft high; it took over a month, under the direction of an American expert specially flown in,

---

[2] EP 1531/709G.

to quell this eruption.

The meeting of June 20, contrary to the proposal of the Foreign Office, provisionally agreed that withdrawal from the oilfields should be gradual. It was considered better to let the Persians themselves run the machine to a standstill rather than for the company to halt operations; though it was recognised that this decision might have to be reconsidered. Sir William Fraser further made the important statement that other oil companies had informed him that they would not pay the Persian Government for oil. The meeting agreed that the Anglo-Iranian Oil Company for its part should in no circumstances make any such payment, but that if necessary tankers should be withdrawn.[3]

Thus, after only 10 days, the Persian presence at Abadan, backed by governmental determination at Tehran, was threatening to compel a dual British withdrawal from either flank of Abadan, a withdrawal of staff from the inland oilfields of supply, and of tankers for maritime export. In an endeavour to stem such developments the meeting of the Ministers took the impeccable decision to apply immediately to The Hague Court for an interim injunction against the Persian Government. Notice of this was given to the court next day. This move was backed by another precautionary decision taken at the meeting on June 20: reversing a decision of June 4, 12 further Hastings aircraft were now to be made available for Operation Midget. Field-Marshal Slim said that this operation could now be carried out at 36 hours' notice.[4]

On the economic side the Chancellor of the Exchequer represented at the meeting of June 20 that an immediate decision was required concerning possible Persian attempts to convert their holdings of sterling into dollars. The Ministers agreed that this should if possible be prevented but that a further decision concerning possible prohibition of British exports to Persia, notably of steel rails, should be deferred. The Minister of Fuel and Power said he was submitting a memorandum on the overall position of oil supply if supplies from Persia ceased.

Mr Noel-Baker in fact produced a memorandum on that day of June 20. He explained that of the 32-33 million tons of crude oil annually produced in Persia, 7½ million tons were exported to refineries in the United Kingdom, Europe and the Western Hemisphere, and the remainder refined at Abadan to yield 22 million tons of products (cf p. 130). If Persian oil ceased flowing the problem of supplying India, two-thirds of whose supplies came from Persia, would be especially serious, more particularly since she was considered to be the country most likely to enter into dealings with the Persian Government: a weak spot for Britain developed from the former base of her Asiatic power. The other main problem would be high-grade aviation spirit. It now appeared, however, that such were the facilities for quick expansion of output of both crude and refined products by British companies operating outside Persia (notably along the Arabian coast) and, above all, by American ones, that the ultimate annual deficit was reckoned at 1 million tons of crude and 3 million tons of refined products, or only some 2 ½ percent of world consumption outside North America.[5] A critical factor in practical terms would be cooperation with American oil companies for the most economical use of tankers.

---

[3] EP 1531/711.
[4] *Ibid.*
[5] EP 1531/710.

Those companies would need to concert emergency action and to be covered by the Department of Justice in respect of the anti-trust laws (cf p. 207).

The Minister of Fuel and Power further[6] estimated that, at any rate initially, British oil companies would be dependent on the Americans for 75 percent of the oil needed to replace Persian supplies: the key to so much in the policy of His Majesty's Government in the Persian crisis of 1951, even when it considered that, as Mr Gaitskell remarked at the meeting on June 20, 'the United States attitude throughout these difficult negotiations had been far from helpful'.[7] And it was estimated that the contemplated drawings on American oil supplies would cost about $350 million f.o.b. per annum. This figure was roughly equivalent to the gold and dollar balance earned by the sterling area in the first quarter of the year; during the current quarter, however, this balance was reduced to $54 million by growing weekly deficits which portended the financial crisis looming towards the autumn.

After allowing, however, for the obviously adverse factors, one can still appreciate the feeling then current in Whitehall that the position regarding oil supply was better than had been expected. This perhaps prompts the question whether a more thorough and ruthless consideration of the problem some months earlier, in the light of the latest world developments in oil production and refining, might perhaps have qualified to some extent the initial insistence upon the absolute indispensability of Abadan to the British economy, and so facilitated a more flexible and realistic approach to the problem in terms of economics. The opening for any such criticism would, however, seem to be distinctly limited since the Ministry of Fuel and Power was now, in effect, skilfully making the best of what promised to be a very bad job, such as could not earlier have been contemplated with any equanimity in view of the magnitude of the issues. Lately, a radical consideration of the effects of stoppage in Persian oil had, perhaps fortunately, been stimulated by the strikes at Abadan in April. As matters now stood the Foreign Secretary was at least able to give the House of Commons relative reassurance concerning oil supplies and to describe the reimposition in Great Britain of petrol rationing, only terminated in May 1950, as 'exceedingly unlikely'.[8]

On June 20, 1951, after the ministerial meeting, the Foreign Secretary in the House of Commons had referred to the 'most serious disaster to life and limb' liable to result from inexpert interference with the installations at Abadan, and reiterated that 'His Majesty's Government are not prepared to stand by idle if the lives of British subjects are in jeopardy'.[9] Mr Morrison, however, still would not go further, as regards protection of British property, when Mr Eden requested an assurance against any British evacuation. The Opposition asked for a debate, which was fixed for the following day.

On June 21 the Cabinet again considered a large military operation to hold the refinery at Abadan but, as it had done on May 10 (cf p. 168), again noted the political risks: the United States would oppose and general support in the Commonwealth and Security Council seemed unlikely; and there would be delay in mounting a large operation. The need for one might, however, perhaps be averted by a show of force

---

[6] EP 1531/768.
[7] EP 1531/711.
[8] Parliamentary Debates, 5th Series, H. of C., Vol. 489, col. 831.
[9] *Ibid*, col. 522.

in the vicinity of Abadan:[10] in effect by a policy of bluff.

In view, more particularly, of the Cabinet conclusion regarding Commonwealth support for intervention in Persia, it is perhaps noticeable that no consideration was apparently given to the possibility of taking soundings for such support at the conference of Commonwealth Defence Ministers which opened in London that same day of June 21. Though the meeting was held in London, instead of in Malta as originally proposed, for fear of further disturbing 'the very delicate situation in Persia'.[11] And the first of the conference's 'conclusions on strategy' began: 'The defence of the Middle East is vital to the security of the Commonwealth nations',[12] and Commonwealth reinforcement for British forces in the Middle East was a standing interest of the British Government (cf p. 70).

The debate on Persia in the House of Commons on June 21, 1951, was opened by Mr Eden, who notably declared: 'There are far, far wider implications about this business than what eventually happens about nationalisation or otherwise in the immediate Persian oil problem . . . What happens in Persia will have its immediate repercussions throughout the Middle East and beyond. This, indeed, has been very very obvious for a long time, and many will feel that once again failure to anticipate the future has bedevilled the present . . . In my view, evacuation would be disastrous. It would be an abject surrender to the threat of force.'[13] This opinion was echoed from the Government benches by the Member for Wednesbury, Mr S.N. Evans, who said: 'If we voluntarily abdicate the effect on British prestige from the Suez to Shanghai, from Abadan to the Falklands, would be disastrous.'[14]

Speaking before Mr Evans, Mr Duncan Sandys, Conservative Member for Streatham, had stressed the importance of denying Persian oil to Russia (though it might take her four or five years to construct oil pipelines from Abadan to the Caspian)[15] and had envisaged the possibility of British military intervention even at the cost of a Russian retort in kind. 'I submit to the House', continued Mr Sandys, 'that if we should be faced with the unhappy choice of dividing Persia or of leaving the Russians to dominate the whole of that country, I have no doubt in my mind that the lesser of these two evils is partition. Our policy in the past has rightly been to promote a free and independent Persia. If through the folly of the Persians we are compelled to give up that policy, it will certainly not be Britain's fault.'[16]

In this searching debate the Conservative Member for Lanark, Lord Dunglass (later Earl of Home), probed the immediate issue when he asked the Foreign Secretary to 'say that it is . . . policy to maintain the Abadan refinery under British management . . . that the protection which His Majesty's Government give will not only be if the lives of the British people in Abadan are threatened, but will extend to them if the Persians try to take physical control of the refinery and interfere with them in their legitimate duties'.[17] And from the Labour side the Member for Gloucestershire West, Mr Philips Price, who had personal knowledge of Abadan,

---

[10] EP 1531/760G.
[11] ZP 19/1G.
[12] ZP 19/7G.
[13] Parliamentary Debates, 5th Series, H. of C., Vol. 489, cols 747-52.
[14] *Ibid*, col. 767.
[15] *Ibid*, col. 809,
[16] *Ibid*, cols. 763-4.
[17] *Ibid*, cols. 770-1.

extended the Foreign Secretary's warning of the previous day concerning Persian interference by opining that 'one cannot draw a line between lives and installations'.[18]

The gravity of the crisis for the fortunes of Great Britain to an appreciable extent overrode party divisions even in the keenly divided parliament of 1951. Though there were naturally some sharp differences. Mr Richard Crossman, for example, took issue with Lord Dunglass and held that to land British troops in Persia to protect oil installations would amount to aggression against a friendly Power. In the same speech Mr Crossman criticised the alleged unfriendly 'activities of the American oil companies',[19] and also singled out by name, for their unhelpfulness, Mr McGhee and Mr Thornburg. Only the day before, His Majesty's Consul-General in Philadelphia had in fact reported that Mr Thornburg had publicly accused the Anglo-Iranian Oil Company, backed by His Majesty's Government, of intriguing in Persia.[20] As for Mr McGhee, even some months later he was still concerned to justify himself against Mr Crossman's criticism.[21] Though the latter was not the only Labour Member to animadvert against Mr McGhee, especially in relation to his recent tour of the Middle East. (Mr George Wigg: 'What I think Mr McGhee did was that in Persia he gave the Persians the impression that if we got out American technicians would go in.')[22]

In winding up the debate the Foreign Secretary said in the above connexion: 'There have been some people, not of outstanding importance, who were associated or have been associated with the American oil industry, who have said some foolish, unwise and perhaps dangerous things in the course of their travels through the Middle East. I am dealing with people who have been or are associated with the American oil industry. I think it would not be fair to hold the American oil companies responsible for their activities in this respect. It is only fair to say that we have had a good deal of help and cooperation from the State Department. I am saying 'as a whole', because I know the point to which my hon. Friend referred about one gentleman, and I do not wish to pursue it, but, as a whole, we have had considerable help and cooperation from the American State Department, and my Right Hon Friend the Minister of Fuel and Power assures me that, as far as the American oil companies are concerned, as companies in their corporate capacity, there is no evidence whatever that they have been conspiring against us; on the contrary they have given a good deal of help and assistance.'[23]

In the same speech the Foreign Secretary said as regards the main issue that the Opposition evidently held 'that something big and strong ought to be done about it', without being too specific. Mr Morrison argued: 'We are not in a period now when we can colonise countries which have reached the stage of self-government. We cannot do in the 20th century what was not uncommonly done in the 19th century. Moreover, we are part of the United Nations, and hon. Members opposite have to face the fact that the imperialism upon which they were brought up is dead. *Mr Eden*: I do not wish to interrupt the Foreign Secretary, but I have not heard one single

---

[18] *Ibid*, col. 809.
[19] *Ibid*, col. 775.
[20] EP 1531/855.
[21] EP 1531/1696.
[22] Parliamentary Debates, 5th Series, H. of C., Vol. 489, col. 801.
[23] *Ibid*, cols. 832-3.

speech in any part of the House which suggested colonising any part of Persia. Most of us know that Persia was a State even before Britain.'[24]

The Foreign Secretary went on to give the House of Commons the important intimation that the Government of the United States had favoured British acceptance of the principle of Persian nationalisation and 'were most anxious that every avenue should be explored . . . Let there be no mistake about the line of the United States Government in this matter. Therefore, I think it would be fair to say that they are in general accord with the policy of His Majesty's Government',[25] and agreed as to the necessity of protecting British lives. Mr Morrison would not go further towards answering the question posed by Lord Dunglass.

In the course of his speech the Foreign Secretary qualified Dr Musaddiq—not without a reservation from Mr Eden—as 'not a left-wing socialist or anything like that; he is a reactionary'. The Persian Government had diverted oil revenues which it was supposed to spend on social development under the Seven-Year Plan. 'It is not the first time in history', said Mr Morrison, 'that members of the upper classes and of extreme reactionary views have diverted . . . the attention of the working classes by preaching to them to have the foreigner . . . It may be that Dr Musaddiq has sown the wind and will reap a Communist whirlwind.'[26] This warning may conceivably have been not wholly uncongenial to Dr Musaddiq, who was to prove adept at playing upon American fears, in particular, that the only likely succession to himself would be Communism in Persia.

In conclusion the Foreign Secretary observed: 'In the Persian Government, we are dealing with an extraordinary Government, and it is somewhat difficult to follow them from day to day. There is the hope that they, having moved about so unexpectedly from day to day, may possibly one of these days move in the right direction. At any rate, let us sincerely hope so . . . We shall be only too pleased to cooperate with them . . . I am perfectly sure that an amicable settlement can be reached on the basis of the principle of nationalisation' as distinct from 'the letter of the law of the Majlis, which indeed, is little more than a series of resolutions'.[27] This optimistic conviction, however, would not appear to have brought full reassurance to the House of Commons as a whole. The Foreign Secretary was not specifically questioned, however, on the relation of his present formulation regarding British acceptance of the principle of nationalisation to the original one of May 19 (cf pp. [171-76) which had included the 'qualification to which His Majesty's Government attach importance' that any oil-settlement must prove satisfactory in other respects. Henceforth this qualification, originally thus emphasised by Mr Morrison himself, tended, in specification if not by presumption, to recede. In any case British acceptance of the principle of nationalisation, with its potential bearing on the British application of May 26 to the Hague Court (cf p. 191), was now, despite the failure of the Jackson Mission, not withdrawn.

On the day of Mr Morrison's speech, June 21, 1951, Mr Jackson, before leaving Tehran after the failure of his mission, addressed a letter to the Persian Minister of Finance warning him that the latest Persian measures against the Anglo-Iranian Oil

---

[24] *Ibid*, cols. 822 and 827.
[25] *Ibid*, col. 832.
[26] *Ibid*, cols. 825-6.
[27] Parliamentary Debates, 5th Series, H. of C., Vol. 489, col. 833.

Company risked provoking mass resignations from it, which would in turn necessitate closing down operations. This would be an expert and dangerous process and Mr Jackson requested that members of the Persian Temporary Board should be present at it for verification and, in effect, protection against accusations of sabotage. Sir Francis Shepherd transmitted a copy of this letter to the Persian Prime Minister and, when he rejected the communication as relating to domestic issues, to the Foreign Minister. On June 25 the latter sent a sharp reply denying that His Majesty's Government had grounds for interfering in the matter, holding that its non-recognition of the term 'ex-Anglo Iranian Oil Company', employed by Dr Musaddiq, was irrelevant, and alleging British provocation. Sir Francis Shepherd did not, in turn, return this note, and in the Foreign Office there was some satisfaction that the acid exchange remained unpublished.[28]

Meantime the Persians at Abadan on June 23 backed out of a temporary compromise on the key issue of tankers' oil receipts whereby Mr Drake had allowed them to be signed in favour of the National Iranian Oil Company subject to an endorsement by himself reserving the rights of the Anglo-Iranian Oil Company. He refused to permit signature of the Persian receipts otherwise. On the same day Mr Drake received a letter, signed by all three directors of the Persian Temporary Board, informing him that he was therefore guilty of sabotage. This menacing development was reported by His Majesty's Consul-General at Khorramshahr to His Majesty's Ambassador at Tehran, who on June 24 transmitted an authorisation from Mr Jackson to Mr Drake, in the present case of duress, to sign, under protest, any documents demanded; but only provided that all charges against him of sabotage were withdrawn. Otherwise, in view of the possible capital penalty, Mr Drake should forthwith leave Abadan for Basra. In the same telegram Sir Francis Shepherd instructed Major Capper to protest in the strongest terms to the local Persian authorities and to accompany Mr Drake when he visited the Persian Temporary Board 'in exercise of your established right to protect British subjects'.[29] This telegram was, as usual, repeated to the Foreign Office, where it was received, without minuted comment, at 6.35 pm on June 24.

At a meeting on the morning of June 25, 1951, the Persian Temporary Board refused to speak to Mr Drake in the presence of His Majesty's Consul-General. When Mr Drake was left alone with the board, it refused to withdraw the charge of sabotage against him. Mr Drake thereafter, without the knowledge of the Temporary Board, followed his instructions and immediately left Persia for Basra. The head of the huge organisation of the Anglo-Iranian Oil Company at Abadan had been forced to quit.

In London this information was given by the Foreign Secretary to a meeting of the ministerial committee on Persia held at four o'clock that afternoon. Mr Morrison described the precipitate departure of the General Manager as 'a most disquieting development, which clearly foreshadowed the disintegration of the AIOC organisation at Abadan'.[30] Some doubts were expressed whether this departure had been necessary; but suggestions that Mr Drake might in some manner return from Basra to Abadan were subsequently not pressed.

---

[28] EP 1531/769, 770, 894.
[29] EP 1531/708.
[30] EP 1531/848G.

Sir Francis Shepherd, who on June 25 protested to M. Kazimi against the accusation of sabotage against Mr Drake, for his part telegraphed to the Foreign Secretary at five o'clock that afternoon that 'Drake's departure would certainly have a bad effect on the morale of British staff'.[31] There is perhaps room for regret that His Majesty's Ambassador had not sent this warning and requested instructions before agreeing on the previous day to transmit the critical message from Mr Jackson to Mr Drake—it is uncertain whether Mr Jackson had himself previously consulted his management in London. As it was, instructions sent from Tehran to Abadan on the authority of the Anglo-Iranian Oil Company but with the endorsement of His Majesty's Ambassador had contributed to a further grave deterioration of the British position. As against such considerations of policy, the concern for the personal safety of Mr Drake is only too comprehensible, if perhaps in some degree premature since the Anti-Sabotage Bill, as Mr Morrison indicated in the House of Commons on June 26, was in any case as yet only laid before the Majlis, but not passed by it. What had happened was, however, evidently accepted, with no recorded criticism, in the Foreign Office, and was upheld in Parliament by the Foreign Secretary.

2. The possibility for British diplomacy, June 20-25

The measures which had been adopted by His Majesty's Government in consequence of the Foreign Office recommendations of June 20 were, so far as they went, well adapted to the more critical phase following the failure of the delegation of the Anglo-Iranian Oil Company in Tehran. This applied more particularly to the measures of military (Operation Midget) and legal precaution (application to the International Court). They had, however, proved insufficient in themselves to arrest a further serious decline in the British position in the dispute. This may have reflected a certain weakness in evaluating what remained the central, political, issue, and in trying to devise extraordinary means, if necessary, in order to counter the persistent hostility and erratic activism of what the Foreign Secretary justly termed 'an extraordinary Government'. To seek its overthrow, as was henceforth done in favour of M. Sayyid Zia, was indeed an obvious and vigorous expedient, if also perhaps a somewhat extreme and double-edged one, as the Americans regularly represented. It was also unlikely to be quick. Whereas it was evidently becoming urgent to halt and swing back the increasingly adverse and dangerous trend against British interests in Persia which had been steadily building up, month after month, jostling them back from one position after another. By then, however, this reversal would require such effort as to call for determined and even aggressive British thinking, in terms of purposeful precision. Nor were opportunities to this end wholly lacking.

In the Persian crisis of 1951 His Majesty's Government suffered from notable handicaps and weaknesses. As one Member of Parliament (Mr Mott-Radclyffe) put it in the debate on June 21, 'the actual issue of nationalisation forced His Majesty's Government to bat on a rather difficult wicket'.[32] No longer an imperial Power in India, with a programme of rearmament only just getting under way, Great Britain was suffering from military weakness—and from economic weakness, which brought one back to dependence upon the United States. But the Persian Government

---

[31] EP 1531/728.
[32] Parliamentary Debates, 5th Series, H. of C., Vol. 489, col. 783.

was much weaker militarily, economically and even politically. In such a situation such factors as the skill and determination upon either side could weigh heavily in the balance.

On June 21, 1951, a circular telegram, giving valuable guidance for publicity, had been sent to British missions abroad in elaboration of the Foreign Secretary's statement of the preceding day in the House of Commons concerning the physical dangers of inexpert interference in the installations at and around Abadan. The telegram, however, stated that it was important that these dangers should not be stressed in detail by any recognisably British organ of propaganda 'lest we should be represented as preparing sabotage and the Persians should be moved to make a quick grab at the installations'.[33] This prudential consideration was of evident relevance. It was swiftly to be demonstrated, however, that the Persians would not in fact need even such a pretext in order to prefer charges of sabotage if it suited them. One may wonder whether, things having gone so far, this was not perhaps the occasion for a bold decision, if necessary at a high level, to accept a calculated risk and mount a crash-campaign to bring out the physical dangers of Persian interference at Abadan by a drumfire of publicity in British and foreign, especially American, organs.

Such a propaganda campaign could have had the important political object of blurring the distinction between protecting lives and protecting installations at Abadan, roughly along the line of argument suggested by Lord Dunglass and Mr Philips Price in the debate of June 21. It was presumably natural that only the speech of the Foreign Secretary (with interventions) in that debate was included in the Persian Confidential Print of the Foreign Office. The present instance, however, perhaps illustrates the potential value of careful consideration by departments of arguments advanced by back-benchers on both sides in a debate on foreign affairs, even though in many cases they are probably already familiar. Such consideration helps to correct the constitutional danger that, despite such devices as question-time in Parliament and correspondence with Parliamentary Ministers, it may sometimes, in practice, be rather more difficult for a Member of Parliament than for a civil servant to stimulate fresh thinking and channel it effectively.

On June 18 a letter from the active-minded Sir Donald Fergusson of the Ministry of Fuel and Power to General Sir Kenneth McLean had begun an important revision of thought in Whitehall along lines which might have coincided very well with propaganda concerning the installations at Abadan. Sir Donald Fergusson argued that, contrary to previous supposition, there might well be important economic advantage, even after withdrawal from the outlying oilfields, in holding the refinery at Abadan and running it on oil from Kuwait.[34] But over and above such an economic consideration, which led on to a military one, there remained the political factor of prime importance: since the Government of the United States would only support British military intervention at Abadan for the protection of lives, any success towards assimilating that to the protection of installations against lethal risks would be, potentially, a cardinal gain towards safeguarding British interests.

Publicity concerning the protection of installations at Abadan obviously led through to the explosive issue of sabotage. On June 26 a further circular telegram

[33] P 10151/34.
[34] EP 1531/671G.

instructed British missions that the Persian Anti-Sabotage Bill 'should be treated as clear evidence that Persian Government fully expect accidents to be caused by the clumsiness of their nominees and are preparing to make scapegoats of British staffs':[35] an ingeniously telling line so far as it went. There is no recorded suggestion that from there it might be possible to take a bold step ahead and try to turn the Anti-Sabotage Bill to positive British advantage. For its capital threat to British subjects, crudely and relentlessly levelled against Mr Drake, might seem to offer another valuable opportunity, after that of physical danger from the installations, for somewhat extending the scope for legitimate British intervention to protect British lives. No doubt the Legal Adviser of the Foreign Office and the Law Officers of the Crown would need to have been carefully consulted as to the position under international law; meanwhile there could perhaps have been valuable political study, with military and economic collaboration as necessary, of precise implications and possibilities, especially as to fall-back positions and breaking points in regard to inadmissible degrees of Persian interference with British installations and threat to British lives. Whereas in fact the relative absence of clear formulation by the Foreign Office, in consultation with His Majesty's Embassy in Tehran, of fall-back positions and breaking-points during the crisis, especially in regard to local Persian encroachment at Abadan, forms something of a contrast to the adept diplomacy, for instance, whereby Sir Miles Lampson (later Lord Killearn), also serving a Labour Government and dealing with an oriental one, had negotiated the surrender of British extra-territoriality in China in 1919-31.

Towards the end of June 1951 a determined drive in British diplomacy and propaganda to turn the tables on the intransigent Persians by advancing a close case for intervention at Abadan to protect British lives on broad grounds might well, one might think, have proved considerably successful so that the prospect of resolute action might have prevented its necessity. Not only would such a policy have commanded strong support in Great Britain, where public opinion was increasingly looking for something of the kind, but in introducing the Anti-Sabotage Bill Dr Musaddiq, as he himself quickly and cleverly realised, had for the first time overstepped the mark so as to alienate neutral and American opinion. This took some days, but by June 27 Mr Steel was reporting that in conversation with Mr McGhee he had remarked that if the Persians were to arrest British subjects under the Anti-Sabotage Bill, 'I should not be surprised if we were obliged to tell the Persians to release them or take the consequences. Rather to my surprise, McGhee said he quite understood and that they would do their best for us. My impression was that this anti-sabotage business has opened their eyes to the fact that protection of British lives may be a more real issue tha[n] they had imagined.'[36] Such was the measure of British opportunity.

There is some evidence that the Foreign Secretary was at that time somewhat critical of aspects of the official functioning and that in this connexion he addressed a minute to the Prime Minister. On a summary of the latest position in regard to Persia, submitted by Mr Furlonge on June 25, Mr Morrison minuted to the Permanent Under-Secretary: 'Not too hot!' In the same minute the Secretary of State noted 'a bad delay' in seeking a visa for Mr Zaehner's journey to Persia, and added:

---

[35] P 10151/38.
[36] EP 1531/756.

'The machine needs tuning up . . . We need to be as efficient as a military operation in war.'[37]

3. Expanding British military planning and limited American support, June 25-30

The only military operation then in readiness was the most limited one, to cover temporarily a British evacuation of Abadan, Operation Midget. That, however, could by June 25 be mounted in 36 hours, or less if the forces were assembled in advance. And the Cabinet decided that day that they should be immediately, in Egypt, and that the American Government be informed; also that, in case of urgent necessity, the operation might be authorised forthwith by the Prime Minister in agreement with Mr Morrison and Mr Shinwell. At the same meeting the Chief of the Imperial General Staff reminded the Cabinet that the safety of the British staff in the outlying oilfields could not be guaranteed;[38] no decision to accelerate the withdrawal to Abadan of these 'hostages to fortune' was, however, taken. That afternoon the Ministerial Committee on Persia was further reminded that Operation Midget was planned on the basis of obtaining Persian agreement in the first instance (it does not seem entirely clear, however, how this related to previous planning assumptions: cf pp. 164 and 197); only in case of clear necessity for the protection of British subjects would His Majesty's Government act without it (cf p. 198).[39]

Nevertheless there was already a trend towards renewed military, if not political (cf above) planning for some operation stronger then Midget. Sir Donald Fergusson's previously noticed letter of June 18, suggesting that the island and refinery at Abadan should be held, had been considered at a meeting of the Chiefs of Staff on June 22. It was agreed that this would amount to an extension of the rejected Plan X, and should be studied.[40] This study subsequently produced Operation Lethal for the seizure of Abadan island after evacuation of the company's staff. At another meeting of the Chiefs of Staff three days later Air Marshal Sir Arthur Sanders, Deputy Chief of the Air Staff, further proposed that consideration should be given to the possibility that Persian resistance might collapse if Operation Midget were executed: British plans should be flexible enough for Abadan to be retained if necessary. This produced a plan for Midget Reinforced. Mr Furlonge, attending for the Foreign Office, supported this view, and the meeting agreed that '*ad hoc* decisions would have to be taken at the time and in the light of circumstances. The fact that no detailed plans existed was not likely to affect our ability or inability to build up Midget.'[41]

On June 24, 1951, the Foreign Secretary had minuted with reference to Operation Midget: 'We just must not be late. I wish we cd. do bigger things.'[42] Leaflets in Persian had been prepared for air-dropping if Midget were undertaken; they included an assurance that British troops would leave after British subjects had been evacuated. On June 25 Mr Morrison minuted on this point: 'Is this right? Not very

---

[37] EP 1015/259G.
[38] EP 1531/847G.
[39] EP 1531/848G.
[40] EP 1015/256G.
[41] EP 1531/777G.
[42] EP 1192/32G.

bold.'[43] In the subsequent event, in accordance with planning development, new leaflets omitting the assurance were printed.

Meanwhile, on June 23, the interdepartmental Working Party on Persian Oil produced a paper on 'Economic Pressure on Persia'. This paper, like most emanating from that body, was a cautious document, and Mr Ramsbotham summarised its recommendations as follows: 'The full range of His Majesty's Government's [economic] sanctions should not be imposed. Many of them could in fact be evaded. They would be likely to alienate free world opinion and possibly be countered by American offers of dollar aid. It would be better to let the major hurt to Persia flow from their [*sic*] own action in ejecting AIOC without having the excuse of blaming His Majesty's Government for the failure of their enterprise.'[44] On the same day Mr Bowker minuted that if these recommendations were approved it would be all the more difficult to act on a point raised by the Minister of Defence and ask the Government of the United States to apply a sanction by instructing the American Military Mission in Persia not to supply her with military advice or equipment in present circumstances. Mr Bowker, following up a minute by Mr Furlonge, recommended that it was inadvisable to take the matter up with the American Government. This breeding of prudence out of prudence did not appeal to the Secretary of State, who minuted: 'Of course, if we are pussyfoot we can't complain of Americans'; and again: 'I'm not impressed by all this . . . We really must have guts . . . We need urgently, I fancy, a fighting programme.'[45] In the Ministerial committee on Persia on the afternoon of June 25 the Foreign Secretary secured agreement that it might be necessary to reconsider the decision to confine military action to Operation Midget.[46]

Three days earlier, Mr Herbert Morrison had said it was time he sent a further message to Mr Dean Acheson, who had on June 20 made public what the Foreign Secretary regarded as a weak statement regretting the breakdown of the oil negotiations in Tehran. On June 23 the Minister in the American Embassy in London, Mr Julius Holmes, told Sir William Strang that 'the State Department were cudgelling their brains, but had not been able to think of any useful course to suggest . . . The Shah was deeply depressed and could not see what he could do at the present.' Sir William Strang told Mr Holmes that 'we counted on the maximum of United States collaboration and support in this crisis which seriously affected both Governments'.[47] Mr Holmes threw out the personal suggestion that, if only for purposes of propaganda, it might be useful if His Majesty's Government could propose that the oilfields and refinery at Abadan be entrusted to a caretaker administration, comprising perhaps one Englishman, one Persian and one neutral such as a Swede or Swiss; they might act as trustees, perhaps under the International Court, while attempts were being made to reach agreement. Sir William Strang undertook to consider this suggestion but it does not, for instance, appear to have been referred to the Working Party on Persian Oil.

On the afternoon of June 25, 1951, a telegram was despatched to Mr Steel in Washington (Sir Oliver Franks was on leave in England) by the Foreign Secretary,

---

[43] EP 1015/240G.
[44] EP 1156/17.
[45] EP 1192/36.
[46] EP 1531/848G.
[47] EP 1531/884.

who cited Mr Acheson's statement of June 20 as a further illustration of the tendency of the State Department 'to put us and the Persians on the same footing . . . The American attitude is surely short-sighted in view of the grave threats to the strategic potential of the Western Powers.' Mr Morrison felt it essential to make 'one further attempt' to induce the American Secretary of State to take a more positive line in public, and Mr Steel was instructed to transmit to him as soon as possible a personal message reasoned to that effect. Mr Morrison therein assured Mr Acheson: 'We are not contemplating the use of force unless the safety of the lives of British nationals in the oil areas is in jeopardy. Nor do I wish to impose those methods of economic pressure which the Persians already seem likely to impose on their own economy.' The Foreign Secretary went on to ask Mr Acheson to consider earnestly whether the Government of the United States could not express approval and support for the Anglo-Iranian Oil Company's proposals of June 19, and 'utter a stern warning to Musaddiq and his Government of the consequences of their present actions, indicating that the United States Government stand fully in line with His Majesty's Government in resisting these actions. It is for consideration whether the other North Atlantic Treaty Organisation Powers represented at Tehran might not also be asked to make similar communications.'[48]

At the meeting of the ministerial committee on Persia on the afternoon of June 25 the Foreign Secretary had further been invited to consult with the Minister of Defence as to whether the American Government should be approached with a view to the United States Navy making its presence felt in the neighbourhood of Abadan; and Mr Morrison in turn had invited the views of the Chiefs of Staff. At a meeting next morning they reverted to the idea, suggested to the Americans as early as the preceding autumn, and expressed the view that there was much to be said for having an American aircraft-carrier at the head of the Persian Gulf. One was available in the Mediterranean whereas the British carrier nearest to Abadan was in Norwegian waters. This appears to have been acceptable, presumably because the bases of the Royal Air Force in the Middle East, notably Iraq, were fully sufficient to provide any air-cover required at Abadan, where Persian anti-aircraft defences were rudimentary. The Chiefs of Staff considered, however, that the most effective American military assistance, which would substantially improve the build-up for Midget and any extension thereof, would be provision of transport aircraft, especially for heavy equipment: there were about 60 in Germany.[49]

If American aircraft and aircraft-carriers in practice remained remote from Abadan, the Foreign Secretary on that day of June 26 informed Parliament that a British cruiser, HMS *Mauritius*, was to steam thither—she cast anchor off Abadan two days later. Mr Morrison also intimated that, in view of the unacceptable Persian requirement concerning oil receipts, British tankers at Abadan were now being instructed to leave forthwith, if necessary after unloading any oil already on board. After this announcement, a third important decision was finalised at a meeting of the committee of Ministers, held at 5 o'clock that afternoon and attended by the Prime Minister, Mr Morrison, Mr Gaitskell, Mr Shinwell, Mr Noel-Baker, Lord Jowitt, Sir William Fraser, Field-Marshal Slim and Admiral Lord Fraser of North Cape, First Sea Lord. This third decision, recommended (like that on tankers) by the Working

[48] EP 1531/746.
[49] EP 1192/43G.

Party on Persian Oil, was that, following on from the provisional decision of June 20 (cf p. 216-7), the staff of the Anglo-Iranian Oil Company in the outlying oilfields should now be withdrawn as operations closed down.[50] The dual withdrawal from the flanks of Abadan to landward (Fields staff) and to seaward (tankers) was thus now decided.

The Working Party on Persian Oil had further recommended that the company should 'make arrangements for the subsequent evacuation of the whole of their British staff' from Abadan;[51] and Sir Francis Shepherd was instructed that the plans for evacuating all personnel from Abadan, 'if and when the local situation should necessitate', must be overhauled to allow for their being kept together in nearby territories against a possible return.[52] The withdrawals of staff and tankers had previously been opposed by the Minister of Defence, who argued that thereafter any return would be difficult; he and the Chiefs of Staff would have preferred to compromise on oil receipts and try again to negotiate with the Persians, preferably at ministerial level.[53] The fine balance of arguments here was perhaps complicated by a tendency, to which Mr Morrison had already drawn attention in the parliamentary debate of June 21, towards some possible confusion between total withdrawal from Abadan as a whole, the ultimate defeat, and preliminary withdrawal of outlying staff to Abadan island, which could be a purposeful concentration and elimination of untenable positions: 'reculer pour mieux sauter'.

The ministerial meeting on the afternoon of June 26 had further agreed that the Foreign Secretary should send a message of commendation and support to the resolute staff of the Anglo-Iranian Oil Company at Abadan where, that same day in the aftermath of the departure from Abadan of Mr Drake, they collectively refused to work for the National Iranian Oil Company. Whatever the pros and cons of the dual withdrawal now decided, this spelt the early cessation of oil production in South Persia. Whereas that very morning the First Sea Lord had considered that 'our real object was to keep the oil flowing'.[54] Such was the adverse pace of events that the main object for British policy looked like becoming at once narrower and broader: to cling to a foothold in the silenced refineries and, by resolutely ruling out and bending back adversity, to confirm the menaced prestige and power of Great Britain throughout the Middle East.

The stakes were piling up. On the afternoon of June 26 the Chief of the Imperial General Staff told Ministers that Operation Midget could now be executed within 21 hours. But it might run into trouble, and a larger operation would take six weeks to mount after ministerial decision, unless the Chiefs of Staff were now authorised to take up the shipping necessary for troop transport: which would at once become publicly known. This authorisation was promptly given. Renewed planning for something larger than Midget was to extend into preparations.[55]

On June 27, 1951, the Prime Minister, Foreign Secretary, Chancellor of the Exchequer and Minister of Defence held a private meeting with the leaders of the Opposition, Mr Winston Churchill and Mr Eden. Mr Churchill said, notably, that he

---

[50] EP 1531/788G.
[51] EP 1531/849G.
[52] EP 1531/782.
[53] EP 1531/849G and EP 1192/43G.
[54] EP 1192/43G.
[55] EP 1531/788G and EP 1192/45G.

had never thought that the oilfields in South Persia could be held by force but that the island of Abadan was 'quite another matter'.[56] He considered that the moral case for using force to protect property of the Anglo-Iranian Oil Company in the general interest was a strong one, at any rate till the International Court gave a decision.

On the same day another meeting was being held, at Ismailia, between the British Commanders-in-Chief, Middle East, and a secret visitor, Mr Drake on his way back to England. The Commanders-in-Chief telegraphed that Mr Drake 'has sought hard to obtain from us some ray of hope that we will provide in the last resort the element of force which in his opinion can alone save the situation'. The Commanders-in-Chief were impressed by considerations advanced by Mr Drake but replied that they were only authorised to assist with evacuation of staff. They now suggested, however, that they might in fact be able to do more 'even at this late hour'[57], if authorised.

This telegram from the Commanders-in-Chief, Middle East, was referred to in a Foreign Office minute of June 28 by Mr Furlonge, who wrote: 'In planning for these operations the Chiefs of Staff are being very cautious, no doubt rightly, since their primary task is not to jeopardise their forces in a militarily unjustifiable operation. Many time[s] during World War II (notably in the suppression of the Iraq Revolt of 1941) such risks were successfully taken, on that occasion I believe because the War Cabinet overruled Lord Wavell.' Mr Furlonge cogently advocated, in particular, the dropping of a prior undertaking to withdraw after completion of Operation Midget, and suggested that recent Persian actions might have modified the disapproval with which the Foreign Office had assumed that world opinion would regard an operation not only to seize but to hold Abadan island. He concluded: 'The political risks are obviously great, but so are the stakes involved not only in Persia but in the Middle East generally.'[58] Mr Bowker thought there was much to be said for dropping this undertaking, while underlining the risks since announcement of subsequent withdrawal was not only the assurance upon which the Iraqi Government had agreed to British military use of Shaiba for the operation, but was also a strong inducement to the Persians not to resist, to the Russians not to intervene and to the Americans to grant support. On June 29 the Chiefs of Staff instructed the Commanders-in-Chief, Middle East, to plan for Operation Midget reinforced (cf p. 226).

Bolder British military planning was getting under way. Larger than Operation Midget Reinforced was Operation Lethal, now also envisaged. On June 29 the Chiefs of Staff also instructed the Commanders-in-Chief to plan for the seizure and indefinite holding of Abadan island only (Operation Lethal); the assumptions were now to be that Persian forces would be hostile, Iraqi facilities, but not forces, would be available, and no Russian opposition; the planning should exclude forces for Operation Midget, which must be available for their role of evacuation.[59] Next day the Commanders-in-Chief, Middle East, represented in reply that in their view they must simplify their planning down to one basic plan suitable for any contingency and capable of last-moment adjustment. Whereas 'if we continue to work on a number of separate plans it is impossible to take suitable preparatory measures for

[56] EP 1531/870G.
[57] EP 1015/250G.
[58] EP 1192/42G.
[59] EP 1015/254G.

all of them'. The complications of an assault-landing in the Shatt-el-Arab had led them to conclude that 'the basic plan for any operation against Abadan should be in the form of an advance through Iraq by troops landing by air at Shaiba or by sea at Kuwait'.[60]

All this British military planning was pursued, as usual, under shadow of the American angle. The Foreign Secretary's plea of June 25 for American support was that same day transmitted and vigorously expounded by Mr Steel to Mr Acheson in the presence of Mr McGhee, who 'of course at once' produced a pessimistic telegram from Dr Grady saying that nothing whatever could be done. The American Secretary of State nevertheless evinced sympathy for the British case, as did his friendly Ambassador in London when the Foreign Secretary made a similar representation to him on June 26.[61] That day, however, Mr Acheson made in public what Mr Steel criticised to Mr McGhee on June 27 as 'very anodyne' remarks on the Persian issue.[62] That afternoon Mr Acheson issued to the Press an admonition, indeed, to the Persian Government to reconsider its intransigent and economically dangerous attitude. This fell far short, however, of any declaration of solidarity with His Majesty's Government or stern warning to the Persian[s]. On the contrary, Mr Acheson recalled that the American Government had 'repeatedly and publicly' sympathised with Persia's wish to control her oil resources; also mentioned was the strong desire of the United States to see the Persians 'realise their national aspirations'.[63]

4. British contacts with friendly Powers and propaganda to Persia

On the same day of June 27 Mr Winston Churchill, at his meeting with the Cabinet Ministers, said that he was 'rather shocked' at the American attitude.[64] He also emphasised the importance of securing support for the British case in the Middle East, notably in Iraq and Turkey. Next day Mr Furlonge despatched a previously drafted letter in reply to letters of May 24 and June 11 wherein Mr Scott Fox, Counsellor at Ankara, had conveyed the generally friendly views of the Turkish Foreign Minister on the Persian dispute. Mr Scott Fox was now requested to 'thank M. Köprülü for the counsels of moderation he has been urging on the Persians and tell him that we much appreciate having his views',[65] which were generally in line with those of the Foreign Office.

As regards support from other friendly nations, Mr Morrison's recent suggestion to Mr Acheson that Anglo-American representation in Tehran might perhaps be supported by other NATO Powers (cf p. 227) followed an earlier suggestion in that general sense from Sir Francis Shepherd[66] and, more recently, in a letter of June 22[67] to Sir Pierson Dixon from Sir Frederick Hoyer Millar, United Kingdom Deputy on the North Atlantic Council. Subsequently this proposal was carefully considered in the Foreign Office; but an inclination, supported by Eastern Department, to adopt it

---

[60] EP 1015/255G.
[61] EP 1531/736 and 789.
[62] EP 1531/756.
[63] EP 1531/762.
[64] EP 1531/870G.
[65] EP 1531/732.
[66] EP 1531/360.
[67] EP 1531/1204.

for evident political reasons was countered by Economic Relations Department, which represented the Foreign Office on the Working Party on Persian oil. Economic Relations Department feared, with reason, that the obvious argument as to the effect upon Western Powers generally of a breakdown of Persian oil supplies would encourage what it was desired to avoid, namely, pressure on His Majesty's Government from other NATO Governments for reassurances in regard to making good such deficiencies. Other fears here included the possibility that discussion of the problem of Persian oil in NATO might occasion renewed attempts, hitherto resisted, to discuss oil shortage in the OEEC; whereas, since the major suppliers were American or British, the British preference was for Anglo-American discussions such as those which were held in Washington early in July (cf p. 272).

While the technical and procedural difficulties of a British attempt to secure vigorous NATO support in the Persian dispute may be fully recognised, it possibly remains an open question whether a determined effort to overcome them might not yet have been worth while on broader political grounds, especially in view of the notable goodwill towards the British case already being evinced by such Governments as the French and Italian. British policy naturally had primary regard to support from the United States, which held the material trumps. At the same time it was perhaps possible to discount to excess the moral, and even practical, advantage of mobilised support of British policy by the other Governments of Western Europe in its effect upon the recalcitrant Persian Government and, not least maybe, upon the faltering American Government: an aspect on which consideration is not recorded. In the event Sir Frederick Hoyer Millar's proposal of June 22 affords another illustration of the length of time then liable to elapse in dealing with issues relating to Powers less directly involved in the urgent press of the Persian crisis. His letter was answered, and then in a temporising sense, in a letter,[68] approved by Sir William Strang, of August 2.

The previously noticed fears of Economic Relations Department were early stimulated by a conversation which Mr J.A. Turpin, Assistant Head of that Department, had on June 26, 1951, with M. Labouret, Second Secretary in the French Embassy. M. Labouret sought to elicit whether His Majesty's Government had a plan for alternative oil supplies if Persian ones dried up, and suggested that the question might be referred to the Oil Committee of OEEC. Mr Ramsbotham thereafter put in hand consultations with the Ministry of Fuel and Power and the interdepartmental Working Party; these produced an Intel of July 4 giving reassuring guidance on the matter to posts abroad. Though on June 27 Sir Roger Makins had minuted that M. Labouret had been 'over-inquisitive'.[69]

On the same day of June 27 the Secretary of State had a general conversation regarding Persia with the French Ambassador. Mr Morrison said that 'the Americans were now behind us', and 'expressed appreciation of the support we had received from the French Government, and which I hoped would continue'.[70] M. Massigli had gained an impression of the imminence of 'evacuation of the Anglo-Iranian Oil Company'—seemingly as a whole rather than only from the outlying oilfields, though the record is not specific. Mr Morrison replied that 'we had no wish to

---

[68] EP 1531/1204.
[69] EP 1531/888.
[70] EP 1531/773.

evacuate but unless the Persians changed their tune there seemed no alternative. We could not take risks with the lives of British subjects who were living under a very real threat. We were not *trying* to evacuate; evacuation was being forced on us. The situation was very worrying and I could not see how it could be solved with the present Persian Government in power.' The perceptible contrast in tone, here as elsewhere, between the public or official statements of the Foreign Secretary, and his secret minutes and observations, may suggest something of the strain and complexity of the Persian crisis for those whose bitter duty it was to endeavour to surmount it.

On the following day of June 28, 1951, as the Foreign Office was promptly informed, a leading article on the Persian crisis in the Swedish liberal organ, *Dagens Nyheter*, commented that 'despite warnings—not only from the Opposition—that an evacuation would be regarded in the whole of the Middle East as a sign of weakness, responsible circles in Britain seem to regard this as the most likely solution. The alternative is a military occupation of the oil installations but the prospects of such an enterprise are unattractive from several points of view.' After referring to the evident danger of Russian intervention in North Persia under cover of the Soviet-Persian treaty of 1921 the Swedish journal continued: 'Even the armed intervention which London seems to have in mind is now described in Tehran as an act of war. But if this entirely legitimate protective measure—doubly justified after the Persians have faced the British subjects with an imminent threat through the new Anti-Sabotage Law—is carried out quickly and finally, the danger of further military complications will not be unduly great.'[71] It is not clear how far the Foreign Office may have been impressed by this friendly testimony from neutralise Sweden to the strength by now of the British moral position as regards possible military action at Abadan.

The Swedish article appeared the day after Mr Steel had reported on the somewhat comparable effect which the Persian Anti-Sabotage Bill had produced in Washington (cf pp. 224-5). In Washington, however, His Majesty's Embassy continued to be severely critical of the propagandist failure of the company, which, wrote Mr Gore-Booth on June 27, left its weakly-staffed office in New York 'complete lack of discretion' in interpreting policy.[72] And as regards the general presentation of the public image of the company, Sir William Strang had occasion to record on the same day of June 27 that Sir William Fraser had told him that he thought that on June 28 he would have to publish the company's profits for 1950: extraneous factors combined to make them 'very high indeed'.[73] Sir William Strang had expressed the view to Sir William Fraser that when the results were announced a good deal of Press preparation would be needed in view of Persian representation of the company as 'bloodsuckers'.[74] Sir Edward Bridges, with whom Sir William Fraser had also communicated, telephoned to Sir William Strang, however, to say that the Chancellor of the Exchequer was much perturbed at the prospect of this publication. Sir William Strang now felt sure that the Foreign Secretary would share these misgivings. He did. The announcement was prudently postponed till towards

---

[71] EP 1531/798.
[72] PG 14537/11.
[73] EP 1531/793.
[74] *Ibid.*

the end of the year.

Meanwhile steps were being taken, with evident effect, to intensify British propaganda to Persia. While in Tehran Mr Jackson had been impressed by the need for better facilities for presenting his company's case, and had suggested that it should acquire a newspaper. Here the Foreign Office agreed with Sir Francis Shepherd that the company should be left to 'paddle their own canoe'.[75] His Majesty's Embassy at Tehran had, however, reversed its standing policy by at last allowing its Daily News Bulletin, at risk of suppression, to cover Persian news, including British editorials on the oil crisis. His Majesty's Embassy significantly reported at the end of June that 'this polemical use of the Bulletin has not prevented a strong increase in its circulation'.[76]

On June 29, 1951, however, Sir Francis Shepherd reported on the discouraging prospects for effective publicity through the biased Persian Press as compared with the Persian broadcasts of the BBC.[77] Two days earlier Mr C.F.R. Barclay of Information Policy Department of the Foreign Office had minuted that he wished to make certain that the Persian service of the BBC had been used to the utmost effect in endeavouring to influence Persian opinion.[78] It would indeed appear that criticism on this service of the Anti-Sabotage Bill produced telling effect and may have contributed to the subsequent retreat of the Persian Government in the matter. Mr Barclay consulted with Mr Gordon Waterfield, head of the Middle Eastern services of the BBC; they, together with Colonel Wheeler and Dr Lambton, agreed that the best hope of appealing to Persian commonsense and traditional friendliness towards the West would be by a broadcast by the Prime Minister—Mr Barclay suggested, possibly by Mr Churchill also. After careful consideration, however, Eastern Department concluded that such an appeal at that time would stand no chance of success. In his despatch of June 29 Sir Francis Shepherd advised that during 'the first fever of nationalisation . . . I do not think the Persians will be susceptible to logic and reason'.[79]

In the same despatch on publicity His Majesty's Ambassador at Tehran took up much the same theme as Mr Churchill had advanced two days earlier. Sir Francis Shepherd wrote: 'It is important that we should consolidate our position in the remaining countries of the Middle East. This is necessary not only to compensate for the temporary loss of our influence in Persia, but, if carried out quickly and effectively, it will bring home to the Persians, as can nothing else, the practical advantages to be derived from continued association with the British people. Hajji Baba still represents the average Persian and there is no argument he understands so well as the inducements of self-interest.' An Ambassador confronted with a crisis may naturally look for support from his colleagues in neighbouring countries; though Sir Francis Shepherd's admirable prescription was not easily applied, for instance, in Egypt. Anglo-Egyptian relations, strained by abortive discussions regarding revision of the treaty of 1936 and notably the Canal Zone (cf p. 413) were to be further aggravated on July 1 by the Egyptian arrest in the Gulf of Aqaba of the *Empire Roach*, a British vessel carrying arms to Jordan. In Iraq, however, British

---

[75] EP 1681/2G.
[76] PG 1344/3.
[77] PG 13437/17.
[78] PB 1049/16.
[79] PG 13437/17.

policy was consistently preoccupied with the Persian issue, especially with ensuring that the Iraqi Government would not object to British troop movements in the country in accordance with treaty stipulations.

As regards propaganda His Majesty's Ambassador in Tehran subsequently reported, somewhat countervailingly perhaps, that likely material on the Persian crisis culled from the foreign Press was less effective from Middle Eastern countries than from others. Nevertheless, the Foreign Office was to write, for instance, on July 21 to His Majesty's Embassy at Ankara, seeking to secure the introduction of more material concerning Persia into the Turkish Press and also enquiring, perhaps none too soon, whether the Turkish wireless service to Persia was being helpful.[80] On the broader issue raised by Sir Francis Shepherd concerning British consolidation in the Middle East, it does not appear that the Foreign Office felt it opportune to take special measures on the spot to coordinate British policy, in order to survey and if possible mitigate the Persian crisis in a broader setting, as by a special meeting of His Majesty's Ambassadors in the area, or a tour by a Minister or high official somewhat on the lines of that made by Mr Furlonge before the crisis had become acute. The Foreign Office was, however, alive to the need for general consideration of Middle East problems and on June 29 Sir William Strang held a meeting for this purpose.

At the meeting of June 29 in the Foreign Office the presence of Sir Oliver Franks, on leave from Washington, suggested the extent to which the new American assistance programme (cf p. 194) was likely to influence British planning. Both he and Sir William Strang emphasised the need for a renewed British effort to implement Mr Bevin's broad policy of promoting economic and social development in the Middle East, so that British influence should not suffer, either in the Middle East or in America, by comparison with the American contribution. It was suggested that the Secretary of State should ask the Chancellor of the Exchequer to review the possibilities of British assistance, though Sir Roger Makins pointed out that the balance of payments had deteriorated. The United States were now ready to agree to a peacetime Middle East Command under a British Supreme Commander. The meeting agreed that it was necessary to expand the Development Division of the British Middle East Office in Cairo, and was informed of Mr Morrison's wish for consideration of the possibility of some imaginative action by the British and American, and possibly French, Governments in connexion with Middle East oil. Sir William Strang recalled the abortive Shinwell-Ickes Agreement (cf p. 54) and Sir Roger Makins the Anglo-American declaration proposed by Mr McGhee, in favour of the 50-50 formula (cf p. 136). It was agreed that the possibility of some such joint action should be examined.[81]

5. British reactions against the Persian Government about the end of June

In relation to Persia herself the Foreign Office had been consulting Sir Francis Shepherd as to the policy to be pursued in the light of Mr Drake's expulsion. His Majesty's Ambassador proposed the presentation to the Persian Government of a further note, indicating readiness to make a final effort to reach agreement; but in this connexion he argued cogently against the possible expedient of his own

---

[80] PB 1049/13.
[81] E 1024/36G.

235

withdrawal, which would depress British morale shortly after the departure of Mr Drake.[82] It may well have been for sufficient reasons, such as the approach of HMS *Mauritius*, that consideration was apparently not given to the contrary and conceivably worthwhile course of seeking to reaffirm the British presence in Abadan itself by a visit from His Majesty's Ambassador in person.

On June 27, 1951, Sir Francis Shepherd repeated information from Khorramshahr that Persian interference in the oil industry at and around Abadan was 'assuming serious proportions'.[83] Continued deadlock regarding tanker sailings had forced pumping from the Agha Jari field to stop. M. Makki was earning his designation by Sir Francis Shepherd as 'the Senior Crusader against the AIOC'.[84] He was responsible, among other things, for preventing transmission of aviation spirit to Basra and for 'intolerable delay in customs formalities'.[85] Persian military on No. 8 jetty at Abadan were preventing embarkation of stores and equipment for offlying shipping. The Persians thereafter instituted searches for arms. M. Makki demanded for himself Mr Drake's car and the launch in which he had departed to Basra: failing which, M. Makki threatened to stop all local car movement and to evict British staff from their houses. On June 28 Mr A.E. Mason, Acting General Manager since Mr Drake's departure, was in fact evicted with his staff from the company's general office at Khorramshahr. His Majesty's Consul-General there telegraphed on June 30: 'May I request that urgent steps be taken to curb M. Makki's actions as the results may be very serious.'[86]

On the same day of June 30 in Tehran the Persian authorities entered and searched the house of the chief representative of the Anglo-Iranian Oil Company, Mr Seddon, sealed all his papers including cyphers and subsequently compelled him to surrender the keys of his safe. Mr Seddon and Sir Francis Shepherd protested to the Persian Government. It was seemingly alarmed at the prospect of losing all the British oil staff, and representation by Dr Grady in particular further helped to secure suspension of consideration by the Majlis of the Anti-Sabotage Bill. A contemporary suggestion linked this significant Persian retreat with the strong British action in sending a cruiser to Abadan.

Whatever the considerations previously, it does not appear certain that this juncture might not perhaps have afforded an opportunity for the return of Mr Drake to Abadan. As it was, however, he was already on his way back to England on a temporary visit, largely with a view to urging that the recent decision to evacuate the British staff from the outlying fields should be reversed, and that they should stay put. Mr Drake did not rate the dangers of disorders high since the Persians were anxious in their own interests to prevent them and, as he told Mr Bowker on June 30, 'now had in Abadan two soldiers to every British member of the staff and forces were being steadily moved into the oilfields'.[87] Mr Bowker explained the cogent reasons for the decision to evacuate outlying British staff, but was much impressed by Mr Drake's argument and recommended that this evacuation should be slowed down; there was no allusion to the potentially adverse bearing of this upon Mr

---

[82] EP 1531/739.
[83] EP 1531/755.
[84] EP 1013/29.
[85] EP 1531/740.
[86] EP 1531/813.
[87] EP 1015/267G.

Drake's own plea three days earlier at Ismailia for British military intervention.

Meantime, at the interparty meeting on June 27, 1951, Mr Eden had suggested a joint Anglo-American approach to induce the Shah to dismiss Dr Musaddiq, which might involve a *coup d'état*. Next day the Foreign Secretary told Mr Gifford that he was considering this possibility. Also on June 28 Sir Francis Shepherd telegraphed his views that a new note to the Persian Government (cf pp. 235-6) would no longer be appropriate, that opposition to Dr Musaddiq was developing and should be encouraged by British refusal to negotiate with him. His Majesty's Ambassador had no doubt that such negotiation would prove unfruitful: 'In short, I feel that we must now do all we can to hasten Musaddiq's departure.'[88]

During their conversation on the morning of June 28 the American Ambassador expressed to the Foreign Secretary the regret of the State Department concerning the recent publication of an alleged statement by Dr Grady, which he now denied, regarding the possibility of the Persian oil industry being taken over by an international company. This was not in fact American policy. Mr Gifford further put to Mr Morrison a proposal from the Government of the United States whereby Dr Grady should suggest to Dr Musaddiq a moratorium in the oil dispute and then the adoption for 60 days of interim arrangements between Persia and the British interests, which would permit operation and shipments to continue till more permanent arrangements could be worked out. This American proposal was viewed unenthusiastically by the Cabinet; the terms were in substance only what the Anglo-Iranian Oil Company had already offered without success; and such an American approach might prejudice the application of His Majesty's Government to the International Court for an interim injunction, which was to be heard at The Hague on June 30. Nevertheless, the Cabinet did not think it judicious to discourage the American proposals. The next item, incidentally, considered at that meeting of the Cabinet was the anxious economic situation of the United Kingdom; the internal financial position was disquieting, and the external balance of payments much less favourable than expected.[89]

There ensued an exchange of British and American views concerning the terms in which the American proposal should be presented to the Persian Government. The Americans evinced some reluctance to go so far as His Majesty's Government desired regarding phraseology which would ensure that the moratorium would be based upon a return to the *status quo ante* and that the Anglo-Iranian Oil Company would resume effective control of operations during the interim. On the afternoon of June 29 a meeting of the Ministerial Committee on Persia decided to take this opportunity to request Mr Dean Acheson to postpone further consideration of his proposal at any rate for a few days: the present moment was not considered entirely suitable for it in view of indications (growing Persian opposition; suspension of the anti-sabotage law) that Dr Musaddiq's Government might be weakening.[90]

At the meeting of British Ministers on June 29, 1951, Mr Gaitskell expressed the view that the American Ambassador in Tehran was in any case a thoroughly unsatisfactory channel, and that he must not act as an 'honest broker'. His Majesty's Ambassador in Tehran was in fact already reporting that same day that Dr Grady,

---

[88] EP 1531/778.
[89] EP 1531/825G, UEE 65/21G.
[90] EP 1531/802 and 850G.

though without instructions to do so, had spoken to the Persian Premier on the lines of the projected American proposal, only to find Dr Musaddiq 'as completely intransigent as ever'.[91] The Foreign Office informed Mr Steel in Washington of its surprise that Dr Grady should have acted so.[92] Furthermore, the Foreign Secretary on June 29 drew Mr Gifford's attention to a report that Dr Grady 'had assured Dr Musaddiq that if the threat of the Anti-Sabotage Bill was withdrawn "the British might attempt to persuade oil technicians to remain at work".' Mr Morrison said such a remark, if correctly reported, was 'altogether inappropriate' and asked that Dr Grady should be 'particularly careful to refrain from making any statement calculated to encourage Dr Musaddiq'.[93] Sir Francis Shepherd commented that during that June: 'United States policy has been more than usually inconstant and clumsy'.[94]

Also on June 29 His Majesty's Embassy in Washington asked the State Department to consider whether the American Military Mission in Persia could be instrumental in supplying her with moderating advice rather than with modern armaments.[95] Thus was the point raised earlier by the Minister of Defence (cf p. 227) taken up. With reference, however, to the broader ministerial decision of June 25 (cf p. 228), the Chiefs of Staff agreed on July 4 that 'any approach to the Americans for assistance in connexion with military action in Persia could be made only on a political level and was, moreover, at present likely to prove abortive'.[96]

Meantime, His Majesty's Government was pursuing legal rather than military means against Persia. On June 30, 1951, the International Court of Justice at The Hague heard the British application for an indication of interim measures of protection against the Persian Government pending the court's substantive judgment of the dispute on the British application of May 26. Leading for Great Britain were the Attorney-General, Sir Frank Soskice, the Legal Adviser of the Foreign Office, Sir Eric Beckett, and Professor H. Lauterpacht. The Persian Government was unrepresented, having by a notification of June 29 rejected the competence of the International Court in a dispute which, it was represented, was one to which the British Government was not a party, and one within the domestic jurisdiction of Persia.

On the same day of June 30 His Majesty's Ambassador at Tehran remitted to Dr Musaddiq a further British note, this time in stiff terms proposed from London. This note regretted the Persian failure to reply to the British *aide-mémoire* of May 19 or respond to the repeated offers to negotiate made both by the Anglo-Iranian Oil Company and by His Majesty's Government. Persian interference, it was explained, had compelled the announced withdrawal of British tankers from Abadan and, temporarily, of 'the British personnel in the oilfields . . . into Abadan as and when their presence in the fields is no longer required'.[97] His Majesty's Government placed on record that the progressive closing down at Abadan resulted solely from the attitude of the Persian Government, and rejected in advance any suggestion that

---

[91] EP 1531/796.
[92] EP 1531/803.
[93] EP 1531/802.
[94] EP 1013/29.
[95] EP 1192/31G and 38G.
[96] EP 1192/40G.
[97] Cmd 8425, p. 44.

accidents due to interference in the company's operations could be ascribed to sabotage, The Persian Government was reminded of its responsibility under international law for the protection of all British subjects in Persia. His Majesty's Government found it difficult to believe that the Persian Government 'even at this late hour, will not recognise the unwisdom of their intransigence'. The note, on the proposal of Sir Francis Shepherd, contained no other suggestion in the direction of further negotiation.

The firm and somewhat minatory British note of June 30, 1951, was in tone the expression of a Government determined to pursue a strong policy against Persian intransigence. In practice military preparation for anything more than Midget, the operation for evacuation, was only effectively beginning. Yet the possibility of further negotiation with the Government of Dr Musaddiq was discounted. This pointed towards the inception of a rather dangerous dichotomy which became latent in British policy towards Persia, with serious results later in the crisis. His Majesty's Government was looking to a middle way: not only, at that juncture, to legal support in an interim injunction from the International Court: but also, thenceforth, to political relief from the fall of Dr Musaddiq. His influence was to be undermined while the Persians, as the Foreign Secretary told the American Ambassador on July 3, were to be allowed 'time to appreciate that we do not intend to give way . . . The British public are not in a mood for further concessions.'[98]

Proposals for the replacement of Dr Musaddiq by another Persian politician were then being urged from several quarters. From the Persian side, one of the proposals from opponents of Dr Musaddiq which secured most British attention had been made on June 22, 1951, to the Minister of Labour, Mr Alfred Robens, during the conference of the International Labour Office at Geneva; at which, incidentally, the Persian Workers' Delegate, M. Mochaver, made a speech that was in substance more critical of the Persian Administration and wealthy classes than of the Anglo-Iranian Oil Company.

Trades unions in Persia were recent and weak but it was a leading Persian trades unionist, M. Kaivan, who then assured Mr Robens that Persian workers, especially those employed by the Anglo-Iranian Oil Company, were opposed to oil nationalisation and believed, rightly or wrongly, that it had been inspired by American business circles. Instead of fruitlessly negotiating with Persians who only cared for their sectional interests, the Shah should be presented with a British ultimatum that unless the position were improved His Majesty's Government would not hesitate to land troops. Real evidence of British determination would be liable to swing many timid Persians. M. Kaivan listed Persian Deputies who might be induced to speak out against Dr Musaddiq, and prominent personalities with influence on the Shah such as M. Taquizadeh, the Speaker of the Senate, and M. Sayyid Zia, the sincerest friend of Britain. Outside the Majlis, the Minister of the Interior, General Zahedi, who had helped M. Kaivan to reach Geneva, was eager to become Prime Minister and could split the National Front. Both he and General Arfa might be good for a *coup*, though the Shah feared them both. Provincial disturbances should be fomented, though M. Kaivan reckoned that the Qashqai 'were in the pocket of the Americans'. Substantially the same communication was made by M. Kaivan in

---

[98] EP 1015/276G.

Geneva to a representative of the Anglo-Iranian Oil Company.[99]

On June 25 the Minister of Labour reported to the Cabinet on the programme advanced by M. Kaivan. At about the same time the qualifications of M. Qavam-es-Sultaneh, then in Switzerland for medical treatment, to succeed Dr Musaddiq were being urged upon the Foreign Office by various unofficial mouthpieces, including a former agent of the Shah and an experienced English businessman. The latter was one of two rather strikingly concordant proponents of the view that M. Makki could and should be bribed to desert Dr Musaddiq. This Englishman also reflected somewhat upon the capacity of His Majesty's Ambassador at Tehran as compared with his predecessor who, the informant said, 'had a great position with the Persians' and should be sent out as a special envoy. This suggestion reached the Prime Minister,[100] but was scouted by the Foreign Secretary in supporting Sir Francis Shepherd to Mr Attlee. Mr Morrison alluded to His Majesty's Ambassador's preference for 'quiet methods'[101] while referring to his own encomium of June 15 (cf p. 210).

Another Persian lobbyer was in touch with three conservative Members of Parliament, Brigadier Fitzroy Maclean, Mr Soames and Mr Julian Amery, who on July 5 transmitted the recommendation of M. Qavam to Mr Bowker. The latter replied that the Foreign Office was not convinced that M. Qavam had a strong following in Persia—some days later Mr Logan minuted: 'He is now old and in poor health and is not a man in whom we could have confidence.'[102] In fact the decision had already gone in favour of M. Sayyid Zia. He was told at the end of June 1951 that His Majesty's Government were prepared to give him full support with a view to his replacing Dr Musaddiq. In this connexion M. Sayyid Zia's principal, and standing request was that his Majesty's Government should take a firm line towards Dr Musaddiq,[103] as in its note of June 30.

On the same day that the three conservative Members of Parliament spoke on behalf of M. Qavam to Mr Bowker, he wrote to Sir Francis Shepherd in order to submit to his judgment the alternative proposals of M. Kaivan. Any action on them should, advised Mr Bowker, be 'carefully coordinated with other plans'.[104] The claims of M. Qavam were, however, discussed in London with Mr Zaehner and, subsequently, the Secretary of State, who minuted on July 5: 'I much want to get a move on to change the [Persian] Govt. for the better'. In this connexion Mr Bowker further wrote to Sir Francis Shepherd on July 7 that Mr Morrison had agreed that care must be taken not to cross wires: 'our attitude to Qavam and any action taken with regard to him should depend entirely on other plans which are now in hand',[105] in favour, evidently, of M. Sayyid Zia.

In his letter of July 5 to His Majesty's Ambassador in Tehran, Mr Bowker had written: 'We have now been forced to the conclusion that there is little to be hoped for from the Shah.'[106] On the previous day Mr Fry had reminded the Foreign

---

[99] EP 1015/271G and EP 2181/14.
[100] EP 1531/1171G.
[101] Confidential/General/415.
[102] EP 1015/273.
[103] EP 1015/383.
[104] EP 1015/271G.
[105] EP 1531/914G.
[106] EP 1015/271G.

Secretary of American opposition to an approach to the Persian ruler,[107] such as Mr Eden had recently suggested. His Majesty's Ambassador in Tehran had had a long conversation with the Shah on June 30, the day on which the latest British note was presented to the Persian Premier. The Shah, who was incidentally about to undergo an operation for appendicitis, remained of the opinion that Dr Musaddiq could only be evicted when the failure of his policy had been amply demonstrated. Here, somewhat ominously, he seemed to think that the stoppage of tankers would not be enough 'but that probably the closing of the refinery was also needed'.[108] The Shah advocated propaganda against Dr Musaddiq and even that emphasis be placed upon a futile promise of his that oil nationalisation would yield Persia £300,000 a day: a suggestion which the Foreign Office duly followed up. The Shah further said that he had agreed to the formation of a new party by M. Sayyid Zia.

In the same conversation the Shah alluded to the parliamentary speech made by Mr Duncan Sandys on June 21 and particularly to his suggestion of a partition (cf p. 219). 'In this connexion the Shah said that if Great Britain took military action as a result of such a policy he did not see how the Persians could refrain from resisting. Any military action of this nature was dangerous because he felt that the Russians would use it to install a Communist Government for the whole of Persia rather than attempt to occupy Azerbaijan militarily.' His Majesty's Ambassador explained away Mr Sandys' reference to partition 'as best I could' and emphasised that Mr Sandys was speaking as a member of the Opposition.[109] An alternative line for Sir Francis Shepherd might have been to take the opportunity to press home Mr Sandys' warning to Persia by emphasising sternly to the Shah the risk and peril in which he was placing his country by permitting the continuance of a Government so erratic and intransigent that it might well compel British military intervention in sheer self-protection; this in turn might indeed provoke the kind of dangers which the Shah feared, however little these were desired by His Majesty's Government which, of course, had no kind of thought or desire for any partition of Persia. The idea of a special approach to the Shah (cf pp. 188-9) had, however, not borne fruit.

The Foreign Office and also Lord Alexander of Hillsborough, Chancellor of the Duchy of Lancaster, were concerned at the implication made by Mr Sandys and also by Mr Crossman in the same debate, that British intervention in South Persia would justify Russian in North. On July 5 the State Department was informed of a possible parliamentary statement based on the official British view, communicated to it in April (cf p. 151), that under Article 6 of the Soviet-Persian Treaty of 1921, which must be interpreted by the Rotstein letter, Russian intervention in Persia would only be justified by action there to promote the restoration of the Czarist régime. The State Department, which had not replied to the earlier Foreign Office paper, now agreed with the proposed statement but suggested adding that such Soviet intervention would violate the Charter of the United Nations (Articles 2(3 and 4), 33 and 37), which in any case superseded the treaty of 1921 under Article 103 of the Charter.[110] The Foreign Office Legal Advisers did not agree that the Charter superseded this treaty, but in any case no parliamentary statement was made.

---

[107] EP 1531/915G.
[108] EP 1015/261.
[109] *Ibid.*
[110] EP 10338/18.

Over and above these particular considerations the political and military advisers of His Majesty's Government were agreed in thinking that it was not certain that British intervention in Persia would lead to a Russian one, at any rate to the extent of unleashing a major conflict.[111] Apart from the usual Soviet propaganda to Persia, there had been a rather noticeable absence in Russia of explicit political or military reactions to the Persian crisis, which was judged to be going nicely anyway for the interests of the Soviet Union. Such was the broad setting to further British military planning in regard to South Persia, and with direct relevance to the question of evacuating British staff from the oilfields into Abadan itself.

6. Questions of British withdrawal from the Fields and intervention at Abadan, July 1-5

On July 1 the Foreign Office transmitted a telegram from Mr Elkington of the Anglo-Iranian Oil Company to Mr Mason at Abadan concerning the pace of the gradual withdrawal of British staff from the outlying oilfields, as decided on June 26 and indicated in the British note of June 30. Mr Elkington enquired whether it would not be better to effect an orderly transfer to the National Iranian Oil Company at Naft-i-Shah and Kermanshah rather than to ask the British staff to hang on as long as possible in remote places where their security was not to be compared with that to be found in Abadan.[112] This viewpoint rather than the more sanguine estimate of Mr Drake (cf p. 236) evidently approximated to that held locally. Mr Middleton from His Majesty's Embassy at Tehran visited Abadan in company with the British Military and Air Attachés, and on July 2 they conferred with Mr Capper and Mr Mason. Their unanimous opinion was that the situation in Khuzistan was likely to deteriorate. They envisaged an early start to the transfer to the Persians of installations and stores in the oilfields, and on the following day the Military Attaché arranged with the Persian military for due protection of withdrawing British staff.[113]

Meanwhile in London the general manager who had returned from Abadan continued to argue against the withdrawal thither of outlying British staff. Mr Drake impressed the Foreign Office, the Chiefs of Staff and the Cabinet, which was told by him that such a withdrawal 'would lead to final surrender of the company's position in Persia'.[114] Mr Drake emphasised to the Cabinet that these were his personal views and that he had not consulted his directors. On the same day Mr Drake accompanied Sir William Fraser to a meeting of the Chiefs of Staff whereat Sir William Fraser notably stressed that 'the official view of the Anglo-Iranian Oil Company was that the company could not continue to run its operations in Persia surrounded by British troops. Their operations could be conducted only on a peaceful basis of cooperation between the 2,500 British staff and the 75,000 Persian personnel and not on the basis of a British colony in South Persia.'[115] The evident soundness of this view was in danger, however, of becoming somewhat academic in that deepening crisis wherein the importance, for instance, for the general British position in the Middle East, of some affirmation of the British presence in South Persia was coming to transcend, for the present, that of the efficient continuation of the company's operations.

---

[111] EP 1015/208G.
[112] EP 1531/767.
[113] EP 1531/929 and EP 1202/6G.
[114] EP 1015/268G.
[115] Cabinet file 14/41/8.

After hearing the views of Mr Drake the Cabinet on July 2, 1951, modified the decision of June 26. Withdrawal of staff from the outlying oilfields was now to be discontinued for the time being, and the Anglo-Iranian Oil Company should decide whether staff already withdrawn should actually return to the fields. This change of policy won the approval of the conservative opposition, if not of those in Persia most closely concerned.

On July 4 Mr Mason telegraphed to Sir William Fraser through His Majesty's Consul-General at Khorramshahr and the Foreign Office that previous announcements had prepared the British staff for evacuation from the fields: 'Any change of policy must now have adverse effect on morale unless adequate objectives can be given.'[116] The same message reported that interference by the Persians 'is daily becoming more serious' at Abadan, where they now refused to recognise the existence of the general management of the Anglo-Iranian Oil Company. The Persians had been unimpressed by the withdrawal of tankers—since the beginning of the month the whole port of Abadan had lain almost empty, with only the impressive silhouette of HMS *Mauritius* as a steadying factor, admitted, despite protests, even by the local Persian authorities. All British wives and children were gone by now. 'The atmosphere', reported Mr Middleton, 'has become one of siege. In extreme heat of July nerves are frayed and British staff left are obviously under great tension.'[117]

It was the British oilmen who, while Cabinets debated and diplomatic wirelesses were congested with secret messages concerning the Persian crisis, had to sweat it out that summer in temperatures that were exceptional even for that torrid region. On July 13, 1951, the shade temperature was 123°F, the hottest for five years at Abadan.[118] In this 'huge, tubed town, streamlined and reeking new', in the words of Mr Dylan Thomas, the poet, who had been there scriptwriting a film for the company, 'the waste oil burns night and day, at the top of thin chimneys: little flags of smelly fire'.[119] In this setting, in the face of Persian provocation and petty persecution, the staff of the Anglo-Iranian Oil Company had commanded admiration by their patient staunchness, increasingly tinged though it now was by the bitterness of frustration. They felt, reported Mr Middleton, that they were being 'used as pawns in the game of international politics'. He closed his appreciation of July 4 by indicating that, now that closure of fields and refineries was near, 'it is important to make and keep to a definite and known programme'.[117]

On the same day of July 4, 1951, Mr Bowker minuted in the Foreign Office: 'The position about withdrawal from the fields is now somewhat confused.'[120] This confusion was thrown into relief by the sharp reactions of Mr Capper and Mr Mason at Abadan, as also of Sir Francis Shepherd in Tehran, to a broadcast that afternoon in the General Overseas Service Bulletin of the BBC, wherein its diplomatic correspondent stated that British policy was now 'to sit tight in Persia even if the flow of oil were to cease entirely'.[121] Sir Francis Shepherd represented on July 5 that the Persians 'are watching for signs of firmness from us. They do not believe that

---

[116] EP 1531/861.
[117] EP 1531/854.
[118] EP 1212/34.
[119] PG 13437/3.
[120] EP 1531/915G.
[121] EP 1531/872.

we will evacuate British staff . . . The BBC announcement will certainly strengthen Musaddiq's hand and weaken his opponents. It has already had a deplorable effect.'[122] His Majesty's Ambassador at Tehran now felt that 'evacuation ought to take place immediately'. He explained his view that 'the Persians have by their conduct enabled us to withdraw British employees of the AIOC as an act of strength instead of weakness. The stoppage of tankers followed by the temporary withdrawal of British subjects is a useful form of counter-attack to Persian intransigence. We should be in a fairly strong position to make conditions for the return of British employees.'[123]

The complexity of the crisis now centred upon the remote region of Abadan was evident in that of the arguments and distinctions which needed to be adduced in evaluating it, as at that juncture. The policy of sitting tight throughout the British oilfields in South Persia was outwardly one of obvious strength but inwardly much less so in view of the military considerations—repeated by the Chiefs of Staff to Mr Drake on July 2—which called for concentration of British staff inside Abadan if a truly strong policy was to be pursued. Mr Drake, however, was emphatic that withdrawal of staff from the Fields to Abadan would break their morale and render a general evacuation inevitable. Despite this assessment, which was subsequently proved incorrect, withdrawal from the outlying fields remained in itself a different proposition from total withdrawal from Abadan, though it was not entirely clear from Sir Francis Shepherd's latest telegrams how far he may have had this in mind. As regards total British withdrawal, certainly it was liable to jolt the inefficient Persians; but basically it would be a weak form of counter-attack; because withdrawal in itself is weak and would here be bluff; because the real British interest from every point of view was to remain at Abadan; and it would be a dangerous bluff since the Persian Government might easily call it by not being so eager as might be hoped to recall the British, whom, on the contrary, it really wanted to kick out.

Such considerations were doubtless so familiar to the Eastern Department of the Foreign Office that no basic formulation was prepared. In a letter of July 7 to Sir Francis Shepherd, however, Mr Bowker recognised the 'two schools of thought': His Majesty's Ambassador and representatives in Persia of the Anglo-Iranian Oil Company favouring withdrawal of staff in order to bring the Persians to reason, as against opinion in London that 'once the company left it would probably not be able to return'.[124] On the immediate issue of withdrawal from the outlying fields, the Cabinet on July 5 endorsed the view of the Foreign Secretary that the decision of July 2 suspending withdrawal should stand, subject to discretion of the company's local representatives, and to moderate-scale withdrawal of non-essential staff meanwhile; though it was recognised that this decision might have to be reconsidered very soon because of the effect of Persian interference upon the morale of the hard-tried British staff at Abadan.[125] Often during that crisis British policy appeared to hinge upon events which were under Persian impulsion.

On July 2 the Cabinet had not only altered its decision of June 26 regarding withdrawal from the Fields but had also in effect modified the authorisation given

---

[122] EP 1611/39.
[123] EP 1611/40.
[124] EP 1531/1010.
[125] EP 1531/938G and 873.

that day by Ministers to the Chiefs of Staff to take up shipping for Operation Lethal. The Cabinet on July 2 confirmed that planning for this should proceed but ordered that no preparatory action likely to become publicly known should be taken before the International Court had given its interim decision,[126] expected in a few days: whereas the Chiefs of Staff had emphasised on June 26 that the taking up of shipping would promptly become public. The prudence of not risking any prejudice to the decision of the court was evident; though this consideration was, of course, not new but had presumably been potentially operative since His Majesty's Government had on June 21 notified the International Court of its application, made next day.

In reaching its decision on July 2 against publicised military preparations for Operation Lethal, the Cabinet had before it a memorandum from the Chiefs of Staff—CP(51)172[127]—stating that if preparations were authorised that day, leading elements of the proposed force from units in the Middle East (1st Infantry Division less one brigade, 16th Parachute Brigade, one armoured regiment) could reach Abadan about August 19, that is, in rather more than the six weeks already specified on June 26. The decision against any publicity was evidently liable to complicate and delay preparations as regards shipping and also, for instance, the prepositioning of units at Shaiba, though the Defence Committee on July 2 authorised that of minimal stores and advance parties.

With reference, however, to the view expressed on June 30 by the Commanders-in-Chief, Middle East, that any operation against Abadan should be by advance through Iraq (cf p. 231) Mr Saner, who was to succeed Mr Fry as Assistant Head of Eastern Department, had told the Chiefs of Staff on July 2 that while there would probably be no difficulty in employing Iraqi facilities for Operation Midget, it was 'most unlikely' that the Iraqi Government would permit unrestricted use of its territory for operations against Persia such as the seizure of Abadan island. (Difficulty here regarding use of Kuwait and Bahrein was not anticipated.)[128] Although it was recognised that this involved an important modification to the planning instruction of June 29 from the Chiefs of Staff (cf p. 230), the Commanders-in-Chief, Middle East, were accordingly informed on July 2 that they should now plan Lethal on the alternatives of use or not of Iraqi facilities. It was further recognised that this would militate against the appreciated desire of the Middle East Command for amplified planning.[129]

In view of the critical importance just then of Iraqi goodwill as regards military facilities it was somewhat unfortunate that on the same day of July 2 Sir John Troutbeck had to represent to the Foreign Office from Baghdad that he, let alone the Iraqi Government, had not been officially informed that HMS *Mauritius* had entered Iraqi waters off Abadan. The Iraqi Acting Foreign Minister had complained of this to His Majesty's Ambassador who subsequently received a note asking for an explanation. On July 5 a telegram from the Foreign Office expressed regret at the failure to inform Sir John Troutbeck and instructed him to explain to the Acting Foreign Minister that the movement of HMS *Mauritius* had been made in accordance with the Anglo-Iraqi Treaty of 1930, and that no prior notification had been required

---

[126] CM(51)48th Meeting.
[127] EP 1192/41G.
[128] EP 1192/40G.
[129] EP 1015/258G.

245

since there was then no question of a visit to an Iraqi port.[130]

Military preparations were among the matters discussed at a further meeting which the Prime Minister and the Foreign Secretary held on July 4 with Mr Churchill, Mr Eden and Lord Salisbury, as recorded by Sir William Strang. Mr Morrison outlined the latest developments, including 'the possibility of a change of Government in Persia'.[131] Mr Churchill observed that the situation had deteriorated and held that while in the last resort it might prove necessary to withdraw the British staff from the oilfields 'and indeed even from Abadan', they should not be dispersed but should be held ready to go in again. The Prime Minister agreed. Mr Eden said that while it was no doubt prudent to make no overt military moves pending a ruling from the International Court, 'there would be positive advantage in making overt moves after that. These might in fact be for the purpose of preparing for the safe evacuation of British subjects, but there would be no harm if an impression were created that they were for some wider purpose.'

7. British resistance to American pressure, July 4-5

In the same conversation of July 4 Mr Churchill looked forward to receiving a reply to the message which he had sent on June 29 to President Truman, who had just received a further appeal, of no very novel content, from Dr Musaddiq. In his own 'strong appeal' for the President's help, Mr Churchill had written: 'The question of commercial oil is minor compared to the strategic and moral interests of our two countries and the United Nations. Short of an invasion of Western Europe I cannot think of any Soviet aggression more dangerous to our common cause than for the region between the Caspian Sea and the Persian Gulf to fall under Russian-stimulated Tudeh-Communist control. If this area fell behind the Iron Curtain it would be a serious blow to Turkey, for whom you have made great exertions. Iraq would inevitably follow suit and the whole Middle East, both towards Egypt and India, would degenerate. Limitless supplies of oil would remove the greatest deterrent upon a major Russian aggression . . . Now that he [Musaddiq] has appealed to you I beg you to reply by word and action so as to lighten the burdens which press upon us all.'[132]

The leader of the Opposition had sent a copy of this message to the Foreign Secretary, who thought it very helpful. The Prime Minister substantially agreed. If they entertained, they did not express, any doubt whether this striking communication might perhaps, in its broad emphasis upon the Communist peril, coincide almost too closely with that American thinking which tended to deduce therefrom that particular British interests in Persia were by comparison expendable, and that Dr Musaddiq at any rate provided some safeguard, however imperfect, against an even less desirable régime.

On July 2, 1951, the Embassy of the United States in London intimated to the Foreign Office that the State Department might be considering whether President Truman, in his reply to Dr Musaddiq, should refer to the previously mooted 'moratorium proposal'. Mr Bowker drew the Embassy's attention to Dr Grady's unauthorised initiative and failure in this direction, and scouted a revival. Sir

---

[130] EP 1212/29 and 31.
[131] EP 1531/916G.
[132] EP 1531/914G.

William Strang minuted that day: 'I think that we should firmly discourage the Americans from saying any more to the Persians at the moment. They are certain to say the wrong thing, and will do nothing but harm.'[133] Next day the Secretary of State told the American Ambassador 'that I did not think there was much more which the United States could do for the present'.[134]

To silence the Americans was easier said than done. In Tehran Dr Grady persisted in restlessly futile soundings with the Persian Government regarding some accommodation over tankers' oil receipts and even, apparently,[135] envisaged detailed proposals on the basis of the Anglo-Iranian Oil Company's rejected offer of June 19. More seriously, Sir Oliver Franks, returning from leave in England, reached New York on July 4 to find a message from Mr Dean Acheson asking him to fly at once to Washington to meet him urgently about Persia. They met after lunch that day in the presence of Mr W. Averell Harriman, Special Assistant to President Truman, and Mr H. Freeman-Matthews, Deputy Under-Secretary of State, together with Mr McGhee. The American Secretary of State expressed his grave concern over the Persian situation and asked His Majesty's Ambassador 'whether we foresaw a risk of having to use British troops': a pointer, perhaps, to the extent to which the American Government itself now admitted such a possibility. In reply Sir Oliver Franks referred to the protection of British lives in Persia and made it clear 'that we could not possibly bind ourselves in all circumstances not to use force. Acheson then reverted to the catastrophic potentialities of the situation.'[136]

The American Secretary of State, reported Sir Oliver Franks, then advanced the proposal 'that the President might ask one of his most intimate advisers, for instance the Secretary of the Interior, or possibly Harriman, to talk with the Persians and with ourselves to see whether any road to a solution could be found . . . I said that the value of this suggestion must depend upon the constructiveness of the ideas in the mind of the President's adviser . . . It emerged that the only constructive idea Acheson had was the possibility on the one hand of accepting the Persian thesis on nationalisation, but on the other insisting that the management of oil production and refining in Persia should be carried out by a British company, either the AIOC under another name, or a subsidiary of it. The management fee should be such and clearly understood to be such that a reasonable share of the profits of the operations should accrue to the managing company . . . this would mean, he admitted, carrying our acceptance of the principle of nationalisation further than we had hitherto been willing to go.'

Sir Oliver Franks replied that he could not forecast the response of Mr Morrison but thought that he would attach importance to two points. 'The first was that there had been an impression in London that the Americans considered the British stake in Persian oil as in the end expendable. Acheson at once intervened to say this was not so. The loss of the British connexion with Persian oil meant the collapse of Persia with all that implied for both of us. The second point was that we had already partly in deference to American advice gone a long way in modifying our proposals to meet Persian tastes. Now the Americans were asking us to go further. How could we feel

---

[133] EP 1531/906.
[134] EP 1531/869.
[135] EP 1531/930.
[136] EP 1531/864G.

sure that this was not an unending process so that ultimately we should have to give way on all points and Musaddiq get what he wanted? Acheson said this would not be the case. If this experiment were tried and failed, the failure would greatly influence American public opinion, which was still not very favourable to the British case, and the United States administration would agree with us that we could go no further.'

The prudent and vigorous reply of Sir Oliver Franks to the proposal of Mr Dean Acheson was justified by the initial and generally adverse reaction of the Cabinet on July 5, 1951, to American mediation along such lines. At the same meeting the Cabinet approved a statement which the Foreign Secretary made in the House of Commons that afternoon regretting that the Persian withdrawal of the Anti-Sabotage Bill had been offset by the latest moves against the Anglo-Iranian Oil Company in Tehran and in Abadan. These now included the closure of the company's information offices from which, as from Mr Seddon's residence, documents were removed. Some from the information offices had been published by the Persians and, explained, Mr Morrison, 'distorted to suggest that they were incriminating'.[137] In fact, one at any rate of the company's documents, which was claimed by the Persians on insufficient grounds to establish bribery and espionage in Persia, was subsequently admitted in the Foreign Office to be genuine and to need 'some explaining away'.[138] Fortunately, however, other alleged documents published by the Persians were rank forgeries so that informed Persian opinion was soon somewhat confused and sceptical of their value.

In concluding his Parliamentary statement on July 5 on the Persian position, the Foreign Secretary said: 'It is clear that conditions are becoming intolerable. Our attitude remains the same. The company has no desire to withdraw . . . Yet this, with all the disastrous consequences to Persia that would ensue, is what the Persian Government appear bent on forcing the company to do.' This caused the Unionist Member for East Renfrewshire, Major Guy Lloyd, to enquire: 'Is the House to understand that, however intolerable the position becomes, the attitude of the government will remain the same?'[139]

In the House of Lords that day a repetition of Mr Morrison's statement by the Lord Chancellor provoked a stronger reaction from the Marquess of Salisbury. He said that he had 'formed a most unhappy impression of it, and especially of that portion dealing with evacuation . . . I could not help feeling that it was deplorably weak.' After referring to the 'odious pressure' upon British staff in the oilfields, Lord Salisbury urged that His Majesty's Government 'must say—and the sooner the better—that they are strongly opposed to the evacuation of the British oil personnel in Persia, and that they will take all steps necessary, if the situation requires it, to protect them. If that is not done, I believe that the whole situation will slip away and a position will arise in the Middle East which none of us would wish or hardly dare to contemplate . . . I am sure that I represent a very large body of opinion in this country.'[140]

---

[137] Parliamentary Debates, 5th Series, H. of C., Vol. 489, col. 2493.
[138] EP 1531/958.
[139] Parliamentary Debates, 5th Series, H. of C., Vol. 489, col. 2496.
[140] Parliamentary Debates, 5th Series, H. of L., Vol. 172, cols. 681-2.

8. The interim injunction of the International Court, July 5

Some hours after these Parliamentary exchanges of July 5, 1951, the Foreign Office learnt that the International Court of Justice had that day delivered its interim decision, the preamble of which incidentally confirmed its recognition of the *locus standi* in the dispute of His Majesty's Government, which 'has adopted the cause of a British company and is proceeding in virtue of the right of diplomatic protection'. The Court did not, indeed, concede the interim measures specifically requested by His Majesty's Government. But by the opinion of 10 judges to two (Judges Winiarski and Badawi Pasha of Poland and Egypt respectively) it 'indicated'—the legal term—five 'provisional measures which will apply on the basis of reciprocal observance' pending final decision of the proceedings instituted on May 26: first, the British and Persian Governments should ensure that no action was taken which might prejudice the rights of the other party as regards the execution of any subsequent decision by the Court on the merits, or, secondly, which might aggravate or extend the dispute or, thirdly, which was 'designed to hinder the carrying on of the industrial and commercial operations of the Anglo-Iranian Oil Company, Limited, as they were carried on prior to May 1, 1951'; fourthly, the company's operations in Persia should continue under the direction of its management as constituted before that date, 'subject to such modifications as may be brought about by agreement with the Board of Supervision' of the fifth measure: 'that, in order to ensure the full effect of the preceding provisions, which in any case retain their own authority', there should be established by agreement between the British and Persian Governments a Board of Supervision composed of two Government-appointed British members, two Persian, and one from a third State to be chosen by agreement between the two Governments or, in default and upon the joint request of the parties, by the President of the International Court. The Board of Supervision would have the duty of ensuring that the company's operations were carried on as specified above. The Board would audit the revenue and expenses and ensure 'that all revenues in excess of the sums required to be paid in the course of the normal carrying on of the operations and the other normal expenses incurred by the Anglo-Iranian Oil Company, Limited, are paid into accounts at banks to be selected by the Board on the undertaking of such banks not to dispose of such funds except in accordance with the decisions of the Court or the agreement of the parties.'[141]

---

[141] Cmd 8425, pp. 47-8.

CHAPTER IX

BRITISH DELIBERATIONS AND AMERICAN ACTION ON THE PERSIAN REJECTION OF THE INTERIM INJUNCTION OF THE INTERNATIONAL COURT OF JUSTICE, JULY 5-15, 1951

1. Initial British reactions to the interim injunction, July 5-7

The interim injunction delivered by the International Court of Justice on July 5, 1951, was the first event for months in the Persian crisis that was strongly favourable to Great Britain. The Foreign Office justly considered that it had 'scored heavily' and that in the circumstances the injunction was 'the best for which we could have hoped'.[1] As the Legal Advisers of the Foreign Office specified, it included 'recommendations which do precisely what we want' in prohibiting hindrance to the operations of the Anglo-Iranian Oil Company as before May 1 of that year, and under the company's management as theretofore.

Such signal vindication of the British application to the Court for an interim injunction might be regarded as a testimony not only to the justice of the British case but also to the skilful pleading at The Hague by the Attorney-General, Sir Eric Beckett and their assistants: more especially, perhaps, in view of the grave and subsequently justified doubts which existed then, as in 1932 (cf p. 40), concerning the valid jurisdiction of the International Court at all in the substantive case which His Majesty's Government had brought before it on May 26; and the consequent doubts, now proved incorrect, whether in these circumstances the International Court would agree to grant such an interim injunction (cf pp. 191-2). This grant was a strikingly fortunate development. Its exploitation to the uttermost was now the task of British diplomacy.

There ensued a phase of intensive British deliberations wherein appreciable divergencies of opinion emerged. In the light of its correct conviction that the Persian Government would reject the finding of The Hague Court, the Foreign Office gave prompt and full consideration to the position, producing three major memoranda on July 6. One of these was by the Legal Advisers, who had cleared it, in its general line, with the Attorney-General. The legal experts suggested that the attention of the Persian Government should be drawn to the restoration of the *status quo ante* of May 1 by the interim injunction. 'On this basis, we can make a specific request to the Persians, eg, to withdraw from Abadan the members of the Persian Board who have been interfering in the management, to cease requiring tanker masters to sign the Persian form of receipt, etc. It seems desirable to seize the opportunity formally to request the Persians to desist, in the light of the finding of the Court, from all those specific actions which, in our view, have been hindering operations or which constitute an interference with the management of the company.' The Legal Advisers cogently argued further: 'If, of course, the Persians flatly reject the recommendations, refuse to cooperate in setting up the proposed Board, they would not be in a position to quote these recommendations against us, but until the position is clearer, we should avoid anything which might give the Persians a handle for saying that we were not ourselves complying with the recommendations',[2] such as

---

[1] EP 1531/937G.
[2] *Ibid.*

overt military preparations or further withdrawals of staff, which might be represented as an aggravation of the dispute. The Legal Advisers did not consider the underlying, but seemingly important, question as to how far it might be judicious, in the light of the interim injunction, for His Majesty's Government to maintain its recognition of the principle of oil nationalisation.

This legal memorandum became an annex to a more general memorandum—CP(51)192—giving the 'preliminary views of Foreign Office officials' on the political implications of the interim injunction. These views coincided with those of the Legal Advisers against action which might be contrary to it, such as further withdrawal of British staff in South Persia: 'The Court's ruling now requires the AIOC to continue operations. This, it is suggested, must be decisive for the present.' Having accepted the injunction, His Majesty's Government should nominate its members of the Board of Supervision and possibly suggest a name or names for the fifth member. The political memorandum did not specifically endorse, or indeed refer to, the proposal of the Legal Advisers for definite demands on the Persian Government. Nor did it suggest other lines of action. On the Persian side, it was argued, 'it is no light matter for any country to flout the decision of the highest legal authority in the world', and the judicial organ of the United Nations. Successive Persian Governments, including the present one, had expressed entire adherence to the United Nations, under whose aegis they had extricated themselves from their trouble with the Russians in 1946. The political memorandum concluded: 'The Court's interim injunction will now be officially cognisant of the dispute. We are now in a strong moral position, and it would seem unwise to jeopardise it by premature or overt action [such as military movements] outside the United Nations. If, despite the Court's ruling, the Persians take further action against the company, it would be for consideration whether we should at once appeal to the Security Council, or both appeal and take simultaneous military action to protect the installations.'

The possibility of an appeal to the Security Council had been considered at length in the third Foreign Office memorandum of July 6, prepared by Mr C.C. Parrott, Head of the United Nations (Political) Department, in consultation with Mr Fitzmaurice. The interim injunction of the International Court had supervened since Sir Gladwyn Jebb, in a telegram of June 30, had further argued that there was 'every advantage in not ourselves taking the initiative in the Security Council'[3] unless to forestall a Persian appeal against British military action. A British resolution calling on the Persian Government to refrain from taking possession of the oil installations might possibly get the requisite majority of seven votes, though the attitude of India and Turkey was uncertain; in any case Russia would veto the resolution which would thus have no more than moral authority. Whereas once the matter was raised before the Security Council, the Persian Government might find it more difficult to make concessions since their prestige would be more openly involved; also the hands of His Majesty's Government would be largely tied and it would be more difficult to take military action at short notice.

These arguments of Sir Gladwyn Jebb were substantially included in Mr Parrott's memorandum, which further considered the merits of applying to the Security Council either under Chapter 6 of the Charter ('the pacific settlement of disputes'),

---

[3] EP 1531/815.

when Great Britain as an interested party would lose her vote and potential veto, or alternatively, avoiding this, under Chapter 7 ('action with respect to threats to the peace, breaches of the peace, and acts of aggression'). Mr Parrott advised: 'We might perhaps try and distinguish the initial grounds of dispute from the subsequent consequences and say that the latter constituted a situation, but it would not be convincing',[4] especially in view of the British reference to the International Court. Mr Parrott agreed with Sir Gladwyn Jebb that it would not be in British interests to raise the matter in the Assembly of the United Nations 'in view of the greater strength of anti-imperialist feeling than in the Security Council, the absence of the veto, and the lack of binding force in Assembly resolutions'. The memorandum concluded that if His Majesty's Government were compelled to take military action the initiative in the Security Council should not be left to the Persians; and 'if we are not compelled to use troops in the near future, we might still consider raising the matter in the Security Council either to bring additional pressure to bear on Persia to comply with the Court's findings on interim measures, or to forestall Persian action in the Assembly if we thought that likely'.

Mr Parrott had warned that it 'appears that practically everything depends' on the attitude of the United States at the United Nations. Mr Paul Mason, Assistant Under-Secretary of State superintending the United Nations departments, minuted on Mr Parrott's memorandum on July 6 that if recourse were had to the United Nations, 'the chances of getting an agreed solution between the Persians and ourselves will presumably recede at any rate for some time to come. I should imagine, therefore, that a further move by us now to the United Nations would be unpalatable to the United States, who appear to be desperately keen on trying to work for an agreed solution.'[5] Mr Parrott's memorandum was subsequently considered at a departmental meeting in the Foreign Office. Meanwhile the main Foreign Office memorandum CP(51)192, with the legal memorandum annexed, was considered by the ministerial committee on Persia on the same day of July 6, and three days later was before the Cabinet.

The ministerial committee on July 6, 1951, decided that British acceptance of the interim injunction of the International Court should be announced forthwith in terms which 'should make it clear that AIOC were willing to continue operations in Persia in accordance with the ruling, in so far as the Persian authorities permitted them to do so'[6]: phraseology which might perhaps seem suggestive of a rather wan acquiescence in advance in Persian flouting of the injunction. A British note of July 7 to the Persian Government, however, stated that His Majesty's Government, on the assumption of Persian acceptance of the full recommendation of the court, hoped very shortly to communicate the names of the two British representatives on the Board of Supervision and to make suggestions regarding its fifth member. Persian reciprocity here would be appreciated. The British note concluded: 'His Majesty's Government will be making a further communication to the Imperial Government about the detailed implementation of the Court's recommendations, particularly about measures to be taken to make possible the resumption of the company's

---

[4] EP 1531/1209G.
[5] EP 1531/1209G.
[6] EP 1531/927G.

operations on the basis proposed by the Court.'[7] When Sir Francis Shepherd remitted this note on July 7 to M. Kazimi, he intimated that the Persian Government did not regard the injunction of the International Court as valid. A statement to this effect was issued the same day by the Persian Ministry of Foreign Affairs.[8] This rejection of the competence of the Court was further repeated in a curt Persian reply of July 12[9] to the British note of July 7.

On July 6 the ministerial committee had decided that the names of the two British representatives on the Board of Supervision 'should be communicated to the Persian Government without delay, if possible, after approval by Ministers, on July 9.[6] The Ministers considered that one representative should be drawn from the Anglo-Iranian Oil Company, but subsequently Sir Edward Bridges and Sir William Strang agreed that its board was not a strong panel from which to choose. On this the Foreign Secretary minuted on July 8: 'Which is to our discredit—must be altered if we come through.'[10] In the event the Foreign Office advised against drawing a representative from the company but, if decided otherwise, would, after consultation with Sir William Fraser, recommend Mr Jackson. In the Foreign Office it came to be suggested that two names be chosen from the following: Sir Francis Wylie, former Governor of the United Provinces in India, Marshal of the Royal Air Force Lord Douglas of Kirtleside, and General Sir Neil Ritchie. Some consideration was also given in the Foreign Office to names for the neutral fifth member of the Board of Supervision, notably to those of Count Carafa and—especially favoured—Mr Walter Levy.

The meeting of British Ministers on July 6 had further decided to maintain for the time being the policy determined by the Cabinet on July 2 and 5 as regards both military preparations for possible intervention in South Persia and maintenance of British staff in the oilfields there. It was thought, in addition, that it would be advantageous for Mr Drake to return to Abadan in accordance with the interim injunction. The Foreign Office requested the views of Sir Francis Shepherd. It was six days later, on July 12, that His Majesty's Ambassador replied that the Persians had banned Mr Drake's re-entry and that there was no hope of securing it.[11] This was apparently accepted as conclusive.

2. British failure to prevent American proposal for intervention by Mr Harriman, July 7-8

On July 7 Mr Herbert Morrison sent a message to Mr Dean Acheson in reply to his proposal of July 4 to Sir Oliver Franks (cf p. 247). The Foreign Secretary observed that it differed but little from the proposal made on June 19 by the Anglo-Iranian Oil Company and rejected out of hand by the Persian Government, which refused to consider anything but the full implementation of their nationalisation laws. Mr Morrison continued: 'I must tell you that one of our main difficulties in dealing with this intractable problem has arisen from a belief persistently held by many Persians that there is a difference of opinion between the Americans and the British over the oil question and that America, in order to prevent Persia being lost

---

[7] Cmd 8425, p. 51.
[8] EP 1531/917.
[9] Cmd 8425, p. 52.
[10] EP 1531/1047.
[11] EP 1531/1003.

to Russia, will be ready to help Persia out of any difficulties which she may encounter as a result of the oil dispute. Influential and friendly Persians themselves have told us this, and stressed that it is an important factor in encouraging Dr Musaddiq's present intransigence. An approach by a representative of the President as you suggest would, I fear, merely encourage Dr Musaddiq in this belief. The danger of this would be all the greater since the decision given by The Hague Court, which has introduced a new and most important factor in the situation.'[12]

The Foreign Secretary's rejection of Mr Acheson's proposal closed with the words: 'I feel most strongly that what is wanted from you now is not an offer to mediate, but a firm and categorical statement that it is up to Persia to accept and follow the recommendations of The Hague Court. Such a statement, making it clear once and for all that the United States of America can give no sympathy or help to a country which flouts a decision of the world's highest legal authority, would be of the utmost value at the present critical juncture.' This message, if perhaps somewhat bluntly phrased in places, constituted a vigorous statement of the British position and of Mr Morrison's strong feelings, expressed to Sir Oliver Franks, that the suggested American intervention at that state 'would be most unfortunate'.[13]

Sir Oliver Franks gave the Foreign Secretary's message to Mr Dean Acheson on the same day of July 7. 'After considerable discussion' the latter gave up his suggestion that one of the President's principal advisers should mediate between the British and Persian Governments. He agreed that the pronouncement of The Hague Court was an important new factor, and, ultimately, that the United States should emphasise to Dr Musaddiq its impartial authority and urge him to give it his most serious consideration. 'At the same time Acheson felt in view of the attitude already taken up by the Persians to the jurisdiction of The Hague Court in this dispute that it was essential for the matter not to be left there. What was needed was to get the recommendations or advice of the Court translated into something which actually applied to the oil situation and therefore gave a *modus vivendi* under which an approach to negotiation could be found.'[14] The danger from the British point of view that this translation might involve some watering down was emphasised by Mr Acheson's feeling that it should be proposed that Mr Harriman go to Persia to try to get Dr Musaddiq 'into line with the recommendations of the Court'. Mr Harriman's purpose would be to arrange for them 'to be put into practice subject to any minor modifications which he might find necessary in the circumstances in order to achieve the main object'.

A reply embodying the above elements, from President Truman to Dr Musaddiq's recent message, would be approved by the President and Mr Acheson at luncheon on Sunday, July 8. 'I hope', added Sir Oliver Franks, 'that you will feel most of your purpose has been achieved. We have got rid of the suggestion of mediation: Harriman's job will be with Musaddiq and not between the two parties . . . I do not know whether you will feel the personal follow up by Harriman to the President's letter is likely to help or not. In any case I was unable to deflect Acheson from this proposal.'

In a telegram approved by Mr Attlee and despatched at 1.12 pm on July 8 the

---

[12] EP 1531/864G.
[13] EP 1531/864G.
[14] EP 1531/913G.

Foreign Secretary replied that he would not wish to stand in the way of Mr Acheson's latest proposal 'as long as it is made quite clear to the Persians that Mr Harriman's role in Tehran would be to induce Musaddiq to accept the recommendations of The Hague Court and not to mediate . . . It is most important that Musaddiq should not be given the impression that there is a possibility of selling his acceptance of The Hague's recommendations in return for concessions by us or that with American assistance he can get the recommendations modified to suit his purpose. I am therefore uneasy over the reference to the possibility of 'minor modifications' . . . A resumption of the company's operations on the basis of The Hague's recommendations (i.e. under the company's management) and a cessation of all Persian interference is an absolute *sine qua non* for the opening of any negotiations. His Majesty's Government were sceptical of ever reaching agreement with Dr Musaddiq and it was 'vitally important that nothing should be done at this critical juncture to strengthen his position . . . I would earnestly beg Mr Acheson to see that the President's message to Musaddiq contains a statement of unqualified support for The Hague recommendations, and not merely a reference to the 'authority and impartiality' of the Court's pronouncement.'[15]

On July 9 Sir William Strang minuted from the House of Commons to the Foreign Secretary: 'Mr Churchill says he does not dissent from the line you have taken with Mr Acheson about Harriman. He does not want mediation. He thinks Harriman will be on our side.'[16] Meanwhile, on July 8, pressure of time had compelled His Majesty's Ambassador at Washington to convey the substance of the British reply, with all due emphasis, to Mr Acheson by telephone. Sir Oliver Franks pointed out to him 'that anything which allowed Musaddiq to gain the impression that he could use American concern to exert further pressure on us, was something to be most carefully avoided'.[17] Mr Acheson appreciated the British reply and said he would do his best to render President Truman's letter to Dr Musaddiq consonant with the British views expressed.

President Truman's letter was sent to Tehran on the same day of July 8, 1951. It assured Dr Musaddiq of 'our sympathetic interest in this country, in Iran's desire to control its natural resources. From this point of view, we were happy to see that the British Government has, on its part, accepted the principle of nationalisation.'[18] The President wrote further: 'Technical considerations aside, I lay great stress on the action of the [International] Court . . . Apart from questions of jurisdiction, no one will doubt the impartiality of the world court . . . I earnestly commend to you a most careful consideration of its suggestion. I suggest that its utterance be thought of, not as a decision, which is or is not binding, depending on technical legal considerations but as a suggestion of an impartial body dedicated to justice and equity.' After a further reference to 'this great court', the President mooted the despatch to Persia of Mr Harriman 'to talk over with you this immediate and pressing situation'. If the tone of this letter, with its reservations regarding the jurisdiction of the International Court, and reduction of its decision to a suggestion was still scarcely liable to be completely satisfactory to His Majesty's Government, no representation on this head

---

[15] *Ibid.*
[16] Confidential/General 415, M/72.
[17] *Ibid.*
[18] *Department of State Bulletin*, Vol. XXV, p. 129.

was made to the Government of the United States.

3. Fluctuating British counsels, July 8-12

On the same day of July 8 Mr Fry, in the absence of Mr Furlonge, submitted a minute with recommendations for action in the face of an expected Persian rejection of the injunction of the International Court. He veered back from the recent policy of delaying the evacuation of British staff from the outlying oilfields and recommended that the International Court be notified that, owing to Persian action, it was impossible for His Majesty's Government to observe the court's ruling; they had accordingly decided to withdraw the staff—precisely how far was unspecified. Secondly, Mr Fry recommended that His Majesty's Government should at the same time seek a resolution in the Security Council of the United Nations calling upon the Persian government to observe the recommendations of the International Court. Thirdly, Iraqi agreement should be sought to the immediate despatch of British troops to Shaiba on grounds of urgent need to be ready to protect British nationals during withdrawal from South Persia; and similarly for the early stationing of troops at Kuwait and Bahrain. Mr Fry, however, marshalled the familiar arguments, including the Attorney-General's opinion of May 25, against military intervention in Persia, and argued that since the International Court was now seized of the dispute it would, if anything, seem to 'the lay mind' that His Majesty's Government had 'less right than ever to use force'. Mr Fry considered that in the final analysis American and world opinion 'may well be the deciding factor in this affair'.[19]

Mr Parrott minuted on July 9 on Mr Fry's paper that in connexion with a British appeal to the Security Council, military measures should so far as possible be limited or postponed. Mr Fitzmaurice agreed that such an appeal 'should certainly *not* be coupled with military measures'. He also agreed with Mr Parrott's view that any reference to the Security Council should be preceded by full consultation with the United States. In general, Mr Fitzmaurice minuted regarding Mr Fry's somewhat debatable proposals: 'All this seems to me premature.'[20]

Also on July 9 Mr Fry explained his paper of the previous day to a meeting of the Chiefs of Staff and expressed his personal opinion 'that it would in no circumstances be politically possible to use armed force for any purpose other than to cover evacuation',[21] which was the limit of military action envisaged in his proposals. This provoked a strong reaction from the representative of the vigorously minded Royal Air Force, Air Vice-Marshal MacFadyen. This Assistant Chief of the Air Staff said that if that was the view of the Foreign Office there had been a waste of time, money and effort in planning for Operations Midget Reinforced and Lethal and taking such preliminary action as assembling aircraft and tank-landing craft. He maintained that the Foreign Office 'had never before put forward these views which seemed in fact to be contrary to those expressed at ministerial meetings'. There was general agreement in the meeting with Air Vice-Marshal MacFadyen and also with Major-General McLeod, who argued that the prepositioning at Shaiba of only a token British force would be 'wholly undesirable'; another factor was that 'forces were simply not available to allow them to be placed in Shaiba and the Persian Gulf

---

[19] EP 1531/982G.
[20] EP 1531/982G.
[21] EP 1192/55G.

Sheikhdoms simultaneously'. The Foreign Office was invited to take account of the views of the Chiefs of Staff in revising the paper under consideration.

On the same day of July 9 the Leader of the Opposition sent a letter to the Prime Minister, with copy to the Foreign Secretary, indicating some stiffening of attitude in a generally contrary sense to the latest paper prepared in the Foreign Office. Mr Winston Churchill argued that the staff of the Anglo-Iranian Oil Company should be encouraged to remain in Abadan, if not in 'the mountainous oilfield. We understood that this was your policy, but that in addition, should it be decided to withdraw the personnel, they would be kept concentrated and intact at Shaiba and upon a liner. We think it would be a disaster if our personnel were justled and bullied out of Abadan', and worse again if they were dispersed and scattered. The Opposition, wrote Mr Churchill, had been led to hope in their first conversation of June 27 with leaders of the Government 'that military movements would be continuous so as to secure ample forces, naval, air, and army, on the spot to meet any emergency'. Mr Herbert Morrison noted here: 'This is my own view but I'm not sure it's the Govt.'s or that it was said.' Mr Churchill continued: 'We also asked that if the worst came to the worst the Government should not exclude the possibility of a forcible occupation of Abadan and we were told that plans for this contingency were in preparation. We have made it clear that should such regrettable measures be forced upon you, you could count on our support. As it seems to us, the judgment of the Hague Court greatly strengthens our world position should such action become necessary.' Mr Morrison minuted: 'Generally I agree with Mr Churchill's letter but see notes. Govt. must make up its mind.'[22]

In the House of Commons that same afternoon the Foreign Secretary reported that Persian interference in the operations of the Anglo-Iranian Oil Company continued to increase. The company's superintendent of communications at Abadan had been ordered by the Persian Temporary Board to hand over his work to one of its members unless he was prepared to serve it. Mr Morrison reiterated that 'our view is that our people should stay there as long as it is practicable, and that remains our policy'.[23] This induced Mr Eden to ask whether the Foreign Secretary had seen a report in the *Daily Herald* of that morning attributing to a member of the British Embassy at Tehran 'a statement that there is a good chance that the lads will be home in time for Goodwood'.

From the Opposition benches, also, Lord Dunglass established the Government's dilemma as follows: 'I think the Foreign Secretary said that it was the Government's wish that the employees should stay in Abadan; but all the statements which the right hon. Gentleman has made at question time and in debate have been in the context of eventual evacuation . . . It seems to me that the policy he is pursuing might simply provoke the Persians to go on increasing their acts of provocation, and that if only he could say almost at once that it is the Government's policy to maintain a staff, even if it is a skeleton staff, in Abadan, that might easily bring a settlement of the problem very much nearer.'[24]

At a cabinet meeting on the same day of July 9 the Lord Chancellor passed to the Foreign Secretary a note which began: 'Damn this legalism. The time *may* come

---

[22] EP 1531/1022G.
[23] Parliamentary Debates, 5th Series, H. of C., Vol. 490, cols. 35-8.
[24] *Ibid*, col. 38.

when you may have to say to the Persians something like this. "This dispute which has gone on all too long can only be settled in one of two ways—either by the use of reason or by the use of force. It is for you, Persians, to decide . . . Whilst on the one hand we are prepared to go all the way to meet the appeal to reason, we are not prepared to stand by and see our people insulted and our property put out of action."'[25] Mr Fitzmaurice minuted on this to Sir William Strang: 'I wish the Lord Chancellor would discuss the matter with the Attorney General who holds very different views about the use of force. Personally I am more in agreement with the Lord Chancellor on the subject and have had a memorandum prepared [and] written to the A-G about it . . . Naturally I have only gone into the purely legal aspects.'

In his long letter of July 10 to Sir Frank Soskice, Mr Fitzmaurice enclosed a memorandum by Mr D.H.N. Johnson, Legal Member of Research Department, on 'the right to intervene in Persia'. Mr Fitzmaurice explained that he himself differed somewhat from the view of the Attorney-General that in the last resort it would be legitimate to use force in Persia to protect British lives, but not property. Mr Fitzmaurice felt some difficulty in finding a logical basis of distinction between the two cases, and it did not seem to him 'necessarily to follow from the Charter [of the United Nations] in all circumstances that the use of force for purposes other than strict self-defence was invariably excluded',[26] notably by paragraphs 3 and 4 of Article 2. With reference to Article 1, setting out the purposes of the United Nations, Mr Fitzmaurice argued that what its Charter was intended to rule out 'was the *illegal* or aggressive use of force'. He suggested that 'if under international law a right to use force in certain specified circumstances and under proper safeguards is recognised, then it cannot be contrary to the purposes of the Charter to use force in those circumstances'.[27] And Mr Johnson showed that under international law before the Second World War a general right did exist to take forcible action to protect the lives of one's citizens abroad and even in certain circumstances national property abroad.

Mr Johnson, in particular, now elucidated the fact that the Second Hague Convention of 1907 specifically provided for military intervention by one Power against another Power which had refused arbitration to its nationals in respect of a debt. The principle of military intervention in certain circumstances had been endorsed in 1910 by the former American Secretary of State, Mr Elihu Root; though such precedents might carry limited weight, as was appreciated in the Foreign Office with reference to the 180 American military interventions on foreign territory up to 1934.[28]

Mr Fitzmaurice concluded his letter to the Attorney-General: 'A case for the limited use of force for the protection of British property in Persia might well be made out notwithstanding any provision of the Charter', and *a fortiori* as regards British lives.[29] Mr Bowker recorded on July 16 that Mr Fitzmaurice had discussed his letter with Sir Frank Soskice, who 'was inclined to agree that we might have a right to send in troops to safeguard lives in danger', but not property.[30] A copy of

---

[25] EP 1192/82.
[26] *Ibid.*
[27] *Ibid.*
[28] EP 1192/26 and 83G.
[29] EP 1192/82.
[30] EP 1192/83G.

Mr Fitzmaurice's letter was subsequently sent to Lord Jowitt.

Such were the legal differences of opinion behind the political ones regarding the possibilities of British military intervention in South Persia. And there remained, basic, the strictly military difficulties. On July 5 the Commanders-in-Chief, Middle East, had telegraphed that if Iraqi facilities were available Operation Lethal could be carried out via Basra with 41 ships of various categories in nine weeks; if such facilities were not available, the operation by direct assault on Abadan would require 78 ships and 13 weeks. Next day the Chiefs of Staff replied that they were 'somewhat disturbed at the timings and shipping requirements . . . as both these show a considerable increase on previous estimates'.[31] By July 9, however, the Chief of the Air Staff was able to inform a meeting of the Defence Committee that, by sending all available transport-aircraft to the Middle East, Operation Midget could be reinforced so that three battalions could arrive at Abadan by D-day, two more on D + 4 and one, making six in all, on D + 6. By July 21 the guns and tanks loaded in the tank-landing ships would be on the spot. Sir John Slessor stated that the Commanders-in-Chief, Middle East, now considered 'that this force assuming it be successful in occupying Abadan should be adequate to hold it', granted arrangements for continuous maintenance and supply. The success of the operation would depend upon the timely evacuation of civilians from the Fields into Abadan.[32]

At a meeting of the Chiefs of Staff two days later, on July 11, 1951, the point was made that, 'if it was officially confirmed that Midget reinforced could both seize and hold Abadan island, Lethal would become a redundant plan only to be undertaken in the event of a complete reverse for Midget'.[33] This advantageous trend in planning development was underlined by a telegram of the same date wherein the Chiefs of Staff conveyed to the Commanders-in-Chief, Middle East, their preliminary view that planning should assume that Iraqi facilities would be available for Operations Midget and Midget Reinforced but not for Operation Lethal. Already on the previous day, indeed, the codeword Midget, operating since May 9, had been cancelled and replaced by Buccaneer as the codeword for an operation in two phases: first to move forces to Abadan to cover the evacuation of British subjects in the face of Persian military opposition; secondly, to remain in Abadan to safeguard British lives and property.[34] Henceforth, till the end of the Persian crisis, Buccaneer was to hold the field outlined by British military planning.

The initiative towards more enterprising military planning, which had been given in the latter part of June by such advisers as Sir Donald Fergusson and Air Marshal Sir Arthur Sanders, had by July 10 produced Operation Lethal, and now Operation Buccaneer. On July 11 Mr Fry submitted a memorandum, agreed with the main departments of the Foreign Office, the Legal Advisers and the secretariat of the Chiefs of Staff, and entitled 'Political Implications of Armed Intervention in the Persian Oil Dispute'.[35] This memorandum argued that in the United Kingdom, despite some shocked opposition to forceful action outside the United Nations, in the main 'public opinion might be expected to favour using force' to protect British property as well as lives, as recently indicated by Lord Salisbury. The likely benefits

---

[31] EP 1192/47G.
[32] EP 1192/50G.
[33] EP 1192/60G.
[34] EP 1015/274G.
[35] EP 1192/52G.

accruing from successful intervention for British interests throughout the Middle East (as against threats of nationalisation of foreign interests, as in Iraq, and of the Suez Canal in Egypt) were explained, if not particularly emphasised, word for word as in Mr Fry's corresponding memorandum of May 21 (cf pp. 181-2). The earlier memorandum was also closely followed as regards likely reactions to British intervention in Persia from the Commonwealth and, more strongly adverse, from the Soviet Union, the United States and the United Nations. The general conclusion was: 'There can be little doubt that world opinion, at all events at the outset, would be against us. It was generally unfavourable to us when the dispute began, but has swung steadily in our favour', a trend strengthened by British acceptance of the interim injunction of the International Court and by Persian rejection of it. This rejection was notified to the United Nations and the court on July 9 in a Persian note which also withdrew Persian acceptance of the Optional Clause. Dr Musaddiq told Dr Grady that President Truman's message was thus too late, and he appeared to discountenance the proposed mission of Mr Harriman.

Mr Fry subsequently minuted that in the light of his above memorandum and of the Cabinet decision of July 12 (cf pp. 263) he could really think of nothing more to say in regard to a suggestion made to the Minister of State in the Foreign Office in a letter of July 11 from Mr Harold Watkinson, Conservative Member of Parliament for Woking, supported next day by the Conservative Member for Chelsea, Commander Noble, on behalf of Mr Eden. This suggestion was that all British staff at Abadan should be withdrawn to Iraq and replaced by a small party of strictly technical troops in order to close down the refinery and retain it on a care and maintenance basis, not as a military operation but as the most convenient means of carrying out the interim injunction of the International Court pending its final judgment. Mr Saner minuted on July 17 that this plan would be open to all the political objections to use of force in Persia plus the additional disadvantage of military weakness: 'It is possible that the Persians might take the opportunity afforded by their being only "technical troops" to avoid fighting, but it would be impossible to count on this.' Next day Mr Furlonge minuted: 'I agree. The suggestions appears to me to have no merits at all.'[36] What was recognised in the Foreign Office as 'a concerted approach by PMs' had, however, been overtaken by certain developments in governmental deliberations.

The arguments pro and con British use of force in Persia to protect property as distinct from lives had been briefly recapitulated in yet another memorandum, CP(51)200 of July 11, signed by the Foreign Secretary and circulated to the Cabinet. The adverse arguments were listed as the Attorney-General's opinion of May 25, alienation of world opinion, danger to British staff in the oilfields 'before we could extricate them', danger of damage to the refinery and oilfields and 'the even more serious consideration that an attempt to maintain the Company in Persia with British bayonets would prejudice the Persians permanently against the Company'.[37] Mr Morrison had considered the question with the Prime Minister and they had therefore concluded 'that force had better be ruled out' for the protection of British property. As regards alternative, non-military action, the argument of the remainder of Mr Morrison's memorandum closely followed that of Mr Fry's memorandum of July 8

---

[36] EP 1531/1104.
[37] EP 1531/2380G.

(cf p. 256). The Foreign Secretary concluded with four recommendations: first, announcement 'that a phased withdrawal of the Anglo-Iranian Oil Company British personnel would be put into operation forthwith', beginning with the men in the oilfields as distinct from Abadan; secondly, that the President of The Hague Court be notified of this; thirdly, 'that the matter should be taken to the Security Council'; fourthly, 'that we should inform the United States Government of the action we are taking, and seek their support in the Council'. Sir Oliver Franks was indeed already being instructed to inform the American Government accordingly, more particularly regarding that British recourse to the Security Council against which the British representative at the United Nations had strongly advised on June 30 (cf pp. 251-2). Since then the Foreign Office had not further sought the opinion of Sir Gladwyn Jebb. The Foreign Secretary's memorandum did, however, embody the conclusion of a meeting in the Foreign Office, attended by Mr Fitzmaurice and Mr Parrott, to consider the latter's memorandum of July 6 regarding reference to the United Nations (cf pp. 251-2). No draft of the Foreign Secretary's memorandum has been traced. It is possible that such a draft, unlike that for Mr Fry's memorandum, may have carried comments by the Permanent Under-Secretary. Otherwise, in this crisis of opinion as also probably at other times, any views which he may have expressed personally were presumably conveyed orally.

Before the Foreign Secretary's memorandum of July 11 was considered on the following day by the Cabinet, the Foreign Office received a first intimation that Dr Musaddiq had artfully reversed his initial objection to Mr Harriman's mission and had now accepted it, with reservations as to the Persian position in the dispute. In a brief of July 12 for the Cabinet meeting, Mr Fry advised that the development should not affect any of the recommendations in Mr Morrison's memorandum: 'There seems little hope that the Harriman mission will come to anything and, if it does not, there will have been delay at a time when it seems desirable that His Majesty's Government, after much restraint, should take some initiative.' To this argument, of much cogency in itself, Mr Fry added: 'Dr Musaddiq's belated acceptance of the Harriman mission probably means that he is hoping to play the Americans off against us.'[38]

Mr Fry had already dictated the above when a telegram of July 11 was received from Sir Oliver Franks wherein he reported that—rather, one imagines, as would have been anticipated—Mr Acheson 'very much hoped' that Mr Morrison would not find it necessary immediately to proceed with his proposal to go to the Security Council, which would almost certainly render ineffective the other, preferably prior, expedient of Mr Harriman's mission. Mr Acheson alluded to the terms of Dr Musaddiq's reply of July 11 to Mr Truman and thought that, 'while maintaining the positions previously taken up', they 'did not exclude a little room for manoeuvre. He had the feeling that Harriman might not find that he was up against a blank wall.'[39] In fact, as Sir Francis Shepherd stressed in a telegram of July 12, Dr Musaddiq's letter repeated four times that he would only consider discussions within the terms of the Persian laws for oil nationalisation. This, as Sir Francis Shepherd represented, was 'at complete variance'[40] with the conditions under which the

[38] EP 1112/43G.
[39] EP 1531/964.
[40] EP 1531/975.

Americans had offered Mr Harriman's mission and with the views conveyed by Mr Morrison in his telegram of July 8 to Washington. It would not appear, however, that Sir Oliver Franks raised, or was instructed to raise, this important point with Mr Acheson, or that he questioned that Mr Harriman would in any case proceed to Tehran.

Sir Oliver Franks' telegram caused Mr Fry to reverse one part of his brief for the Cabinet meeting. He now swelled the somewhat fluctuating counsel regarding recourse to the Security Council by advising against it. American support for it could better be secured if Mr Harriman's mission had failed. This, Mr Fry now suggested, outweighed his earlier contentions that application to the Security Council should have a sobering effect on Persian opinion, and that delay might lessen the soundness of the British case. Mr Fry concluded: 'It is nevertheless recommended that the proposed announcement of a phased withdrawal, and the despatch of a letter to the President of The Hague Court, should go forward.'[41]

As regards Mr Harriman's mission, the Cabinet meeting of July 12 invited the Foreign Secretary to do, in effect, what he had already done: namely, to inform the American Government that His Majesty's Government did not regard it as appropriate that Mr Harriman should act as a mediator, and considered acceptance by the Persian Government of The Hague ruling to be 'the necessary basis for a settlement of the dispute'.[42] It would rather appear, however, that the Cabinet contemplated that Mr Harriman's mission would take place in any event now that Dr Musaddiq had accepted it upon his terms, as opposed to the British ones.

In Cabinet discussion on July 12, 1951, of the possibility of negotiating with the Persian Government, the Prime Minister thought it unsafe to assume that 'if we succeeded in upsetting the present [Persian] Government their successors would be less unsatisfactory, and we should risk identifying ourselves with support of an equally undemocratic régime'. He further considered that 'we must not alienate genuine nationalist feeling in Persia by clinging to the old technique of obtaining concessions and insisting upon exact compliance with their terms'. In the discussion 'attention was drawn to the need for considering how far we should be willing to go to enable the Persian Government to avoid making concessions which they regarded as humiliating. We had no legal right to interfere with Persian expropriation and operation of their oil industry, but we had the right to require compensation for the AIOC, and the Persian Government could only pay this compensation if the industry was profitably operated. Mr Harriman might be able to impress this point upon the Persian Prime Minister, and it might also be desirable to make it clear to the United States Government that we should not insist on the withdrawal of the nationalisation law if amendment would make it workable.'

In the light of Mr Harriman's mission the Cabinet decided to take no action for the present on any of the positive recommendations in the Foreign Secretary's memorandum of July 11: as regards not only prompt recourse to the Security Council, against which Mr Morrison himself now advised, but also the proposed phased withdrawal of British staff from Persia. Some Ministers held that this was bound to be interpreted as a sign of weakness; it was, however, also pointed out that withdrawal, at least from the Fields, could not be deferred much longer and 'it must

---

[41] EP 1112/43G.
[42] EP 1531/1089G.

be represented as an act of deliberate policy when it took place'.[43] As regards recourse to the Security Council, Sir Gladwyn Jebb on the same day of July 12 telegraphed further argument of his earlier advice against it. On which the Prime Minister commented on July 13: 'I think that this telegram gives very strong reasons for not going to the Security Council.'[44]

At the same meeting on July 12, 'in discussing the possibility of military intervention in Persia, the Cabinet were reminded that they had at one stage asked the Chiefs of Staff to consider the military implications of seizing Abadan and holding it, if necessary, against Persian opposition, for the purpose of refining there crude oil brought from Kuwait. The Cabinet were, however, impressed by the arguments developed in . . . CP(51)200 against the use of force for the protection of British property . . . they agreed that military action in Persia, on a larger scale than that necessary for the protection of British lives, should not be contemplated unless there were some far-reaching change in the general situation, such as the fall of the present Government and the establishment of a Communist régime in Persia.' This relegation of Operation Lethal left the field to Operation Buccaneer. Such was the political tendency towards increased caution at the same time as military preparations were progressing. On the following day the Chiefs of Staff informed the Commanders-in-Chief, Middle East, of this Cabinet decision and commented that it meant that for the present Buccaneer in both phases was the only plan to keep in mind and in immediate readiness; preparations for that operation could in no way be relaxed.[45]

The relegation of Operation Lethal to some extent cut both ways. On the one hand it reflected the circumspection of His Majesty's Government about preparing the strongest military action against Persia: action which would involve not only grave complications and hazards abroad, but stern measures at home; such as taking up 40 to 50 ships, calling up 30,000 reservists and two territorial divisions, and chartering of civil aircraft. In some measure Buccaneer represented a retreat from Lethal: militarily, Buccaneer was likely to be the more hazardous operation; politically, its basis was the more circumscribed. On the other hand it was a considerable planning advance that the Commanders-in-Chief, Middle East were now prepared to underwrite the risk of holding Abadan with the relatively light forces earmarked, and promptly ready, for Buccaneer and so cut out those preparations for Lethal, which, as may well have been inevitable, would be militarily cumbersome and slow, and therefore politically dangerous. Since in time of peace, more even than in war, a military stroke, to be successful, most often needs to be swift.

Also on July 12 Mr Fry addressed to Lieutenant-Colonel R.G.V. Fitzgeorge Balfour, Assistant Secretary to the Chiefs of Staff Committee, a letter which incidentally indicated certain criticisms of the minute recording the opposition of the meeting of the Chiefs of Staff on July 9 to his opinion regarding the political implications of the use of force in Persia (cf p. 256)—an opinion, stated Mr Fry, which had in fact been endorsed by Lieutenant-General Sir Kenneth McLean. Mr Fry observed that the implications in question had long been known and discussed:

---

[43] EP 1531/1089G.
[44] EP 1531/1000 and 1072.
[45] EP 1192/51G.

'the position simply is that Ministers nevertheless wished certain plans to be drawn up, and so directed the Service authorities. The Foreign Office official view in this, again so far as I am aware, has not varied and is set out, once more,'[46] in Mr Fry's memorandum of July 11. This memorandum had largely recapitulated the suppositions in that of May 21 (cf p. 181-2) without, however, going so far towards recommending the use of force. The possible advantages of such use of force had not been underrated in the Foreign Office (cf pp. 129, 181-2, 183, 230). It had also, however, given all due weight to the serious political repercussions liable to result, more especially, from any large and slow operation (cf Plans X and Y and Lethal) on a scale greater than Operation Midget (cf pp. 185, 230, 256).

4. The British failure to exploit the interim injunction, July 5-12

It may be judged both natural and correct that the Foreign Office should in principle have been reluctant to countenance or counsel military measures towards a solution of the stubborn problem of Persian oil. Force, after all, most often spells the failure of diplomacy. In time of peace, especially, military action is apt to be easy to initiate, difficult to terminate—an open-ended risk. And all the more so in such complex circumstances and in the face of the likelihood, prudently assessed in the Foreign Office, that such British military action would provoke predominantly hostile or critical reactions in the rest of the world, in the United Nations and, especially, in the United States. Yet by the time the Foreign Office had been driven to pursuing the highly dangerous possibility of stimulating a governmental reversal in Persia, the scope, indeed the hope, for successful negotiation by normal methods was becoming almost desperately small. Malignant and increasing Persian pressure upon British civilians in Abadan, with all that implied for the British presence throughout the strategic and oil-bearing Middle East, underlined the stark alternatives, at last, of surrender or resistance. That was what the British people largely sensed. In this pass it was the evident duty of those advising His Majesty's Government to seize upon every solid advantage to the British cause and seek to exploit it resolutely, perhaps even ruthlessly, in building up a strong policy which might politically justify and underpin, even if it did not actually succeed in replacing, use of force in the ultimate extremity. And the greatest and solidest advantage then to Britain was the interim injunction of the International Court.

It may have been the interposition of Mr Harriman's mission to Tehran, amid so many complications and anxieties, which restrained His Majesty's Government from ever following up the lines indicated in its apposite note of July 7 to the Persian Government regarding the recommendations of the International Court. The promised 'further communication' regarding the due resumption of the operations of the Anglo-Iranian Oil Company upon that basis was not sent before, or after, receipt of the negative Persian reply of July 12 (cf p. 253). Whereas it might have seemed most desirable to act without delay, for any reason, upon the recommendations for specific demands upon the Persians regarding Abadan which the Legal Advisers of the Foreign Office had generally cleared with the Attorney-General and submitted on July 6 (cf pp. 250-1). In practice these important recommendations appear to have been rather quickly lost to sight or overlaid. If, on the other hand, the Persian Government had been promptly presented with a formal

---

[46] EP 1192/55G

and specific British demand for the cessation of all unwarranted Persian interference at Abadan, the reinstatement of Mr Drake and general restoration of the company's operations as before May 1 in accordance with the indication of the International Court, that would, at the least, have provided an excellent legal platform for all subsequent British measures in the event of Persian recalcitrance.

The more that Persian rejection of the international ruling could thus be nailed down, the better for the British cause in the international forum. Henceforth every further Persian action at Abadan against British interests could be legitimately denounced as a blow, not merely against an allegedly imperialist Power and capitalist company, but against those foundations of international law and order upon which a weak and precariously situated country like Persia must especially depend. Since His Majesty's Government had virtually abandoned hope of fruitful negotiation with Dr Musaddiq, there would appear to have been every advantage in making the most of this gift to British propaganda.

Within such a context it might have proved possible to give special effect to the hope expressed by Sir Francis Shepherd on July 4, that the widest publicity was being given in London to reports from Abadan, 'which display the outrageous attitude of the Persian authorities'.[47] On the same day General Sir Brian Robertson represented from Fayyid to the Vice-Chief of the Imperial General Staff that inadequate publicity was being given to the indignities inflicted upon British subjects in South Persia. General Robertson wrote: 'I submit that we ought at this time to be building up our case and not belittling it.'[48] Over a month later, on August 7, Mr Bowker commented to Lieutenant-General Brownjohn that, among other things, 'as it is our policy to remain in the fields and Abadan, it hardly seems desirable to paint too lurid a picture of the suffering of our people in the area, as this would be liable to increase popular agitation for military intervention while Ministers were still unwilling to authorise it.'[49] It came back to that.

A vigorous follow-through from the interim injunction by British propaganda might have been the more effective since one has the impression that, as regards media for Persia (eg the Embassy news bulletin and the BBC), it was at last working at concert pitch. The inauguration by the BBC on June 27 of the additional broadcast to Persia (cf p. 206) was followed on July 5 by the inception of a system of relay via Bahrein. Such broadcasts from the Persian Gulf had been mooted earlier by Sir Francis Shepherd, who presumed they would avoid any suggestion of covert activities.[50] His Majesty's Embassy in Tehran reported that the BBC broadcasts were admirable and that, with the extra times and wavelengths, they were having considerable effect.[51]

The ground, too, was propitious just then for a stern concentration of British propaganda on the reckless recalcitrance of the Persian Government and the menacing possibilities latent in its provocation of His Majesty's Government, with potential openings for Russian intervention. Dr Musaddiq's flouting of the injunction of the International Court had weakened his Government and aroused considerable concern in Persia, with opportunities for M. Sayyid Zia. In the Majlis

---

[47] EP 1531/868.
[48] EP 1531/1043.
[49] EP 1531/1332.
[50] PB 1041/21.
[51] EP 1531/1015.

on July 8 M. Azad, a Deputy formerly supporting the National Front, had compared Dr Musaddiq to Herr Hitler, seeking to distract the people's attention from unaccomplished reforms in the face of 'anarchy and ruin'.[52] In other countries the effect was corresponding. The American Press produced a crop of 'excellent editorials' from the British point of view. (On July 17 the Foreign Office sent copies to the BBC for its use.)[53] A Turkish newspaper warned Persia of Soviet machinations and Professor Nihat Erim, recently Deputy Turkish Prime Minister, wrote on July 12 that she would have only herself to blame if she had to face the combined hostility of Great Britain, the United States and France.[54] If, unhappily, that did not quite occur, the French Government of its own accord instructed its Ambassador in Tehran to protest against the Persian attitude to The Hague ruling.[55] Nor was it due to British initiative—the Foreign Office was indeed sceptical of its achieving anything—that King Abdullah of Jordan sent personal messages urging moderation upon both the Shah of Persia and Dr Musaddiq.[56] This was one of King Abdullah's last acts of policy before his assassination on July 20, 1951, which further weakened British influence in the Middle East.

From beyond the Middle East the Australian Government was meanwhile urging great caution upon the Government of the United Kingdom in reaching a decision to withdraw British staff from South Persia.[57] On the other hand it may or may not have been due to some defect of coordination that Mr Fry, in his memorandum of July 11 (cf pp. 259-60), followed that of May 21 in including Canada in his statement that the Old Commonwealth would probably support British military intervention in Persia. Two days earlier, on July 9, Mr Logan of Eastern Department had initialed a minute of July 3 by Mr P.M. Johnston, Head of Commonwealth Liaison Department, referring to two curtailed conversations which the Foreign Secretary had had in the last week of June with Mr Lester Pearson, Canadian Secretary of State for External Affairs. For these conversations Mr Morrison had been briefed that Canadian officials had not been very appreciative of British difficulties regarding Persian oil; Mr Morrison had sought Canadian sympathy, but had gathered from Mr Pearson 'that Canadian interest in the oil dispute was not sufficiently strong to warrant any direct expression of sympathy with our point of view'.[58] Mr Johnston had minuted on this that it was perhaps a pity that the Foreign Secretary had been unable to interest Mr Pearson 'more strongly in Persia, particularly in view of unfavourable Canadian Press comment'.

Canadian Press comment on the Persian crisis, at any rate before the decision of The Hague Court, had been less favourable than the American to the British case. Except for conservative organs at Toronto, Canadian editors, including those normally very favourable to Great Britain, had been uniformly critical of the British position; and the *Globe and Mail* of Toronto had referred in this connexion to the 'failure' of British propaganda.[59] The Commonwealth Relations Office attributed

---

[52] EP 1531/926.
[53] PB 1048/15.
[54] PG 13437/17.
[55] EP 1531/1004.
[56] ET 10334/2 and EP 1531/1019 and 1120.
[57] EP 1531/1089G.
[58] B 31/31.
[59] AU 1021/7.

the tone of the Canadian editors to their being initially less well informed than the American concerning the facts and implications of the Persian situation. At the request of the Foreign Secretary this had been explained in a memorandum[60] by Mr J.N.O. Curie, Assistant Head of American Department, of which the Head had recently defected. With that unhappy background, it is not clear from Foreign Office records whether any sustained effort was made through the Commonwealth Relations Office to stimulate an improvement in Canada at a time when the unity of the Old Commonwealth, at least, might be of critical importance in relation to the Persian crisis and potential military action.

A circular telegram of July 7, 1951, from the Foreign Office had requested British missions abroad to try to stimulate comment on The Hague ruling along prudent lines which included the argument that the injunction was 'not a one-sided victory for us'[61] since it subjected the Anglo-Iranian Oil Company to a mixed Supervisory Board with control of finance and Persian representation. As regards this by no means inconsiderable sop to the Persians, one rather wonders whether it might not have been possible for British diplomacy, by supplementing firmness with adroitness, to have turned it to positive advantage so as to save British, as well as Persian, face. On the one hand The Hague decision afforded His Majesty's Government a *locus standi* for upholding the operating rights of the Anglo-Iranian Oil Company, in accordance with its terms, more firmly than before. On the other hand it was by now (July 6) recognised in the Foreign Office that 'dislike of the company is general in Persia'.[62] While the crisis centred upon the company, which evidently needed to be sustained by His Majesty's Government, the particular form of the Anglo-Iranian interest had, however unfairly, in practice become a diplomatic millstone, heavily prejudicing progress towards an ultimate solution. By pressing its acceptance of the Supervisory Board, no less than of the advantage to the company under the rest of the interim injunction, His Majesty's Government might conceivably have been able to initiate a graceful retreat, under the best conditions, from too strict and stultifying association with the company in working towards an eventual solution: compare the Prime Minister's warning of July 12 against 'clinging to the old technique' (cf p. 262). Such a retreat might have helped to cover one, on the other hand, from too rigid British admission, now, of oil nationalisation (cf p. 251).

In such a context it might not, perhaps, have been impossible for His Majesty's Government to intimate discreetly that Persian accommodation regarding what were, after all, only provisional operating rights for the Anglo-Iranian Oil Company under the interim injunction, would be repaid by British accommodation regarding Persian interests in any final settlement along imaginative lines, to which the mixed composition of the Supervisory Board might already seem to point. The strikingly close approximation of the Supervisory Board to the body suggested by Mr Julius Holmes to Sir William Strang on June 23 (cf p. 227) was a most interesting feature, though it apparently provoked only slight contemporary comment. In any case there might have been great advantage in hastening to follow up the British note of July 7 to the Persian Government by notifying to it, if possible before Persian rejection of

---

[60] *Ibid.*
[61] P 10151/41.
[62] EP 1531/937G.

the interim injunction, not only the two British nominations to the Supervisory Board but also the British proposal for the fifth, external member; especially if the latter had been Mr Walter Levy; especially since Mr Berthoud minuted on July 9 that the State Department would welcome 'his entry into the Persian arena'.[63] It might have advantaged the British case to have exploited this circumstance to the uttermost, thereby perhaps gratifying the influential Mr McGhee and presenting to the American Government a constructive alternative to the Harriman Mission in the deployment of Mr Levy at the rather more hopeful, and less embarrassing, technical level.

Nor, conceivably, need this have proved a purely empty manoeuvre. Even in the face of Persian rejection of the ruling of the International Court, His Majesty's Government had every right, if not duty, to adhere to it so far as might be. It might well have been advantageous at least to consider, and if possible announce, unilateral British implementation of the interim injunction in so far as it might lie with His Majesty's Government; and more particularly with regard, precisely, to the provision most obviously favourable to the Persians; the setting up of the Board of Supervision with control of the Persian revenues of the Anglo-Iranian Oil Company. Such a practical initiative from His Majesty's Government towards meeting the Persian viewpoint by mitigating the company's autonomy might, with a vigorous push from British propaganda, have produced a highly favourable response abroad, even, ultimately, in Persia. For if judiciously exploited, such a move might have made it considerably harder for Dr Musaddiq to maintain that stand against the interim injunction as a whole which was already arousing criticism and anxiety in his country.

Without Persian cooperation, any functioning of the two British representatives on the Board of Supervision would not, of course, have had legal effect under the ruling of the International Court. But it might well have had practical effect, especially if they had been joined by Mr Levy as a third member. The United States Government might well have been reluctant to go so far, but it might possibly have been made awkward for it to reject a firm British appeal, perhaps even in public, for cooperation in implementing the rule of international law and in adjuring the Persian Government to do likewise. Furthermore, it might have been worth large material concessions by Great Britain to get the United States firmly lined up with her on the impeccable issue of The Hague ruling, and to put a full stop to the Persian game of playing off the Anglo-Saxon Powers against one another. American participation in the board of Supervision might conceivably have been presented as the introduction to a bold and imaginative plan, likely to appeal to Americans, for the entry of American commercial interests into the Persian oil industry; so that in future the Persian Government would have to reckon, and collaborate, with an Anglo-American partnership. Mr Harriman was later to say that if a British proposal for American participation had been made that summer, it might have influenced Persian thinking and led to a more satisfactory situation. Mr Anthony Eden thought the same.[64]

The concession to the United States at that stage of an interest in Persian oil would have been a heavy step, implying a decline in British influence in Persia. But

[63] EP 1531/1058.
[64] Sir Anthony Eden, *Full Circle* (London 1960), p. 202.

it had already declined so far that the evident alternatives for Great Britain were liable to be graver still. And a judicious British initiative towards cutting her losses by bringing in the United States might possibly have secured positive advantages even in the economic field, for instance by including the Persian issue in that wider problem of oil in the Middle East, in connexion with which Mr Morrison had already suggested imaginative Anglo-Franco-American action (cf p. 235). The possibility of such action was given preliminary examination in the Foreign Office, but was overlaid during the rapid development of the Persian oil crisis that summer.[65]

Mr Morrison was conscious of the need for 'an overall policy for the Middle East'.[66] He was to write, as suggested (cf p. 235), to Mr Gaitskell on July 31 that 'recent events in the Middle East, particularly in Persia, make it urgently necessary for me to examine whether anything can now be done to make our Middle East policy more effective',[67] especially by economic action. Mr Gaitskell, with his heavy responsibility of protecting the pound, stated in interim reply on August 10 that he was 'very doubtful whether we can take anything more on; our economy is heavily overstrained, and it is no use our partnership with the United States involving us in heavier and heavier burdens'.[68] But if there was to be a partnership, Great Britain would have to play her part, and the cession of a share in Persian oil might conceivably have constituted that British contribution which Sir Oliver Franks had seen as essential for the maintenance of British influence (cf p. 194). Politically such an accommodation would have formed part not of a weak, but of a strong and now greatly strengthened, British policy towards Persia and in the Middle East generally.

With firm American support at last His Majesty's Government might well have underpinned its policy by firm insistence upon the legal advantage of The Hague ruling. If Dr Musaddiq disregarded formal summons to comply with it, he could be persuasively presented as bearing the responsibility for any British military action which might subsequently be required in order to uphold the rule of international law. Such a policy might have coincided admirably with British support for M. Sayyid Zia; and might have encouraged the Foreign Office to give greater stimulus to the Shah, either through Sir Francis Shepherd or conceivably through the friendly and perhaps somewhat neglected Persian Ambassador in London.

As it was, Sir Francis Shepherd had an audience of the Shah on July 12, 1951. On his way in, the Persian Master of Ceremonies, M. Pireira, gave the view that the Minister of the Interior, General Zahedi, considered that a change of Persian policy was needed (cf pp. 240). The Shah expressed to His Majesty's Ambassador his conviction 'that Dr Musaddiq must be got rid of as soon as possible. He did not seem very clear as to how this should be done but said that he had encouraged M. Sayyid Zia to revive his National Will Party. He had also received most affectionate letters from Qavam-es-Sultaneh, who evidently wished to be received back into favour and to re-enter political life. The Shah wondered whether MM. Qavam and Sayyid Zia could not work together in order to get rid of Dr Musaddiq.'[69] The Persian monarch, however, was rather apprehensive about M. Qavam's weakness for having something in the nature of a private army. Sir Francis Shepherd replied that this 'was

---

[65] UES 15332/1G.
[66] E 1192/133G.
[67] E 1103/11.
[68] E 1103/12.
[69] EP 1015/281.

certainly something to be guarded against'.

Despite the British support of M. Sayyid Zia, His Majesty's Ambassador apparently did not exploit the opening offered by the Shah on July 12 further than to say that he thought that opposition to Dr Musaddiq was growing—perhaps Deputies might soon summon enough courage to vote him out of office; that things looked more hopeful than a week ago but that time was very short. In the Foreign Office it was thought that MM. Qavam and Sayyid Zia would not work together, and Mr Bowker minuted on July 24: 'There is no evidence here that the Shah is prepared to do more than wait on events.'[70] On the same day Mr Furlonge had minuted that a failure of Mr Harriman's mission obviously due to Dr Musaddiq's intransigence might greatly assist M. Sayyid Zia. The latter had, however, been 'handicapped and depressed'[71] by the despatch of so important an American mission to confer with Dr Musaddiq so soon after his flouting of the International Court. Though it might perhaps have been still worth while for His Majesty's Government to accept this drawback and support the Harriman mission if the American Government continued to press for it and provided that His Majesty's Government firmly refused to be led away from the interim injunction. In which case the short period before the failure of the Harriman mission might have served constructively not only to swing the American Government into closer support but also to gain the necessary time till British evacuation from the outlying Fields and preparations for the second phase of Operation Buccaneer were complete.

5. Preliminaries and economic background to the Harriman Mission

In the Foreign Office Mr Averell Harriman was considered to be fundamentally well-disposed towards Great Britain and was described, for the benefit of Sir Francis Shepherd, as 'reserved in manner, inarticulate and not very forthcoming in conversation. He also has a strong streak of personal vanity and is susceptible to attentions of all kinds.'[72] Sir Francis Shepherd was highly sceptical of the value of Mr Harriman's mission if it were based upon the terms indicated by Dr Musaddiq to Mr Truman. His Majesty's Ambassador telegraphed on July 12 that he regarded it as of the 'utmost importance'[73] that Mr Harriman should not arrive in Tehran under any misapprehensions. In accordance with the Cabinet decision of that day the Foreign Secretary tried to prevent this by a telegram to Washington; though it now only expressed the 'hope that the main objective'[74] of Mr Harriman's mission would be to induce Persian acceptance of the interim injunction. It was somewhat unfortunate that on the same day of July 12 the United Press agency reported President Truman as expressing the hope in Washington that Mr Harriman 'will succeed in mediating the British-Iranian oil dispute'.

The *New York Herald Tribune* of July 13, 1951, printed this United Press message immediately beneath a report of a press conference given on the previous day in Tehran by His Majesty's Ambassador, described as 'looking flushed and irritated'. Sir Francis Shepherd referred to the basis of Mr Harriman's mission and said that there was 'not much point' in his coming. His Majesty's Ambassador

[70] *Ibid.*
[71] EP 1015/383.
[72] EP 1531/1049G.
[73] EP 1531/975.
[74] EP 1531/964.

subsequently held that he had been misrepresented and issued a statement to rectify what the Foreign Office described to him at the 'unfortunate impression that we are cold-shouldering Harriman'.[75] This impression caused Mr Winston Churchill to telephone to the Foreign Office his concern and his view that it was 'a mistake for Ambassadors or Generals to give news conferences'.[76] Sir Francis Shepherd explained privately that on the previous evening in Tehran 'there was very nearly a free fight between the British and American journalists at the Ritz bar . . . The former demanded in strong language to know why the Americans did not keep their fingers out of our affairs.'[77]

Sir Francis Shepherd considered that 'the misrepresentation of my remarks is however pale and insignificant [compared] with what the United Press thereupon attributed to Harriman': namely contradictions of the alleged British views that Dr Musaddiq was activated by personal interest and that the oil dispute could not be settled while he was in power. The United Press subsequently disclaimed this message and it was suggested that it had been invented in Tehran. A public denial of it was not, however, issued, presumably because it appeared only in Tehran. Such was the inauspicious inauguration of the Harriman Mission.

President Truman's special envoy proceeded to Tehran via Paris where, on the morning of the holiday of the Quatorze Juillet, he had a long and friendly conversation in secret with the Chancellor of the Exchequer, then visiting Paris for a meeting of the Organisation for European Economic Cooperation. This talk had been suggested by Mr Gaitskell, who knew Mr Harriman, in order to impress upon the latter 'that we have strongest objections to any idea of mediation or negotiation'.[78] Mr Harriman assured Mr Gaitskell that 'he appreciated that the attitude of His Majesty's Government was quite firm and that our proposals [of June 19] contained no margin for bargaining. On the financial side he even thought they went too far. He would not wish to appear to push us along if only because the eyes of all the American oil companies were on him . . . He may try to adapt our proposals without change of substance so as to save Musaddiq's face.' The Chancellor of the Exchequer further reported that Mr Harriman's whole attitude was likely to be influenced by his anxiety not only to deny the oil in South Persia to the Russians but also to keep them away from the oil areas in the North.[79]

The Chancellor of the Exchequer had on July 9 proposed, and the Cabinet had agreed, that the Memorandum of Understanding with Persia could justifiably be suspended should legislation by the Majlis enable her to convert her note cover of sterling exchange into dollars at British expense. Persian refusal to accept the interim injunction would give His Majesty's Government adequate justification for such action.[80] It appears that on the following day the Prime Minister and the Foreign Secretary strongly favoured the immediate adoption of this sanction. A conversation with the Governor of the Bank of England, however, induced Mr Gaitskell, and on July 12 the Cabinet, to reverse this view: suspension of the Memorandum of Understanding would constitute a clear breach of agreement between two central

---

[75] EP 1531/990.
[76] EP 1531/1060.
[77] EP 1531/1130.
[78] EP 1531/987G.
[79] *Ibid.*
[80] EP 1531/1066G.

banks and might destroy the confidence of other countries holding gold and sterling in London. The Cabinet on July 12 yet did instruct the President of the Board of Trade to arrange, so far as possible with no publicity, that for the time being scarce materials, notably steel rails and sugar, should not be exported to Persia. In his brief to Mr Morrison for that meeting of the Cabinet Mr Fry had observed that 'at first sight the withholding of steel rails from Persia would not seem effective unless the Memorandum is suspended at the same time'[81] so as to prevent Persia, if she wished, from buying such rails in, perhaps, the United States with dollars provided by Great Britain. In practice, however, the Board of Trade did not prevent ships laden with rails and sugar for Persia from sailing from Britain a day or two later. The Board was informed on July 14 that the Prime Minister felt 'that greater ingenuity might have been shown in finding some excuse to detain them'.[82] Thus, although the Prime Minister, the Chancellor of the Exchequer and the Foreign Secretary had all felt that some economic sanctions against Persia were by then justified, none were taken at that time.

On July 4, 1951, Mr Gaitskell had given to a Press conference the gross figure of $350 million a year for British replacement of Persian oil[83] (cf pp. 218); this was rather more than the total of all British exports for dollars in 1950. Only on the day before Mr Gaitskell's announcement had Mr Kenneth Younger in the Foreign Office set on foot an enquiry into whether there were other regions besides Persia where British commercial interests might be resented and threatened. The Foreign Secretary here expressed concurrence with Mr Younger's conviction that there was some justice in 'a very general feeling, reflected both in Parliament and in the Press, that the present Persian oil crisis might have been avoided if the Government and the Anglo-Iranian Oil Company had shown more imaginative understanding of the Persian attitude in the last two or three years . . . I should like to feel sure that we cannot be caught unawares on any future occasion.'[84]

July 5 saw the first meeting of a Cabinet Oil Working Party with Mr Flett of the Treasury again as chairman, and Mr Ramsbotham representing the Foreign Office. The new working party was at the request of Mr Gaitskell, to prepare an urgent appreciation of the long-term effects upon the United Kingdom of a total loss of Persian oil. It was recognised that the fundamental problem would be whether the sterling area could afford the dollar drain in order to retain the many advantages of the maintenance of the British share in the international oil trade, which was the largest single British earner of foreign currency. Close contact with the oil companies would be maintained.[85] A week later the working party agreed that the Foreign Office should advise against the previously noticed suggestion of June 22 from Sir Frederick Hoyer Millar for marshalling Britain's allies under the North Atlantic Treaty by emphasising the general effect of the loss of Persian oil (cf pp. 231-2).

On the day after the Cabinet Oil Working Party began work in London there was held in Washington the first meeting of the Foreign Petroleum Supply Committee, representing the American oil companies and corresponding to the recently

---

[81] EP 1112/43G.
[82] EP 1156/20G.
[83] *The Times*, July 5, 1951, p. 6.
[84] UES 15320/25.
[85] UES 15314/16.

constituted British Oil Supply Advisory Committee (cf p. 207). British representation on the American committee and its sub-committees was accepted, and the first meeting of the Foreign Petroleum Supply Committee was attended by Mr Harold Wilkinson, President of the Asiatic Petroleum Corporation. This first meeting was regarded as satisfactory, and some days later the chairman of the American committee, Mr Stewart Coleman, a director of the Standard Oil Company of New Jersey, said that he was hopeful that oil supplies to friendly nations, formerly dependent on the Persian oilfields, could be maintained. The collaboration between British and American oil interests, thus inaugurated, was to be of considerable importance for the future of the industry and constituted a practical step towards that kind of cooperation which the Shinwell-Ickes Agreement had failed to achieve.

Meanwhile, however, Dr Musaddiq was significantly coupling his rejection of the ruling of the International Court with a bill to authorise acceptance at long last of the proposed $25 million Export-Import Bank loan from the United States. In a telegram of July 10 Mr Herbert Morrison assumed that there could be no question of the United States giving financial or other assistance to Persia while she was flouting The Hague Court, and requested Sir Oliver Franks to speak urgently to Mr Acheson.[86] Mr McGhee, to whom His Majesty's Ambassador spoke, replied, however, that the State Department was bound to attach greater importance to the danger of driving Persia into the Russian camp; and to state now that the loan was no longer available would, apart from the long-range effects, prejudice the mission of Mr Harriman.[87] Mr Furlonge described this reply as 'somewhat unsatisfactory' and the Foreign Secretary felt a good deal more strongly than that, minuting on July 17: 'Please take or prepare to take all necessary & emphatic steps to stop US from rewarding sin agst. UK. I shall be very very cross if they do & shall not hide my anger under a bushel. Make clear to Sir O. Franks, anyway for his infn. Shd. I see US Ambassador?'[88] This question was not answered in writing and does not seem to have been pursued.

All this argument and deliberation was related, in the first analysis, to the position on the ground in the parched district of Abadan. There the burning question remained: how much longer could or should the British staff stick it out. Sir Francis Shepherd had telegraphed on July 11, 1951: 'There seems to be some conflict between decision that staff should remain as long as possible and actual instructions given to the company's manager on the spot . . . It looks therefore as if decision to retain British staff as long as possible is likely to be overtaken by events.' His Majesty's Ambassador commented: 'Persian Government are still convinced that we are bluffing (Musaddiq said in a private conversation two days ago that he was convinced of this) and that we shall not abandon the oilfields and our present policy lends colour to this belief . . . Maximum political effect will only be obtained by complete withdrawal with no reference to retention of a hard core.'[89]

The above telegram from Sir Francis Shepherd was minuted by Mr Fry on July 14, two days after the Cabinet decision not to announce a withdrawal of staff for the present. Mr Fry agreed with His Majesty's Ambassador's view that an unannounced

---

[86] EP 1531/936.
[87] EP 11345/14.
[88] EP 11345/15.
[89] EP 1531/973.

and 'filtered' withdrawal would still produce no effect on the Persians but considered that there had been no alternative to holding up an announced withdrawal in view of Mr Harriman's mission and an appeal from Mr Acheson on July 12 that it should not be prejudiced by the 'strong action' of such a withdrawal.[90] American pressure was spoiling whatever chance there might have been of presenting the withdrawal as a sharp shock in execution of a determined policy rather than as a gradual submission to the Persian impulsion of events.

On July 12 Air Marshal Sir John Baker, British Commander-in-Chief, Middle East Air Forces, and Major-General F.R.G. Matthews, designated commander of Operation Buccaneer, Phase One, held a meeting at Shaiba to concert arrangements with the Senior Naval Officer, Persian Gulf, His Majesty's Consul-General at Khorramshahr and Mr Drake, who had returned to the Middle East. Air Marshal Baker reported: 'the Persians are playing their waiting game with oriental skill and cunning. Only the departure of British employees will bring about the chaos we all fear and Drake still believes that force alone will break the stalemate.'[91] Major Capper reported, however, that the same meeting considered that 'the time is passing, if it has not already passed, when it was to our advantage to keep a foot in the field areas under the existing conditions'.[92] They were again deteriorating. The Persians were attempting to assume executive control. In Abadan the British staff were being stopped and searched, were having their houses robbed wholesale and were then being accused of engineering the housebreaking in order to discredit the Persians. His Majesty's Consul at Khorramshahr was, as usual, protesting strongly to the Persian authorities and on July 16 had a helpful conversation with the able General Mir Jalali, who had succeeded General Shahbakhti in command of Persian troops in Khuzistan, and the ineffective Brigadier Kemal, the Garrison Commander at Abadan. They both seemed anxious to assist within their limited scope. In the fields, however, the Persians were becoming increasingly truculent and 'conditions . . . are fast becoming unbearable for British staff'.[93] Their morale was sinking, though Mr Seddon, who then paid a short visit to Khuzistan, reported on July 15 that in general it remained 'astonishingly high'.[94]

On July 16 M. Makki informed a local Press conference that the patience of the Persians was nearly exhausted and that they intended to take over the refinery at Abadan before the outlying oilfields.[95] By that date Mr Seddon and Mr Mason were agreed that 'we should make a very early announcement of complete withdrawal at least from all the field areas', at least so soon as Mr Harriman might have failed in his mission. The Foreign Secretary minuted on this telegram on July 17: 'Can we get a really considered view on this? We are drifting.'[96]

Meantime in Tehran the American Ambassador, resuming his favourite role of candid critic, announced publicly on July 14 that he considered that the Persians were mistaken in rejecting the Jackson proposals, and that the British were mistaken in disregarding his recent suggestions for an interim solution (to Persian advantage)

---

[90] EP 1531/997 and 1471.
[91] EP 1192/51G.
[92] EP 1611/41G.
[93] EP 1531/1024.
[94] EP 1531/1026.
[95] EP 1531/1032.
[96] EP 1531/1026.

of the question of tanker receipts (cf pp. 247). Dr Grady further volunteered that the problem of Persian stability was as much a concern for the American Government as for the British and (almost approximating to the apocryphal quotation of Mr Harriman by United Press) that Dr Musaddiq had the Persian people behind him and was the man to deal with in coming months.[97] Dr Grady himself however would not be there. On the same day of July 14 *The Times* quoted a spokesman at the White House to the effect that Dr Grady had undertaken his Embassy for one year only and had again asked the President to accept his resignation; it was understood that Dr Grady would be succeeded by Mr Loy Henderson, American Ambassador to India. Meanwhile, however, Dr Grady's remarkable intervention somewhat offset Mr Harriman's own diplomatic explanation that he came for discussions but not as a mediator. This statement was made by Mr Harriman upon his arrival in the Persian capital on Sunday, July 15, 1951.

Mr Harriman had flown in with his wife, Mr Rountree of the State Department and Mr Levy. Their arrival coincided with a Persian pro-communist demonstration in Tehran, organised by the Association for the Struggle against Imperialist Oil Companies. In the Majlis Square the demonstrators clashed and fought with members of the Toilers Party of rival extremists supporting the Government. The police proved quite inadequate and the square was only cleared by troops with tanks after some 20 people had been killed and over a hundred injured. Such was the troubled inauguration of the Harriman Mission to Tehran.

---

[97] *The Times*, July 16, 1951.

CHAPTER X

THE MISSION TO TEHRAN OF MR AVERELL HARRIMAN, JULY 15–AUGUST 3, 1951

1. Reactions to recommendation by the British Commanders-in-Chief, Middle East, of military action at Abadan, July 16-25

In the House of Commons on July 16, 1951, the Foreign Secretary drew attention to the arrival of Mr Harriman in Tehran and welcomed American interest in the Persian problem. Mr Maurice Edelman, Labour Member for Coventry North, asked: 'May we take it that Mr Harriman's function is not to mediate but to reinforce Britain's stand there?'[1] Mr Herbert Morrison, showing greater caution than Mr Harriman himself in disclaiming any mediation, thought it better that he 'should not particularise' on that. Nor would he be drawn by a request from Mr Duncan Sandys for an assurance that His Majesty's Government would not let go of the interim injunction of the International Court. Brigadier Ralph Rayner, Conservative Member for the Totnes Division, enquired whether the Foreign Secretary did not appreciate 'that every successive statement he makes to the House reeks of weakness? Could he not make a statement with a bit of guts in it?'[2]

On the same day of July 16 Mr Bowker, in confidential conversation with Mr J.F. Root of the American Embassy, referred to the 'very reasonable recommendations'[3] of The Hague Court and suggested, with regard to Dr Grady's ideas, that undue attention was now being given to the question of tanker receipts. When, however, Mr Root said he thought that Mr Harriman would raise that question, Mr Bowker agreed and said that His Majesty's Government would consider his suggestions. In fact Mr Harriman was finding his first conversations with Dr Musaddiq 'completely unfruitful'.[4] If, meanwhile, there was on the civil side already a certain relaxation of British insistence upon the connexion between the Harriman mission and The Hague ruling, the military side now produced an important initiative towards a stronger policy.

On July 16, 1951, the Commanders-in-Chief, Middle East, despatched to the Chiefs of Staff a signal, No. 476/CCL,[5] which noted the Cabinet decision of July 12 that any military operations should now be confined to the protection of British lives. The Commanders-in-Chief presumed, however, that this did not mean that no action would be taken till British lives had actually been lost. They considered that the danger of Persian violence against British staff was mounting (though in subsequent fact it produced no fatalities). They wished 'to record emphatically that neither by "Buccaneer" nor by any other means at our disposal can we prevent the loss of British life should such violence be offered. We can only shut the stable door after the event unless we anticipate the event itself. If, therefore, His Majesty's Government wish to assume the protection of British lives in Abadan we recommend most strongly that a date should now be fixed for introducing British troops to Abadan for this purpose under operation "Buccaneer".'

---

[1] Parliamentary Debates, 5th Series, H. of C., Vol. 490, col. 841.
[2] *Ibid*, col. 842.
[3] EP 1531/1094.
[4] EP 1531/1048.
[5] EP 1531/1068G.

The Commanders-in-Chief presumed that the date for action should not be before the Harriman Mission had failed. Other factors were that as the Persians at Abadan tightened their stranglehold upon such resources as communications and river craft, those available for a British landing were correspondingly diminishing; but—very important—two British tank-landing ships containing tanks and guns would not reach Basra till July 25. Therefore the date of launching Operation Buccaneer should not be earlier than July 27, but preferably not later. Meantime it would be very important to build up the British case by propaganda. In conclusion the Commanders-in-Chief, Middle East, drew attention to 'steadily increasing evidence' of Communist activity in Persia, including release of Communist prisoners, infiltration of the public services and army, and the demonstration which had greeted Mr Harriman. And behind loomed the secular danger of 'the advance of Russian influence and power to the headwaters of the Persian Gulf'.

The Commanders-in-Chief, Middle East, reinforced this striking and collective message by a private and identic telegram from each of them, from Sir Brian Robertson to the Chief of the Imperial General Staff, from Rear-Admiral I.M.R. Campbell to the First Sea Lord and from Air Marshal Sir John Baker to the Chief of the Air Staff. This telegram alluded to the ordeal of the staff of the Anglo-Iranian Oil Company 'in face of every form of indignity, injustice and provocation'.[6] The three Commanders-in-Chief continued: 'Throughout the informed rank and file, as well as the officers in the three services of our Command, all are solidly against the idea of evacuation. The flouting of The Hague Court decision by the Persians has finally convinced us all that we are facing an issue in which our whole position and prestige as the responsible Allied defence authorities in the Middle East is at stake. We are confident that we now have the power and resources to intervene effectively and take control of the refinery area against whatever opposition the Persians can muster . . . Our failure to stand firm in Persia would be interpreted throughout this area as a sign of fundamental weakness and give immediate impetus to widespread neutralist and nationalistic influences . . . We do *not* believe that there is any single Government in the Middle East, possibly excluding Jordan alone, which would be able to withstand the political pressure to withdraw from our defence associations which such a solution will produce.'

If the last consideration was, for instance, subsequently to prove exaggerated and if the recommendation to execute Operation Buccaneer was one of obvious gravity and risk, yet history may judge that in that crisis, having regard to the information and circumstances then obtaining, the three British Commanders-in-Chief in the Middle East, from the military standpoint, worthily upheld their trust in that region by issuing their cogent and ringing call to action which they themselves would have to execute. As from July 16, 1951, at least, any responsibility for the subsequent British debacle at Abadan and beyond was not theirs.

On the same day of July 16 an advance copy of part of the collective signal No. 476/CCL from the Commanders-in-Chief, Middle East, though apparently not their private telegrams to the Chiefs of Staff, was briefly discussed at a meeting of the Vice-Chiefs of Staff. According to a minute of July 17 by Mr Furlonge, who attended the meeting, the provisional view was that the recommendation of the Commanders-in-Chief that a date be fixed for the introduction of British troops into Abadan was

---

[6] EP 1531/1068G.

unacceptable: the decision was a grave one which could be taken only if the local circumstances fully justified it; indeed it might well be that such action, if the lives of British staff were not immediately threatened, would endanger rather than protect them.

Mr Furlonge stated in his minute of July 17 that from the point of view of the Foreign Office it seemed that the best answer for the Chiefs of Staff to send to General Headquarters, Middle East, would be on the lines, first, of the above provisional view of the Vice-Chiefs of Staff, and secondly that: 'Unless Mr Harriman's visit produces a radical change in the situation it is probable that as soon as its results are known His Majesty's Government will announce at least the evacuation of the oilfields personnel into Abadan and possibly, depending on circumstances, the evacuation of Abadan itself.'[7] The arguments in favour of withdrawing the 500 men concerned from the outlying oilfields appeared to Mr Furlonge to be 'overwhelming'.[8] In this minute, which was initialled by Sir William Strang on July 17, Mr Furlonge noted that the Chiefs of Staff would be considering the representation from the Commanders-in-Chief, Middle East, at a meeting which he would be attending, at 4.15 pm on that day of July 17.

In opening the discussion of the Chiefs of Staff that afternoon Admiral Lord Fraser of North Cape 'said that he thought we should order withdrawal from the oilfields into Abadan now . . . We should then immediately be prepared to put Buccaneer into effect if necessary . . . He was horrified at the idea which now seemed to be prevailing that whatever the success of Buccaneer we should inevitably evacuate and withdraw our troops. In the last three weeks the situation had greatly changed; The Hague Court had given its ruling; the Persians were becoming increasingly impossible, intolerable and impudent; and it was indeed time, in his opinion, that we should take a very strong line. As to the United Nations, he felt that it should not be impossible to justify military action on the basis of enforcing the ruling of The Hague Court. The Chiefs of Staff should press Ministers to agree that if Buccaneer was put into operation the forces should stay at Abadan and not withdraw, and that it should be made clear that, from a military point of view, this was possible. Furthermore, withdrawal would lead to a great outcry from the British public who were tired of being pushed around by Persian pipsqueaks . . . Firm action would give everyone a fillip and dispel the dumps and doldrums into which they were rapidly falling. A gesture was needed such as the immediate embodiment of a Territorial Division and the despatch of the Home Fleet into the Mediterranean. He realised that the United States might not support armed action in Persia, as things stood at the moment, but we should not be diverted from our purpose by this. It would of course be easier in this respect if Mr Harriman had received a rebuff from the Persians before any action was taken.'[9]

The Chief of the Air Staff agreed generally with the forthright statement of the First Sea Lord, while observing that the question of holding Abadan Island was largely a political matter, and questioning the opportuneness of ordering evacuation of the oilfields till the outcome of Mr Harriman's mission became clear. Field-Marshal Sir William Slim, however, thought that the latter action would probably

---

[7] EP 1192/67G.
[8] EP 1531/1123G.
[9] EP 1192/67G.

strengthen Mr Harriman's hand by proving to the Persians that his Majesty's Government were not bluffing. Sir John Slessor then gave a careful analysis of time-factors, including the following: pending the optimum date of July 27 Buccaneer could, as an emergency measure, still be mounted at any moment so that the troops would arrive at Abadan within 24 hours; whatever date for Buccaneer was selected, evacuation from the oilfields should be ordered from London six days before; the Commanders-in-Chief, Middle East, could not be given the fixed date for Buccaneer for which they asked 'unless Ministers were prepared to authorise the mounting of the operation whatever now took place. He suggested that the Chiefs of Staff ought not to recommend this course to Ministers *unless* they (Ministers) were prepared to agree to carry out the operation and to stay on in Abadan.'

The Chief of the Imperial General Staff agreed generally with the Chief of the Air Staff. It seemed to Sir William Slim 'that the best course now would be to seize and hold Abadan Island after the oilfields had been safely evacuated . . . He confirmed that, as a result of the preparations of the last few weeks, the seizure and holding of Abadan with the Buccaneer forces now seemed a practical proposition, though some additional reinforcement possibly up to the Lethal strength would perhaps be required later . . . It might be objected that the tying-up of forces in Persia was playing the Russian game; it was an equally and perhaps more valid answer that the weakening of our position in the whole Middle East . . . and the very serious loss of prestige in the Arab countries, with all the long-term consequences, would even more be playing into the hands of the Russians.'

The Chiefs of Staff decided to represent the main purport of their discussion to the Ministerial Committee on Persia and, in particular, to recommend that a definite date should now be fixed for the execution of Operation Buccaneer and that evacuation from the oilfields should be ordered on July 21; also, that the object of Operation Buccaneer should be changed to the seizure and holding of Abadan Island. If Mr Furlonge had explained to the Chiefs of Staff the contrary considerations which he had minuted earlier that day, this was not recorded. The meeting was also attended by Sir Roger Makins, though it is uncertain whether he was present for the discussion on Persia. The presence of a senior representative of the Foreign Office at this important discussion was liable to be advantageous, especially since it would seem that there may subsequently have been some uncertainty in the Foreign Office about one, at least, of its conclusions. Mr Bowker, in a submission to the Foreign Secretary on July 18 in preparation for the meeting of Ministers that day, noted that the fixing in advance of a date for Operation Buccaneer raised 'obvious difficulties . . . and it is understood that the Chiefs of Staff will themselves recommend against it'.[10] Mr Bowker commented that the confidence expressed by the Commanders-in-Chief, Middle East, in their capacity to hold Abadan Island was a 'radical change from the views which the Chiefs of Staff have previously expressed': presumably Mr Bowker can have been referring here only to the views they had expressed before about July 10, though this was not specified. Despite all the previous memoranda and discussions, Mr Bowker advised that the implications of Operation Buccaneer 'in the eventuality of a Persian attempt to take over the refinery need further consideration'. He suggested that the Foreign Secretary should recommend to the Ministerial Committee on Persia that it should that day take no decision on this

---

[10] EP 1531/1068G.

question which should be urgently studied for further consideration by the full Cabinet. The constitutional appropriateness of this advice on so important an issue is beyond question. There are some suggestions that the Cabinet may in general have been inclined towards a more cautious policy, again, than the Ministerial Committee on Persia.

At 11 am on July 18, 1951, the Prime Minister, Foreign Secretary, Minister of Defence, Chancellor of the Exchequer and Minister for Fuel and Power attended the Ministerial Committee on Persia. Also present were Field-Marshal Sir William Slim, Marshal of the RAF Sir John Slessor, Admiral Sir George Creasy, Sir Edward Bridges, Sir William Fraser and Mr Bowker. The Ministers first considered that vexed question of withdrawal from the outlying oilfields, upon which, as Mr Herbert Morrison observed, a decision had previously been postponed 'for various reasons'.[11] It was now agreed that this withdrawal should 'be carried out in as short a time as possible in order to minimise danger from possible Persian obstruction. Should the Persian Government intervene to prevent the withdrawal we should be fully justified in taking all available forcible action.' Sir William Slim observed that for military reasons, since July 27 would be the best date for Operation Buccaneer if it was required to protect British lives, it would be best that the instructions for evacuation should not reach the staff of the Anglo-Iranian Oil Company before July 21, with the withdrawal beginning on July 23.

Notification to the above effect regarding 'the complete and rapid withdrawal of the British personnel from the fields'[12] was accordingly telegraphed on the night of July 18 to Sir Francis Shepherd with instructions to inform the Persian Government on the morning of Friday, July 20. His Majesty's Ambassador was further apprised, for his own information, that the Commanders-in-Chief, Middle East Forces, had been authorised to take all necessary measures to ensure that Operation Buccaneer 'can be mounted immediately and in the greatest possible strength, in the event of the concentration of the AIOC personnel resulting in disturbances provoked by either Nationalist or Tudeh elements. These measures include the flying-in of about three battalions of British troops to Shaiba where they should arrive by July 26.' In the latter connexion Sir John Troutbeck was informed that Ministers had decided that 'any possible Iraqi objections must be overridden'.[13]

Sir Oliver Franks was instructed to inform Mr Acheson as soon as possible of the decision to withdraw from the fields in view of the deterioration of the situation there in recent days: 'There is of course no question of withdrawal from Abadan itself in present circumstances.'[14] His Majesty's Government would have preferred not to make this announcement till the results of Mr Harriman's mission had become clearer, but was by no means certain that it might not in fact be helpful to him in the way previously suggested by Sir William Slim.

These telegrams to Tehran, Baghdad and Washington were previously approved by the Prime Minister. On the following day of July 19 the Foreign Office notified agreement with a representation from Sir Francis Shepherd that to announce the withdrawal to the Persian Government on a Friday would cause additional irritation

---

[11] EP 1531/1132G.
[12] EP 1531/1026.
[13] *Ibid.*
[14] *Ibid.*

and that he would prefer that the announcement be made on Monday, July 23, and the withdrawal begun on July 24.[15] This further postponement of withdrawal, on top of that which Sir William Slim had advocated, was, however, to allow more time for other developments and complications.

The ministerial decisions were also communicated to Mr Churchill, Mr Eden and Lord Salisbury at a meeting with Mr Attlee, Mr Morrison and Mr Gaitskell in the House of Commons on the same evening of July 18. 'Mr Churchill', recorded Sir William Strang, 'said the Opposition did not object to the withdrawal of British personnel from the outlying oilfields. But at least a skeleton or nucleus should be maintained at all costs in Abadan. If necessary financial inducements should be offered. If all British staff left Abadan there would be no personnel left for us to protect and we should have the less excuse to send troops in. He urged that in the announcement about withdrawal from the outlying fields, to be made in the House, it should also be stated that there was no intention of bringing the essential nucleus away from Abadan. If this could be said, there would be no difference between Government and Opposition. *The Prime Minister* said he would consider this. Much would depend on the comment we received from Tehran. *Mr Churchill* wondered whether withdrawal from the fields could not be deferred until the battalions were in position in Shaiba. The two acts would then make maximum impact on the Persian Government. *The Prime Minister* thought this would be running too great a risk with British lives.' When Mr Eden asked whether the despatch of the battalions to Shaiba could be squared with the Anglo-Iraqi Treaty Mr Morrison 'admitted that it would mean stretching the Treaty'. Sir William Strang noted here: 'It is, in fact, in the view of the Legal Adviser, not justifiable under the Treaty. But we are banking on the Iraqis at worst acquiescing: they may in fact not be, at heart, displeased to see their ally taking vigorous action, even at their expense.'[16]

The Ministerial Committee on Persia had on July 18 also considered the recommendation of the Commanders-in-Chief, Middle East, for fixing a date for Operation Buccaneer. In presenting their telegrams, while the Chief of the Imperial General Staff did not specifically put forward the recorded resolutions adopted by the Chiefs of Staff the day before, he observed that the grounds for the anxiety of the Commanders-in-Chief 'about the British military position throughout the Middle East, if we failed to stand firm in Persia, were explained in the telegrams before the meeting, and this anxiety was fully shared by the Chiefs of Staff'.[17] The meeting decided that the Foreign Secretary should prepare yet another paper, after CP(51)200 of July 11, more specifically now on the use of Operation Buccaneer for more than the protection of British lives. This memorandum would be considered by the Cabinet on Monday, July 23, when Persian reaction to the announcement of British withdrawal from the fields would be known—though the interval of five days at such a time was perhaps rather striking.

After this meeting the Chiefs of Staff telegraphed to the Commanders-in-Chief, Middle East: 'Ministerial opinion is at present undecided as to whether Buccaneer should stay at Abadan or should be launched for any other purpose than protection

---

[15] EP 1531/1077.
[16] Confidential/General/415, M. 76.
[17] EP 1531/1132G.

of lives.'[18] Pending further ministerial consideration the military build-up was, however, to continue. Deployed for Phase I of Operation Buccaneer was a force comprising 2 cruisers (HMSs *Mauritius* and *Euryalus*), 4 destroyers (HMSs *Chequers, Chieftain, Chivalrous, Chevron*), 1 frigate, 3 tank-landing ships, 3 battalions of infantry (Loyals, Lancashire Fusiliers, Camerons), a squadron of tanks, a detachment of artillery, 90 transport aircraft plus a squadron of Brigand aircraft providing air support from Shaiba.[19] This compact British striking-force of the three arms would operate, if it did, under the command of Major-General F.R.G. Matthews with Major Capper acting as his adviser on civil affairs.[20]

At a meeting of the Chiefs of Staff on July 20, however, Sir John Slessor said that he had now decided that the prepositioning of British troops at Shaiba would be inadvisable unless Operation Buccaneer was certain to follow shortly thereafter, which was not then the case. Admiral Creasy and General Brownjohn agreed, and the Commanders-in-Chief, Middle East, were instructed accordingly. This decision of evident prudence was naturally liable to be welcome in the Foreign Office, especially since it was underlined there on the following day that the flying-in of troops to Shaiba could only with difficulty be reconciled with the Anglo-Iraqi Treaty of 1930.[21] Such, however, was already the brake of political uncertainty upon military preparation.

Nevertheless at the meeting on July 20 the Chiefs of Staff, in considering a draft of the new Foreign Office paper for the Cabinet, decided that additional emphasis should be given to passages indicating the broad advantages which the execution of Operation Buccaneer might be expected to procure for British interests throughout the Middle East: 'in the opinion of the Chiefs of Staff a display of determination on our part would have nothing but a wholesome effect on the Middle East, particularly since the Arabs respected strength alone.'[22] The Foreign Office was asked to consider this view among others in redrafting its memorandum.

Three days later, on the same day that the Cabinet met to consider the Foreign Secretary's memorandum, the Chief of the Air Staff had a long conversation at luncheon with the former American Ambassador, Mr Lewis Douglas, then visiting London. About a fortnight previously Mr Douglas had indeed told the Foreign Secretary that he would be very glad to do anything he could to help His Majesty's Government concerning the Persian crisis, and gave Mr Morrison the impression that he thought that the American Government had not given sufficient backing. The Foreign Secretary had told Mr Douglas that the British Government would be pleased to receive stronger American support—Mr Morrison had in fact, on July 3, expressed the hope to General Eisenhower, Supreme Commander of the Allied forces in Europe, that he might stimulate it.[23] Mr Morrison, however, was not sure that there was anything which could be done by Mr Douglas, who naturally did not wish to trespass upon the preserves of Mr Gifford. But Mr Morrison thought that Mr Douglas' offer was worth bearing in mind. Mr Bowker had advised on this on July 15 that in his view there was nothing specific which Mr Douglas could do except

---

[18] EP 1192/67G.
[19] EP 1192/78G.
[20] EP 1023/9G and 10G.
[21] EP 1192/81G and 73G.
[22] EP 1192/81G.
[23] WU 1198/256.

take every opportunity of urging the Government of the United States to afford His Majesty's Government wholehearted support and not to be led into mediating.[24] It is not clear whether this last point, in particular, was in fact conveyed to Mr Douglas. It was, however, to Mr Bowker that Sir John Slessor now wrote on July 23 of his conversation that day with Mr Douglas concerning Persia.

Mr Lewis Douglas, wrote Sir John Slessor, 'was critical of the United States Government's action in the matter—indeed he was critical of ours too . . . but his attitude to the whole affair had many points in common with that of the Chiefs of Staff. In his view the situation in Persia itself, the loss of oil, the dollar exchange and balance payments problems that it may involve, etc, are chicken-feed. The real point in his view is the effect on the British position in the Middle East which he described as the gateway to *Africa*, the last continent this side of the Atlantic where we may yet have a chance of keeping Communism out—or under. He agreed with me that there was one other major consideration in this affair, namely Anglo-American unity . . . He fully accepts that we may have to intervene forcibly and does not underrate the difficulties and disadvantages of that *vis-à-vis* United States opinion.'

Sir John Slessor continued that Mr Douglas had, however, said to him: 'I think you ought to serve notice on our Administration *now* that, while you will go, and indeed have nearly gone, to the limit of concessions, circumstances may well arise soon when you will have to use force; and you should tell them exactly why—ie the effect on the Middle East as a whole. You should not give anyone the opportunity of saying that you acted unilaterally without giving the United States Government plenty of notice in advance.' The Chief of the Air Staff concluded to Mr Bowker that Mr Douglas 'was very emphatic about that, and I thought your Secretary of State might be interested to know his view privately'.[25]

Sir William Strang initialled this letter without comment on July 24, 1951. On the following day the Foreign Secretary asked that consideration be given to Mr Douglas' proposal for a prompt British approach to the American Government with a full and candid warning concerning possible use of force in Persia. It does not appear that such consideration produced any quick or specific result or that the potentially valuable offer of assistance from Mr Douglas was, however, diplomatically, ever taken up. Already, however, by the time that the Foreign Secretary had made his request on July 25 much more counsel and deliberation, much of it in a contrary sense, had been brought to bear upon the stubborn problem of British military intervention in South Persia.

By July 20 Mr Herbert Morrison's further memorandum for the Cabinet—CP(51)212[26]—had been prepared. It began by drawing attention to the 'revised military opinion' according to which it was now feasible to occupy and hold Abadan at short notice instead of 'as a result of extensive preparations spread over several weeks'. It was suggested that in view of this factor coupled with continued Persian intransigence, the probable failure of the Harriman Mission and the interim ruling of The Hague Court, Ministers might wish to re-examine as soon as possible all the implications of an operation to protect British property as well as lives. The memorandum continued—and the Chiefs of Staff did not query this: 'It is not

[24] EP 1531/1071.
[25] EP 1531/1173G.
[26] EP 1192/65G.

possible to forecast the exact circumstances in which the operation might be contemplated, but one obvious possibility is that it should be carried out if and when the Persian authorities announce their intention of occupying the refinery.'

In the Foreign Secretary's memorandum the well-worn pros and cons of such military action were cogently restated, if with rather less emphasis upon the broad considerations regarding the Middle East than the Chiefs of Staff desired or than might have seemed politically justifiable. Though as regards the possibility of Russian intervention it was notably observed: 'The risk of the Russians occupying Northern Persia might be worth accepting provided that we retained full control of the Abadan refinery.' In this connexion the Foreign Secretary was to express the view on July 24 to the South African Minister of Labour, Mr Schoeman, that 'as regards the danger of war . . . even if we sent troops it was not certain that the Russians would intervene and that even if they did the result might be a sort of joint occupation which would be nothing new in Persia'.[27]

Mr Morrison concluded in his memorandum of July 20 that, if it were necessary to execute Operation Buccaneer in order to protect British lives, it seemed desirable that His Majesty's Government should not publicly commit itself to withdrawing British forces 'in case circumstances might make it desirable to retain them in order to ensure the operation of the refinery'.[26] That was the only specific recommendation either way in the memorandum of July 20.

If, on the main issue of intervention on behalf of property, the memorandum of July 20 listed rather more objections than advantages, and listed the objections last, yet its general tenor evidently differed from the rejection of such military action in Mr Morrison's memorandum CP(51)200 of July 11. Notably, the reference in the earlier memorandum to the Attorney-General's opinion of May 25 was not now repeated. In the memorandum of July 20 it was indeed pointed out that if Great Britain took the action in question there might a majority in the Security Council of the United Nations for 'a resolution enjoining us to remove our troops forthwith. In this event His Majesty's Government would be obliged either to comply or to use the veto (a course they have hitherto never adopted)'. The memorandum now continued, however: 'On the other hand I am advised that it might be possible to sustain a case in international law on the following lines: the nationalisation laws which the Persians are endeavouring to implement are in our view illegal. The Persian attempt to implement them has led to a highly inflammatory situation in which irreparable damage might be done to the company's property and the lives of the British staff endangered. In such cases there is nothing in International Law or in the United Nations Charter which necessarily prevents a State from taking its requisite protecting action to preserve life and to prevent irreparable injury to its interests.'

The background to that paragraph, with its swing to the thesis of Mr Fitzmaurice, was continued argument between him and the Attorney-General. On July 17 Mr Fitzmaurice had addressed another long letter to Sir Frank Soskice, reinforcing his letter of July 10, citing precedents regarding British interventions in China in the nineteen-twenties, and arguing that as regards national interests in a foreign country, 'the right of protection (provided the circumstances justify its exercise and the amount of force used is proportionate to those circumstances) is really an aspect, a

---

[27] E 1057/2.

special case, or legitimate extension, of the right of self defence'.[28]

On the following day of July 18 the Foreign Secretary was sent a letter by the Attorney-General who appreciated that Mr Morrison 'was anxious not to be impeded unduly by unnecessary legal niceties', but thought it 'my duty to remind you of the possible practical dangers of proceeding upon a too liberal interpretation of such rules of international law as can be said to have been formulated with any precision'. These dangers were that if Great Britain infringed the sovereignty of other countries she might be ha[u]led before the Security Council or the International Court. Sir Frank Soskice considered that the standing British policy of supporting those bodies logically implied 'that we should do our best to remain within the law although quite obviously this does place us often in a most unfairly disadvantageous position with regard to other countries which are not so scrupulous'.

The Attorney-General remarked that he had not been asked for an opinion as to the extent to which military intervention in Persia would be justified. He was sure that the Foreign Secretary would bear in mind the explained risks 'involved in transgressing principles of international law so far as they can be said to be formulated with regard to such matters'. Sir Frank Soskice explained he was 'fully conscious of the very great pressure to which you are being subjected to take what are very irresponsibly described as "strong measures"'. Mr Herbert Morrison minuted on this letter on July 19: 'I have been warned.'[29]

The letter of the Attorney-General did not mention the interim injunction of the International Court. Mr Fitzmaurice minuted on July 20 that the Persian refusal to comply with it or to negotiate with His Majesty's Government on any reasonable basis, and the resultant practical dangers at Abadan, were the right reasons to advance in support of any military action. It would be more important to avoid suggesting that Great Britain was taking the actual settlement of the dispute into her own hands or was ultimately seeking to prevent enforcement of the Persian nationalisation law: for it might then be very difficult to avoid being in breach of paragraph 3 of Article 2 of the Charter of the United Nations, prescribing peaceful settlement of international disputes.[30]

On the same day of July 20 the Chiefs of Staff expressed a view similar to that of Mr Fitzmaurice, recording their agreement 'that we should have a good case for sustaining our actions under international law by arguing that since The Hague Court had directed us to keep normal operations going as part of their interim decision, and since it was no longer possible to do this in the oilfields, it was at least possible to keep the refinery going. We should therefore have some right to send forces into Abadan to protect the British who were going about their lawful occasions as directed by The Hague Court.'[31]

The nub of this issue in international law, as argued on the one hand by Mr Fitzmaurice and the Chiefs of Staff and on the other by the Attorney-General, was brought out some days later by a former Lord Chancellor who had also been Foreign Secretary. In a debate in the House of Lords on July 31, 1951, Viscount Simon remarked: 'If you substitute acceptance of the rule of law for your own decision,

---

[28] EP 1192/83G.
[29] EP 1192/120G.
[30] EP 1192/86G.
[31] EP 1192/81G.

what is important is to secure that you really get the rule of law applied and accepted . . . What prospect is there of the Persian Government accepting the rule of law?'[32]

Meanwhile a long summary of the Foreign Secretary's memorandum of July 20 had been telegraphed, with request for comments, to Sir Oliver Franks, Sir Gladwyn Jebb and Sir Francis Shepherd. This telegram was repeated to Sir John Troutbeck in Iraq, but not to Sir Ralph Stevenson in Egypt, despite the heavy bearing of the issues upon the whole British position in the Middle East, and in Egypt in particular. On the same day of July 20 a contemptuous reference to 'British bluffing' had appeared in the Egyptian Press, which observed that 'the Persians have succeeded in compelling London and Washington to recognise their nationalisation of the oil company. Their nerves have withstood the cold war waged against them. We have been galvanised in the same alembic.'[33]

In reply to the request for his views regarding possible use of force in Persia, Sir Gladwyn Jebb telegraphed on the evening of July 21, 1951, a reiteration of his opinion two months earlier (cf p. 182) that it could not legally be harmonised with the charter of the United Nations 'except in circumstances involving the obvious collapse of the Persian State . . . It is true, of course, that there is no specific Charter Article which debars a State from taking such protective action but it would be, in my opinion, extremely difficult to argue convincingly here in favour of what would amount to the seizure of a piece of foreign territory because it happened to have on it some British property which was being damaged.'

Sir Gladwyn Jebb concluded: 'To sum up what I feel is this. It may well be that an act of force of the kind indicated by you would, if successful, have a most healthy effect on the whole situation in the Middle East. It may well be also that it would not result in any Russian intervention in Northern Persia. Finally it could quite well result in the fall of Musaddiq and his replacement of [*sic*] a Prime Minister more amenable to our views. But unless the United States are prepared to approve our action wholeheartedly and without reserve it is likely that we should have to pay a very heavy price for our 'forward policy' in the United Nations. Many Americans would say that we were deliberately wrecking that institution; and if this view should be shared by the Administration our enemies all over the world might seek to profit from our embarrassment and confusion.'[34]

This telling telegram from New York was substantially reinforced that same evening by another from Washington. Sir Oliver Franks advised that if Mr Harriman failed in his mission 'in circumstances as favourable as possible to us, we should have to reckon with the strong probability the State Department would consider the use of force by us in any circumstances would strengthen the position of Musaddiq'. Any such British action 'should so be presented to the United States and the world as to minimise the considerable opposition it will meet . . . It should take place because of a definite incident or provocation and, if possible, be presented as maintaining the *status quo* on the lines of the Hague Court decision pending final settlement of the dispute.' Sir Oliver Franks further made the same point as had Mr Lewis Douglas concerning the high importance of giving Mr Dean Acheson timely warning of any proposed military action.

---

[32] Parliamentary Debates, 5th Series, H. of L., Vol. 173, col. 133.
[33] Cited, P. Calvocoressi, *Survey of International Affairs 1951* (Oxford 1954), p. 276.
[34] EP 1192/65G.

Sir Oliver Franks concluded: 'To sum up, the operation you are considering will meet with opposition in any event from the Administration and from the American public. It would be lessened if Harriman failed in circumstances wholly favourable to us, if the public presentation of our action was as favourable as one could hope, if we had prepared the mind of Acheson in advance, and if the operation achieved quick and decisive success. Otherwise the pressure on Anglo-American relations would be very considerable.'[35]

On the following day of July 22 Sir Francis Shepherd put forward the same argument as that which Sir Oliver Franks expected from the State Department: that any British military action in Persia 'in the present conditions would have the effect of strengthening Dr Musaddiq and uniting the country behind him. The disadvantages would in fact heavily outweigh the advantages unless the situation were far more ominous than it is now. I would be strongly against any such action unless the Harriman mission fails and unless conditions deteriorate a good deal further than they have as yet.'[36]

His Majesty's Ambassador in Tehran advised that any British military action should be preceded by an ultimatum to Persia in the light of Persian criticism of the lack of one before the British intervention 10 years earlier. Sir Francis Shepherd thought it probable that a British attempt to run the refinery at Abadan on imported oil under a military régime would initially occasion labour disorders but that the Persian workers 'would probably knuckle under'. The telegram concluded: 'I consider that this operation should only be considered if the situation in Persia and prospect of rehabilitating the oil industry becomes virtually hopeless.'

Mr Furlonge noted of the three ambassadors consulted regarding military intervention in Persia that 'all were unfavourable for varying reasons'.[37] The Foreign Secretary explained this important fact to the Cabinet on July 23 when it considered his memorandum of July 20. The Attorney-General observed that the previously noticed argument there of the position under international law, in general accordance with the views of Mr Fitzmaurice, 'did not in his view correctly present the legal position'.[38] Sir Frank Soskice considered that the minimum use of force in Persia to protect actually endangered British lives 'was the most we could hope to justify in international law; and even this could not now be said with certainty to be permissible in view of Article 2(4) of the United Nations Charter'.

The Cabinet agreed on July 23 to defer consideration of the use of force to hold and operate the refinery at Abadan. Two days later the Chiefs of Staff instructed that all forces for Operation Buccaneer could stand at 24 hours' notice instead of the three hours' notice of the last three weeks. In this connexion the Chiefs of Staff informed the Commanders-in-Chief, Middle East: 'Continual unavoidable changes of policy with regard to military action in Persian [*sic*] have recently led us to send you so many various instructions about Buccaneer that there appears to be some risk of confusion . . . We can now give you no indication as to the likelihood or possible timing for carrying [out] Buccaneer on our own initiative. In *no* circumstances is Buccaneer to be mounted except on our direct and express authority.'[39] This was the

---

[35] *Ibid.*
[36] *Ibid.*
[37] EP 1531/1153.
[38] EP 1531/1180G.
[39] EP 1192/79G.

beginning of the end of Operation Buccaneer. This tendency had been encouraged by important developments meanwhile in the mission to Tehran of Mr Averell Harriman.

2. The Harriman Formula

In Tehran Mr Harriman's uphill mission had begun, remarked Sir Francis Shepherd, as 'not so much a fact-finding as a fact-providing one'.[40] It was 'pounding away at repeating to the Persians' much of what Sir Francis Shepherd and, lately, Count Carafa had been urging upon them: notably their prospective difficulties in marketing any oil in the face of Anglo-American opposition and the risk for Persia of losing her market permanently once the stoppage of her oil had been made good by working up supplies elsewhere. In this Mr Harriman received what His Majesty's Ambassador termed 'the tireless aid of Mr Levy', who 'relentlessly attacked' M. Kazem Hasibi, a Persian engineer who was an Under-Secretary at the Ministry of Finance and was regarded as a fanatical force behind Dr Musaddiq's policy of oil-nationalisation. Sir Francis Shepherd thought he perceived evidence that 'in this Persian Hunting of the Snark it may be the case that "what I tell you three times is true"'.[41] Some days later Mr Herbert Morrison wryly described 'the difficulty of doing business with a Government which did not seem to care if it ruined its own country'.[42]

For Persia, as for other emergent countries of the East, economic considerations were, as Lord Mountbatten had warned (cf pp. 139-40), not the only, nor even the main ones: especially, perhaps, when landowners like Dr Musaddiq were themselves economically remote from oil. In origin the oil dispute was indeed economic and here the Persian Government had not been without legitimate grievances (cf pp. 56, 95-6, 174, 391) which had not always received very forthcoming recognition from the British side. The economic growth of the Anglo-Iranian Oil Company, congenial to the Treasury, had outrun its political awareness in Persia (cf pp. 48-9, 56-7, 60, 132). Sir Francis Shepherd had tended to sympathise with Persian resentment at the lack of control over their main source of revenue (cf p. 105), which was in effect administered by a foreign monopoly, rather strictly controlled from London. This resentment tended towards alignment with anti-colonialist stirrings against Western imperialism, caught up in the cold war. In this Dr Musaddiq, socially conservative but with unusual popular support, was trying to combine a policy of neutrality with the assertion of frustrated Persian nationalism against the Western, if not the more frightening Eastern, occupying Powers of a decade earlier. If the economic issues were the immediate ones, in the last resort they were by now subordinate.

By July 20-21 Mr Harriman thought that Dr Musaddiq 'was moving towards a point to [*sic*] where he would be prepared to negotiate on a basis of the principle of nationalisation without insisting on the acceptance of the nationalisation laws':[43] the Persians made out that their understanding was that there had previously been no British acknowledgement of the principle of oil nationalisation in Persia (cf, however pp. 177, 211, 214, 221).[44] In this connexion Sir Francis Shepherd reminded

---

[40] EP 1013/36.
[41] EP 1531/1217.
[42] E 1057/2.
[43] EP 1531/1099.
[44] EP 1531/1105.

Mr Harriman on July 20 'that a crucial point to which His Majesty's Government attached great importance was a return in the south to the *status quo* . . . Harriman seemed to think that a British Government Mission should come in advance of any undertaking by the Persians to this effect.'[43] He urged that the announcement of withdrawal of British staff from the oilfields should if possible be postponed for a few days.

On July 19, 1951, however, the Persian Government had withdrawn the residence-permit of Mr Seddon and ordered him to leave the country. His recent visit to Abadan was alleged to have been suspicious and in order to arrange the disorders in Tehran on July 15. The preferment of this 'ridiculous and insulting charge' during Mr Harriman's visit was justly regarded by Sir Francis Shepherd as provocative. It inclined him to reverse advice he had telegraphed earlier that same day and now 'to think that we should go ahead with the announcement to withdraw, whether or not the Persian Government give way about Seddon. I apologise for these rapidly succeeding opinions but the Persian Government's actions are unpredictable and do not seem to be governed by any perceptible logic.'[44]

Mr Harriman followed up a British protest to the Persian Government, which speedily restored Mr Seddon's residence permit. Sir Francis Shepherd on July 22 nevertheless further protested to the Persian Foreign Minister against the action and accusation against Mr Seddon, coupling this with a complaint against Persian activities against British staff in South Persia: 'I intimated that this state of affairs could only be remedied by withdrawal of Makki and a virtual return to the *status quo*. I have no great hopes that these representations will be effective.'[45] Mr Harriman, however, was encouraged by the Persian retreat regarding Mr Seddon and continued to urge postponement of withdrawal of British staff from the oilfields.

At the meeting of the Cabinet on July 23 the Foreign Secretary advised delaying for 'a further day or two' the announcement of the long-debated withdrawal even though 'it was disquieting that the Persian Prime Minister had so far given no evidence of a change in his attitude'.[46] The Cabinet decided accordingly and also noted that the Chancellor of the Exchequer had decided upon a similar delay in issuing an Order in Council now prepared for the limitation of Persian facilities in using sterling, in reply to a Persian Bill tabled by Dr Musaddiq on July 12 for the release of £14 million held as note cover (cf p. 271). British exports to Persia were, however, still to be delayed and if necessary prevented. It would appear that Mr Gaitskell took a prominent part in discussion at that meeting of terms upon which His Majesty's Government might agree to that resumption of negotiations with the Persian Government which Mr Harriman was seeking. It was in pursuance of a suggestion from Mr Gaitskell that Sir Francis Shepherd was instructed to advise Mr Harriman of the repercussions which the Persian crisis was having in Iraq, where the Iraq Petroleum Company with its American participation had with difficulty reached a basis of an agreement on 50-50 principles with the Iraqi Government on the previous day of July 22.[47] In accordance with the discussion in the Cabinet on July 23 the Foreign Office and the Treasury collaborated that day in drafting instructions to Sir Francis Shepherd. At the wish of the Foreign Secretary, Sir William Strang

---

[45] EP 1531/1115.
[46] EP 1531/1180G.
[47] EQ 1015/8.

explained the position to Mr Winston Churchill, who 'said he hoped that we should not, in our response to Mr Harriman, give up our position'.[48]

The instructions of July 23 to Sir Francis Shepherd explained that His Majesty's Government were not over-impressed by the Persian withdrawal of 'the outrageous charges' against Mr Seddon, and were somewhat concerned lest the trend of Mr Harriman's discussions 'should result in our being placed in the position of having to reject a wholly unacceptable basis for discussions'.[49] Before His Majesty's Government could send a mission to Tehran for discussions on the basis of an acceptance of the principle of oil nationalisation, four 'essential prerequisites' must be met: first, the Anglo-Iranian Oil Company must be allowed to resume operations under its own management, and interference with its staff must cease; secondly, no attempt (for instance, by new forms of tanker-receipts) to prejudice the legal possession of the company during discussions; thirdly, negotiations to be with the Persian Government and not with members of the Oil Commission; fourthly, no Persian insistence upon prior British acceptance of the terms of the nine-point nationalisation law of May 2.

The four conditions omitted any reference to the interim injunction of the International Court in accordance with the view expressed in the Cabinet that day that this should not be too much stressed provided that negotiations could be resumed substantially upon that basis. Sir Francis Shepherd was further instructed to indicate to Mr Harriman that Mr Jackson's rejected proposals of June 19 were likely to represent in substance the British limit. This marked the first British retreat, during the Harriman mission, from the authority of the interim injunction of the International Court, coinciding with the retreat from Operation Buccaneer.

The British instructions of July 23 crossed Sir Francis Shepherd's communication (received around noon on July 24) of what subsequently became known as the Harriman Formula. This stated that the Persian Cabinet, meeting on July 23, had approved a formula as follows. The Persian Government would be willing to negotiate with representatives of His Majesty's Government 'on behalf of the former company' if His Majesty's Government, on that behalf, had previously made a formal statement of its consent to 'the principle of nationalisation of the oil industry'. By that was meant 'the proposal which was approved by the Special Oil Committee of the Majlis and was confirmed by the law of Esfand 29, 1329 (March 20, 1951), the text of which proposal is quoted hereunder: "In the name of the prosperity of the Iranian nation and with a view to helping secure world peace we the undersigned propose that the oil industry of Iran be declared as nationalised throughout all regions of the country without exception, that is to say, all operations for exploration, extraction and exploitation shall be in the hands of the Government".'[50]

The Persian Oil Commission told Mr Harriman that in the last clause the phrase 'in the hands of' could be translated 'under the authority of'.[51] This important gloss remained, however, verbal. Sir Francis Shepherd commented, in general, that the above-cited text was quite different from that of the law of March 20, as known to

---

[48] EP 1531/1138.
[49] *Ibid.*
[50] Cmd 8425, p. 52.
[51] EP 1531/1127.

him. His Majesty's Ambassador subsequently reported that the text cited in the Harriman Formula appeared to be that of a manifesto issued by the National Front on November 6, 1950 (cf p. 90).[52] It was the Foreign Office which, in reply to Sir Francis Shepherd, pointed out that the text in question was very similar to the proposal introduced by the National Front in the Majlis Oil commission on November 29, 1950 (cf p. 90), as recorded in proceedings of the commission received from His Majesty's Embassy on July 4. The telegram from the Foreign Office commented that the resolution adopted by the Majlis and Senate on March 15-20 (cf pp. 123, 126, 132) was evidently 'carefully drafted to revive this proposal and to present it as having been accepted and approved' by the Oil Commission.[53]

In conclusion the Persian communication of July 23, 1951, reiterated the rejection of Mr Jackson's proposals but stated that the Persian Government was willing to negotiate the manner in which the law of March 20, 1951, was carried out in so far as it affected British interests. Although these proposals from the Persian Government became known as the Harriman Formula, Mr Harriman had begun by refusing to transmit them on the ground that he was not a mediator, but had later, after discussion, agreed to do so.[54] *The Times* of July 25, 1951, described Mr Harriman as not very enthusiastic about the proposals. On the other hand, Sir Francis Shepherd had reported the day before that Mr Harriman 'considered that the present was a very favourable if not the only opportunity for starting negotiations and strongly recommended that His Majesty's Government should accept this opportunity'. When His Majesty's Ambassador had reiterated 'that a *sine qua non* of negotiations would be a return to the *status quo* in the south, Harriman said that, although this was very much in his mind, he did not feel he could go into details on this point with the Persians. The considerations involved were rather more concrete than his terms of reference permitted.'[55] Concrete those considerations certainly were.

In the same conversation of July 24 with Sir Francis Shepherd regarding the Persian formula, 'Harriman emphasised the need for some elasticity on our part in order to take account of the state of public opinion in this country, and I pointed out that similar considerations applied to British public opinion'—let alone that of the British sufferers at Abadan. On the same day Sir Francis Shepherd, who was evidently making a considerable diplomatic effort to relieve his compatriots in the south, briefly emphasised to M. Bushihri, the Persian Minister of Communications, 'the need for drastic and immediate action'[56] to remedy the situation there. M. Bushihri said that a lot of foolish things had been done and that they would be remedied immediately. His Majesty's Ambassador proposed to ascertain 'whether anything in fact is being done', and returned to the charge with the Foreign Minister.[57] On the Persian side, however, most of the doing continued to be at Abadan, against the British.

On the same date of July 24, 1951, Mr Mason, bearing the burden and heat of the day in South Persia, telegraphed to Sir William Fraser through His Majesty's

---

[52] EP 1531/1155.
[53] *Ibid.*
[54] EP 1531/1196G.
[55] EP 1531/1129.
[56] *Ibid.*
[57] EP 1531/1140.

Consul-General at Khorramshahr to confirm that his general management could not remain alongside the Persians much longer unless M. Makki, the Temporary Board and their subordinates were withdrawn. Offices, records, communications, cars, launches had been seized from the Anglo-Iranian Oil Company by the Persians. Mr Mason commented: 'The British and the company's prestige has inevitably sunk to a very low level in the eyes of the Persian [?and] Arab communities. The game of cat and mouse has been in progress for a month with the British staff being mice.'[58] Mr Mason emphasised that this was not a complaint, that all his sore-tried staff were in good heart and prepared to carry on as long as possible.

A leak just then in the British Press of the previous decision of His Majesty's Government, now suspended, for the withdrawal of British staff from the outlying Fields did not, however, improve their morale. Major Capper reported on July 25 that Mr Mason was not prepared to ask his field-staff to remain indefinitely in 'degrading and exasperating conditions'.[59] From Tehran Mr Seddon fully supported Mr Mason and on July 25 reported to Sir William Fraser, through Sir Francis Shepherd, that, unlike Mr Harriman, he was sceptical as to the latter having now built up a fund of Persian goodwill. This, considered Mr Seddon, was 'based entirely on considerations of Persian self-interest resulting from a dawning appreciation of the difficulties of their position. Withdrawal would surely underline these considerations rather than dispel them . . . For various reasons entirely sound in themselves, we have constantly postponed taking any final and definite decision on this matter of withdrawal. I question whether it has strengthened our position. It is true that we have maintained a foothold in the south but this has been at the expense of a disastrous loss of prestige . . . The initiative still rests largely with the Persians and so far the only serious attempt to wrest it from them has been made by the Americans rather than ourselves.'[60]

Sir William Fraser replied to Mr Mason on July 25 that 'every effort is being made to obtain complete withdrawal of interference as a prerequisite to discussions'[61] with the Persians. Sir Francis Shepherd reported on the same day that Mr Harriman would put the four British conditions of July 23 to the Persians, but was reluctant to discuss them as being outside the scope of his activities[62]—unlike, evidently, the Persian conditions. Meanwhile in Washington the British Embassy had been urging support for the British requirements upon the State Department, where Mr McGhee was 'exceedingly optimistic', while maintaining that 'it was essential that no one should go better than the 50-50 arrangement, or the position of all the companies in the area would be in jeopardy'.[63] Fear for the American 50-50 formula (cf p. 144) was henceforth to assume increasing prominence in American thinking and, if only rather tentatively, in British calculations as to how to influence that thinking.

Gingered up just a little by Mr Christopher Steel, the State Department on July 25 emphasised to the Persian Ambassador in Washington that the Persian Government would be 'well advised to take no action which would jeopardise

---

[58] EP 1531/1107.
[59] EP 1531/1137.
[60] EP 1531/1136.
[61] *Ibid.*
[62] EP 1531/1140.
[63] EP 1531/1142.

successful negotiations'. Which incurred from Mr Herbert Morrison the pregnant comment: 'We want them to leave off!'[64] In London on the same day of July 25 the American Ambassador was observing to Sir William Strang that if His Majesty's Government sent a Minister to Tehran for sincere negotiations, which then failed, 'the blame, if any, would lie rather with the Americans than with the British; on the other hand, if we insisted upon unnecessarily rigid conditions before agreeing to despatch a mission, he thought that the blame would fall on us rather than on the Americans'.[65] Mr Gifford, like Mr Harriman, hoped that, in return for the Persians not insisting upon the nine-point law of May 2, His Majesty's Government would not allude to the ruling of The Hague Court. This tacit bargain, with all that it implied in derogation of British interests, was to assume importance.

Mr Furlonge noted in a brief of July 25 for the Foreign Secretary that it would appear that the Persians had, in effect, accepted two of the four British conditions of July 23: namely that the Persian Government should negotiate with His Majesty's Government and should not insist upon the nine-point law of May 2. The Ministerial Committee on Persia that afternoon considered that this latter advance, and absence of Persian reference to Persian control of the international marketing of oil, constituted 'a very substantial concession' by Dr Musaddiq. At the same time 'there could be no question of our agreeing to send a mission to Persia until the Persian Government had taken effective action to end their interference with the company's property and staff.'[66]

That evening the Foreign Secretary communicated to the American Ambassador the substance of this justified and necessary proviso and also stipulated, presumably with reference to the second unfulfilled British condition regarding such devices as tanker receipts, that 'there should be a working arrangement to keep the oil flowing while the talks went on'.[67] In response to a request from Mr Gifford, Mr Morrison assured him that if Ministers should find difficulty in sending a mission to Tehran on the basis of the Persian proposals, he would be given an opportunity of making representations before a final decision was reached. The American Ambassador went to the perhaps rather surprising length of handing the Foreign Secretary a rough draft of a reply from His Majesty's Government which, he considered, might be acceptable to the Persian Government: as indeed it might since it merely spelt out British acceptance of the principle of Persian oil nationalisation and was innocent of any stipulation regarding Persian practices at Abadan.[68]

Next day, July 26, 1951, Mr Root of the American Embassy showed Mr Saner at the Foreign Office a telegram from Mr Harriman listing seven points upon which he considered that he had secured a Persian advance: the two British desiderata regarding governmental negotiations and no prior acceptance of the nine-point law; thirdly and fourthly, readiness to negotiate the execution of the first law of March 20, and for a foreign-owned company to operate as agents for the National Iranian Oil Company; fifthly, recognition of the necessity of the goodwill of foreign companies for shipping and marketing oil; sixthly, readiness to negotiate 'even after clear and repeated statements by Mr Harriman that they cannot expect greater

---

[64] EP 1531/1279.
[65] EP 1531/1168.
[66] EP 1531/1161G.
[67] EP 1531/1186.
[68] EP 1531/1201.

financial returns than those received by other countries in comparable circumstances'[69] (the 50-50 formula); seventhly, Persian acceptance of the principle that they would have to deal with the Anglo-Iranian Oil Company in working out the above arrangements, and any *modus vivendi* for operating the oilfields pending negotiation of a new agreement. If any of the points in this considerable list were subsequently repudiated Mr Harriman, said Mr Root, 'would regard himself as having been deceived'.

Also on July 26 Sir Francis Shepherd reported on a discussion of the four British conditions which he had had on the previous day with the Persian Foreign Minister: who subsequently sent His Majesty's Ambassador his tendentiously inaccurate record of the conversation[70]—an illustration of the kind of difficulties encountered in dealing with, and trusting, the Persian Government. Sir Francis Shepherd suggested the withdrawal of M. Makki from Abadan for a start and presented as 'official alternatives' a return there to the *status quo* or acceptance of the ruling of The Hague Court. His Majesty's Ambassador, however, was not hopeful that the Persians would produce anything acceptable on that. He also felt that there was nothing to be gained regarding the second unfulfilled British condition concerning such Persian devices against the Anglo-Iranian Oil Company as tanker receipts: 'The Persians are both suspicious and muddled about it, and I would strongly recommend that we should not insist on it.'[71] This advice was speedily to be adopted. This marked the second British retreat on negotiating terms during the Harriman mission.

The Foreign Secretary informed the Cabinet on July 26, 1951, that 'the offer by the Persian Government to reopen negotiations . . . was a most encouraging development'.[72] He now 'felt that on balance we should demand only one such [prior] condition, namely the undertaking to end interference with the staff'. Some Ministers felt that before a British Minister went to negotiate at Tehran, as Mr Harriman desired, the Persian Government should give a definite undertaking, and afford evidence, that interference at Abadan had stopped. The question of tanker receipts was again raised, and it was argued that negotiations could not be conducted satisfactorily till the Anglo-Iranian Oil Company had resumed control of its operations: while His Majesty's Government could not hope for a complete return to the *status quo*, they could insist, as a condition of resuming negotiations, that the Persian Government should conform to the principles of the interim ruling of the International Court. On the other hand it was argued that the Persian offer, under American pressure, to negotiate should not be missed and that a British mission might proceed to Tehran if the Persians undertook to send immediate instructions to terminate interference at Abadan; though it was recognised that such instructions might not be fully carried out. On the whole this latter school of thought prevailed as regards the terms of the British reply to the Persian proposal.

On the evening of July 26 Sir Francis Shepherd was instructed to present at once to the Persian Government a note on the following lines: His Majesty's Government recognised 'the principle of nationalisation of the oil industry in Persia' and agreed to send a Minister to negotiate in Tehran. But 'before His Majesty's Government

---

[69] EP 1531/1279.
[70] EP 1531/1228.
[71] EP 1531/1146.
[72] EP 1531/1181G.

can consider the despatch of a mission they must request that the Persian Government should send instructions to the competent authorities to ensure that the present interference with the company's operations and the present vexations to the company's staff are discontinued'.[73]

Sir Francis Shepherd was further instructed that when presenting this note to the Persian Government he should 'make it plain that His Majesty's Government's acceptance of the principle of nationalisation does not in any way imply acceptance of the law of May 2. You should also emphasise that the question of the treatment to which the company and the company's staff are being subjected to [*sic*] is of crucial importance and that it would be quite impossible for a mission to start negotiations . . . as long as these conditions continue. His Majesty's Government will expect that if instructions are sent by the Persian Government on the lines requested they will result in an immediate and concrete improvement in this respect'. In the event of a subsequent deterioration, 'the mission would have to be immediately withdrawn'.

It was explained to Sir Francis Shepherd that 'Ministers do not wish to specify at this stage the precise conditions regarding the cessation of present interference and vexations which they would regard as satisfactory'. He was, however, to make clear to the Persian Government 'that we cannot accept the present position under which the whole of the company's operations are being brought to a standstill', and he could doubtless quote specific instances in support. His Majesty's Ambassador was to 'stress most strongly' that the earnest of Persian goodwill especially desired was the withdrawal, even if unobtrusive, from Khuzistan of M. Makki and other leading trouble-makers.

Before presenting the note to the Persian Government, His Majesty's Ambassador was to inform Mr Harriman and explain that His Majesty's Government had been largely influenced by the results, gratefully acknowledged, of his able and patient work in Tehran. 'But', these long instructions continued, 'Mr Harriman must appreciate that public opinion in this country is much exercised over the indignities to which a British company and British nationals are being subjected and would regard the despatch of an official mission to Tehran, headed by a senior British Minister, in present circumstances as a complete surrender to the Persian Government's aggressive and intransigent tactics. It is therefore of the greatest importance that there should be a radical improvement in the situation before the mission starts, and we rely on him to use his utmost influence with the Persian Government in support of your representations to secure this.' Mr Harriman should be made aware that British Ministers had been greatly impressed by the recent telegrams from Mr Seddon and Mr Mason, and by the difficulty of prolonging the stay in the fields of the company's staff, who 'are of course in the front line for Britain'.[74]

The detailed instructions to Sir Francis Shepherd faithfully reflected the discussion in the Cabinet and by their strong tone helped to counterbalance, if they could not conceal, the fact that the wording of the note to the Persian Government, requiring the despatch of instructions to discontinue interference in the operations of the Anglo-Iranian Oil Company, represented a weakening from the British conditions of only three days before, with their insistence upon the company's

---

[73] EP 1531/1198.
[74] EP 1531/1198.

resumption of operations under its own management as the first of the 'essential prerequisites'. This was the third British retreat on negotiating terms during the Harriman mission.

At its meeting on July 26, 1951, the Cabinet, on the proposal of the President of the Board of Trade, had also agreed to some relaxation as regards British exports to Persia. On the same day Mr Fitzmaurice advised, regarding his difference of opinion with the Attorney-General concerning the legality of British military action in Persia, that if the Foreign Secretary felt he might still wish to take such action 'it is unwise to saddle yourself in advance with a formal Law Officers' Opinion . . . that you are not entitled to do so'.[75] On the other hand Mr Fitzmaurice emphasised that 'the Attorney-General is the principal legal adviser to the Government and his view necessarily prevails over that of any departmental lawyer'. Some months later Sir William Strang was to note that the view held by the Attorney-General was the 'more widely supported'[76] of the two; and Mr Fitzmaurice himself stated at the time that he was not sure that his own view 'would be agreed to by all my legal colleagues here':[75] rather later, in another but somewhat related connexion, it was noted in the Foreign Office that it was not unusual for the Legal Adviser, Sir Eric Beckett, to view things differently from his deputy, Mr Fitzmaurice.[77]

Mr Fitzmaurice concluded that, despite his personal views, 'we must assume, in any action we may take, that we shall only be able to justify it legally if it is clearly necessary for the purpose of saving life'.[78] The opposite contingency of military action even if British lives were not endangered was ruled out of consideration for the moment in a telegram of July 28 from the Foreign Office to Sir Gladwyn Jebb. This telegram (which resulted from a departmental meeting held on July 24 by the Minister of State and attended by Mr Paul Mason, Mr Parrott, Mr Furlonge and Mr Fitzmaurice) judiciously proposed that in the event of British intervention to protect lives His Majesty's Government should forestall a Persian appeal to the Security Council by itself promptly making a communication to it.[79] Sir Gladwyn Jebb entirely agreed but could not 'disguise the fact that if we take unilateral action—even in the event of British lives being obviously endangered—we are in for a rough passage'.[80] After discussing procedural modalities under the Charter of the United Nations, Sir Gladwyn Jebb concluded his telegram of July 29: 'As a last reflection, may I just add that the only thing which would really worry me would be a situation here in which we were obviously opposed by the Americans.' Within the last few days a rather sharp Anglo-American divergence regarding policy towards Persia had indeed occurred, if in a less dangerous context.

3. The journey of Mr Harriman from Tehran to London, July 27-28

His Majesty's Ambassador in Tehran, even before receipt of his instructions of July 26, 1951, had been continuing his persistent endeavours to secure some improvement in conditions in South Persia. He spoke of it to M. Martin Daftari and, on July 26, to the Shah; but, as usual with the latter, with no conclusive effect. By

---

[75] EP 1192/120G.
[76] EP 1531/2147.
[77] EP 1531/1158.
[78] EP 1192/120G.
[79] EP 1192/65G.
[80] EP 1192/80G.

contrast Mr Harriman's assistant from the State Department, Mr Rountree, was that evening strongly urging upon Sir Francis Shepherd what was now the American line: that, reported the latter, the opportunity for negotiations with the Persians 'should not be prejudiced by any condition on our part which the Persians might fight it difficult to accept . . . Politically it would be impossible for the Persians to make substantial move towards the restoration of the *status quo*.'[81] In London the American Ambassador, when informed by Sir William Strang of the new instructions to Sir Francis Shepherd, queried the reference in the proposed British note to Persian interference with the operations of the Anglo-Iranian Oil Company. Mr Gifford thought that there was room for misunderstanding by the Persians. They might interpret it as a demand for a return to the *status quo* as laid down by The Hague Court. Sir William Strang, however, thought that the instructions were clear enough.[82]

Mr Harriman reacted more strongly than Mr Gifford to the instructions of July 26, 1951, to Sir Francis Shepherd. The latter received them when he was with Mr Harriman, who declared that they would mean 'the end of his efforts'.[81] His Majesty's Ambassador telegraphed at 10.25 am on July 27 that he was inclined to agree, and suggested, whether or not at the instance of Mr Harriman, that they should both fly to London. The Press could be told that the visit was in connexion with a British desire, expressed by Mr Morrison in the House of Commons on July 25, for clarification of the Persian proposals for negotiation. This telegram was received in the Foreign Office just after half past eleven that morning.

At 3.15 pm that day Mr Attlee, Mr Morrison, Mr Gaitskell, Mr Shinwell and Mr Noel-Baker attended a meeting of the Ministerial Committee on Persia. The meeting agreed with the Foreign Secretary that the proposed visit of Mr Harriman and Sir Francis Shepherd would serve no useful purpose. Mr Harriman, as Mr Morrison observed, was not a mediator and a visit by him then to London would make the Persians conclude that he was seeking to put pressure on His Majesty's Government on their behalf. It was further held that 'it was important to distinguish between interference with the Anglo-Iranian Oil Company's staff, which must be stopped, and the Persian refusal to allow the Company to continue their operations, which might be dealt with by the mission in their negotiations'.[83]

At 5.10 pm on July 27 a short telegram to Tehran, *en clair* for speed and designated 'Emergency', informed Sir Francis Shepherd that instructions were being sent to him advising against the visit he proposed.[84] Less than a quarter of an hour later a telegram[85] was received from Sir Francis Shepherd reporting that a spokesman of the Embassy of the United States in Tehran had given the Press the statement suggested in His Majesty's Ambassador's telegram of that morning. At 5.30 pm in the Foreign Office a telegram, embodying the ministerial decision against the proposed visit, was sent through to be encyphered. This telegram generally restated the previous position of His Majesty's Government, while observing that it did not wish to lay down meticulous conditions nor to insist on the resumption of full working in the oil industry in South Persia. By contrast, however, with the

[81] EP 1531/1163.
[82] EP 1531/1210G.
[83] EP 1531/1210G.
[84] EP 1531/1163.
[85] EP 1531/1167.

ministerial view expressed that afternoon, the telegram, for whatever reason (conceivably subsequent consultation with Sir William Fraser), explained that it was impossible to draw a clear distinction between interference with operations and with staff since some aspects of the former were just as exasperating to the staff as personal indignities. The growing indiscipline of the Persian staff due to orders being given over the heads of the competent officials was a case in point.

At 5.55 pm the Foreign Office received a further telegram from Sir Francis Shepherd, *en clair*, in reply to the warning telegram outward of 5.10 pm. His Majesty's Ambassador represented that he could not expect to receive his cyphered instructions before Mr Harriman's aeroplane left Tehran for London. Sir Francis Shepherd would accompany him unless he received definite instructions, *en clair*, by emergency telegram by 6 pm Greenwich Mean Time.[84] Such instructions were not sent. The instructing telegram which had been sent for cyphering at 5.30 pm, with designation 'emergency', was not despatched till 7.10 pm. Such is the story told by the official telegrams and documents. Sir Francis Shepherd flew to London that night with Mr and Mrs Harriman, Mr Rountree and Mr Levy.

When Sir Francis Shepherd reached London on the morning of July 28, 1951, he presumably gave the Foreign Secretary a fuller, unrecorded, account of the lively events in Tehran wherein he had been caught up on the preceding day. The *New York Herald Tribune* indicated on July 28 that His Majesty's Ambassador had the day before discussed his latest instructions with President Truman's special envoy in 'a futile two-hour conference'. According to the *Baltimore Sun* of the same day Mr Harriman complained to Sir Francis Shepherd that the instructions which he was receiving from London 'were both leisurely in transit and obscure in content'. After the conversation 'although there were the customary denials of discord, Harriman had fire in his eye' and he then 'accepted the view of other American authorities that the British were deliberately stalling'. Mr Harriman thereafter saw both the Shah and Dr Musaddiq.

According to the *New York Herald Tribune* Mr Harriman was influenced by the fact that Sir Francis Shepherd 'never appeared to give more than lukewarm support to Mr Harriman's mission . . . In deciding to go over the head of Sir Francis, Mr Harriman did not wait for a specific invitation from London. When he began the mission, the Foreign Office said it would be glad to see Mr Harriman at any time . . . . Evidently Sir Francis left the meeting with no inkling that Mr Harriman would fly to London.' *The Times* reported on July 28: 'The Ambassador was still awaiting instructions from London on whether he was to travel or not after Mr Harriman had boarded his aircraft. A despatch from London was then delivered to him at the airfield by a breathless First Secretary. Sir Francis Shepherd read it to the accompaniment of the photographers' flashlamps and boarded the aircraft, which took off shortly before midnight.'

Mr Harriman's determination to fly from Tehran to London in the face of objection by His Majesty's Government with regard to critical negotiations may seem somewhat remarkable in one who had himself maintained that he was not a mediator between the British and Persian Governments. That fiction to cloak American intrusion was now swept away. The Foreign Secretary recorded that he subsequently told the American Ambassador that 'I had been somewhat taken aback by Mr Harriman's announcing at a Press conference that he would come to London before we had been able to give our approval; in fact, I had been doubtful of the wisdom of the visit, though in the event it has proved useful. Mr Gifford said that at the time he shared my doubts as to the advisability of the visit.'[86]

4. Discussions in London with Mr Harriman and Mr Levy, July 28-30

The Ministerial Committee on Persia, with the Prime Minister in the chair, held its 17th meeting at 4 pm on July 28, 1951. In addition to the Foreign Secretary, the Chancellor of the Exchequer and the Minister of Fuel and Power there were also present Sir Francis Shepherd and Mr Richard Stokes, the Lord Privy Seal who, it was proposed, would be the Minister to negotiate with the Persians if that course were adopted. This proposal had been made by Mr Stokes in a letter of July 24 to Mr Herbert Morrison. The proposal prevailed over a respectful representation by Sir William Strang, in concert with Sir Edward Bridges, that it would be gambling to send Mr Stokes, who perhaps scarcely possessed quite the necessary experience or cool temperament: a Minister of the standing of Mr Gaitskell might be more of a match to Mr Harriman in so important a mission.[87] Sir Francis Shepherd now represented that if its despatch was agreed 'without first obtaining any assurance from the Persian Government that they would take steps to improve the situation in the south the effect on the staff would be very serious indeed'. Mr Noel-Baker expressed the view that 'the Persian Government could without difficulty put a stop to these intolerable conditions if they wished to do so'.[88]

At 4.30 pm the meeting was joined by Mr Gifford, Mr Harriman and Mr Rountree. Mr Harriman stated that 'the Persian Government were now genuinely anxious to find a solution . . . It was his considered opinion that His Majesty's Government should impose no prior considerations for the despatch of a ministerial mission: conditions in the South were undoubtedly deplorable, but it would be extremely difficult for the Persian Government to give any specific undertaking' to improve them before negotiations began. Dr Musaddiq had told Mr Harriman the day before that he would send instructions in that sense, and his 'intention to take effective action would certainly be strengthened' by an immediate British acceptance of negotiations.

Several British Ministers represented to the American special envoy that 'public opinion in this country would resent what appeared to be a complete surrender to Persian demands. Moreover the position of a mission led by a Cabinet Minister would be most humiliating if the intolerable interference with the staff was maintained after the mission's arrival.' There ensured a discussion of the terms of a British reply to the Persian offer in place of that which Mr Harriman had taken against. This led to the proposal by the Prime Minister of a formula forming the basis of a new British note which Mr Harriman now agreed to transmit to the Persian Government. This text, repeating British willingness to recognise the principle of nationalisation and to negotiate, whittled the precondition down to a request for an assurance that the Persian Government recognised that negotiations 'can be conducted in a satisfactory manner only if the present tension which exists in the South is relieved',[89] and that it would enter into discussions in that spirit. This was

---

[86] EP 1531/1256.
[87] Confidential/General/415, M.87.
[88] EP 1531/1211G.
[89] EP 1531/1211G.

the fourth British retreat on negotiating terms during the Harriman Mission.

The proposed British note was transmitted as a draft to the Persian Government from Mr Harriman by Dr Grady, and His Majesty's Embassy in Tehran was not required to take any action on it.[90] American mediation could now scarcely be more direct. Sir Francis Shepherd was not alone in considering that Mr Harriman's activities had much strengthened and encouraged the Persian Government. On July 28 a Persian paper published an interview with M. Husein Fatimi, the Prime Minister's influential Parliamentary Under-Secretary, which apparently advanced the nine-point law of May 2 as the basis for any negotiations.[91] On the following day Dr Musaddiq handed Dr Grady a reply expressing the Persian Government's belief 'that no tension exists in Khuzistan'.[90] The Premier further stated[92] that the British negotiator should understand from the outset that the principle of nationalisation of oil meant that its 'exploration, extraction and exploitation' should be in the hands of the Persian Government and that the conditions of sale would have to conform to the nine-point law. Proposals similar to the rejected ones of Mr Jackson could not be discussed.

Dr Grady told Dr Musaddiq that this meant a return to the position of three months earlier. The Counsellor of the American Embassy in Tehran who related this to the British Embassy said that Mr Harriman must not know that His Majesty's Government knew these supplementary particulars 'as Harriman has been "playing cards close to his chest"'.[93] On July 30 Mr Middleton further telegraphed from Tehran that even Dr Grady's 'strictly personal view is that the essential basis of goodwill is lacking on the Persian side and that Musaddiq is as intransigent as ever'.[94] Dr Grady was, however, content to leave the running to Mr Harriman, who had so gravely misled His Majesty's Government as to the Persian attitude. Mr Harriman now refused to deliver formally to His Majesty's Government the Persian reply, which was characterised by the Cabinet on July 30 as 'entirely unacceptable'.[95] Mr Harriman returned to Tehran from London that day and was seen off at the airport by the Lord Privy Seal and Air Marshal Sir John Slessor, described in the Press as an old friend of Mr Harriman.

Not the least fruitful aspect of Mr Harriman's unsolicited visit to London had been discussions which the resourceful Mr Levy had been holding at a more technical level with members of the Working Party on Persian Oil. Mr Levy substantially confirmed what Mr Root had told Mr Saner on July 26 regarding the seven points on which Mr Harriman believed, somewhat over-optimistically as it now appeared, that he had secured Persian concessions. Mr Levy, however, felt that negotiations with the Persians would be in vain unless they were met on three main points: first, the Anglo-Iranian Oil Company should not be reintroduced in disguise as the exclusive operating company; secondly, no foreign monopoly holding in Persia; thirdly, whilst recognising Persian dependence upon the Anglo-Iranian Oil Company's shipping and marketing services outside Persia, that company should not be the exclusive customer for Persian oil. Mr Levy suggested that His Majesty's

---

[90] EP 1531/1234.
[91] EP 1531/1174.
[92] EP 1531/1177.
[93] *Ibid.*
[94] EP 1531/1189.
[95] EP 1531/1212G.

Government might renounce its shareholding in the Anglo-Iranian Oil Company in favour of foreign oil companies which would represent the other major customers for Persian oil.

In the above connexion Mr Levy explained at a meeting at the Ministry of Fuel and Power on July 29, 1951, with Mr Victor Butler of that Ministry, Mr Ramsbotham of the Foreign Office, Mr Flett of the Treasury and Mr Gass of the Anglo-Iranian Oil Company, 'that the Persians had asked for American participation but Mr Harriman and himself had discouraged this and said that no American company would wish to take over from AIOC. If, however, the operating company was on a mixed basis it might well advance His Majesty's Government's long-term interests to have a percentage of United States participation in the Persian company. Perhaps AIOC could take some 40 per cent of the shares'[96]—a strikingly prescient suggestion, which, however, was to take some three years yet to materialise.

Other interesting points made by Mr Levy, as recorded by Mr Ramsbotham, were, first, that he thought it would be possible to meet the specified requirements 'within the framework of the nine-point law'; and, secondly, and significantly, that 'his instructions were not to upset the 50-50 formula'. Mr Levy was surprised here at the 'low figure' of 57 cents a barrel estimated as profit-share to the Persians under a 50-50 agreement on 1950 tonnage, and felt that they might expect something near 70 to 80 cents a barrel as under the Venezuelan formula which he had been ventilating with the Persians. Whereas, as Mr Levy had previously been informed from the Treasury, 57 cents was almost exactly what the Saudi Arabian Government had received in 1950:[97] which perhaps suggests the limitations of American arguments from the Venezuelan formula based upon Gulf of Mexico prices.

It may perhaps be some measure of the distinctly evolutionary quality of British economic thinking on the subject hitherto that Mr Ramsbotham should have written on August 1, 1951: 'Mr Levy has somewhat revolutionised our thinking.' Mr Ramsbotham, however, proceeded to argue: 'We should not quietly accept Mr Levy's assessment of the Persians' minimum "conditions" without first testing them out on a revised version of the *aide-mémoire* of June 19.' Sir Roger Makins agreed.[98] Though Sir William Strang had already minuted on July 29 to the Foreign Secretary: 'I am pretty sure that if we are to maintain the flow of oil from Persia and to preserve the operations as a British interest, something on the lines suggested by Mr Levy will be necessary. This will cause a major row with Sir William Fraser and his Board who are very competent, but very stubborn and not very broadminded people. There will have to be a kind of revolution in management, and I don't think that Sir William Fraser is the kind of man either to conduct it or even to recognise its necessity.'[99] Mr Herbert Morrison minuted the same day: 'Why ever wasn't Mr Levy's startling idea ab. new company brought up Sat. [July 28, by Mr Harriman]? Looks as if suspicions of US were well founded if they are to come in.'[100]

The technical ideas of Mr Levy, however, exerted an evident influence upon the notes on the economic and organisational aspects of the oil problem which were prepared at about that time by the Treasury and the Working Party on Persian Oil

---

[96] EP 1531/1290.
[97] EP 1531/1108.
[98] EP 1531/1291.
[99] EP 1531/1236G.
[100] EP 1531/1221.

for the prospective mission of the Lord Privy Seal. The main brief for Mr Stokes observed in particular: 'A 50-50 basis is the one major point on which, for their own good reasons, consistent American support is likely to be forthcoming. While some tactical advantage might be achieved, in case of need, by suggesting to the Americans that we would prefer to accept something worse than 50-50 rather than make some other undesirable concession, in practice any such arrangement would be most dangerous because of (i) the immediate effect on our balance of payments, (ii) the probable repercussions elsewhere, eg, in Iraq.'[101] In comments on this brief, sent to Tehran on August 11, the Anglo-Iranian Oil Company felt 'that there are circumstances in which they would prefer to go more than 50-50 in order to secure other points'.[102] It was felt in Whitehall, however, that 'repercussions elsewhere would be embarrassing though it is true that the principle of 50-50 does not seem to have the same appeal for Arabs (eg, Iraqis and Kuwaitis) as it does for Americans'.[103] Though the company's readiness to exceed a 50-50 division in certain circumstances scarcely went beyond the contemplation of the Ministry of Fuel and Power, back in June, of a 60-40 split (cf pp. 202). The potential bargaining advantages of such a formula were evident, if only as a veiled threat, in endeavouring to clinch American support on other issues. Throughout the crisis, however, British diplomacy apparently made no attempt to play this card.

It may be noticed that the Anglo-Iranian Oil Company apparently only commented on the official notes for Mr Stokes a week after they had been written and he had left for Tehran. The company had not participated in their drafting. At a meeting of Ministers and officials held by the Chancellor of the Exchequer on July 31 the Lord Privy Seal had expressed the view 'that, if Mr Levy's assessment of the Persian mind was correct, there might be advantage in his being able to inform the Persians that AIOC as an entity would be eliminated from any settlement'. It was generally felt at the meeting, however, 'that the mission should, if possible, leave the details of the constitution of the proposed operating company either until the negotiations had progressed some way or for subsequent negotiation between the oil companies concerned. As regards tactics, the mission would only be discussing general principles on behalf of the company.'[104]

On behalf of the Anglo-Iranian Oil Company, Sir William Fraser selected Mr Gass as its chief representative to accompany Mr Stokes if he went to Tehran. Mr Levy thought that in that case 'Mr Stokes might just as well not go to Tehran. For Mr Gass to go to Persia would be like Mr Levy, a Jew, going to Saudi Arabia.'[105] This view had been expressed on July 29 to the other members of Mr Stokes' proposed mission, Mr Flett, Mr Butler and Mr Ramsbotham. It was considered in the Foreign Office that nobody less than the Prime Minister could make Sir William Fraser change his choice. In the event the company was represented on Mr Stokes' mission by Mr Elkington. On the diplomatic side, the Lord Privy Seal wished to take with him Sir Horace Seymour, who had been His Majesty's Minister in Tehran from 1936 to 1939 and of whom the Foreign Secretary also evidently held a high opinion. It was understandably represented, however, that such a course might seem to the

---

[101] EP 1531/1267G.
[102] EP 1531/1308.
[103] *Ibid.*
[104] EP 1531/1292.
[105] EP 1531/1236G.

Persians to imply lack of confidence in His Majesty's Ambassador at Tehran.[106] When the Lord Privy Seal subsequently left for Tehran he was not accompanied by Sir Horace Seymour or, perhaps regrettably in all the circumstances, by any diplomatic adviser of comparable seniority.

5. Announcement of intention of His Majesty's Government not to withdraw entirely from Abadan, July 30-31

While the stimulating ideas of Mr Levy were being secretly discussed in Whitehall the sombre position throughout the Middle East was hotly debated on July 30 in what proved to be the last discussion of the Persian crisis in the House of Commons before it went into summer recess and was then prorogued, with a view to a general election, on the same day as the main crisis terminated in the British relinquishment of Abadan, on October 4, 1951.

In view of the still uncertain success of Mr Harriman's mediation it was perhaps natural that in the debate in the House of Commons on July 30 the Foreign Secretary should have tried, as he had told the Cabinet he would, to prevent discussion of the position in Persia.[107] Mr Winston Churchill replied in debating fettle to Mr Herbert Morrison's opening speech, generally surveying the problems for British policy in the Middle East; this was described by Mr Churchill as 'an able and agreeable parade of bland truisms and platitudes'.[108] The Leader of the Opposition ascribed 'the decline of our influence and power throughout the Middle East' to the loss of the Indian Empire, 'the mistakes and miscalculations' in withdrawing from Palestine in such a way as to earn almost equal Arab and Jewish hatred, and 'the impression which has become widespread throughout the Middle East that Great Britain has only to be pressed sufficiently by one method or another to abandon her rights and interests'.

Mr Churchill proceeded to deliver a personal attack upon the Foreign Secretary as 'a caucus boss' and one who 'dwells below the level of events'.[109] Nor did Mr Churchill spare the Foreign Office, which, with particular reference to its failure to secure success in Persia in 1949-50, he described as having 'fallen into . . . disarray' during the illness of Mr Bevin, and having failed 'to benefit from the accumulated experience of the old Foreign and Political Department of the Government of India, whose personnel they had absorbed'.[110] (It may perhaps be recalled that such was the former career of both Mr Fry and Mr Saner, Assistant Heads of the Eastern Department.)

Mr Churchill remarked of Mr Harriman's mission to Persia: 'Naturally he was not, in our view, going as a mediator, still less as an arbitrator. We rightly take our stand upon the judgment of The Hague Court. That was the attitude of His Majesty's Government.'[111] Mr Churchill concluded with a warning: 'If the Government so manage this affair as to lead in the end to the total evacuation of the British oil personnel from the Abadan refinery, it will be our duty to challenge them here and in the country by every means in our power. The issue between us—which I trust

[106] EP 1531/1237G.
[107] EP 1531/1212G.
[108] Parliamentary Debates, 5th Series, H. of C., Vol. 491, col. 978.
[109] *Ibid*, cols. 998-9.
[110] *Ibid*, col. 991.
[111] Parliamentary Debates, 5th Series, H. of C., Vol. 491, col. 993.

will not arise—is the total evacuation, in any circumstances which are at present foreseeable, of the Abadan refinery by the nucleus of British personnel. We request that if this decision is taken, and if possible before it is taken, Parliament should be recalled in order that a clear issue may be presented . . . If they [the Government] use their precarious and divided majority to cast away one of the major interests of the nation . . . then I say the responsibility will lie upon them for this shameful disaster, diminution and impoverishment of our world position; and we are quite certain that in the long run justice will be done to them by the British people.'[112]

The Conservative criticism of the Government was wound up by the Member for Bromley, Mr Harold Macmillan. In particular, he cut through with an enquiry: 'Would it not have been possible to adopt a consistent and coherent policy of partial evacuation, of evacuation perhaps of the mountain oil fields . . . or even evacuation of the greater part of the staff in Abadan leaving a small, selected team of men to maintain the refinery? That would have brought upon Persia all the economic pressure of the policy of total evacuation that some people have thought attractive. It would also have maintained the principles of the continuity and the reality of our connexion. By limiting the number required to stay and by making frequent reliefs, the physical and moral pressure on the staff could have been reduced . . . Such a policy of non-evacuation, or of only partial evacuation, involves a policy of protection. It means that measures must be taken to secure the safety and reasonable comfort of these men while they are carrying out the duty of protecting British rights and, incidentally, the decision of the International Court.'[113]

In conclusion, Mr Harold Macmillan stated: 'It is perhaps natural, at a time when parties are so nicely balanced in the House and when a fresh appeal to the country is perhaps so near that we should all watch each other with more than usual anxiety and keenness, each trying to see where a shrewd blow can be struck at some chink in our opponent's armour, that some electoral advantage can be obtained by charges, imputations or insinuations that one party—which, after all, represents at least half of our fellow countrymen—is seeking, or would thoughtlessly risk, the frightful dangers and sufferings of war . . . I beg of Ministers not to repeat these monstrous charges against their fellow countrymen. Though we may differ in the means to achieve those ends—peace and freedom—which far transcend our minor differences, let us at least be generous enough to believe that we are each and all united in this: that we seek these common purposes in sincerity and good faith. At this moment our people, after all their efforts, are in these great affairs distracted, confused, even disillusioned. It is surely our duty to sustain their courage. Let us disdain to exploit their fears.'[114]

In winding up the debate at just on nine o'clock on the night of July 30, 1951, the Prime Minister very much welcomed the note struck by Mr Harold Macmillan and contrasted it with that sounded by the Leader of the Opposition: in replying to whom, Mr Attlee incidentally remarked that it was 'quite wrong' to say that an impression of weakness had been given in the Middle East, 'because we were not weak . . . But it is really no good jobbing backwards.'[115] On the Persian issue, he mentioned among

---

[112] *Ibid*, col. 995.
[113] *Ibid*, cols. 1059-60.
[114] *Ibid*, cols. 1061-2.
[115] Parliamentary Debates, 5th Series, H. of C., Vol. 491, cols. 1064-5.

other things American pressure for the principle of nationalisation. Shortly thereafter Mr Harold Macmillan interjected: 'What about evacuation?' Mr Attlee answered: 'There may have to be withdrawal from the oil wells and there may have to be withdrawal from some part of Abadan, but our intention is not to evacuate entirely.'[116]

With that reply to an interjection the Prime Minister thereupon ended his speech and that heavy debate. It appeared that the potential issue between His Majesty's Government and the Opposition, which Mr Churchill had raised, no longer existed; and that the policy of partial evacuation, advocated by Mr Macmillan, was now agreed between them.

On the following day of July 31, 1951, in a debate on foreign affairs in the House of Lords, the Marquess of Salisbury took up some of the themes developed by Mr Winston Churchill regarding the Persian 'storm area', and more particularly the Government's failure in that direction to 'grasp the nettle earlier. By that, I do not mean in the last few weeks; but months, and perhaps years, ago.'[117] Lord Salisbury, however, cited and welcomed the Prime Minister's assurance of the previous evening, while nothing 'the unorthodox manner of so important a declaration'.

'But', continued Lord Salisbury, 'I would ask further: Do His Majesty's Government accept all the implications of that statement? Are they prepared to make it possible for these employees to remain in Abadan? At present, those men are, as I see it, in the situation of a man who is hanging on by his finger-nails to a ledge of rock half way down the cliff. It is not much good saying to a man in that situation: "It is my policy that you should stay there." You have got to give him some evidence that you are prepared to help him. Is it the policy of the Government, if necessary, to give that support? I hope very much that it is . . . A declaration of that kind, in amplification of what the Prime Minister said yesterday, would, I believe, go far to steady the situation.'[118]

Replying for the Government, Viscount Jowitt, the Lord Chancellor, stated: 'I have no authority to go beyond what the Prime Minister has said. He announced yesterday, and I am not attempting to add to anything he said, that we should stay in Abadan. I would announce to the noble Marquess that, in saying that, we accept all the implications that follow from that decision.'[119] At the close of the debate the Marquess of Salisbury compared the wording of the assurances of the Prime Minister and of the Lord Chancellor and rather preferred the latter: 'For I think it more accurately represents the possibilities of the situation—with the further stress which was put on it to-day, that the Government accept all the implications of that statement . . . why did they not say it sooner?'[120]

Lord Jowitt in turn asked Lord Salisbury if he suggested 'that we ought to have occupied Abadan? *The Marquess of Salisbury*: The answer I give to that is this: Does the noble and learned Viscount suggest that in any circumstances we should now occupy Abadan—because that is exactly what he has pledged the government to do? *The Lord Chancellor*: I certainly do. I maintain that we have the right to protect the lives of our citizens. Whatever it is necessary to do, that we shall do.' Viscount

---

[116] *Ibid*, col. 1072.
[117] Parliamentary Debates, 5th Series, H. of L., Vol. clxxiii, col. 29.
[118] *Ibid*, col. 34.
[119] *Ibid*, col. 63.
[120] *Ibid*, col. 150.

Alexander of Hillsborough, Chancellor of the Duchy of Lancaster, interjected that 'what the Lord Chancellor has just said has been said quite openly by the Government for weeks . . . *The Marquess of Salisbury*: But they did not say that they would stay in Abadan, and protect British lives for that purpose.'[121] Now, at all events, that formulation was not contradicted from the Government benches.

On the following day of August 1, the Foreign Office despatched two circular telegrams to British missions abroad, valuably citing the statements by the Prime Minister and the Lord Chancellor and giving the following confidential guidance on the line to be adopted if these statements were taken to indicate a British intention to maintain the British staff in Abadan by the use of force, namely: 'His Majesty's Government contend that, in view of the interim decisions of The Hague Court, the AIOC has a *prima facie* right to maintain its staff in Abadan in order to continue its operations, and that the Persian Government ought to permit this. The staff, or as many as are needed for the purposes of these operations, will accordingly remain in Abadan. Whilst they are there, the Persian Government are under an obligation to ensure their protection. Should they fail in their responsibility in this respect, and still more should they indulge in forceful measures liable to endanger the lives of British personnel, His Majesty's Government would have an undeniable right at International Law to take measures for their protection. Should they be compelled to do so, the Persian Government alone would be responsible.'[122]

6. Anglo-Persian agreement on the despatch to Tehran of a British official mission, August 1-3

While the policy of His Majesty's Government was being hardened and tempered in the heat of parliamentary debate a somewhat opposite influence was again being brought to bear through the American special envoy, back in Tehran. The Foreign Secretary informed the Cabinet on August 1 that thanks to further discussions with Mr Harriman the Persian Government would now in general accept the draft British note of July 28 except that it should refer to relieving, not 'the present tension . . . in the South', but merely 'the present atmosphere'; in its reply to this the Persian Government would recognise 'the essentiality, in the interests of the success of the negotiations, of both Governments creating the best possible atmosphere'.

As Mr Morrison told his colleagues, 'this placed us in a difficult position. The communications would now contain no specific reference to an improvement in the conditions in South Persia.'[123] Mr Harriman, however, advised acceptance of the Persian conditions and on balance the Foreign Secretary agreed. In discussion in Cabinet some Ministers 'drew attention to the disadvantages of accepting the proposal: the attitude of the Persian Government which it revealed did not hold out much hope for successful negotiations, and its acceptance would have an adverse effect on the morale of the Company's staff in the south . . . The general view of the Cabinet was, however, that although there were serious disadvantages in accepting the proposal we should be in a still more difficult situation if it were rejected.' Such was the ultimate dilemma of going along with the American mediation.

The Cabinet agreed that the Persian proposal for the despatch of the British

---

[121] Parliamentary Debates, 5th Series, H. of L., Vol. clxxiii, col. 151.
[122] P 10151/48.
[123] EP 1531/1238G.

mission should be accepted. The British agreement was tied down as subject to three understandings: first that in the Persian 'formula for negotiations' (the proposed new wording) the phrase 'in the hands of' in the law of March 20 would be rendered 'under the authority of', as specified to Mr Harriman on July 24; secondly, that the basis for British acceptance of Persian oil-nationalisation was the law of March 20; thirdly, that the reference to relieving 'the present atmosphere' related particularly to the then situation in the South.[124] The Persian Government confirmed these three understandings to Mr Harriman[125] but they were not embodied in any of the eight formal documents exchanged between the British and Persian Governments on August 3 as the basis of the mission which the Lord Privy Seal was now to lead.[126]

This was the fifth and final British retreat on negotiating terms during the Harriman Mission. Great Britain had been pushed right down the line. In diplomacy Mr Averell Harriman had displayed qualities, if not always quite of statesmanlike wisdom, yet of determined address and initiative which were scarcely equalled on the British side, more awkwardly and weakly situated. The interim injunction of the International Court seemed receding. The British 'essential prerequisites' of July 23 had now vanished. The evacuation of the Fields, once agreed for July 23, then deferred for one day, then postponed for 'a further day or two' (cf pp. 280-1, 289), was still unaccomplished. The Persian 'effective action' of relief in the south, till which there had on July 25 been 'no question' of sending a British mission, had not been taken, or even promised. That 'radical improvement' at Abadan which had still been 'of the greatest importance' to His Majesty's Government on July 26 had not begun, if it ever would. The British Government was once again, as during the Jackson mission (cf p. 208), entering into negotiations while acquiescing in Persian refusal to secure improvement of conditions at Abadan; though it might seem that such a demand could now have been reinforced by reference to the interim injunction of The Hague Court. As it was the very reference to tension in the south had, in the official documents, been dissolved into 'the atmosphere'.

The atmosphere at Abadan (still over 120 degrees in the shade) was heavy and, so far from improving, again deteriorating, as might indeed by then have been expected. Persian 'interference in company administration continues to increase'[127] reported Major Capper on July 29. At that time the expulsion at short notice of three more of the company's British staff was ordered on various pretexts by the Persian Temporary Board. When an approach about that was made to M. Makki, still malevolently ensconced at Abadan, he 'stated that he would oppose anything requested by his Majesty's Consul-General and His Majesty's Embassy'.[128] Production at the refinery, which had been tapering off throughout July, ceased altogether on the last day of that month, less than a week after the Foreign Secretary had posited to the American Ambassador an 'arrangement to keep the oil flowing' (cf p. 293). Now, so far as purely British oil-working at Abadan was concerned, it was finished, for good—the end of a great British enterprise.

On the black day of July 31, 1951, at Abadan the unhappy British staff were, however, cheered by the arrival, to join the cruiser *Euryalus*, of HMS *Chevron* and

---

[124] EP 1531/1182.
[125] *Ibid.*
[126] EP 1531/1307.
[127] EP 1531/1248.
[128] EP 1531/1136.

by the passage to Basra of her three sister destroyers. The Persian watchers were 'sullen and reflective'.[129] By August 2 the British Chiefs of Staff had 'clear evidence'[130] that the Persians there intended to oppose with force any British landing: delay naturally assisted the defensive build-up. But the main attention now was focused not upon Operation buccaneer but upon the Stokes Mission.

The Lord Privy Seal had made it clear to Mr Harriman that if the Persian Government continued to be unreasonable he was prepared to accept a breakdown of his negotiations; 'in that event the Musaddiq Government would probably fall'.[131] And the Shah told Mr Harriman that it must go in such a case.[132] Only for the present the prospect of a further British negotiating mission naturally strengthened Dr Musaddiq further against that opposition which M. Sayyid Zia, with British support, had been mobilising with some success against him. Indeed the Shah himself threw the ranks of M. Sayyid Zia into 'some disarray' by intervening against their obstruction of the Bill to release some £14 million held as note-cover (cf p. 289), for which the impecunious Persian Government accordingly secured approval in the Majlis: the Shah had argued that the Government should not be weakened as it was about to embark upon oil negotiations.[133] Clearly, the Stokes Mission did not tally very closely with the standing British objective of securing the fall of Dr Musaddiq. Though such complexities in pursuing that kind of aim were perhaps only to be expected.

A potentially significant development, however, in Persian politics was the resignation on August 1, 1951, of the Minister of the Interior, General Zahedi. Mr Logan minuted three days later that the general, though apparently supporting the National Front, had been critical of it and might now be openly so: he had favoured a settlement of the oil dispute.[134] The available evidence, at all events, does not indicate that special interest was otherwise shown, either in the Foreign Office or in His Majesty's Embassy at Tehran, in this political departure at that critical juncture; or that any attempt was made to set it against the suggestive report supplied some weeks earlier by M. Kaivan (cf p. 240) regarding the eagerness of General Zahedi to succeed Dr Musaddiq, as he was in fact to do in 1953.

As regards encouraging opposition against the Government of Dr Musaddiq, however, the Foreign Office doubtless had good reason not to lend itself to the active lobbying, just then, of Prince Hamid Kadjar, the 33-year-old employee of Socony Oil who was the heir to the old Qajar dynasty evicted by Reza Shah. Prince Hamid, who was in close touch with Persian affairs, suggested a rising in his interest by the Qashqai tribesmen, which might be held to justify a British landing at Abadan. In a minute of August 1 Mr Logan resolutely discounted the feasibility and desirability of such action—though indeed the possibility of tribal risings had also been proposed by other Persian lobbyers, including M. Kaivan (cf p. 240), and it was evidently not a little feared by the Persian Government. Mr Logan argued with evident force that matters had not changed from 10 years earlier when Sir Reader Bullard had advised against a Qajar restoration because there was no considerable demand for it. There

---

[129] EP 1212/39.
[130] Cabinet file C 14/41/8, part 3, 27.
[131] EP 1531/1238G.
[132] EP 1531/1222.
[133] EP 1015/285.
[134] EP 1015/288.

was general agreement in the Foreign Office with Mr Logan's estimate.[135]

Closer to the realities of the then situation—perhaps rather uncomfortably close—was the subject of a minute of August 2, 1951, by Mr Fitzmaurice to Eastern Department, complaining that he had not been consulted before the formula of British recognition of the principle of oil nationalisation had been communicated to the Persian Government. (Mr Herbert Morrison, in his speech in the Commons on July 30, had reiterated: 'We have agreed to accept the principle of nationalisation.'[136]) Mr Fitzmaurice made the not unimportant point that it would have been more prudent to preface such recognition with some such words as 'for the purpose of these negotiations'. For 'we do not want to have it argued that we have in effect admitted the legality of the Persian nationalisation of the company's undertaking, as this might affect our case before The Hague Court'.[137] Mr Fitzmaurice did not refer to the position here in relation to the interim injunction.

Mr Furlonge replied to Mr Fitzmaurice on August 3 that he appreciated his argument, but it was doubtful whether Mr Harriman, still less the Persians, would have accepted his proposed addition. The British text in question had been 'worked out by Ministers during their discussions with Mr Harriman, and Ministers were clearly anxious to run no risk of alienating Mr Harriman, and the United States Government, by standing out for something which he regarded as unacceptable.'[138]

Mr Logan minuted on the same day of August 3 that it appeared that 'the importance of the forthcoming negotiations will be: (*a*) to attract American support for our case in future, should the negotiations fail. (*b*) To show moderate opinion in Persia just how far we are prepared to meet the Persian demands'.[139] The first of these arguments was a somewhat ominous repetition of that used earlier in support of the Harriman Mission; and by then the second was perhaps open to a fairly obvious and countervailing answer. It was not, however, made. As for hope that the negotiations might not merely exert indirect influence upon American and moderate Persian opinion, but actually advance the British cause with the Persian Government, Mr Logan concluded: 'If they lead to an agreement, so much the better.'[140]

On that Friday, August 3, 1951, there were exchanged the formal documents of Anglo-Persian agreement on the despatch of a British official mission to Tehran. The Lord Privy Seal left London that day.

---

[135] EP 1015/292.
[136] Parliamentary Debates, 5th Series, H. of C., Vol. 491, col. 912.
[137] EP 1531/1311G.
[138] *Ibid.*
[139] EP 1531/1222.
[140] *Ibid.*

CHAPTER XI

FAILURE OF THE MISSION TO TEHRAN OF THE LORD PRIVY SEAL, AUGUST 3-23, 1951

1. The Mission of the Lord Privy Seal up to his presentation of the Eight-Point Proposals, August 3-13

The Lord Privy Seal, accompanied by Sir Donald Fergusson, Mr Flett, Mr Ramsbotham and Dr Nuttall, arrived in Tehran on Saturday, August 4. Sir Francis Shepherd also flew back to Tehran. The representatives of the Anglo-Iranian Oil Company, led by Mr Elkington, travelled separately. Mr Stokes' party was accommodated by the Persians in the Sahebgharanieh Palace, the Palace of the Ill-Omened King, disused since the Qajars, set in delicious gardens with a cascading stream, flower-bordered terraces beneath great plane trees, and pavilions for a harem. This idyllic milieu was described by Mr Ramsbotham as being 'without office accommodation, half an hour by car from the Embassy in Tehran and with the most erratic telephone system'.[1] Mr Harriman and his staff were, however, housed within the same luxurious compound, which Mr Stokes found 'most convenient'.[2] Whereas Sir Francis Shepherd, from his distance, described the arrangement as 'very unfortunate . . . The Mission is sitting in the laps of the Americans.'[3] These circumstances possibly lent importance to the absence from Mr Stokes' mission of a diplomatic adviser of senior standing.

The Lord Privy Seal had had the benefit of briefing discussions and a memorandum of guidance (cf pp. 301-2), but did not carry specific instructions; he enjoyed latitude for negotiation, subject to reference to the Cabinet. On the morning of August 5 the Lord Privy Seal had a preliminary conversation with the Persian Prime Minister, who observed among other things that 'any arrangement that might be made with His Majesty's Government would be a model on which Russia might base demands in respect of northern oilfields. Such demands Persia was in no position to resist though she would never abandon her independence whether Russia threatened her directly or indirectly through Communism':[4] perhaps an indication of Dr Musaddiq's standing, and possibly exploitable fear of the Russian factor. Against the words 'Persia was in no position to resist', the Foreign Secretary noted: 'Significant for us if we had been stronger?'

Dr Musaddiq further said that 'all he asked was that His Majesty's Government should let Persia enjoy the same benefits, social and economic reforms, which the Labour Government had introduced in the United Kingdom. I said', reported Mr Stokes, 'that the two cases were hardly comparable. The first reform in Persia should be measures to oblige the rich landowners to share their wealth with the peasants.' Against the statement by Dr Musaddiq in the above quotation the Foreign Secretary noted 'Untrue', and against that of Mr Stokes, 'Good'.[5]

The Lord Privy Seal lunched on that day of August 5 with the Shah, who incidentally did not appear to rate the Communist danger in Persia very high. In

---

[1] EP 1531/1391.
[2] EP 1531/1265.
[3] EP 1531/1344.
[4] EP 1531/1250.
[5] *Ibid.*

emphasising to His Majesty the danger for Persian oil of loss of foreign markets, Mr Stokes 'said that in fact the power exercised by the international oil companies was rather frightening. If the circumstances made it necessary they could kill the Persian oil business stone dead.' The Shah for his part warned Mr Stokes that his Prime Minister 'was a difficult person to deal with because he would agree to a point one day and retract his agreement the next'.[6] But the Shah thought it best to settle with Dr Musaddiq, who 'must fall of his own weight'.

It was on the advice of the Shah that Mr Stokes that evening 'spoke to Dr Musaddiq more forcibly about the practical issues'.[7] In replying to Mr Stokes' emphasis upon the necessity for an equitable settlement, 'Dr Musaddiq, adopting a humorous tone, declared that he had always been himself solicitous for the health of the [Anglo-Iranian Oil] Company: so much so that he had performed a surgical operation on the company. The Lord Privy Seal interposed to say that we must now do something to help the company in their convalescence. He added that he wished Dr Musaddiq to take seriously what he said . . . Dr Musaddiq said that under the two nationalisation laws the Persian Government had successfully divorced the company. The Lord Privy Seal said it was a curious arrangement for a man to divorce his wife and then attempt to starve her to the point where she is obliged to kill him. Dr Musaddiq very much enjoyed these humorous exchanges. Adopting a more serious vein he declared it was impossible for his Government to go outside the nationalisation laws.'[8] It is not recorded that the Lord Privy Seal protested against this bracketing of the Persian nationalisation law of March 20, which His Majesty's Government had accepted, with that of May 2, which it had specifically rejected, as one of the three agreed understanding upon which Mr Stokes had gone to Tehran. This was the first of the understandings which Dr Musaddiq in effect repudiated.

The Persian Premier went on to propose, as regards the security of British technicians to be employed by the National Iranian Oil Company, that a statute for it 'should be devised providing for a "conseil d'administration"',[7] with a majority of neutral foreigners, for the direction and administration of all aspects of the industry. Mr Stokes replied that by the time an efficient organisation of that kind were established, Persia would be bankrupt; furthermore, the British staff would not remain except under an experienced operating company. Dr Musaddiq said that all practical questions could be discussed by Mr Stokes' mission with the sub-committee of the Oil Commission which he had established for discussions with the Harriman Mission. This sub-committee comprised members of the Senate, the Majlis and the Government, including the Ministers of Finance and of Communications. An initial meeting with this sub-committee was held on the following day of August 6. Mr Stokes summed up: 'Despite the readiness to compromise which undoubtedly exists amongst the Persians, and which he himself probably feels, Musaddiq himself in his meeting with me appeared no less intransigent than he has been in the past.'[9]

On the same day that Mr Stokes in Tehran was holding his first conversations with the Persian monarch and prime minister, Major Capper at Abadan gave a press

---

[6] EP 1531/1338.
[7] EP 1531/1251.
[8] EP 1531/1339.
[9] EP 1531/1260.

conference. He was reported to have expressed his personal views that Persian restoration to the Anglo-Iranian Oil Company of seized property, such as houses and cars, should be insisted upon, that Mr Drake should return to Abadan, and MM. Makki and Mazda, described as dangerous elements, should leave it.[10]

The Lord Privy Seal complained to the Foreign Secretary that His Majesty's Consul-General had been 'maddeningly indiscreet'.[11] Mr Stokes thought that Major Capper should be recalled.[12] On August 9 Mr Morrison agreed, in reply, that the latter had been indiscreet, 'but Makki is enough to madden anyone. What I think about Makki is nobody's business . . . I should be most reluctant to withdraw Capper and I hope that Persians will be wise enough not to ask for this.'[11] They did ask for it but the request was parried and Mr Stokes telegraphed on August 10: 'After discussion with Shepherd, I am not pressing for Capper's withdrawal.'[13]

Major Capper's controversial press conference of August 5 formed an unfortunate prelude to the visit of the Lord Privy Seal to Abadan two days later, as previously arranged with a view to maintaining the morale of the British staff there. This valuable assertion of the British presence coincided with a visit of Mr Harriman to Abadan. It was generally felt that Mr Stokes' visit did much good. He formed a 'tremendously favourable' impression of the British staff at Abadan, 'who I am sure will stay on until the end of the negotiations and thereafter . . . Makki is a stupid fellow and causes the main trouble.'[14] The Lord Privy Seal assured the Staff Consultative Committee of the Anglo-Iranian Oil Company at Abadan 'that it was His Majesty's Government's intention in any settlement to see that there should be a 100 percent efficient, predominantly British staff organisation'.[15]

While Mr Stokes and Mr Harriman were paying their flying visits to Abadan on August 7, back in Tehran the fertile brain of Mr Levy 'floated a new suggestion which he says he has reason to think would be well received by the Persians'.[16] Accepting that the National Iranian Oil Company would own all assets within Persia, there should be constituted a separate purchasing company, 'either 100 percent AIOC or a consortium on the Levy Model', which would conclude a long-term contract with the National Iranian Oil Company; the purchasing company would guarantee to buy specified amounts of oil for a period of something like 25 to 30 years. In this commercial contract the purchasing company would be able to insist, under threat of resort to Kuwait or elsewhere, that it must be assured that the stipulated quantity and quality of oil would be forthcoming in Persia upon agreed financial terms. In order to provide such assurance the Persians would have to accept a British-controlled operating company, which would not participate in profits but would be remunerated by a nominal fee. The price which the purchasing company would pay to the National Iranian Oil Company 'would be ascertained on 50-50 principles since these terms are available from other sources . . . this price would be cost plus 50 percent of excess proceeds over costs.'[17]

---

[10] EP 1531/1293 and 1362.
[11] EP 1531/1275G.
[12] EP 1531/1283.
[13] EP 1531/1303.
[14] EP 1531/1269.
[15] EP 1531/1340.
[16] EP 1531/1259.
[17] *Ibid.*

The previous proposal for a British-controlled operating company under the National Iranian Oil Company was thus now elaborated by Mr Levy into one for two new interlocking companies, for operating and for purchasing, with novel emphasis upon the latter and possibilities for attractive presentation to the Persians. Regarding the constitution of the purchasing company 'Levy continues to harp on the need to abolish the monopoly position of AIOC if we are to carry the Persians with us', and proposed a consortium. The British mission, however, was not yet convinced that on this 'Levy is correctly interpreting Persian feelings',[18] and its immediately following telegram expressed the intention that both the purchasing and the operating companies should be British.[19]

On his return from Abadan the Lord Privy Seal on August 8, 1951, in discussing with the Persian sub-committee the general principles for preliminary agreement, stated in particular that the staff of the Anglo-Iranian Oil Company insisted 'that day-to-day management of the industry must be in British hands . . . This did not mean that the overall control of general policy would not be Persian.'[20] On the following day, however, Mr Stokes found that in interpreting the Harriman Formula Dr Musaddiq was 'adamant that phrase "in hands of" . . . could not mean "under authority of", which interpretation was apparently agreed between Harriman's staff and Oil Commission though not, I understand, by Musaddiq himself.'[21] Mr Stokes now secured the latter's permission for him to refer the point to Mr Harriman 'as there had clearly been a misunderstanding'.[22] The Lord Privy Seal, however, reported to Mr Morrison: 'In any case I do not think this matters greatly as we are not committed to Persian interpretation of this formula.'[21] Thus did Dr Musaddiq repudiate the second of the three agreed understandings upon which the Lord Privy Seal went to Tehran. The third understanding, regarding the reference to conditions in South Persia, was of so platonic a character as to render repudiation or the reverse somewhat irrelevant.

On the same day of August 9 an explanatory statement on the practicalities of nationalisation was made to the Persian negotiators by Sir Donald Fergusson, who had earlier been introduced to them by Mr Stokes as 'a man of wide experience of the nationalisation of industries in the United Kingdom'.[23] Sir Donald Fergusson now said 'that in considering the question of nationalisation the British Mission naturally thought in terms of the United Kingdom's experience in nationalising certain large industries since the war', more particularly coal, comparable to oil in Persia. 'For many years there had been bitter feelings in the Labour Party about the activities of the private coal companies.'[24] Sir Donald Fergusson explained the difficult process of nationalisation, the necessary distinction between governmental control of general policy and executive management of the business, and arrangements for compensation: although in the case of the British coal companies that compensation had been financial; whereas that same morning 'the Lord Privy Seal had reminded the [Persian] Prime Minister again that the [Anglo-Iranian Oil]

---

[18] EP 1531/1259.
[19] EP 1531/1261.
[20] EP 1531/1277.
[21] EP 1531/1282.
[22] EP 1531/1341.
[23] EP 1531/1334.
[24] EP 1531/1336.

Company was not interested in a cash compensation',[22] which Dr Musaddiq regularly proposed, but in payment in oil.

The central question of nationalisation clearly involved complex and delicate considerations for His Majesty's Government with regard not only to the Persian Government but also to the Anglo-Iranian Oil Company. On the same day that the Lord Privy Seal had left London for Tehran the Treasury was asking for a legal opinion whether His Majesty's Government could 'by virtue of its majority holding compel the company to accept a solution of the Persian dispute which the present Board of Directors (other than the Government nominees) regard as unacceptable'.[25] Mr C.S. Evans, an Assistant Treasury Solicitor, replied on August 7 that the Government Directors' power of veto was a negative power. The only course, short of legislation, for His Majesty's Government to pursue in order to compel acceptance would be to secure the appointment of a new board. This would require such public and controversial action at a General Meeting of the company that in the Foreign Office Mr Rothnie regarded it as 'almost unthinkable . . . In any case the company is well aware of all this.'[26]

On August 8 Sir Eric Beckett, in reply to an enquiry from Mr Logan following up the previous argument of Mr Fitzmaurice (cf p. 309), advised that the British case against Persia before the International Court of Justice would not be impaired by any British proposals made in Tehran to the Persian Government provided that they were made without prejudice, so that His Majesty's Government's basic position would remain unaffected if no agreement on a compromise was reached. On August 9, however, Mr Saner minuted that the conference at Tehran was liable to be chilled by repeated use of the formula 'without prejudice'.[27] No telegram regarding the importance of this phrase was sent to the Lord Privy Seal from the Foreign Office before it learnt, on August 11, that he had in any case introduced it into his submission to the Persians.

The Persian background to the Lord Privy Seal's communication of August 11 had been the departure at long last from Abadan of M. Makki, on a short visit to Tehran, after a final splutter of 'offensive remarks' against Major Capper, whom he described as 'a colonist and a cowboy'.[28] On August 10 Mr Stokes telegraphed to the Foreign Secretary that he did not think that the presence of British warships at Abadan was necessary while his mission was in Tehran. The Lord Privy Seal hoped that they would be withdrawn on condition that there was an improvement in the tone of the Persian Press and that Dr Musaddiq would undertake to give instructions for Persian officials in the oilbearing areas to show a more friendly attitude. (Smaller concessions regarding conditions in the south than those originally proposed in London as preconditions for the despatch of Mr Stokes' mission were thus now proposed as the price of the withdrawal of British naval units.) The Lord Privy Seal thought that such a naval withdrawal to Basra would have an excellent effect, especially if attributed to his intervention.[29]

It appears that on August 11, 1951, Mr Stokes had a meeting, which he did not immediately report, with M. Kashani, the fanatical extremist. According to Persian

---

[25] EP 1531/1305.
[26] EP 1531/1305.
[27] EP 1531/1319.
[28] EP 1531/1300.
[29] EP 1212/41.

press reports of the meeting, cited by Sir Francis Shepherd on August 14, M. Kashani told Mr Stokes that if Dr Musaddiq deviated from the Nine-Point Law of May 2 even he would risk the fate of General Razmara; and the same applied to M. Kashani himself.[30] Whereas the Soviet Press had hitherto shown no sign of direct interest in Persian affairs, on August 17 all Russian newspapers carried a Tass report of the Stokes-Kashani conversation. Although M. Kashani had said that the Persians were not Communist, His Majesty's Embassy in Moscow cited a report in *The Economist* that he had been openly helping Soviet propagandists. According to Tass a remark by Mr Stokes that Persian poverty was the fault of big landlords was exploited by M. Kashani to attack British support of them and Czarism in general.[31] Some months later Dr Lambton was recorded by Mr Berthoud as commenting that in visiting M. Kashani on August 11 'without reference to the Embassy' Mr Stokes had made a 'disastrous mistake . . . This greatly confused Persian public opinion. Dr Kashani has received large sums of money from somewhere. There is no evidence that it comes from the Russians.' Dr Lambton thought it not impossible that there was some American secret source, outside the State Department, 'who may for some time have been supporting Dr Musaddiq and M. Kashani as their answer to Communism'.[32]

On the same day of August 11, 1951, a British memorandum was communicated informally, on behalf of the Lord Privy Seal, to M. Bushihri, the Minister of Communications, who was acting as official host to Mr Stokes and Mr Harriman. (M. Bushihri-Dihdashti had been in Germany for some time after 1939, had been under arrest in Persia as a suspect from 1943 to 1945, and was described in a British assessment as 'a lightweight with little influence'.[33]) The intention was for M. Bushihri to sound Dr Musaddiq on the desirability of the memorandum being formally tabled at an early meeting of the negotiating committee. This procedure reflected Mr Stokes' difficulties with a Persian adaptation of the tactics of Tweedledum and Tweedledee. 'The Persian delegation', Mr Stokes later explained, 'had been unwilling that anything they said should be regarded as definitive until they had referred back to the Cabinet, and the Persian Prime Minister . . . had declared that he could not discuss or reply to proposals because by doing so he would be usurping the functions of the Persian delegation.'[34]

The first of the six paragraphs of the British memorandum of August 11 stated that it was submitted 'without prejudice to any parties concerned'.[35] Three days later the Foreign Office expressed gratification 'that you intended to establish that our proposals are made without prejudice' and commented: 'If no agreement is ultimately concluded, His Majesty's Government will revert to their position before the negotiations took place . . . The principle of nationalisation was recognised by His Majesty's Government as a preliminary to the opening of negotiations but it has not been accepted even as a principle for any other purpose.'[36]

The British memorandum of August 11 further reiterated acceptance of the Harriman Formula and it was explained that 'the British delegation now wish to

---

[30] EP 1531/1315.
[31] EP 1531/1374.
[32] EP 1531/2095G.
[33] EP 1012/1 of 1952.
[34] EP 1531/1486G.
[35] EP 1531/1294.
[36] EP 1531/1319.

submit . . . [an] outline of a possible arrangement which might be found suitable': and in relation to which the present document was in the nature of a preliminary covering memorandum. The last paragraph of the memorandum stated that the outline of specific suggestions which was to follow 'should be regarded as being governed by the principle that the Anglo-Iranian Oil Company will cease to exist in Persia and that the Persian Government will acquire full authority over exploration'.[35]

The British memorandum of August 11 had been drafted with the assistance of the representatives of the Anglo-Iranian Oil Company. Two days later Sir Francis Shepherd, however, wrote to Mr Bowker that it had been agreed with Mr Harriman and given to Mr Bushihri before he himself had seen it. His Majesty's Ambassador commented that in view of the isolation of the mission from the Embassy 'the tendency has not unnaturally been that the Americans get their word in first and this combined with Stokes' own impetuosity has made things sometimes a little awkward'. Sir Francis Shepherd hoped, however, 'that things are now somewhat better organised'.[37]

At 3.15 pm on August 12 the Foreign Secretary telegraphed to the Lord Privy Seal with reference to the last paragraph of his covering memorandum: 'We assume that the words "name of" which are quoted by Reuter as having been included in your press statement have been omitted before "Anglo-Iranian Oil Company". We regard their insertion as essential.'[38] With reference, further, to the draft of the specific proposals which Mr Stokes had also telegraphed to the Foreign Office the day before. Mr Morrison now observed to him that they 'differ substantially from those considered before your departure and, as you have pointed out, once they have been put forward it is unlikely that you will be able to withdraw from them. Ministers must therefore have time to consider them.' So must the board of the company. Mr Stokes was asked to defer presentation 'at least' of the specific proposals till he had received their views on, it was hoped, the morrow. The Foreign Secretary had not yet received from the Lord Privy Seal a telegram of August 12, only despatched at 5.24 am on August 13, wherein he further reported that he had taken it upon himself to communicate, also, to M. Bushihri a copy of the draft of the specific proposals, to secure the preliminary reaction of Dr Musaddiq.[39]

The Lord Privy Seal replied to Mr Morrison's telegram of August 12, in a telegram received in the Foreign Office at 8.45 am on August 13, that he now proposed, when submitting the specific proposals, to omit the covering memorandum and to incorporate its gist in an introductory verbal statement. He felt that if, in this introduction, the phrase regarding the Anglo-Iranian Oil Company were qualified by reference only to its name, that 'would destroy the positive effect of statement. Elkington agrees.'[40] Mr Stokes, however agreed to a revision such that the final wording ran, 'the AIOC as such would cease to operate in Persia'.[41] He felt, further, that it would be quite impossible to refrain, beyond that night of August 13, from presenting the proposals to the Persians. Mr Harriman agreed. They would therefore be tabled unless contrary instructions were received by 4.30 pm.

[37] EP 1531/1344.
[38] EP 1531/1296.
[39] EP 1531/1298.
[40] EP 1531/1299.
[41] EP 1531/1425.

Mr Stokes explained: 'This is not normal negotiation allowing time for careful consideration at each stage in London. The Persian politicians are negotiating in fear of their lives.' He also emphasised that Mr Harriman must be fully satisfied that Mr Stokes had done everything reasonably possible and had been thwarted by Persian irresponsibility: 'Harriman has seen the draft and approves of it. To substitute an alternative at this stage would risk loss of Harriman's support which in the long term I believe will be of paramount importance.'[40]

A telegram from the Foreign Secretary and the Chancellor of the Exchequer was despatched at 2.55 pm on August 13 to inform the Lord Privy Seal that they and the Anglo-Iranian Oil Company agreed that the proposals in question should be put to the Persians subject to certain drafting amendments, including an important one regarding compensation to the company, noted below. Mr Stokes subsequently reported that these instructions had reached him in time for the proposals to be presented to the Persians, but not for the amendments to be included in them.[42] The instructions to Mr Stokes had further stipulated that he should do his best to secure Mr Harriman's 'positive support' for the proposals and that there should be no weakening upon three points: first, day-to-day operations to remain in British hands; secondly, the new purchasing company to be 100 percent subsidiary of the Anglo-Iranian Oil Company and managed and controlled in the United Kingdom; thirdly, no arrangement should give Persia more than 50 percent of the net profits.[43]

Such was the background to the British communication to the Persian negotiators, after some rather barren sparring regarding their preliminary acceptance of the general principle of Anglo-Persian cooperation, of what became known as the Eight-Point Proposals of August 13, 1951. On the same day the Iraqi Government authorised signature of the new agreement with the Iraq Petroleum Company[44] (cf p. 289).

The first of the Eight-Point Proposals was that compensation by the National Iranian Oil Company to the Anglo-Iranian Oil Company for the assets in South Persia 'would be included in the operating costs of the oil industry in the area',[45] with separate provision for compensation for the assets previously used for distribution and marketing within Persia. The instructions of August 13 to the Lord Privy Seal had stipulated, in vain, that this paragraph should be modified to Persian advantage so that in compensation for its assets in South Persia the Anglo-Iranian Oil Company should only receive 'the benefits of the purchasing and operating arrangement',[43] rather than a special levy upon the operating costs.

The Eight-Point Proposals proceeded to follow closely those of Mr Levy for separate purchasing and operating companies, contracting to the National Iranian Oil Company. Apart from the main, long-term contract of the 'Purchasing Organisation' with the Persian Company (point 2), the latter 'would be able to make additional sales of oil subject to the normal commercial provision that such sales should be effected in such a way as not to prejudice the interests of the Purchasing Organisation'[45] (point 3). Under point 4 the Purchasing Organisation 'will agree with the National Iranian Oil Company an Organisation which, under the authority of the

---

[42] EP 1531/1309.
[43] EP 1531/1299.
[44] EQ 1537/108.
[45] Cmd 8425, p. 54.

National Iranian Oil Company, will manage on behalf of the National Iranian Oil Company the operations of searching for, producing, transporting, refining and loading oil within the area. The Purchasing Organisation will arrange from current proceeds the finance necessary to cover operating expenses.'

Point 5 proposed that 'the Purchasing Organisation would buy the oil from the National Iranian Oil Company at commercial prices f.o.b. Iran less a price discount equal in the aggregate to the profit remaining to the National Iranian Oil Company after allowing for the discount and for the costs of making the oil available to the Purchasing Organisation'. There would be Persian representation on the board of directors of the Operating Organisation, 'which will of course only employ non-Iranian staff to the extent that it finds necessary to do so for the efficiency of its operations' (point 8).

On August 15, 1951, *The Financial Times*, before learning particulars of the Eight-Point Proposals, asked what might become of the British case in international law, based upon the Anglo-Iranian Oil Company's concession of 1933: 'At best it would seem to have been badly muddled: at the worst betrayed entirely.' On the following day, however, the same journal found it difficult to see how Mr Stokes could have offered better terms than the 50-50 arrangement which was understood to be implied in the Eight-Point Proposals. Though it was not clearly formulated by them despite the fact that Sir William Fraser, perhaps with the fate of the complex Supplemental Agreement in mind, had enjoined in a telegram of August 11 to Mr Elkington: 'The paramount need is for simplicity in any arrangement concluded so long as it is fair.'[46]

The Times described the Eight-Point Proposals as 'extremely ingenious',[47] as they certainly were. Subsequently, however, it was increasingly appreciated that they did not possess such attractive simplicity, nor even perhaps such financial attractions for Persia, as Mr Jackson's proposals of June 19: which the Persians, however, had flatly rejected. Criticism in the Majlis fastened upon the fact that whereas the earlier British proposals were for a straight split of profits, 50-50, the Eight-Point Proposals envisaged, in addition to this split, deduction of compensation from the operating costs of the National Iranian Oil Company. Mr Ramsbotham scarcely exaggerated in subsequently observing that 'it was perhaps unfortunate'[48] that the British delegation in Tehran had not received in time from the Foreign Office the amendment of August 13 to the first point of the proposals which would precisely have met this Persian objection: more particularly since, as Mr Flett was later to remark on his return to the Treasury from Tehran, 'the company have never expected that they would be able to secure any substantial compensation payment as such'.[49] Mr Stokes himself was to comment on August 25 to Sir Donald Fergusson regarding the Eight-Point Proposal: 'I think we all agree that it suffered from being a joint adventure. Somewhat like the Atlantic Charter!'[50]

Whatever the precise merits of the Eight-Point Proposals of August 13, 1951, there was little illusion in the Foreign Office but that the main, and highly dubious, question was whether any proposals whatever stood a chance with Dr Musaddiq

---

[46] EP 1531/1302.
[47] *The Times,* August 20, 1951.
[48] EP 1531/1408.
[49] EP 1531/1473.
[50] EP 1534/1546.

who, as *The Times* was to observe, had 'almost a vested interest in the continuance of this dispute'.[47] Mr Ramsbotham wrote to Mr Logan, on the day that the Eight-Point Proposals were presented, that from talks with M. Sayyid Zia, still the British protégé, and with His Majesty's Embassy, 'it is extremely unlikely Musaddiq will be prepared to negotiate a settlement'.[51] The Lord Privy Seal subsequently told the Shah that on August 12 he had three times 'been cheered by small children in the streets'. The Shah agreed with Mr Stokes 'that this was significant'.[52] There was less certainty in the Foreign Office.

On the same day that the Eight-Point Proposals were presented, M. Makki returned to Abadan. On the following day of August 14 the Foreign Secretary informed Mr Stokes that he was 'not happy'[53] about his proposal of August 10 for the withdrawal of British warships from Abadan. (This view was strongly shared by the Chiefs of Staff.)[54] Mr Morrison referred to the continuing risk of Communist disorders there and stated: 'I should regard it as an essential prerequisite for a withdrawal of the warships (as distinct from occasional visits to Basra) that the attitude of the Persian officials, as well as the tone of the Press, should have markedly improved, and not merely that Musaddiq should have given an undertaking to send instructions to this effect. You will no doubt appreciate that once the ships are withdrawn it would be difficult to send them back without appearing provocative, even if the Persian officials again became truculent, unless there were actual disorders.'[53]

2. Persian negation of the Eight-Point Proposals, August 14-19

On the evening of August 14 the Lord Privy Seal opened a conversation with the Persian Prime Minister by stating that he was 'bitterly disappointed on three accounts'.[55] First, 'despite promises made conditions at Abadan were deteriorating'. Complaints of Persian interference were increasing from the British staff, who had reached the end of their tether. Mr Stokes said that he 'could not remain as the guest of the Persian Government unless steps were taken forthwith to control matters . . . Makki was almost exclusively responsible. Musaddiq said that Makki was a deputy and could not be chased from Abadan.' The Premier had heard of no complaints from there but undertook to examine the list of grievances which Mr Stokes undertook to send him.

The Lord Privy Seal's second complaint to Dr Musaddiq was that M. Hasibi, though only a technical consultant, had been giving misleading press interviews on the substance of the Anglo-Persian discussions. 'Musaddiq declared that Hasibi had a perfect right to do so. He would like our discussions to be made public.'[56] Thirdly, Mr Stokes complained that, despite an invitation from himself, the Persian negotiating delegation had not wished to meet that day to hear his explanation of the Eight-Point Proposals. 'Musaddiq declared that they could never accept our proposals because they were completely outside the formula on which we had agreed to negotiate, and he repeated the phraseology of the 20th March Law.'

---

[51] EP 1531/1347.
[52] EP 1531/1382.
[53] EP 1212/41.
[54] EP 1192/92G.
[55] EP 1531/1316.
[56] *Ibid.*

Mr Stokes sought to controvert Dr Musaddiq's latter point, while expressing his willingness to consider any suggestions which might improve his proposals in relation to the law: 'but in view of the Prime Minister's attitude, I saw no alternative but to go home. This immediately caused Musaddiq to say that I should ask Harriman's opinion. He would judge whether the proposals conformed with the formula. The Persians would accept them if he pronounced in the affirmative.' The report of this important statement, happily secured by the firm language of the Lord Privy Seal in that stiff conversation, was received in the Foreign Office in the early hours of August 15. At 2.25 pm that day the following telegram was despatched to Mr Stokes: 'We assume you are endeavouring to get Harriman to make a statement in support of our proposals. We attach great importance to this.'[57]

On August 15, 1951, the Persian authorities, despite undertakings to the contrary, released the text of the Eight-Point Proposals. Mr Stokes replied that day by putting out a full explanation of them; it pointed out among other things that 'there is plenty of oil in the world and unless Persian oil is competitive no one will buy it. Because Persian oil is further away from the most important markets it costs more to carry to those markets.'[58] In the Foreign Office, however, Mr Rothnie commented that the hand-out was 'not too good in that it did not bring out the profit-sharing arrangement'.[59] On August 15 the Lord Privy Seal further explained the proposals to the Persian negotiators, as well as strongly repeating his representations regarding conditions in the South: which evoked from Dr Shayegan a hot denial of any interference with the British staff.

With regard to the crucial issue of support from Mr Harriman, Mr Stokes replied to Mr Morrison that at a dinner which Mr Stokes gave to the Persian delegation on the evening of August 15 'Harriman avoided giving any indication of support for our proposals. While he intends to speak firmly to Musaddiq today [August 16], he considers it too early to come out in public support. The situation is somewhat confused.'[60] Mr Ramsbotham subsequently referred to Mr Harriman's 'weak speech'.[61] Mr Stokes did not report what attempts he may have made to induce Mr Harriman to adopt a more friendly and satisfactory attitude in support of proposals which the latter had approved beforehand, which had been drafted in concert with himself and had indeed been very largely originated by his own advisers; and which had been put forward in pursuance of a negotiation keenly pressed by Mr Harriman upon His Majesty's Government, who had agreed to it with little hope but largely with a view, precisely, to securing from him that open support which was not now forthcoming.

The Lord Privy Seal did record that on August 15, 1951, M. Sayyid Zia said to him 'that agents of the Standard Oil of New Jersey and, on my suggestion, Socony, had been working against us for a long time, backed up by officials of the American Embassy (?Wells) and by the Ambassador.'[62] The Shah told Mr Stokes the same thing.[63] The Lord Privy Seal, in accordance with the advice of M. Sayyid Zia,

---

[57] EP 1212/45.
[58] EP 1531/1324.
[59] EP 1531/1368.
[60] EP 1531/1330.
[61] EP 1531/1568.
[62] EP 1531/1381.
[63] EP 1531/1533G.

mentioned the matter to Mr Harriman who both dismissed it as nonsense and said he would look into it. In the Foreign Office Mr Berthoud subsequently minuted that the Americans named 'might have been working against us but certainly not in my view at the instigation of these two very friendly and reputable oil companies'.[64] On August 18 Mr Stokes recorded a conversation with M. Ghulam Ebtehaj, brother of the Persian Ambassador in Paris and described by Mr Rothnie as 'not a trustworthy character'; in this record Mr Stokes wrote: 'It appears that Grady has been working quite openly against us and encouraging Prime Minister to continue his resistance to our proposals.'[65] Sir Francis Shepherd subsequently related an incident suggesting that Mrs Grady, at all events, spoke to Dr Musaddiq somewhat in that sense.[66]

Despite the heavy developments of recent days the Lord Privy Seal on August 16 returned to the charge regarding withdrawal of British warships from Abadan. Reporting that M. Makki had made a moderate speech on his return to Abadan and had shown friendliness to British employees, Mr Stokes now proposed, in agreement with Mr Elkington, that one of the two British warships at Abadan should be withdrawn; the other could follow if conditions continued to improve.[67] On the spot, however, both Major Capper and Mr Mason considered that there had been no noticeable improvement. By August 17 M. Makki was already back to his old verbal form (specimen: 'The oil exploiters had made Khuzistan a barren land for their own ends. Khuzistan could provide enough food for 25 million people but now it could not provide enough for the population of Abadan.')[68] Recognition of Persian negation of Mr Stokes' proposal had already been implicit in the precautionary order issued by the Chiefs of Staff on the same day of August 16 that the forces for Operation Buccaneer should by August 18 be brought back from 72 to, at most, 24 hours' notice.[69]

It was, rather significantly, not till August 17, 1951, when the situation in Tehran was confused by lack of Anglo-American solidarity, that the Persian Government formally requested the withdrawal of His Majesty's Consul-General at Khorramshahr on account of circumstances in the aftermath of his Press conference of August 5[70]—a demand which was, in the event, successfully resisted by His Majesty's Government. On the same day of August 17 the Lord Privy Seal, in a last effort to prevent formal Persian rejection of the eight-Point Proposals, issued a statement that they were his best offer and that the amendments to them which he could consider would be slight.

In repeating his statement next morning Mr Stokes further announced that Mr Harriman had been kept fully informed at all stages in the formulation of the proposals and that he, Mr Stokes, had every reason to believe that Mr Harriman fully approved them and regarded them as coming within the Harriman formula.[71] Sir Francis Shepherd telegraphed on that day of August 18: 'Persian attitude towards the Lord Privy Seal's Eight-Point Proposal is being largely conditioned by the belief

---

[64] *Ibid.*
[65] EP 1531/1460G.
[66] EP 1015/305.
[67] EP 1212/45.
[68] EP 1531/1358.
[69] EP 1192/75G.
[70] EP 1531/1351.
[71] PB 1048/33.

that there is still a difference of opinion between ourselves and the Americans and that this can be exploited . . . It is probable that this Persian belief can only be dispelled by a clear and unequivocal statement by Harriman.'[72] But he published no statement.

At an informal meeting in Tehran of the British and Persian delegations on the evening of August 18 the Persians remitted their formal reply, 'tantamount to a rejection', to the Eight-Point Proposal. Mr Stokes reported: 'Harriman joined the meeting and in a short statement declared that in his view the proposal formed a good basis for a settlement and that arrangements could be worked out within the framework of the nationalisation law. But the manner in which he said this must have left the Persians in some doubt whether he wholeheartedly supports our proposals.'[73]

Mr Stokes' assistant, Mr Ramsbotham, subsequently wrote that Mr Harriman's assistant, 'Walter Levy, who is 100 percent with us, has been magnificent'; and that it was due to Mr Levy's 'overnight efforts' on the night of August 18-19 that Mr Harriman, at a further meeting with the Persians on the morning of August 19, 'came out with his admirable statement'.[74] He now spoke most forcibly in favour of the Eight-Point Proposals, as conforming to the Harriman formula, and told the Persians that publication of their reply would adversely impress world opinion and that collapse of the negotiations would spell further misery for the Persian people.[75]

In reply the Persian Minister of Finance disagreed with Mr Harriman regarding the consonance of the proposals with the formula, but observed: 'Mr Harriman's statement had come as a complete surprise to his delegation and had created a new situation.'[76] As His Majesty's Ambassador pointed out, however, Mr Harriman had still made no statement in public in support of the Eight-Point Proposals. There was much force in Sir Francis Shepherd's judgment that Mr Harriman's strong statement to the Persian delegation 'to my mind should have been made publicly and at least a day earlier'.[77] As it was, lack of full and evident Anglo-American solidarity in a critical phase may have been responsible for loss of the last real chance, however slender, of rescuing something by negotiation before the British eviction from Abadan.

3. British policy with regard to the failure of the Mission of the Lord Privy Seal, August 20-23

On the morning of August 20 Mr Stokes and Mr Harriman attended a two-hour meeting with Dr Musaddiq. Any hope which this new procedure may have encouraged was liable to be quickly dispelled by Dr Musaddiq's reversion to limiting negotiations to the three topics on which he had regularly insisted since the passage of the nationalisation law of May 2. These were recapitulated in substance by his claim now that the Lord Privy Seal was competent only to negotiate regarding terms of purchase of Persian oil by His Majesty's Government, arrangements for retention

---

[72] PB 1048/24.
[73] EP 1531/1355.
[74] EP 1531/1391.
[75] EP 1531/1357.
[76] EP 1531/1384.
[77] EP 1531/1396.

of British staff, and compensation to the Anglo-Iranian Oil Company.[78]

Sir Francis Shepherd commented on the same day of August 20: 'It seems to me fairly clear that Musaddiq only agreed to the sending of a [British] mission to negotiate on the Harriman formula as a result of American pressure and that his mental reservations were such that he had in fact no intention of retreating from his original position.'[79] This diagnosis of the intentions of Dr Musaddiq, with its implications of grave error in Mr Harriman's earlier assessment of them as the basis for the British mission, was to be substantially confirmed by the Persian prime minister himself. Dr Musaddiq informed the Majlis on September 9, 1951: 'Mr Harriman came, and as I was sure that the negotiations of the British Delegation would lead to no result I said that we would arrange a formula on which our negotiations should be based.'[80]

At the tripartite meeting of August 20, 1951, in Tehran Dr Musaddiq impressed Mr Ramsbotham, who was in attendance, by his diplomatic skill. Mr Ramsbotham accurately forecast that Dr Musaddiq would employ the 'negative and feminine tactics of avoiding either rejection of acceptance of our proposals' and would 'try to push us along point by point, making concessions as we go'.[81] In particular, Dr Musaddiq on August 20 broached the question of the employment of British staff. He could not accept a separate operating agency but would consent that a majority of the directors of the National Iranian Oil Company should be neutral foreigners. Under them, the heads of the separate sections of the industry, such as exploration, production and refining, would be British. These British heads of section could be given full powers on behalf of the National Iranian Oil Company to conclude individual contracts with the staff.[78]

A telegram from Tehran to the Foreign Office interpreted this proposal by Dr Musaddiq as a return to his original idea that all foreign technicians should be directly employed by the National Iranian Oil Company. This was described as clearly unacceptable unless it could be transformed into something very different, perhaps through the introduction of a small British management committee under a British manager.[82] And the immediately following telegram of August 20 from Tehran suggested other, commercial, concessions to the Persians.[83]

In a telegram received in the Foreign Office just before nine o'clock on the morning of August 21 the Lord Privy Seal requested comments on the above suggestions by that afternoon. He described this as essential since the Majlis was to meet on August 23 and he might have to withdraw his offer of the Eight-Point Proposal before then. Mr Stokes explained that British views in Tehran upon the right course to follow were somewhat divided. The view of the Embassy was in fact that Dr Musaddiq had no intention of agreeing to anything not fully in agreement with the Nine-Point Law, and that firm resistance should be made to his attempt to extract successive British concessions in the belief that His Majesty's Government would not risk the breaking of negotiations. Mr Stokes himself, however, considered that Dr Musaddiq was genuinely ready for an agreement embodying the substance

[78] EP 1531/1363.
[79] EP 1531/1396.
[80] EP 1531/1591.
[81] EP 1531/1391.
[82] EP 1531/1364.
[83] EP 1531/1365.

of the Eight-Point Proposals provided that they were accompanied by enough British concessions, in addition, to enable him to present the proposals to the Majlis as falling within the Nine-Point Law. Mr Stokes favoured, and thought Mr Harriman would support, such concessions 'without weakening in any way our fundamental position'.[84]

In London the concessions proposed by Mr Stokes were considered by the official Working Party on Persian Oil after discussion with the Anglo-Iranian Oil Company. The resultant views were embodied in an unsigned note by the Foreign Office of August 21. It was held that the concessions were open to strong objections, of which 'the overriding one' was that relating to the position of the company's British staff. Moreover, 'there seems no evidence to support the view advanced by the Lord Privy Seal that by making some further concessions we shall increase the possibility of reaching an acceptable settlement'. Previous concessions to the Persians had been 'primarily necessitated by the need to secure American support. Now that Mr Harriman has apparently expressed open support of our proposals, we feel that we can at last make a firm stand.' This, it was recognised, might well 'lead to a breakdown in negotiations. In our view, however, it would be far preferable that such a breakdown should come from the Persians rather than from ourselves. We do not therefore recommend that the Lord Privy Seal should, as he suggests, withdraw our existing offer.'[85]

The note of August 21, 1951, by the Foreign Office was prepared for a meeting of the Ministerial Committee on Persia which the Prime Minister called for that afternoon. Before it could meet, at just before half past two, the Foreign Office received a message from the Lord Privy Seal to the Prime Minister, who was also acting as Foreign Secretary in the absence of Mr Morrison on what he described as a 'much needed abbreviated holiday'.[86] Mr Stokes reported without further explanation in that telegram of August 21: 'I have withdrawn my Eight-Point Proposals and told the [Persian] Prime Minister that if he decides to accept before mid-day tomorrow the principles I outlined which would make it possible for British staff to remain in the refinery and oilfields, I shall be prepared to resume discussions.' Otherwise he would promptly leave Tehran. Mr Harriman entirely agreed.[87]

A telegram from the Foreign Office asked Mr Stokes what were the principles he referred to. He replied that they were principles mentioned in a telegram subsequent to his preceding message as having been put to Dr Musaddiq without commitment at their meeting that morning, notably to the effect that on the question of British staff, 'I was prepared to consider a British managing committee or general manager in place of the proposed operating organisation'.[88] Before the meeting, which was attended by Mr Harriman, Dr Musaddiq had told Mr Stokes that 'he hoped that I would give him 100 percent of what he asked for'.[89] The Persian Premier proceeded to reject Mr Stokes' proposed concession as impossible and made it clear that he 'was not prepared to agree to anything which the British staff could possibly be

---

[84] EP 1531/1366.
[85] EP 1531/1401G.
[86] Confidential/General/415, M. 113.
[87] EP 1531/1370.
[88] EP 1531/1372.
[89] EP 1531/1453.

expected to accept'.[90]

The Lord Privy Seal told Dr Musaddiq at that meeting on August 21 that he could not agree to the Eight-Point Proposals being submitted to the Majlis unless Dr Musaddiq 'made a positive recommendation supporting them. If the Prime Minister would not himself take the responsibility, I could negotiate no further and must withdraw my Eight-Point Proposals'[89]: as he did directly after the meeting in a letter to Dr Musaddiq in the terms which he had telegraphed to Mr Attlee. It 'had come as a great surprise' to Mr Stokes that, after what appeared to be a useful conversation with Dr Musaddiq on the previous day, the latter 'should have become so intransigeant and inflexible the very next morning'.[89]

The Lord Privy Seal made the latter admission to the Shah when, as Mr Stokes recorded in a brief 'History of events on August 21, 1951',[89] he and Mr Harriman visited the monarch just before 1 o'clock. Mr Stokes told the Shah 'that I thought it was almost impossible to arrive at any settlement with the Prime Minister as he constantly had in his mind the Nine-Point Law whereas I was negotiating on the basis of the 20th March Law and the practical application of nationalisation'. That was the crux: the Nine-Point Law *versus* the Eight-Point Proposals.

Mr Stokes also told the Shah that one of the difficulties with regard to management of the Persian oil industry was 'the terrible dishonesty of his people'. When the Shah asked the Lord Privy Seal what he thought he ought to do, Mr Stokes said 'I thought he should get rid of Musaddiq and get a man of greater vision and one who was not himself a fanatic nor surrounded by people who were'.[89]

The accomplished fact of the Lord Privy Seal's withdrawal of his proposals and ultimative demand upon Dr Musaddiq confronted Mr Attlee, Mr Kenneth Younger and Mr Douglas Jay, Financial Secretary to the Treasury, who were the only three Ministers to attend the meeting of the Committee on Persia at 5 o'clock that afternoon. Among the officers and officials in attendance were Sir John Slessor, Sir William Strang, Sir Leslie Rowan, recently appointed Second Secretary at the Treasury, and Sir Frank Lee of the Board of Trade; Sir William Fraser also joined the meeting. There it was agreed that 'it was of the greatest importance that in the event of a breakdown, responsibility should be seen clearly to lie with the Persians'.[91]

The telegram from Mr Attlee to Mr Stokes resulting from the meeting of the Committee on Persia stated that 'if we had had time' the Government would have expressed critical views on his proposed concessions, substantially in accordance with the note by the Foreign Office. If Dr Musaddiq accepted Mr Stokes' 'new proposals', the latter should offer no further concessions without reference to His Majesty's Government. If the proposals were rejected Mr Stokes 'should come home direct' and should press Mr Harriman to make a public statement supporting the British proposals.[92]

Mr Harriman on the evening of August 21 did address a letter to Dr Musaddiq and release it to the Press. President Truman's envoy dwelt at some length upon the economic dependence of the oil industry in Persia upon foreign cooperation. He did not, however, specifically endorse the Eight-Point Proposals or censure the Persian

---

[90] EP 1531/1372.
[91] EP 1531/1402G.
[92] EP 1531/1370.

attitude towards them. What Mr Harriman did write was: 'The British delegation handed to the Iranian Government for discussion an outline of proposals for settlement. Under the proposals, however, it was contemplated that negotiations take place through which fair and practical detailed arrangements could be worked out in accordance with the formula submitted through me. I have been informed by the British delegation that since the Iranian Government read into these proposals concepts that were not intended, the proposals have been withdrawn.'[93] The support Mr Harriman gave in public to the British proposals, which the Americans had largely suggested as being acceptable to the Persians, was not only late but also lukewarm.

Nor was the background in Washington regarding Persian affairs reassuring to the Foreign Office. On August 20 Sir William Strang had approved a telegram instructing Sir Oliver Franks to inform the State Department as soon as possible of the grave concern of the Foreign Office at an intimation which it had just received that the State Department, acting on advice from Mr Harriman and Dr Grady, now intended to announce that the Export-Import Bank was prepared to discuss implementation of its proposed loan to the Persian Government, though no money would be immediately available since many arrangements were still necessary. Such an announcement at such a moment would seem to conflict with the strong language which Mr Harriman had used to the Persian negotiators on August 19, would revive Persian ideas of Anglo-American differences and would have a most unfavourable effect on British public opinion. It was earnestly hoped that the State Department would not act, at least till the results of Mr Stokes' mission were known.[94]

His Majesty's Ambassador in Washington on August 20 mentioned this matter briefly to the Secretary of State, who said that it should be discussed with the officials concerned but stated that it would be made plain to the Persians that the Americans were dragging their feet and that no money would be quickly available. The Office of Iranian Affairs in the State Department later said that no announcement regarding the loan was intended but that any Press enquiries would be answered in accordance with the information which had disturbed the Foreign Office. The American representatives in Tehran had evidently advised that unfriendly remarks regarding the prospects of the loan would lessen chances of a settlement. Nor could the British arguments budge the State Department. 'We emphasised', reported Sir Oliver Franks, 'that you would greatly regret the Department's views and that British public opinion would frankly not understand them.'[95]

The ominous divergence of the British and American attitudes regarding developments in Persia was underlined by the fact that just at that time the possibilities of economic sanctions against Persia were again being discussed in Whitehall. It was decided that no action of that kind should be taken immediately; when subsequently, on August 23, Mr Stokes saw references in a telegram to contemplated economic measures he expressed himself as most anxious that no such action should be taken pending his return to London.[96]

The overriding question for His Majesty's Government, regarding possible action

---

[93] EP 1531/1454.
[94] EP 11345/14.
[95] EP 11345/20.
[96] EP 1531/1398.

if the Persian negotiations failed, remained, however, that of military action and the complementary issue concerning the evacuation or retention of the British oil men in South Persia. As regards the latter, Mr Mason at Abadan was continuing to apply the policy of the Anglo-Iranian Oil Company for the thinning out of British staff pending a final decision. It would appear that the company was for practical reasons not very keen on concentrating in Abadan staff withdrawn from the outlying fields. Sir William Fraser told the Ministerial Committee on Persia on August 21 that the 300 British staff still in the fields were being reduced. If Mr Stokes' negotiations broke down he proposed to evacuate the remainder there as quickly as possible, in about five days. The meeting agreed and considered that such staff should be evacuated to Basra as soon as possible rather than concentrated in Abadan.[97]

Behind these immediate measures there loomed, inexorably, the military problem. Of the alternatives open to His Majesty's Government, 'none is very attractive' observed Mr D.R. Serpell, an Assistant Secretary in the Treasury, in an important minute of August 20 to Mr A.M. Allen, Private Secretary to the Financial Secretary, Mr Jay, for the latter's attention. (A copy of this minute was received in the Foreign Office.) Mr Serpell stated: 'His Majesty's Government's present policy, as announced in the House of Commons, is that the company should not withdraw entirely from Persia. Barring other developments this policy might lead to a situation in which the Persian Government withdrew the residents' [?residence] permits of those AIOC employees who remained in Abadan.'[98] If His Majesty's Government decided that they should nevertheless remain there, their protection would necessitate Operation Buccaneer. 'This, however', wrote Mr Serpell, 'envisages only a brief incursion on to Persian soil, the collection of the employees in question and a quick withdrawal': a statement which was strictly accurate only in relation to Buccaneer Phase I, though an extension on to Phase II had in fact been prepared and envisaged (cf pp. 259 and 278-9]).

In a separate minute written in the Foreign Office on the same day of August 20 Mr Furlonge similarly observed that if the Persians withdrew residence permits 'or if conditions became otherwise intolerable, the only means of carrying out the present Government policy of hanging on to Abadan would be to use force'.[99] Unlike Mr Furlonge, however, Mr Serpell in his minute carried his consideration further, recapitulating the 'political dangers' of British military action with regard to the United Nations and observing that 'on the military and economic sides too there would be serious disadvantages'.[98] Once British troops were in Abadan there would be no reason, wrote Mr Serpell, to withdraw them till a settlement was reached. Meanwhile His Majesty's Government would bear the responsibility for provisioning the whole of Abadan, with a population of about 100,000, and doubtless, in order to minimise unrest, for continuing to pay wages at the current rate of a total of some £1½-2 million a month. 'Further, it is doubtful, to say the least, whether, once we have brought AIOC or something like it, back into Persia by the use of force the company could ever again lead a settled and orderly existence.'

In conclusion Mr Serpell listed three possible courses: '(i) AIOC can hang on as long as possible in Abadan', but accept any Persian withdrawal of residence permits:

---

[97] EP 1531/1402G.
[98] EP 1531/1528G.
[99] EP 1531/1385.

'this would mean that our disappearance from Persia was somewhat ignominious'; (ii) to forestall the Persians by not delaying to withdraw the British staff from Abadan; Mr Serpell explained that 'AIOC themselves say they can see no commercial reason for leaving them there once the Stokes Mission has been withdrawn'; he considered that this step, particularly if accompanied by other, economic measures, 'might have some effect from the point of view of prestige and propaganda'; (iii) 'We can insist on keeping AIOC alive in Persia, sending British troops to Abadan to safeguard British life and property . . . This would secure us some supplies of oil, earn some money and save us some dollars; but might bring us greater odium in Persia and the Middle East.'

Mr Serpell commented upon this choice of evils: 'It is unpalatable, but probably true, that we shall probably only get a settlement with Persia that is in any degree satisfactory with United States assistance. The matter needs further (and early) consideration. I myself feel, however, that the Americans are most unlikely ever to accept our *holding* Abadan by armed force, and I feel therefore that the alternatives open to His Majesty's Government are only (i) and (ii) above. Of these my vote would go to (ii).'[100] In concluding his lucid minute Mr Serpell thus advised, in effect, in a sense which might involve a reversal of the policy of His Majesty's Government as announced in Parliament, more particularly in the light of American considerations. Of the American Press at that period the *Christian Science Monitor*, indeed, briefly observed that Great Britain could not do less than prepare to defend the refinery at Abadan if necessary. More typical, however, of the American temper, if particularly blunt, was the observation of the *Philadelphia Inquirer*: 'Let it be plainly stated that we will provide neither oil nor loans if Britain persists in using force.'[101] And by August 18 the weekly gold and dollar balance of the sterling area had dipped to its largest deficit that summer, amounting to $110 million.[102]

Mr Serpell's minute, generally advancing considerations against military implementation of the policy of His Majesty's Government announced in Parliament, evidently came before the Working Party on Persian Oil, which on August 22 submitted a note on 'Action Consequent upon the Withdrawal of the Stokes Mission',[103] if that should occur. The Working Party noted that 'Mr Harriman must bear some responsibility for a breakdown in negotiations' owing to the now evident inaccuracy of the basis upon which he had persuaded His Majesty's Government to enter into them without insisting upon an improvement in the oilfields. It was recommended that a further attempt should be made to induce the reluctant Americans to come out publicly in support of the attitude of His Majesty's Government.

The Working Party advised that if the Stokes Mission failed it would be for consideration, 'in the light of the undertakings given to Parliament', which of the three courses previously listed by Mr Serpell should be adopted. It was submitted that if the British staff, in case of need, was not to be retained at Abadan by British use of force, then their withdrawal forthwith was preferable, 'as involving less loss of prestige', to retaining them there unless and until the Persians demanded their

---

[100] EP 1531/1385.
[101] EP 1531/1422.
[102] UEE 7/8G.
[103] EP 1531/1403G.

withdrawal. The Working Party recalled the advice given by Sir Oliver Franks and Sir Gladwyn Jebb as to the likely adverse effects, in regard to the United States and the United Nations, of British military intervention at Abadan except to cover the evacuation of endangered British nationals (cf p. 286), 'which we are advised', stated the Working Party, 'is also the only course defensible in international law'. The Working Party did not recall the strong representations in the opposite sense from the Chiefs of Staff and the Commanders-in-Chief, Middle East, more particularly with regard to the maintenance of the whole British position in the Middle East. This consideration was also a most serious one politically for the Foreign Office but if its representative had emphasised this to the Working Party, it was not apparent in its note to Ministers.

The Working Party, however, did not go so far as Mr Serpell in directly giving an indication against British use of force. The Working Party's 'Summary of Conclusions and Recommendations' began as follows: '(1) That once the British staff have been withdrawn from the fields, they should either: (*a*) be withdrawn completely from Abadan forthwith; or (*b*) be maintained in Abadan, even in the face of a Persian demand for their withdrawal, if necessary by the use of force. (2) That Operation Buccaneer should be put into effect: (*a*) if the lives of British staff in Abadan are clearly in danger; or (*b*) if course 1(*b*) above is decided upon in order to maintain them in Abadan if the Persian Government demand their withdrawal.'[104] The first alternative put forward by the Working Party thus involved the abandonment of the undertaking given by the Prime Minister to the House of Commons on July 30 and confirmed on the following day by the Lord Chancellor to the House of Lords. The one course rejected by the Working Party was that of just hanging on at Abadan till the Persians might turn out the British staff.

The note submitted by the Working Party on Persian Oil on August 22, 1951, was considered at four o'clock that Wednesday afternoon at the nineteenth meeting of the Ministerial Committee on Persia. As regards Ministers, it was a small one. The four Ministers present were the Prime Minister, Mr Alfred Barnes, the Minister of Transport, Mr Kenneth Younger from the Foreign Office and Mr Douglas Jay from the Treasury. In attendance from the Foreign Office were Sir William Strang, Mr Bowker and Mr Furlonge; from the Treasury, Sir Leslie Rowan and Mr Serpell. Also present were Sir Frank Lee from the Board of Trade and Sir Laurence Watkinson of the Ministry of Fuel and Power. The secretaries were Sir Norman Brook and Mr J.A. Atkinson.

After discussion the meeting agreed that every effort should be made to keep the British staff in Abadan 'for the time being, though military force could not be used unless their lives were in danger'. If used for any other purpose it must be assumed that neither the United Nations nor the United States Government would support His Majesty's Government. It was recognised that if a nucleus of British staff remained at Abadan, the Persian Government might cancel their necessary permits: 'in that event they might have to be withdrawn'. The preference of the Working Party for earlier and voluntary withdrawal was noted. 'On the other hand, it was the view of the meeting that great importance must be attached to preserving British assets in Abadan for as long as possible; that the retention of British staff in Abadan would be in accordance with the ruling of the International Court; and that, even if the total

---

[104] EP 1531/1403G.

evacuation of British staff contributed to a change of government in Persia, no new Persian Government was likely to feel strong enough to invite the British staff to return once they had all left Persia.'[105]

The Ministerial Committee on Persia on August 22 accordingly: '(1) Agreed that the withdrawal of British staff from the oilfields, and of less essential British staff from Abadan, should continue, but that the "hard core" at Abadan should not, at present, be withdrawn. (2) Agreed that Operation Buccaneer should be put into effect only if the lives of British staff in Abadan were clearly in danger.'[106] The meeting also, in the light of the views previously expressed by Sir Gladwyn Jebb, 'agreed that the dispute with Persia should not be referred to the Security Council, but that the Security Council should immediately be informed in the event of Operation Buccaneer being put into effect'. These three decisions all had a somewhat negative implication as regards taking any fresh or early action. A telegram sent that night from the Foreign Office to inform Sir Francis Shepherd of these decisions stressed the critical second one, observing that 'there can be no question of using military force merely to secure the retention of this ["hard core"] personnel in Abadan'.[107]

On August 22, 1951, Ministers were scattered on holiday, Mr Herbert Morrison in Scandinavia, Mr Gaitskell in the Channel Islands, Mr Shinwell in the Netherlands, Mr Noel-Baker also abroad, while Lord Jowitt was in Australia. The Prime Minister was the only Cabinet Minister present at that meeting of the Ministerial Committee on Persia which decided, in effect, to exclude military implications from 'all the implications' which, as Lord Jowitt had assured the House of Lords on July 31, His Majesty's Government accepted as following from the policy, announced by the Prime Minister in the House of Commons on the previous day, of not withdrawing entirely from Abadan. This important modification of British policy, as regards military action, was made primarily on the basis of a paper from the Working Party on Persian Oil, which does not appear to have included representatives from the Ministry of Defence or from any of the three Service Departments. Nor were any of these Ministries or Services represented, either ministerially or officially, at the meeting of the Committee on Persia on the afternoon of August 22.

On the morning of August 22 British military action at Abadan had again been considered at a meeting of the Chiefs of Staff attended by Marshal of the Royal Air Force Sir John Slessor, Admiral Creasy, Lieut.-General Brownjohn and Mr Furlonge. The question more particularly under consideration was a hypothetical and tactical one as to how far, if Abadan island were occupied and held by British forces, it might be necessary to throw out defences or patrols on the mainland, perhaps to a depth of 10 miles. Mr Furlonge thought that such operations might slightly aggravate the task of publicity, but observed: 'The really big decision was to move troops into Persia at all, compared with which a decision on whether to confine our activities to the island would be merely a drop in the bucket.'[108] Sir John Slessor agreed but was more concerned lest 'we should gradually be drawn on to increase the scope of our operations with the consequent demand for more troops and so on; he recalled that the fear that this would occur had been expressed by the Prime Minister'.[109]

---

[105] EP 1531/1420G.
[106] *Ibid.*
[107] EP 1531/1387.
[108] EP 1192/99G.
[109] *Ibid.*

At the same meeting of the Chiefs of Staff Admiral Creasy expressed the hope that they were not 'unduly underestimating the staunchness of the Persian troops'. Sir John Slessor observed that the Commanders-in-Chief, Middle East, seemed quite happy about their ability to carry out Operation Buccaneer, Phases I and II, with the forces at their disposal. In reporting this meeting to Sir William Strang, Mr Furlonge minuted that the Chiefs of Staff had assured him that they quite understood that none of these operations had been authorised by Ministers. The Chiefs of Staff evidently thought it unlikely that they ever would be. This minute of August 22 was initialled by Sir William Strang.[110]

As from August 22, however, the forces for Operation Buccaneer were activated to readiness at six hours' notice in view of the threatening course of political events in Tehran.[111] Next day the British Senior Naval Officer, Persian Gulf, telegraphed a suggestion that from the military point of view 'time is definitely not on our side'[112] at Abadan. If the Lord Privy Seal's negotiations broke down General Mir Jalali, commanding Persian troops in the province of Khuzistan, proposed to move from Ahwaz into Abadan,[113] where it was confidently expected that Persian security measures would be promptly reinforced.

The Lord Privy Seal on August 22, 1951, telegraphed a reply to the Prime Minister regarding his animadversions upon the proposals which Mr Stokes had put to Dr Musaddiq on August 21 (cf pp. 324-5). Mr Stokes said he shared Mr Attlee's misgivings about them but had felt justified in making them in the circumstances. Mr Stokes thought it 'essential that if we are to break off negotiations we should do so because of Persian insistence on management arrangements which neither the British staff nor any other staff in similar discussions could possibly be expected to accept'.[114] He subsequently explained, further, that 'in framing this new proposal he had been careful to hedge it round with sufficient safeguards to ensure that if circumstances required it could later be developed in such a form as to make it unacceptable to the Persians'.[115]

The Foreign Office and the Working Party on Persian Oil had certainly considered that the objections to Mr Stokes' concession regarding management, let alone to Persian desiderata, were overriding. It would rather seem, however, that the Lord Privy Seal may still not have attached the same procedural importance as did Ministers and officials in London to placing the onus for the act of discontinuing negotiations clearly upon the Persians. As it was, Dr Musaddiq on August 22 did not comply with Mr Stokes' ultimative demand, and at a meeting that evening with him and Mr Harriman, declined to give satisfactory assurances, as requested. Mr Stokes reported that he had therefore informed Dr Musaddiq 'that I had no alternative but to suspend our negotiations and return home but that the Harriman formula still stands and the door is open for the resumption of negotiations on that basis'.[116]

Towards the end of that meeting of August 22 in Tehran the Persian Prime Minister handed the Lord Privy Seal a longish letter in Persian, restating the Persian

[110] EP 1192/98G.
[111] EP 1192/94G.
[112] EP 1192/102G.
[113] EP 1991/14.
[114] EP 1531/1386.
[115] EP 1531/1486G.
[116] EP 1531/1389.

position in reply to Mr Stokes' letter of the preceding day, withdrawing the Eight-Point Proposals. Mr Stokes then learnt that the Persian reply was published in Tehran while their meeting was actually in progress. The Lord Privy Seal told Dr Musaddiq that he was shocked at this behaviour; 'Harriman was also shaken'.[117] Thus was the unhappy position reached wherein the Lord Privy Seal's negotiations in Tehran were discontinued by himself.

It was not until after their return to London that Mr Stokes and Mr Ramsbotham, in fuller accounts of the last working meeting with Dr Musaddiq on August 22, explained that the latter had asked the Lord Privy Seal whether he would prefer his earlier proposal for an operating organisation or his new proposals for a British manager. When Mr Stokes said he would prefer the earlier proposal, Dr Musaddiq said he was prepared to accept it subject to agreement on the other matters in dispute, notably the sale of oil and compensation to the Anglo-Iranian Oil Company. To Mr Stokes, however, 'it had soon become clear that Dr Musaddiq did not realise what he was accepting and that the organisation he proposed for the oil industry was fundamentally different from anything we could accept'.[115] Mr Ramsbotham thought that Dr Musaddiq's offer 'was probably a gambit to force a break on the financial aspects rather than on the British staff. In the course of this discussion Musaddiq said that he understood the Lord Privy Seal had also suggested the possibility of a Management Committee consisting of two Persians, two British and two foreigners. Mr Stokes denied he had ever made such a suggestion and went on to say that in his view it would be unworkable since responsibility must rest in one man's hands.'[118]

The practical importance of the issue of management in regard to the British oilmen was evident, and the *Financial Times* may have gone rather far on August 15 in describing the unrest among them as 'in a sense an unfortunate side-issue' in relation to the central problem of agreeing new terms for the marketing of Persian oil. Mr Berthoud, however, minuted a week later in a somewhat similar sense, suggesting that the most important point was to avoid any concession to the Persians 'which would involve our giving up a fair share of the production profit to which AIOC are entitled on any reckoning'.[119] Whereas Mr Stokes stressed to Mr Harriman on the following day of August 23 that the company should not increase their demands on any Government succeeding that of Dr Musaddiq. 'I feel very strongly about this', recorded Mr Stokes.[120] Mr Harriman subsequently expressed the view, with which Sir William Strang agreed, that Mr Stokes had made a mistake in becoming involved in discussion of the issue of management.[121]

At half past seven on the morning of August 23, 1951, the Lord Privy Seal, in his own words, 'took a very genial farewell'[120] of the Persian Prime Minister. The conversation was 'limited to pleasantries', during which Mr Stokes told Dr Musaddiq that he 'regretted that the big bone seemed likely to tear open his stomach!' At nine o'clock Mr Stokes had a long conversation with the Shah. He asked the Lord Privy Seal to stay and, recorded the latter, to 'see the Prime Minister with him, but I told him that I did not think that would be any use as I was now suspending the discussions on firm ground and on a good wicket which would hurt

---

[117] *Ibid.*
[118] EP 1531/1408.
[119] EP 1531/1444.
[120] EP 1531/1481.
[121] EP 1531/2022.

nobody whereas if we shifted on to more material matters such as the share in the profit, etc, negotiations would break down once more from lack of understanding on [*sic*] the facts of life on the part of the Prime Minister'. The Shah, recorded Mr Stokes, 'said that after my explanation he thought I was right to continue my plan to leave Tehran at once'.[122]

The Shah told Mr Stokes that he thought that he himself was left with three possible courses: first, to try to continue with Dr Musaddiq's Government while trying to 'weed out some of the more undesirable elements, which he thought would be difficult but would be worth trying'—Mr Stokes gave the Shah 'the names of the people who I thought ought to be got off the scene if Musaddiq was to succeed in coming to an arrangement'; secondly, the Shah might have recourse to a weaker Government, which Mr Stokes said 'would be disastrous'; the third possibility was 'a strong Government which would mean martial law and putting in prison all the agitators'. Mr Stokes expressed to the Shah his own belief that in the end that was what he would have to resort to. The Shah pointed out the seriousness of this course, which would probably mean martial law for two years. Mr Stokes 'said it would probably take that time too'.[123] It is not recorded that he spoke specifically in favour of M. Sayyid Zia, then the British hope in Persian politics.

Mr Harriman decided to leave Tehran shortly after Mr Stokes. Before leaving, both issued statements indicating that the negotiations were suspended but not broken off. On August 23 Mr Harriman drove with Mr Stokes to see him off at the airport of Tehran. During the drive, recorded the latter, Mr Harriman 'emphasised that he thought that either the United States or the United Kingdom, or both, might well have to come to the aid of Iran financially within the next few months. I said I hoped he would talk to the Prime Minister about that during his visit to London.'[124] Mr Stokes thus did not express agreement with Mr Harriman; but his reply would seem to have contrasted in tone with the strong representations which His Majesty's Embassy in Washington had, on instructions from the Foreign Office, just been making to the State Department; and, as the committee of ministers was informed on August 24, Mr Stokes agreed with Mr Harriman that, as regards economic measures, 'they would urge the United States and United Kingdom Governments to take no immediate steps which might prejudice the present position'.[125]

At a press conference in Washington on the same day of August 23 President Truman expressed disappointment at the suspension of negotiations in Tehran, but stated: 'It has been clear during the course of negotiations that both Persia and Great Britain sincerely desire a settlement and in view of this fact I am confident that an arrangement can ultimately be worked out.'[126] On the evening of the day on which the American President saw fit thus to underwrite Persian sincerity in the negotiations, Mr Attlee addressed to him a personal message wherein the Prime Minister pointed to Persian insistence on the letter of the Nine-Point Law, contrary to the indications which Mr Harriman had remitted to His Majesty's Government. Mr Attlee also observed that throughout the negotiations the Persians had done nothing on the crucial question of improving the atmosphere in South Persia. He was

---

[122] *Ibid.*
[123] *Ibid.*
[124] EP 1531/2022.
[125] EP 1531/1486G.
[126] EP 1531/1405.

convinced 'that the absence of agreement can be attributed solely to the blind intransigence of Dr Musaddiq and his extremist followers, and to the intimidation which they have been able to practise on the Deputies and Senators'.[127]

Mr Attlee continued in his message to President Truman: 'We entirely share the apprehensions which we know are felt in the United States Administration regarding the possibility of Persia falling under Communist domination as a result of the disruption of her economy which the present situation is causing. Our information indeed suggests that under the present régime the Tudeh Party has made significant progress amongst the population, due largely to the mistaken leniency which Dr Musaddiq has practised towards them. It must be only too clear that the longer the present standstill in the oil industry continues the greater the danger that the Tudeh Party will be able to exploit the consequent distress.'

His Majesty's Government, said the Prime Minister, were convinced that there were many sensible Persians who were either openly opposed to Dr Musaddiq's policy or else were wavering in their attitude. British information suggested that the way to swing the waverers into open opposition was to convince them that there was no exploitable divergence between the British and American Governments on the oil issue. Mr Attlee stated in conclusion of his powerful plea: 'I would therefore urge with all the earnestness at my command that the United States Government should now make plain that they fully support the stand which His Majesty's Government has been compelled to make in this matter; that they regard the breakdown in the oil negotiations as solely the fault of the present Persian Government; and that the disaster which now threatens Persia is due only to the policy of that Government.'[128]

On the same day of August 23, 1951, the News Department of the Foreign Office issued a full statement of 'the circumstances under which the Lord Privy Seal, with the full approval of His Majesty's Government, has felt compelled to suspend the negotiations . . . His Majesty's Government must now take their stand on the interim decision given . . . at The Hague on July 5 . . . As a result of the stoppage of its operations in the oilfields consequent on the action of the Persian Government, the AIOC has been compelled to withdraw its personnel from these fields; it has, however, instructed a nucleus of its personnel to remain in Abadan, in order to be ready to carry on the company's operations, in accordance with The Hague Court's decision, whenever the Persian Government make it possible for them to do so.' If the Persian Government were to fail in its obligation under international law to ensure the safety and protection of this British personnel, His Majesty's Government, as previously stated, 'would be obliged to take the necessary measures to protect them'.[129]

The press-release of August 23 proceeded, as in Mr Attlee's message to Mr Truman, to express deep gratitude 'to Mr Harriman for the untiring efforts which he has made to create and maintain a basis for negotiation'. In conclusion the parting assurance which Mr Stokes had given to Dr Musaddiq was confirmed: His Majesty's Government 'remain prepared at any time to reopen negotiations on the basis of Mr Harriman's formula . . . They will continue to pursue their application to The Hague

---

[127] EP 1531/1409G.
[128] EP 1531/1409G.
[129] EP 1531/1387.

Court for a definitive judgment in this dispute.'[130]

It was appreciated both in London and in Tehran that the brunt of the breakdown of negotiations would fall, once again, upon the long-tried British staff at Abadan. The Lord Privy Seal, before leaving Tehran on August 23, telegraphed to Mr Mason: 'I hope it may be possible to resume negotiations before long. Meanwhile I consider it absolutely essential that you maintain a foothold in Abadan.'[131] On the same day Mr Attlee telegraphed a message to Mr Mason, for the staff of the Anglo-Iranian Oil Company, announcing withdrawal, at last, from the outlying oilfields and reduction of the staff in Abadan itself. But some 'will be asked to stay in Abadan to show that the British oil industry is not deserting Persia'. The Prime Minister expressed the admiration felt for the conduct of the staff under 'exasperating conditions'. He and Sir William Fraser knew that the hardships would be borne by those still remaining, supported as they were by 'the legal authority of an order of the International Court and by the mass of public opinion in this country'.[132]

After the failure of the Stokes mission the reversion of His Majesty's Government to taking its stand upon the interim injunction of the International Court represented a consequent development of policy (cf p. 315) and was evidently the correct decision in itself. That stand, however, was now doubly weakened. In the first place it was logically open to His Majesty's Government to summon the recalcitrant Persian Government solemnly to comply with the terms of the interim injunction and to cease all interference with the management of the company as before May 1. Such a crack of the whip in accordance with the neglected legal advice of July 6 (cf p. 250) might still have proved salutary, or at least precautionary for the future. Whereas in practice the Foreign Office statement of August 23 might seem to have gone perilously far towards condoning, almost, previous Persian flouting of the injunction, and accepting that its execution should depend upon the unlikely exercise of Persian goodwill. In this connexion the withdrawal of British staff from the outlying oilfields, determined at last, assumed an air of weakness.

A second potential weakening of the British stand upon the interim injunction was threatened by the forthcomingness of British adherence, still, to the Harriman formula. There was much to be said for this in itself. It was politic in relation to America and also, at least to some extent, in regard to Persia since it demonstrated continued British good faith and helped to fasten upon Dr Musaddiq the blame for the breakdown of negotiations. While, however, the interim injunction and the Harriman Formula, recognising the nationalisation law of March 20, were strictly compatible, their implications were divergent. British adherence to both of them, even as alternatives, was liable to be difficult and to require careful coordination, especially on the juridical side.

The Harriman Formula had led on to the British Eight-Point Proposals. Their withdrawal now was, one would suppose, intended to include that of Mr Stokes' introductory statement with its assurance that the company as such would cease to operate in Persia (cf p. 316). It was perhaps regrettable, though, that greater explicitness had not been given to the withdrawal of this important statement, standing in evident contradiction to the basis of both the interim injunction and the

---

[130] *Ibid.*
[131] EP 1531/1399.
[132] *Ibid.*

substantive British application of May 26 to the International Court. Reconciliation
—if that were indeed possible—of some continuity of the concession of 1933 with
some acceptance of the principle of nationalisation remained the central difficulty
for Great Britain, as throughout the crisis. That had underlain Sir Eric Beckett's
advice of August 8 (cf p. 314), and Mr Fitzmaurice had earlier given his not wholly
reassuring opinion that acceptance of the principle of nationalisation 'within the
context of the invitation to negotiate [in the Harriman formula] does not perhaps
damage our legal position though if the recognition were quoted out of its context it
might be damaging'.[133]

The previously noted criticism in *The Financial Times* of the handling of the
British case in international law (cf p. 318) would seem to have been at any rate not
entirely beside the point. A comprehensive review of the legal aspects of the political
issues might have helped to clarify them despite the evident difficulties. As it was,
the abortive mission to Tehran of the Lord Privy Seal had resulted in His Majesty's
Government being pushed, yet again, further down the line. The Persian Government
had effectively conceded nothing. His Majesty's Government had indeed formally
resumed its stand upon the interim injunction of the International Court. But it was
a belated and weakened one. The situation for the hard-tried British oilmen, now
pressed back upon Abadan, was anything but improved. More time had elapsed, and
also, perhaps, some resolution.

All this might yet have proved worth while had it been, as hoped, the purchase
price at last of solid and wholehearted American support for the British cause. That,
however, was evidently not the case. The most that was achieved was, in the words
of Sir Donald Fergusson, 'that the mission had served a useful purpose in educating
the Persians and the Americans on the basic facts of the oil dispute'.[134] Mr Harriman
recognised the intransigence of Dr Musaddiq and henceforth the American Press was
inclined to be more critical of him. This was a real but marginal advantage by
comparison with the further British setbacks.

[133] EP 1531/1319.
[134] EP 1531/1486G.

CHAPTER XII

FAILURE OF BRITISH PRESSURE AGAINST DR MUSADDIQ, AUGUST 24-SEPTEMBER 17, 1951

1. The Expectant Pause, August 24-September 1

On his arrival at London airport on the morning of Friday, August 24, 1951, the Lord Privy Seal made a Press statement along the general lines of that given before his departure from Tehran. Mr Stokes in particular expressed 'confidence that with some good will on both sides there was no reason why a satisfactory conclusion should not be reached'[1] with Persia. That afternoon, however, in reporting on his mission to a meeting of the Ministerial Committee on Persia, Mr Stokes stated: 'In the unlikely event of a complete change in Dr Musaddiq's entourage it might be possible to negotiate successfully with him. Otherwise the only hope lay in a change of Government in Persia.'[2] On the following day Mr Bowker minuted, and Sir William Strang agreed, that 'at some moment it may be necessary to tell the Shah in firm language that he must dismiss Musaddiq and appoint a strong Prime Minister in his place. For this it is essential that the Americans should act with us.'[3]

For the present the Committee on Persia went along with the view expressed to it on August 24 by the Lord Privy Seal that 'we should allow a few days' time' for the grave implications of the departure of Mr Stokes and Mr Harriman from Tehran to sink into the Persian Government. Such a waiting pause would also afford time for consultation with Mr Harriman who would shortly be passing through London on his way back to Washington.

Meanwhile, the Lord Privy Seal told the Committee on Persia on August 24, 'he was concerned at some of the Press stories which spoke of [British] naval activity and the possibility of other measures'. After hearing a brief report from the Vice-Chief of the Naval Staff the Ministers 'agreed that no move to reinforce the naval force off Abadan should in present circumstances be taken'.[4] As regards economic measures, it was agreed that the proposed Sterling Control Order, denying Persia the special financial facilities enjoyed under the Memorandum of Understanding, should not be made till after discussion with Mr Harriman, unless Persia attempted large-scale conversion of her sterling into dollars. Cargoes and export licences for Persia were, so far as practicable, to be delayed administratively but no overt action of denial should be taken for the present.

Also on the afternoon of August 24 the Shah sent for His Majesty's Ambassador and told him that the departure of Mr Stokes and Mr Harriman had indeed been a shock to Dr Musaddiq. The latter was willing to accept the Lord Privy Seal's desideratum of a British managing director. Following up his discussion with Mr Stokes on August 22 of a mixed management committee of six, Dr Musaddiq now proposed that one of the two British members of it should be the managing director. After discussion with Mr Harriman and Mr Levy, Sir Francis Shepherd commented: 'It seems to me that this does represent an apparent advance on the part of Musaddiq.

---

[1] *The Times*, August 25, 1951.
[2] EP 1531/1486G.
[3] EP 1531/1434.
[4] EP 1531/1486G.

I am, however, very doubtful whether it represents a genuine attempt to find a quick solution . . . The suggestion, as outlined to me by the Shah, is vague, but I do not wish to ask Musaddiq for a preliminary qualification or even confirmation, because that would give him opportunity of claiming that negotiations had already been restarted.'[5] This estimate was discussed by Sir William Strang with Mr Stokes and was approved.

Sir Francis Shepherd further telegraphed privately to Sir William Strang on August 25 that the Lord Privy Seal's press statement at London airport was 'having unfortunate effect here. It has both strengthened the Government's position and has mystified and discouraged the Opposition.'[6] After consulting Mr L.F.L. Pyman, his Oriental Counsellor, and also Mr Zaehner and Colonel Wheeler, His Majesty's Ambassador in Tehran strongly recommended that, in order 'to counter the impression that we are still weak and ready to flirt with Musaddiq',[7] the BBC should broadcast an unequivocal statement that His Majesty's Government had no further hope of reaching agreement with the existing Persian Government. Sir Francis Shepherd added: 'If I may say so we have had too much waffling and something lapidary is now needed.'[8]

Sir William Strang replied the same day to Sir Francis Shepherd, explaining the policy, adopted by the Committee on Persia on August 24, of a waiting pause for a few days: 'at any rate until situation has been reviewed with Harriman, it is not intended to take any step which could be represented as retaliatory or provocative . . . It may be that tougher line will then be taken, in word and act.'[9] Meanwhile, explained Sir William Strang, the British line was that negotiations were suspended or adjourned, but the next move was up to the Persians and discussions could only be reopened if they put forward reasonable proposals.

Sir Francis Shepherd replied on August 26 to Sir William Strang by cogently observing that he did not see how the Persians could be expected to put forward further proposals in view of Dr Musaddiq's proposal to Mr Stokes on the eve of his departure, and of the subsequent approach through the Shah, both discounted on the British side and, in His Majesty's Ambassador's view, rightly. His personal opinion was 'that there is now no more chance of reaching a reasonable agreement with Musaddiq than ever there was and that the moment has come for us to try to get him out. The opportunity may not last.'[10]

Most informed Persians were shocked by Dr Musaddiq's failure to maintain negotiations with Mr Stokes and Mr Harriman, and the Persian Premier's position was weakened. On the same day of August 26 an attack against him in the Majlis was forcibly led by M. Jamal Imami, who had actually proposed Dr Musaddiq for the premiership and was one of the most influential members of the Oil Commission. Sir Francis Shepherd now urged that British organs should at least refrain from suggesting any hope in the existing Persian Government, and should make it clear that its attitude had hitherto been unsatisfactory. He concluded his telegram of August 26 to Sir William Strang: 'We cannot afford to continue to be conciliatory. I

---

[5] EP 1531/1408.
[6] EP 1531/1463.
[7] EP 1531/1414.
[8] EP 1531/1464.
[9] EP 1531/1428.
[10] EP 1531/1429.

fear this view may not be shared by the Lord Privy Seal or Harriman but it is supported by the history of the development of this dispute since the murder of Razmara.'[11]

The fear of Sir Francis Shepherd was correct. Mr Stokes explained his disagreement with him to the Committee on Persia on August 27, before a meeting with Mr Harriman. The Lord Privy Seal 'believed that we should continue to await events',[12] and that British attacks on Dr Musaddiq or sanctions against Persia would be likely to strengthen his position. And on the same day Sir William Strang minuted to the Prime Minister: 'While it is certainly desirable that Dr Musaddiq should be removed from office as soon as possible, I am not convinced that direct attacks on him by the BBC or in official statements by His Majesty's Government would be best designed to achieve that purpose. On the other hand, I think that our public line should be toughened up if in two or three days' time there is still no sign of a change of line or a change of Government in Tehran. Meantime, our action against Dr Musaddiq should be indirect and behind the scenes. You will have noticed an encouraging growth of opposition to him in the Majlis itself.'[13]

On the preceding evening of August 26 Mr R.M. Hadow, Private Secretary to the Minister of State in the Foreign Office, had had a long conversation with M. Hamzavi, the Persian Press Counsellor of long standing in London, who sought Mr Hadow's personal impressions of Mr Stokes' mission. Mr Hadow pointed out that he 'was not in any way connected with the Foreign Office's handling of Persian affairs but from what I gathered Mr Stokes had got on extremely well with all the eminent Persians he had met from the Shah downwards. He was optimistic that a settlement could be found, as could be seen from his statements since his return. Hamzavi asked if he really thought Musaddiq could come to any reasonable agreement. I said that provided the more sinister pressures behind him could be removed, the impression seemed to be that he would like to get out of the mess he was in.'[14]

Mr Hadow emphasised to M. Hamzavi 'how extremely unimportant Persian oil in fact was. Even if we lost the refinery and the fields, their loss could be made good in almost no time . . . I was now no longer worried about the effect on Britain the quarrel would have, but I was a friend enough of Persia's to feel sad that the Persians themselves were now going to be in such a jam.'

The Persian Press Counsellor, recorded Mr Hadow, 'was greatly agitated by all this and said . . . but surely we could not go and leave Persia in the lurch. "What about the Lord Chancellor's statement in the Lords?" I said that as far as I knew all this meant was that we would safeguard the lives of British personnel in Abadan and possibly the installations while the personnel were present, if damage to the installations might entail danger to the personnel. But once all the personnel had gone, I did not see why we should enter into a costly and dangerous operation merely to support an industry which was of more importance to the Persians than to us.'[15]

At the end of the conversation M. Hamzavi said he thought his Ambassador should try to act with M. Sayyid Zia 'but, unfortunately, Soheily was showing

---

[11] *Ibid.*
[12] EP 1531/1437G.
[13] EP 1531/1429.
[14] EP 1531/1498.
[15] *Ibid.*

increasing signs of wanting to wash his hands of the whole business'. Mr Hadow formed the impression that both M. Hamzavi and M. Soheily had decided that if the worst came to the worst they could afford to live comfortably outside Persia. In the Eastern Department of the Foreign Office Mr Rothnie minuted that Mr Hadow's line regarding the comparative unimportance of Persian oil had subsequently been 'very happily' repeated by Mr Harriman to M. Soheily. The latter was taking quite a sensible line and might make a useful supporter of M. Sayyid Zia, though not himself a Prime Minister.

The Eastern Department did not comment upon the seemingly important initiative which Mr Hadow had taken in giving a Persian official, however friendly, an interpretation of the Lord Chancellor's critical statement which tended to raise some doubt regarding the Prime Minister's public assurance that the British intention was not to evacuate Abadan entirely. These declarations of July 30-31 had not been withdrawn, whatever the bearing on them of the secret decisions of the Ministerial Committee on Persia on August 22 (cf pp. 329-30).

August 26, 1951, saw the completion of what Sir William Fraser termed the 'difficult and distressing operation'[16] of withdrawing all British staff from the outlying Fields to Abadan. The Persian staff in the Fields would not after the end of the month be paid by the Anglo-Iranian Oil Company. The question of continuing payment to the Persian staff in Abadan itself was among those considered at an augmented meeting of the Committee on Persia which Mr Attlee called on August 27 so that he might be assisted by senior Ministers in the discussion with Mr Harriman which was to be held later that afternoon. The meeting of the Ministerial Committee on Persia at 3.30 pm was attended by the Prime Minister, the Lord President of the Council (Lord Addison), the Chancellor of the Duchy of Lancaster (Lord Alexander of Hillsborough), the Home Secretary (Mr Chuter Ede), the Minister of Defence, the Secretary of State for Scotland (Mr Hector McNeil), the Lord Privy Seal, the Parliamentary Under-Secretary for Foreign Affairs (Mr Ernest Davies) and the Economic Secretary of the Treasury (Mr John Edwards). The officials in attendance included Sir William Strang, Mr Bowker, Sir Leslie Rowan, Sir Frank Lee and Sir Donald Fergusson.

The augmented Committee on Persia took note that 'some 40,000 people depended on the continuance of wage payments in Abadan and if these were to stop considerable trouble might be expected with danger to the lives of British personnel still remaining there, and with the consequent risk that Operation Buccaneer might have to be mounted. It was argued on the one hand that a show of force might bring the Persians to their senses, but that, on the other hand, this would get very little sympathy from the United States in the United Nations and from the Asian members of the Commonwealth. It might also have the effect of uniting the country behind Dr Musaddiq, and it was therefore important that we should do nothing to provoke trouble in Abadan.'[17] The meeting agreed that Persian employees in Abadan should continue to be paid for the present. On the same day the British Commanders-in-Chief, Middle East, reported that the forces for Operation Buccaneer were reverting to 24-hours' notice instead of six, and four days later the Commanders-in-Chief were

---

[16] EP 1531/1410.
[17] EP 1531/1437G.

given discretion to stand down the operation to 72-hours' notice.[18]

The interdepartmental Working Party on Persian Oil recommended on August 27 that British publicity regarding Persia should be strengthened by laying down firm conditions for the resumption of negotiations, notably that there could be no question of any further British governmental mission going to Persia till the Persians had not only made reasonable proposals but had demonstrated their genuine desire for accommodation in preliminary discussion with His Majesty's Embassy. The Ministerial Committee on Persia, however, that day rejected this recommendation regarding firm conditions and also decided against intimating that His Majesty's Government could not expect to negotiate successfully with Dr Musaddiq.

The Working Party on Persian Oil had also recommended 'that every attempt should be made to convince Mr Harriman of the necessity for unequivocal and public United States support for the British case and to induce him to represent this strongly in Washington'.[19] Here also the Ministers somewhat moderated the emphasis of the Working Party. The Committee on Persia held that in view of Mr Attlee's strong and still unanswered appeal of August 23 to President Truman, 'we could not ask Mr Harriman to do more than support the Prime Minister's request on his return to Washington, and there could be no question of Mr Harriman himself making any further statement at the present time'.[20] If Mr Harriman was asked, as agreed, to support Mr Attlee's request it was apparently in private conversation, not at the meeting which British Ministers held with him at 10 Downing Street at 4.30 pm on August 27, 1951.

Mr Averell Harriman expressed to the British Ministers views which were in broad accordance with those of the Lord Privy Seal: 'No agreement could be reached with Dr Musaddiq so long as he was surrounded by his present advisers . . . The Shah did not know where to turn. Nevertheless it was with the Shah that we should now deal . . . He should however be encouraged rather than forced . . . Mr Harriman said that his general recommendation was that the situation should be allowed to simmer . . . We should . . . work quietly behind the scenes and see whether the Persians could be encouraged to come forward with more reasonable proposals.'[21]

On the economic side, however, the Prime Minister represented to Mr Harriman the importance of timing, which might be a question of days rather than weeks or months: 'The company could not go on indefinitely paying the Persians in Abadan. His Majesty's Government could not go on letting the Persian have dollars or scarce commodities like steel or sugar when they themselves were being placed in balance of payment and other difficulties by Persian action. The Americans should understand our difficulty in view of their own feelings about exports to the Soviet Union and satellites. When the House of Commons reassembled there were certain to be questions about this, and His Majesty's Government would have to show that they were taking some action and were not tamely acquiescing. The action we took would not be economic sanctions or retaliation but measures to protect our own position . . . It was pointed out that if we did not react our situation in the Middle East as a whole would suffer.' Mr Harriman felt unable to express a view about the

[18] EP 1192/94G and 105G.
[19] EP 1531/1437G.
[20] EP 1192/94G and 105G.
[21] EP 1531/1466G.

supply of steel or sugar, 'but anything in the nature of economic sanctions or military pressure would tend to stiffen the Persian attitude . . . Military action, except for the purpose of securing the safe evacuation of British nationals, would have a disastrous effect.'[22]

Mr Harriman, while apparently not directly pressed for support by the British Ministers, was asked whether the Persians still thought there was an Anglo-American difference of view. Mr Harriman replied 'that he had made it quite clear to the Persians that the Americans were not prepared to save them from their folly'. At a press conference in London on the following day Mr Harriman made friendly references to the potential value, previously, of the rejected Eight-Point Proposals and firmly denied extensive press reports of differences between himself and Mr Stokes. In the Foreign Office, however, Mr Rothnie observed in this connexion that Mr Harriman 'has not so far said in so many words that he was 100 percent behind the ultimatum [presented by Mr Stokes]. I doubt whether he can be induced to do so now.'[23]

In the privacy of his meeting with the British Ministers Mr Harriman said that the two embassies in Tehran were not working closely enough together and that 'the United States Ambassador and Sir Francis Shepherd differed in their views as to the prospect of a change of Government',[24] Dr Grady holding that there was no practicable alternative to Dr Musaddiq. Dr Grady was now due to be replaced in a few weeks by Mr Loy Henderson, described by Mr Frank Roberts, who had worked with him in New Delhi, as 'an absolutely reliable and loyal colleague'.[25]

Mr Harriman's criticism of Anglo-American cooperation in Tehran came a fortnight after a proposal from the State Department for a joint Anglo-American appreciation of nationalist feeling in Egypt. The Foreign Secretary had been inclined to agree to this suggestion, though with some caution since, as he had minuted to the Prime Minister on August 14, 'there is a danger lest this joint appreciation might be the thin end of the wedge and might eventually lead to American efforts at mediation between us and the Egyptians, on the Persian model, but resulting in pressure on us to make compromises which would be unacceptable because dangerous to our vital interests. We know that the Americans are anxious that we should take a less "rigid" stand in regard to Egypt.'[26] As regards Persia Sir William Strang wrote on August 28 to Sir Francis Shepherd, urging him and all his staff to 'make a deliberate and self-abnegating effort to get on terms of confidence with your United States colleagues, however difficult this may be'.[25] In reply His Majesty's Ambassador underlined this difficulty owing to the Americans' 'suspicion of the colonialist and imperialist attitudes of British policy in all parts of the East . . . They are certainly ambitious of increasing American influence in this country and regard us as their chief rival.'[27]

It was apparently Mr Harriman, rather than Mr Stokes, who now suggested to British Ministers that it would be useful if an expert in international oil, as well as in the working of British nationalisation, were attached as an adviser to Sir Francis

---

[22] *Ibid.*
[23] EP 1531/1499.
[24] EP 1531/1466G.
[25] EP 1901/11.
[26] JE 1051/183G.
[27] EP 1025/1.

Shepherd. The presence in Tehran of representatives of the Anglo-Iranian Oil Company may hitherto have forestalled such an arrangement, which might otherwise seem rather an obvious one. Mr Harriman's suggestion was pursued in Whitehall but to a negative conclusion so far as any action went before the climax, or nadir, of the crisis at Abadan.

Mr Walter Levy, who accompanied Mr Averell Harriman through London, on August 28 expressed to Mr Berthoud 'undiluted praise' for all the official members of the mission of the Lord Privy Seal, while coinciding with Sir Francis Shepherd's judgment regarding the impulsiveness of its head. Mr Levy further opined that 'Sir William Fraser had learned absolutely nothing from past events and was completely out of touch with the position. The same applied, in his view, to many of the other Directors and senior staff, including Mr Seddon, who should be replaced . . . It would help towards the solution of the whole Persian problem if, during this brief lull, Sir William Fraser were removed.'[28] On the same day Sir Donald Fergusson asked Mr Furlonge to represent to the Foreign Office his strong conviction in the same sense. (The view in the Foreign Office was rather that Sir William Fraser was 'chastened and cooperative'.)[29] Sir Donald Fergusson explained that it was difficult for him to put this view forward himself since the Ministry of Fuel and Power should by rights be defending the Anglo-Iranian Oil Company.

Shortly afterwards Sir Donald Fergusson, accompanied by Sir Leslie Rowan of the Treasury, went to see Sir William Strang in the above connexion. Sir Donald Fergusson, recorded Sir William Strang, said that 'the Anglo-Iranian Oil Company, though an efficient industrial and commercial organisation, had mismanaged the political side of their relations with the Persian authorities. The organisation was too highly centralised, all important decisions having to be referred to London . . . Sir William Fraser had no other thought but to secure the integral execution of the agreement of 1933, whatever the political circumstances, and to squeeze the last possible pound out of the Persians . . . Sir William Fraser should cease to be chairman of the company.'[30] Similar misgivings had been expressed to Sir Donald Fergusson, notably by the Governor of the Bank of England. Sir Leslie Rowan said that since he was new to his post all this was fresh to him but he would look into the position, especially the question of the Government's relationship to the company.

In the event Sir William Fraser continued to be chairman of the Anglo-Iranian Oil Company. It was in any case almost certainly too late by then to secure his replacement, had that proved feasible in itself, before the final rundown at Abadan. It was later learnt in the Foreign Office that the Anglo-Iranian Oil Company 'were much upset at the manner in which they were brushed aside'[31] during Mr Stokes' negotiations. On the other hand the Lord Privy Seal was inclined to take a critical view of the company's financial dealings in Persia (cf pp. 332, 365, 391-2).

Mr Averell Harriman told British Ministers on August 27, 1951: 'As regards future action, it would be desirable to forget the past and start afresh.'[32] It does not appear that Mr Harriman was specifically taken up on this advocacy of a clean slate when, for Great Britain, the slate was anything but clean: Persian violation of the

---

[28] EP 1531/1468.
[29] EP 1537/10G.
[30] EP 1537/10G.
[31] EP 1531/1695.
[32] EP 1531/1466G.

concession of 1933 and unilateral nationalisation of Britain's greatest single commercial investment overseas, Persian rejection of the Jackson Proposals, Persian rejection of the interim injunction of the International Court, Persian rejection of the Eight-Point Proposals, Persian persistence in oppressing British staff and stifling British industry at Abadan. In so far, however, as Mr Harriman's rather jaunty advice related to the technical elaboration of fresh British suggestions for economic accommodation with Persia, British official thinking was by then far from clinging to old stereotypes.

Sir Donald Fergusson laid bare the central dilemma in a letter of September 5, 1951, to Sir William Strang: 'The Persians are not far wrong when they say that all our proposals are, in fact, merely dressing up AIOC control in other clothing. This is inevitable if Persian oil is to be produced and sold efficiently in large quantities and any real concession on this point is therefore impossible.'[33] Four days earlier, however, Mr Berthoud had minuted: 'In this whole dispute, we should clearly distinguish between the national interests and those of AIOC. In so far as they are not synonymous, it is fair that AIOC should subordinate themselves. Perhaps they are willing to do so. The national interest, as I see it, is that we should continue to secure large quantities of oil in Persia for sterling at the cheapest possible price and that the arrangements should not upset our other world-wide commitments.'[34]

Mr Berthoud's reading of the national interest was clearly correct so far as it went, and it was natural and proper that he should deal with the economic aspect. Perhaps this affords another instance, however, of a certain tendency in the Foreign Office, possibly promoted by staffing arrangements, to factorise a dispute which was indeed economic in origin too much in those economic terms which were naturally the prime concern of other Ministries such as the Treasury and the Ministry of Fuel and Power. However serious the economic issues, as then in regard to the British investment in Persian oil, the main concern of the Foreign Office, and not of the other Departments, must always remain political: in that case, more particularly, the critical bearing of the Persian crisis upon the whole future of British influence and power in restive Egypt and throughout the strategic area of the Middle East, the land bridge between Russia in her aggressive communism and Africa in her emergent nationalism. This overriding consideration of geopolitics, which the Chiefs of Staff and the British Commanders-in-Chief in the Middle East had so strongly represented, was certainly not ignored in the Foreign Office. But it was not emphasised there, for instance, in any special memorandum to the Cabinet, as might perhaps have been expected in view of the political magnitude of the challenge to British statesmanship in seeking to maintain, if not strengthen, the world position of the United Kingdom at the head of the Commonwealth and Empire.

On the economic side, however, Mr Berthoud was already looking ahead with prescience towards some sort of consortium in Persia (cf p. 301). As regards the Purchasing Organisation of the Eight-Point Proposals, he minuted on September 1, 1951: 'There is no reason of policy as I see it, why this company should not be a mongrel mixture of AIOC, Royal Dutch Shell, Burmah Oil and even the American companies.'[35] Meanwhile the Eight-Point Proposals were being clarified and recast

---

[33] EP 1531/1545.
[34] EP 1531/1500.
[35] EP 1531/1500.

in Whitehall in what was dubbed a 'Child's Guide Edition'. Of the 11 points which now constituted a 'Revised outline of suggestions to form basis of new agreement', the ninth, in particular, began as follows: 'The Operating Organisation shall have a board of six directors, two of whom shall be Iranian, two British and two neutral— one of the British shall be Managing Director':[36] an acceptance of what Dr Musaddiq had offered through the Shah to Sir Francis Shepherd on August 24.

There was every reason by now for distrusting the sincerity of Dr Musaddiq as a negotiator. Nevertheless the fact that British official circles were prepared to envisage agreement upon the proposals which he had made on the issue on which Mr Stokes had broken off negotiations, but were not prepared to let Dr Musaddiq know this, constituted a sad commentary on the diplomatic *impasse* which had been reached—just the barren situation which a negotiator must above all seek to avoid, whenever possible, by one means or another. As it was, all this economic thinking in Whitehall was a long-term exercise of future application. The immediate reality was that by August 29 both Sir Francis Shepherd and Mr Zaehner in Tehran and the Persian Ambassador in London, at luncheon with the Lord Privy Seal, were intimating that His Majesty's Government should seek to secure the overthrow of Dr Musaddiq.[37]

On August 30, 1951, a Foreign Office telegram to Sir Francis Shepherd indicated that the expectant pause of a week in British policy towards Persia was to be terminated in the light of his advices and 'in view of Musaddiq's failure to make any advances since the departure of the Lord Privy Seal's Mission . . . Though reluctant, the Lord Privy Seal agrees with the course we now propose as the only sensible alternative.'[38] His Majesty's Ambassador was asked to comment upon new instructions to himself which were under consideration. These were that he should so soon as possible deliver to the Shah a message which would begin by referring to Dr Musaddiq's continued intransigence. Furthermore 'his actions are fast ruining the economy of the country and threaten if continued to create those conditions of which the Tudeh Party can best take advantage. His Majesty's Government have therefore reluctantly come to the conclusion that it will not be possible to negotiate a settlement so long as Musaddiq remains in power. They therefore urge His Majesty to consider seriously whether the interests of his country do not demand that he should now take resolute action to replace this régime by one more capable of pursuing those interests.'

Sir Francis Shepherd would further indicate to the Shah the likely necessity for certain British economic measures against Persia, which 'could of course be revoked in the event of an acceptable settlement on the oil question being in sight'. His Majesty's Ambassador would have discretion to convey to M. Sayyid Zia the sense of the message to the Shah, after delivery. The BBC would be asked gradually to intensify pressure against Dr Musaddiq.

These proposed instructions were warmly welcomed by Sir Francis Shepherd, who had indeed to a considerable extent anticipated them on August 29 in a conversation with the Shah, telling him that 'we had no desire or intention to enter into vague discussions with Musaddiq which would almost certainly turn out not to

---

[36] EP 1531/1473.
[37] EP 1015/296.
[38] *Ibid.*

be genuine but which would merely have the effect of wasting time'. His Majesty's Ambassador recalled to the Shah 'the talks which we had had about the position of the monarchy in Persia and the need for definite intervention by the Shah at the appropriate moments'. With his support, argued Sir Francis Shepherd, the replacement of Dr Musaddiq 'could be brought about very quickly', and His Majesty's Ambassador 'suggested that Sayyed Zia was the best candidate'.

'The Shah', reported Sir Francis Shepherd, 'said that he had seen both Sayyed Zia and Qavam that morning and he had encouraged them to continue organising their party. I expressed surprise that Qavam should appear to be active since I heard he was definitely failing in health. The Shah said that on the contrary his impression was that Qavam had taken a new lease of life and was definitely active . . . It was evident that as between Sayyed Zia and Qavam he preferred the latter for the purpose of settling the oil question . . . Qavam was not in a state of health to remain in office for very long. One of his objections to Sayyed Zia was that as an Anglophile he would probably require greater concessions from us than an impartial Prime Minister would.'[39]

After this conversation the Shah elusively took to the hills on holiday, 'rather surprisingly'[40] in the view of Sir Francis Shepherd. The latter further reported that Dr Grady was convinced there was nothing to be hoped from Dr Musaddiq but 'did not think drastic action was needed by the Shah at the moment. Grady would be glad to see a change of Government but was not proposing to support any particular candidate.'[39] Sir Francis Shepherd, however, proceeded to suggest that his proposed instructions be strengthened by a specific recommendation of M. Sayyed Zia to the Shah.

Mr Bowker represented in a minute of September 2 to the Prime Minister: 'Sir Francis Shepherd points out that the nomination of Qavam would mean a return to reaction and corruption and he would certainly not be especially friendly to us. Moreover, once he became Prime Minister it might be difficult to get him out again . . . We regard Sayyed Zia as the one man who would be able, and anxious, to get a reasonable oil settlement with us, and at the same time adopt a long-term policy of development and reform which is essential for Persia's future stability . . . There would be little possibility of Qavam and Sayyed Zia working together.'[41] Mr Attlee approved this argument and Sir Francis Shepherd was instructed to stiffen his message to the Shah 'by warning him specifically against the risks of appointing a reactionary Prime Minister and of [*sic*] leaving him in no doubt of my view that the interests of his country would be best served by the appointment of Sayyed Zia.'[42]

The correspondent of *The Times* in Tehran reported on September 2, 1951, that M. Qavam and M. Sayyed Zia, the most obvious successors to the criticised Dr Musaddiq, had no popular support, though officials of the British Embassy thought that M. Sayyed Zia had plans for social reform. The correspondent concluded, more cautiously than His Majesty's Ambassador, more in accordance with the views of Dr Grady: 'Little as the opinion of the general public may count in the immediate workings of Persian politics, it is still doubtful whether nationalist zest has waned

---

[39] EP 1531/1462.
[40] EP 1013/38.
[41] EP 1015/298.
[42] *Ibid.*

sufficiently to enable its symbol, Dr Musaddiq, to be overthrown in the immediate future or, even if he were, to enable a successor to reach an oil agreement which would at the same time satisfy both the British public and the Persian.'[43] On September 3 M. Sayyed Zia told Sir Francis Shepherd, in the context of his possible premiership, that he would wish to find a *modus vivendi* in regard to oil for six months or a year but not on the lines of the interim injunction of the International Court (though he himself did not object), because of the propaganda in Persia against it.[44]

2. Mounting Anglo-Persian tension before the British representation to the Shah and Anglo-American conversations in Washington, September 1-11

On September 1, 1951, Dr Musaddiq had made an intransigent broadcast and his extremist Under-Secretary, M. Fatimi, told a press conference that the Persian Government would no longer wait upon the discussions with Great Britain but would make contact with countries offering to buy crude oil from, and supply technicians to, the National Iranian Oil Company. Asked whether His Majesty's Government would be able to prevent the transport of oil on the basis of the interim injunction of The Hague Court, M. Fatimi replied: 'No, because the British Government recognised the principle of nationalisation after The Hague Court had given its judgment. The Hague Court decision has lost all value.'[45] This report by Sir Francis Shepherd of this grave statement was received in the Foreign Office two days later, on Monday, September 3.

It was recognised in the Foreign Office that it was 'important to disabuse the Persians of the idea that we have in any way rendered The Hague Court decision invalid',[46] and Sir Eric Beckett was consulted. The Foreign Office forthwith invited the BBC to broadcast to Persia a refutation of M. Fatimi's thesis: His Majesty's Government had accepted the principle of nationalisation of the Persian oil industry 'without prejudice', solely as a basis for discussions when Mr Stokes was trying to reach a settlement out of court; unless and until a settlement with Persia was reached by agreement such British acceptance of the principle had no legal effect. In transmitting this to Mr Waterfield of the BBC on September 4 Mr Barclay wrote, as a corollary, that pending a change in the Persian attitude His Majesty's Government continued to base their position on the interim injunction of the International Court.[47] Clear and accurate as the British legal refutation was, so far as it went, it was unfortunate that by then it should have been necessary. This consideration was pointed by the mild terms in which the BBC duly broadcast the refutation on September 5.

On September 3 the Persian Ambassador in London, on instructions from his Government, asked Mr Bowker at the Foreign Office whether His Majesty's Government were proposing to make any new proposals. Mr Bowker replied that His Majesty's Government were still waiting for the Persian Government to make the next move since 'the so-called "new proposals" which Dr Musaddiq had made to Mr Stokes just before he left were . . . merely a repetition of the proposals which

---

[43] *The Times,* September 3, 1951.
[44] EP 1531/1536.
[45] EP 1531/1485.
[46] *Ibid.*
[47] PB 1048/41.

had been already put to Mr Stokes previously and found quite unacceptable'. M. Soheily said he would report to his Government and added his personal view that it 'could not last much longer'.[48]

M. Fatimi's threatening remarks of September 1 incited the Anglo-Iranian Oil Company to publish on September 6 a statement that the Persian Government was trying to sell oil in defiance of its obligations and of the interim injunction of the International Court; the company was confident that no reputable person would accept or carry such oil and threatened legal action against any who did. This stiff warning lay along what was perhaps the most successful line of British action in the whole crisis. Because for once the power realities rested with the British, valuably supported by the Americans in the economic, as they were not in the political, aspect of the Persian dispute. Anglo-American cooperation between oil companies and near-monopoly in tanker tonnage made the British threat, this time, a real one (cf p. 421).

The declaration of the Anglo-Iranian Oil Company had been approved by the Cabinet on September 4 at a meeting which was attended by the Foreign Secretary, back from his holiday for a few days in his office before flying across the Atlantic to attend the San Francisco Conference on the Japanese Peace Treaty, tripartite meetings of Foreign Ministers in Washington, and a meeting of the North Atlantic Council in Ottawa. The Cabinet on September 4 also considered a memorandum by the Chancellor of the Exchequer arguing that 'it is becoming increasingly difficult to justify further delay' in issuing the proposed Sterling Control Order. This would 'nullify the "Memorandum of Understanding" arrangements by removing Persia from the Transferable Account Area . . . By leaving Persia in the . . . area, we ourselves are according to her the means of receiving payment for the oil denied to us. Our dollar situation is deteriorating rapidly' (cf p. 360) and Persia was taking dollars of the order of 850,000 a week. Issue of the Sterling Control Order 'may even succeed in hastening the fall of Dr Musaddiq'.[49] The Cabinet approved Mr Gaitskell's recommendation that, unless Persian financial pressure forced action meanwhile, the American Government should be informed of the British intention to make the order and, unless their reaction against it were very strong, it should be issued immediately thereafter.

The Foreign Secretary informed the same meeting of the Cabinet that Mr Seddon at Tehran had recommended that wages to Persian employees in Abadan should now be stopped. Sir Francis Shepherd agreed since 'the Persians were determined to ensure the protection of British personnel in order to give us no excuse for landing British forces there. Nor did he think the termination of these payments would of itself lead the Persians to cancel the residence permits for the British staff.'[50] The Cabinet, however, asked that a full appreciation of the risks involved be prepared for subsequent consideration.

On the following morning of September 5 Dr Musaddiq, presumably after he had had received M. Soheily's account of his negative conversation with Mr Bowker, sharpened things up in a speech in the Persian Senate wherein he threatened that unless His Majesty's Government were prepared within a fortnight to reopen

---

[48] EP 1531/1505.
[49] EP 1112/91G.
[50] EP 1112/91G.

negotiations on a basis acceptable to the Persian Government he would cancel the residence permits of the British staff at Abadan. That ultimate and latent Persian threat was now out in the open. The term of a fortnight may possibly have held some significance in relation to the fact that the Royal Firman for elections to the 17th Majlis was due on September 21. With possible ways out by now so impeded, if not blocked, the Persian threat edged the crisis closer to the crunch when His Majesty's Government would have to knuckle under or take the consequences or compel the Persians to take them in terms of force.

On his return to the Foreign Office Mr Herbert Morrison had found a letter addressed to him at the end of August by the Attorney-General, reiterating his views regarding the possibility of British military action in Persia: 'the absolute maximum would be something in the nature of a rescue operation to protect life . . . If we undertake anything beyond this, I feel that there is no chance of successfully justifying it before The Hague Court': against which the Foreign Secretary cogently noted, 'But Persia defying the Court'.[51] During Mr Morrison's absence Sir William Strang had on September 1 sent the Prime Minister a copy of Sir Frank Soskice's letter, but it was left to the Foreign Secretary to minute highly critically upon what he termed the 'simple politics' of its argument. This ran further: 'We really would be in the most disastrous position . . . if we ourselves refused to obey the order of The Hague Court or attempted to exercise a veto in the Security Council'. His own position, explained the Attorney-General, would then be 'one of the very greatest difficulty . . . Not only would world opinion swing against us but I think amongst our supporters there would be very great dismay if any such course were undertaken.' This consideration was, indeed, bound to carry much weight with a Cabinet which had to rely for its narrow parliamentary majority upon the support of the Labour Party with its diverse and radical elements, including the followers of the recently resigned Mr Aneurin Bevan.

On September 5 the interdepartmental Working Party on Persian Oil, in briefly considering Dr Musaddiq's new threat that morning, provisionally concluded, in particular: 'If, as is to be assumed from the Attorney-General's letter, the use of force to maintain the staff in Abadan is precluded, it would be better in replying to Dr Musaddiq's ultimatum when it comes to state that unless he withdraws his threat, we propose ourselves to take the staff out forthwith.' (Marginal comment by Mr Morrison: 'Sense and policy may supersede A-G's law.') 'This course would at least be less undignified than leaving the staff to be ejected piecemeal after the "ultimatum" had expired.' Against this Mr Morrison noted: 'It would be denounced with some justice as scuttle & surrender.' He had also minuted on the same paper: 'HMG should consider force. Confiscation, in spite of an agreement & Hague Court decision, plus expulsion is very serious to lie down to. Alternative is probably ineffective appeal to UN.'[52]

The Working Party also thought it would be 'essential to deal with' some specific and unhopeful points which Dr Musaddiq had apparently raised regarding the basis for resuming negotiations. The Foreign Secretary here noted: 'Not very impressive with an angry public opinion.' In amplification of an earlier point made by the Working Party, Sir William Strang recorded on the same day of September 5 that it

---

[51] EP 1192/110G.
[52] EP 1531/1532G.

had 'considered whether it would not be possible for us to tell the staff in Abadan to stay, whatever the Persians might do, and then, if the Persians mishandled them, we might set "Buccaneer" going. The Working Party, however, came to the conclusion, on the strong advice of the company, that this was not feasible, since the Persians could find a number of ways of making conditions completely unbearable for our staff (eg by cutting off water) without in any way physically molesting them.' Sir William Strang concluded: 'We must do our utmost to get Musaddiq out before the fortnight is up.' On which the Foreign Secretary wrote: 'By all means—if you can.' In conclusion Mr Morrison on September 5 minuted to Sir William Strang on the same paper: 'You may inform PM of my feelings. See *private* notes on A-G's letter. Most of it policy—not law.'[53] On the following evening of September 6 Mr Morrison left for San Francisco.

All this minuting was before receipt on September 6 of the comment of His Majesty's Ambassador in Tehran on the Persian Prime Minister's threat. Sir Francis Shepherd considered it of the first importance that it should be countered by a brief and forthright British official statement. This, he proposed, should state that Dr Musaddiq's speech had shown that no further negotiations with the present Persian Government could produce any result. The negotiations of the Lord Privy Seal were no longer suspended but broken off. The statement would conclude, in Sir Francis Shepherd's draft: 'As regards threat to withdraw residence permits of British company employees, His Majesty's Government consider[s] this as an ultimatum with which it has no intention of complying. Any attempt made by Persian Government to evict British employees from Abadan by force would be contrary to decision of The Hague International Court.'[54]

On the same day of September 6 Sir William Strang redrafted in his own hand the statement proposed by Sir Francis Shepherd. The redraft reproduced almost verbatim the first part of the original draft, regarding the severance of negotiations. In place, however, of the last two sentences proposed by Sir Francis Shepherd, the new text read: 'As regards the threat to withdraw the residence permits of the British company employees, it is evident that any attempt made by the Persian Government to evict them would be a further breach of the interim decision of The Hague International Court.'[55] This text was approved by the Prime Minister and the statement was issued by the Foreign Office that day in that form.

In view of the critical weakening of the statement proposed by His Majesty's Ambassador in Tehran it may be worth noticing a letter which Mr Raymond Blackburn, a former Labour supporter but now Independent Member of Parliament for the Northfield Division of Birmingham, wrote on the following day of September 7 to *The Times*, where it was published on September 10. Mr Blackburn quoted the last clause of the Foreign Office statement of September 6 and compared it with the assurances given to Parliament by the Prime Minister on July 30 and by the Lord Chancellor on July 31. Mr Blackburn commented: 'Surely the Government are bound by their commitments to Parliament to add that British technicians remaining in Abadan will continue to enjoy full protection from this country.'

On the same day of September 6 on which the Foreign Office issued the British

[53] EP 1531/1532G.
[54] EP 1531/1513.
[55] EP 1531/1540.

reply to the latest Persian threat Sir Donald Fergusson asked Sir William Strang if he had any objection to, or else any comments on, a minute which Sir Donald Fergusson proposed to submit to the Minister of Fuel and Power. Sir Donald Fergusson argued that if His Majesty's Government were to contemplate a settlement, or even negotiate further, on anything like the terms on which Dr Musaddiq insisted they would, first, be jeopardising 'all other British interests and assets in nearly every country of the world'; secondly, would destroy the prospect, dear to the Americans, of investment in backward countries to combat Communism; thirdly, would 'strike a fatal blow to the authority of the International Court of Justice and the principle of the rule of international law. As I see it therefore we have not only the right but the duty in the light of the decision of The Hague Court to stay in Abadan and to use force to protect our people there and to move the oil from the tanks, paying the proceeds into an account under the jurisdiction of The Hague Court as recommended by that Court.'[56]

Sir Donald Fergusson concluded his powerful minute to Mr Noel-Baker: 'You will remember that the Prime Minister stated in Parliament quite definitely that we were going to remain at Abadan and I suggest that probably the best way of forcing the Shah to act and bring down the Musaddiq Government and avoiding the actual use of force would be to make it clear that we propose to act on the lines indicated above.' On the same day of September 6 Sir William Strang told Sir Donald Fergusson that so far as he, Sir William Strang, was concerned, he might put in his minute; and Sir William Strang sent Sir Donald Fergusson a copy of the Attorney-General's latest letter to the Foreign Secretary. The Permanent Under-Secretary of State for Foreign Affairs did not record that he gave Sir Donald Fergusson an indication of the Foreign Secretary's strongly critical reaction to that letter; or that he, Sir William Strang, made any personal comment to Sir Donald Fergusson upon his minute.

The view expressed by Sir Donald Fergusson at the end of his minute was, in substance, also advanced on the same day of September 6 by His Majesty's Ambassador in Tehran. Sir Francis Shepherd telegraphed that he thought that in delivering the proposed message to the Shah, who was, however, still absent from Tehran, 'I should explain that any attempt by the Persian Government to evict British subjects from Abadan would not only cause anger in the United Kingdom but would create a dangerous situation on the spot which might well necessitate the use of force by us . . . If it became necessary to land British troops on Persian soil this would greatly transform the existing situation both in Persia and abroad and if this were to be avoided, it was essential for steps to be taken to summon a more reasonable Government in the immediate future . . . Perhaps you or Washington could take action in support. It is most likely that the Shah may seek American advice and it is most important that we should speak with one voice in this matter.'[57]

Mr Furlonge promptly minuted, on September 6, on Sir Francis Shepherd's proposal, that without necessarily deciding whether, and in what precise circumstances, British troops should go into Abadan, 'it seems worth considering whether the argument might not be employed with the Shah in any attempt to ginger him into action. He must fear that if for any reason British troops landed in Abadan

---

[56] EP 1531/1547.
[57] EP 1015/304.

the Russians would invade Azerbaijan; and the argument might be decisive in inducing him to find the necessary resolution to dismiss Musaddiq. It could not be used with Musaddiq, as he would probably call our bluff, which the Shah would seem unlikely to do. In general I should be inclined to recommend giving Sir Francis Shepherd the authority to act as he proposes, and to do our utmost to rally the Americans in our support.'[58]

Sir William Strang discussed this cogent minute by the Head of the Eastern Department with its author. Thereafter, on September 6, the Permanent Under-Secretary minuted to the Prime Minister that he did not think it possible to go so far as Sir Francis Shepherd suggested. Sir William Strang recommended avoidance of use of the phrases 'necessitate the use of force by us' and 'necessary to land British troops on Persian soil'. He suggested that Sir Francis Shepherd should confine himself to saying that any Persian attempt to evict British subjects from Abadan would engender not only British anger but also a dangerous situation on the spot: that His Majesty's Government, as repeatedly stated, 'have a right to protect the lives of our citizens',[59] and that if such a situation was to be avoided it was essential to take prompt steps to summon a more reasonable Persian Government.

The Prime Minister minuted on this on September 7: 'I think it necessary to give Shepherd very clear instructions as to how far he may go. He appears to contemplate military action as a possibility even without danger to lives of British citizens affording the reason. We should not threaten to use force unless we mean to do so and we do not. The Shah must be perfectly alive to the possibilities of the situation. I think it would be enough to stress the obvious danger of the course Musaddiq is following and the imperative need for a change of Government.'[60] This was the written text of a message which, in a slightly variant form, Mr Attlee had dictated by telephone to Sir William Strang. Instructions in the above sense were accordingly sent to Sir Francis Shepherd in a telegram shaped by Sir William Strang on the same day of September 7. Action proposed by His Majesty's Ambassador in Tehran to counter the Persian threat to withdraw the residence permits of British subjects at Abadan had thus been significantly weakened, in relation to possible use of force, at the highest level in London in regard not only to the public British declaration but also, now to the proposed communication to the Shah.

It was on September 7, 1951, the day after Sir William Strang had minuted to Mr Attlee in the above connexion, that the Permanent Under-Secretary further minuted to the Prime Minister, with reference to the subject of the Foreign Secretary's previously noticed minute of September 5: 'Mr Morrison (who has now left for San Francisco) has instructed me to give you his view on the Attorney-General's letter. He agrees that the question whether the action could be justified as in accord with international law is important . . . On the other hand Persia is clearly ignoring international law and is ignoring an Order of The Hague Court. The law is not being observed on the other side. Consequently Mr Morrison considers that, though the legality of the action is important it is not the only aspect to be taken into account and the political aspect is highly important.'[61] It may, however, be worth noticing

---

[58] EP 1015/308.
[59] EP 1015/298G.
[60] *Ibid.*
[61] EP 1192/110G.

incidentally that Mr Emanuel Shinwell subsequently commented on the relations between Mr Morrison and Mr Attlee: 'I think it doubtful whether Morrison, even when he was Foreign Secretary, was asked for his opinion very often, and on those occasions it seldom affected the Prime Minister's decision.'[62]

On the afternoon of September 7 there was received in the Foreign Office a telegram of warning from His Majesty's Ambassador in Tehran that the British declaration in reply to Dr Musaddiq's threatening speech might possibly lead him to withdraw residence permits without further notice since some members of his Government had apparently favoured that course even before his speech. With regard to this grave warning after the operative event Sir Francis Shepherd, who had not yet received the latest telegram from the Foreign Office, commented: 'I presume that we should refuse to withdraw the remaining employees. If so we ought to be ready with an announcement. In addition to The Hague Court argument we could of course point out that . . . the Persians are attempting inexcusable confiscation . . . that forcible action by the Persian Government might oblige us to respond with force. Since this possibility would thus become more practical we should, I suppose, consider again whether the matter should be brought before the Security Council.'[63]

On September 8 Sir William Strang submitted to the Prime Minister a draft reply to Sir Francis Shepherd under cover of a minute wherein Sir William Strang reiterated the conclusion of the Working Party on Persian Oil that any retention of British staff at Abadan against Persian injunctions would have to be by British military intervention in view of the non-violent pressure, such as stopping water supplies, which the Persians could otherwise exert. The Permanent Under-Secretary continued to the Prime Minister: 'On the other hand the Working Party recognise the serious blow to British prestige throughout the Middle East if we acquiesce in a piecemeal eviction of the British staff. In this connexion, *The Times* this morning, in an article from their diplomatic correspondent, expressed the view that His Majesty's Government, in the light of the assurances already given in Parliament, should take action to secure the retention of the British staff. It has been ascertained that *The Times* are fully aware that this does not represent present governmental policy and were expressing their own view of what ought to be done in view of the outcry which they anticipate in this country if it is not. If, however, it is nevertheless decided that force cannot be used for the purpose . . . the best method of reducing the blow to British prestige' would, in the view of both the Working Party and Sir William Strang, be to meet 'an official threat or a decision by Dr Musaddiq' to evict British staff by withdrawing them all forthwith. Sir William Strang added that he did not think that the arguments against recourse to the Security Council of the United Nations, which had hitherto prevailed, 'have any less force now, and I do not think we should adopt it'.[64]

Instructions to Sir Francis Shepherd in general accordance with the above minute were embodied in the draft telegram which Sir William Strang submitted to Mr Attlee. The draft stated in particular that it did not seem practicable to refuse to withdraw the British staff from Abadan, if it came to that, 'since we are not prepared to use force. I recognise the harm that will be done to British prestige in Persia and

---

[62] Emanuel Shinwell, 'The Anatomy of Leadership', *The Sunday Times,* October 2, 1960.
[63] EP 1531/1517.
[64] *Ibid.*

elsewhere by an apparent acquiescence in the Persian Government's action, but I consider that this would on balance be less than the harm which would be caused to the United Kingdom in the international field generally if we were to resort to measures which could be represented as being contrary to the United Nations and which would be difficult to defend in international law.'

The preceding passage was one of those deleted when the telegram was recast on September 8 on the instructions of the Prime Minister. Sir Francis Shepherd was informed, instead: 'I should prefer not to anticipate course we shall pursue if Musaddiq actually withdraws residence permits or proceeds to evict company's staff in Abadan. There are so many unknown factors and I wish to base a decision on facts rather than suppositions. It is possible that your communication to the Shah may alter the situation.'[65] Once again the decision was to wait upon events rather than to formulate policy in anticipation of them. Still standing, however, was the intimation of the previous day to Sir Francis Shepherd that 'His Majesty's Government have not (repeat not)' come to a decision to employ military action at Abadan 'even when British lives are not in danger'.[66] He was now further informed: 'I do not think that a recourse to the Security Council at this stage would serve any useful purpose.'[65]

Leaving aside any theoretical possibility of some further British application to The Hague Court, since its interim injunction was unobserved and unenforced while its hearing of the substantive plea was still pending, there were five main courses still open to His Majesty's Government in the Persian dispute: first, further negotiations, direct or indirect, with the Persian Government; secondly, use of military force; thirdly, recourse to the Security Council; fourthly, acquiescence in eviction from South Persia; fifthly, securing the overthrow of the existing Persian Government. Of these five possible courses His Majesty's Government had for most practical purposes, by September 8, 1951, rejected the first three. That left only the last two, the extreme alternatives of either knuckling under to British eviction or else evicting Dr Musaddiq himself. From a diplomatic point of view this situation was excessively precarious for Great Britain, representing, indeed, a bankruptcy both of regular diplomacy and of military resource.

The chances of a change of government in Persia were considered by Sir Francis Shepherd in an important despatch of September 4, analysing the political situation there. Sir Francis recognised that 'Dr Musaddiq himself, aided by clever propaganda, has captured the imagination of the Persian people to a considerable extent . . . Unlike all other Prime Ministers since 1923, Musaddiq is not an obvious nominee of the Shah or of one or another great Power.' The frail and nationalistic Premier appealed to Persian 'sentimental mysticism' while, at the other extreme, the National Front had intimidated Deputies and Senators, who were apt to follow 'the age-old tendency of the Persians to take the line of least resistance'.[67]

On the other hand, wrote His Majesty's Ambassador, 'I believe that as a movement the National Front is largely devoid of positive content. It has not taken any firm hold on the small minority which can be said to possess any political consciousness.' Nepotism was rife and 'corruption, on a scale equal to anything in recent Persian history, is alleged against such leading figures of the National Front

---

[65] EP 1531/1517.
[66] EP 1015/304.
[67] EP 1015/305.

as Dr Fatimi and Makki'. Therefore, concluded Sir Francis, there was 'now a good prospect that the Opposition will shortly overturn the present Government'.[68] The judgment was, perhaps, somewhat stronger than the supporting evidence, and was, as Mr Furlonge noted, 'very different from Mr Grady's and Mr Rountree's'.[69]

Mr Furlonge minuted on Sir Francis Shepherd's despatch: 'It must be remembered that during the last 18 months at least, if ever there were two possible courses of events in Persia, the course less favourable to our interests was also one which eventuated; and that we have constantly been in the position of being advised to do something, or nothing, in the hopes that the situation would evolve favourably for us; and this has never occurred. It may be that this was in effect a tidal set which has been running all one way, and which in the natural course of events may at some stage turn and run the other. This, to some extent, seems to have been what happened over Azerbaijan [? in 1946]. But if not, we may eventually have to cut our losses lest worse befall.'[70] This apposite minute rather recalled Mr Furlonge's own meteorological argument, put to the Americans back in April, that Persian 'pressure behind nationalisation was more of a gust than a prevailing wind', and Mr McGhee's rejoinder that 'time had worked against the United Kingdom' (cf p. 143).

As regards pressure against Dr Musaddiq, His Majesty's Ambassador in Tehran had pointed out on September 6 that there His Majesty's Government was 'generally credited with having influenced the appointment of all Prime Ministers in Persia and my inclination is to use Sayyid Zia's known friendliness for us boldly. There seems to be no reason why in these circumstances we should cold-shoulder our friends for the sake of time-servers . . . Sayyid Zia . . . is a far better card to play against Russia than any of the old guard of politicians.'[71] On the following day the correspondent of *The Times* in Tehran on the contrary expressed the view, held by the Americans, that the public knowledge that M. Sayyid Zia was the candidate of the British Embassy was a handicap to him. A similar fear was voiced in the Foreign Office on September 10 by Mr Ernest Davies.[70]

On September 8 Mr Philip Noel-Baker had revived the by now familiar but somewhat forlorn idea, not favoured by the Foreign Office, of a coalition between M. Sayyid Zia and M. Qavam. Sir William Strang replied on September 12 in a minute to the Prime Minister copied to the Minister of Fuel and Power: 'The main objection to any association of Qavam with the new Government is undoubtedly the reputation he has for corruption and reaction, which would tend to increase the risk of the Tudeh Party extending their influence amongst the people during any such régime. We must aim not only at a solution of the oil question, but at the development in Persia of a stable and progressive régime.'[72] However desirable the latter might be as a long-term and ideological objective, yet it might seem, as regards immediate importance in that crisis, to be strictly subordinate to the former aim. But by then Sir William Strang was apparently thinking in terms not merely of a new Persian Government but of 'the new Government' of M. Sayyid Zia.

The Lord Privy Seal had written to the Foreign Secretary on September 6 to convey his views on possible political solutions in Persia (cf pp. 332, 337, 362, 366).

---

[68] *Ibid.*
[69] EP 1015/313.
[70] EP 1015/313.
[71] EP 1015/304.
[72] EP 1015/335.

Mr Stokes opined in particular that 'the Embassy in Tehran overestimates the willingness of any of the alternatives to Musaddiq to risk their neck'.[73] Mr Morrison minuted on this letter: 'Inclined to think LPS not far wrong.' The Persian Opposition had indeed on September 6 successfully played its traditional and characteristically negative gambit of preventing the attendance in the Majlis of a quorum to endorse Dr Musaddiq's latest positioning against His Majesty's Government. But two days later Sir Francis Shepherd was reporting that unless the elusive Shah returned soon from his holiday, the Opposition was 'in danger of ebbing'.[74] On September 9 Dr Musaddiq, 'jocular rather than emotional',[75] treated the Majlis to a speech wherein he boasted of his bad faith regarding the Stokes Mission, accused His Majesty's Government, perhaps understandably, of seeking to install a new Persian Government, and delivered a backhander against the Shah by alluding to talk of a Persian republic. Sir Francis Shepherd ruefully concluded that 'far from taking account of the realities of the situation, Dr Musaddiq has become more and more extremist as time goes on'.[76]

The extremist agitator, M. Kashani, had on September 7, 1951, organised a demonstration of his Fighting Muslims (Musalmanan-i-Mujahid) in Tehran 'to express solidarity with the Egyptians and abhorrence of the "colonialist" Security Council's vote in the Suez Canal dispute'.[77] The reference was to current difficulties in Anglo-Egyptian relations (cf Chapter XV, Section 1) and the adoption on September 1 by the Security Council (with Russian abstention) of a resolution calling upon Egypt to end its embargo on shipping bound for Israel (cf p. 207). M. Kashani's open-air meeting expressed both solidarity with the Egyptians and 'support for Dr Musaddiq in his struggle against British colonialist policy'. The repercussions of the conflict at Abadan were spreading in widening rings.

At Abadan and Khorramshahr crowds of Persian unemployed were by now gathering almost daily to demand work of M. Makki, who was roughly handled in a small demonstration on September 4. Major Capper suggested to Sir Francis Shepherd that this incident had value for propaganda but in the Foreign Office Mr Rothnie thought it better to leave it to the Opposition Press in Tehran.[78] There was doubtless a good deal to be said for that as for most cautious courses, but it is rather difficult not to regard it as also a small instance of habitual reluctance to exploit ruthlessly even the most favourable opportunities for propaganda, even in support of such a ruthless policy as the overthrow of the existing Persian Government. Whereas ruthless policies mildly executed are apt to be among the worst: 'willing to wound, and yet afraid to strike'.

As tension mounted at Abadan, the Persian Temporary Board there was becoming, in Mr Mason's words, 'active and aggressive'.[79] He had, for instance, been compelled to surrender to the Persians the keys of certain hangars and aircraft stores. Sir William Fraser instructed Mr Mason on September 5 to lodge a written protest but four days later the latter reported that he had not done so since if he had

---

[73] EP 1015.310.
[74] EP 1112/76.
[75] EP 1531/1521.
[76] EP 1531/1591.
[77] EP 1015/318.
[78] EP 1212/50 and EP 1531/1518.
[79] EP 1531/1494.

it would very probably have provoked Persian withdrawal of residence permits.[80] That was the Persian Sword of Damocles now suspended over the British staff at Abadan. They must obey Persian behests and even to protest was becoming too dangerous. Mr Ross, the General Manager of the Abadan Refinery, was acting similarly to Mr Mason.

His Majesty's Consul-General at Khorramshahr rather pointedly telegraphed on September 10, 1951: 'I suggest that the stage is approaching when some definite line of policy might be indicated'.[81] He considered that the Temporary Board intended to pursue their take-over of Abadan irrespective of governmental policy in Tehran. Two days later Sir William Fraser instructed Mr Mason that he should play for time and that his policy should be 'neither to comply nor defy':[82] not exactly easy. And time was running out.

On September 11 the Persian Opposition, headed by such Deputies as MM Imami, Ibtihaj and Taimurtash, published a manifesto denouncing Dr Musaddiq for having accomplished nothing in regard either to the question of oil or to the financial predicament of the country, while permitting corruption and intimidation to prevail. This was very likely, in part, a measure of British success in bracing the Persian Opposition. The declaration was regarded in the Foreign Office as 'surprisingly brave', though it was observed that it was entirely negative since no alternative policy was proposed.[83]

On the same day of September 11 Sir Francis Shepherd wrote somewhat ominously to Sir William Strang: 'The Deputies are so averse from taking anything in the nature of positive action that they may still prefer to let things slide for a little longer. If that happens the possibility of some kind of *coup d'état* becomes more likely . . . At a given moment political opinion may reach a point where it will seem quite natural for the Shah to dismiss the Government and dissolve the Majlis in which case he would seem to have little alternative except to appoint Sayyid Zia and allow him to establish a mild form of dictatorship. We must do what we can to secure a change of Government by constitutional means, but the Persian political character may lead them from sheer lack of initiative to procrastinate until the second alternative becomes inevitable.'[84] Whereas Sir Francis Shepherd had been specifically instructed on September 7, in rejection of a suggestion of his, that in making his forthcoming representation to the Shah 'you should not (repeat not) refer to the possibility of his dismissing the Majlis and ruling by decree'.[85]

British policy in regard to the Persian crisis was running into some danger of operating in a vacuum. On September 8 a paper which the Working Party on Persian Oil had tentatively drafted on an 'Approach to a New Persian Government' was remitted by Sir William Strang to the Prime Minister. This paper was drafted 'in view of the possibility that Dr Musaddiq and his Government might at any moment be dismissed by the Shah or forced to resign, and that they might be replaced by a Government headed either by Sayyid Zia or by some other more reasonable

[80] *Ibid.*
[81] EP 1531/1531.
[82] EP 1531/1542.
[83] EP 1015/312 and 321.
[84] EP 1015/324.
[85] EP 1015/304.

politician'.[86] This possibility certainly existed and might prudently be anticipated. And earlier reports from Tehran may, despite such sober appreciations as that of Mr Furlonge, have encouraged some measure of wishful thinking. But whereas the favourable possibility remained strictly contingent, the stubborn reality was the persistence of the régime of Dr Musaddiq.

No doubt further negotiation with Dr Musaddiq would, as Sir Francis Shepherd consistently represented, strengthen him and weaken the shakily reviving Opposition. A pause wherein to seek to promote the downfall of the Persian Premier might well be justified as an extreme expedient even though, if it failed, it would evidently prejudice any remaining chance of a settlement. But that failure was another possibility, however disagreeable, which the Working Party, and especially the Foreign Office, needed to envisage. Here, in the grim straits to which British policy was being reduced, it might seem to be for urgent consideration whether, even at so late and unhopeful a stage, some alternative kind of diplomatic pressure upon, or negotiation with, the Persian Government should not still be attempted, if only to buy time pending the fruition of other measures. Any further diplomatic dealing with Dr Musaddiq was indeed almost bound by now to be bad for Britain. But, in default of military resolve, it might yet be a question of diplomatically steering the least bad course which still appeared open, in order to avoid a worse outcome.

Even then it might not have been wholly impossible to seek to inject some new diplomatic or political factor to loosen the deadlock with Dr Musaddiq. For instance it might have been worth exploring the possibilities for His Majesty's Government of threatening really severe financial pressure against the Government of Dr Musaddiq; whereas a telegram of September 5 from the Foreign Office to Sir Oliver Franks explained that in issuing the Sterling Control Order it was proposed to announce that since 'the intention is to withdraw only the exceptional facilities which can no longer be justified the powers conferred by the Order will normally be exercised in such a way as to allow all transactions [by Persia] except conversions into United States dollars and the payment and receipt of sterling by Persia in respect of oil transactions'.[87]

Mr Ramsbotham later explained to Mr Serpell that it had always been felt in the Foreign Office that economic measures taken against Persia 'should not be extended to include punitive measures in the absence of a decision by Ministers to impose full economic sanctions against Persia, with all the consequences that such a decision would entail'.[88] The Prime Minister, however, appeared rather more disposed towards taking economic measures against Persia, and some consideration of their intensification might have been particularly appropriate since the chairman of the Working Party on Persian Oil was normally Mr Flett of the Treasury.

On September 4 Mr John Walker, Commercial Counsellor in Tehran, had written to Mr Flett that fortunately M. Ibrahim Zand, who was showing obstinacy in resisting Dr Musaddiq, might continue as Governor of the Persian national bank, the Bank Melli. The honest M. Zand was strongly supported by his recently appointed Vice-Governor and mentor, M. Ali Nasir. The latter now told Mr Walker that the Persian

---

[86] EP 1531/1604G.
[87] EP 1112/67.
[88] EP 11112/2.

Government was 'groping about blindly'[89] with no economic or financial plan for tiding over while it resisted an oil settlement along the lines proposed by the British. The Government harboured the illusion that it could draw freely on the Bank Melli, which was however determined to protect its own position and good name. Some days later M. Nasir further told Mr Walker that he personally readily appreciated the reasons for the Sterling Control Order and that moderate Persians like himself 'were rather surprised that we had not already taken some such action'.[90]

M. Nasir was subsequently described by the British Embassy in Tehran as 'honest, frank, very friendly and has a charming personality. He goes out of his way to keep on the best of terms with the Bank of England.'[91] Even though MM Nasir and Zand may have lacked the ultimate in backbone, yet such a singularly favourable situation for British interests at the Persian national bank might perhaps have rewarded closer attention and exploitation in that crisis than it apparently received. And while stringent British financial pressure against Persia was undoubtedly liable to arouse American opposition, yet skilful indications of the possible necessity for such action might even have proved a card in British dealings with the United States.

Another resource for British policy, which was in fact later considered (cf p. 405) might have been some adaptation of M. Sayyid Zia's recent suggestion of a temporary *modus vivendi* (cf p. 347): though that would doubtless have been much harder to achieve with Dr Musaddiq, especially if based upon the interim injunction of the International Court, for which the Working Party was still hoping, in relation to M. Sayyid Zia, in the draft paper submitted on September 8. In this connexion it might have proved profitable to take most secret soundings, such as Mr Berthoud had earlier suggested and Mr Zaehner was involved in, more particularly with the Shah—he might prove more responsive than in regard to such strong action as the dismissal of Dr Musaddiq. The British need to negotiate even under adverse conditions corresponded to her overriding need to retain a toehold at Abadan by exorcising the Persian threat to withdraw residence permits. And a temporary standstill along imaginative lines might perhaps have been easier to achieve initially than a permanent agreement, especially if ingeniously combined with economic or financial sweeteners of one kind or another. The Government of the United States would almost certainly have welcomed such a course and might really have supported it.

Intensification of British financial pressure and a strong push for an interim solution favourable to Persia and just good enough for Great Britain were doubtless only two possibilities among others. But perhaps some combination of them, or of something like them, might have stood some chance at any rate of swinging both the Shah and the Americans into putting more efficacious pressure upon Dr Musaddiq. This possibility might have been considerably strengthened if reinforced by the third expedient, still, of a broad and imaginative British approach to the Americans. This could conceivably have been tougher than anything hitherto in resolutely defending the strong British case in Persia, while at the same time being more practically generous, even in the direction of American participation at Abadan, as Mr Berthoud was already contemplating.

---

[89] EP 1112/82.
[90] EP 1112/83.
[91] EP 1051/15 of 1952.

Any such British approach to the United States would, however, have been inevitably made from a position of financial weakness. In terms of international finance the British position had been gravely deteriorating through the summer of 1951, with the loss of Persian oil as an aggravation. The gold and dollar balance of the sterling area went sliding down through 1951 from holdings of $360 million in the first quarter, to $54 million in the second, plunging into a deficit of $638 million in the third quarter which would be ending that September. The Chancellor of the Exchequer had left for talks in Washington on September 4. On September 13 a message from the Treasury to its representative with Mr Gaitskell in Washington warned that the British position regarding gold and dollars was likely to be 'even worse' during the last two quarters than Mr Gaitskell had forecast to the American Secretary of the Treasury; and even so the deficit for the third quarter was underestimated at $525 million. The Treasury feared a weakening of confidence in sterling. The telegram added: 'Present performance of oil companies suggests that rather more dollars will be spent on replacement of Abadan oil than was thought likely a little while ago.'[92]

The simultaneous presence in Washington, however, of the Chancellor of the Exchequer and the Foreign Secretary might possibly have afforded an exceptionally good opportunity for a broad and concerted approach to the American Government. Conceivably it might not have proved impossible to devise a handsome economic offer to the Americans regarding Abadan and present it in an advantageous form so as to secure not only real American support in Persia but also the prospect of some appreciable alleviation of the dollar crisis for Britain. And within the context of a concerted British policy towards both America and Persia the prospect of particular economic measures against the latter might perhaps have been employed positively as a bargaining counter instead of their being applied somewhat piecemeal as rather belated acts of retaliation.

As it was, a leakage in the British Press, notably the *Daily Telegraph,* induced the Prime Minister, in a few minutes talk with the Economic Secretary to the Treasury as guests were assembling for lunch on September 10, to instruct him to issue immediately the Sterling Control Order and Export Control Order regarding Persia.[93] That afternoon Mr Attlee told Sir William Strang 'that he was not prepared to accept the Foreign Office view and wished the requisitioning of steel rails and sugar now on their way to Persia to be effected . . . Public opinion in this country would not understand that, having made the Export Control Order, we now allowed cargoes of valuable products to reach Persia . . . He did not consider that in this instance we should be deterred by American views.'[94] Such was the overruling of cautious advice from the Foreign Office against the requisitioning of British cargoes for Persia, having regard, more particularly, to international law and to opposition from the State Department. (The Treasury had also expressed doubts.)[95] On the same day of September 10 the Prime Minister approved the stoppage by the Anglo-Iranian Oil Company of pay to Persian workers at Abadan. These economic measures were adopted before Sir Francis Shepherd had delivered the British representation to the

---

[92] UEE 7/9G.
[93] EP 1112/87.
[94] EP 1157/19.
[95] EP 1157/18.

Shah and just as the Foreign Secretary was beginning his conversations in Washington.

When consulted in advance regarding the British issue of the Sterling Control and Export Control Orders the United States Government had felt that it was a question which His Majesty's Government must decide for itself. If it felt compelled to take action, the State Department hoped that his Majesty's Government would inform the Shah in advance and in detail, and suggested that no public announcement be made so that the Persians would be left to discover for themselves the results of British administrative action.[96] The hope of the State Department was not fulfilled, and its suggestion was not adopted.

On September 10, 1951, the Foreign Secretary began his conversations in Washington. It was subsequently felt on the British side that these had brought British and American policies much closer, particularly in regard to the Middle East. 'It is clear', concluded a Foreign Office summary, 'that the Americans have now reached the conclusion that our two countries can no longer afford to pursue independent policies in the Middle East and that if the whole area is to be saved for the West, they must give us their full support in Egypt and elsewhere.'[97] That, however, only applied with reservations to Persia, though the summary recorded, a little surprisingly perhaps, that 'on Persia, the Foreign Secretary's object was not to reach decisions; that would not have been possible in a fluid and changing situation'.[98] On Persia there was what Sir Pierson Dixon, who accompanied Mr Morrison, termed 'a somewhat unsatisfactory exchange of views'.[99]

Sir Pierson Dixon recorded that 'when the Secretary of State made it plain that a serious situation would arise if the Persians were to take active steps to expel our nationals from Abadan', Mr Dean Acheson was 'discouraging'. He reiterated the standing American opposition to British military intervention in Persia except in case either of danger to British lives or of a Communist *coup* in Persia. Indeed Mr Acheson and Mr Harriman 'did not think that there was any vigorous action which could be taken without worsening the situation'. Yet in the next paragraph, headed 'The Personal Element', Sir Pierson Dixon wrote that 'so long as Mr Acheson is at the State Department, and whatever trimming of his policies he may be forced to resort to in the face of public criticism, we can feel confident that American foreign policy will be conducted by a man who understands the British position and sympathises with the British approach to international affairs'.[100]

The possible vigorous action of His Majesty's Government in Persia which the Americans scouted included not only armed intervention but also 'pressing the Shah too hard for the removal of Mussadiq'[101]: a somewhat depressing repetition, and at a much more advanced and serious stage, of previous American opposition to such a potentially important initiative (cf pp. 188-9). The State Department had already on September 7 refused a British request that Dr Grady be instructed to support Sir Francis Shepherd in his representation to the Shah for the removal of Dr Musaddiq. Instead the American Ambassador would be instructed 'to reply to the Shah if

---

[96] EP 1112/73.
[97] ZP 23/29G.
[98] *Ibid.*
[99] ZP 23/26G.
[100] ZP 23/26G.
[101] ZP 23/29G.

approached on Musaddiq's dismissal that he must decide for himself. If, however, the Shah showed an inclination to dismiss the Prime Minister he should *not* discourage him.'[102] On September 10 Mr Harriman justified this to Mr Morrison, observing that he personally felt that the instructions to Sir Francis Shepherd were likely to worsen rather than improve matters.

Mr Harriman recognised that in Persia 'we were dealing with completely unreasonable people' and 'he had reached the conclusion that it was impossible to make a deal with Musaddiq and his advisers'.[103] On the other hand 'The United States Government did not believe that matters would in fact be improved by a sudden change of government' in Persia. Mr Harriman emphasised the danger inherent in the receipt by the British and American Governments of quite different political appreciations from their Embassies in Tehran (cf p. 342), and urged closer cooperation between them. None of the Americans in Tehran and none of the Persians, including the Shah, to whom Mr Harriman had spoken, believed that M. Sayyid Zia was capable of governing.

It became clear that Mr Harriman favoured M. Qavam as a possible successor to Dr Musaddiq. Mr Harriman expressed himself to the Foreign Secretary as strongly against his including in the British message to the Shah a reference by name to M. Sayyid Zia. The Foreign Secretary telegraphed to the Foreign Office: 'This change in the message seems worth while in order not to forfeit American goodwill. This was said by Harriman in the context of the vital necessity of ourselves and the Americans marching in step in all our moves in Persia.'[104] Only it was evidently the British who were to keep in step with the Americans.

A telegram of September 11 instructed Sir Francis Shepherd as the Foreign Secretary proposed. The Lord Privy Seal, who was on holiday in Cornwall, subsequently minuted that he disagreed with the approach to the Shah in this form unless he assured Sir Francis Shepherd that he would introduce martial law. Mr Stokes held the view towards which Sir Francis Shepherd was inclining, that M. Sayyid Zia could not govern without martial law.[105] While Mr Harriman, as noticed, thought that he could not do so in any case. It was against this background of doubt that His Majesty's Ambassador on September 11 at last delivered to the Shah, only a few minutes after his return to Tehran from his inconvenient holiday, the British representation against the continued governance of Dr Musaddiq in accordance with the instructions of August 30 to Sir Francis Shepherd and subsequent modifications.

With whatever relevance to the questionably sincere proposal made by Dr Musaddiq through the Shah on August 24, the British message to the latter on September 11 stated that since the departure of the Lord Privy Seal from Tehran the Persian Premier had not only failed to put forward any constructive proposals but had been trying to represent the statement handed to Mr Stokes before he left 'as "new proposals" which called for a reply from His Majesty's Government'.[106] Sir Francis Shepherd did not mention the name of M. Sayyid Zia as a possible successor to Dr Musaddiq but the written text of the verbal message which His Majesty's Ambassador communicated, purposely in draft form, to the Shah stated: 'His

---

[102] EP 1015/307.
[103] EP 1024/1.
[104] EP 1015/309.
[105] EP 10155/335.
[106] EP 1015/332.

Majesty's Government are impressed with the disadvantages of the appointment of a reactionary Prime Minister and are convinced that the best interests of Iran would be served by the appointment of someone possessed of the will and ability to get the oil flowing again and to reach a reasonable oil settlement, and also to adopt the long-term policy of development and reform which is essential to Persia's future stability.'[107] The message concluded with what was now a retrospective, instead of premonitory, explanation of the economic measures against Persia adopted by His Majesty's Government.

Sir Francis Shepherd reported of this interview: 'The Shah was as gentle and friendly as usual but his expression while listening to the message was quite ferocious and made me think of his father. If this means anything it is a good sign.'[108] His Majesty's Ambassador, however, did not elaborate this optimistic assessment. Since the Shah showed a desire to study this delicate message Sir Francis Shepherd even went so far as to leave the draft text of it with him. As the Shah was obviously somewhat out of touch with the latest developments His Majesty's Ambassador 'thought it best to leave him to digest the message without launching into discussions'. The absence of verbal persuasion and reinforcement of the British message was perhaps unfortunate since the Shah gave Sir Francis Shepherd the impression that he doubted whether his influence would be strong enough to counter the intimidation of Deputies which Dr Musaddiq, aware of the strength of the Opposition, was apparently working up again. His Majesty's Ambassador, however, asked the Shah if he could see him again in a day or so, and proposed to arrange this.

3. American rebuffs to Dr Musaddiq and the Shah's refusal to dismiss him, September 11-17

On September 12 the Foreign Office was notified that three days earlier Dr Musaddiq had asked the Italian Ambassador in Tehran to transmit to London a message that he was prepared to negotiate an oil settlement 'in sections',[109] but apparently on terms no more favourable than before. Dr Musaddiq told Signor Cerrulli that he would be sending a communication to Mr Harriman which the latter might object to passing on to His Majesty's Government. In this letter to Mr Harriman, sent on September 12, the Persian Premier called for a resumption of negotiations upon his same old three points, terms of employment of British staff, compensation to the Anglo-Iranian Oil Company and sale of oil to His Majesty's Government. If negotiations were not resumed within 15 days of receipt of the proposal by His Majesty's Government, the Persian Government would cancel the residence-permits of the British staff in South Persia. That ultimate threat was now made in writing though the fortnight's grace was, in effect, pushed forward from September 5 by about a week.

Mr Averell Harriman commented to Sir Oliver Franks that Dr Musaddiq's letter was 'just the same old stuff'.[110] In a long reply of September 15, 1951, to the Persian Premier Mr Harriman observed: 'In some respects the [latest Persian] proposals in fact represent a retrogression from the positions taken during the discussions' in

---

[107] *Ibid.*
[108] EP 1015/315.
[109] EP 1531/1543.
[110] EP 1531/1730G.

Tehran, notably as regards Persian 'willingness to consider a long-term contract for the sale of Iranian oil to an organisation acting on behalf of former purchasers of the products'.[111] Mr Harriman pertinently reminded Dr Musaddiq as regards compensation to the Anglo-Iranian Oil Company: 'There must be more than a willingness to pay; there must be the ability to do so in an effective form', as might be ensured by suitable arrangements with Great Britain regarding oil for the future. It was considered in the Foreign Office that Mr Harriman's letter 'states so admirably many of the points which we have been making to the Persians over recent months'.[112] In conclusion Mr Harriman fulfilled Dr Musaddiq's anticipation by refusing to transmit the latter's letter to His Majesty's Government, particularly in view of the threat which it contained.

Three days earlier, on September 12, Mr McGhee had intimated that in accordance with a promise by Mr Acheson to Mr Morrison, American policy regarding the long-mooted loan to Persia by the Export-Import Bank had at last been revised. Dr Grady had informed Dr Musaddiq that it was impossible to proceed with it. The latter had expressed great indignation and had accused the Americans of applying sanctions. The Foreign Office was gratified by this 'slap in the face' for Dr Musaddiq. It perhaps suggested that His Majesty's Government's own economic measures against Persia, over which the Foreign Office had been somewhat exercised as regards American opinion, had not unduly antagonised it but possibly even the reverse.

The American withdrawal of the Export-Import Bank Loan, together with Mr Harriman's rebuff to Dr Musaddiq, were hopeful pointers towards the implementation of what was perhaps the most important statement which the Foreign Secretary had secured in Washington from the American Secretary of State: that 'the United States Government would continue to hammer home to the Persians on all possible occasions that Persia could not hope to solve the oil problem except by agreement with the United Kingdom and that they could expect no help from the United States or from anybody else unless they were prepared to cooperate with us'.[113] The difficulty subsisting with the American Government regarding possible use of force in Persia was, however, brought out again in Washington on the morning of September 14 when it came to drafting a communiqué on the general conversations held by the three Western Foreign Ministers, Mr Acheson, Mr Morrison and M. Schuman.

One sentence in the draft communiqué read: 'The three Ministers, on behalf of their Governments and peoples, restate their fidelity to the principle contained in the United Nations Charter that international differences must be resolved by peaceful processes and not by force or threat of force.' Mr Herbert Morrison reported that he had proposed an amendment 'since it occurred to me that this might prove embarrassing in the event of our wishing to resort to force in Persia. I suggested a wording which would, in fact, have been more in accordance with Article I of the Charter but both Mr Acheson and M. Schuman thought that this wording would look very weak and they clearly did not understand why I should see any objection to the existing text. Since it was impossible to explain what I had in mind before such a

---

[111] EP 1531/1594.
[112] EP 1531/1618.
[113] EP 1024/1.

large company, I eventually acquiesced in the wording of the draft.'[114]

The Foreign Secretary added in his telegram: 'I presume, in fact, that in any eventuality in which we might have to use force in Persia we should be justified by the right of inherent self-defence contained in the Charter. After agreeing to drop my suggested amendment, I brought my anxieties privately to the notice of Mr Acheson.'[115] The statement in which Mr Morrison had acquiesced, and which was published the same day could scarcely help affording some reassurance to Dr Musaddiq and, perhaps not less important just then, to the Shah, being almost the opposite of that pressure upon him regarding possible British use of force which Sir Francis Shepherd had proposed. No attempt, evidently, had been made to bring pressure to bear upon Mr Acheson by winning the support of the French Government, as might have been possible, for British military intervention in Persia, with its implications for the Middle East in general and the Suez Canal in particular. Already noticed, however, is the extent to which, in the then existing power-relationships, British policy in that area tended to play down the French factor. And in that instance it was in any case as well, perhaps, that the Foreign Secretary did not try to mobilise French support in view of the ruling which the Prime Minister had reiterated on September 7 against political employment of force in Persia by His Majesty's Government. It is not clear how far the Foreign Secretary on his travels may have been informed of this ruling to any greater extent than might be inferred from the telegrams which had been accordingly despatched from the Foreign Office to Tehran.

The wide dispersal of British Ministers during that critical September, as latterly in August, may have contributed towards somewhat disjointed counsels, if not policies, regarding Persia. From Cornwall the Lord Privy Seal on September 14 transmitted to the Prime Minister, mainly residing at Chequers, a letter which the Aga Khan, who had both British and Persian nationalities, had addressed to him four days earlier from Paris concerning the crisis. The Aga Khan argued more particularly that the 50-50 principle was in itself insufficiently attractive to Persia, having regard to the very large profits which the Anglo-Iranian Oil Company had made in earlier years, unless its assets in South Persia were made over without compensation; otherwise 'they should suggest something like 60-40'.[116] Mr Stokes thought that this chimed with his own views which, as expressed in his covering letter of September 14 to Mr Attlee, were decidedly critical of the company's high profits—Mr Stokes mentioned that Sir William Fraser had lately refused him a copy of the company's balance sheet for 1950. This balance sheet, published on November 28, 1951, in fact showed that the company's net profit for 1950, after deduction of over £50½ million for British taxation, was still nearly £34 million, as compared with £18½ million in 1949. (Compare also the earlier estimates: p. 96). This gross profit of over £84½ million was after deduction of £16 million paid to the Persian Government as royalties under the concession of 1933, as compared with about £33 million payable under the Supplemental Agreement. The difference was set aside in a special account.

The Lord Privy Seal now explained to the Prime Minister: 'Ever since I began to

---

[114] ZP 23/34G.

[115] *Ibid.*

[116] Cited, Francis Williams, *A Prime Minister Remembers* (Memoirs of Earl Attlee: London 1961), p. 253.

learn some of the facts concerning the oil business whilst I was in Tehran I have been very uneasy in my mind . . . I cannot help but feel that we are being rushed into insisting on an arrangement which is ungenerous to Iran having regard to all the facts, in order to maintain a 50-50 arrangement which may well be vital to America but is not vital to us where the cost of production is so much less.'[117]

The idea of going beyond the American 50-50 fixation in the direction of 60-40 might have had much to commend it in itself (cf pp. 301-2). In fact, however, it might perhaps be thought that it was rather Mr Stokes himself who had been rushed by the Americans, notably Mr Harriman, into tabling the abortive Eight-Point Proposals of August 13, 1951. In substance this was evidently the arrangement which Mr Stokes was now inclined to consider ungenerous to Persia in his second thoughts induced by the facts about oil which he had only learnt in Tehran. In particular, it may seem rather surprising that the Lord Privy Seal was apparently unaware that at the time at which he had made the Eight-Point Proposals, in closer concert with Mr Averell Harriman than with the Anglo-Iranian Oil Company, the latter was already to a large extent virtually in agreement with both the alternatives now proposed by the Aga Khan: namely surrender of physical assets in South Persia against little or no compensation (cf pp. 317-9), or a 60-40 split if other arrangements were satisfactory (cf pp. 301-2).

In his letter of September 14, 1951, Mr Stokes, seemingly in a critical mood during his Cornish holiday, informed the Prime Minister that 'I have *no respect* for Shepherd's judgment'. The Lord Privy Seal thought it important to realise that 'the Shah and most competent Iranians I have spoken to consider the *best* settlement can be made with Musaddiq and that it is in the best interest of their country that we should attempt it. I don't myself believe that the old gang Zia-Qavam are any use . . . . Although Zia has come out into the open, the Shah does not yet seem to be supporting him.'[118]

In Tehran on the evening of September 13, 1951, M. Sayyid Zia had launched a new National Will Party with the impeccable, if somewhat diffuse, objectives of 'everything for people and everything by people. Free speech for everybody and free thought for everybody.'[119] This revival of the Persian Opposition owed something to British stimulation at considerable financial cost. On the other side, M. Makki had temporarily returned from Abadan to help whip up a quorum for Dr Musaddiq in the Majlis; the Opposition prevented this on September 16 but did not induce the Majlis to vote against him. On the previous day Sir Francis Shepherd had telegraphed: 'I understand the Shah has authorised a member of the Court to say, on his behalf, that the next Prime Minister should be M. Sayyid Zia. The Shah still seems to be undecided as to what method to employ to get rid of Musaddiq, whose popularity he regards as a considerable difficulty. It does not seem that the Majlis will be in a position to vote against Musaddiq tomorrow, but the Opposition is confident that there will not be a quorum. In view of this and the uncertainty [as yet] about Harriman's reaction to Musaddiq's note, I have not thought it wise to nag the Shah . . . This delay is irritating but not specially dangerous, though time is getting

---

[117] Francis Williams, *A Prime Minister Remembers*, pp. 249-50.
[118] *Ibid*, p. 250.
[119] EP 1015/320.

short.'[120]

During the critical phase in Persian politics after the British representation of September 11, 1951, to the Shah, His Majesty's Ambassador, departing from his intention on that date, thus did not see His Majesty again for six days, till 5 o'clock on the afternoon of September 17. The Shah then intimated to Sir Francis Shepherd that despite Mr Harriman's rebuff and the refusal of the Majlis to constitute a quorum, Dr Musaddiq had no intention of resigning: 'instead he played upon the Shah's fears and threatened to appeal to the people over the heads of the Deputies'.[121] The Shah 'thought that Musaddiq was now desperate and was anxious to make an agreement'. He had offered to the Shah to agree to annual purchase by His Majesty's Government of 15 million tons of oil; the Purchasing Organisation would be allowed to place orders for Persian oil from any other purchasers; there could be a British general manager.

The Shah thought that these terms were very substantial advances, offering a basis for further discussions. When he suggested that His Majesty's Ambassador might accept his assurances that the new proposals were genuine, Sir Francis Shepherd replied that there was the greatest objection to His Majesty intervening in the matter. It would drag him embarrassingly into the political arena. Sir Francis Shepherd further reported that he said: 'The furthest I could go was that if Musaddiq had any new proposals he should make them to us in writing. If he did so they would of course receive consideration. I reiterated, however, that I suspected this move to be precisely the same as the other moves made by Musaddiq and it was merely designed to gain time and discourage the Opposition . . . The Shah said he would see whether Musaddiq would make the proposals in writing . . . and would let me know at once. I did not disguise my dissatisfaction with this approach and pressed the Shah as hard as I could.'[122]

His Majesty's Ambassador represented to the Shah that 'it was clear that the Opposition were only waiting word from His Majesty as to the composition of the next Government before voting this Government out. The Shah evinced scepticism on this point and said that even supporters of the two possible prime ministerial successors had spoken to him of the dangers of defeating the present Government.' Sir Francis Shepherd now advanced the claims of M. Sayyid Zia by name, arguing among other things that the Shah's own example of social reform, as in his decision in January 1951 to transfer to the peasants the Pahlevi Foundation lands, 'had not been followed and it was essential that there should be a Government which would give effect to the sort of policy which he himself had always advocated'. But the Shah said he was not in the least convinced that either M. Sayyid Zia or M. Qavam could control the situation 'and that in his position he was not entitled to take unnecessary risks'.[123]

Sir Francis Shepherd commented: 'It is clear for the moment Musaddiq has succeeded in making the Shah more frightened of encouraging a change of Government than of letting Musaddiq remain. This is most disappointing but I am doing what I can to resolve the position.'[121] But His Majesty's Government for its

---

[120] EP 1015/319G.

[121] EP 1015/325.

[122] EP 1015/333.

[123] *Ibid.*

part was evidently not frightening the irresolute Shah. The British attempt to resolve the Persian crisis in that phase by securing the fall of Dr Musaddiq had failed.

CHAPTER XIII

BRITISH REJECTION OF THE PERSIAN PROPOSALS OF
SEPTEMBER 19 AND PERSIAN ANNOUNCEMENT OF EXPULSION OF
BRITISH OIL WORKERS IN SOUTH PERSIA, SEPTEMBER 18-25, 1951

1. Political developments in Great Britain and in Persia, September 18-19

On September 18, 1951, the Oriental Counsellor in His Majesty's Embassy in Tehran, Mr L.F.L. Pyman, wrote to Mr Furlonge that three days earlier Dr Musaddiq had told a supporter in the Majlis that 'it was quite clear to him [Dr Musaddiq] that the Labour Government wished to settle this [oil] question with him personally; the affability shown by Mr Stokes on arrival proved this. The fact that Mr Stokes left with the question unsettled would not really affect the final outcome.'[1] But, the Persian Premier made out, during Mr Stokes' visit the British Labour Party had decided to hold a general election and feared that they would lose it if they had concluded an agreement with him. The Labour Government had therefore decided not to hold further negotiations till after the election, when it would come to terms with Dr Musaddiq. Mr Pyman commented that this was typical of Persian reasoning, and in the Foreign Office Mr Rothnie noted on September 22 that reports in *The Times* rather confirmed that Dr Musaddiq might be thinking that way.

On September 19 Mr Clement Attlee announced in a broadcast that a general election would be held on October 25. On September 20 *The Times* published a Financial Survey entitled The First Year of Rearmament. Headlines read: 'Wages and Prices. Breakdown of Stabilisation Policy', 'External Deficits Again. Big increase in cost of imports'. A leader in *The Times* on 'Effects of Rearmament' observed the same day: 'For Great Britain recent months have been disquieting on account of the continuous rise in prices, an internal inflation, and the grave turn in the balance of payments.' The recent visit to Washington of the Chancellor of the Exchequer had not been successful in resolving this financial predicament which, on the economic side, lay behind British policy in the Persian crisis, as did the Korean War on the military side. Mr Shinwell subsequently suggested that 'Gaitskell's forecasts of an economic decline' may have influenced Mr Attlee towards a decision to go to the country in October; though, according to Mr Shinwell, this was 'unexpected by his colleagues', and the announcement had been made despite a request from Mr Morrison and Mr Shinwell in North America that it should be delayed till they could discuss it with Mr Attlee.[2] Mr Shinwell later commented that 'in 1951 a tired Prime Minister led a tired party into a campaign which very few people in the country believed we could win'.[3]

In Tehran the political situation was described by Sir Francis Shepherd on September 19, in a somewhat ominous phrase, as 'confused and rather tense'.[4] He was not very strongly impressed by the Shah's fears of the effects of dismissing Dr Musaddiq, and commented: 'A timorous Court is of course an invitation to the use of mob pressure.'[5] The Persian Opposition was inclined to be discouraged. The

---

[1] EP 1531/1595.
[2] Emanuel Shinwell, 'The Anatomy of Leadership', *The Sunday Times*, September 25, 1960.
[3] *Ibid, The Sunday Times*, October 2, 1960.
[4] EP 1015/326.
[5] EP 1015/331.

previous day had brought the dismissal of the Governor-General of the strategic province of Azerbaijan, M. Iqbal, an anglophile who was resolutely anti-communist and equally opposed to the National Front. This dismissal, His Majesty's Ambassador subsequently reported, was 'generally regarded as another victory over the Shah for Dr Musaddiq'.[6]

In the Foreign Office Sir Roger Makins was now officiating temporarily in place of Sir William Strang, who had recently gone on holiday, while the Foreign Secretary was still absent. Sir Roger Makins minuted to the Prime Minister on September 19 that the Working Party on Persian Oil had that morning reviewed the position in Tehran. The general feeling was that it 'looked to be worse than our reports from Tehran had led us to expect, and that there was considerable risk in letting it drag on much longer in the hopes that a favourable development would occur. We had frequently done this in the past and it always got worse rather than better. On the other hand no very obvious steps to remedy the situation suggested themselves.' Further economic measures such as the freezing of sterling against Persia would, assumed Sir Roger Makins, perhaps somewhat readily, 'merely increase the risk of Persia going Communist and would thus not necessarily bring Musaddiq to heel. There therefore appeared to be nothing for it but a further approach to the Americans . . . if only to see whether they had anything constructive to suggest.'[7]

Such was the impasse which British policy towards Persia had now reached. The expert advisers of His Majesty's Government could only suggest another approach to the equivocally friendly Americans. If, as Sir Roger Makins suggested, the American viewpoint regarding Persia was 'now closer to ours than it had been for many months past',[8] yet it remained questionable what that might amount to in terms of effective support from the United States, especially since, as Sir Roger Makins reminded the Prime Minister, Mr Truman had still not seen fit to reply to Mr Attlee's urgent request for it in his personal message of August 23 to the President. If, however, His Majesty's Government could think of nothing to propose on its own account towards resolving the deadlock, the Persian Government now modified it by making the next move.

2. British rejection of the Persian Piece of Paper, September 19-22

On the evening of September 19, 1951, M. Husein Ala, the Persian Minister of Court, called on His Majesty's Ambassador and left with him a paper which, reported the latter, 'purported to be fresh proposals by the Persian Prime Minister referred to by the Shah in my conversation with him on September 17'.[9] Sir Francis Shepherd pointed out to M. Ala that this document was neither signed nor dated: on leaving M. Ala asked that the paper be regarded as being dated September 19. A subsequent examination of the original Persian text showed that it was typed on plain paper with no official marking. This became known as the Persian Piece of Paper. Dr Musaddiq subsequently explained[10] that after receiving Mr Harriman's letter of September 15 he had represented to the Shah the need for expediting a solution of

---

[6] EP 1015/345.
[7] EP 1015/325.
[8] *Ibid.*
[9] EP 1531/1580.
[10] EP 1531/1654 and 1759.

the oil question; the Shah thought that before sending an 'ultimatum' direct to His Majesty's Government an attempt should be made to find a basis for conciliatory discussions towards a settlement; the Persian Government 'had no alternative but to obey', drew up the Piece of Paper and submitted it to the Shah for private remission to Sir Francis Shepherd.

In the Piece of Paper the Persian Government gave 'the outline of its final views'.[11] Sir Francis Shepherd observed to M. Ala that they did not seem to him to constitute an advance. The three invariable subjects proposed by Dr Musaddiq for negotiation were restated under four heads: first, compensation to 'the former oil company' and claims of the Persian Government; secondly, sale of oil to His Majesty's Government; thirdly, conclusion of contracts with foreign experts; fourthly, transport of oil.

On the following day of September 20 Mr Furlonge in the Foreign Office, unlike Sir Francis Shepherd, recorded his recognition that the Piece of Paper 'admittedly hints at the acceptance of a single purchasing organisation, the omission of which in Musaddiq's letter to Harriman no doubt promoted the latter to describe Musaddiq's letter as "in some respects retrogressive". Furthermore, as regards compensation the Persian suggestion is no doubt meant to be more reasonable than their previous offers; but as Mr Harriman has pointed out, this would be of no avail unless the industry could be enabled to function effectively. It is in this respect that the document is wholly unsatisfactory, since the main retrogressive step is the new suggestion of a foreign technical adviser or liaison officer between foreign technicians and the Board of Directors. Even if this official were British (of which Sir Francis Shepherd is, no doubt rightly, suspicious) he would not even be a "General Manager".'[12]

His Majesty's Ambassador in Tehran had drawn attention to the fact that the Piece of Paper did not include either of the terms mentioned to him by the Shah regarding the annual British purchase of 15 million tons of oil, and a British general manager. M. Ala, however, told Sir Francis Shepherd verbally that he could give him an assurance on behalf of the Shah that the proposed liaison officer, described in the Piece of Paper as 'technical director of foreign nationality',[13] would be British. His Majesty's Ambassador commented: 'Musaddiq has only too obviously evaded putting this in writing and the manner in which the démarche has been made is evidence of its insincerity'.[14]

The Persian communication of September 19 stated in conclusion that the Persian Government 'is waiting to hear your views, in case you agree to the opening of negotiations on the basis of this communication, so that the said negotiations may start after the lapse of one week from the date of the transmission of this communication'.[13] Neither in the British Embassy in Tehran nor in the Foreign Office does it appear to have been remarked particularly that this term of one week, proposed on September 19, coincided closely, and perhaps ominously, with that of 15 days mentioned in Dr Musaddiq's letter of September 12 to Mr Harriman. Sir Francis Shepherd reported, however, that in remitting the Piece of Paper the Persian

---

[11] EP 1531/1584.
[12] EP 1531/1640.
[13] EP 1531/1584.
[14] EP 1531/1580.

Minister of Court 'emphasised the danger that would attend a change of government and pointed out that if this démarche were not accepted by us Musaddiq would certainly withdraw residence permits of the remaining British employees'.[14] That was now the crunch. His Majesty's Ambassador proceeded to suggest in the same telegram that he should return the Piece of Paper to M. Ala under cover of a reasoned letter of rejection.

Mr Furlonge, in his minute of September 20 on the Piece of Paper, agreed with Sir Francis Shepherd that it made 'no acceptable advance on Musaddiq's usual position'[12] and that it was probably a further manoeuvre by the latter to enable him, in the Majlis on Sunday, September 23, to discourage the opposition by suggesting that he had resumed negotiations with His Majesty's Government. 'We have therefore', wrote Mr Furlonge, 'no hesitation in recommending that the [Persian] document should be rejected as a basis for negotiations; the Treasury and Ministry of Fuel and Power agree'.[15] Sir Donald Fergusson later minuted to Mr Noel-Baker in full and retrospective support of this recommendation, more particularly having regard to Persian retrogression on the 'decisive issue'[16] of the operating management of the oil industry.

On the same day of September 20, however, Sir Oliver Franks telegraphed in very strong support of a representation from the State Department that His Majesty's Government should send no negative reply to Tehran without previous Anglo-American consultation.[17] Sir Francis Shepherd reported that on that day, also, M. Ala had given the American Chargé d'Affaires a copy of the Piece of Paper and had urged that Mr Harriman and the Government of the United States should persuade His Majesty's Government to negotiate upon it. The American Chargé d'Affaires pointed out that the document 'represented no apparent advance'. His Majesty's Ambassador very much hoped that the Americans would stand firm and 'not be stampeded by Ala's cries of alarm. Internal situation here is undoubtedly deteriorating but it will not be improved by surrender to Musaddiq.'[18]

The negative reaction which the Persian Piece of Paper evoked in the British Embassy in Tehran and in Whitehall was not shared by the Lord Privy Seal. He informed Sir Roger Makins that he did not agree with recent recommendations by the Working Party on Persian Oil, and considered that the Shah's intimations on September 17 and the Piece of Paper indicated that Dr Musaddiq had advanced a long way. Mr Stokes argued with considerable force that no settlement was possible without the Shah's backing, which had not been secured for a change of government. More questionable, perhaps, was Mr Stokes' belief that a better settlement could not be obtained from another Persian Government.[19]

The Lord Privy Seal elaborated these views on the following day of September 22 in a memorandum entitled 'Notes on Iranian Oil situation'.[20] Mr Stokes guessed that the Shah, 'who is as progressive as most labour members here', shrank from supporting either M. Sayyid Zia or M. Qavam because they 'represent all the old reactionary elements' and could not govern without martial law. Mr Stokes thought

---

[15] EP 1531/1640.
[16] EP 1531/1936.
[17] EP 1531/1588.
[18] EP 1531/1589.
[19] EP 1531/1639.
[20] EP 1531/1616.

that one should 'desist from the silly slogan that "we can't negotiate with Musaddiq".' If he had indeed made the proposals advanced by the Shah, 'we are nearly home in form'. The Lord Privy Seal considered that His Majesty's Government should put to the Shah a scheme embodying these points and based upon the Eight-Point Proposal, 'which needs redrafting into English anyway'. The Shah should be left 'to handle his own politicians. Mucking about with discredited old men who don't even begin to understand what is happening will get us nowhere.' Apparently, however, Dr Musaddiq was by implication excluded from this category of old men.

Sir Roger Makins had noted on September 21 that the views of the Lord Privy Seal were 'directly contrary' to the recommendations of the Eastern Department of the Foreign Office, in agreement with the Treasury and Ministry of Fuel and Power, in favour of rejecting the Piece of Paper. This recommendation was embodied in a draft telegram instructing Sir Francis Shepherd that he should actually strengthen the proposed wording of his letter of rejection. The draft telegram represented it as essential that Sir Francis Shepherd should not, as he had proposed, specify the suggestions put to him by the Shah but not included in the Piece of Paper, 'in order to avoid giving the impression that had these been included the document might have been acceptable as a basis . . . Paragraph 3 of your draft should be strengthened in order to make it clear to the Shah that (except in the unlikely event of a complete change of heart on the part of Musaddiq) His Majesty's Government are not prepared to envisage negotiations with him.'[21] Sir Francis Shepherd was informed, however, that it seemed doubtful whether it was advisable actually to return the Persian document to M. Ala; though this was left to the discretion of His Majesty's Ambassador.

It was apparently Sir Roger Makins who first advanced the grave consideration that if the course indicated in the draft telegram to Sir Francis Shepherd was adopted, 'we shall be forcing the issue. Either Musaddiq will fall, which on present evidence seems doubtful, or we shall be inviting an ultimatum, and the government will at once be faced with the decision to withdraw from Abadan or to stay there by force.'[22] Sir Roger Makins advised that Ministerial discussion was necessary before Sir Francis Shepherd acted, and referred to the question of ascertaining American views. The latter point was alluded to by Sir Francis Shepherd in a personal telegram, received in the Foreign Office at one o'clock on the afternoon of September 21, wherein he also transmitted the following important information: 'The Shah has now sent me a message that he is convinced of the need of getting rid of Musaddiq and is now only concerned as to how best it can be done.'[23]

Sir Francis Shepherd telegraphed, in continuation, that his delicate and difficult task was almost impossible if the Americans insisted upon high level consultation at every step. He was fully convinced that the Persian overture of September 19 'should be summarily rejected and I do not think we should give it exaggerated importance by consulting the Americans about it'.[24] His Majesty's Ambassador in Tehran had indeed had much to endure from the Americans, but this advice would suggest that

---

[21] EP 1531/1581.
[22] EP 1531/1639.
[23] EP 1531/1633G.
[24] *Ibid.*

the potential gravity of a British rejection of the Piece of Paper was not so fully apparent to him as it was to Sir Roger Makins and, probably, to others.

On that morning of September 21 *The Times* had opined in a leader that the attitude of Dr Musaddiq made a serious Persian offer on oil unlikely. It was argued that His Majesty's Government now needed to determine urgently and precisely the action necessary to prevent a Persian expulsion of the residual British staff at Abadan. Mr Attlee's parliamentary statement of July 30 was again recalled, together with Lord Jowitt's acceptance next day of its implications on behalf of His Majesty's Government. 'One "implication"', noted *The Times*, 'is inevitably the use of force . . . To use force would not be in any way a solution; but it would register—for the attention of all, in Persia, or outside—the British determination, once the process of negotiation is halted, not to surrender interests in face of plain threats.'

Both in *The Times* and in Whitehall there was some canvassing of the idea that the Government should seek to agree with the opposition to exclude Persia as an electoral issue. Mr Kenneth Younger minuted on this suggestion: 'I am afraid I consider this a non-starter. Our Middle East policy has been the main target of Tory criticism, and the Foreign Secretary has replied by accusing the Tory back benchers of trying to start up two wars! Personally I don't think election nonsense will have much effect on either of these issues [Persia or Egypt] unless the Prime Minister or Foreign Secretary or Mr Churchill or Mr Eden personally say things which would subsequently tie their hands. Surely they can be left to look after that aspect of things themselves.'[25]

Mr Younger on September 21 discussed with Sir Roger Makins the latter's minute of that day regarding the Piece of Paper and subsequently rang up the Prime Minister, who was attending the Scottish Labour Party Conference at North Berwick. Mr Younger explained to him the existing position, including indications received from the Shah and the Persian Embassy in London of their attitude, and 'emphasised the importance of keeping in line with the Americans'.[26] The Prime Minister agreed that, subject to advice from Washington, Sir Francis Shepherd should be instructed as proposed by the Foreign Office. In particular, recorded Mr Younger, Mr Attlee 'felt that it was impossible to reopen conversations on the basis of a document produced in this hole-and-corner manner without authentication'. He agreed with Mr Younger that the latter should hold a meeting with Mr Philip Noel-Baker and the dissenting Mr Stokes. The Prime Minister told Mr Younger that 'he was not disposed to share the Lord Privy Seal's optimism about the possibility of doing a deal with Musdaddiq, having previously got rid of the extremists around him'.[27]

The Prime Minister informed the Minister of State in the Foreign Office that it might, without further reference to Mr Attlee, instruct Sir Francis Shepherd, as proposed, to reject the Piece of Paper, provided the Americans agreed. The previously drafted telegram of instructions to Sir Francis Shepherd was despatched at 9 pm on September 21, but with a concluding injunction that he should suspend action on it pending further instructions in relation to consultation with the American Government.[28] He was referred to a telegram of even date to Sir Oliver Franks,

---

[25] EP 1531/1642.
[26] EP 1531/1624.
[27] *Ibid.*
[28] EP 1531/1581.

agreeing to await the reactions of the State Department. In view, however, of the suspected manoeuvre of Dr Musaddiq with regard to the meeting of the Majlis on September 23, it was considered most important for Sir Francis Shepherd to act before that date. It was hoped that, for the reasons which appeared to be appreciated by the American Chargé d'Affaires in Tehran, the State Department would not suggest anything but rejection of the Persian approach of September 19.[29]

On the evening of September 21 Sir Oliver Franks had a long talk at the State Department with Mr McGhee, who on the previous day had briefly intimated to Mr Herbert Morrison, at a session at Ottawa of the North Atlantic Treaty Organisation, that if Dr Musaddiq made some new proposal he, Mr McGhee, 'hoped we should not be too rigid but would play along with him.'[30] Mr McGhee now informed Sir Oliver Franks that, in conversation with the American Chargé d'Affaires in Tehran, 'Ala had said that he was confident that Musaddiq would be willing to send negotiators with full powers to London. Mr McGhee said that this possibility had also been mentioned to His Majesty's Embassy at Tehran in conversation by a court official.'[31]

Mr McGhee then handed His Majesty's Ambassador a paper explaining the views of the State Department. This began by urging that if the Persians confirmed their offer to send a delegation with full powers to London, His Majesty's Government should agree to receive it. If considered useful, Mr Harriman would be prepared to come to London during the negotiations. The memorandum observed: 'While it does not appear that specific terms of the present [Persian] proposal would be acceptable to the British, we do not believe that this is necessarily a reason for rejecting the Persian overture . . . Musaddiq apparently is anxious to reach an agreement . . . We believe it highly advisable for the British to remain in a negotiating posture, and fear that negative reaction to present developments may make a settlement impossible, at least for a long time to come. We realise there is a possibility that resumption of discussions may assist Musaddiq in remaining in office, but summary rejection of his offer might strengthen his Government . . . He could then place complete blame for failure to reach a settlement on the British . . . We attach great importance to the Shah's attitude in this matter and believe that since the present approach is fully backed by him it should be given considerably more weight than otherwise.'[32]

Mr McGhee proceeded to explain to Sir Oliver Franks that 'the State Department had, as we knew, shared our views that it was hopeless to negotiate with Musaddiq. They were n[o]w convinced, however, that the Shah would not dismiss Musaddiq; they were nervous of what might in any case happen after he went . . . There was a chance of Musaddiq yielding to pressure and being ready to negotiate constructively . . . We were not far from a basis for settlement except on the question of the profits split.'[33] Mr McGhee wondered whether, instead of returning a negative reply in writing to the Persian proposals, His Majesty's Government could not concentrate its reply on the more favourable aspects of what the Persians had said to British and American representatives in Tehran.

---

[29] EP 1531/1588.
[30] EP 1015/336.
[31] EP 1531/1598.
[32] EP 1531/1599.
[33] EP 1531/1598.

The gist of Sir Oliver Franks' reply to Mr McGhee was that, in order to prevent Dr Musaddiq claiming in the Majlis to be negotiating again with His Majesty's Government on the basis of the Piece of Paper, a written reply pointing out its inadequacy must be sent at once. His Majesty's Ambassador further reported for the Foreign Secretary that he had argued to Mr McGhee: 'You would be surprised at the rapid change of front on the American side on the possibility of negotiating with Musaddiq at all. We had been let down by him so often, when he had made statements in conversation which he had later quite failed to fulfil, that you would need something very definite to convince you that he had really changed his spots. The various remarks made hitherto in conversations were inadequate.'[32]

Sir Oliver Franks observed to Mr McGhee that nevertheless the Persian offer to send a mission to London 'seemed a new factor of some importance'. There ensued a somewhat speculative discussion, wherein 'McGhee was trying to force the pace', regarding the assurances which His Majesty's Government might require before being willing to accept such a mission. In accordance with an assurance which he had given to Mr McGhee during this conversation, His Majesty's Ambassador concluded his report of it with the following recommendation: 'I realise the difficulty for you in accepting any possibility of negotiation without a change of Government, nevertheless, since it now seems that this may not take place as soon as we had hoped owing to the Shah's nervousness, and in order to keep the Americans firmly with us, I recommend that we should, while replying on the lines of your present instructions to Ala's Piece of Paper, at the same time by constructive verbal remarks leave the door open for the development of the possibility of new and more realistic proposals. We shall have achieved our immediate object of preventing Musaddiq saying that he is in negotiation. Moreover if it all comes to nothing and the Persians fail to firm up on their remarks to us and the Americans, we shall have lost nothing; and if it does come to something, we may have gained a great deal.'[34]

On September 22, 1951, Mr Furlonge minuted on this message from Sir Oliver Franks that the attitude of the State Department was to some extent based upon misapprehensions. On the technical side, Mr McGhee was wrong in supposing that the main difficulty with the Persians was the question of splitting profits from oil, though it was a major one. The main difficulty concerned the functions of British technicians, upon which the Persian proposals were quite inadequate. More importantly, Sir Francis Shepherd had not reported a Persian offer to send a delegation to London. From what had been gathered from the Embassy of the United States in London, it was more probably that the American Embassy in Tehran had suggested this course to M. Ala, who said he would think about it. It was not until September 25, in a Saving telegram received in the Foreign Office two days later, that Sir Francis Shepherd reported the important fact that there had been some talk in Tehran of the possibility that the next time Anglo-Persian negotiations took place it should be in London, and that in the previous week this had been mentioned to Mr Middleton by M. Human of the Persian court. This suggestion had, however, been 'apparently contingent'[35] upon British acceptance of the Piece of Paper as a basis for negotiations and therefore had not been resumed.

The result was that as regards the muffled suggestion of a Persian mission to

---

[34] EP 1531/1599.
[35] EP 1531/1645.

London the Foreign Office was apparently, if anything, under more of a misapprehension than the State Department. The most important, however, of the misapprehensions attributed by Mr Furlonge to the State Department was that the Shah was unwilling to dismiss Dr Musaddiq; whereas his message to Sir Francis Shepherd, reported by the latter on September 21, showed, wrote Mr Furlonge, that the 'Shah is determined to do just this'.[36] This view was not shared by the Lord Privy Seal.

It was in the office of the Lord Privy Seal that a meeting was held on the morning of September 22, 1951, in London in order to decide what reply should be returned to the Persian proposals of September 19. The meeting was also attended by the Minister of Fuel and Power and the Minister of State in the Foreign Office; the Treasury too was represented.[37] It is suggestive not only of the urgency and delicacy of the consultation but also, perhaps, of some procedural relaxation in the absence of both the Foreign Secretary and the Permanent Under-Secretary that no minute of this critical meeting, held by Mr Stokes, is apparently preserved in the Foreign Office. It is from the minute of a meeting of the Cabinet Committee on Persia three days later, on September 25, that one learns, from an observation there by Mr Stokes, that at the meeting on September 22 'he had made it clear that in his view, it was most unlikely that the message [to Sir Francis Shepherd regarding the dismissal of Dr Musaddiq] would prove to give a correct account of the Shah's intentions'.[38] This was confirmed by Mr Stokes in a letter of October 3 to Mr Morrison.

Mr Furlonge went to the heart of the matter on September 25 in commenting that delicate political issues in Tehran could not be handled beyond a certain point from London; the Foreign Office must in general be guided by the advice of His Majesty's Ambassador in Tehran so long as he remained there, which in itself presupposed that the Foreign Office had full confidence in him.[39] The Foreign Office felt obliged to maintain that confidence whereas the Lord Privy Seal no longer shared it. The view of the Foreign Office nevertheless prevailed at the meeting in Mr Stokes' office on September 22. A broadcast that morning by Tehran radio that Dr Musaddiq had put forward new proposals to His Majesty's Government seemed to confirm the suspicions entertained both in the Foreign Office and in His Majesty's Embassy in Tehran that they represented an insincere and tactical manoeuvre for purposes of Persian internal politics.

It was in the light of the Shah's message to Sir Francis Shepherd regarding the dismissal of his Prime Minister, 'which appeared to alter the basis on which the American advice had been given',[40] that the interdepartmental meeting on September 22 decided to ignore that advice. Sir Francis Shepherd was instructed that afternoon to deliver to M. Ala his written communication, as previously agreed, in rejection of the Persian Piece of Paper. Nor was he to accompany it with any constructive oral communication such as Sir Oliver Franks had proposed. His Majesty's Ambassador was, however, to inform the Shah at the same time, if possible by personal contact, that 'we were anxious to anything possible which would assist him in getting rid of Dr Musaddiq and are ready at any moment to

---

[36] EP 16531/1736.
[37] EP 1531/1649G and 1827.
[38] EP 1531/1649G.
[39] EP 1531/1644.
[40] EP 1531/1598.

consider proposals for a settlement from a Government which is sincerely anxious to find a solution and in which the Shah has confidence. To this end we should be prepared to consider any suggestions which His Majesty might personally wish to make.'[41]

At the same time, in reply to the Persian broadcast on the morning of September 22, the following official statement, approved by Mr Noel-Baker, Mr Stokes and, subsequently, Mr Younger, was issued and put out over the Persian service of the BBC: 'His Majesty's Government have received a further communication from Dr Musaddiq, which, however, constitutes no advance on his previous attitude and does not provide any basis on which negotiations should be resumed. The Persian Government are being so informed.' That Government reacted, in a broadcast of September 23 by M. Fatimi, by denying that Dr Musaddiq had sent any note, and announcing that in view of the failure of its endeavour 'to create, by indirect means, an atmosphere of mutual good understanding . . . it has now been decided to take direct action'.[42] M. Fatimi then referred to 'the expulsion of British technicians'. His tone rather suggested that the British rejection of the Piece of Paper may not have come amiss to Dr Musaddiq who, in accordance with British suspicions, may not have sincerely wished to associate himself with the Shah's initiative towards further soundings.

On September 24 Mr Stokes wrote to Mr Younger that he did not object to the telegram sent to Sir Francis Shepherd as a result of the meeting two days earlier but, he continued, 'I simply cannot understand why people will insist on the phrase "getting rid of Musaddiq"'. He, unlike his entourage, was, in the opinion of the Lord Privy Seal, 'quite tractable'.[43] On the following day the Ministerial Committee on Persia directed that Sir Francis Shepherd should be asked as to the channelling and estimated significance of the critical message from the Shah which had promoted the British rejection of the Piece of Paper but had not convinced the Lord Privy Seal. His Majesty's Ambassador replied on September 26 that the message had reached him through M. Perron, the Shah's Swiss private secretary, and Mr Zaehner. Sir Francis Shepherd added: 'I am sure it is perfectly genuine and represents the Shah's view. As the message indicated, the Shah is still perplexed about how to get rid of Musaddiq, and I think he is much influenced by Ala who wants to exhaust every chance of revising (? resuming) negotiations with Musaddiq. The Shah of course clutches at every straw to postpone or avoid action, and he is much afraid of the consequences'[44] (cf pp. 160-1).

This not very reassuring gloss upon the earlier message was to appear, if anything, still less so in the light of a despatch which Sir Francis Shepherd had sent on the previous day (cf p. 382); this, and subsequent developments, went far towards justifying Mr Stokes' scepticism of it, even if his opinion of Dr Musaddiq's tractability was wide of the mark. If such importance was going to be attached in the first place to the brief and unelaborated message from the Shah it might perhaps have been preferable to have checked back on it before rather than after basing a critical decision to a considerable extent upon it. This decision to break with Dr Musaddiq,

---

[41] *Ibid.*
[42] EP 1531/1612.
[43] EP 1531/1641.
[44] EP 1015/341.

without making the most strenuous attempt to throw the responsibility for a rupture back upon the Persians, represented a serious departure from the position of the Foreign Office a month earlier at the close of Mr Stokes' mission to Tehran (cf p. 325). The present decision was taken at a meeting whereat Mr Stokes was the only Cabinet Minister present, after telephone consultation of the Prime Minister, who had authorised such a course without further reference to him provided that the Americans agreed with it. But they had opposed it. There is no record, however, that Mr Attlee was consulted again before the critical decision to reject the Piece of Paper was implemented. Such further consultation may or may not have taken place.

On September 22 a member of His Majesty's Embassy in Washington explained to Mr Rountree, in the absence of Mr McGhee, the British rejection of the latest Persian overture. Mr Rountree regarded the critical message from the Shah to Sir Francis Shepherd as 'not significantly new'. Mr Rountree said that the 'State Department would be greatly disappointed at our action, which he interpreted as a flat rejection'[45] of the Persian approach. Mr Furlonge subsequently minuted in this connexion that Mr Rountree's attitude was, however, well known and that there was no special reason to believe that the State Department as a whole, and particularly Mr Acheson, shared his somewhat defeatist attitude.[46] Events were nevertheless to indicate that this important issue of the rejection of the Persian proposals of September 19 had to a considerable extent now come between the British and American Governments.

3. Deterioration in Persia and the Persian announcement of expulsion of British oil workers in South Persia, September 22-25

On September 22, 1951, the Head of the Eastern Department of the Foreign Office minuted: 'The Prime Minister is understood to have informed the Minister of Fuel and Power that he wished the Working Party to prepare a detailed survey of the question of the line to be adopted once a more reasonable Persian Government was in the saddle.'[47] That an instruction from the Prime Minister upon so important a question of foreign policy should apparently only have come indirectly to the knowledge of the competent department of the Foreign Office is perhaps one illustration of the disadvantage of both the Foreign Secretary and the Permanent Under-Secretary being absent at a critical time; and also, perhaps, of a tendency for questions with a grave political bearing to be treated too much in terms of economics, however important those might be in themselves, in the Working Party on Persian Oil under the chairmanship of the Treasury.

On the previous day of September 21 the Working Party had accordingly produced a revised and expanded version of its draft paper of September 8 on an 'Approach to a New Persian Government'. The Working Party advised that one should first negotiate with a new Persian Prime Minister for a temporary *modus vivendi* regarding oil, somewhat as M. Sayyid Zia had himself suggested. In considering what form such a *modus vivendi* might take the Working Party noted that 'there is a growing difference of view between His Majesty's Government and the [Anglo-Iranian Oil] Company on a number of important issues in respect of the

---

[45] EP 1531/1606.
[46] EP 1531/1644.
[47] EP 1531/1604G.

political and commercial aspects of the problem. The Board of AIOC is becoming restless',[48] apparently fearing that His Majesty's Government might make an agreement with Persia which the Board would consider to be unworkable, unacceptable to the British staff and commercially unattractive.

There was active awareness in the Foreign Office of the resentment at the top of the Anglo-Iranian Oil Company regarding its subordinate role in the negotiations of the Lord Privy Seal. Sir Roger Makins echoed a representation from Mr Victor Butler of the Ministry of Fuel and Power in minuting on September 26 to the Prime Minister: 'We feel that there is a risk of losing sight of the necessity of bringing the Company, and its staff, along with us in any negotiations which are undertaken.'[49] Sir Roger Makins supported a suggestion by the Working Party for early discussions at a high level between the Government and the Company. Some days previously Mr Furlonge had commented: 'All this . . . ties up with the question of Sir William Fraser's position. If it is decided to take steps to secure his retirement (for which the present time may not be wholly suitable) it might be easier to keep the Company in closer touch with whatever negotiations are begun.'[50] Mr Bowker agreed. But it was in any case too late now to do anything effective regarding the position of Sir William Fraser before the swiftly developing crisis reached its culmination.

Mr Furlonge, whose minuting in that critical month of September usually attained a high order of clarity, commented on the Working Party's contingent study of September 21: 'The Lord Privy Seal is likely to take the line, as he already has on the earlier paper, that the Working Party are indulging in wishful thinking.'[49] Next day, September 23, Mr Furlonge did not specifically mention Mr Stokes in writing to Sir Francis Shepherd that it would be helpful to have any additional ammunition to counter criticism that the policy of backing M. Sayyid Zia to supplant Dr Musaddiq rested upon wishful thinking because the Shah would not bring himself to impose M. Sayyid Zia, because even if the latter did attain office he would lack sufficient popular support, and because he would not in any case be able to offer better terms than Dr Musaddiq.[51]

Meantime the British Embassy in Tehran continued to run the criticised policy. On September 20 Sir Francis Shepherd had sent the Foreign Office material for a talk on the Persian Service of the BBC on the lines that Dr Musaddiq had lost support in Persia: 'the people and particularly the Senate and the Majlis are only waiting for a sign from the Shah to end this period of false promises and illusions'.[52] It was only after His Majesty's Ambassador had complained on September 24 that this had not been used that he was informed from the Foreign Office that doubts had been entertained regarding the propriety of such a public hint to the Shah, especially since the BBC 'felt that they could not successfully put over the line that the text represented the views of neutral and impartial sources'.[53]

Sir Francis Shepherd complained in a letter of September 26 to Mr Bowker that this reply was disappointing since abnormal times demanded unusual measures; and also that an adapted broadcast which had been given the day before had concluded

[48] EP 1531/1610.
[49] EP 1531/1604G.
[50] EP 1531/1695.
[51] EP 1531/1624.
[52] PB 1048/52.
[53] PB 1048/57.

with a suggestion that there were still hopes in London of some sort of arrangement with Dr Musaddiq through the good offices of Mr Harriman: this was 'of course damaging and unhelpful'.[54] On the other hand Mr Barclay had written two days earlier to the Press Attaché at Tehran: 'We are anxious not to give colour to the idea which I am afraid is spreading throughout the world that the BBC is the official mouthpiece of His Majesty's Government. The BBC is by its charter independent, and is very jealous of this.' Though its overseas services were amenable to guidance from the Foreign Office, 'we must hide this from the outside world as much as possible'.[55]

Mr Scott replied to Mr Barclay that in Tehran the BBC was indeed regarded as the mouthpiece of His Majesty's Government and that it was precisely its success which gave its mistakes enormous importance. 'On the whole . . . the BBC has done a good job for Britain in this country. Had they shown more readiness to respond to advice they would have done a better.'[56] The independence of the monopolistic BBC, though it might on occasions be adapted by agreement in the overseas services, was, as the Foreign Office appreciated, a precious extension of British freedom of the Press. One can, however, also understand the feeling in the hard-pressed Embassy in Tehran that in an acute crisis this freedom could be purchased at a high price in terms of the national interest abroad.

At Abadan itself the crisis deepened and darkened. The piecemeal surrender of British interests to Persian authorities at Abadan necessarily exercised a debilitating influence upon British personnel. On September 21 the Senior Naval Officer, Persian Gulf, asked the Admiralty for the fullest publicity to counter misunderstandings regarding the intentions and obligations of British warships at Abadan. It should be explained, in particular, that the risk of a serious incident affecting British lives did not justify the use of force to prevent the Persians removing miscellaneous craft of the Anglo-Iranian Oil Company which were not wearing the Red Ensign 'and which present similar case to other item[s] of company property such as aeroplanes, cars, houses, etc, already requisitioned by Temporary Board'.[57] Thus is compliance apt to breed compliance (the Law of Let Go). With the return to Abadan of M. Makki the general situation deteriorated further. Power was passing from the Anglo-Iranian Oil Company to the National Iranian Oil Company.

The long-suffering Mr Mason telegraphed from Abadan on September 23, 1951, that if his British staff was asked to stay on indefinitely they must be given 'a more specific call'[58] to raise their spirits and provide a clear objective. He envisaged the possibility of a policy of passive resistance, with the British technicians leaving their jobs to sit in their houses. This interesting idea was in response to an intimation from the Persian Temporary Board to the Anglo-Iranian Oil Company that British personnel working in departments from which it had laid off Persians would be deprived of their houses and all amenities. So the Persian game of cat and mouse with the humiliated British as mice, as Mr Mason had earlier remarked (cf p. 292), went on at Abadan.

Next day, September 24, His Majesty's Consul-General at Khorramshahr

---

[54] PB 1048/70.
[55] PG 13452/3.
[56] *Ibid.*
[57] EP 1212/51.
[58] EP 1531/1570.

reported that a Persian take-over of the Communications, Transport and Shipping Departments of the Anglo-Iranian Oil Company at Abadan would render the execution of Operation Buccaneer more difficult.[59] It was all very well for Sir William Fraser to adjure Mr Mason, as he did on September 25: 'While we do not wish you to adopt a provocative attitude . . . we must not hand over any control voluntarily'.[60] Mr Mason, in his very difficult and exposed position, may on occasion have been at fault in the extent of his compliance with Persian instructions; but the distinction between voluntary and involuntary surrender might seem to be becoming somewhat academic for the British staff at Abadan, deprived of resolute succour and support, whether military or diplomatic. On September 24, following the British rejection of the Persian proposals of September 19, a spokesman of the Persian Government said that it regarded negotiations with his Majesty's Government as being definitely broken off.[61]

On September 25, 1951, Sir Francis Shepherd reported in a despatch received in the Foreign Office two days later: 'The situation has become still further confused owing [to] the vacillation of the Shah. It is known that while not liking Musaddiq he is afraid to get rid of him.' The dismissal of M. Iqbal, a friend of the Shah, and 'the sudden departure for Europe of his twin-sister, Princess Ashraf, against whose interference in politics Dr Musaddiq is known recently to have protested, have contributed to the impression that the Shah is no longer able to stand up to Dr Musaddiq'.[62] His Majesty's Ambassador did not comment upon this negation of his report of four days earlier which had critically promoted the British rejection of the Piece of Paper by suggesting that the Shah intended to dismiss Dr Musaddiq. It was only on September 26, the day after the despatch cited above, that Sir Francis Shepherd transmitted the not very reassuring explanation (cf p. 378) of his message of September 21.

Sir Francis further reported in his despatch of September 25 that since the Shah was thought to believe that there was too great a risk in replacing Dr Musaddiq by the anglophile M. Sayyid Zia, the latter had informed his sovereign that he did not wish necessarily to be regarded as a candidate for the immediate succession to the Premiership. This had further confused matters, giving new hope to the partisans of M. Qavam-es-Sultaneh, who had made it clear that he was very much a candidate, and of M. Husein Ala. The British protégé in Persian politics had bent till he became a broken reed. Mr Furlonge subsequently minuted on Sir Francis Shepherd's despatch: 'the final collapse of the S.Z. policy.' Mr Bowker added: 'I fear Mr Furlonge is right'.[63]

The policy of promoting M. Sayyid Zia against Dr Musaddiq had proved unsuccessful. The doubts about it expressed by the Lord Privy Seal and by the State Department had been justified. Sir Francis Shepherd reported at the same time that the decree for fresh elections to the Majlis had been issued. The two Prime Ministers in that Anglo-Persian crisis, Mr Attlee and Dr Musaddiq, were both seeking fresh mandates from their electorates. And on the afternoon of September 25, 1951, the Persian Government announced that it had instructed the Temporary Board at

---

[59] EP 1192/114G.
[60] EP 1531/1621.
[61] EP 15531/1620.
[62] EP 1015/346.
[63] *Ibid.*

Abadan to inform British technicians that, since they had refused to serve the National Iranian Oil Company, they must leave Persia within one week from Thursday morning, September 27. Their residence-permits would be withdrawn. At last the Persian cat had pounced.

CHAPTER XIV

BRITISH APPEAL TO THE UNITED NATIONS AND RELINQUISHMENT OF ABADAN, SEPTEMBER 25-OCTOBER 4, 1951

1. The Prime Minister's exchange with President Truman and the decisions of the British Cabinet, September 25-27

Shortly after the Persian announcement of the intended expulsion of British oil workers from South Persia, at 5.30 pm on the afternoon of September 25, 1951, Mr Attlee presided over the 22nd meeting of the Ministerial Committee on Persia at No. 10, Downing Street. Other Ministers present were Mr Gaitskell, Mr Stokes, Mr Noel-Baker and Mr Ernest Davies. Representatives of the Chiefs of Staff were in attendance together with high officials, Sir Roger Makins and Mr Bowker from the Foreign Office, Sir Leslie Rowan and Mr Serpell from the Treasury. In the face of the latest Persian move the meeting evidently recognised the heavy import of having relied, evidently in error, upon the Shah's message of September 21 regarding the dismissal of Dr Musaddiq.

The Committee on Persia once again went over the well-worn pros and cons of British military action at Abadan. The Chief of the Imperial General Staff confirmed that 'with the naval and air support available it should be possible for the Buccaneer force to get ashore and dominate Abadan'.[1] On his advice it was decided that force should forthwith be brought forward to the shortest possible notice. The Prime Minister, however, enjoined that no action be taken which would prejudice the decision of the Cabinet which was to meet on Thursday, September 27. It alone could authorise military action in Persia for any purpose other than the protection of British lives.

Meanwhile His Majesty's Ambassador in Tehran was forthwith instructed on September 25 to make representations to the Persian Foreign Minister against the latest Persian decision and to warn him that 'His Majesty's Government reserves full liberty of action'.[2] Sir Francis Shepherd was also to deliver to the Shah an oral message from Mr Attlee. The Prime Minister expressed understanding of the Shah's previous hesitation to intervene, 'but he must appreciate that a political situation has now arisen which he alone can redress, and that if he does not act now the situation may well be beyond his or our power to control or repair. I therefore trust that he will take immediate action to ensure that the expulsion measures against the company's staff are not carried out.'[3]

At the same time Mr Attlee sent a further personal message to Mr Truman, who had still vouchsafed no reply to his previous appeal of August 23. The Prime Minister represented to the President: 'To submit to an eviction of British staff would in the view of His Majesty's Government have the gravest consequences not only for the United Kingdom interests in Persia, but for United States as well as United Kingdom interests throughout the Middle East. Further it would represent a blow to British, and I believe to Western, influence and prestige in an area which, as we have both recognised, is a weak spot in our containment wall . . . On the other hand, for

---

[1] EP 1531/1649G.
[2] EP 1531/1619.
[3] *Ibid.*

His Majesty's Government to seek to maintain the British staff in Abadan by armed intervention would clearly run serious risks, quite apart from its legal aspect. You will appreciate, however, that public opinion in this country will find it difficult to understand why a decision of The Hague Court cannot be enforced and its violation by the Persian Government prevented.'[4]

On the crucial issue, this message, which was drafted in the Foreign Office and approved by the Prime Minister, thus did not ask for American support for British armed intervention at Abadan. Nor did it seek to extract from Mr Truman a really strong and effective measure of diplomatic support by threatening such British intervention as a likely alternative. On the contrary, such a possibility, though raised, was rather diffidently scouted. Mr Attlee concluded with an appeal that the United States Government should 'stand firmly with us in opposition to this [Persian] procedure by ultimatum and that your representative in Tehran will be instructed to associate himself with the representations which Sir Francis Shepherd is making. I am sure that the only chance of preventing grave damage to the interests of both our countries and to the long-term interests of Persia itself lies in our taking firm joint action and letting the world know that we are doing so.'[5]

Already on the afternoon of September 25 the British Embassy in Washington had received a call to the State Department from Mr Rountree. He said, in particular, that the American Administration appreciated that His Majesty's Government might need to take very quick decisions but '"expected to be consulted" before there was any decision to use force against the Persians outside the present understanding, which was that we should employ it only to save British lives in danger'.[6] The Foreign Office replied that the Americans were being consulted but that Sir Oliver Franks might have an opportunity of mentioning to Mr Dean Acheson that it took 'strong exception to being given a message in such terms by a junior State Department official'.[7]

Sir Oliver Franks had what he described as 'a friendly but difficult meeting'[8] with Mr Acheson and Mr Harriman before President Truman considered the Prime Minister's message on September 26. Whereas Mr Julius Holmes in London told Sir Roger Makins that day that he thought the message 'a very just appreciation of the position',[9] Mr Averell Harriman began by referring Sir Oliver Franks to the difference in the British and American assessments of the Persian situation; from this, felt Mr Harriman, 'the differences in policy so largely followed'.[8] He later told His Majesty's Ambassador privately that he agreed that a settlement could not be reached with Dr Musaddiq but did not agree with the apparent British tactics of 'bringing increasing pressure to bear on Musaddiq and letting it be a matter of public knowledge in Persia and generally that this was what we were doing'.[10]

On the same day of September 26 Mr Truman sent Mr Attlee a brief interim reply. The President acceded to the Prime Minister's request for diplomatic support at Tehran where the American Ambassador was to express grave concern at the

---

[4] EP 1531/1619.
[5] *Ibid.*
[6] EP 1024/3.
[7] *Ibid.*
[8] EP 1531/1631.
[9] EP 1531/1632.
[10] EP 1531/1630.

proposed Persian action, without going so far as to demand withdrawal of the expulsion order. Mr Truman explained: 'We feel that to reach a satisfactory solution of the problem in Persia, and in all probability even to secure a lifting of the expulsion order, some new element must be injected into the situation', as by a British initiative in making 'some suggestion which would provide a basis for the Persian Government's assuming a more amenable attitude'. The Persian threat, in fact, should be conjured by further British appeasement. Whereas the President observed: 'I am very glad to note . . . that you recognise the very grave consequences of using force to maintain the British staff at Abadan because, as you know, this Government could not consider support of any such action'.

If the United States was the great and friendly Power in the West which had acquired a determining influence upon British policy, that policy was already coming to attach considerable importance to the views in the East of newly independent India, formerly the base for British enterprise in South Persia. Now, as regards the Persian crisis, the views of the two great republics were perhaps not very far removed. When Sir Girja Bajpai, KCSI, KBE, Secretary-General of the Indian Department of External Affairs, represented to the High Commissioner of the United Kingdom the risks of using force in Persia, General Sir Archibald Nye, as he reported on September 26, 1951, observed to Sir Girja Bajpai 'that indeed the arguments for and against the use of force had been under daily consideration for months'.[11] But that day of September 26 was the last one for such consideration before a final decision was at length reached. And even in that last reckoning notable new fluctuations of opinion came lapping through to swell those intricate permutations and vacillations of counsel which enmeshed British policy and complicated its execution in the Persian crisis of 1951.

In some contrast to the advice which Sir Francis Shepherd had tendered on September 6 (cf p. 350), he telegraphed on September 26 that in discussing with Mr Middleton that morning 'the effect in Persia of the use of force, we came to the conclusion that the disadvantages would considerably outweigh the advantages. My present feeling is that our most effective course might be to withdraw the British personnel . . . We should not do more than use the Royal Navy to prevent unauthorised export of oil from Persian ports.'[12] Sir Francis did not explain his important conclusion against the use of force (cf, however, p. 287) but said that Mr Middleton would report their conversation: he was flying to London in accordance with instructions in order to be available to advise the Cabinet on September 27.

On the same day of September 26 the intensification of the Persian crisis produced an opposite evolution of thought in the Foreign Office. In the continued absence of Sir William Strang, Sir Roger Makins minuted to the Foreign Secretary, who was due back in London that day: 'It seems almost certain that we shall be faced with a choice of withdrawal under threat or armed intervention, since the Shah looks like a broken reed. The decision is to some extent subject to what the lawyers say about the international law complications and what the Americans say about the general position. But faced with Hobson's choice, my own inclination is for the bolder course, though, in the short run, this carries the greater danger.'[13]

---

[11] EP 1192/119.
[12] EP 1015/343.
[13] EP 1531/1808.

Sir Roger Makins' incisive and important minute was the first political recommendation of the use of force in Persia from any of the permanent staff of the Foreign Office, at any rate since May 21-22 (cf pp. 183, also pp. 230 and 263-4). The earlier recommendation had, of course, been made at a lower level than the present one since Sir William Strang had at no time made such a submission to the Foreign Secretary as that now tendered by Sir Roger Makins. Some such consideration, together with the familiarity of the arguments by then, may conceivably have been partly responsible for the fact that no memorandum was prepared in the Foreign Office in support of the important advice now tentatively offered by Sir Roger Makins. Such a memorandum might nevertheless have been valuable in view of the new acuteness of the crisis and of the fact that the Foreign Secretary had not impressed his personal and standing inclination towards strong measures upon previous papers prepared by his department.

The allusion by Sir Roger Makins to legal advice referred to the fact that the Ministerial Committee on Persia had decided at its meeting on September 25 that the question of using force at Abadan should, as Sir Roger Makins explained to Mr Herbert Morrison, be given 'further urgent consideration by the Law Officers'. The Foreign Secretary noted against this: '? Pity'.[14] In accordance with the committee's decision Mr Fitzmaurice telegraphed to Sir Eric Beckett, who had accompanied the Attorney-General to The Hague hearings in the International Court of the Anglo-Norwegian fisheries dispute; Mr Fitzmaurice asked that Sir Frank Soskice be consulted again on the issues which had already been thrashed out, but not agreed, between them in July (cf pp. 258 and 284).

Mr Fitzmaurice substantially reiterated his previous opinion regarding possible legal justification for the use of force, and now argued in particular: 'Whereas at an earlier stage the landing of troops at Abadan in circumstances other than danger to life would have been clearly directed to preventing the Persians enforcing the nationalisation law, similar action now could be represented as being the only action capable of preventing the whole purpose of the Court's injunction from being irremediably frustrated.'[15] Among a number of other legal arguments Mr Fitzmaurice referred, however, to 'the difficulty arising from the question whether a decree of interim measures is binding on the parties in the way that a final decision on the merits is': an important, though perhaps rather submerged difficulty (cf, however, p. 192), whatever the moral force of an injunction. Mr Fitzmaurice now continued: 'Also Article 94 of the [United Nations] Charter, though probably not directly applicable to interim measures, may be held to imply that the correct course is not self-help but appeal to the Security Council. The landing of troops could, however, be accompanied by simultaneous reference to the Council.'[16] Sir Roger Makins argued in a second minute of September 26, after consulting Mr Fitzmaurice, that such a simultaneous procedure would have to be justified 'on the grounds that emergency action in face of an ultimatum was necessary. There is a precedent for this in the United States action in going into Korea before going to the Security Council, though of course the circumstances were very different.'[17]

---

[14] EP 1531/1808.
[15] EP 1192/117G.
[16] *Ibid.*
[17] EP 1531/1807.

The Attorney-General replied to Mr Fitzmaurice's message on the same day of September 26 that he adhered to his previous opinion and that 'the Court's statute makes it clear that all questions arising in connexion with non-compliance with such an [interim] order are matters for the Security Council, and I think it will be hopeless to try to excuse resort to force because of such non-compliance, if no recourse had been had to the Security Council'.[15]

At roughly the opposite extreme to the opinion of the Attorney-General stood the minute, also of September 26, which Brigadier R.W. Ewbank, Secretary of the Chiefs of Staff Committee, addressed to the Minister of Defence by way of brief for the meeting of the Cabinet next day. The general tenor of this minute broadly corresponded to that of a personal letter which Brigadier Ewbank further addressed on September 27 to Mr Furlonge at the Foreign Office. Brigadier Ewbank there wrote: 'As you know, the Chiefs of Staff have repeatedly emphasised their concern at the effect of our eviction from Persia on British prestige in the Middle East, the consequent weakening of our positions throughout that area, and the encouragement which our enemies will receive from seeing us so apparently feeble as to be unable or unwilling to defend ourselves against barefaced robbery, even by a Power whose standing among her own Middle Eastern neighbours could hardly be described as high . . . I think you would agree with me that there is every indication that we shall tamely allow ourselves to be kicked out of Abadan subject to a few wordy and futile protests, if only because we shan't be able to make up our minds to any other course of action in the short time available.'[18]

Brigadier Ewbank proceeded to propose to Mr Furlonge that British propaganda to the Middle East should already be building up for whatever explanation might be decided on in order to minimise the blow to British prestige there. In conclusion Brigadier Ewbank emphasised that his letter was not written on behalf of the Chiefs of Staff, 'so you need take it no more seriously than as my personal view'.[19] He was taken at his word. Nobody in the Foreign Office answered his letter in writing.

Such was the last line-up, after months of debate, on the critical issue of British use of force to maintain British interests at Abadan. This was now favoured by the Chiefs of Staff and Commanders-in-Chief, Middle East, and on the whole by Sir Roger Makins and, apparently, Mr Fitzmaurice of the Foreign Office in accordance with the standing inclination of the Foreign Secretary. This inclination was shared by strong elements of the Conservative Party and, probably, by the majority of the British public. The French Government, among others, was likely to be sympathetic to British military intervention but was not specifically consulted on this. The use of force had not been advised by Sir William Strang, was probably not favoured on the whole by the Treasury and had been opposed by the Prime Minister. In this he was supported by other Ministers besides the Attorney-General and, probably, by a strong section of his own party. The United States Government was in general opposed to British use of force, as were the Indian and other Eastern Governments together, probably, with a preponderance of world opinion as reflected in the United Nations. The arguments on both sides were strong and difficult.

On the back of the second minute on Persia which Sir Roger Makins addressed to him on September 26 the Foreign Secretary scribbled in pencil:

[18] EP 1531/1703G.
[19] *Ibid.*

'Aga Khan
US—Imposs. without Military
Blow up
Shah, 50-50
Later—after British out
Dip.   action
         Sanctions
         + Security Council
         ? withdraw
H. of C.—US.'[20]

This rough annotation was almost a kaleidoscopic epitome of the heavy and intricate issues in the last phase of the Persian crisis of 1951. They were to be settled at last at the Cabinet Meeting held at 10 am on Thursday, September 27, 1951. It sat for two and three-quarter hours. In contrast to the recent dispersal of the Government, this Cabinet was attended by all its 17 members except the Minister of Education, who was convalescent. The Foreign Secretary was accompanied by Mr Younger and the meeting was joined by Mr Noel-Baker, Mr Strauss, the Minister of Supply, and by the Solicitor-General and the Minister of Food.

The Prime Minister told the Cabinet that in view of the American attitude he did not think it would be expedient to use force to maintain the British staff in Abadan. That course could not expect to find much support in the United Nations. Mr Attlee recognised, however, that if the remaining British staff were expelled it would be humiliating for Great Britain. The Foreign Secretary agreed with the latter point and thought that, in such a case 'Egypt might be emboldened to take drastic action to end the military treaty and possibly to bring the Suez Canal under Egyptian control, and British legal rights in many other parts of the world would be placed in jeopardy. In these circumstances he was inclined to think that the Persian Government should be told that the United Kingdom could not tolerate the expulsion of the remaining staff from Abadan and would, if necessary, take the necessary steps to ensure that they were not expelled.'[21]

The Cabinet noted that Operation Buccaneer could now be mounted in 12 hours but also that the Law Officers had advised that 'unless the Security Council had sanctioned the use of force by the United Kingdom, military operations designed to seize Abadan would in present circumstances be illegal'. Some doubt was expressed whether this opinion took sufficient account of the rights of self-defence, but the general view in the Cabinet was that force could not be employed as proposed since 'we could not afford to break with the United States on an issue of this kind . . . In any event, the use of force would not necessarily bring nearer a solution of the dispute.'[22]

There was also general agreement in the Cabinet that 'every endeavour' (except, presumably, military endeavour) should be made to prevent the expulsion of the British staff from Abadan since, if that occurred, the prospects of establishing British management of the Persian oil industry would be greatly lessened. It was pointed out that the British public expected some effective action to be taken though not

---

[20] EP 1531/1807.
[21] EP 1531/1704G.
[22] *Ibid.*

necessarily by the use of force. It was still the general view that no concessions should be offered to Dr Musaddiq as distinct from a more reasonable Persian Government. The Cabinet accordingly agreed in conformity with a summing up by the Prime Minister that, after a preliminary intimation to the United States Government, His Majesty's Government should immediately refer the Persian dispute to the Security Council of the United Nations, which should be asked to consider as a matter of urgency what steps could be taken to compel the Persian Government to respect the interim injunction of the International Court.

Thus did the Cabinet decide, not without some doubts, upon that reference of the Persian dispute to the Security Council which had been under previous consideration but had been advised against by the Foreign Office and by the United Kingdom Representative to the United Nations, and had been shelved by the Cabinet on July 12 (cf p. 262). Nor had the omens recently improved. The Egyptian Government was not paying the slightest attention to the call of September 1 from the Security Council for the termination of its selective embargo in the Suez Canal (cf p. 356). It was on September 5 that the Foreign Secretary had forecast that the alternative to British use of force at Abadan 'is probably ineffective appeal to UN' (cf p. 349).

Immediately after the meeting of the Cabinet on the morning of September 27 the Prime Minister entertained at luncheon M. Tran Van Huu, the Prime Minister and Foreign Minister of Vietnam. The French Ambassador telegraphed to his Government that after this luncheon Mr Attlee told him that 'failing results from our, and American, representations in Tehran, we should be obliged to intervene in Abadan'.[23] It is unclear whether or not this apparently striking statement may perhaps have represented some misunderstanding by M. Massigli of something that the Prime Minister said. Some such doubt may possibly—but uncertainly—have prompted M. Le Roy, Counsellor in the French Embassy, to show to Mr Bowker next day a copy of M. Massigli's telegram. Mr Bowker told M. Le Roy 'that Ministers had no present intention of using force at Abadan, except for the protection of British lives'.[24]

In accordance with the instruction of the Cabinet the American Government was promptly informed of the decision to go immediately to the Security Council. The Foreign Secretary told Sir Oliver Franks: 'I should be glad to know urgently if they have any comments. I naturally hope for the full support of the United States representative in proceedings before the Security Council.'[25] On the same day of September 27, however, the President of the Board of Trade sent the Foreign Secretary a copy of a letter which he addressed to the Prime Minister after the Cabinet meeting to express his continuing concern regarding policy towards Persia. Sir Hartley Shawcross, who had attended the Cabinet, wrote, in particular, to Mr Attlee: 'I entirely agree with your view about the inexpediency of using force at this stage . . . We should not completely dismiss the possibility that the certainty of a final crisis might stiffen the States into some action. If we go straight to the Security Council we not only step ahead of the United States without knowing what their reaction will be or what further action that had themselves contemplated but we leave the Persians with no time or opportunity of modifying their position . . . Moreover,

---

[23] EP 1531/1720.
[24] *Ibid.*
[25] EP 1531/1629.

from the electoral point of view, I think a reference to the Security Council taken alone is not likely to be a very convincing measure.'[26]

Sir Hartley Shawcross proposed that the Shah and Mr Truman be told at once that if the Persian decision to expel British nationals was not withdrawn His Majesty's Government would simultaneously with the expulsion, take three measures: first, go to the Security Council as already decided; secondly, withdraw diplomatic representatives; thirdly, 'cut off all economic relations, and stop all supplies'. The Cabinet had considered and rejected the second expedient as offering no sufficient advantage. On the economic issue the Cabinet had gone so far as to decide that Sir Francis Shepherd, when informing the Shah that the Security Council was being approached forthwith by His Majesty's Government, should say to him that while the latter 'might find it possible to improve the offer which they had so far made if they were dealing with a reasonable Persian Government, he must expect that serious financial and economic consequences would follow the expulsion of the remaining British staff from Abadan'.[27]

Sir Hartley Shawcross now further proposed that the Shah and Mr Truman should also be told that His Majesty's Government was not finally bound to a 50-50 profit-sharing but 'would consider the matter at large with any [Persian] Government prepared to enter into serious negotiation'.[26] This course had been advocated by some Ministers in the Cabinet that day but it had been pointed out that 'any higher percentage would have serious repercussions . . . and would almost certainly be opposed by the United States Government'[27] —the by now familiar debate (cf pp. 301-2). The President of the Board of Trade wrote to the Prime Minister that Mr Stokes agreed with his letter, and he rather thought that Mr Shinwell might do so, and probably Mr McNeil.

On the following day of September 28 Mr Stokes wrote to Mr Attlee confirming Sir Hartley Shawcross' statement for his part but adding to it in the light of further correspondence from the Aga Khan and his own renewed criticism of the high profits extracted from Persia in earlier years by the Anglo-Iranian Oil Company[28]— criticism which was not accepted without question in the Foreign Office or, apparently, in the Ministry of Fuel and Power or the Treasury. Though the Ministry of Fuel and Power had recently produced figures showing that during the period 1932-50 His Majesty's Government had drawn slightly more from the company in income tax alone (£103,250,000) than the direct payments of all kinds made to the Persian Government (£102,800,000). This latter figure compared with a grand total of dividends and taxation to His Majesty's Government of over £194 million, nearly twice as much. During the period, however, £92 million had been invested in Persia, and the company had set aside £40 million to pay to Persia under the Supplemental Oil Agreement.[29] In this connexion Mr Stokes informed Mr Attlee: 'As I explained to the Cabinet yesterday, I did not appreciate these figures when I was in Tehran and I am bound to tell you I think the Treasury were wrong in not placing them before me. Had these big differences been alive in my mind, I certainly would have suggested something beyond a mere 50-50 arrangement.'[28] On this point Sir Donald

---

[26] EP 1531/1706G.
[27] EP 1531/1704G.
[28] EP 1536/29
[29] EP 1531/1764.

Fergusson was to represent in a cogent and forceful letter of October 3 to Mr Stokes in reply to the Aga Khan's criticism: 'I do not believe that any better financial terms that it would be possible for us to give would satisfy him [Musaddiq]. It is not more money, but other objectives that he is really interested in.'[30] This was most likely true, although it might yet, perhaps, have been profitable earlier, to have given greater consideration to the diplomatic possibilities of exploiting something like a 60-40 offer in relation, if not to the Persian Government, then to the American.

The Foreign Secretary for his part minuted on his copy of Mr Stokes' letter of September 28 to Mr Attlee: 'Getting a bit tired of his lecturing me. Let his PS know.'[28] The considerations advanced by Mr Stokes evidently went beyond those of Sir Hartley Shawcross. Whatever the merits of the substance of the latter's proposals at that stage, his suggestion of a more deliberate timing might perhaps have deserved careful consideration as affording scope for greater flexibility and pressure. But the fact that the new suggestion was made just after the Cabinet had reached important decisions may have told against it; the instructing telegrams to Sir Oliver Franks and Sir Francis Shepherd were approved on September 27 in accordance with the decisions of the Cabinet.

The two ambassadors were informed, in particular, that the Cabinet was not prepared 'at this stage' to authorise use of force: the British staff at Abadan should still remain at their posts, 'and the question whether they should withdraw or wait to be expelled should be considered at the end of the period of warning given by the Persians'.[31] The latter decision had been adopted despite recognition of the fact, represented more than a month earlier by the Working Party, that prompt withdrawal would avoid the humiliation of expulsion. The prompt action now determined upon was, however, British recourse to the Security Council in the hope that it might yet simplify the long-deferred but now impending decision regarding withdrawal from Abadan. Though squarely faced now by that humiliation, British policy still seemed to be playing for time after the eleventh hour.

2. British appeal to the Security Council and decision to withdraw from Abadan, September 27-October 1

Meanwhile in Tehran the Majlis was due to meet on the morning of September 27, 1951. A last representation was telegraphed from the Foreign Office to urge the disappointing M. Sayyid Zia to take effective action and, in particular, prevent the Majlis from endorsing Dr Musaddiq's decision to expel the British staff at Abadan. This was achieved by ensuring once again that there was no quorum. Whereupon Dr Musaddiq treated the crowd assembled outside the Majlis to an anti-British oration. The negative and technical gambit of the Persian Opposition achieved only limited effect in face of the popular passions which the demagogic old premier and his confederates were whipping up—on the previous day, for instance, a Persian newspaper connected with M. Kashani had published an article odiously gloating over the mortal illness, recently announced, of King George VI. From Abadan Mr Mason had complained on September 26 that he and his senior staff were in a most invidious position owing to lack of directives. Next day the great British refinery passed completely under Persian control with a Persian military guard. Considerable

[30] EP 1531/1839G
[31] EP 1531/1662.

392

Persian reinforcements moved into Abadan.

In Persia the key-figure remained the Shah, weakly enigmatic, isolated and suspicious, tortuously well-intentioned but fearful of action, opposed to Dr Musaddiq and often inclined to be helpful to Great Britain, but—it came to be suspected—[32] perhaps cherishing some deeper resentment against her for the events 10 years back which had brought down his father. (Britain, blamed for most things in Persia, was thus subject to criticism from the Shah for the eviction of Reza Shah and from Dr Musaddiq for his promotion: cf p. 203). Any resentment felt by the Shah may have been heightened by his alleged displeasures at the British rejection of the Persian offer of September 19 which he had sought to promote. Sir Francis Shepherd explained the reason for this in an audience of the Shah on the afternoon of September 27 and then gave him Mr Attlee's message of September 25. The Shah, who was nervous, demurred at the suggestion that he had not hitherto intervened in events and said he thought that the British staff at Abadan should leave Persia— 'most unsatisfactory'[33] commented a telegram from the Foreign Office instructing His Majesty's Ambassador to deliver to the Shah the further message agreed by the Cabinet on September 27.

On the evening of September 29 Sir Francis Shepherd delivered the second message to the Shah, who still seemed 'completely undecided as to what to do next' but gave Sir Francis the impression that 'our resort to the Security Council was not unpalatable'.[34] The Shah thought that the expulsion-order might be rescinded if, but only if, the Security Council so ordered. Sir Francis accordingly concentrated on trying—in vain as it transpired—to induce His Majesty to secure a postponement of the order, impressing upon him the dangers of the situation.

Sir Francis Shepherd had been instructed to threaten the Shah with 'stringent measures' of an economic nature. These were considered in a memorandum written by Mr Ramsbotham in the Foreign Office on September 28. He had attended a meeting at the Treasury, whereat the Board of Trade and the Bank of England were also represented, in order to consider economic sanctions against Persia. In his subsequent memorandum Mr Ramsbotham reviewed, and found arguments of expediency against, such sanctions, ranging from banning trade with Persia—which would be easy—to blocking Persian sterling. This latter, wrote Mr Ramsbotham, 'would be a serious blow to Persia, but there would certainly be evasions and undercover sterling deals through intermediaries . . . The British Bank [in Tehran] would have to withdraw and might never return . . . Sanctions . . . might drive Persia into Russian arms . . . It would be a serious precedent . . . to apply punitive sanctions against a small country without the backing of the Security Council.'[35]

Mr Ramsbotham appreciated that 'we shall need to explain carefully why Persia can flout international law without our being able to retaliate . . . Assuming that public opinion in this country can be guided, all the arguments suggest that full economic sanctions would be most unwise. But we should urgently explore the legal position as regards a naval blockade of Abadan'[36] to prevent Persian export of oil: the measure advocated by Sir Francis Shepherd and, now in London, by Mr

---

[32] EP 1015/422.
[33] EP 1531/1662.
[34] EP 1531/1678.
[35] EP 1112/92G.
[36] *Ibid.*

Middleton. Mr Ramsbotham's prudently negative arguments and conclusions against full economic sanctions were substantially reiterated the same day by Mr Flett's Working Party on Persian Oil, generally addicted to moderate and safe, if also weak, courses. The Working Party's cautious conclusions, contrasting with the strong economic policy advocated by the President of the Board of Trade, were elaborated in a memorandum of October 4. This memorandum appreciated, among other things, that 'with a largely agrarian economy and with a low standard of living, Persia has an undoubted capacity for muddling through. But if she is left to her own resources the collapse of her economy must be only a matter of time.'[37] The Working Party's memorandum was accepted by the Chancellor of the Exchequer and, in general, by the Foreign Secretary.

Another moderation in British policy towards Persia had, perhaps, become manifest on September 27 in regard to a further approach to the Lord Privy Seal from the Aga Khan, who proposed to write secretly in a generally emollient sense to Dr Musaddiq. In accordance with the reiterated British refusal to treat with him further, Mr Stokes told the Aga Khan that His Majesty's Government could not authorise him to hold out hope to Dr Musaddiq of a successful solution regarding Persian oil. The Prime Minister, however, wrote to the Lord Privy Seal on September 27: 'I see no reason why the Aga Khan should not say that he is confident that with goodwill and common sense on both sides a successful solution of the problem could be found.'[38] The Aga Khan telegraphed to Dr Musaddiq accordingly. Mr Herbert Morrison minuted: 'I don't mind.' (Subsequently, on October 2, Mr Stokes, on the basis of prolonged interdepartmental consideration, also replied at last to the Aga Khan's letters to him of September 10—cf p. 365—and later dates and treated him to a vigorous and cogent defence of the past record of the Anglo-Iranian Oil Company. The tone of this letter to the Aga Khan contrasted rather markedly with those which Mr Stokes had sent Mr Attlee on September 14 and 28.)

A somewhat different inflection in the fluctuating counsels of His Majesty's Government was liable to flow from a personal message from the Attorney-General to the Foreign Secretary, transmitted from The Hague on the morning of September 28, with copies to the Prime Minister and the Lord Chancellor. Sir Frank Soskice now telegraphed, further to his opinion sent to Mr Fitzmaurice and considered by the Cabinet: 'I think International Court would not consider Persian expulsion order as a justification for British forcible intervention in Abadan. However, situation wholly unprecedented and in practice unlikely International Court would ever have to decide this. If Anglo-Iranian case comes to trial this action would prejudice us unless we had at least been to the Security Council. It is more likely that His Majesty's Government would have to defend British action before Security Council and possibly General Assembly. If so, it would be infinitely easier if we had obtained vote authorising us to use force blocked by Soviet veto. Principles of international law relating to self-help admittedly not certain. I think policy considerations must be ultimately deciding factor.'[39] This important message represented an appreciable modification of the Attorney-General's opinion of September 26 and indeed throughout preceding months. But his new advice was despatched only the day after

---

[37] EP 1165/25.
[38] EP 1531/1698.
[39] EP 1192/117G.

the Cabinet had taken its decisions regarding Persia.

On the morning of September 28, 1951, a meeting of the Ministerial Committee on Persia was attended by Mr Attlee, Mr Morrison, Mr Gaitskell, Mr Shinwell, Mr Noel-Baker, Sir Hartley Shawcross, Mr Stokes and Lord Pakenham, who had succeeded Lord Hall as First Lord of the Admiralty. Those in attendance included Admiral Sir George Creasy, Mr Bowker, Mr Middleton, Sir Leslie Rowan and Mr Flett. The Prime Minister first reported that he had informed the leaders of the Conservative and Liberal Oppositions of the decisions of the Cabinet on the previous day. The Liberal leaders strongly supported the reference to the Security Council, which they felt was overdue. The Conservative leaders, reported Mr Attlee, 'had attempted to maintain that the Government were committed to the use of force in order to prevent the expulsion of the AIOC staff from Abadan, and he had explained to them that his statement in the House of Commons on July 30 meant no more than it said, namely that the Government's intention was not to evacuate entirely'.[40] (The Prime Minister apparently did not allude to the Lord Chancellor's statement in the House of Lords.) The Conservative leaders, unlike the Liberals, did not favour a debate on Persia when the House of Commons met on October 4 for prorogation before the general election. The Committee on Persia decided that if possible no statement on Persia should be made in the House when it reassembled.

The Committee on Persia further considered the prevention of Persian export of refined oil. The Prime Minister said that 'it was the view of the Lord Chancellor that we had the right in international law to protect our property in refined oil from Abadan, and that we should probably have a good case for using force to prevent its alienation . . . A decision to instruct His Majesty's ships to intercept tankers on the high seas must, however, be considered in relation to our reference of the dispute to the Security Council.'[41] The President of the Board of Trade was supported by Mr Middleton in advising that instructions for such interception should be issued and announced at once, before actual reference of the Persian dispute to the Security Council. The meeting decided accordingly.

A statement of British policy issued by the Foreign Office late in the evening of September 28 included an allusion to the above decision, but in a modified and vague form. This afforded scope for those second or third thoughts which so often supervened in the determination of British policy throughout the Persian crisis of 1951. Sir Roger Makins minuted to Mr Herbert Morrison on September 29 that at a meeting at the Foreign Office that morning the Service Departments had pressed strongly that British warships in the Persian Gulf be instructed to carry out the interception agreed upon the day before; whereas the Ministry of Transport considered that it would constitute a completely new precedent in international trade and one liable to injure British merchant shipping; Mr Fitzmaurice gave an opinion coinciding with one which Sir Eric Beckett had indeed delivered as long ago as the previous May,[42] denying the legal validity of forcible interception of tankers of third States; and the political implications might be serious.[43] There would appear to have been insufficient exploration and coordination of views at the official,

---

[40] EP 1531/1705G.
[41] *Ibid.*
[42] EP 1531/447.
[43] EP 1531/1753G.

interdepartmental level before the important issue of intercepting tankers came before Ministers for their decision.

On October 2, 1951, Sir Roger Makins telephoned a further minute regarding the interception of tankers to the Foreign Secretary who was attending the Labour Party Conference at Scarborough. Sir Roger Makins agreed with the arguments of Mr Fitzmaurice and held that such naval interception was an unacceptable risk at least while the British case in the Persian dispute was before the Security Council, as it already was by then. Mr Attlee and Mr Morrison decided to suspend action regarding interception.[44] This decision was confirmed on October 4 by the Committee on Persia.[45] The reasons for this revised decision were, in themselves, strong. The fact remained, however, that it represented an abandonment of the measure put forward by Mr Ramsbotham and Mr Middleton as a substitute for full economic sanctions, themselves already a possible substitute for use of force. It was another weakening chain-reaction (the Law of Let Go).

It is rather difficult to resist the impression that the interception of tankers had been snatched at somewhat too hastily as a plausible substitute for other action, as also, perhaps, had recourse to the Security Council: which, in turn, was to cut across naval interception as well as other lines of British policy. At the meeting of the Committee on Persia on September 28 the Foreign Secretary, who had seen Sir Hartley Shawcross' letter of the previous day to Mr Attlee, yet advised that 'we should not delay taking the necessary steps to summon an urgent meeting of the [Security] Council . . . Public opinion in this country would expect immediate action of some kind, and the United States Government could not dispute our right to bring before the Security Council the obvious failure of the Persian Government to observe the interim ruling of the International Court.'[46] The meeting agreed that the necessary steps at the United Nations should be taken forthwith.

On the last item considered by the Committee on Persia on September 28, the Prime Minister said that, in order to avoid giving the Persians any early indication of British intentions regarding the withdrawal of staff from Abadan, it would be preferable to remove them, 'if removal proved necessary', across the river to Iraq on British warships rather than to fly them home. Sir William Fraser, who had joined the meeting, said he thought that the company's staff would be willing to fall in with this. It was 'agreed that the AIOC should inform the staff that if it was necessary to withdraw them from Abadan, appropriate arrangements would be made by His Majesty's Navy'.[47]

The background here was that Sir William Fraser had told the previous meeting of the Cabinet Committee on September 25 that if the British staff at Abadan were deprived of reasonable amenities he saw no course open but to withdraw them. Just after the next meeting of the committee on the morning of September 28 there was received in the Foreign Office a telegram from Khorramshahr transmitting a message wherein Mr Mason informed Sir William Fraser: 'We consider that evacuation can be delayed but *not* cancelled' now that nearly all the British staff were extruded from their offices. They had 'prepared to depart next week, and they will *not* be prepared

---

[44] EP 1531/1756G.
[45] EP 1531/1804G.
[46] EP 1531/1705G.
[47] *Ibid.*

to wait for forcible expulsion which might mean emergency evacuation rather than withdrawal with a degree of dignity'.[48] Mr Mason, after consultation with Major Capper, recommended evacuation by aircraft from October 1 to October 4.

No announcement regarding evacuation from Abadan, which His Majesty's Government was still hoping to avert, was to be included in the statement of British policy which, the Committee on Persia decided on the morning of September 28, was now to be published. This statement described the Persian expulsion order as 'a final flouting of the findings of the International Court'. This had 'created a situation which might well be thought to justify the use of force . . . His Majesty's Government would, however, be reluctant to take any action which might have the effect of weakening the authority of the United Nations, on whose principles their policy is based. They have, therefore, decided that the right course in present circumstances is to bring the situation urgently before the Security Council . . . His Majesty's Government will request the Council to call upon the Persian Government to comply in all respects with the order of the International Court, and in particular to permit the continued residence at Abadan of the staff affected by the expulsion orders.'[49] Such was the tenor of the British draft resolution to the Security Council, as communicated to the State Department.

When Sir Roger Makins told the American Minister in London on September 28, 1951, that His Majesty's Government looked for full American support for their reference to the Security Council, 'Mr Holmes replied that he felt certain that this would be forthcoming'.[50] Mr Holmes was wrong. Sir Oliver Franks telegraphed that he was not certain that the State Department (it may have been Mr Acheson himself) 'will consider the proposed action in the Security Council as compatible with the new approach which they have in mind',[51] and which, he reported later on September 28, included some proposals 'which would be very difficult for us'.[52] Sir Oliver Franks presciently advised that His Majesty's Government would get nowhere in the Security Council without American support and, speaking urgently on the telephone to Sir Roger Makins that evening, begged him not to issue at once the official statement of British policy which had just been drafted and approved by the Foreign Secretary at 7 pm on September 28. But the gist of it had already percolated to press circles in London and New York. Mr Morrison, rung up by Sir Roger Makins, 'said that if the statement were not issued there would be chaos and we must, if humanly possible, get it out'.[53]

In further telephoning that evening Sir Roger Makins pointed out to Sir Oliver Franks that His Majesty's Government were consulting the United States Government on the handling of their case at the Security Council, not on the substance of the decision to resort to it; on that they had not anticipated any criticism. The British statement of policy was issued at 10.30 pm, embargoed till midnight, and the United Kingdom Delegation to the United Nations was instructed to take formal action with the President of the Security Council. Thus it was yet again under ominous auspices for Anglo-American relations in the Persian crisis, recalling the

---

[48] EP 1531/1621.
[49] *The Times*, September 29, 1951.
[50] EP 1531/1725.
[51] EP 1531/1656.
[52] EP 1531/1719.
[53] *Ibid.*

warning of Sir Hartley Shawcross against precipitate action, that His Majesty's Government, baffled of other expedients and nearly cornered, took their case to the Security Council of the United Nations.

Early on the morning of September 29 there was received in the Foreign Office a long message from the State Department expanding President Truman's proposal for some British appeasement of the Persian Government and reiterating the standing American concern at the 'imminent danger' that Persia 'will be lost to the Western world . . . The Department believes it highly advisable that the British Government maintain constant efforts to convince the Iranian people that it is trying in good will to find a solution which will be acceptable to Iran.'[54] In pursuance of this somewhat irritating advice an informal feeler to the Shah was proposed and, if so desired, the American Ambassador in Tehran would indicate to him 'the United States willingness to endeavour to obtain undertakings from the British along certain lines' as a basis for negotiating. These included 'the substitution of Anglo-Dutch interests for the provision of management of operations' within Persia, 'with a Dutch or other neutral manager'; also British purchase and transport of oil from Abadan while paying half of its value to the National Iranian Oil Company.

The long American homily concluded: 'The United States will continue to use its full influence in an endeavour to bring about a peaceful solution.'[55] The idea of a just solution had somewhat receded. Whatever the intrinsic merits of the American proposals, and they were not negligible, they indicated how far the United States Government was from sharing the view, for instance of the anglophil *Christian Science Monitor* that it was almost inconceivable that the British would not stand fast at Abadan, and that America should reciprocate British support in Korea. The proposals of the State Department, however, were in any case now superseded by the British plump for the Security Council. That was at any rate peaceful enough, but still incapable of winning that ever elusive reward, firm American support.

The State Department lost little time in roundly condemning the proposed British resolution for the Security Council, and even authorised the American delegation to the United Nations to tell enquirers that the Department saw some difficulty in it and were thinking along different lines. The Americans were very doubtful whether the British resolution would secure the necessary seven votes in the Security Council, apart from the likelihood of a Russian veto. So, indeed, was Mr John Coulson, then acting for Sir Gladwyn Jebb at the United Nations. The reason that Mr Coulson's advice had not been sought before going to the Security Council may, perhaps, have been that Sir Gladwyn Jebb was then in England and could presumably reiterate his advice of June 30 as to the risks of such a course: risks which had now been accepted; though scarcely in the expectation, presumably, that they would include an American counter-draft for a resolution which, as Sir Oliver Franks told the State Department, 'put us into the dock with Persia'.[56] The Security Council would thereby call upon the British and Persian Governments to resume negotiations at the earliest and to refrain from any action aggravating the situation or prejudicing the position of the parties concerned. This draft was considered in the Foreign Office to be

---

[54] EP 1531/1663G.
[55] *Ibid.*
[56] EP 1531/1667.

'pusillanimous to the point of disaster'.[57]

Sharply contrasting with the attitude of the strong and courted American Government was that of the weak and somewhat neglected French Government. On September 28 M. Parodi, Secretary-General of the French Ministry of Foreign Affairs, told Mr William Hayter, the British Minister in Paris, that the 'French Government felt that their interests in this dispute were bound up with ours, both on general grounds and also because of the reactions which successful Persian seizure of the oil would have on French interests in the IPC, Suez Canal, &c.'[58] He had suggested that the French Government should make representations to the American Government in support of the British case and enquired if there was any other French action which would be welcome, as at the Security Council. The French Embassy in London made a similar communication. His Majesty's Government conveyed its warm appreciation to the French Government, and Sir Gladwyn Jebb would be keeping in close touch with his French colleague at the United Nations.

The Dutch attitude towards the British case in the Persian dispute was similar to the French. Italy, while not a member of the United Nations, was also inclined to be friendly. The Indian Government, like the American, favoured continued negotiations, while instructing its representative at the United Nations to support measures designed to dissuade the Persians from expelling the British staff from Abadan. Sir Girja Bajpai, however, told Sir Archibald Nye that 'his Government felt considerable doubts about the wisdom of the degree of emphasis we were placing on the decision of The Hague Court, the more so since negotiations had been conducted since this decision without very much regard to the rulings which had been given'.[59] These doubts were almost precisely shared by the Turkish Government.[60]

Now coming home to roost were the results of what was, perhaps, the gravest single mistake in the British diplomatic handling of the Persian crisis of 1951: failure to prevent the Harriman mission from prejudicing the effective exploitation of the notable British success in securing the interim indication of The Hague Court with its high moral, and potentially practical, value, despite its strictly juridical limitations (cf pp. 264-5 and 387). However technically valid the British juridical reservations in the negotiations with the Persians after the interim injunction (cf pp. 309, 314-6, 334-6, 347), it was now too late in practical terms to turn the clock back to that decision, at least without the use of force. Nor can one easily believe that there was in Whitehall any person concerned with the crisis who did not in his heart of hearts know that this was so. That was the inner emptiness of the procedural device of referring the case to the Security Council.

By contrast, His Majesty's Government does not appear to have given thought to the possibility of demanding strong Turkish diplomatic support in Tehran in return for British support at Ottawa, despite previous reluctance, for Turkish adhesion to the North Atlantic Treaty in accordance with the urgent desire of the Turkish Government.[61] Though in any case the Turkish Government went rather further than the Indian in urgently instructing its Ambassador in Tehran to urge the Persian

---

[57] EP 1531/1665G.
[58] EP 1531/1659.
[59] EP 1531/1723.
[60] EP 1531/1708.
[61] WU 11923/103, 118, 159, 260 and WU 1198/294G.

Government to postpone the entry into force of its expulsion order. With so much spontaneous goodwill, it is not easy to understand why His Majesty's Government did not make a special and strong effort to induce all friendly Governments to support the British cause not only in the Security Council, as was done, but also by most vigorous, and preferably collective, diplomatic action at Tehran to induce the Persian Government to postpone, if not cancel, the expulsion order, now the last hope at the last hour. Even without the obvious backing of a threat of British military action as the alternative, such a course might conceivably have yielded valuable results: especially if British diplomacy had skilfully managed to trade a British threat of military action for an American threat of economic or other sanctions or displeasure in a more ominous American representation to the Persian Government than that ordered by Mr Truman in response to Mr Attlee's appeal of September 25. *The Times* reported that on September 29 the new American Ambassador had a long private conversation with the Shah but did not seem to have given him any special message from the President; Sir Francis Shepherd reported only that Mr Henderson had presented his credentials to the Shah.

The gravity by then of the Abadan crisis evidently made it most difficult to take any effective measures by diplomacy within the scope of the policy of His Majesty's Government. Though it might almost seem that British diplomacy at that juncture preferred to use blunt instruments rather than sharp ones. Even within the Foreign Office the amount of constructive and original thought devoted to fresh methods of diplomatic technique to try to loosen the stubborn crisis might seem rather small by comparison with that given to possible refinements of economic solutions. Whereas the second were perhaps not likely to be much good without the first. One might think, however, that His Majesty's Embassy in Tehran for its part might on occasions have displayed rather greater diplomatic ingenuity. Certainly, one would imagine that Sir Francis Shepherd would have welcomed some concerted support from friendly Embassies in his difficult and bitter task—Sir Roger Makins telegraphed to him on September 29: 'We all appreciate the way in which you are standing up to the continuing crisis.'[62]

On the afternoon of September 30, 1951, His Majesty's Ambassador in Tehran had a conversation with the Persian Minister of Court. On instructions from the Shah, M. Ala had tried to induce Dr Musaddiq to rescind or postpone the expulsion order. The Premier would only postpone it if there was some gesture of British goodwill such as the resumption of negotiations on the basis of his last proposals or possible conversations on assessment of compensation to the dispossessed Anglo-Iranian Oil Company. Sir Francis Shepherd 'pointed out to Ala that we had in fact made a number of gestures of goodwill all of which had been rebuffed . . . and that expulsion order itself was an expression of ill will. It was expecting rather much that we should submit to this kind of blackmail.'[63] This spirited retort was not validated by an equally spirited British policy. So that for Britain it was almost becoming a choice of submitting to blackmail in Tehran or submitting to humiliation at Abadan.

Sir Francis Shepherd told M. Ala, however, that he would try to see Dr Musaddiq before he left to represent Persia before the Security Council and would make a last effort to induce him to take a reasonable view. Subsequently M. Ala informed His

---

[62] EP 1531/1828.
[63] EP 1531/1661.

Majesty's Ambassador that 'Dr Musaddiq had said he would be delighted to see me to discuss any question except oil'.[64] The Persian Prime Minister, like the Shah, was, with good reason, no longer afraid of Britain. The effect of her appeal to the Security Council had been to consolidate the Majlis and the Senate for the time being behind Dr Musaddiq and, as came to be recognised in the Foreign Office, to strengthen his position. It was probably rather more than coincidence that it was on September 29, the day on which British resort to the United Nations was announced, that the Persian Government at last withdrew the exequatur of His Majesty's Consul-General resident at Khorramshahr who, in the words of Sir Francis Shepherd, 'had been tireless in his attempts to defend British interests and the personal status of the British staff'[65] at Abadan. Major Capper was next to be appointed Ambassador to Liberia.

On the same day of September 29 Mr Mason telegraphed that his staff had been informed that if necessary transport for evacuation would be arranged (cf p. 396-7). He reported: 'There have naturally been criticisms and resentment that no aircraft programme has been arranged. They wish to make it quite clear that they are *not* prepared to remain in Abadan after Wednesday, October 3'[66] except on two conditions: first, that they resumed their jobs then taken over by Persians and, secondly, that the Persians had a complete change of heart so that there was no risk of the British staff being deprived of essential services. They were evidently sick of being pushed around and left without effective succour. Next day Major Capper telegraphed that if the Persians were not given three days' notice they might refuse to permit the use of His Majesty's ships for the withdrawal of the staff on the grounds of insufficient time to make arrangements:[67] an almost inverted fear that the Persians might raise difficulties about the execution of their own ultimate threat. To such a pass had things now come.

On the morning of September 30 the question of evacuation was discussed in London yet again at an interdepartmental meeting whereat the Foreign Office, Admiralty and Treasury were represented. It was agreed that whatever happened at the Security Council the British staff could not remain at Abadan after October 3: even if the Council did call on Persia in time to withdraw the expulsion order, the Persian Government most probably would not recognise the resolution: another revelation of the inner emptiness of British resort to the Council. It was further represented at the interdepartmental meeting that if evacuation from Abadan was, as previously decided, to be effected by the Royal Navy, it would be necessary to ask permission of the Persians, who might well refuse; this would be particularly embarrassing in view of the British resolution before the Security Council. The interdepartmental meeting was accordingly unanimous in recommending that the decision taken only two days earlier by the Committee on Persia for a naval evacuation should now be reversed; and that evacuation should be by commercial aircraft, as desired locally: another wobble in British counsels.

The conclusions of the interdepartmental meeting on September 30 were telephoned by Sir Roger Makins to Mr Herbert Morrison, who was that day engaged

---

[64] EP 1531/2018.
[65] EP 1013/40.
[66] EP 1531/1621.
[67] EP 1611/52.

on the National Executive of the Labour Party at Scarborough in approving its election manifesto. At six o'clock that evening Mr Leishman, his assistant private secretary, telephoned from Scarborough to Sir Roger Makins that the question of evacuating Abadan had been considered at a meeting attended by the Prime Minister, the Foreign Secretary, the Chancellor of the Exchequer, the Minister of Defence and the First Lord of the Admiralty. In the light of the recent messages from Abadan Mr Attlee and Mr Morrison both thought that the staff there of the Anglo-Iranian Oil Company had reached the end of its tether and would not stay on. The meeting decided to withdraw the British staff at Abadan and to announce this decision at 12.5 a.m. on October 2, without specifying the means or date of withdrawal. This was transmitted from the Foreign Office that evening in telegram No. 1334[68] to Tehran and No. 431 to Khorramshahr. The immediately preceding telegram from the Foreign Office, No. 1333[69] to Tehran and No. 430 to Khorramshahr, had, however, issued instructions that Sir Francis Shepherd, Major Capper and Commodore Wallis were to decide how to notify the Persian authorities of the evacuation; in accordance with the ministerial decision, the company's staff should be informed on October 1 that they would be withdrawn on October 3—by warships.

On the method of evacuation the Ministers at Scarborough had rejected the unanimous advice of the interdepartmental committee and had adhered to the decision adopted by the Committee on Persia on September 28 (cf p. 396). The Ministers correctly estimated that it was very unlikely that the Persians would in fact object to the use of British warships, which, in the event, were to accomplish their task successfully. At the same time their use not only ran counter to the strong wishes of the hard-tried British staff at Abadan but, as it were, rubbed in the British humiliation, coming as it did on top of the previous ministerial rejection of interdepartmental advice that the ultimate humiliation should be avoided by timely evacuation before Persian eviction. Now it had come to that. His Majesty's ships, the proud and traditional guarantors of British policy and sea power, and hitherto stationed in that role in the crisis at Abadan as in others, were now at Persian behest to remove the British castaways from that great wreck which they had just had to watch and accept. And the local representative of British authority, His Majesty's Consul-General at Ahwaz resident at Khorramshahr, was to leave with the last of them, sent packing by the Persians. Such was to be the British withdrawal from the sweltering shores of Abadan, ordered at long last from the bracing coast of Yorkshire.

On the same day of September 30, 1951, Sir Roger Makins had made a last representation regarding the use of force in a minute to the Foreign Secretary: 'I think you must now decide what action is to be taken, if the action in the Security Council is frustrated . . . The alternatives remain intervention or withdrawal. In view of the local situation at Abadan, the latter may have to take place before the proceedings at New York have terminated.'[70] One senses that the writer himself may have felt that was conscientiously posing a decision which had virtually been taken already. British military intervention at Abadan was now out. The action of the Foreign Secretary was to be diplomatic.

---

[68] EP 1611/50.
[69] *Ibid.*
[70] EP 1531/1815.

A telegram of September 30 from the Foreign Office to the British delegation at New York explained: 'The fact is that the staff are being withdrawn, not principally on account of the expulsion order but because the Persians have made conditions in Abadan intolerable.'[71] It is rather difficult to resist the impression that this was something less than the whole truth; and that the argument approximated dangerously to running away from one's own decisions. True enough, the long-enduring British staff at Abadan was at last, as Ministers correctly appreciated, just about at the end of its tether. But that was, very largely, because His Majesty's Government had, for however good reasons of policy, withheld from them that effective succour which they on their side had good reason to expect, if not from the obligations of a Government towards its nationals abroad, then from the interim injunction of the International Court of Justice. The British official announcement of September 28, scouting the use of force, may well have been the last straw for the oilmen at Abadan. To seek to impute the final decision to evacuate to their immediate position or to any failure of their staunchness can scarcely appear a worthy argument. By then the whole set of British policy was in any case in the opposite direction to resistance to the Persians.

The same telegram of September 30, 1951, to New York recognised that the decision to withdraw in any case from Abadan complicated the presentation to the Security Council of the British resolution, which precisely and urgently sought to prevent such withdrawal, and which was still to be pressed. Such was the complication, not to say confusion, in which British policy found itself, that it was coming dangerously close to pursuing two contraries. Well might Sir Gladwyn Jebb agree that his task in the Security Council, which was to meet on October 1, would now be more difficult since the decision to evacuate, to be announced at 6.5 pm New York time, when the Council would be actually in session, 'will to some extent invalidate the argument as to urgency'[72] of the Security Council acting on the British resolution. Gravest of all, the complication of British policy was to introduce further reservations into relations with the United States.

British recourse to the Security Council had superseded the American proposals, received in the Foreign Office on September 29, for further discussion of terms with Dr Musaddiq, to which His Majesty's Government 'in any case see strong objections'.[73] Sir Oliver Franks was so informed in a telegram of October 1, approved by both Mr Morrison and Mr Attlee. Agreement was expressed with American emphasis upon the importance of the Shah, but the Foreign Secretary doubted whether he really understood British efforts to reach a settlement 'or whether the implications, for example, of the eight-point proposals have ever been fully explained to him'.[74] (Whose fault that was, remained, perhaps, a question.) As to the American suggestions for particular proposals, Sir Roger Makins had advised that they 'do not really offer a new approach but are variations on a theme'.[75] He considered that the important one regarding the substitution of Anglo-Dutch interests for Anglo-Iranian 'has basic difficulties in that the AIOC would never willingly accept and it would probably not be acceptable to Anglo-Dutch'. Such difficulties

---

[71] EP 1611/57G.
[72] EP 1531/1682.
[73] EP 1531/1663.
[74] *Ibid.*
[75] *Ibid.*

were certainly liable to be formidable but Mr Berthoud, following up Sir William Strang, had already suggested the dilution of the Anglo-Iranian Oil Company into a consortium, though not the company's supersession (cf pp. 300-1, 344-5—It was subsequently reported that the American oil companies were veering back from recent consideration of arrangements to replace the Persian working of Anglo-Iranian Oil Company, which had unfavourably impressed Mr Harriman.)[76] These issues, while seminal for the future, were yet academic for the present. On the immediate one of the divergent British and American resolutions proposed for the Security Council the Foreign Secretary had on the previous day of September 30 sent a personal appeal to the Secretary of State.

Mr Herbert Morrison informed Mr Dean Acheson that he was 'deeply concerned' by the implications of the American draft resolution. 'I feel rather strongly', wrote the Foreign Secretary, 'that it is out of harmony with the friendly and understanding talks we had in Washington. We have honourably abided by The Hague decision and I do not like . . . being put into the dock together with Dr Musaddiq. You know full well the efforts I have made in this country towards a close alignment of the policies of our two nations—and at times it has been a difficult task—and there is no doubt that British public opinion would strongly resent the imputation in the United States resolution if they heard of it. I ask you most earnestly, as friend to friend, to take this into account and to reconsider the United States proposal. America will surely not refuse to stand together with us in seeking to uphold through the United Nations the rule of law which has been our guiding principle in this issue.'[77]

It is difficult not to sympathise with the rather injured tone of Mr Morrison's appeal and, indeed, not to regret that some similarly powerful British representation had not been made to the Americans at a rather earlier stage. By now things had gone so far that even the issue of American support for the British case was no longer quite so straightforward as one might suppose.

On the same day of September 30 the State Department told His Majesty's Ambassador that they were wondering whether they should try to arrange for President Truman to send a personal message to Dr Musaddiq in order to back up one which, it was hoped, he would be receiving from Dr Carlos Muniz, the Brazilian delegate on the Security Council, who would be its President in October; this would ask the Persian Government to delay the expulsion of the British staff from Abadan pending consideration of the question by the Council. In the event Dr Muniz refused to send such a message on his own responsibility since he was afraid of being criticised like his Russian predecessor, M. Malik, for undue 'freewheeling'. The State Department, however, remained 'most anxious to be helpful on this point'[78] and asked whether the Foreign Secretary would think that, if it could be arranged, President Truman should still send such a message upon the critical issue of expulsion.

A telegram despatched from the Foreign Office at 4pm on October 1 replied to Sir Oliver Franks that the position had been altered by the decision to withdraw the British staff in any case on October 3: 'this does not in our view substantially affect the position in regard to the Security Council resolution but it does suggest that a

---

[76] EP 1531/1889.
[77] EP 1531/1815.
[78] EP 1531/1666G.

message from President Truman in the sense suggested . . . would not now serve a useful purpose. Musaddiq would in any case almost certainly reject it.'[79] (Though perhaps even that might have been to British advantage.) Sir Oliver Franks was accordingly to 'express some doubt' to the State Department regarding the usefulness of such a message from Mr Truman, and to express a preference for concentrating on obtaining from the Security Council an authorisation for Dr Muniz to send a similar (and presumably equally ineffective) message to Dr Musaddiq: 'A message from Mr Truman is we feel a weapon to be reserved for the most favourable moment.'[80] Such was the British reply approved for despatch by Sir Roger Makins before submission to Mr Morrison who did not comment.

When one is fighting with one's back to the wall it can be rather a luxury to reserve a formidable weapon for a more favourable moment. But British diplomacy almost seemed to be no longer really fighting, but indulging in shadow-boxing. Even in such a matter as that of stimulating helpful messages to Tehran, it now preferred the weaker course. The face-saving British appeal to the Security Council to restrain the Persian Government from expelling the British staff at Abadan inevitably acquired a certain air of unreality in relation to the substantive British decision to have done at long last and to withdraw in any case from Abadan.

British diplomacy, however, was still not wholly without further resource. The above instructions to Sir Oliver Franks further commented, in accordance with a submission by Sir Roger Makins, approved by Mr Morrison and Mr Attlee:[81] 'a possible element for inclusion in a Council resolution might be a clause calling upon the two parties to work out by negotiation a *modus vivendi* based on the interim decision of the Hague Court. This would be preferable from our point of view to a clause simply calling on the two parties to negotiate . . . we have already devoted considerable thought to this possibility'[82] (cf p. 359). While it was recognised that this interesting proposal was unlikely to be 'particularly palatable to Musaddiq',[83] it was yet seemingly worth pursuing if only as a possible bargaining counter in bidding for effective support from the United States and in the United Nations. Whereas in practice when Sir Gladwyn Jebb suggested the idea to the American delegation to the United Nations, they could not see any future for it and commented so as to provoke Sir Gladwyn Jebb to protest against such a 'defeatist attitude which would in effect imply that we must let the Persians get away with everything'.[84] A considerably diluted reference to the interim injunction was subsequently included in a subsequently further diluted draft resolution (cf p. 416) for the Security Council.

On October 1, 1951, *The Times* published a report from its correspondent in Washington that hardly anyone there 'is inclined to credit Britain with even the first glimmerings of statesmanship during recent months' as regards Persia; 'whatever happens now, American faith in British diplomacy has received a shock from which it will take a long time to recover'. The State Department, still anxious to mediate in the dispute, was reluctant to be forced out openly on the side of Great Britain by her resort to the Security Council after 'a series of unparalleled diplomatic blunders'.

[79] *Ibid.*
[80] *Ibid.*
[81] EP 1531/1762.
[82] EP 1531/1666G.
[83] *Ibid.*
[84] EP 1531/1739.

Some days later Sir Oliver Franks reported that the State Department 'feel that we have behaved all along as though we had the alternative of using force available as a last resort to maintain our position in Abadan. For a variety of reasons this was not done; therefore our tactics have, in their view, been mistaken.'[85]

It was not only in Washington that British diplomacy came under fire. On September 29 a leader in *The Times* had claimed that the country had been misled by its reading of the Government's statements of July 30 and 31; and the rejection of the Persian proposals of September 19 was particularly criticised. *The Times* proceeded to administer a little lecture on diplomacy: 'It is one of the first rules of diplomacy not to sever negotiations until some alternative policy is settled . . . The Government wasted time, and pursued a vain hope in banking on the downfall of Dr Moussadek.' *The Times* returned to the theme on October 5 in a leader which was entitled 'Faults in Diplomacy', and which observed: 'It appears that almost every simple diplomatic rule was broken.' On the same day Mr Eden observed that in the oil dispute the British Government had 'tried everything and followed through in nothing'.[86]

In so far as His Majesty's Government had banked on effective support from the Security Council of the United Nations—and perhaps it was not really so very far— it was doomed to further disappointment. At the meeting of the Council on October 1 the Russian delegate, M. Tsarapkin, objected to the adoption of the provisional agenda regarding the Persian dispute as constituting an intervention in the internal affairs of Persia. This objection was overruled by nine votes to two (Russia and Yugoslavia). Sir Gladwyn Jebb thereupon made a strong statement of the British case against the 'insensate actions' of the Persian Government. He referred to the British decision to evacuate on October 3 but argued that it did not 'detract in the slightest from the urgency of the situation' and that the Security Council ought to indicate to the Persian Government that 'its latest arbitrary action [regarding expulsion] should . . . be rescinded before the ultimatum expires'.[87]

The Persian delegate to the United Nations, Dr Ardalan, replied that he had no authority to take part in the discussion, and requested an adjournment of 10 days to enable Persian representatives to reach New York. Sir Gladwyn Jebb expressed a preference for a very brief delay but the Turkish delegate, for instance, observed that many delegations had not yet received instructions. The Council decided on a postponement of 10 days, or less if the President, after keeping in touch with the Persian delegation, found that that would be practicable. By this simple and not unforeseen device did the Persian delegation postpone substantive discussion and decision in the Security Council till a week after the expiry of the ultimatum for the expulsion of the British from Abadan. Meanwhile the idea that Dr Muniz should be authorised to send a restraining message to Dr Musaddiq was evidently not pressed or adopted.

British resort to the Security Council had so far achieved nothing substantial and for the future the prospect was anything but bright. Not only the Americans but Sir Gladwyn Jebb himself continued to consider, as he was to telegraph on the night of October 2-3, 'that the necessary majority for our resolution as at present drafted is

---

[85] EP 1531/1770.
[86] *The Times*, October 6, 1951.
[87] EP 1531/1737.

improbable . . . I can conceive of little worse than a failure to obtain the necessary votes in the Security Council.'[88] In reply the 'provisional comments at official level' from the Foreign Office were inclined to insist upon the British thesis, based on the Hague ruling, 'even at the risk of not securing seven votes . . . As things are the United Nations stand to lose more than the United Kingdom from the failure of a resolution on these lines.'[89] In reply to this perhaps imperfectly realistic argument Sir Gladwyn Jebb, who personally favoured resumption of negotiations with Dr Musaddiq (cf pp. 410-11), argued in a message of October 4 to Sir Roger Makins that 'to press on with this obviously very moral resolution . . . could simply mean that we should make the worst of all worlds'.[90]

3. The British relinquishment of Abadan, October 1-4

By October 2, 1951, British policy in regard to Persia was in some disarray, with a tendency towards recrimination not only with the American Government on the one hand but, on the other, with the Anglo-Iranian Oil Company. Mr Mason had reported in a telegram of about 1.45 pm on October 1 from Khorramshahr that when he had that afternoon informed his staff of the arrangements for evacuation by the Royal Navy to Basra, 'they became suspicious that they would be held there, otherwise they argued why cannot aircraft come into Abadan for passengers equally well as into Basra'.[91] On October 3 the Foreign Secretary minuted on this telegram: 'I'm a bit fed up with AIOC & its staff. Are they playing politics? Tell Chairman I doubt whether company has any leadership.'[92]

The above minute probably reflected the embarrassment caused to His Majesty's Government by Mr Mason's announcement of the evacuation to local press correspondents at 1 pm on October 1, nearly 12 hours before the hearing in the Security Council of the urgent British appeal against expulsion. His action was questioned from the Foreign Office with reference to telegram No. 431 to Khorramshahr (cf p. 402), giving the terms, which were only general, of the public announcement of evacuation, which was only to be made early on October 2. The reply of October 3 from Khorramshahr explained Mr Mason's action in accordance with the instructions in telegram No. 430 to Khorramshahr. As instructed, Major Capper had informed the local Persian authorities of the proposed evacuation at approximately noon on October 1. Mr Mason had duly been informed of it, with the particulars as to date and transport, at about 9 am that morning and had told his staff about noon. Since the British staff lived with the British press correspondents they too heard the news, and when they asked about 1 pm for confirmation Mr Mason had felt bound to admit the facts.[93]

While Mr Mason's handling of the local Press might conceivably have been rather more perspicacious, he had received no instruction that the information regarding evacuation was to be given to his staff in confidence, even though the communication was to be both earlier and more detailed than the proposed public announcement. It would appear that the source of the muddle was imperfect

---

[88] EP 1531/1714.
[89] *Ibid.*
[90] EP 1531/1767.
[91] EP 1531/1686.
[92] *Ibid.*
[93] EP 1611/50 and 58.

coordination of the instructions issued in the two telegrams of September 30 from the Foreign Office. The importance of this confusion was enhanced by the fine timing whereby His Majesty's Government had sought, so far as might be, to reconcile its divergent decisions to appeal to the Security Council against expulsion from Abadan and in any case to evacuate it. Complicated policies tend to produce complications.

As it was, after Mr Mason's announcement at Abadan on October 1, Sir Roger Makins had telephoned to Mr Morrison at Scarborough and advised that the decision to evacuate be announced in London that afternoon. After consulting Mr Attlee and Mr Shinwell the Foreign Secretary agreed to such publication provided, still, that no indication of the method of evacuation was given.[94] (Yet, whether or not owing to some further confusion, the Admiralty issued an announcement on that evening of October 1 regarding naval evacuation.)[95] It was held in the Foreign Office that Mr Mason's statement 'was to some extent at least responsible for the Council refusing our plea of urgency'.[96] The British official announcements of September 28 and of October 1 had both been awkwardly hurried out largely owing to advance leaks of one kind or another. And the latter instance tended to exacerbate the rather strained relations between His Majesty' Government and the Anglo-Iranian Oil Company now that their long and proud partnership in Persia was drawing to a somewhat ignominious close.

At 6.15 pm on October 2, 1951, a telegram from the Foreign Office to Khorramshahr transmitted the following message from Sir William Fraser to Mr Mason: 'At this time when you and your staff are leaving the great industry which has been built up by you and your predecessors I and my co-directors . . . join in tribute to your courage and tenacity in the face of the most difficult situations which have ever confronted the management and staff in the company's history. You have the satisfaction of knowing that you have all fulfilled your duty in a manner which has been a source of pride to the British people.'[97]

The Foreign Secretary minuted on the above message: 'I may want to see Fraser ab[ou]t AIOC men's doubtful propaganda in Abadan.'[98] As a pendant to this one may perhaps cite an observation by Colonel H.G. Dunn, the British Military Attaché from Tehran who attended the evacuation of the company's staff from Abadan: 'The cry was not "Home for Goodwood" [cf p. 257), but "Home for the Election"'.[99] During it, reported Colonel Dunn, the staff wished to criticise the Government. The correspondent of *The Times* reported: 'The attitude of the staff on leaving was one of depression. Although they were tired of staying on with no work to do, they had hoped to be able to remain, and looked forward to an agreement.'[100] It is said that the oil men enlivened the tense interim of the last few days before evacuation by staging a revue entitled 'Stand Firm, You Cads!'

It was on the evening of October 2, 1951, that Mr Winston Churchill opened the Conservative election campaign in a speech at Liverpool Stadium. He read out the

---

[94] EP 1611/61.
[95] *The Times*, October 2, 1951.
[96] EP 1611/50.
[97] EP 1531/1686.
[98] EP 1531/1686.
[99] EP 1611/67.
[100] *The Times*, October 4, 1951.

'solemn undertaking' regarding the British presence in Abadan which Mr Attlee and Lord Jowitt had given in Parliament on July 30-31, and commented: 'I do not remember any case where public men have broken their word so abruptly and without even an attempt at explanation . . . We have been expelled . . . in defiance of the ruling in our favour of the Hague Court.' The Foreign Secretary and his associates, said Mr Churchill, no doubt hoped 'to cover up their failure by saying that the Tories want war . . . But this is not now a living issue . . . We have fled from the field even before the parleys were completed.' Dr Musaddiq, he continued, had realised that His Majesty's Government's show of armed force was only bluff and 'shrewdly chose the moment of the election, knowing what they would be thinking about then. And so this chapter is finished.'[101] Mr Herbert Morrison replied next day at Scarborough, reiterating that the Prime Minister had not undertaken to use force to keep our people at Abadan, referring to 'the semi-hysteria of the bulk of the Tory backbenchers', and challenging Mr Churchill to 'say whether in his judgment the Government should have gone to war with Persia or not'.[102] ('Whose finger on the trigger?', asked the *Daily Mirror*.)

The Times commented on October 3 that in Persia His Majesty's Government 'have suffered a humiliating defeat'. While in England the responsibilities for that defeat were being hotly argued in electioneering exchanges, in Abadan the consequences of it were being played out in practical and human terms. There was a certain tendency among the British staff there, as earlier perhaps in the company's board in London, to criticise the higher British executives in Abadan, in their very difficult and invidious position, for being too friendly with the usurping Persians. On the evening of October 2 some of the British executives actually dined with M. Makki, perhaps with a long view to future relations when the Anglo-Iranian Oil Company might return to Abadan. But at present, after decades of splendid enterprise there, it was being thrown out.

The early morning of Wednesday, October 3, 1951, found almost all the remaining British staff at Abadan, about 320 of them, waiting in their bungalows for buses which carried them to the Gymkhana Club. There they passed through the Persian customs, which expedited formalities. Among the few British women still to be evacuated were nurses, now carrying large hams. They were included in the 40 who were to leave that morning by air. The remaining 280 were to go by sea to Basra. Some of the British staff had with them dogs, tennis rackets, golf clubs—their yachts they had to leave behind, unsold. By 9 am nearly all were ready to leave.

The area was strongly cordoned by Persian troops. The Persian determination was, as throughout recent weeks, to afford no pretext for British intervention. Courteously correct now, but unyielding to the last, the Persian authorities had refused to allow His Majesty's Ships to moor alongside but insisted that the departing British be ferried out to HMS *Mauritius*, lying in the Shatt-el-Arab, not in the company's craft but in Persian naval launches. Three of them operated a shuttle service. Mr Mason was concerting arrangements with the Senior Naval Officer, Persian Gulf, aboard HMS *Mauritius*. Mr Ross stood on the jetty bidding farewell to the staff, who were given copies of Sir William Fraser's last message to Mr Mason, together with one from Sir Francis Shepherd: His Majesty's Government as such had

---

[101] *Ibid*, October 3, 1951.
[102] *Ibid*, October 4, 1951.

sent no official adieu to those who had for so long borne the physical heat and burden of the crisis. The scene was watched by all senior Persian officials at Abadan (except M. Makki) and by numbers more who had come from Tehran for the occasion. Watching from Number One Jetty were Colonel Dunn and Major Capper. His Majesty's Consul-General, speaking on behalf of his staff, said in farewell to the evacuees: 'We wish you *bon voyage*, and a well-deserved leave and speedy return.'[103] But speedy their return to Persia was not to be.

The ferrying out to HMS *Mauritius* was inclined to be slow. The British Military Attaché from Tehran estimated, however, that the traditional hospitality of the Royal Navy might to some extent compensate the British oil men for their disappointment at not being flown direct to England. Only 10 British men including Mr Mason and Mr Ross, along with Major Capper, remained in Abadan pending their final departure on the morrow. At about 1.30 pm, at high tide, on that day of October 3 HMS *Mauritius*, carrying the 280, cast off. As she passed the great refinery and the house of Mr Ross 'the oil employees cheered lustily'[104]—an interesting demonstration since Mr Ross was one of those who was said to have incurred some criticism for his friendliness with the Persians. The warship was accompanied by the last five remaining sea-going tugs of the British Tanker Company, flying the Red Ensign. As HMS *Mauritius* steamed upstream to Basra all hands were on deck and her ship's band was playing. The tune was 'Colonel Bogey'.

Such was the immediate outcome of British diplomacy in the Persian crisis of 1951. Colonel Dunn reported that in a last, pathetic piece of wishful thinking the departing British staff had thought that British military forces would assault Abadan after they had left. The military planning staff had indeed for some while past represented that from a strictly military standpoint the best time to launch Operation Buccaneer would be after the bulk of the company's staff had withdrawn; and on September 19[105] the Chiefs of Staff had overruled a representation from the Commanders-in-Chief, Middle East, that the readiness of Buccaneer should be reduced in the light of the menacing situation in Egypt (cf pp. 313f). The ripples from trouble at Abadan were already lapping through the Middle East. On the same day of October 3 Sir John Troutbeck was writing from Baghdad to Mr Furlonge regarding 'the prevalent mood of speculation here as to how far we shall allow ourselves to be pushed around in Persia without hitting back'.[106]

Also on October 3 Sir Gladwyn Jebb was advising a resumption of negotiations with Dr Musaddiq—'purely intellectual exercise though this is likely to be'—on the grounds that 'only by so doing are we likely to get willing American support for those methods of coercion which will almost undoubtedly be necessary if we are to arrive at any settlement consonant with our prestige and our interests'.[107] It was still the same, familiar theme: His Majesty's Government should at present take a more conciliatory line with the unyielding Persian Government in order to be able to take a stronger line later with that support from the United States Government which in fact was never effectively forthcoming.

The attitude of the French delegation had differed markedly from that of the

[103] *The Times*, October 4, 1951.
[104] *Ibid.*
[105] EP 1192/115G.
[106] EP 1192/123.
[107] EP 1531/1740.

American in the debate in the Security Council on October 1, and only the French delegate had gone out of his way to support Sir Gladwyn's plea of urgency. On the same day the French Ambassador in London told Sir Roger Makins that the French Government was very much disturbed by a report from its delegate in New York: 'the United States Government did not seem to be alive to the realities of the situation'.[108] Sir Roger Makins said that His Majesty's Government 'regarded the American attitude as deplorably weak'. M. Massigli thought that the State Department was anxious to uphold the United Nations but was overruled by the Pentagon, which was obsessed by the fear of Persia falling to Russia. In a further conversation two days later Sir Roger Makins stated in reply to a question from M. Massigli that he thought it was still the British view, as it always had been, that although the Russians could deny Great Britain the use of Persian oil, they could not use it themselves. In any case the Persians would probably be unenthusiastic about working their oil industry with Russians.

The French Ambassador opined to Sir Roger Makins on October 1 that 'if the United States persisted in their attitude the whole Western position in the Middle East would collapse'.[109] In their second conversation on October 3 M. Massigli said that the United States Government had shown displeasure that the French Government had agreed to support Great Britain in the United Nations before having heard the American view. The latter was now being actively represented to the French Government. Sir Roger Makins 'stressed the importance of the Americans, ourselves, the French and the Dutch standing together in this matter. Our position and our interests in the Middle East and in other parts of the world were in jeopardy. We must make it clear that we upheld the rule of law in these matters and that we would not allow the Persian Government to profit from their course of action. Once the Persians were convinced that we were in earnest it might be easier to negotiate.'[110]

The French Ambassador expressed a wish to discuss the matter with the Foreign Secretary—once again, even at that crux for Britain, the initiative came from the French side. Mr Herbert Morrison minuted on October 4: 'Yes. I propose to ask him to stiffen up US and not be squeezed by them. Here's a chance for Anglo-French pressure on US. Let us be stiff with US.'[111] There might have been a considerable amount to be said earlier for such a policy, despite the limited strength of France. Hitherto, however, the possibilities for Britain of such a policy seem to have been somewhat neglected. They might still be not negligible. But it was much too late now to avert the debacle at Abadan. British cooperation with other Western Powers regarding Persian oil was in future to take the form, mainly, of bringing them into the previously British industry.

At half past five on the afternoon of Thursday, October 4, 1951, the 24th meeting of the Cabinet Committee on Persia was attended by Mr Attlee, Mr Morrison, Mr Gaitskell, Mr Shinwell, Mr Noel-Baker, Sir Hartley Shawcross, Mr Stokes, Lord Pakenham and Mr Barnes, the Minister of Transport. In attendance were Vice-Admiral Guy Grantham, Vice-Chief of the Naval Staff, General Brownjohn, Air

---

[108] EP 1531/1788.
[109] *Ibid.*
[110] EP 1531/1757.
[111] *Ibid.*

Marshal Sir Arthur Sanders, Sir Roger Makins, Mr Bowker, Sir Donald Fergusson, Sir Leslie Rowan and Mr Flett—nearly all of them long versed in that bitter crisis. The committee decided that the forces for Operation Buccaneer should be released for other duties. Their protracted vigil and unimplemented menace was at an end. It was also decided (cf p. 396) that for the present British warships should not intercept tankers carrying oil from Abadan.

At that meeting of the Committee on Persia the Prime Minister 'said that the position adopted by the United States Government had embarrassed us throughout the course of the dispute, and their unwillingness to support us now in the Security Council was quite unjustifiable. It would, however, be impracticable to put forward our original resolution to the Council without United States support, and further discussions with the United States Government about a compromise text would have to go on.'[112] The Lord Privy Seal observed that 'even if the decision of the Council was ultimately in our favour, the Persian Government would certainly not conform with it'. The Foreign Secretary intimated that 'the United States Government were now thinking of a joint operation of the oil industry in Persia, representing British, United States, and possibly Dutch and French interests'.[113] The new pattern of the future was already emerging on the day on which the finest chapter of British industrial enterprise in Persia, indeed in any foreign land, was brought to an unhappy close.

At ten o'clock on the morning of October 4, 1951, the Temporary Board of the National Iranian Oil Company had bidden farewell to Mr Ross, who was to be the first of the last to leave. He was presented by M. Makki with a Persian carpet. Mr Ross is said to have commented: 'Would you call that a fair exchange?'[114] However he shook hands with M. Makki and M. Barzargan, the Chairman, and drove away to cross over to Basra. Two more cars drew up to convey Mr Mason and his staff. The Persians turned their backs and walked off, refusing to the end to recognise the general administration of the evicted Anglo-Iranian Oil Company. Major Capper stayed till the last. Expelled from Persia, His Majesty's Consul-General in Khuzistan left by consular launch that afternoon. This completed the British relinquishment of Abadan in 1951.

---

[112] EP 1531/1804G.

[113] *Ibid.*

[114] Norman Kemp, *Abadan* (London 1953), p. 249.

CHAPTER XV

AFTERMATH AND RECOMMENCEMENT,
OCTOBER 5, 1951-AUGUST 5, 1954

1. Repercussions in Egypt

The gravest and most prompt repercussion of the British eviction from Abadan occurred in Egypt with special significance for the British position on the Suez Canal. In the later words of Lord Avon: 'The troubles fomented on the Shatt al Arab, festered on the Nile.'[1]

Since the beginning of 1950 the nationalist Wafdist Government of Nahas Pasha had held power in Egypt. The two big, brooding questions outstanding on the Anglo-Egyptian agenda were the maintenance in the Canal Zone of the great British military base and British Middle East Headquarters and, directly related, the revision of the Anglo-Egyptian Treaty of 1936. This 20-year treaty provided, in particular, for reconsideration at the end of its term, in 1956, of the stationing of British forces in the Canal Zone to ensure its defence in cooperation with Egyptian forces. The two central questions were complicated by two others: on the one hand the mounting Egyptian demand for Sudanese union with Egypt in the incipient aftermath of British imperialism; and on the other the reiterated but fruitless British demands, reinforced now by the Security Council, that Egypt should raise her selective embargo in the Suez Canal on shipping bound for Israel, and notably the British refinery at Haifa (cf pp. 207, 213-4, 356, 389).

Such were the unpropitious conditions in which His Majesty's Government had on April 11, 1951, communicated to the Egyptian Government new proposals for the solution of the two main issues between them. His Majesty's Government had indicated its readiness to revise the treaty of 1936 in accordance with its Article 16; this had notably stipulated that revision should 'provide for the continuation of the Alliance'. Such revision would cover the early withdrawal of British troops from their base in the Canal Zone; this would henceforth be guarded by Egyptian forces, tended by 'essential British civilian personnel'[2] and operated under an Anglo-Egyptian control board. On April 24 the Egyptian Government had rejected these proposals as insufficient, 'in toto and in detail'.[3]

This critical British difference with Egypt had festered on through the summer. Relations were exacerbated by the incident of the *Empire Roach* (cf p. 234-5) and menaced by the Persian example. On the morning of October 4, even as the last British subjects were leaving Khorramshahr, the acting chief of the Egyptian Royal Cabinet told His Majesty's Embassy in Cairo that 'with the example of the events in Persia before them it was very difficult for the country to accept anything less from the [Egyptian] Government than formal abrogation'[4] of the Anglo-Egyptian Treaty of 1936. In the same despatch Sir Ralph Stevenson reported that the Egyptian Press deduced from the eviction of the British from Abadan that 'it had been proved that

---

[1] Sir Anthony Eden, *The Memoirs of the Rt Hon Sir Anthony Eden: Full Circle* (London 1960), p. 195.
[2] Cmd 8419, *Anglo-Egyptian Conversations on the defence of the Suez Canal and on the Sudan, December 1950-November 1954*, p. 24.
[3] *Ibid*, p. 25.
[4] JE 1051/365. The editorial insertion of 'Egyptian' in the original of this memorandum may perhaps be in error for 'British'.

the British could not stand up to force'. On October 8, 1951, Nahas Pasha laid before the Egyptian Parliament Bills for the unilateral abrogation of the Anglo-Egyptian Treaty and of the Sudan Condominium Agreements. Among the precedents which he cited in alleged justification of such unilateral abrogation of treaties were the abrogation by the German Government of Herr Hitler of Part V of the Treaty of Versailles, of the Pact of Locarno, of the German-Polish declaration of non-aggression, of the Anglo-German Naval Convention of 1935.

Thus swiftly justified was the warning which the Foreign Secretary had given to the Cabinet on September 27, 1951, as to the likely repercussions in Egypt of British acquiescence in eviction from Abadan. This probable correlation had naturally been taken into account at the higher levels, at least, in the Foreign Office. Yet when all allowance is made for the time-saving convenience of verbal consultation within the Office, one is still rather surprised to notice how few papers during the Persian crisis of 1951 were marked and minuted in joint consultation between Eastern Department, responsible for Persian affairs, and African Department handling those of Egypt. There was some danger that the Suez Canal might prove to be almost more of a real divide departmentally, on paper, than it was politically, on the spot.

Despite the Egyptian defiance of October 8 His Majesty's Government five days later joined with those of the United States, France and Turkey in a joint proposal to the Egyptian Government to participate in the establishment of an interallied Middle East Command, wherein Australia, New Zealand and South Africa were also willing to participate. This would supersede arrangements under the Anglo-Egyptian Treaty of 1936. This spacious and constructive proposal had already been adumbrated to the Egyptian Government in the days of Mr Ernest Bevin; since then work on it had actively proceeded and the inclusion of Turkey, in particular, reflected the recent satisfaction of a Turkish demand (cf pp. 399-400) when the North Atlantic Council, meeting at Ottawa on September 20, 1951, had agreed to invite Turkey and Greece to accede to the North Atlantic Treaty Organisation.

Egypt replied on October 15, 1951, by enacting the bills of abrogation tabled a week earlier. The Egyptians suspected, perhaps understandably, that the four-power proposals were a dodge to perpetuate and consolidate British occupation. And the Wafdist organ *al-Balagh* had earlier observed: 'No one waits for far-reaching proposals from a weak [British] Cabinet on the eve of an election campaign in which it is doomed to defeat.'[5] The outgoing Labour Government in fact did its best to offset the debacle in Persia by displaying resolution in Egypt. One of its last acts was to reinforce the British garrison in the Canal Zone by two brigades. That was their destination, rather than Abadan.

After becoming Foreign Secretary on October 27, 1951, Mr Eden sent the Egyptian Government a stiff notification of British refusal to accept Egypt's unilateral denunciation of the Anglo-Egyptian treaty, which contained no provision for such a procedure. 'If', he represented, 'the principle were accepted that one party to such a treaty were entitled to denounce that treaty unilaterally, no reliance could be placed on any international agreement, and the whole basis and structure of international relations would cease to exist.[6] His Majesty's Government accordingly intended 'fully to maintain their rights'. They needed to. On October 16, 1951, the

---

[5] Cited, P. Calvocoressi, *Survey of International Affairs 1951*, p. 281, note 4.
[6] Cited, Sir Anthony Eden, *op. cit,* p. 226.

day after Egypt broke her treaties with Great Britain, large parties of Egyptian students from Cairo arrived in the Canal Zone and proceeded to incite celebrations in the form of attacking and looting British property. Lieutenant-General Sir George Erskine, General Officer Commanding British troops in Egypt, took vigorous counter-measures.

Throughout the autumn of 1951 the situation in the Canal Zone deteriorated into a war of nerves, pinpricks and sniping affrays. By the end of the year the British forces had lost the services of 93 per cent of its Egyptian civilian labour. From January 4, 1952, British tanks were in action against houses harbouring snipers, and on January 25 they stormed police headquarters at Ismailia; the Egyptian police, refusing a British summons to disarm, fought it out till some 40 of them had been killed. Next day Cairo endured 'Black Saturday'. Vengefully nationalistic mobs swept through the city, killed over 20 people—about half of them British—burned and looted some 700 premises including Shepheard's Hotel, and did millions of pounds worth of damage.

On the morning of the following day, January 27, 1952, King Farouk dismissed the Government of Nahas Pasha for failing to maintain order. This, by an ironical outcome, was to prove the end of the long ascendancy in Egyptian politics of the corrupted Wafd. But henceforth Egypt was steering towards a revolutionary course, soon fatal to its indulgent king and, in the long run, even more damaging to the interests of Great Britain than that nationalist eruption in Persia with which she was still confronted.

2. British failure at the Security Council and Anglo-American Conversations in Paris

It was rather natural during a general election that some recriminations regarding what Mr Eden described on October 5, 1951, as the 'resounding and humiliating defeat'[7] at Abadan should have dragged on in its wake. Mr Herbert Morrison became involved in some public contention with returning personnel of the Anglo-Iranian Oil Company regarding the extent to which its local advisers had influenced His Majesty's Government to order evacuation. The Diplomatic Correspondent of *The Times* summed up: 'It seems clear that as a whole the members of the staff at Abadan had become restive, not at the difficulties or danger of their situation, but rather at the length of time which they had to spend without knowing whether the Government would withdraw them or hold the position by force.'[8]

Within the Foreign Office both Sir William Strang and Sir Roger Makins tended to be critical of the Anglo-Iranian Oil Company, described by the latter on October 30 as 'bankrupt both in men and ideas'.[9] The company, however, was in the long run liable to be braced by the new men and new ideas introduced five days earlier into His Majesty's Government by the general election wherein a Labour overall majority of 6 had been converted into a Conservative majority of 17. A general charge might indeed still lie against the company for having earlier pursued unduly slow, rigid and unimaginative policies in Persia. Yet there was more than a little, for instance, in what Mr Rothnie of the Eastern Department of the Foreign Office wrote on

---

[7] *The Times*, October 6, 1951.
[8] *Ibid.*
[9] EP 1531/2061.

November 3, 1951, regarding the company's discharge of its social obligations for local Persian welfare: 'There was nothing much wrong with what AIOC did in this direction—except that they did it in a remote corner of Persia and thereby got the worst of both worlds; incomprehension of what they had done and resentment that they had done it.'[10]

As regards the other main target for criticism, if not resentment, in Whitehall, Mr Eden, the new Foreign Secretary, on October 31 initialled an observation by Sir William Strang that 'the Americans bear a substantial responsibility for recent events in Persia'.[11] After the arrival of Dr Musaddiq in New York on October 8 to attend the resumed session on Persia of the Security Council, the American Government had continued to urge His Majesty's Government to negotiate with him. Whereas, as Mr Herbert Morrison had remarked on October 5 in a conversation wherein he strongly renewed to the American Ambassador complaints against American policy regarding Persia: 'We had no wish to be made fools of once more or find ourselves in another blind alley.'[12] Against this background the State Department continued to be considerably reluctant even in its support of the British resolution for forthcoming presentation to the Security Council. As Sir Oliver Franks reported on October 6: 'There seems to be no very great appreciation among Americans as a whole of the importance of maintaining the rule of law to protect international trade and investment.'[13]

On October 9, 1951, His Majesty's Government agreed to an amended text of an American draft for a watered-down British resolution to the Security Council. In this the Security Council, 'noting the action taken by the International Court of Justice on July 5, 1951', and 'conscious of the importance' of upholding the court's authority, called for the early resumption of negotiations 'in accordance with the principles of the provisional measures indicated by the International Court of Justice', failing mutually agreeable arrangements consistent with the United Nations Charter; and for the avoidance of any action which would further aggravate the situation or prejudice 'the rights, claims or positions of the parties concerned'.[14]

It became evident, however, that even this diluted text was unlikely to obtain the necessary seven votes in the Security Council. This was mainly due to the attitude of those whom Sir Gladwyn Jebb described as 'the chief wobblers',[15] the representatives of India and of Yugoslavia. The vote of Ecuador was also important and uncertain. This was one example among many of the high, perhaps dangerously high, price for the liberalisation of international relations through the United Nations which was being exacted in terms of rather unedifying lobbying by the Great Powers concerned of the governments of small and remote countries. Apart from the great-power veto, the undifferentiated importance of votes in the United Nations was tending to render the settlement of international issues referred to it increasingly precarious and unrealistic. On October 16 His Majesty's Government reluctantly agreed to weaken further the text of its resolution to the Security Council by accepting amendments to it proposed by the Yugoslav and, especially, Indian

---

[10] UES 15327/31.
[11] EP 1015/366.
[12] EP 1531/1762.
[13] PG 13437/45.
[14] EP 1531/1822.
[15] EP 1531/1938.

Governments. These notably deleted all reference to the interim injunction of the International Court of Justice.

The Persian debate had been resumed in the Security Council on October 15, 1951. Sir Gladwyn Jebb rebutted an attack by Dr Musaddiq on the Anglo-Iranian Oil Company but reported of the contribution of the American representative to the proceedings on the following day: 'I cannot fail to draw your attention to the lamentable intervention of Gross at the end of the meeting . . . He implied that the whole United States attitude was based on the desire to show maximum friendship to both parties and I fear the final impression may have been one of appeasement at any price . . . His very indecisive statement caused considerable surprise among friendly journalists.'[16]

In the continued debate in the Security Council on October 17 the representative of Ecuador, M. Quevedo, diverged from the attitude of the United States to indicate that he could not vote for the British resolution even with the Indian and Yugoslav amendments. M. Quevedo expatiated upon the question of domestic jurisdiction and held that it would be inadmissible for the Security Council to pronounce on the Anglo-Persian dispute before The Hague Court had delivered its main decision as to whether it had jurisdiction in the dispute; which would be months ahead. The Yugoslav delegate wobbled backwards against even the emasculated British resolution. After discussion between Mr Attlee and Mr Morrison, approval was given to Sir Gladwyn Jebb's suggestion for avoiding an unfavourable vote on the resolution by proposing adjournment of the discussion in the Security Council pending the judgment of the International Court; and it was suggested that some other delegation should be induced to move this. When Sir Gladwyn asked the Indian representative, Sir Benegal Rau, to sponsor this eminently innocuous motion he declined on the grounds that he might thereby commit himself. Sir Gladwyn Jebb had to turn to the representative of Britain's firmest friend throughout the crisis, France, and 'to recruit Lacoste instead'.[17]

The French motion for adjournment, to what proved to be the Greek Kalends, was adopted by the Security Council on October 19, 1951, by eight votes against one, the Russian, with two abstentions, by Great Britain and Yugoslavia. Such was the wan expedient to which British policy was reduced. In the Security Council, scarcely less than in South Persia, His Majesty's Government had been humiliatingly driven back to ever weaker expedients, not a little owing to pressure from the two great republics of America and India. The vote of October 19 in the Security Council concluded the coda in the United Nations to the previous orchestration by the Labour Government of its policy in the Persian crisis of 1951. The earlier advice from Sir Gladwyn Jebb and from Sir William Strang (cf pp. 251-2, 353) against resort to the Security Council had been fully vindicated.

Sir William Strang commented on October 23, 1951, on 'the anti-colonial and anti-imperialist majority in the United Nations. Sir Eyre Crowe foresaw in 1918 that the creation of the League of Nations would in some respects be inimical to the survival of the British Empire and to the status of the United Kingdom as a great Power. Our experience of the United Nations confirms the pertinence of that view. The recent lamentable proceedings at the Security Council where the Netherlands

---

[16] EP 1531/1923.
[17] EP 1531/1965.

and France almost alone gave us consistent and active support, shows that the United Nations has scant concern for the rule of law and is showing the way to international anarchy.'[18] The irresolute resolution of the Security Council on Persia represented, in the later words of the incoming Mr Eden, 'a dismal failure to measure up to events'.[19]

Sir William Strang's pregnant denunciation of the failure of the United Nations occurred in 'Some Notes on the Persian Oil Dispute and its Implications',[18] which he wrote two days before the general election. The Permanent Under-Secretary noted that 'the fate of long-term agreements with immature and nationalistic Middle Eastern Governments . . . is discouraging'. During the 18 years' operation of its 60-year concession of 1933 the Anglo-Iranian Oil Company had indeed 'made vast profits and a great contribution to the Exchequer . . . They have squeezed every pound they could out of Persia.' Was it better, Sir William Strang asked, thus to make hay while the sun shone or 'to make more flexible and perhaps rather shorter term agreements? . . . Were His Majesty's Government wise to take up a majority of the shares of the company, and yet to limit the powers of the directors nominated by them and to persist in the policy of non-intervention in the commercial operations of the company, rigidly insisted upon by the Treasury until a few months ago? . . . Ought the policy for the extraction, refining and marketing of that [Middle Eastern sterling] oil to be determined so fully as at present by private corporations?'

In the same paper Sir William Strang expressed little doubt that only by British occupation 'by military force . . . could the withdrawal from Abadan have been prevented'. He concluded, however: 'I suspect that whatever we or that company had done, either at an earlier period or in recent months, the Persians being what they are, the issue would have been the same sooner or later, namely the unlawful dispossession of the company . . . If it had not happened in 1951 it would have happened a year or two later. Indeed, had the company done what so many people now say they ought to have done, namely offer the Persian Government more favourable agreements in times past, it is at least possible that the dispossession would have accelerated . . . It may well be that, unless means can be found to enforce international law in these matters the best defence against illegal invasion of foreign oil rights in the Middle East may be a concerted approach to the negotiation of agreements with Middle Eastern Governments by Western Governments and oil companies.' The hopeful initiative in that direction of the Shinwell-Ickes Agreement had already foundered upon American opposition. An imaginatively fresh and ultimately successful attempt to achieve real coordination with America regarding Persian oil was now, however, to be made by the new British Government.

Upon reassuming office Mr Eden, with the approval of Mr Winston Churchill, lost little time in reconstituting, in effect, the previous Ministerial Committee on Persia as a smaller Ministerial Committee under his own chairmanship. Sir William Strang then proposed, on November 1, 1951, that the recast Ministerial Committee should be served by an 'informal official committee', the Persia (Official) Committee, also under Foreign Office chairmanship, in replacement of the Working Party on Persian Oil: Sir William Strang now opined, in a judgment with which one may well agree, that the Working Party was 'not a very satisfactory body and has

---

[18] EP 1531/2147.
[19] Sir Anthony Eden, *op. cit,* p. 195.

not shown the necessary drive'.[20] The new inter-departmental committee would, under the chairmanship of Sir Roger Makins, function upon a higher level than the Working Party. If this important reform of the official machinery in Whitehall had been made some months earlier it might perhaps have considerably improved its handling of the Persian crisis as a whole. The new set-up notably strengthened and restored the influence of the Foreign Office to what one might think was its proper primacy in the determination of foreign policy regarding Persia. Both committees were now under Foreign Office chairmanship in place of the previous arrangement whereby the Ministerial Committee had habitually sat under the Prime Minister, and the Working Party under a representative of the Treasury. Lieutenant-General Sir Kenneth McLean was now to attend meetings, as required, to provide military liaison.

On November 1, 1951, Mr Eden held in his room at the Foreign Office an important meeting foreshadowing the new Ministerial Committee on Persia, comprising Mr R.A. Butler, Chancellor of the Exchequer, Lord Leathers, Secretary of State for Coordination of Transport and Fuel and Power, and Mr Selwyn Lloyd, Minister of State in the Foreign Office. Also in attendance were Mr Anthony Nutting, Parliamentary Under-Secretary of State for Foreign Affairs, Sir William Strang and members of the future official committee, Sir Roger Makins, Sir Leslie Rowan and Sir Donald Fergusson. The meeting was completed by Sir Francis Shepherd, back from Tehran for consultations, Mr Furlonge and Mr Ramsbotham as secretary.

The new Foreign Secretary expressed the view that during the Persian crisis 'the American reading of the situation had been more correct than our own'.[21] There was undoubtedly much to support this view. To a considerable extent, however, the divergent British and American assessments of political force in Persia harked back, fundamentally, to that argument which Sir Oliver Franks and Mr Furlonge had had with Mr McGhee back in April as to whether the wind of change blowing through Persia was 'more of a gust than a prevailing wind' (cf p. 144). And, as often, which view was right depended largely upon the time-scale employed. In the short run the American assessment of gale-force had proved the more correct, as it might again be proved, one day, in the very long run. Meanwhile the British reduction of the Musaddiq experience to a gust, while dangerously over-sanguine in the short run, as had just been expensively demonstrated, was yet to prove the more accurate in the middle perspective of practical politics, over the coming year or two. The American contention that the only alternative to Dr Musaddiq was Communism in Persia was to be proved incorrect, but not nearly so quickly or easily as in British anticipations.

After Dr Musaddiq had got away with his grab of Abadan before the Security Council at New York he had, at the invitation of the United States Government, proceeded to Washington, where he met President Truman and held discussions. The Americans continued to try to find a basis for negotiations between His Majesty's Government and the untreatable Persian Premier. They now proposed that the National Iranian Oil Company should manage the oilfields, but the Abadan refinery should be denationalised and sold by the Anglo-Iranian Oil Company to Royal Dutch Shell, which would sell the refined products to a purchasing organisation formed by

---

[20] EP 1531/2075G.
[21] EP 1531/2045G.

Anglo-Iranian. No compensation would be paid to the Anglo-Iranian Oil Company and British technicians would be excluded from Persia.[22]

At Mr Eden's meeting on November 1 it was agreed that 'while the structure of the proposed organisation in the American scheme was reasonable, it contained a number of provisions which were quite unacceptable when considered against His Majesty's Government's three main interests',[21] namely prestige, finance, and economic repercussions elsewhere. In this connexion Sir William Strang minuted two days later to Mr Eden that it had been thought that the Americans 'would stand firm on their sacred principle of "50-50", but now it appears that they are prepared to sacrifice even this, though by fudging they pretend that they are not doing so. In the early stages of this dispute the Americans urged us to "make a deep bow in the direction of nationalisation"' (cf p. 144). They are now asking us formally to ratify an act of expropriation at the expense of British interests. They do not seem to see that this will strike a blow at the security of foreign investments everywhere, theirs as well as ours.'[23]

Mr Eden observed at the meeting on November 1 that 'we must have an alternative policy if we were to reject the American plan . . . He was doubtful whether the right policy was simply to wait for Musaddiq to fall. It might be harder to reach a satisfactory arrangement in the future, especially if the Persians were in the meantime able to sell some of their oil.'[21] In reply *Sir William Strang* desired 'answers to the following two questions: (*a*) whether a bad agreement with Persia was better than no agreement at all; (*b*) whether a reasonably satisfactory agreement was possible with any Persian Government. *Sir Francis Shepherd* said that there was a better chance of reaching a satisfactory settlement with a successor Government than with Dr Musaddiq . . . *Sir Donald Fergusson* suggested it would be better to have no agreement than to negotiate one with Dr Musaddiq on the lines of the American proposals.' In the course of further discussion Mr Eden incidentally 'said that he doubted whether the AIOC could ever return to Persia in any form except by the use of force. Sir Francis Shepherd said he was not convinced on this point.'[24]

By contrast with so much of the previous development of the Persian crisis, the opinion of those British officials who had borne the burden of it in London and in Tehran was now to be happily vindicated in the longer run. This was in good measure due to two basic causes. First, the ultimate humiliation of the eviction from Abadan, while gravely damaging the whole British position in the Middle East, yet paradoxically strengthened the British bargaining position in direct relation to Persia. Because in Persia Britain now had virtually nothing left to lose. Now at last, as never previously, time, that great ally, was on the British side for a spell. The British, traditionally good at making the best of a bad job, now really could afford to sit back, for some months at least, work for the fall of Dr Musaddiq and let the Persians stew in their own oil, which they could not market. That was the second basic factor. In that oil crisis of 1951 Britain had already taken her dose of punishment. Now it was the Persian turn. This was some reflection of the two fundamental and over-sanguine miscalculations, one on either side, which had largely conditioned the whole of the crisis: the over-optimistic estimate, earlier, by His Majesty's Government and, still

---

[22] EP 1531/2032G.
[23] EP 1531/2080G.
[24] EP 1531/2045G.

more perhaps, by the Anglo-Iranian Oil Company of the extent of Persian dependence upon oil revenues from Abadan; and the over-optimistic estimate, throughout, by the Persian Government of the extent of British dependence upon oil supplies from Abadan.

The British failure to induce the Persian Government to act in time to prevent the damage to Persia which would result from British relinquishment of Abadan was at once both emphasised and alleviated by the extent to which, thereafter, the tide of events, sure enough, began at long last to turn and flow in the British direction. In the first place Persia on her own, at that time, could not market or have transported significant quantities of oil; and the rest of the world could almost do without it. Anglo-American domination of the tanker-shipping of the world—always the strongest ultimate weapon against Persia—was now brought to bear. The employment of this weapon depended upon support of British interests by the American oil companies. This was secured with notable success, though it obviously heightened British dependence upon American goodwill. The Anglo-Iranian Oil Company took keen legal action against the few tankers which did still attempt a run from Abadan (cases of the *Rose Mary*, of the *Miriella*). In all Dr Musaddiq sold only about 130,000 tons of oil.

The long-term trends within the oil industry were also against the Persians. On the one hand it was just at this time that production from the oilfields of the Arabian peninsula went soaring up: whereas the production of crude oil in the Middle East in 1950 was 86.6 million tons of which Persia contributed 31.75, total production in 1952, despite the Persian stoppage, was 104.44 million tons. On the other hand there was an economic trend towards the location of refineries close to consuming areas, sometimes under pressure from their Governments, rather than at the source of production. From this point of view, even before the crisis of 1951, the magnificent refinery at Abadan with its brand new catalytic cracker was already tending to conform to an obsolescent pattern. In 1945, 85 percent of all the oil refined in the eastern hemisphere was processed in the Middle East; by 1953 this figure was 19 percent. European refineries in 1945 processed only 6 percent of this total of oil; by 1953 they were processing 63 percent.

Such was the economic setting which was to condition the whole of the Anglo-Persian oil dispute from the winter of 1951 to the summer of 1954. By then, indeed, the blockade against tankers plying to Abadan had for various reasons begun to weaken seriously; but the broad trends continued to run against any easy re-entry by a recalcitrant Persia into the oil markets of the world. During the same period from 1951 to 1954 the diplomatic setting was also to remain largely constant, in accordance with a personal telegram which Sir William Strang was already addressing on November 4, 1951, to Sir Oliver Franks in Washington in a follow-through from the meeting held three days earlier by the Foreign Secretary. That meeting had been in preparation for discussions which Mr Anthony Eden proposed to hold with Mr Dean Acheson in Paris, where they would both be attending a meeting of the Assembly of the United Nations.

Sir William Strang telegraphed to Sir Oliver Franks that before leaving for Paris on that day of November 4 the Secretary of State has 'asked me to send you the following outline of his view on the Persian oil question. There are two main differences between the American appreciation of the situation and our own. They fear that the only alternative to Musaddiq is Communism and to save Persia from

Communism they are ready to sacrifice the interests of the Anglo-Iranian Oil Company and those of His Majesty's Government. We may be wrong but we think that a backward and loose-knit political and economic organisation like Persia would not be likely to collapse as soon as all that and that once it had become clear that he [Musaddiq] could not wring further concessions from His Majesty's Government there would be a fair chance that an alternative and less xenophobic Government would appear. Without United States encouragement we doubt whether Musaddiq would have survived so long. Again the Americans believe that it would be better for us to make a bad agreement with Persia and make it quickly than to make no agreement at all. We do not think so . . . The conclusion is that in their own interests no less than in ours they [the Americans] would do well to join us in taking a stiffer line with Persia than they have been willing to do in the past. The Secretary of State will express his views to Mr Acheson in Paris.'[25] Mr Churchill later commented on this telegram: 'I like all this so much.'[26]

The British and American viewpoints regarding Persia were too strongly held and too divergent to be quickly reconcilable. At the end of their discussions in Paris, on November 13, 1951, Mr Eden and Mr Acheson had to agree to differ about the future of Persia. But in other respects the seeds of that real Anglo-American cooperation which alone could solve the oil problem had been sown, and the Americans had been headed off insistence on negotiations with Persia at any price by the time that Dr Musaddiq left the United States for Tehran via Cairo on November 18.

In response to a request from Mr Eden in Paris for briefing on British 'minimum requirements',[27] Sir Donald Fergusson and Sir Leslie Rowan had arrived there on November 7 with important new instructions which had been agreed at a meeting held by Lord Leathers, and were approved in general by the Prime Minister and later by the Cabinet. It was in accordance with these instructions, and also with what Mr Eden had already said to Mr Acheson, that Sir Donald Fergusson and Sir Leslie Rowan, at a meeting between Mr Eden, Mr Acheson and Mr Harriman at the British Embassy in Paris on that evening of November 7, argued effectively against the unacceptable American proposals regarding Persian oil. When Mr Acheson asked about an alternative, Mr Eden proposed what he believed to be the only way of stopping the Persian game of playing off the United States against the United Kingdom. This was the seminal suggestion from His Majesty's Government for—in the words of a subsequent report by Sir Leslie Rowan of Mr Eden's statement—'a consortium of United States and British oil interests, together with perhaps oil interests from elsewhere. If a consortium of this sort were established the American oil companies might be prepared to concede some share in the oil of Saudi Arabia to British companies.'[28] This followed the lines of a brief prepared for Mr Eden in Paris on November 6;[29] whereas the instructions brought next day from London had stipulated 'as an essential element, that in return for American participation in Persia, AIOC should have some share in Saudi Arabia. This would provide a basis on which His Majesty's Government could agree that the AIOC as such should cease to

---

[25] EP 1531/2056.
[26] EP 1531/2124.
[27] EP 1531/2059.
[28] EP 1531/2138.
[29] EP 1531/2161.

operate within Persia.'[30]

Mr Dean Acheson, however, represented the previously expressed and proper reluctance of the American Government to benefit from British misfortune in Persia. 'It appeared', reported Mr Eden of this meeting, 'that Mr Harriman was slightly less negative. He thought that if this proposal had been made last summer, it might have . . . led to a more satisfactory solution.'[31] Mr Eden later added: 'So did I, though I did not say so.'[32]

In accordance with a request from Mr Acheson to Mr Eden, and at the latter's direction, Sir Leslie Rowan, Sir Donald Fergusson and Mr Flett prepared a formula comprising the general principles on which His Majesty's Government would be prepared to negotiate with any Persian Government. These principles were endorsed in London at the level of a meeting with Sir Roger Makins and Sir Leslie Rowan held on November 8 by Lord Leathers, who felt, however, that the proposal for American participation should be pressed before alternatives were discussed. Lord Leathers also drew attention to the important discrepancy regarding British participation in Saudi Arabia and said that he would telephone to Mr Eden that afternoon and would 'explain that Ministers had had it in mind that the handing over of some British oil interests in Persia to the Americans would be matched by some concession of American interests in Saudi Arabia to British companies. He would tell the Foreign Secretary that he would be prepared, if necessary, to go to Paris on the following morning.'[33] It would appear, however, that Lord Leathers did not go to Paris. Some days later the Persia Official Committee included among possible proposals for a settlement either a partnership between the Anglo-Iranian Oil Company and Aramco in Persia and Saudi Arabia or a consortium of companies for Persia. Mr Ramsbotham did not believe that Aramco would ever accept the first alternative and the second was deemed generally the most satisfactory in the Foreign Office. Mr Eden agreed and thought that Lord Leathers did not appreciate 'how low the name of Anglo-Iranian' had fallen.[34]

On the evening of November 8 Mr Eden put to Mr Acheson and Mr Harriman the four principles just endorsed in London: first, fair compensation for nationalisation; secondly, as Mr Harriman had specified in his letter of September 15 to Dr Musaddiq, security for payment of effective compensation; thirdly, and clearly to American as well as British interest, Persia should not secure better terms than other concessionary Governments which had respected their contracts; fourthly, 'His Majesty's Government cannot negotiate on a basis of discrimination involving the exclusion of its own nationals'.[35] These principles were maintained in substance throughout the subsequent negotiations to solve the stubborn problem of Persian oil.

Immediately, however, the British statement of policy was cautiously received by the Americans and Mr Dean Acheson reiterated his scepticism as to American participation in the Persian oil industry. Though not all other Americans, apparently, were so scrupulously guarded. A month earlier, on October 9, Sir Francis Shepherd had talked in Tehran with a visiting Congressman, Representative John Kennedy of

---

[30] EP 1531/2059.
[31] Ep 1531/2082.
[32] Sir Anthony Eden, *op. cit,* p. 202.
[33] EP 1531/2138.
[34] EP 1531/2192, 2193.
[35] Sir Anthony Eden, *op. cit,* p. 199.

Massachusetts. His Majesty's Ambassador had reported that, in relation to the Communist menace and the need to keep Persian oil flowing, the 34-year-old Mr Kennedy had asked him whether he did not think that, if the Anglo-Iranian Oil Company failed to agree with the Persian Government, 'it would be a good thing for American concerns to step into the breach. The possibility was being discussed in Congress circles in Washington.'[36]

Sir Francis Shepherd had told Mr Kennedy that he thought that Dr Musaddiq would object to any form of foreign organisation for oil in Persia. This view was endorsed by the Foreign Office.[37] So far as it went, it may well have been correct. But now, looking beyond the horizon of Dr Musaddiq—and also perhaps of some of his British opponents hitherto—the large idea of an oil consortium with American participation in Persia was gradually to gather fruitful strength. Henceforth an improving, if still imperfect, Anglo-American collaboration regarding Persia might look, or perhaps glance sideways, to the possibility of a real community of economic interests. In terms of power-politics, if Britain was to get back into Persia she needed, to some extent, to sell out to America. This was the deeper set to counteract further deterioration of the situation in the short run and on the surface of events.

3. Stalemate in Persia

Dr Musaddiq opened the New Year of 1952 by expelling from Persia all British consular officers on grounds of alleged interference in internal affairs, mainly in the year 1920, and of the superfluity, since the termination of the Indian Empire, of the 11 British consular establishments in Persia. His Majesty's Government complied with this demand under protest against Persian contravention of the Anglo-Persian Treaty of March 4, 1857. On January 22, 1952, the day after the British consulates had to close, the Persian Government refused its *agrément* to the appointment of the Hon R.M.A. Hankey as His Majesty's Ambassador in succession to Sir Francis Shepherd. Mr Hankey's previous service in His Majesty's Embassy under Sir Reader Bullard was apparently held against him. No new Ambassador was therefore appointed. His Majesty's Embassy was to be entrusted to the Counsellor, Mr Middleton, as Chargé d'Affaires. After a farewell interview on January 27 with Dr Musaddiq, who 'honoured the occasion by having put on his clothes',[38] Sir Francis Shepherd terminated his troubled embassy of one year and ten months in Tehran. He was appointed His Majesty's Ambassador in Warsaw, transferring from the southern to the western confines of the Soviet Union.

In the first quarter of 1952 Dr Musaddiq was strengthened against the domestic opposition by discussions with representatives of the International Bank, which had tentatively suggested that it might act as trustee and set up an organisation to manage the Persian oil industry and finance its restoration to full working order. Mr Eden told the American Ambassador he had 'some hopes'[39] from those activities. But the blinkered way in which Dr Musaddiq rebuffed this approach and stultified the discussions went far towards confirming earlier British doubts as to whether he would tolerate any kind of foreign operation of the oil industry in Persia. The

---

[36] EP 1531/1837.
[37] EP 1531/1905.
[38] EP 1051/17.
[39] EP 1531/2263G of 1951.

stubborn old Persian Premier, never one to help foreigners to help him, alienated the International Bank that spring as he had done the American Government in the preceding autumn.

On March 20, 1952, the State Department announced refusal of the long-sought American loan to Persia since 'it is most difficult to undertake additional commitments to a country which has the immediate means of helping itself'.[40] A month later an American announcement of continuation of the previous commitment of military aid to Persia was indeed made in a form which Mr Eden regarded as 'deplorable';[41] this, however, was not much more than a ripple on the surface of gradual Anglo-American rapprochement regarding Persia. It was estimated that during the financial year 1952-53 American military aid to Persia was worth something under $25 million. About the same figure represented, for the same period, the total of American technical and economic aid to Persia under the Point-Four Programme. This was earmarked for such estimable purposes as irrigation, public baths, disinfectants and improving the breed of hens. The sums involved were chicken-feed in relation to Persia's financial straits. She went plunging into the red financially if not politically 'down the Communist drain',[42] as President Truman expressed the standing American fear for Persia to Mr Churchill in August 1952. Nevertheless Persia justified British anticipations of the previous autumn as to the extent to which she would be able to scratch along somehow on her low-level economy.

The barren policy of Dr Musaddiq stimulated opposition to him in the Persian Parliament and Press that summer until two developments in July 1952 combined to strengthen him once again. A period of particularly tortuous political intrigue, even by Persian standards, and of obscure manoeuvring by the Shah, culminated on July 16 in the latter refusing Dr Musaddiq's demand that he should become Minister of War with control of the armed forces, of which the Shah was head. Dr Musaddiq resigned and on July 17 the Majlis nominated, and the Shah confirmed, M. Qavam-es-Sultaneh as Prime Minister. But in the face of demonstrations and, later, riots by the gangs of Dr Kashani, the National Front and the Tudeh Party, the Shah refused to sanction M. Qavam's resolute policy of dissolving the Majlis and arresting M. Kashani. The weak Persian monarch was, reported Mr Middleton, 'in the grip of fear' and of pusillanimous advice from M. Husein Ala. On July 21 the Shah accepted M. Qavam's resignation, apparently 'with alacrity and relief'. Next day the Majlis duly nominated Dr Musaddiq to be Prime Minister again by 61 votes to none, with three abstentions. Mr Middleton concluded that in this crisis the Shah 'did not live up to his own responsibilities or exercise his powers . . . and it is only poetic justice that his own position should as a result have been seriously weakened'.[43] This swift collapse of a constitutionally managed alternative to the Government of Dr Musaddiq formed a suggestive pendant to the British policy a year earlier of banking upon the replacement of Dr Musaddiq by M. Sayyid Zia with the support of the Shah.

On the same day that Dr Musaddiq triumphed back to power, by what Mr Middleton wryly termed 'a happy coincidence',[44] the International Court at The

---

[40] *Department of State Bulletin*, Vol. XXVI, p. 494.
[41] EP 1192/7.
[42] EP 15316/5.
[43] EP 1015/189.
[44] EP 1015/189.

Hague at last delivered judgment regarding its juridical competence to entertain the substantive plea against the Persian Government in the oil dispute which His Majesty's Government had entered over a year before, in May 1951. By nine votes (including that of the British judge, Sir Arnold McNair) to five the International Court decided, against the British pleading, that it did not enjoy jurisdiction in the dispute after all. It held, contrary to British legal argument, that the conditions under which Persia had accepted the Optional Clause in 1932 restricted the jurisdiction of the International Court to treaties concluded thereafter by Persia, and that the Anglo-Iranian Oil Company's concession of 1933 was not an international treaty of convention. The interim injunction of July 5, 1951, accordingly lapsed.

In the autumn of 1951 the notable failure of British recourse to the United Nations, in contrast to the successful invocation of the League of Nations in 1932, had gone far to justify the prior legal recourse to The Hague Court in the Abadan Crisis. Now, however, the legal advice given in 1932 against resort to The Hague Court was proved in the long run, despite changed circumstances, to be still substantially valid. Even though, as a temporary measure, the interim injunction of the International Court had certainly been more potentially valuable from the British point of view than anything subsequently produced by the United Nations. Now the International Court, like the Security Council, had proved a broken reed for the legitimate defence of British interests. The attempt to shift the onus of British policy on to international institutions had in this instance proved a failure. As regards the possible alternative of British use of force, Sir William Strang later observed, in relation to differences with America regarding policy in Arabia: 'Abadan might have been saved if we could have thrown forces into it, though the operation would have been of doubtful legality and politically most explosive.'[45]

On July 25, 1952, three days after Dr Musaddiq had returned to power under the encouraging auspices of the decision of The Hague court, but also under the clamp of what he himself termed 'a desperate financial situation',[44] he initiated with Mr Middleton a sounding in the direction of further negotiations. The Americans as usual were all in favour of that. But when Mr Winston Churchill, who was in charge of the Foreign Office in the absence of Mr Eden on his honeymoon, suggested to Mr Truman that they should address a joint message to Dr Musaddiq the President at first scouted the proposal as possibly implying that Great Britain and the United States were ganging up on Persia. Mr Churchill replied to Mr Truman on August 23, 1952: 'I thought that it might do good if we had a gallop together such as I often had with F.D.R. . . . I do not myself see why two good men asking only what is right and just should not gang up against a third who is doing wrong. In fact I thought and think that is the way things ought to be done.'[46]

The Churchillian touch carried the day. On August 30, 1952, joint proposals from Mr Truman and Mr Churchill were officially delivered to Dr Musaddiq. These were for submission to the International Court of the specific question of compensation for the nationalisation of the Anglo-Iranian Oil Company; and negotiations between the company and the Persian Government for making arrangements to resume the flow of Persian oil; if the Persian Government agreed to these two proposals it would be understood that: first, the company would seek to move and pay for oil already

---

[45] EA 1084/465 of 1952.
[46] EP 1534/259.

stored in Persia; secondly, British restrictions on exports to Persia and Persian use of sterling would be relaxed; thirdly, the United States Government would immediately grant the Persian Government $10 million 'to assist in their budgetary problem'.[47]

Mr Middleton subsequently commented: 'A year ago the joint Anglo-American proposals would have been greeted as a great victory for Persia and, I believe, accepted without much demur. Today Persian opinion, such as it is, is unanimous in rejecting the offer.'[48] Dr Musaddiq, fortified by feelers from the controversial American oilman, Mr Alton Jones, and by the opinion of the visiting Dr Schacht that the Persian premier was one of the wisest statesmen he had ever met, proceeded to tender counter-proposals which represented no material advance upon his previous obduracy. They were garnished with a demand that within a time-limit of 10 days the Anglo-Iranian Oil Company should pay over, in convertible sterling, £49 million which Persia would have received had she not rejected the Supplemental Agreement. This impertinent ultimatum was by now merely unrealistic except, conceivably, in relation to American fear of communism. President Truman did indeed inject a further plea from Mr Churchill for another joint note in reply to the Persian Government. In general, however, the United States Government stood with Her Majesty's Government in its adherence to the Truman-Churchill proposals as against the ridiculous Persian proposition. This provoked Dr Musaddiq to sever diplomatic relations with Great Britain on October 22, 1952.

Shortly before withdrawing from Persia Mr Middleton was still reporting: 'If the idea that the Americans are working against us and are supporting Dr Musaddiq and the National Front could be eradicated from the Persian mind, this would be the greatest single blow that could be dealt to Dr Musaddiq.'[49] For the basic difference in the British and American evaluations of the Persian problem still largely persisted. In this connexion Sir Anthony Eden later commented: 'It was very much to the credit of the President and Mr Acheson that, despite these firmly held [American] opinions [on Persia] and the natural desire to make progress with a vexing and much debated international topic in an election year, they never took an initiative which we would have considered highly damaging to our interests.'[50] That was the reassuring context which minimised the effect of various less reassuring American tendencies at the end of 1952, during the 'lame duck' administration of President Truman in the last days before the newly elected President Eisenhower assumed office.

The British Petroleum Attaché in Washington reported in the first week of December 1952 that Mr Dean Acheson was discussing with the five major American oil companies the possibilities of their purchasing large quantities of Persian oil and of forming a non-profit-making company to produce and refine it. But the American oil companies, perhaps in their own interests, as usual evinced greater regard than the State Department for British susceptibilities. On December 6 the State Department, after previous warnings to Her Majesty's Government, published its view that the purchase of Persian oil was best left to individuals or firms, which must

---

[47] Cmd 8677: *Correspondence between Her Majesty's Government in the United Kingdom and the Iranian Government, and related documents, concerning the joint Anglo-American proposals for the settlement of the Oil Dispute*, p. 3.
[48] EP 1534/259.
[49] EP 1015/251; cf Sir Anthony Eden, *op. cit*, p. 208.
[50] Sir Anthony Eden, *ibid.*

weigh the legal risks; it believed, however, that the moving of relatively small quantities of oil would not provide, and had at times seemed likely to hinder, a solution of the main problem. The State Department would continue to address itself to this 'so that the essential international principle of adequate and effective compensation may be given effect and Iran may again benefit from the large scale resumption of its oil production'.[51] The Foreign Office went so far as to characterise this statement publicly as being helpful, whereas the American *Journal of Commerce* called it shocking and said that none of the big American companies would buy stolen Anglo-Iranian oil. A fortnight later a strong representation from Mr Eden probably contributed towards a decision by Mr Acheson not to proceed with the State Department's proposed authorisation, at last, of the ever-pending $25 million credit from the Export-Import Bank to the Persian Government.

The first quarter of 1953 brought further fruitless negotiations with Dr Musaddiq, as usual under the impulsion of the American Government, though now the Republican one—President Eisenhower, reported Mr Eden from Washington to Mr Churchill, 'seemed obsessed by the fear of a Communist Persia'.[52] After the Persian Premier had yet again, in the words of the Foreign Office, refused 'to face up to our proposals',[53] Mr Eden reported further: 'The difficulty of this situation remains that the Americans are perpetually eager to do something. The President repeated this several times. I reminded him that in response to American pressure we had modified our terms over and over again for a settlement. For my part I had many times felt in the last two years that if we could just stay put for awhile the chances of settlement would be improved.'[54]

The Foreign Secretary headed the United States Government off the idea of sending American technicians and machinery to Abadan. Then in April 1953 Mr Humphrey, the American Secretary of the Treasury, put to Mr R.A. Butler, the Chancellor of the Exchequer, a proposal which Mr Humphrey, apparently supported by Mr Foster Dulles, had been discussing with the American oil companies: that they should form an American syndicate to take over the Persian interest of the Anglo-Iranian Oil Company, which would become a customer of the syndicate. Mr Butler was politely unresponsive. The persistent Mr Humphrey told him: 'I hate to drop the matter entirely at this stage.'[55] But he had to.

Meantime in Persia Dr Musaddiq's precipitate career had become headlong. By the beginning of 1953 one of his two main props, the extremist Dr Kashani, had significantly deserted him and encouraged the Majlis, of which he was then president, to active opposition. And M. Makki went along with Dr Kashani. In February Dr Musaddiq openly challenged the Shah and, becoming increasingly unpopular, headed towards extremities. This was, perhaps, to prove his costliest mistake, if not even in terms of Persian politics, then in terms of American support, hitherto, despite its qualifications, his second main prop. Dr Musaddiq had now begun a process whereby the American Government at long last came to join the British in viewing him as a dangerous extremist instead of as a patriotic stay against Communism. In July 1953 President Eisenhower published his letter of June 29 to

---

[51] *Department of State Bulletin*, Vol. XXVII, p. 946.
[52] E 1022/4G: cf Sir Anthony Eden, *op. cit,* p. 212.
[53] P 10154/6G.
[54] Cited, Sir Anthony Eden, *op. cit,* p. 213.
[55] EP 1531/266.

Dr Musaddiq in which he withdrew support from, and refused to give more aid to, Persia or to buy her oil.[56] By the end of the month Mr Dulles was expressing concern at the Persian Government's toleration of the growing activities of the Communist Tudeh Party.[57] This stimulated the Persian Opposition, now promoted by General Zahedi, into full cry, including a telegram to the Secretary-General of the United Nations protesting against Dr Musaddiq's rigging up a referendum in the interests of a dissolution of the Majlis which the Shah refused to grant.

On August 15, 1953, Dr Musaddiq, in defiance of the royal prerogative, declared the Majlis dissolved. This ushered in a further instalment of the swift crisis of a year before and another Persian Day of Dupes, only this time in reverse. The Shah fled to Baghdad, to Rome. But in Tehran General Zahedi headed a remarkable royalist revulsion, seized control on August 19 and three days later welcomed the Shah back. Dr Musaddiq was arrested, charged with treason and ultimately condemned to three years' solitary confinement. The erratic old man was finished as an active politician.

At long last, and at how heavy a cost, the British contention that Dr Musaddiq was a political eccentric, and not the only alternative to Communism, had for the present been proved correct as against the Americans. Only in the event it was the latter who largely proved it, to whatever extent the downfall of the doctor was indeed promoted, as has been maintained,[58] by the American Central Intelligence Agency. In any case few things are more striking in the whole Persian crisis than the quick puncture of 'Musaddiq's extraordinary buoyancy' (Foreign Office memorandum of January 1954)[59] once the American Government really came out against him. Doubtless, however, the prime causes of Dr Musaddiq's fall were his own mistakes and growing unpopularity in Persia. Yet even after making all due allowance for the difference in Persian[60] circumstances in 1953 as compared with 1951, one is left with the impression that if a mark of the greatest among great Powers be the capacity to influence the government of smaller Powers by its extreme displeasure then, in relation to Persia, that greatest Power, over against Russia, was now the United States and no longer Great Britain as in the days of her recently relinquished Indian Empire.

4. Settlement of the Anglo-Persian oil dispute by the constitution of an international consortium

The fall of Dr Musaddiq and advent of General Zahedi to power in Persia rendered possible a settlement of the Anglo-Persian oil dispute; though it was to take just on a year still to steer it home, through American snags as well as Persian ones. Early in September 1953 the British Petroleum Attaché in Washington was again reporting that at recent meetings with the main American oil companies and Mr Alton Jones the State Department had apparently 'pressed for the formation of an all-American company to buy out the Anglo-Iranian but . . . the American companies were insistent upon the idea of an Anglo-American combine'. The Foreign Office, then in charge of the Marquess of Salisbury after Mr Eden had had an operation, expressed its concern that the State Department, without awaiting British views,

---

[56] *Department of State Bulletin,* Vol. XXIX, p. 74.
[57] *Department of State Bulletin*, Vol. XXIX, p. 178.
[58] Cf Andrew Tully, 'CIA—the Inside Story', *The Sunday Times*, February 25, 1962.
[59] EP 1016/1 of 1954.
[60] EP 15316/8; cf Sir Anthony Eden, *op. cit,* p. 214.

should thus have been discussing plans which still seemed based on that of Mr Humphrey, and which 'are so different from the joint proposals'[61] previously presented by the British and American Governments to the Persian. The Foreign Office held closely to them but the State Department on September 25 expressed the view that they were open to serious objections, while intimating in particular 'that it was difficult to see how the 50-50 principle could be applied to Persia except by means of an arrangement for the operation of the industry on Persian territory which would, in fact, amount to a new concession, however it might be camouflaged to make it acceptable to Persian public opinion'.[62]

The day after he returned to the Foreign Office on October 5, 1953, Mr Eden sent a message to Mr Dulles wherein he sought to delimit and define the scope of a special mission to Tehran which, the State Department proposed, should now be undertaken by Mr Herbert Hoover, junior, adviser to Mr Dulles on problems relating to world-wide petroleum affairs, in order to supplement the diplomacy of Mr Loy Henderson, to whose helpfulness Mr Eden paid warm tribute. While welcoming Mr Hoover's exploratory mission in general terms, the Foreign Secretary added: 'But I feel strongly that our immediate aim should be to re-establish [Anglo-Persian] diplomatic relations. You will not misunderstand me I am sure if I say that negotiations through intermediaries, however trusted and well briefed, can be no completely satisfactory substitute for direct contact.'[63]

At the beginning of November 1953 Mr Hoover returned from Tehran via London. On November 4 he circulated to a meeting held in the Foreign Office, with Sir Pierson Dixon in the chair, a secret and unsigned document wherein the Persian Government had outlined to him possible principles for a settlement of the oil dispute. According to the minutes of the meeting, 'the document proposed that the NIOC should manage the industry with an international consortium (in which AIOC could have a minority interest) buying and marketing oil: . . . no compensation would be paid by the Persians but the AIOC could make their own arrangements for compensation with the other members of the consortium . . . Persia was to get as much for her oil as other producing countries got.'[64]

Mr Hoover recognised that the Persian document was unsatisfactory as it stood and when, on the following day of November 5, he mentioned it at luncheon with Mr Eden, 'I said at once', the Foreign Secretary recorded, 'that it contained many ideas which were unacceptable; and it is our understanding that Mr Hoover therefore decided that it would be unhelpful to leave the document with us.'[65] That, however, was for Persian consumption: this quotation formed part of the 'formidable instructions' (Mr Eden)[66] given to Mr Denis Wright when he proceeded as British Chargé d'Affaires to Tehran after Anglo-Persian diplomatic relations had been restored exactly a month after Mr Eden's luncheon with Mr Hoover. In practice the unsigned Persian document opened the way towards the negotiation of the oil settlement which was thereafter reached. The role, and reception, of this document contrasted strikingly with those of that other, and so different, unsigned Persian piece

---

[61] Sir Anthony Eden, *ibid.*

[62] EP 1531/31.

[63] Cited, Sir Anthony Eden, *op. cit,* pp. 215-16.

[64] EP 1534/114.

[65] EP 1051/84.

[66] Sir Anthony Eden, *op. cit,* p. 217.

of paper which His Majesty's Government had rejected, with heavy consequences, back in September 1951.

Before a settlement could be reached there was naturally a long way to go, especially for the dispossessed and, in Persia, still highly unpopular Anglo-Iranian Oil Company. Early in the New Year of 1954 Sir William Fraser, in a conversation with Mr Eden, emphasised the gravity of abandoning his company's full claim to a 100 percent return to Persia. Nevertheless, later in that conversation, the Foreign Secretary recorded, 'Sir William Fraser said that he was prepared to admit to me privately, though he begged that this should go no further, that he would prefer an arrangement'[67] whereby his company would make its comeback as the holder of a 50 percent share 'or something near it' in an international consortium with the other main oil companies, and would receive adequate compensation.

Negotiations in London between the oil companies, with the assistance of Mr Hoover, for the constitution of a consortium to operate the Persian oil industry formed the first phase of the negotiations for a settlement in 1954. The companies, recorded Sir Anthony Eden, came to terms 'with remarkable rapidity'[68] so that on April 12, 1954, he could announce agreement on the constitution of the consortium. The Anglo-Iranian Oil Company would control 40 percent, the largest single holding, if a minority one; another 40 percent went to the five participating American companies, Standard Oil of New Jersey, Standard Oil of California, Socony-Vacuum, Gulf Oil and Texas Oil; Royal Dutch Shell got 14 percent and the Compagnie Française des Pétroles the remaining six. Anglo-Dutch interests thus held 54 percent. And the Anglo-Iranian Oil Company was to be paid £214 million by its partners for their 60 percent holding. Mr Hoover subsequently termed this 'the largest private deal in history'.[69]

Two days later, on April 14, 1954, the second phase opened when negotiations with the Persian Government were formally initiated in Tehran. On his arrival there the previous December Mr Wright had been promptly beset by special emissaries from the Shah, 'his sinister secretary Perron' (Mr Wright)[70] and the ever-busy M. Shahrukh, who had vainly tried to inveigle Mr Wright into secret communications with the sovereign behind the backs of General Zahedi and his Ministers; the weak Shah was at his negative game of seeking to strengthen his own position by weakening that of his Government. If Mr Wright's straightforward refusal to play along caused for a time 'a certain coolness on the part of the Shah',[71] it was richly rewarded in the fruitful negotiations with the Persian Government which now ensued.

In February 1954 Sir Roger Stevens had arrived as the new British Ambassador in Tehran and, in the words of Sir Anthony Eden, 'quickly established his authority as our representative'.[72] Sir Roger Stevens found a Persian Government which was unusually well-disposed by Persian standards, which had managed to allay the worst of anti-British feeling in Persia, but which did not itself enjoy strong popular support. Her Majesty's Ambassador, in his maiden despatch of March 13, 1954, from Tehran,

---

[67] EP 1531/15G.
[68] Sir Anthony Eden, *op. cit,* p. 218.
[69] *New York Herald Tribune,* August 9, 1954.
[70] EP 1051/94 of 1953.
[71] EP 1051/12 of 1954.
[72] Sir Anthony Eden, *op. cit,* p. 219.

accordingly tendered the prescient advice that an unusual feature of the forthcoming negotiation with the Persians on oil was that it would be necessary 'to build up the other party's reputation if the agreement is to be ratified and executed. It will therefore be no ordinary trial of wits. I should compare it rather to a meeting of co-executors of the estate of an elderly crank as troublesome in death as in life . . . I believe that this allegory represents something not too far removed from the spirit in which the Persian Government (not, be it said, from altruistic motives) is prepared to approach these negotiations.'[73]

Just five months later, on August 13, 1954, Sir Roger Stevens could report: 'After two and a half years of frustration due to Persian indecision, ignorance, emotionalism and guile, it is pleasant to be able to record that this negotiation was remarkable for the decisiveness, intelligence, realism and rectitude displayed by the Persian delegation.'[74] In this connexion Sir Anthony Eden wrote: 'Full credit must be given to the courage and tireless energy of their brilliant finance Minister, Dr Amini.'[75] Her Majesty's Ambassador found it difficult to write of the latter's performance 'except in superlatives'. [76]

The happy issue at last of the complex negotiations with the Persian Government was all the more so for British interests in view of the anxiety which had been expressed, for instance, in a letter of May 1, 1954, from Mr Roger Allen, Assistant Under-Secretary supervising the Eastern Department, to Sir Roger Stevens: 'We have very little doubt that this is our last chance of getting a Persian settlement . . . Our blockade of Persian oil is now on its last legs . . . There is no doubt whatever that the Persians can themselves produce crude oil, and we estimate that, failing a settlement, we should quickly find them exporting, entirely on their own account, something between 5 and 6 million tons a year. That we think would be sufficient to put the Persian industry as far out of our reach as the Mexican oil industry now is . . . In our view, therefore, it will now have to be a very bad settlement before it is worse than no settlement.'[77] Whereas the oil agreement with Persia announced on August 5, 1954, was, if not a very good one for Great Britain, at least, in the words of Sir Anthony Eden, 'a remarkable improvement on what might have been expected three years before'.[78]

By the agreement of August 1954 the Persian oil industry remained nationalised in the ownership of the Persian Government—the big Persian gain. The National Iranian Oil Company would also continue to operate the Naft-i-Shah field and the Kermanshah refinery for home consumption, and would continue to handle internal distribution of oil products. But effective control of both the refinery at Abadan and the main oil fields in Persia was to be exercised on behalf of the Persian Government and the National Iranian Oil Company by the consortium. This would function through a complex structure of four companies, two of them operating companies registered in Persia and incorporated under Dutch law, with two Persian seats out of seven on each of the boards. The main control was vested in the third company, which was a holding company registered in London and retaining all the shares in

[73] EP 1534/49.
[74] EP 1534/331.
[75] Sir Anthony Eden, *loc. cit.*
[76] *Ibid.*
[77] EP 1534/83.
[78] Sir Anthony Eden, *op. cit,* p. 218.

the two operating companies. Also registered in London was the fourth company for the procurement of supplies and staff for the operating companies.

The effect of the agreement, which was to run in the first instance for 25 years, was to give Persia a 50-50 split of profits, so that she would not do better than other oil-producing countries in the Middle East—the principle which was at least as dear to the United States as to Great Britain. Transactions would normally be settled in sterling, with currency arrangements similar to those in force before 1951. Finally, over a 10-year period beginning in 1957 when production was fully restored, the Persian Government would pay the Anglo-Iranian Oil Company net compensation totalling £25 million.

5. The final reckoning

The smallness of the compensation to be paid by the Persian Government naturally took account of the much larger sum which, as the Persians had long projected, was to be received by the Anglo-Iranian Oil Company from its partners in the consortium. It was substantially the American companies, rather than the Persian Government, which bought the Anglo-Iranian Oil Company out of its dominating position in Persia. In some ways this mutually convenient arrangement might seem fair enough since it was to a considerable extent a financial reflection of the power-position resulting from the long-drawn Anglo-Persian oil dispute. The Anglo-Iranian Oil Company would in effect control something nearly like half the holding of the consortium while the Persian Government would get half the profits of the nationalised industry. The duel between those two antagonists had roughly ended in a draw, with neither anything like fully satisfied, but each, perhaps, able to make some claim to a win on points, depending upon which ones were especially stressed. For British interests in the strictly economic field this vindicated, if in the event only by a rather dangerously narrow time margin, the opinion of Lord Strang in relation to the crisis of 1951 that 'it is usually better to make no agreement than to make a bad one'.[79] But the real winner of the Anglo-Persian oil dispute, to a large extent economically and certainly politically, for a time at least, was the American *tertius gaudens*.

The remarkable quiescence of the Soviet Union throughout the Anglo-Persian dispute had conceivably been artfully designed to weaken the British position as, in a seeming paradox, it quite likely did. But perhaps Russian policy had not been so subtle or deeply laid. In any event it did largely allow the Americans to steer a nice course alongside, and often in between, the British and Persian Governments and to insert themselves economically and politically into the, for them, new field of Persian affairs on the east of the Near East. The participation of America in the oil consortium for Persia denoted an advance in her overall power-positioning in the Middle East. Whereas for Great Britain even her support of the Baghdad Pact and adherence to it in 1955 could not wholly stem that retreat in the Middle East which the crisis at Abadan had accelerated and which further developments over Suez were even then, in 1954, serving to underline.

The Persian eviction of the British from Abadan in 1951 had, as noticed (cf pp. 413ff), stimulated strong political currents in Egypt. They generally worked against British interests and had by 1954 carried Colonel Nasser to power. During the

---

[79] Lord Strang, *Britain in World Affairs* (London 1961), p. 304.

protracted Anglo-Egyptian negotiations regarding the British base on the Suez Canal
Her Majesty's Government was under the usual American pressure to appease its
opponents in the Middle East. Her Majesty's Government reached the commodious
conclusion that, in the later words of Sir Anthony Eden, while 'the Suez Canal
remained of supreme importance, the base was yearly less so . . . an outdated
commitment'[80] since the advent of the hydrogen bomb. On July 27, 1954, 10 days
before the conclusion of the Persian oil agreement, an Anglo-Egyptian communiqué
announced heads of agreement for the complete withdrawal of British forces from
their base in the Canal Zone, with arrangements for its civilian maintenance
thereafter and for British military re-entry in the event of attack from outside on
Egypt, the Arab League or Turkey, but not, to Persian umbrage, Persia. Egypt agreed
to uphold the international convention of 1888 regarding the free navigation of the
Suez Canal.

The debate in the House of Commons two days later, on July 29, 1954, saw the
first substantial revolt of Conservative backbenchers since Mr Churchill had
returned to office. Twenty-six of them voted against this British retreat from Suez
three years after the retreat from Abadan. Their chief spokesman, Captain Charles
Waterhouse, Member for Leicester South-East, recalled Conservative criticism of
Mr Morrison in the electoral campaign when 'we . . . told him that he had scuttled
from Abadan'.[81] Now Mr Attlee said that 'the Opposition entirely agrees with the
evacuation of our troops from Egypt', but he strongly criticised the terms of the
proposed agreement and referred to 'a lot of special pleading'[82] by the Government
in connexion with arguments invoking the hydrogen bomb. This last criticism found
considerable support, including that of Captain Waterhouse who doubted the
strategic logic of moving the British base in the Middle East from Suez to Cyprus,
doubted the value of the Egyptian pledge to uphold the convention of 1888.

On this 'historic occasion' (Mr Attlee) Captain Waterhouse was followed by Mr
Julian Amery, Conservative Member for Preston North. He said: 'It is the end of a
process which has lasted 72 years . . . There is now a withdrawal of British power
from this central position in the Middle East to the perimeter . . . There is a tendency,
fostered I think by some of our Middle Eastern advisers, to forget Egypt's African
role.'[83] Mr Amery proceeded to criticise British diplomatic 'blunders' in failing to
recruit support regarding Egypt from France, Turkey and Israel, and asked whether
there had been 'any effort . . . to see whether we could strike a bargain with the
Americans' for theirs. Mr Amery concluded: 'Fearful mistakes have been made, but
it is not because of such mistakes that we are leaving Egypt. We are leaving because
we are undergoing a certain moral collapse. The responsibility may rest nominally
on the Ministers concerned but it goes far deeper.'[84]

Mr Amery's searching critique was considerably relevant to the conduct of
British policy not only in regard to Egypt in 1954 but also—the earlier instalment—
in regard to Persia in 1951. Then as now the bitterly difficult issues largely, though
not wholly, transcended party differences. In winding up the heavy debate on July
29, 1954, Mr Eden gave a balanced defence of the proposed agreement and drew

[80] Sir Anthony Eden, *op. cit*, p. 260.
[81] Parliamentary Debates, 5th Series, H. of C, Vol. 531, col. 740.
[82] *Ibid*, cols. 731-6.
[83] *Ibid*, cols. 771-8.
[84] *Ibid*, cols. 780-1.

attention to hopeful factors in the Middle East, including the forthcoming oil agreement with Persia as a contribution to 'a bit of rebuilding' there. He went on to ask: 'Does not the House see that through all these things, and finally, most important of all, this agreement with Egypt, we shall be creating a new pattern of friendship throughout these Middle Eastern regions? . . . Of course, it is true that no one can foresee how it will work out in direct terms of our relations with Egypt.'[85] But Mr Eden had asked with reference to the expiry date of the Anglo-Egyptian Treaty of 1936: 'What would happen in 1956 if we had no arrangement?'[86]

An Anglo-Egyptian agreement in the terms previously indicated was signed on October 19, 1954, the third anniversary of the failure of the Security Council of the United Nations to uphold international morality in the crisis arising from Persian nationalisation of the great British stake at Abadan. Within another two years, in 1956, Great Britain was to be locked against Egypt in the still graver, differently developing but similarly influenced crisis arising from Egyptian nationalisation of the cardinal Anglo-French interest of the Suez Canal.

The two great British reverses at Abadan and at Suez, contrasting yet largely complementary, indicated that, within the context of the cold war led by the United States against the Soviet Union for the adherence of the uncommitted and under-developed peoples in the aftermath of the Second World War, Great Britain had not as yet discovered fully satisfactory means of reconciling the decline of her imperial heritage and of European influence with the resurgence of aggressive nationalism in the Middle East and in the continents beyond. Of critical importance one way or the other for this difficult reconciliation would be the newly evolving multi-racial Commonwealth of Nations, potentially the great contribution of British statesmanship to an era of swift transition and international regrouping. But success in this direction might call not only for real cooperation from others within the Commonwealth but also for a British development, in Europe and elsewhere, of keener though perhaps more modest attitudes together with strengthened and bolder convictions.

The implications here might include some revaluation of the basic principles of British foreign policy as laid down, for instance, in Sir Eyre Crowe's celebrated memorandum of 1907. Some such resolute reappraisal could encourage a hope that Great Britain might not only avoid further great relinquishment of power and prestige, as at Abadan in 1951, but might even succeed in consolidating her diminished position as the basis for a more compact and positive policy. If Great Britain were thus able to regain a larger measure of initiative in her foreign policy, she might the more readily command, once more, the support of nations of goodwill for her purposes and policies in world affairs.

---

[85] *Ibid*, cols. 818-9.
[86] *Ibid*, col. 814.

CHAPTER XVI

CONCLUSIONS

The conclusions to be drawn from such a study as that of British policy in the relinquishment of Abadan in 1951 are of three main kinds: political conclusions regarding issues of policy, personal conclusions regarding its execution by individuals, and administrative conclusions as to mechanism for the preparation and conduct of policy. The three sets of conclusions clearly overlap but are roughly separable.

1. Political Conclusions

1. The decision in 1951 to relinquish control at Abadan of the greatest single British investment overseas was one of the heaviest decisions taken by any British Government since the Second World War. Nor has its political importance diminished in subsequent perspective.

2. Throughout the Abadan Crisis of 1951 one adverse factor was Article VI of the Soviet-Persian Treaty of 1921. That treaty may in the future stand out as an early index to the declining power of the British Empire. The Russian Government, however, did noticeably little to exploit the Abadan Crisis, and British policy was more immediately influenced by pressure from the American Government. At the same time, the potential Soviet threat to Persia remained the chief bugbear for the Americans. For them the importance of supporting Persia in the cold war outweighed that of maintaining British control of Persian oil.

3. During the Abadan Crisis a critical weakness in the British legal case was the fact that the Anglo-Iranian Oil Company's concession of 1933 was not an intergovernmental treaty but a contractual agreement. This underlay the ultimate refusal of jurisdiction in the case by the International Court of Justice in 1952.

4. During the Abadan Crisis many Persians from the Shah downwards did not forget that 10 years earlier British forces had invaded their country in concert with the Russians, in what approximated in Persian eyes to an ominous revival of the Anglo-Russian convention of 1907, dividing Persia into spheres of influence. Britain, blamed for most things in Persia, was subject to criticism from the Shah for the eviction of Reza Shah, and from Dr Musaddiq for his promotion.

5. The attitude of His Majesty's Government in 1951 regarding possible use of force at Abadan stood in some contrast to that of 1946. The despatch then of Force 401 from India was the last such use of troops from an undivided India under British rule. The decline of the British Empire, notably in India, lay behind the Abadan Crisis. During it a heavy power-factor for Great Britain was the lukewarmness towards her cause of the two great democratic republics of East and West respectively, India and the United States.

6. British economic and military weakness after the Second World War spelt British weakening in the Middle East, though not its abandonment as suggested by the Prime Minister. The relative British decline and American ascendancy in the Middle East generally (eg, Saudi Arabia, Palestine, Greece, Turkey) extended to Persia and underlay the Abadan Crisis. Its importance in this wider context of the British presence in the Middle East was appreciated, and was at times, though not always, emphasised in the Foreign Office.

7. The potential repercussions of the Abadan Crisis upon the British presence in Egypt and her aspirations towards nationalising the Suez Canal were appreciated at the time in the Foreign Office and elsewhere. An additional complication was the Egyptian embargo on shipping passing through the canal to Israel, especially oil tankers to Haifa. A suggestion by Mr Anthony Eden in the summer of 1951 that a British tanker should be escorted through was opposed, notably in Washington, and was not adopted. In October the British relinquishment of Abadan was promptly followed by Egyptian unilateral denunciation of the Anglo-Egyptian Treaty of 1936 and by a grave crisis in the Canal Zone.

8. It may be that in 1950-51 the background of British power and prestige (eg, Second World War, Indian Empire) was too close to permit a full adjustment to changed circumstances wherein Great Britain might need to reinforce her position of strength in relation to lesser Powers such as Persia by exploiting the techniques of bargaining from weakness with greater Powers such as the United States. Hence, perhaps, the impression sometimes that British policy regarding Persia was at once too rigid and too weak.

9. The Abadan Crisis bore out the anxiety of Mr Ernest Bevin five years earlier regarding possible Persian oil nationalisation. It might have helped towards averting that danger if fuller consideration had been given in 1946 to his concern regarding the status of the Anglo-Iranian Oil Company, and to the logical weakness then of British opposition to nationalisation.

10. The middle of the 20th century found the Anglo-Iranian Oil Company at Abadan technologically in the van but socially somewhat backward. Its economic achievement in Persia had outrun its political awareness. The company suffered from both geographical and political isolation in Persia. By the spring of 1951 the opposed Persian parties of Dr Musaddiq's National Front and the communistic Tudeh were finding common ground in attacking the company as the 'monumental scapegoat' for Persian inadequacies. The direction of the company came to be severely criticised in Whitehall and elsewhere. During and after the Lord Privy Seal's mission to Tehran relations between His Majesty's Government and the company were somewhat delicate.

11. In 1948 the enforcement by the Treasury upon the Anglo-Iranian Oil Company of the general policy of dividend limitation was liable to impair Anglo-Persian relations, and stimulated the abortive Supplemental Oil Agreement. This financially fair agreement was unhappily complicated in form and was politically not forward-looking enough to meet basic Persian resentment against the predominance of a British monopoly in controlling the main source of Persian revenue. This resentment approximated towards anti-colonialist stirrings against Western imperialism.

12. In September 1950 a Treasury brief for financial negotiations with Persia ruled that the importance of Persian oil precluded any British breaking point. This contrasted with the reluctance of the Foreign Office, in accordance with the Treasury, to press the Anglo-Iranian Oil Company to meet the Persians over improvements to the Supplemental Agreement: for some while a seemingly unresolved dichotomy in British economic policy towards Persia.

13. The British attempt to secure ratification of the fair and already signed Supplemental Agreement, rather than embark upon concessions to the sharp Persians, possessed evident advantages during the first half of 1950 and perhaps for

some time even after Sir Francis Shepherd's suggestions in July and September for additional concessions. But Mr Bevin's decision in October, towards pressing the Anglo-Iranian Oil Company to be more forthcoming, appears to have been implemented with excessive caution.

14. Despite the large political implications, the immediate issue of the ratification of the Supplemental Agreement was to a considerable extent a technical and economic one which only occasionally in 1950 reached the level of the Foreign Secretary, let alone the Cabinet. Nor was it of predominant importance for the otherwise much occupied Eastern Department of the Foreign Office.

15. The Treasury was the department directly responsible for the interests of His Majesty's Government in the independently minded Anglo-Iranian Oil Company; the Ministry of Fuel and Power was also closely interested. In dealings with the Persian Government concerning oil interests the Foreign Office tended to be notably handicapped by having to conduct them, so to speak, at one remove, if not two. The views of the Foreign Office and of the Treasury in respect of the company differed seriously at the beginning of 1951.

16. The large profits drawn by His Majesty's Government from the Anglo-Iranian Oil Company constituted a genuine Persian grievance. During 1939-46 British taxation alone was double the Persian royalties: and the secret preferential rate at which the Admiralty paid for its oil aroused particular resentment in Persia. The Foreign Office could only try to rectify such grievances by representations to other departments. But if economic issues were the immediate ones, in the last resort they became subordinate (cf No. 11).

17. In 1950-51 the two governmental directors of the Anglo-Iranian Oil Company were retired public servants whose chief qualifications were perhaps their general experience and distinction. There may have been somewhat insufficient awareness in the Foreign Office in 1950 of the constitutional relationship and powers of His Majesty's Government in regard to the company before they were revised in April 1951. This might suggest some neglect of the historical background and of research facilities. Nor, perhaps, was the preparation of considered memoranda upon issues of high policy always quite sufficient.

18. The American programme of economic aid to Persia in 1950-51 to some extent tended to cut across British interests and was not definitely revised till September 1951. Nor did the Foreign Office succeed in securing wholehearted American support for the Supplemental Oil Agreement, which was torpedoed in December 1950 by Aramco's 50-50 agreement with Saudi Arabia. Insufficient British attention had been devoted to the Aramco negotiations and the State Department had evinced a greater sense of urgency than the Foreign Office regarding the importance of securing early Persian ratification of the Supplemental Agreement.

19. General Razmara proved disappointingly ineffective in steering the Supplemental Agreement through the Majlis and in publicising British concessions. It might perhaps have helped if some British quarter had preceded the generally well-disposed Shah in considering the possibility of trying exceptional and urgent procedures. In 1950-51 notable British caution was displayed regarding any attempt to counter obstruction in the Majlis by, for example, encouraging the Shah towards dissolving it.

20. During the latter half of 1950 His Majesty's Government did not exploit the eagerness of the Shah of Persia for military conversations regarding British defence

of the oil in South Persia in the event of Russian aggression. In such conversations, and perhaps subsequently, it might have been possible to arrange in advance for the all-important Persian request for British intervention in the event of any grave threat to British interests at Abadan.

21. The Korean War stimulated Anglo-American strategic concern for Persia. His Majesty's Government did not, however, use its support of American arms in Korea as leverage in Persia. On the contrary, planning for the defence of British oil interests there tended to become largely, though not exclusively, subordinated to broader planning for the support of Persia and the Middle East generally in the Cold War against Soviet Russia, the main American preoccupation. It appears that that in turn was partly related to a still broader Anglo-American world oil survey so that at times planning for defence of Persian oil perhaps approximated rather dangerously to a vicious circle.

22. Since so much was at stake in Persian oil it seems not inconceivable that the balance of advantage for His Majesty's Government might have lain in the early adoption of an adroitly resolute policy designed to put a bold front on the Russian menace to Persia, and if necessary to play upon Persian fear of it. It would also have been a great gain to set the Americans calculating that, in order to conjure their bugbear of Russian intervention in Persia, it was especially desirable to appease, not the Persian Government, but the British. The absence of such an American calculation was a heavy factor throughout.

23. The handling of Persian questions during 1950 probably suffered to some extent from its being a rather unlucky year for the Foreign Service as regards personnel owing to transfers and to illness, notably the mortal one of the much absent Mr Bevin. His Majesty's Government was also strained by its small parliamentary majority and other political difficulties. Surveying the fortunes of British oil interests in Persia in 1950, it is possible to understand why it largely appears in retrospect as a year of drift and deterioration towards worse to follow.

24. By the first quarter of 1951 the three critical stages in the hostile Persian trend against British oil interests were: (i) the withdrawal of the Supplemental Agreement on December 26, 1950, and subsequent political deterioration in Persia; (ii) the murder of General Razmara on March 7, 1951 (Dr Musaddiq was later reported to be implicated); (iii) the Majlis resolution, in favour of a proposal to nationalise the oil industry, of March 15. The adverse pace was quickening.

25. At the beginning of 1951 the Foreign Office was rightly concerned by the Persian threat of oil nationalisation, but early British reactions were somewhat slow and understandably embarrassed. The Persian demand for nationalisation placed the British Labour government in a logical dilemma which hampered its handling of the crisis. His Majesty's Government was, however, much less inclined towards accepting such nationalisation than was the United States Government, which in 1951 steadily pressed His Majesty's Government towards appeasement of Persia. The British view that Persian pressure for nationalisation was more of a gust than a prevailing wind was to a considerable extent correct in the long, but perhaps too long, term. The American assessment of gale force was more correct on the short term.

26. Between February and April 1951 opinion in the Foreign Office evidently hardened against any considerable admission of Persian nationalisation of the oil industry. The potential gravity of such nationalisation for the British economy,

balance of payments and naval supplies was fully appreciated, as was Persian inability to run efficiently such a highly technical industry so dependent upon export markets. In May the Foreign Secretary and his advisers expressed doubts regarding the measure of British recognition accorded to Persian oil nationalisation; but they were overruled. It was not in the first instance the fault of the Foreign Office that this British measure of recognition was unfortunately communicated to the Persian Government in a somewhat unclear form.

27. The Persian service of the BBC was notably successful on the whole but British publicity in general was running at a low level in Persia in 1950 and early 1951. The Anglo-Iranian Oil Company for long eschewed propaganda in Persia and its publicity organisation was generally disappointing. In Persia the friends of Britain became afraid to profess their friendship. After Dr Musaddiq took office, however, British propaganda upon the whole developed a strong campaign against him. Dr Musaddiq's Government was exceptional, though, in Persia in its strong propaganda and mobilisation of popular support, also by intimidation. Dr Musaddiq exerted a will-power which was not matched on the British side (the Law of Let Go).

28. His Majesty's Embassy in Tehran may possibly have been somewhat lacking in informally non-committal but sufficiently reliable contacts with Persian nationalist circles. The difficulties here are evident, but the Embassy was apparently seldom able to give very specific advice in advance of the manoeuvres and intentions of the National Front. If in general the Embassy's reporting also seems occasionally somewhat incomplete, the advices which it received from the Foreign Office were perhaps not always so full and prompt as might have been desirable. In March-May 1951 the Foreign Office received complaints from several diplomatic and military authorities that they were being kept insufficiently informed of the Abadan crisis. The diplomatic correspondence with Tehran during the crisis did not invariably quite match the level of events. British policy often seemed to be waiting upon, or catching up with, Persian propulsion of events.

29. British expectations that the Majlis Oil Commission's extended, two-month study of oil nationalisation would probably only begin about mid-April 1951 proved over-optimistic in contrast to urgent, and radical, warning from Admiral Earl Mountbatten. It was perhaps unfortunate that no effect was given to his proposal that a special negotiating mission should quickly visit Tehran, or to a somewhat similar proposal subsequently made by Mr Berthoud. The constitution of the mission of the Anglo-Iranian Oil Company to Tehran in June may not have been wholly happy. The Persian Government, though, bore the responsibility for its brusque rejection of the very reasonable Jackson Proposals, which were, however, criticised for being made too late.

30. In the spring of 1951 His Majesty's Government was on the whole unsuccessful in its dealings regarding oil with the stopgap Persian Government of M. Husein Ala. A contributing factor here was probably American support of him and suspicions of British support of M. Sayyid Zia. It may be that during the summer this British support, given in opposition to Dr Musaddiq, was both too open and too optimistic.

31. In March-April 1951 it was the Foreign Secretary and Foreign Office who stimulated military planning to prevent Persian seizure of British installations at Abadan, and were specially inclined to favour protective warship movements. British diplomacy valuably secured conditional Iraqi consent to British use of

military facilities at Shaiba in case of trouble at Abadan. In May the Foreign Office was disposed to consider a small, quick military operation at Abadan but, when that was judged militarily impracticable, it was opposed to a large, slow operation for cogent reasons of policy. Throughout the crisis the Foreign Secretary was inclined towards strong measures, if necessary. By July, however, the Foreign Office was rebutting military criticism of its caution regarding possible use of force at Abadan. That course (Operation Buccaneer) was advocated that month by the British military authorities but was opposed by His Majesty's Ambassadors at Washington and Tehran and by the British representative to the United Nations.

32. The arguments in international law regarding justification for possible British military intervention at Abadan were finely balanced and not fully conclusive. They provoked some disagreement within both the Foreign Office and the Cabinet. A central issue was intervention to protect British property as distinct from British lives. Finely balanced, also, were the heavy political and military arguments for and against intervention. The American Government was in the main consistently against it. The policy of His Majesty's Government was here subject to protracted permutations and shifts of counsel. Probably, as came to be recognised in the Foreign Office, only British military force could at the last have prevented the abandonment of Abadan.

33. The lynching of three British subjects during riots at Abadan on April 12, 1951, afforded a good opportunity, which was not to recur, for British military intervention there to protect British lives. There were strong arguments against that, but it might have been an important gain if British diplomacy had exploited the situation to extract from the alarmed Persian Premier an undertaking to invoke British assistance in the event of further serious deterioration at Abadan. As it was, no British authority appears to have signalled promptly the possible military implication for Britain of relying for security at Abadan upon the introduction of strong Persian forces into precisely that area.

34. Mr McGhee's proposal early in April 1951 for an Anglo-American joint statement in support of profit-sharing in oil concessions throughout the Middle East may have reflected American concern lest, having outbid the Supplemental Agreement in the 50-50 Aramco Agreement, the latter should be overtrumped by Great Britain. This concern might have provided a British lever on the American Government. The decision in Whitehall, against initial recommendations in the Foreign Office, not to take up Mr McGhee's proposal might seem a heavy one.

35. The Anglo-Iranian Oil Concession of 1933 differed from other oil agreements in entitling the Persian Government to participate in the world-wide prosperity of the company, largely derived from investing its Persian profits. This complicated a settlement on the lines of the fashionable 50-50 principle; on the one hand there would be technical difficulties in setting up a Persian subsidiary of the company, and on the other hand the company feared that the Persian Government would refuse to renounce its share in the company's rapidly expanding profits outside Persia, notably from Kuwait. The company could not afford to pay the Persian Government half of its total profit.

36. Behind the Abadan crisis lay Britain's financial dilemma in 1951: serious deterioration of her balance of payments made it increasingly important to retain Persian oil, but at the same time increasingly difficult for His Majesty's Government to resist pressure from the American Government on whose financial aid it might

become dependent. It was also estimated in June 1951 that, at any rate initially, British oil companies would be dependent upon the Americans for three-quarters of the oil needed to replace Persian supplies.

37. The prelude to the Anglo-American conversations on Persia held in Washington in April 1951 was inauspicious. The conversations did not secure solid American support for British policy. They were a failure for British interests and actually made things worse. The Anglo-American exchanges in May were relatively more successful for his Majesty's Government, though they pressed it further towards accepting accomplished facts in Persia.

38. The most important British gain secured from the Anglo-American exchanges in May 1951 was the withholding of American oilmen as possible replacements at Abadan. How far this represented a real American sacrifice to British interests is somewhat doubtful. But the American announcement of this measure created in Tehran, almost for the first time, an impression of Anglo-American solidarity. This, however, did not last. In general the Foreign Office was notably successful in ensuring that other nations did not, except in agreed cases, supply oil experts to the Persian Government. The later British strangulation of Persian oil exports was another major British success.

39. The conduct of relations with Dr Musaddiq, a demagogic xenophobe and fanatical eccentric, presented a problem of exceptional difficulty for His Majesty's Ambassador at Tehran and for British diplomacy generally. Nor were matters always eased by the conduct of the American Ambassador in Tehran. His reading of the Persian situation, though not always inaccurate, differed seriously from that of His Majesty's Ambassador. The latter had comparable differences of view with the Lord Privy Seal during and after his mission to Tehran. Advices from Tehran were not always concordant.

40. After Persian nationalisation of the oil industry on May 2, 1951, notable caution was displayed, partly under American pressure, regarding any British economic sanctions against Persia. In addition, legal and other difficulties prevented British naval interception of tankers carrying refined oil sold by the Persian Government.

41. His Majesty's Government made, but did not always press, initiatives to mobilise support in the Abadan crisis from friendly governments such as France and Turkey. Such initiatives were on occasions notably successful. His Majesty's Government was however conscious, perhaps almost to a fault, that any decisive support must come from the reluctant Government of the United States. Normal contacts with it through His Majesty's Embassy in Washington might perhaps have been valuably supplemented, to a rather greater extent than they were, by such means as grave representations to the American Ambassador in London and personal exchanges at a high level. Though when the latter were effected the results for Britain tended to be disappointing (cf No. 58).

42. Withdrawal of British oil workers from the outlying Fields in South Persia, while possibly a prelude to evacuation of Abadan itself, was yet the essential precondition, for the safeguarding of British lives, to any British military intervention to hold Abadan and in fact prevent its evacuation. The implications of this potentially important distinction between withdrawals from Fields and from Abadan Island needed to be drawn with particular clarity, not always fully achieved. Total British withdrawal from Abadan was certainly liable, as was on occasions

urged, to jolt the inefficient Persians. But basically it was a weak riposte.

43. British appeal to the International Court of Justice against Persian oil nationalisation had to reckon from the beginning with grave doubts whether it would accept jurisdiction (cf No. 3). Somewhat comparable doubts had helped to determine His Majesty's Government in the Anglo-Persian dispute of 1932 to appeal to the League of Nations rather than to The Hague. In 1951, however, there was a considerable consensus of expert British opinion that, despite the legal uncertainty, appeal to the International Court was to be preferred to one to the United Nations. The appeal of May 26, 1951, successfully asserted the standing of His Majesty's Government in the dispute; and the grant by the International Court of an interim injunction on July 5 was a notable success for the British case. Despite these considerable tactical advantages there was little or no prospect of effective enforcement of a favourable verdict of the court in the substantive case if it should ultimately accept jurisdiction, which in fact it did not.

44. In the latter part of May 1951 the Foreign Office in conjunction with other departments undertook a notably comprehensive review, with partial implementation, of political, military, economic, juridical and propagandist measures for the advancement of British interests in the deepening crisis in Persia. By the end of the month, however, British policy had to reckon that the United States Government would, for most practical purposes, disapprove of such British measures as economic sanctions, military intervention or political approach to the Shah. After the earlier negativism of the Anglo-Iranian Oil Company, room for British manoeuvre was now restricted between the negative obduracies of Dr Musaddiq and of the State Department.

45. The supple instructions for local appeasement issued at the beginning of May 1951 by the Anglo-Iranian Oil Company to its Fields Manager in Persia, and subsequently endorsed by His Majesty's Government, were to have major implications for the development of the Abadan Crisis. Early in June there was insufficient British resistance to the despatch to Abadan of the Persian Temporary Board of Directors and the Parliamentary Mixed Commission, or to the latter's initial and critical try-on in hoisting the Persian flag over the company's office at Khorramshahr. The precipitate departure of Mr Drake from Abadan on June 25 was unfortunate. Local conditions thereafter swiftly deteriorated till oil production at Abadan ceased on July 31: the end of a great British enterprise.

46. In mid-June 1951, in general accordance with previous policy, Sir Francis Shepherd advised against concentrating upon unseating Dr Musaddiq. Shortly afterwards, however, efforts in that direction were stimulated (cf No. 30), but without success. In this connexion the Shah appeared to be generally favourable to British interests and opposed to Dr Musaddiq, but he remained a weak and somewhat equivocal figure (cf No. 4). The Foreign Office discountenanced any encouragement of the Qajar dynasty or incitement of the tribes in South Persia.

47. In some contrast to initial insistence in Whitehall upon the indispensability to the British economy of Abadan, it appeared by the summer of 1951 that its loss would leave the position of British oil supplies rather better than expected, and the position of the Persians correspondingly weaker. This was due to expansion of output elsewhere, notably along the Arabian coast and by American companies, in accordance with the latest world developments in oil production and refining. The importance of the loss of Abadan had perhaps been somewhat over-estimated

economically and under-estimated politically. At times the Foreign Office may have been almost too inclined to appreciate the crisis in terms of economics, the special care of other departments, rather than in those of its particular sphere of diplomacy and high policy.

48. The cooperation of American oil companies to assist the British trade to tide over the Abadan crisis, as through the Foreign Petroleum Supply Committee in Washington, was on the whole decidedly good. After the British relinquishment of Abadan such Anglo-American cooperation successfully crippled the Persian export of oil. Nevertheless the basic position was a strengthening of the American companies over against the injured Anglo-Iranian, which they might, and did, to some extent supersede in Persia. Early British recognition of this unpalatable fact, and advantageous offer of commercial partnership to the Americans, might conceivably have been more successful than anything else in securing that solid American support of British policy in Persia which had hitherto been lamentably lacking. Ultimately it was along such lines that a solution was found, with American participation in the international consortium which replaced the Anglo-Iranian Oil Company in Persia in 1954. A suggestion in 1951 that this should be balanced by British participation in Saudi Arabian oil was not pursued.

49. On June 20, 1951, the Foreign Office made clear recommendations for immediate steps in the Abadan Crisis. Nevertheless it may be that British diplomacy and propaganda missed a chance then for facilitating the protection of British interests, if necessary by force, by a crash campaign to exploit both the lethal technical dangers of a shut-down of the oil workings and also the Persian mistake in alienating neutral opinion by introducing an Anti-Sabotage Bill which included the death penalty by military tribunal.

50. Within a fortnight of the arrival at Abadan in June 1951 of the Persian Parliamentary Commission and Temporary Board, Persian pressure was being successfully applied towards compelling a dual British withdrawal from the flanks of Abadan to landward (Fields staff) and to seaward (tankers). For the latter the Persian lever was chiefly insistence upon tanker receipts in favour of the National Iranian Oil Company. The main British objective, from having been the economic one of keeping the oil flowing, became a political one, at once narrower and broader: to cling to some foothold in Abadan in order to ride out the crisis and maintain the menaced prestige and power of Great Britain throughout the Middle East. Here the ultimate Persian riposte was withdrawal of residence permits from the British oil workers (cf No. 600).

51. The staff of the Anglo-Iranian Oil Company in South Persia was 'in the front line for Britain' throughout the crisis. In general the oil men displayed notable fortitude and restraint in very trying conditions wherein they lacked resolute succour and support.

52. The International Court's interim injunction of July 5, 1951, however precisely binding it might be, was the first development for months in the Persian crisis which was strongly favourable to the British cause. British policy did not forthwith exploit this advantage strongly, but came to accept the Harriman Formula, recognising the Persian nationalisation law of March 20. This formula was strictly compatible with the interim injunction, but their implications were divergent. British adherence to both of them, even as alternatives, was liable to be difficult. Similarly delicate was the basis of the Lord Privy Seal's mission to Tehran in relation to the

British application of May 26 to the International Court on the basis of the concession of 1933. The potential legal contradiction compromised a cogent defence of British interests. After the failure of Mr Stokes' mission the British stand on the interim injunction was a belated and weakened one.

53. After the interim injunction of July 5 American policy regarding Persia was clearer and more decided than British policy. The United States Government overcame British resistance in imposing Mr Harriman's mission to Tehran. This mission strengthened Dr Musaddiq and led to successive British retreats from its negotiating positions. Mr Harriman, despite his denial of mediation, exerted pressure in that sense and misled His Majesty's Government as to the Persian attitude. Mr Harriman's visit to London at the end of July was against the inclination of His Majesty's Government. British agreement then, on weak premises, to send the Lord Privy Seal to Tehran was largely a further attempt to procure American support at the cost of pursuing conciliation of Persia to, if not beyond, the limits of desirability.

54. The failure during the mission of the Anglo-Iranian Oil Company to Tehran in June 1951 to secure a practical improvement in conditions for British oil workers in South Persia was unhappily repeated in the negotiation of preconditions for the mission of the Lord Privy Seal in August.

55. On July 30, 1951, the Prime Minister gave the important assurance in the House of Commons, as regards Abadan, that 'our intention is not to evacuate entirely'. Next day the Lord Chancellor added in the House of Lords: 'We accept all the implications that follow from that decision.' The Prime Minister subsequently held that his statement did not commit His Majesty's Government to use of force to prevent British evacuation of Abadan. The Opposition did not accept this. In relation to this question the decision of the Ministerial Committee on Persia on August 22 was of large importance.

56. After the Lord Privy Seal had reached Tehran on August 4, 1951, Dr Musaddiq in effect repudiated all the three agreed understandings upon which Mr Stokes had come for negotiations. Dr Musaddiq got away with this.

57. The arrangements for the accommodation in Tehran of the Lord Privy Seal's Mission, and his liaison with his Majesty's Embassy, were not altogether happy. Nor was his liaison with London regarding the drafting, presentation and subsequent withdrawal of the Eight-Point Proposals. Mr Stokes may not have attached the same importance as was felt in London to placing the onus for discontinuing negotiations clearly upon the Persians. His mission was a failure.

58. The Eight-Point Proposals which the Lord Privy Seal put to the Persians on August 13, 1951, had been largely inspired by the advisers of Mr Harriman and were approved by him beforehand since his support was rightly regarded as most important. Nevertheless Mr Harriman's subsequent support of the proposals was tardy and insufficient. President Truman's unsatisfactory statement upon the failure of Mr Stokes' negotiations induced Mr Attlee to address to him a powerful plea for American support. Mr Truman did not answer this message.

59. By September 8, 1951, His Majesty's Government had for most practical purposes rejected the three possible courses in the Abadan Crisis of, first, further negotiation, secondly, military force, thirdly, recourse to the United Nations. That left only the extreme alternatives of either knuckling under to British eviction or else evicting Dr Musaddiq himself. This situation was excessively precarious for Great Britain, representing, indeed, a bankruptcy both of regular diplomacy and of military

resource. In this predicament British policy tended once again to wait upon Persian impulsion of events rather than to be formulated in anticipation of them. The wide dispersal of British Ministers during August-September may have contributed towards somewhat disjointed counsels. Support from the Americans was alienated by what they considered to be the ineptitude of British diplomacy.

60. In September 1951 the predicament of British policy regarding Persian oil rendered questionable the British rejection of the Persian Piece of Paper, which the Shah had promoted, however unhopeful in themselves the Persian proposals might be. The alternative to their discussion was Persian withdrawal of residence permits from British oil workers (cf No. 50). This last card was played by Dr Musaddiq on September 25.

61. In September-October 1951 it might have been to British advantage to attempt to follow up, even with Dr Musaddiq, the consideration which was given to the possibility of a *modus vivendi* regarding oil in Persia, even if it were not based upon the interim injunction of the International Court. A temporary standstill along imaginative lines might, despite obvious difficulties, have been easier to achieve initially than a permanent agreement and might have secured valuable support from the United States and in the United Nations.

62. The decision of His Majesty's Government on September 27, 1951, to refer the Persian oil dispute to the Security Council of the United Nations was legally impeccable but represented a reversal of earlier expert advice (cf No. 43). The grounds for that advice had not materially altered. The appeal to the Security Council was a procedural device of inner emptiness, confused in execution and ineffectual in result. American support for it was most reluctant and unsatisfactory. The position of Dr Musaddiq in Persia was strengthened by this British ploy.

63. In formulating British policy in late September and early October 1951 it was found difficult to pursue a firm and consistent line regarding resort to the Security Council, naval interception of Persian-exported refined oil, or the method of evacuation of British staff from Abadan. The British decision of September 27 to appeal to the Security Council against the Persian expulsion order was not very easy to reconcile in practice with the decision three days later to withdraw quickly and completely from Abadan in any case. The announcements of both these decisions were rather awkwardly hurried out.

64. During the Abadan Crisis His Majesty's Government constantly found itself pressed into adopting an immediately weaker course towards Persia (recognition of principle of oil nationalisation; Harriman Mission; Stokes Mission) in hope that, in the likely event of its failure, solid American support would thereby have been secured for stronger measures thereafter. This hope was repeatedly proved false. Effective lack of such American support for British policy, despite the Anglo-American agreement of November 1947 regarding mutual support on the Middle East, underlay the whole development of the crisis in 1951 and facilitated the Persian game of playing Great Britain off against the United States. Between 1951 and 1954, however, there was on the whole a marked improvement in this respect.

65. In October 1951 the failure of the British appeal to the Security Council to secure justified redress for Persian breach of engagement and expropriation of British oil workings indicated the dangerously high price which was being paid for the liberalisation of international relations through the United Nations. In the Foreign Office the Permanent Under-Secretary considered that the United Nations was

showing the way to international anarchy. The attempt to shift the onus of British policy on to international institutions (United Nations; The Hague Court) in this case proved a failure.

66. After the withdrawal from Abadan the British view that no oil agreement with Persia was better than a bad agreement was vindicated in 1954, if by rather a narrow margin. After 1951 time was Britain's ally for just long enough, basically because Britain had little left to lose in Persia and because the Persians could not market their oil. This reflected the two fundamental and over-sanguine miscalculations, one on either side, during the crisis: the British estimate, earlier, of the extent of Persian dependence upon oil revenues from Abadan; and the Persian estimate, throughout, of the extent of British dependence upon oil supplies from Abadan.

67. In 1954 the final negotiations, first between oil companies for the constitution of an international consortium in Persia, and secondly with the Persian Government were conducted with such speed, realism and success as to present a happy contrast to the negotiations of 1950-51. On the Persian side much was due here to the Minister of Finance, Dr Amini.

68. The two great British reverses over nationalisation at Abadan in 1951 and at Suez in 1956, contrasting yet largely complementary, indicated that, within the context of the cold war led by the United States against the Soviet Union for the adherence of the uncommitted and under-developed peoples in the aftermath of the Second World War, Great Britain had not as yet discovered fully satisfactory means of reconciling the decline of her imperial heritage with the resurgence of aggressive nationalism in the Middle East and in the continents beyond.

2. Personal Conclusions

Policy must be conducted by individuals. In the present context, however, it would be evidently inappropriate and invidious to attempt any ultimate judgments upon personal conduct in the bitter crisis for British policy towards Persia in 1951. Here especially, if readers of the preceding narrative should seek any conclusions, they must properly draw their own.

Perhaps, however, one general caution as to personnel is reinforced by some suggestions from the Abadan Crisis: that British interests in an increasingly complex and competitive world stand to be endangered if the Foreign Office were to admit any dilution of ability in its recruitment.

Doubtless it is virtually impossible to be equally strongly staffed, in proportion to need, in all posts and departments; and a violent crisis will subject any staff to special stress, which foresight can only minimise. It would, however, even seem preferable, if unavoidable, that the Foreign Service should be somewhat under-staffed and that some marginal activities be sacrificed (perhaps with some welcome saving of paper-work) rather than that it should attempt to undertake too much with personnel of less than the highest calibre and character in relation to each responsibility. An age of broadening democracy and technical elaboration doubtless increases the call for specialised technicians in the Foreign Service but this if anything enhances its primary need, still, for a diplomatic élite.

3. Administrative Conclusions

Any conclusions regarding administration to be drawn from the Abadan crisis relate, of course, to practice at that period. Since then administrative practice in the

Foreign Office has naturally changed in a number of respects and those versed in it will best be able to judge the relevance of any historical conclusions.

A. THE FUNCTION OF THE FOREIGN SERVICE IN WHITEHALL

During the Abadan crisis as at all other times British foreign policy, conducted by the Secretary of State for Foreign Affairs, was the policy of His Majesty's Government, of the Cabinet under the Prime Minister and the authority of Parliament. The official staff of the Foreign Office and of His Majesty's Missions abroad played a very important part as the expert advisers and executants of this policy. In the normal way, however, they were the originators of it, if at all, only in a subordinate sense, in so far as their advice was adopted at the governmental level of policy-making and decision. As always under the British constitution the responsibility for policy was political.

These standing conditions had a special bearing upon British policy in the Abadan crisis, which had to be directed by a Government nearing the close of six arduous years of power and enjoying, or burdened by, the smallest parliamentary majority of the century. This factor, even apart from others, inevitably spelt some weakness. The course of the crisis demonstrated how difficult, if not impossible, it was in such circumstances for the Foreign Secretary and the Foreign Office to promote a strong conduct of foreign policy.

The Foreign Office yet remained the Department of State with the most direct responsibility for meeting the Abadan crisis. But as usual, and even more than usual, the Foreign Office, more than any other department, inevitably had to work under the strain of constantly having others looking over its shoulder. Few administrative changes from the pre-war period are more striking or serious than the formidable growth of interdepartmental work, especially on the economic side, so prominent in regard to Abadan. The fact remains that in any crisis in foreign affairs, whatever its economic or other implications, the efficient direction of policy demands that the Foreign Office should if necessary assert against the Treasury or any other department the primacy of its own responsibility in terms of high policy. The Foreign Office clearly needs to keep fully abreast of relevant economic issues, as it notably did on the whole during the Abadan crisis; but if it diverges too far from its primary, political function to compete in terms of economics it must run the risk, in advising on foreign policy, of reducing itself to one department among others, and not the most expert one at that.

The latter danger was not, one feels, always quite avoided during the Abadan crisis, and the formulation of policy may sometimes have suffered as a result. The interdepartmental organ at official level was the Working Party on Persian Oil which, as was admitted (cf pp. 418-9), did not prove fully satisfactory. As its name implied, it was primarily an economic body, often meeting under a chairman from the Treasury, with the Foreign Office often represented, however ably, from Economic Relations Department. Yet the Working Party was liable to be asked for highly political advice (cf pp. 329, 357-8). This rather lopsided arrangement meant that the Cabinet would draw coordinated, interdepartmental advice on economic issues from the Working party on Persian Oil, and on military issues from the Chiefs of Staff. On the overriding, political issues there were informal consultations between Sir Edward Bridges, Sir William Strang and Sir Donald Fergusson; but no coordinating committee under regular Foreign Office chairmanship, and on a higher official level than the Working Party, to match up to the Ministerial Committee on Persia, itself only constituted on May 1, 1951. This defect on the official level was remedied shortly after Mr Eden became Foreign Secretary in October 1951 (cf pp. 418-9), after Abadan had been relinquished.

Some further considerations regarding the function of the Foreign Office in Whitehall are adduced in Section C below.

B. THE INTERNAL FUNCTIONING OF THE FOREIGN OFFICE

As regards the conduct of policy within the Foreign Office, almost the main impression emerging from the silent stacks of files on the Abadan crisis is the endless rustle of the in-tray. There can have been little or no time for philosophic brooding upon the heavy issues. During the crisis there were few days which did not bring new reports of developments for examination or decision, some fresh angle calling for adjustment, unexpected hitches or complications, procedural or personal problems, more work and more again. All in all, the precision and grip upon this conglomeration of affairs, which was exercised from day to day by those immediately concerned, stands out impressively. It is the picture of a great Department of State in action under pressure. Criticism is relevant only to this highest standard.

Nor was the Foreign Office administratively stagnant. To take but one practical example, in order to cope with the huge and horrid increase in papers, the year 1950 had brought a complete revision of the filing system which had been in use for a generation. The new system in most ways represented a marked improvement in logical classification, enabling any particular topic to be turned up and followed through more easily than before. Though in any particular correspondence an obtuse logic could the more easily, perhaps, relegate a telegram to one file and the reply to another (cf p. 273). Rationalised classification by subject put a premium upon intelligent filing in registries. The call for staff of high calibre (cf section 2 above) applies to Branch B scarcely less than to Branch A.

Nevertheless, so far as is possible from the limited sampling of the Abadan crisis, one might perhaps hazard an impression that the Foreign Office was on the whole less efficient then than it was either earlier or later. Still relevant in 1950-51 was a circular on 'Conduct of Official Business' which Sir Ivone Kirkpatrick had written and Sir Orme Sargent had subsequently circulated in 1948. This began: 'The Foreign Office is not so efficient as it used to be. This is due to a number of factors such as the relative inexperience of many of the staff, greater volume of work, increases in the establishment, which makes it more difficult to follow what is going on, and finally the ever-increasing complexity of our affairs. But it is also due to failure to observe well-established principles.'[1]

It may not be necessary here to recapitulate Sir Ivone's trenchant and timely criticisms under the headings: Submission of Papers (Tidiness: Accuracy: Punctuality: Judgment), Minutes, Drafts, Letters, Telegrams. But some of his comments seem particularly relevant at time to the handling of the Abadan Crisis. For instance: 'There is not enough punctuality or speed in dealing with urgent and important matters. Departments must have enough nous to recognise what is urgent

---

[1] XM 02(6/48): printed by Sir Ivone Kirkpatrick, *The Inner Circle* (London 1959), pp. 207-13, (This circular was recirculated under cover of Office Circular No. 1 of 1960.)

and important . . . The old despatches and official letters had form, which imposed a certain discipline and required clarity of thought and expression. Telegrams and semi-official letters, though seemingly easier to write, trap the unwary into looseness of thought or expression.'[2]

Instead of dwelling, however, upon all those obvious administrative virtues which are especially needed in a crisis, it may be more rewarding to try to pick out, even if a little arbitrarily, one or two noticeable gaps in administration which seem to be suggested by the sad story of Abadan. And, in an attempt to render criticism constructive, to suggest possible arrangements whereby they might have been reduced or remedied.

C. SUGGESTED GAPS AND IMPROVEMENTS

A number of weaknesses in administration suggested by the Abadan Crisis can be roughly grouped in relation to the two cardinal desiderata of continuity and drive.

I. *Continuity*

The greatest organisations of official administration, such as the former Indian Civil Service and the Great German General Staff, have usually won their success and prestige through an imaginative blend of high continuity and efficient flexibility.

A few years before the Abadan Crisis the Foreign Office had promoted a notable increase in flexibility by the amalgamation of the Diplomatic and Consular Services into one Foreign Service. Initially, however, the benefits from this were, perhaps, especially liable to be offset to some extent by breaks in professional continuity, emphasised by the break in regular recruitment during the Second World War. By about 1950 the pendulum had, by a natural impetus, perhaps swung rather too far in reaction to the previous continuity of specialisation in functions or regions as, for instance, in the expert Levant Consular Service. This may have been particularly felt in His Majesty's Embassy in Tehran where a high proportion of the regular staff in 1950-51 were new to Persia.

At the other end, continuity in the conduct of business within the Foreign Office was also liable to be reduced by the inevitably increasing interdepartmentalism in Whitehall, proliferation of departments within the Office and remorseless multiplication of papers (cf sections A and B above). It was something of a feat for an official to hold his own efficiently from day to day in this tossing sea of files, let alone to look around, back to historical precedents and warnings or forward to the remoter but in the long run possible more important implications and consequences of immediate action.

The administrative lessons of the Abadan Crisis include obvious improvements in the organisation through departments and committees of historical research on the one hand and of forward and contingent planning on the other. Such improvements were probably largely introduced in after years so that it may be sufficient here to suggest one or two particular ways in which such improvements might, through individuals, be closely geared into that daily activity of departments upon which all must finally still depend. Two such expedients might possible be working leave and continuity-men.

---

[2] *Ibid.*

(a) Working Leave

A study of the Abadan Crisis leaves the impression that on the whole the various issues were dealt with at the right levels in the Foreign Office, and reinforces the axiom as to the critical importance of the duties of a Head of Department. He remains the administrative linchpin. It might add strength if officials from the rank of Head of Department upwards were permitted or indeed compelled to take working leave, amounting perhaps to not more than a few days once or twice a year. During working leave, which should not count against normal annual leave, an official should absent himself from the Office and should not be encouraged to take away papers to work on. But he would be expected to work hard, by thinking. There might be slightly less excuse then for claiming that the grinding press of administration leaves no time for deeper and constructive thought. The Head of Department or Under-Secretary could broadly review his field of responsibility and perhaps sift and coordinate his recommendations of policy, possibly in a short, conspective paper upon his return. Such mental discipline might prove especially valuable when affairs were working towards some crisis.

(b) Continuity-men

In order to cope with increased efficiency with the kaleidoscopic problems of foreign affairs in the aftermath of Western imperialism, it might possibly be worth while for the Foreign Office to consider taking a leaf out of the book of the modern film industry by maintaining a small number of continuity-men, preferably as additional Assistant Heads in the largest and most important departments.

Such an additional Assistant Head should be an integral part of the departmental machine under the authority of the Head of Department. The Assistant Head should, however, work rather to one side of the machine in a manner somewhat comparable to the functioning of a Counsellor of Embassy or, for instance, of Sir John Pratt in his capacity of Adviser on Far Eastern Affairs in the Foreign Office for 13 years before the Second World War. The Assistant Head would need to keep fully abreast of the current work of his department but should so far as possible be relieved of routine duties of day-to-day correspondence, interviews and committees other than those directly concerning his particular duties. These should be:

(i) Coordination for the department of all (*a*) intelligence, (*b*) research, (*c*) planning. So far as is possible it would be his heavy responsibility, under the Head of Department, to remember, foresee and suggest. It would be one person's responsibility to keep the department fully briefed. Though the Assistant head would, of course, act rather as an intelligence and liaison officer with intelligence, research and planning organs.

(ii) To relieve the Head of the Department of some, at any rate, of the crushing burden of paper work and to speed it by facilitating quick reference and, for instance, by paying special attention to the digestion of long despatches and reports.

(iii) To prepare short, periodical reports on the work of the department, somewhat comparable to those from missions abroad; also to supervise, for instance, the assembling of departmental Confidential Print and any White Papers, etc.

(iv) The Assistant Head could, under the Head of Department, doubtless organise a good deal of his work through junior members of the department. Here it might be a most valuable reform if the Assistant Head was specifically responsible for training juniors in office practice and procedure. It seems likely that the Head of

Department often simply does not have time to perform fully this important function which, if undertaken thoroughly, might do as much as anything to improve the standard and professionalism of work throughout the Office.

A few such additional posts of Assistant Heads might provide valuable outlets for officials with a rather special bent who might not be so usefully employed elsewhere. And, in some cases at least, it would probably be advantageous that such continuity-men should occupy their positions for longer than the usual term of departmental duties. There might obviously be some administrative economy, and possibly other advantages, if they were to work to Under-Secretaries rather than to the Heads of some departments. On balance, however, it seems likely that the advantages of this alternative might be outweighed by the danger of impairing the essential authority of Heads of Departments.

II. *Drive*

Whereas a study of the pre-war archives of the Foreign Office conveys a dominant impression of highly skilled individuals at work, its post-war archives— certainly in the case of Abadan—are even more a register of great departmental machines at work. Though this contrast naturally represents some oversimplification, it yet remains a striking and to some extent disturbing one. One feels that it is appreciably harder than before for individual drive and initiative to cut through to effective action. But greater individual drive is precisely what is needed to propel the enlarged departmental machinery at top efficiency. To prevent these considerations from approximating to a vicious circle is an administrative problem not wholly dissimilar, perhaps, to that of automation in modern industry. A crisis, or even the persistent tension of the Cold War, is obviously liable to intensify the problem.

Something of this probably lay behind a minute which the Foreign Secretary wrote in the thick of the Abadan Crisis: 'We need to be as efficient as a military operation in war' (cf p. 226). Mr Herbert Morrison could also, perhaps, have instanced the organisation of his wartime Ministry of Home Security with its system of alerts for air raids and invasion. It seems possible that the handling of the Abadan Crisis might have benefited if there had been in operation some administrative system of political alerts upon or, still more valuable and more difficult, before the onset of a crisis of exceptional gravity.

The organisation of such a system would evidently raise a number of problems which can only be indicated here, for instance: which high authority should be responsible for issuing a political alert; whether and, if so, how far it should operate throughout Whitehall; how an incipient crisis in foreign affairs should qualify for an alert. Here it may be suggested that the Abadan Crisis would have qualified as involving (*a*) the greatest single British economic investment abroad, (*b*) the possible use of military force. It would clearly be desirable that any system of political alerts should operate not only as simply, but also as rarely, as possible. Otherwise there would be the risk of wasting effort and of crying Wolf, Wolf. Though even occasional test-alerts might have training value.

It may well be asked what would be the real gain, over any existing practice, from adding yet another piece of administrative machinery for political alerts during the Cold War. The answer might in the main be twofold. First, a warning alert should act as a psychological stimulus throughout large parts of the Foreign Office and perhaps, if so decided, in Whitehall. It might provide that kind of extra jerk which, in less complicated days, could more easily be transmitted by a single resolute official or Minister of senior standing. After an alert had geared the administrative machine into overdrive, valid excuses for delays or shortcomings would be strictly limited. In the second place an alert should reduce the chances of shortcomings by making precautions automatic. The issue of a political alert might be a little comparable to the issue of orders, often routine but always urgent, by the captain of a ship heading into a storm. For an efficient department such an alert might come mainly as confirmation of measures already taken. But in any case those measures would be prescribed and taking effect.

Those more particularly versed in current administration will best be able to judge how far the necessary measures are already covered, and which should become automatic under a political alert. The following possible examples are merely suggestions arising from a study of the Abadan Crisis. Upon the issue of the codeword alerting a crisis for British foreign policy in regard to any particular area or issue:

(i) Special designations of priority should speed to the utmost the transmission, decyphering and registration of all correspondence relating directly to the crisis. It would thus be classified apart. Any unauthorised disregard of such priority would be a clear administrative error. Also, all departments in the Foreign Office, and possibly even more widely in Whitehall, even though not directly concerned with the crisis, would be held specially responsible for watching for, and promptly reporting to the department directly concerned, any part of their own business which might seem to have a bearing on the crisis even if only indirectly, for instance by analogy.

(ii) The department of the Foreign Office primarily concerned would become responsible, preferably through the previously suggested Assistant Head, for the prompt production, if not already undertaken, of two related memoranda. The first should be a short, historical memorandum explaining the background and setting of the crisis together with any specially relevant precedents and political, economic, juridical or other angles. The second memorandum should weigh possible courses for British policy in the crisis and should recommend what appeared on balance to be the best one, paying special attention to the clearest attainable definition of maxima and minima, fall-back positions, breaking-points and the like. These two memoranda should, at the least, provide clear yardsticks. With them, all departments concerned and missions abroad should be in the least possible doubt as to the facts they were working on and the aims they were working to.

(iii) There should be a prompt review at high level in the Foreign Office of all major staffing arrangements in departments and missions affected by the crisis. This would naturally include arrangements for leave, including the suggested working leave, which might now be especially valuable. Occasionally, though one would hope not often, it might prove necessary at some levels to operate quick and resolute transfers, as in wartime. A preferable expedient where possible and necessary might, however, be some reversion towards an older tradition in the Foreign Office, when it was much smaller in the 19th century, whereby in a crisis all buckled to and the department directly affected was specially helped by others. It seems important, indeed, that the conduct of the crisis should clearly remain with the relevant department, which should not be subordinated to any special posse of high-powered troubleshooters, as may perhaps be the tendency in a crisis in some foreign administrations. But the temporary injection into the department of even one highly gifted and fresh mind, if only at a relatively subordinate level, might prove really stimulating and worth the obvious risk of causing certain difficulties in personal relations. That risk would need to be borne in mind in selecting an individual for such a special assignment—incidentally a most valuable one for his own training. The risk might be minimised by a straight exchange between the department and the affected mission abroad. It might perhaps, though, even be worth considering whether the department might not occasionally, depending upon the nature of the crisis, be valuably reinforced from the Cabinet Office or another Government Department. Within an increasingly interdepartmental context such exceptional departmental secondment, if it could be arranged on a temporary basis, might bring its own benefits and facilitate smooth liaison in a crisis.

(iv) There should be a prompt review at high level of interdepartmental machinery for meeting the crisis. Any necessary new working parties or committees should be quickly established, with special attention to their being of sufficiently high calibre and efficiently matched on the official level to any Cabinet committee of Ministers. Such special committees should normally be under Foreign Office chairmanship in accordance with:

(v) For the term of the political alert ultimate responsibility for all relevant political decisions should be specifically reaffirmed as resting with the Foreign Office. This would usefully increase the onus upon timely interdepartmental consultation. Because in its absence on account of great urgency or for any other reason, or in case of difference of opinion, the Foreign Office itself would be fully entitled, and indeed required, to take such political decisions and actions as it deemed necessary under the direction of the Foreign Secretary and the Cabinet. Thus, while interdepartmental consultation should be constant and quick, everything should be done to prevent it from bogging down the execution of policy by weakening decisions and delaying action. This creeping danger in administration during a political crisis demanding urgent measures should be reduced by clear definition of the primacy of the political responsibility of the Foreign Office, somewhat though not completely comparable to the primacy of the Ministry of Defence in relation to the Service Departments. Such political primacy should imply that during a crisis responsibility for the coordination of economic, military or other special measures with political implications should in the last resort not be diffused in interdepartmental committees but should be concentrated upon the Foreign Office under the direction of the Cabinet.

(vi) After a political alert had been stood down the next of the suggested periodical reports by the additional Assistant Head of the relevant department of the Foreign Office—cf section I (*b*) (iii)—would naturally take the form of a review of the department's handling of the crisis. Thus a valuable record and set of precedents for future reference would automatically be provided.

Such, very roughly and tentatively, might be the possible working of at any rate one expedient for keying up British foreign policy in a crisis to an administrative drive to match the urgency and gravity of the issues for the nation, such as those at Abadan in 1951.

Commentary by Lord Strang on Mr Rohan Butler's study of 'British Policy in the Relinquishment of Abadan in 1951'[1]

Secret (FO 370/2694)

I. *Introductory*

This case-history of British policy in the relinquishment of Abadan in 1951 is the work of a historian who has an almost unrivalled acquaintance with Foreign Office papers in the inter-war years, and can bring his profound understanding of these to the study of a post-war episode of lasting significance in British foreign policy. It is a postmortem, the purpose of which is to examine how far 'initial judgments and forecasts had stood the test of time', and to enable the present administrator 'to see current problems in perspective as regards both policy and administrative practice'. His narrative of events 'often endeavours to explain not only what happened but why one thing was done rather than another, why in a particular way at a particular time, and what were the frequently conflicting considerations which underlay critical decisions'.

2. The work comprises (1) a short introductory chapter giving the early history of British enterprise in Persia; (2) the main body of the work, being an analytical narrative of events from the negotiation of the Supplemental Agreement between the Anglo-Iranian Oil Company and the Persian Government to the relinquishment of Abadan, October 1947 to October 1951; (3) a short concluding chapter bringing the story down to the solution of the Persian oil problem in August 1954; (4) a chapter of conclusions, political, personal and administrative.

3. The writer of the present memorandum was Permanent Under-Secretary at the Foreign Office from February 1949 to December 1953. He has been invited to read Mr Butler's study and, from his personal knowledge of events during the material period, and from his experience of Foreign Office administration, to draw what lessons he can both as to the conduct of affairs in the circumstances of the time, and as to the possible bearing of these lessons upon the conduct of affairs in the circumstances of today. He feels more competent to attempt the first task than the second, since in the nine years since his retirement much has changed in the content and climate of international affairs and no doubt accordingly also in the organization and methods of the Foreign Service.

4. He proposes to examine and to test Mr Butler's comments and conclusions, and in one important aspect—the personal aspect—to supplement them. Apart from making two general and most useful observations, Mr Butler refrains altogether from attempting 'any ultimate judgments upon personal conduct in the bitter crisis for British policy towards Persia in 1951' since he thinks that this would be 'inappropriate and invidious'. His readers, if they should seek any conclusions, must, he says, 'properly draw their own'. The present writer thinks it right to offer some

---

[1] In a minute of 16 December 1962 Sir H. Caccia, Permanent Under-Secretary of the FO, wrote that with the agreement of the Foreign Secretary, Mr Butler's Abadan memorandum was being sent to Lord Strang, who had been PUS at the time of the crisis. Circulating Strang's comments on 7 February 1963, Mr D.R. Hurd, Sir H. Caccia's Private Secretary, noted that the PUS had promised Lord Strang that his comments would not be 'seen or referred to outside a restricted circle in the Foreign Office, and hopes that great care will be taken to ensure that this is so'. It is clear that his caution was due to the references in his text to officers who might still be serving.

comment on the outlook and performance of some of these, whether Ministers or officials, who were most closely concerned with these events, since this seems to him to be an essential element in any postmortem.

5. He will then deal with Mr Butler's administrative conclusions; and finally, instead of reviewing Mr Butler's voluminous political conclusions, he will take up one fundamental issue which Mr Butler has raised in regard to the conduct of British diplomacy.

II *The Personal Aspect*
(*a*) *Ministerial*

6. During the first nine months of 1950, Mr Bevin was absent abroad or through ill-health for all but a few weeks. During the latter part of 1950 and the early part of 1951 he increasingly bore the marks of the illness which was to prove fatal, and he was much absent from duty. At this time 'British foreign policy . . . lacked strong ministerial direction at the highest level'. Mr Morrison, who succeeded him early in March 1951, and whose period of office almost exactly coincided with the main crisis, was inexperienced in foreign affairs. Not until Mr Eden became Secretary of State at the end of October 1951 did a Minister take over our foreign policy with a strong hand; but by that time we had already been forced to withdraw entirely from Abadan. From then on, our policy was conducted with new energy and resource. Admittedly, this had become easier for us since we now had little left to lose in Persia, and since time was now on our side rather than on that of the Persians, because the Persians could not market their oil. But the change of ministerial direction gave a new impulse which was perceptible throughout the government machine.

7. When Ministers know their own minds and can convey their policies to their officials, the advice tendered by the latter can be more securely based and more clearly expressed than where officials have to try to make up their Ministers' minds for them.

8. Mr Eden immediately took the steps which enabled him to set a new course. In place of the existing Ministerial Committee on Persia under Mr Attlee's chairmanship, he set up, with Mr Churchill's approval, a smaller Ministerial Committee under his own Chairmanship. Secondly, on the recommendation of the Permanent Under-Secretary, he secured the appointment of an interdepartmental Persia (Official) Committee, in place of the lower-level and not fully satisfactory Working Party on Persian Oil under Treasury chairmanship, to serve the Ministerial Committee, under the chairmanship of a Deputy Under-Secretary in the Foreign Office. These steps restored the primacy of the Foreign Office in what was essentially an issue of foreign policy; and ensured a more alert and more coordinated handling of the crisis than had proved possible hitherto.

9. Mr Butler rightly says that these steps might with advantage have been taken earlier. But to this, Mr Morrison himself was an obstacle. Unlike Mr Bevin and Mr Eden, he stood in no position of special authority with his Prime Minister, as his former colleague, Mr Shinwell, was later to observe. That he, instead of the Prime Minister, should have held the Chairmanship of the Ministerial Committee on Persia was, in the circumstances of the time, hardly possible. Then again, unlike Mr Bevin, who was jealous for the primacy of the Foreign Office in foreign affairs, he took a narrow view of the competence of the Foreign Office in Whitehall. The Foreign

Office, he thought, had quite enough work of its own without concerning itself over-much with what other departments might think or do. (This note on Mr Morrison's outlook is based on personal recollection, not upon Mr Butler's narrative. Mr Butler was perhaps unaware of it.) This outlook did not pass unquestioned by Mr Morrison's advisers; but it stood in the way of any proposal that the chairmanship of any new or stronger inter-departmental official committee on Persia should pass into Foreign Office hands. As soon as Mr Eden came in, it was possible to make the desired change.

10. In the Persian crisis, it was the Prime Minister rather than the Foreign Secretary who settled the main course of policy, and, in Mr Attlee's mind, that course meant retreat rather than resort to force. In 1946, he was even contemplating our pulling out from all the Middle East. At the decisive Cabinet meeting on September 27, 1951, 'the Prime Minister told the Cabinet that in view of the American attitude he did not think it would be expedient to use force to maintain the British staff in Abadan. That course could not expect to find much support in the United Nations'. On September 7, he had written: 'We should not threaten to use force unless we mean to do so and we do not'. In taking this view, Mr Attlee relied upon the emphatic opinion of the Attorney-General, Sir Frank Soskice, that we might have a right to send in troops to safeguard lives in danger, but not property; and that 'the absolute maximum would be something in the nature of a rescue operation to protect life . . . if we undertake anything beyond this, I feel that there is no chance of successfully justifying it before The Hague Court'. The Attorney-General's view was repeatedly contraverted by the Second Legal Adviser to the Foreign Office, Mr Fitzmaurice, down to the end, and was only slightly modified towards the close of the crisis. Mr Morrison heartily disliked the Attorney-General's ruling and asserted the claim of policy as against the pretensions of law; but, as Mr Butler remarked, 'the Foreign Secretary had not impressed his personal and standing inclination towards strong measures upon previous papers prepared by his department'.

11. The vitally different relationship ruling between Mr Eden and his Prime Minister, and its beneficent effect upon the conduct of public business, may be exemplified by a minute written by Mr Churchill ('I like all this so much') upon a telegram sent by the Permanent Under-Secretary to H[is] Majesty's Ambassador at Washington, Sir Oliver Franks, at Mr Eden's request, outlining the views on the Persian oil questions which the Foreign Secretary, then on his way to Paris, would express there to the United States Secretary of State, Mr Acheson. The effect of a strong hand and a clear mind at the controls may be seen in the fact that the four principles for a settlement put by Mr Eden to the United States Government within a fortnight of his taking office 'were maintained in substance throughout the subsequent negotiations to solve the stubborn problem of Persian oil', that is to say until 1954.

12. His Majesty's Government were again unfortunate in 1951 in that, when they at last decided to send a member of the Government on a mission to Tehran, they could find no one of higher calibre than Mr Richard Stokes, the Lord Privy Seal. The Permanent Under-Secretary and the Secretary of the Treasury, Sir Edward Bridges, rightly as it proved, advised against this choice, but without avail.

13. Whatever the qualities possessed by the ministers who were in power during the worst of the Persian Oil crisis in 1951, it may well be that no better result could in the end have been achieved (and it was, in the end, not a bad result, thanks largely

to the vigour and skill of the new government). Nevertheless, we might perhaps have avoided some of the grosser humiliations which we had to suffer. But the calibre of the Foreign Secretary himself does matter tremendously, and his relationship with the Prime Minister perhaps no less. He cannot get the best out of his officials unless he can inspire, stimulate and control them. We have only to contrast the course of our foreign policy under less competent Foreign Secretaries, like Aberdeen, Derby, Simon or Hoare with the achievements of Castlereagh, Canning, Palmerston, Salisbury, Grey, Eden and Bevin in his prime.

(*b*) *Official*

14. When we turn now to the official staff, and in particular to the members of the Foreign Service concerned in the Abadan affair, we find that Mr Butler, while refraining from judgment on individuals, states two general conclusions which refreshingly confirm views which are likely to be held by those responsible for the administration of the Service. The first is 'that British interests in an increasingly complex and competitive world would stand to be endangered if the Foreign Office were to admit any dilution of ability in its recruitment'. The second is that 'an age of broadening democracy and technical elaboration doubtless increases the call for specialised technicians in the Foreign Service, but this if anything enhances its primary need, still, for a diplomatic élite'.

15. These are judgments which should be retained and noted for quotation in any discussion about the future development of the Foreign Service.

16. It is to be noted that some of those most closely concerned in the Abadan affair were of consular rather than of diplomatic formation. Sir Francis Shepherd, HM Ambassador in Tehran, and his Counsellor, Mr Middleton, were from the Consular Service. Mr Furlonge, Head of Eastern Department, had been a member of the Levant Consular Service. Others came from outside the Foreign Service: Mr Furlonge's assistants, Mr Fry and Mr Saner, were former members of the Indian Political Service. Of these officers, it may be said that they were steady rather than forceful or brilliant.

17. Sir Francis Shepherd on the whole came quite well out of the ordeal. He was commended, and not as a matter of form, by Mr Morrison on June 15 1951 for his defence of British interests which had been 'both judicious and robust'. It is true that the Lord Privy Seal informed the Prime Minister on September 14 1951 that he had 'no respect for Shepherd's judgment'; but good judgment was not Mr Stokes's own strong point. Shepherd was less effective than his predecessor, Sir J. Le Rougetel, or his successor, Sir Roger Stevens (also a product of the General Consular Service) who, as Sir Anthony Eden later noted, 'quickly established his authority as our representative': but Shepherd was more sorely tried than they were. Shepherd's mild temperament and 'quiet methods' were far removed from the successfully belligerent diplomacy of Sir Reginald Hoare at Tehran in 1932 (a reversion to which Sir Reginald pressed upon the Foreign Office in 1951), or from the adept conduct (highly commended by Mr Butler) of our retreat from extra-territoriality in China by Sir Miles Lampson (later Lord Killearn), who had once drawn from Sir Austen Chamberlain the characteristically exuberant exclamation: 'Bravo Lampson! A man!' Nor was Shepherd able to act as boldly as Le Rougetel had done, under Mr Bevin's instructions, in 1946, when Indian troops were at hand. When Mr Shepherd's appointment to Tehran [was made], it was thought from his recent record in Jakarta, that he would be one to keep his head in a crisis, and a crisis was suspected

in Persia. But perhaps this was not enough. It would have been better if we had appointed a member of the diplomatic élite, but these do not grow on every bush. What difference this would have made in the outcome is anybody's guess. The Hoares and the Lampsons, had such been available, would have found themselves operating in 1950-1 in situations much less favourable for diplomatic exploitation than those which they had known in the early 1930s.

18. The same kind of reservation applies to Mr Furlonge. Heads of department hold key positions and should be outstanding men, if such can be found, and Mr Furlonge was hardly that. His work was highly creditable, but he lacked the grasp and vision of the first-class official. Prospective heads of department should be spotted early in their careers and nursed and tested for later appointment.

19. Mr Michael Wright and his successor, Mr Bowker, were up to standard as Assistant Under-Secretaries in charge of Middle Eastern affairs. On the economic side, Mr Berthoud, the Assistant Under-Secretary (who came from the oil industry and the Ministry of Fuel and Power) and his junior, Mr Ramsbotham, were outstandingly good, being both perceptive and constructive, perhaps because they had more time to think than their hard-pressed colleagues on the political side. Of Mr Furlonge's assistants, Mr Henry Hankey, who served down to August 1950, was hardly the requisite standard. His successor, Mr Fry, who served down to July 1951, was, as his later record has shown, of superior ability, and comes well out of the record. On the organization of the work on Persia within the Office, there will be something to say later.

20. It may be invidious for the Permanent Under-Secretary to speak about himself, but he has been keenly interested in seeing himself through the candid eyes of the historian.

21. Mr Butler regrets that there were not to be found in the files more of the Permanent Under-Secretary's comprehensive minutes on policy, from some of which he quotes. But on one occasion he does surmise, rightly, that 'in this crisis of opinion as probably at other times, any views which he may have expressed personally were presumably conveyed orally'. Such oral communications with Ministers and colleagues must be an essential part of the PUS's practice; but, like others, indeed perhaps more than others, he should have a care to ensure—without being obsessed by it—that, for the sake of the historians, the record should carry as clear an explanation as possible of why things happened as they did, and a fair representation of the part which he himself played. If, in this case, the PUS's record is less complete than it might with advantage have been, it is to be remembered that the Abadan crisis was not the only crisis which the PUS had to handle in the summer and autumn of 1951. Thus, while he could at a pinch leave the Abadan affair in the able Under-Secretaries' hands of Mr Bowker and Mr Berthoud, the defection of Maclean and Burgess, which occurred when the Abadan crisis began to reach its height, was something which he had perforce to handle personally and, for a time, to the exclusion of almost everything else.

22. While he feels that, in point of policy, he might at times have displayed more purpose, vigour and resource, and less acquiescence in the hesitations of Ministers and in the rigidities of the Treasury and the Company, than the record shows, and that in point of administration, as will be noted later, he omitted to take what he now recognizes to have been an important necessary step, he may perhaps claim that his general line was in the event vindicated, although as Mr Butler suggests, by a narrow

margin of time. That line was that the crisis should be played long, that force was no solution, that it was better to make no agreement than to make a bad one, that the agreement to be aimed at was on the basis of a consortium, and that for this to be made possible, Musaddiq must be displaced. But that is not to say that some other policy, and a different kind of diplomacy, had these been in keeping with the sentiment of the government, and had they been resolutely applied in face of all difficulties, might not have been equally, or more successful.

23. Mr Butler comments, with implied criticism, on the fact that in the autumn of 1951 the Foreign Secretary and the Permanent Under-Secretary were both away from the Office at the same time, the former abroad on business, the latter on leave. This is, of course, in principle, undeniable. But if Mr Butler had looked at the dates, he could have seen that the period of simultaneous absence lasted for one week only. Ministers, including Mr Morrison himself, had already been on holiday; and for a very difficult spell the Permanent Under-Secretary had had to handle the crisis with the Prime Minister alone. There is no evidence that the Permanent Under-Secretary's absence had any unfavourable effect on the course of events. It would be an impertinence to think so, since his duties were undertaken by the capable hands of Sir Roger Makins. The one minor criticism which Mr Butler bases on this coincidence (379) is captious in the extreme.

III *The Administrative Aspect*
   (*a*) *Minor Criticisms*
24. A reading of this 300,000-word historical case-study of the Abadan crisis prompts the wry reflection that if public servants wish to stand up to the scrutiny of historians, their first recourse is to put everything down on paper.[2] Try as they will to qualify the thought, historians tend to assume that if something is not set down in writing in the archives it was not said or not done. By usual Foreign Office standards, the Abadan affair was well documented. A powerful Secretary of State and bustling officials will, in time of crisis, take many of their decisions after *ad hoc* meetings, and of such meetings there will often be little record except the action that emerged from them. But Mr Morrison was not apt to work in this way; and the Eastern Department, and notably its head, Mr Furlonge, was bureaucratic rather than bustling, more inclined to write a minute than to hold a meeting. The consequence was that the records deposited were comprehensive enough for Mr Butler to be able to chronicle events almost day by day and step by step. He pays tribute to the 'impressive precision', to the 'prudent skill and devoted work' and to the 'precision and grip' of the Foreign Office. He can commend the Eastern Department for their 'admirable celerity' on one occasion (170) or the Foreign Office for their 'notably comprehensive exploration of expedients' on another, or Mr Furlonge for the 'high order of clarity' of his minutes. But he is at constant pains to make a note when he finds no record of this or that paper having been communicated to other Whitehall departments, or this or that telegram having been repeated to posts abroad; of this or

[2] In a memorandum of 15 February 1963, 'Abadan and After in the light of comment by Lord Strang', Butler responded (para 4) that while a historian could easily compress his story when it was 'of a strong government pursuing a clear and consistent policy', it was much less easy to compress the record of 'weak governments with confused and vacillating policies'. He added: 'In the case of Abadan this factor heavily compounded another which I indicated in my Preface; how much longer diplomatic history is apt to become when one tries to explain not merely what happened, but just how and why.'

that point having been adequately reported by telegram; of this or that clue or suggestion having been followed up; of this or that Persian or American statement or argument having been contraverted; of this or that opening having been exploited; of this or that report having been properly checked.

25. As to these shortcomings, it is fair to say that, given the broad and inexorable sweep of events, they can have had little if any effect upon the outcome. It is fair to add, also, that excess of zeal can create exasperation and waste valuable time, and that too liberal telegraphing can choke the wires. Absence of record does not necessarily mean absence of action. Much that is done informally by word of mouth passes unrecorded. Without the telephone and the informal talk, the machine would break down. If many of the things which Mr Butler finds were not recorded were in fact not done, this may well sometimes be because those responsible thought, rightly or wrongly, that they were not worth doing. If there is no selection, the machine will not work.[3]

26. But it may be admitted that, if there were few serious faults, reporting and inter-communication, though in general adequate, did sometimes fall short of the highest standard. The fault was not however in the general organization and functioning of the mechanism of communication. Had there been serious failures in this respect, Mr Butler would not have failed to note them. Apart from a few lapses, there is little evidence that the conduct of public business was impeded for this cause. The shortcomings derived rather from defects in policy or from the temper in which diplomacy was conducted, than from the work of Communications Department.

27. Two of the minor points made by Mr Butler may be specially mentioned.

28. He refers, justly, to the treatment in the Foreign Office of an important despatch from Her Majesty's Ambassador at Tehran in which he reviewed the whole Persian oil problem and made some specific and far-reaching proposals for the settlement. This despatch was dated December 31, 1950. It was received in the Foreign Office on January 4, 1951 and reached the Eastern Department next day. It was not minuted in the Third Room until January 20 and was not seen by the Assistant and the Head of the Department until January 24. This was a serious lapse in that during this period serious discussions were held with the Treasury, the Ministry of Fuel and Power and the Anglo-Iranian Oil Company on January 16 and 23, and a paper was prepared for the Cabinet and circulated on January 22. Had Sir F. Shepherd sent his report by telegram, this *lâche* would not have occurred, since telegrams are immediately circulated to those concerned. But one can understand how it happened. The junior who received the despatch would want to make a thorough study of it before minuting it, which he would conceive it to be his duty to do; and he may well have found this a difficult task. Meanwhile, the despatch lay hidden while the machine sped on. Clearly, his proper course would have been to send the despatch straight up to his superior, adding, if he wished, that he had retained a carbon copy and would submit a minute as soon as he could.

29. It is important that the impact of formal despatches from Ambassadors upon

---

[3] Butler acknowledged that the Abadan crisis was generally well-documented, but suggested (para 8) that as important gaps tended to occur at the higher levels of the FO, where the work was 'particularly intense, important, and, often secret', it would be good idea for every PUS to be asked, on retirement, to write 'an entirely frank survey of his tenure of office . . . paying particular attention to those confidential considerations, both political and personal, which are least likely to be adequately reflected in the main files'. This would produce a corpus of 'inner history' difficult for any later historian to neglect or controvert.

the minds of the Foreign Secretary and his senior advisers should be immediate and direct, and should not be muffled by misguided adherence to the procedures of bureaucracy. No doubt the need for this has been brought to the attention of the Office from time to time, as occasion has arisen. Mr Butler rather regrets that the file bears no evidence of a reproof akin to the storm which would assuredly have broken around the head of the unfortunate junior had he been serving in the days of Lord Curzon and Sir Eyre Crowe. But archives are not written for the sole delectation of historians,[4] and it can be taken as certain that the delinquent was left in no doubt about the enormity of his offence.

30. Mr Butler's second point is less well founded.

31. He says: 'When all allowance is made for the time-saving convenience of verbal consultation within the Office, one is still rather surprised to notice how few papers during the Persian crisis of 1951 were marked and minuted in joint consultation between Eastern Department, responsible for Persian affairs, and African Department handling those of Egypt. There was some danger that the Suez Canal might prove to be almost more of a real divide departmentally, on paper, than it was politically, on the spot.' Mr Butler recognizes, however, that 'this probable correlation had naturally been taken into account at the higher levels, at least, in the Foreign Office.'

32. As to this criticism, there are several things to be said.

33. Most of the papers on the Persian affair were highly technical. There were quite enough outside people to consult—Treasury, Ministry of Fuel and Power, and the Company. It would have been an intolerable burden upon the two departments and an inexcusable waste of time, if lateral internal consultation by the passage to and fro of papers—in principle a necessary procedure—had been religiously practised. In the vast majority of cases, African Department would have had nothing of value to contribute. On broad matters of policy, or upon other significant developments, they were not left out of the picture. They could follow the course of events from the telegrams circulated to them each day, and could raise their voice if any point occurred to them which might affect their province, as they no doubt did. What is more, the two departments were supervised by the same Assistant Under-Secretary, one of whose prime tasks it was to see that the policies of his departments were, so far as possible, in harmony. There is no evidence that the impact of our handling of the Persian crisis upon our interests in Egypt was overlooked.

(b) More substantial criticisms

34. To pass now from these minor criticisms to more substantial gaps in the archives. Of these, five may be mentioned. Mr Butler notes the absence or delay in the production (1) of a historical study of the peculiar relationship between His Majesty's Government and the Anglo-Iranian Oil Company; (2) of an estimate of the growing movement in Persia for the nationalization of oil, and of its implications for the general outlook of H[is] Majesty's Government upon the nationalization of British property in foreign countries; (3) of an enquiry into the degree of dependence of Great Britain upon Persian oil; (4) of a comprehensive political appreciation for

---

[4] Butler commented (para 6) that he quite appreciated this point, and that if archives were so written 'they would really not be of much use to historians . . . But the remorseless accumulation of enormous masses of paper is in fact apt to fill the modern historian—and certainly this one—with a gloom second only to that of the administrator himself. But once a file is there the conscientious historian, no less than the administrator before him, feels bound to give it such attention as it may deserve.'

the Cabinet on 'the overriding considerations of geopolitics in relation to our handling of the Persian crisis'; and (5) of a recapitulatory memorandum on the use of force at the final, critical stage of the conflict.

35. Of these, the first is the only one which calls for any extended comment.

36. At several points, Mr Butler remarks on the uncertainty which seemed to prevail in the Foreign Office about the character and history of the constitutional relationship between His Majesty's Government and the Anglo-Iranian Oil Company, in which the government held a majority of shares and to whose board the government appointed two directors. Mr Butler perhaps makes too much of this. That relationship was defined in a letter addressed to the board by Sir John Bradbury, Joint Permanent Secretary to the Treasury, on May 20, 1914, in which an assurance was given to the company as to the limits in the field of general policy within which the veto of the government directors would be exercised. The position as seen by Mr Bevin was stated in a letter which he wrote to the Chancellor of the Exchequer and the Minister of Fuel and Power on July 20, 1946 saying that 'as Foreign Secretary I have no power or influence, in spite of this great holding by the Government, to do anything at all'. In October 1950 he thought that pressure might now be brought to bear on the company. The Treasury still maintained that H[is] Majesty's Government could not dictate to the company as to the advances they should pay to the Persians. The Treasury view on this point was put formally to the Permanent Under-Secretary of the Foreign Office by Sir Henry Wilson Smith, a Second Secretary of the Treasury, at a meeting held, at Treasury request, in January 1951, as a consequence of which the former, at a meeting which they both had on January 23 with Sir William Fraser, the Chairman of the Company, refrained from pressing the company to move further or faster than they wished. (The sense of Sir H. Wilson Smith's intervention is based upon personal recollection, not upon Mr Butler's narrative.) In the light of this, it is curious to find Mr Berthoud, early in February and in March, questioning the current interpretation of Sir John Bradbury's letter. He did not think that the Treasury's cautious attitude was justified by the terms of the letter. This view was, however, not supported by the Treasury Solicitor's department. Asked by the Lord Privy Seal, Mr Stokes, for a legal opinion whether H[is] Majesty's Government could 'by virtue of its majority holding compel the company to accept a solution of the Persian dispute which the present Board of Directors (other than the Government nominees) regard as unacceptable', Mr C.S. Evans, the Assistant Treasury Solicitor, replied on August 4, 1951, that the Government Directors' power of veto was a negative power. The only course, short of legislation, for His Majesty's Government to pursue in order to compel acceptance would be to secure the appointment of a new board. This course, the Foreign Office thought, was 'almost unthinkable'.

37. There is little doubt that, on the strict interpretation of Sir John Bradbury's letter, all political considerations apart, Mr Evans was right and Mr Berthoud was mistaken. The Government directors' powers as therein defined were negative, not positive. They could, within a defined field, impose a veto; they could not impose a positive course of action on the company. If this was the right view, on which both the Treasury and the Foreign Office continued to act, no mere historical memorandum could have modified it.

38. Whether it was desirable (and it certainly was) to get away from this basis of relationship was another question. As Mr George McGhee, the Assistant Secretary

at the State Department, had dryly observed to Sir F. Shepherd in March: 'The Foreign Office allowed the chairman of the company to dictate its policy about oil in Persia.' In the event some revision had been made in April 1951 in the relationship between the government and the company, with the acquiescence of the latter. The purpose of the revision, as stated in a paper circulated to the Cabinet by the Foreign Secretary, was to secure that His Majesty's Government should now exercise a close control over the actions of the company since 'this is not a commercial affair but a vital national interest'. The proposed letter to the company, the text of which had been approved by Ministers, was communicated in draft to Sir William Fraser by Sir Edward Bridges at a meeting on April 3, 1951, also attended by the Permanent Under-Secretary of the Foreign Office, when Sir William Fraser said that the proposed change in favour of more intensive consultation would be welcome and not fundamental. In recording this, Mr Butler, without quoting the terms of the draft letter or giving the date of its despatch, observes: 'The minute of this conversation made by Sir William Strang . . . does not record that Sir Edward Bridges followed his brief from the Treasury so far as to raise specifically with Sir William Fraser "the question of the part played in the future by the Government Directors who appear to be allowed to play a very limited role in return for their annual emoluments of £2,950 per annum"'.

39. It may be inferred from this that, while the role of the government directors remained as defined by Sir J. Bradbury, the liberty of the government itself to bring influence to bear was to be extended. (What the letter, in terms, said was that His Majesty's Government were 'to be kept in close touch with the development of the company's general policy', and that there was to be 'mutual consultation in good time, and at appropriate levels'.) This is in fact what happened in practice, to such a point that, in the later stages of the affair, the views of the company come to be increasingly disregarded.

40. Mr Butler's treatment of this subject leaves something to be desired. Sir J. Bradbury's letter to the Anglo-Persian Oil Company of May 20 1914 and Sir E. Bridges's letter to the Anglo-Iranian Oil Company of April 12, 1951, which put a new gloss upon the earlier letter, without amending or superseding it, were key documents in the affair. It would have been useful if Mr Butler had made a careful analysis and comparison of the two letters. Instead of which, he is led off the main track by a rather eccentric view expressed by Mr Berthoud about the meaning of the Bradbury letter, and by the apparent failure of Sir E. Bridges, in his talk with Sir W. Fraser about the new draft letter, to make every point in the brief supplied to him by one of his juniors. The fault of the Foreign Office was not in misunderstanding the Bradbury letter but in not pressing earlier and more strongly for a new relationship between the government and the company to be defined.[5]

41. As regards points (2) and (3) mentioned above, there is some substance in Mr Butler's comment. The studies on the implications of nationalization and on the place of Persian oil in our economy might with advantage have been pursued and brought to a point at an earlier stage. The possible remedy for such shortcomings

---

[5] Butler conceded (para 3) that a detailed comparison of the letters might have been useful, but noted this would be a long business and might hold up the narrative, so he had decided against it. 'This is a good illustration of the risk of justified criticism which a historian runs when he tried to omit or compress material in order to shorten his narrative.'

will be discussed when Mr Butler's own recommendations are considered.

42. The same may perhaps be true as regards point (4). It might well have been useful for the Cabinet to have had papers from time to time placing the Persian oil dispute in the broad context of British interests abroad and of the policies best designed to defend them. Certainly, it would supply a historian with evidence upon which to come to a judgment upon the formulation and conduct of our foreign policy. On the other hand, the nature and bearing of the dispute in relation to the totality of our interests abroad would be obvious to the professional mind within the Foreign Office, and there is no reason to think that these were misapprehended by Ministers. The difficulty was not so much to recognise the character of the problem as to find practicable means of dealing with it. Nevertheless, the definition and analysis of a problem in its widest implications can be enlightening both for the writer and for the reader, and the Foreign Office might well have set itself an exercise on these lines.

43. On point (5), there is less substance in Mr Butler's criticism. The position was that in the final phase of the dispute, at the end of September 1951, when H[is] Majesty's Government were faced with the crucial decision whether or not to resort to armed intervention in order to prevent the expulsion of the company's staff from Abadan, Sir Roger Makins, who was in charge of the Office in the absence of the Permanent Under-Secretary, wrote a minute to the Secretary of State saying, rather out of the blue: 'It seems almost certain that we shall be faced with a choice of withdrawal under threat or armed intervention . . . But faced with Hobson's choice, my own inclination is for the bolder course; though, in the short run, this carries the greater danger'.

44. Mr Butler rightly observes that this was the first recommendation in favour of the use of force made at a high level in the Foreign Office—the Permanent Under-Secretary had at no time made such a submission. He then goes on: 'Some such consideration, together with the familiarity of the arguments by then, may conceivably have been partly responsible for the fact that no memorandum was prepared in the Foreign Office in support of the important advice now tentatively offered by Sir Roger Makins. Such a memorandum might nevertheless have been valuable in view of the new acuteness of the crisis and of the fact that the Foreign Secretary had not impressed his personal and standing inclination towards strong measures upon previous papers prepared by his department.'

45. The fact is that, as Mr Butler indicates, the question of the use of force had been argued backwards and forwards *ad nauseam* for months past, and it was as clear as anything could be that H[is] Majesty's Government were not going to use force on the eve of a general election, whatever anyone might say. The Prime Minister and most of the Cabinet were against it, and so were Sir Gladwyn Jebb at New York, Sir F. Shepherd at Tehran, and the Permanent Under-Secretary in London. The Foreign Secretary was inclined to favour force, but does not seem to have pressed very hard for it. The Governments of the United States and of India, as well as a preponderance of world opinion as reflected in the United Nations, were opposed. (A useful description of the final line-up is given by Mr Butler on p. 388.) If Mr Morrison and Sir Roger Makins had wished to press their view (and Sir Roger's view was, as he had said, no more than an 'inclination'), they could have prepared a paper for the Cabinet re-examining the whole problem and advocating a new decision. If they did not do so, they no doubt thought—and no doubt rightly— that the time for this had passed. The historian may regret, if only for the sake of

tidiness, that a last fight was not made for forceful action; but if the advocates of such action did not think it worth while to put their case formally in writing, this was a matter for themselves and not a just cause of complaint against the Foreign Office.

(*c*) *Suggested Remedies*

46. It is now proposed to look at Mr Butler's administrative conclusions.

47. These are prefaced by a justly admiring reference to Sir Ivone Kirkpatrick's paper on 'Conduct of Official Business' circulated by Sir Orme Sargent in 1948 and re-circulated in 1960. Mr Butler gently suggests that Sir Ivone's 'trenchant and timely criticisms' were not, in 1951, being adequately attended to, and that the Foreign Office in 1951 was 'on the whole less efficient than it was either earlier or later'. This may well have been so, at any rate so far as Eastern Department and the Embassy at Tehran were concerned, the staff of which were steady rather than outstanding in ability. It is to be doubted whether it was true of the Office as a whole. In any event, an examination of the Order Book would show how far those in charge of the administration of the Office were alert to the need for accuracy, economy and expedition in the conduct of business. One of Sir Ivone Kirkpatrick's observations was, in truth, rather wide of the mark, in the circumstances prevailing in 1951. He was always a *laudator temporis acti.*[6] 'The old despatches and official letters', he said, 'had form, which imposed a certain discipline and required clarity of thought and expression. Telegrams and semi-official letters, though seemingly easier to write, trap the unwary unto looseness of thought or expression.' The loose semi-official letter can certainly be a snare, but so also can the orotund official despatch, as contrasted with the crispness of the well-drafted telegram. So essential, indeed, had telegraphic correspondence become that the Permanent Under-Secretary and the Chief Clerk were later to carry on a vigorous and continuous campaign to secure economy and precision in the drafting of telegrams which were threatening to choke the channels of communication.

(i) *Continuity*

48. Mr Butler starts by urging the importance of continuity, as a means of ensuring 'time for philosophic brooding upon the heavy issues' and due attention to 'historical research on the one hand and of forward and contingent planning on the other'. To meet this need, he makes two specific suggestions.

49. The first is additional 'working leave' of a few days once or twice a year for Heads of Department and Under-Secretaries during which, away from official papers, they would think intensively about policy and perhaps write a short paper.

50. There is something in this; but the period, to be useful, would have to be more than just a few days; a week would be the minimum. A hard-pressed officer takes time to unwind; and for him to have to launch into hard thought straight off the treadmill might prove to be an intolerable burden.

51. The next suggestion is for the appointment of 'continuity-men' to the most hard-pressed Departments, with the rank of Assistant Head, acting under the authority of the Head of Department. This Assistant Head would be relieved of routine duties. He would have general departmental duties such as the oversight of intelligence, research and planning, the digestion of long despatches and reports, the preparation of periodical surveys of the work of the department, and the training of juniors. For the sake of continuity, he would serve rather longer than the usual

---

[6] One who praises past times (Horace).

departmental term.

52. Mr Butler compares the situation of the proposed 'continuity-man' to that of Sir John Pratt, who was Adviser on Far Eastern Affairs for 13 years before the Second World War. But this was something quite different. Sir J. Pratt had the rank of Consul General and was equal in status with the Head of the Far Eastern Department. He worked as much to the Assistant Under-Secretary as to the Head of Department. He was a powerful, if rather cranky, expert on China, and on China alone. He had nothing to do with Japan. And he had no general departmental duties such as those proposed for the 'continuity-man'.

53. The idea of a 'continuity-man' is, in theory, a good one, if the necessary staff could be spared; and if the scheme could be made to work, it would be useful. But in practice, as a matter of human psychology, it would be hard to keep the 'continuity-man' to his general duties. In times of heavy pressure, he would tend to be drawn into the day-to-day executive work of the department; and, if he were ambitious and active-minded, he would itch to take part in the submission of action papers to higher authority.

54. But the experiment would be worth trying, if this has not already been done.

(ii) *Drive: The Political Alert*

55. In Mr Butler's mind, the counterpart to continuity is drive.

56. He observes that, whereas before the Second World War the work of the Foreign Office gave the impression of being done by highly skilled individuals, post-war impression was rather of a great departmental machine. The need for individual drive and initiative has therefore become all the greater and the problem, as he sees it, is how best to secure this. His proposal is that, with the arrival or even the threat of an international crisis of exceptional gravity, a political alert should be proclaimed in the Foreign Office and perhaps in Whitehall, much as, in a grave domestic crisis, a state of emergency may be declared. This would provide a 'psychological stimulus' or 'extra jerk' which would gear 'the administrative machine into overdrive' more effectively than an individual Minister or resolute senior official would be likely to do.

57. This would involve priority for all crisis correspondence; the immediate production and circulation by the Department of a background historical memorandum, and a memorandum weighing possible courses of action, with a recommendation of the one which might seem, on balance, to be the best (a tall order, this!); a prompt review of all staffing arrangements in the departments and missions concerned, with a call upon less heavily occupied departments and missions, and the injection of fresh minds from the Cabinet Office or other government departments; a review of inter-departmental machinery; the reaffirmation of the responsibility of the Foreign Office, under the Foreign Secretary and the Cabinet, for all relevant political decisions, in order to ensure that the process of interdepartmental consultation does not put the brake on necessary action.

58. It may be agreed that all these are steps which it might be requisite to take at some stage or other in the development of a crisis; but whether the declaration of an alert, with a kind of 'war-look' for its application, is the best way to secure them is more open to doubt. The onset of a crisis may be gradual rather than sudden. The Persian oil dispute lasted seven years, from 1947 to 1954, but its phase of acute crisis fell within a period of a few months in 1951. It might be difficult to decide at what point to declare the alert; and well before that point it might be better if some of the

measures prescribed in the alert had already been taken as developing circumstances might from time to time have required. The important thing is not so much to declare an alert as to make sure that the Foreign Secretary and his department, and in particular the Permanent Under-Secretary, are themselves alert and fore-sighted enough to ensure that the machine is geared to the tasks which are likely to fall upon it.[7]

59. On the whole, the Foreign Office, as a department, has usually shown itself to be responsive to the demands of changing times, and to be able to adjust itself automatically to the stress of a crisis. But the present writer would be the first to admit that there were shortcomings during the Abadan crisis. Certainly, the Ministerial Committee on Persia and the Persia (Official) Committee set up under Foreign Office chairmanship by Mr Eden as soon as he took office should have been constituted earlier. The reasons for this omission have been noted above (paragraph 9); but the Permanent Under-Secretary would have done well to press for the establishment of the official committee sooner than he did. He might well have controverted the views of the Treasury and of the company more strongly than he seems to have done. He might have more strongly represented the belligerent views of Mr Morrison, irresolute though these were, against the prevailing views of the Prime Minister. But officials, in tendering advice, must have regard to practical possibilities. If they persistently disregard these, they stultify their influence.

60. The choice of Sir F. Shepherd for Tehran and of Mr Furlonge for Eastern Department could perhaps have been bettered,—though neither of them fell down on his job. But one can only draw upon the material that is available. The influx into the diplomatic side of the Service, in the early post-war years, of former consular officers under the amalgamation scheme, and of new recruits from the former Indian Services, did not, in its first impact, strengthen our diplomacy. This would be particularly so in an area, such as Asia, where they would be most likely to be employed. In 1951, the work of education and of assimilation was still going on.

61. Eastern Department could, with advantage, have been more strongly reinforced than it was: Mr Furlonge and his staff, faithful though they were, did not quite measure up to a first-class crisis. But something was done. Mr Furlonge was given a second Assistant in September 1950, one of whom (first Mr Fry and later Mr Saner) concentrated on the affairs of Persia, the Persian Gulf, Saudi Arabia and the Yemen. The number of juniors dealing with Persia and the Persian Gulf rose from two in January 1950 to three in February 1950 and to four in September 1950 and onwards. Some of those appointed to the Eastern Department to deal with Persia and the Persian Gulf were chosen for their experience in the Levant or in other parts of Asia. Mr Furlonge had served at Jedda and Beirut; Mr Fry in the Indian Political Service and later in the United Kingdom High Commission at Delhi; Mr Saner with the Government of India and later with the United Kingdom staff at Madras; Mr Rogers (specialising on the Persian Gulf) in the Indian Civil Service and in Consular posts in South Persia; Mr Cranston (Persian Gulf) in the Indian Political Service and later in the United Kingdom High Commission in Delhi; Mr Logan (Persia) had served at Tehran. On the other hand, Mr Leavett (Persia) had been transferred from

---

[7] Butler, while acknowledging (para 9) that the onset of a crisis might be gradual, said he was still inclined to feel that 'this very difficulty, if it could be successfully overcome, rather underlines the possible advantage . . . of stemming drift by the incisive declaration of a political alert'.

the Customs and Excise; Mr Rose (Persian Gulf) probably the ablest of Mr Furlonge's recruits, who worked in the department from April 1950 onwards, had served at Oslo, Algiers and Copenhagen; Mr Rothnie (Persia and Persian Gulf) had served at Vienna and Bangkok.

62. What Eastern Department somewhat lacked was straight diplomatic experience and skill. It is always tempting to lean to the side of the expert or of someone possessing what is regarded as related experience when making appointments; but the contribution to be made by a man of sheer ability, provided that the necessary expert advice is available to him, can be decisive. This is in line with Mr Butler's insistence on the need for a diplomatic élite (paragraph 14). Those who attended to the staffing of Eastern Department in the looming crisis would have done well to see that either the Head, or the Assistant dealing with Persia, was of this calibre. It might have been difficult to change Mr Furlonge in mid-stream; but, good though Mr Fry was, it might have been better to appoint, instead, one of the very best First Secretaries in the Service, even though he might have had no eastern experience. For this omission, the Permanent Under-Secretary bears ultimate responsibility.

63. But there was one decisive step which the Permanent Under-Secretary himself should have taken. The Abadan affair was handled in the Foreign Office by two Assistant Under-Secretaries, Mr Michael Wright (later Mr Bowker) on the political side, and Mr Berthoud on the economic side. The only officer coordinating their work was the Permanent Under-Secretary himself, and he had the whole of the rest of the work of the Office, political, economic and administrative, to deal with. As Mr Butler's narrative shows, he was not able to give his mind sufficiently to the Persian problem. He now recognizes that he ought, early in 1951 if not sooner, to have committed responsibility for Persian affairs to one of the existing Deputy Under-Secretaries, or even to an additional Deputy Under-Secretary, though to get the extra post would have needed a stiff fight with the Treasury. (In 1951, there were only two Deputies, other than the Chief Clerk:[8] there are now four.) This Deputy would have worked under the Permanent Under-Secretary and over the two Assistant Under-Secretaries. Such a step would in itself have been in the nature of an alert. This is in fact what happened in Mr Eden's time. The chairmanship of the Persia (Official) Committee was held by a Deputy Under-Secretary in the Foreign office, first by Sir Roger Makins and later by Sir Pierson Dixon, and these two officers in turn assumed responsibility for handling the Persian oil problem in all its aspects. Mr Eden's task, difficult though it was, was easier than Mr Morrison's had been: but he owed his ultimate success not only to his own skill and resolution but also to his having been better served by his Office and by H[is] Majesty's Embassy in Tehran (under Mr Denis Wright as Chargé d'Affaires and later under Sir Roger Stevens as Ambassador) than his predecessor had been.

IV *The Political Aspect: the Role of Diplomacy*

64. It is not the purpose of the present paper to argue at length the merits or demerits of British policy in the Abadan affair. We were driven out of Abadan, the

---

[8] Note in original: 'There was in addition, a Deputy Under-Secretary in charge of the very large German Section, dealing with occupation and Control Commission work in Germany. He also worked to the Permanent Under-Secretary.'

greatest single British investment overseas; but in the end we saved a good deal out of the wreck, suffering much loss and humiliation in the process. Mr Butler has carefully and on the whole justly, if at times a shade pedantically, analysed the course of events in his political conclusions on pp 308-318. In the course of his narrative he returns repeatedly to one fundamental aspect of our diplomacy which it is important to examine.

65. Thus he sees a lack of 'diplomatic ingenuity' and of 'adroit and purposeful diplomacy', and he advocates the exploitation of 'techniques of bargaining from weakness in negotiating with great powers like the United States'. He thinks that 'instead of only stringing along with the Americans and acquiescing' in their fear that British military action in Persia might provoke Russian intervention under Article VI of the Soviet-Persian Treaty of 1921, 'British policy might seek to exploit it to its own advantage': that is to say, 'the balance of advantage for His Majesty's Government might have lain in the adoption of an adroitly resolute policy designed to put a bold front on the Russian menace to Persia, and if necessary to play upon Persian fear of it. It would also have been a great gain to set the Americans calculating that, in order to conjure their bugbear of Russian intervention in Persia, it was especially desirable to appease, not the Persian Government, but the British.'

66. He makes the general observation: 'Great Britain remained America's chief ally and, as noticed, was far from possessing no cards even if some of them represented a lead from material weakness. That was a diplomatic art which Great Britain had largely been able to neglect during the 19th and early 20th centuries whereas now conditions called for some revival, perhaps, of techniques familiar enough in the 18th century.' And, in comment on the Persian Anti-Sabotage Bill, with its direct and immediate threat to the safety of the British staff at Abadan, he says: 'One may wonder whether, things having gone so far, this was not perhaps the occasion for a bold decision, if necessary at a high level, to accept a calculated risk and mount a crash-campaign to bring out the physical dangers of Persian interference at Abadan by a drumfire of publicity in British and foreign, especially American, organs.' In general, he says 'British policy regarding Persia was at once too rigid and too weak'.

67. The absence of such vigorous, indeed adventurous, diplomacy, resulted, for example, in a failure to exploit against the Persians, and in the mind of the Americans, the interim ruling of the International Court, so clearly and perhaps unexpectedly in our favour; in what Mr Butler regards as 'the gravest single mistake in the British diplomatic handling of the Persian crisis of 1951', namely 'failure to prevent the Harriman mission from prejudicing the effective exploitation' of the ruling of The Hague Court; and in an inadequately determined mobilization of support for our cause in friendly foreign capitals.

68. Without controverting this thesis, it is fair to record the political and other disabilities under which His Majesty's Government were labouring in this affair at this period, to all of which Mr Butler does justice.

69. The Labour Government had an exiguous majority in Parliament. They were moving into grave balance of payment difficulties. British prestige in the Middle East was already in decline. Having lost the use of the Indian army, His Majesty's Government lacked adequate, immediately available military forces. Their own policy of nationalization inhibited them from developing a full attack upon the Persian position. The Treasury policy of dividend stabilization, tenaciously

maintained, swelled the share of the Exchequer and unfairly restricted the share of the Persians in the company's profits. His Majesty's Government were in conflict with a weak but diplomatically adroit foreign government which was bent upon satisfying anti-foreign nationalistic aspirations even at the price of economic ruin. They were hamstrung by the rigid, unimaginative, reactionary outlook of the Anglo-Iranian Oil Company (Sir William Fraser, its chairman, was an accountant), technologically advanced but socially backward and remote from the life of the Persian people; and, although the government held a majority of shares, they conceived themselves, until very late in the day, to be estopped from influencing the policy of the company by assurances given to the latter at the time of the acquisition of their holding. In view of American aid, they were reluctant to quarrel with the United States Government, notwithstanding that the Americans (*a*) were ready to sacrifice British interests in Persia in order, they hoped, 'to save Persia for the West', a policy which, Mr Butler says, bedevilled the whole Abadan crisis; (*b*) were, as a general policy, currying favour with anti-colonial governments; and (*c*) were pursuing the unavowed, and perhaps even sometimes unconscious, objective of political and economic expansion in the world at British expense.[9] His Majesty's Government were in the dilemma of wishing to contain American economic penetration while yet seeking American political support, which, until very late in the day, was usually withheld. 'Effective lack of such American support for British policy, despite the Anglo-American agreement of November 1947 regarding mutual support in the Middle East, underlay the whole development of the crisis in 1951 and facilitated the Persian game of playing Great Britain off against the United States'. His Majesty's Government were hampered in the free conduct of a foreign policy by a declared devotion to the Charter of the United Nations and an unquestioning respect for the views predominating in the Security Council and General Assembly. One might well ask, as the Permanent Under-Secretary did ask, if one joined the United Nations, what else could one expect? 'The United Nations has scant concern for the rule of law and is showing the way to international anarchy.'

70. If, in the face of these impediments, His Majesty's Government were not able more successfully to safeguard their interests in Persia, it is fair to ask how much more successful the United States has been, although in an infinitely stronger position, in preventing and securing redress for the wholesale confiscation of American property in Cuba. The Americans, so far at any rate, have in fact been less successful. Castro has not yet suffered the fate of Musaddiq.

71. But these were not the only impediments.

72. In a general way, again, His Majesty's Government were hampered in the free conduct of their foreign policy by the obligation or habit of consultation, particularly with some of the other Commonwealth governments, or at least by the discipline of a regular supply of information. They conceived it their duty, too, to consult liberally with the United States government on each important move in the development of the crisis. What is more, they were bound to report from time to time in Parliament on their acts and intentions. In those conditions, it would have been

---

[9] Note in the original: 'This latent, and even overt nationalistic and imperialistic urge is well described and historically analysed by the American Professor R.W. Van Alstyne in *The Rising American Empire*, Blackwell, Oxford, 1960.'

exceedingly difficult to pursue the bold, adventurous, almost blackmailing course which Mr Butler thinks we might have embarked upon.

73. Finally, to do so would have been contrary to the still well-established traditions of British diplomacy, the quiet tradition of Castlereagh, Salisbury and Grey[10] rather than the rumbustious tradition of Canning and Palmerston. That quiet tradition still informs the professional habit and outlook of the Foreign Service. Again and again in Mr Butler's narrative, the mark of our counsel and action is prudence, circumspection, mildness, caution, second thoughts, degenerating at times into over-complication, hesitation, wobble. Both in Tehran and in Washington, through the mouths of Sir Francis Shepherd and Sir Oliver Franks, our words were sometimes muted rather than forthright, and this was not always the fault of their instructions.

74. One further point may be made here. There is a natural tendency among historians to seize upon a cogent or strongly expressed piece of writing for especial praise or notice, and Mr Butler is no exception to this. But he is experienced enough to look behind the words. One is familiar with the man who writes strong minutes and leaves it at that, without the necessary follow-up in action. There is also the man who proposes bold courses without giving thought to the practical means of execution or without foreseeing and providing for the consequences. The minutes and memoranda by officials in the Abadan papers are on the whole free from this kind of nonsense. The members of the Eastern and Economic Relations Departments and the Under-Secretaries were, as a team, gravely concerned for the safeguarding of British interests and were marked by a deep sense of responsibility. Mr Butler, like readers of his narrative, might sometimes think that they need not so unfailingly have kept their feet upon the ground. But they were following an established tradition, and it was not a bad one.

75. The question is whether, in our present international situation, we can any longer afford to maintain this tradition, well suited as it may have been to our more spacious days. In spite of these impediments and predispositions, would it be possible to give our diplomacy a new look? The example is here before our eyes. The French have traditionally employed a highly efficient diplomacy for self-regarding national ends. Unlike ourselves, they have not as a rule thought it to their long-term advantage to cast their bread upon the waters by taking account of the general interest side by side with the national interest. Can we any longer afford, indeed do we now need, to be to this extent altruistic? President de Gaulle has shown how a European Power, alliance or no alliance, can follow an independent, nationally-based policy, paying scant regard to the interest of others.[11] France has shown how to exploit the advantages of the weaker party. As M. Massigli is reliably reported once to have said: 'France, though no longer so powerful as of old, has always a stopping card to play in the game of diplomacy.' She can, and does, make

---

[10] Note in the original: 'For a summary of their views and practice see the author's *Britain in World Affairs*, Deutsch, London, 1961: for Castlereagh, pp 102, 103-4; for Salisbury, p 217; for Grey, pp 269-70.'

[11] Butler commented (para 12) on this apparent reference to President de Gaulle's veto, announced on 14 January 1963, of Britain's application to join the EEC: 'Compared with our position after expulsion from Abadan, that after our exclusion from the Common Market would seem to be potentially much stronger, rich in possibilities for skilfully [*sic*] political and diplomatic exploitation from the platform of all the economic groundwork now valuably accomplished and still to hand . . . we are now more popular and influential in much of Western Europe than for years past, while the Americans genuinely want us in there . . . Here a new and more enterprising look in our diplomacy might be especially timely.'

the most of her nuisance value. Having no effective parliamentary check, and little public sentiment in favour of the United Nations, and a deep scepticism about the reliability of the United States and the effectiveness of NATO, she can follow courses on a number of international issues which one would say are not open to any British Government in the face of prevailing Parliamentary and public opinion. And yet, unless we break free from these shackles, may we not be condemned to relative international impotence? Is it not time, as Sir Ivone Kirkpatrick once asked, for us to force someone to appease *us*, for a change? If we cannot bring about a revolution in our international outlook and procedures, can we not at least make a modest start? We have a Foreign Secretary today who, more than any of his recent predecessors, has the necessary qualities. And might we not, in our training, try to instil into our new recruits some insight into the active game of diplomacy, as the French have shown that it can still be played?[12]

76. That is one of the main queries that is raised by Mr Butler's study.

STRANG

---

[12] The PUS quoted this paragraph in his monthly letter to HM Representatives, sent out on 1 February 1963. The letter began by referring to President de Gaulle's veto, which the PUS described as a challenge as much to the US as to the UK. The French decision, the PUS said, meant a re-consideration of methods rather than long-term objectives, and he asked HM Representatives for comments on Strang's ideas for a new perspective on British diplomacy. In the light of the volume of responses received, however, Butler was asked to make a detailed analysis of the replies and produce a synthesis. The resulting memorandum, 'A New Perspective for British Diplomacy', of 24 May 1963, is reproduced below.

Memorandum by Rohan Butler, 24 May 1963

A New Perspective for British Diplomacy

I. *The origins of a reappraisal of British diplomacy*

1. Early this year Lord Strang wrote a long memorandum commenting upon my recent study of *British Policy in the relinquishment of Abadan in 1951*. Lord Strang concluded with the particularly interesting question: 'Would it be possible to give our diplomacy a new look? The example is here before our eyes. The French have traditionally employed a highly efficient diplomacy for self-regarding national ends', as Lord Strang went on to explain and assess.

2. Sir Harold Caccia cited Lord Strang's enquiry in his monthly letter of February 1, 1963, to HM Representatives abroad, and invited observations. Thirty-four replies were received. The Permanent Under-Secretary commented on them in his monthly letter of March 1 and explained the context of Lord Strang's remarks, for lack of which some of HM Representatives has previously, through no fault of theirs, not fully appreciated the thought of Lord Strang (cf. para. 7). At the same time the replies of HM Representatives regarding the nature and functions of British diplomacy in the modern world were so stimulating as to call for some analysis.

3. In tentatively attempting such an analysis with commentary, the present writer is very conscious of the limitations imposed by the nature of the material and, especially, by his limited competence to assess it. The letters to Sir Harold Caccia represent an incomplete and possibly uneven sample of views since the proportion of HM Representatives who wrote in was about a third; among those who did there was sometimes, though by no means always, a rather natural tendency for the replies to vary in length inversely with the size of the post. The present writer, also, is personally unacquainted not only with most of the correspondents but also with their current despatches which might in a number of cases help to set their views in perspective. One can only try to turn these disadvantages to some positive advantage by hoping that the angle of vision here may be a slightly fresh one, being that, to a considerable extent, of an outsider looking inwards at the problems confronting British diplomacy today.

II *Diplomatic method and the French example*

4. To begin with a conclusion, the present correspondence strikingly illustrates the high value of the Permanent Under-Secretary's monthly letters to HM Representatives and of occasional general discussion by them of broad issues of common interest. The slight danger of falling into undue self-consciousness by looking over one's shoulder can be avoided and is surely outweighed by the value of an expert meeting of minds about such questions as where and how all the everyday work and diplomatic activity is, and should be, leading our country in the second half of the twentieth century.

5. The letters from HM Representatives, taken by and large, constitute a most impressive and perhaps unparalleled corpus of professional thinking about the role of British diplomacy today. The general impression conveyed is of an intellectual

and indeed moral quality of which the nation could justly be proud, did it but know, as is clearly impossible, of such correspondence. This does, however, prompt the hope that it may prove possible to maintain and perhaps strengthen any tendency to encourage selected members of the Foreign Service to deliver occasional public or semi-public lectures at home, take part in academic discussion-groups, etc, as opportunity offers between foreign postings. Ever-growing public interest in foreign affairs renders the cultivation of informed support for our foreign policies increasingly desirable. Whereas, more broadly, Sir Peter Garran (Mexico City) wonders, for instance, whether Her Majesty's Government were 'rather slow in explaining the problem of the Common Market to the public?'

6. In any such cultivation of public relations to mutual benefit, two of the most valuable groups, in my personal view, might be: (i) selected undergraduates and students, at an impressionable and formative age; this, incidentally, might not only benefit recruiting, but provide valuable indications from the younger generation of likely growth-points in British opinion regarding foreign policy; (ii), if ever at all possible, trades unionists. The Foreign Secretary, as well as several of our ambassadors, have recalled Mr Ernest Bevin's plea for more coal to strengthen his diplomatic hand. One wonders whether it might not prove beneficial if it were ever politically possible to make such pleas more directly, for instance in a speech somewhat matching that which the Foreign Secretary delivered last autumn to the Institute of Directors. Workers' representatives, like undergraduates, might possibly be flattered and receptive if occasionally they were specially posted about foreign policy and their potential contribution to it on a broadly patriotic basis. The two approaches might constitute something of a pincer-movement towards trying to fulfil the Secretary of State's wish that 'in this country we had a little less of the intellectual fringe and a little more of the horse-sense of the great majority'.

7. Passing to particular opinions expressed by HM Representatives, almost two-thirds of those who wrote in the first instance came out strongly on the whole in often cogent criticism of Lord Strang's suggestion that lessons might be learnt from the French conduct of diplomacy. The sampling is too limited to draw positive deductions from such facts as that almost the strongest reactions to Lord Strang's ideas either way came from two envoys (against: Sir David Ormsby-Gore; for, Lord Alport) whose early experience had been political rather than diplomatic; or that the only four writers under fifty years of age (Sir David Ormsby-Gore, Mr Hancock—Oslo, Mr King—Conakry, Mr P.M. Foster) were particularly critical of Lord Strang's suggestion. In his subsequent circular letter of March 1, 1963 Sir Harold Caccia, in seeking to hold the balance, explained that Lord Strang's remarks in their context referred to 'the methods and emphasis of our diplomacy rather than to the main lines of policy'. And indeed almost two-thirds of the correspondents had more or less specifically drawn the important distinction, consecrated by Sir Harold Nicolson, between foreign policy and diplomacy.

8. Criticism by our ambassadors of Lord Strang's suggestions in relation to British foreign policy was to some extent balanced by rather strikingly widespread opinions in favour of conducting British diplomacy with:

(i) *Sharper thinking:* ' . . . a need for greater ruthlessness in discarding inherited axioms and sentiments; above all for recalculating at frequent intervals what our essential interests in any part of the world are, and how we should go about ensuring them' (Sir John Maud, Capetown); ' . . . to avoid the drowsiness induced by the hum of a vast international machine, and to approach conventional policies and traditional assumptions with wide-eyed scepticism' (Sir Roger Stevens); ' . . . tendencies which seem to have grown in Great Britain in recent years. One is the abandonment of objective and logical standards in favour of an undigested form of supposedly liberal sentiment' (Sir Paul Grey, Berne).

(ii) *Plainer speaking:* 'There is a tendency at times not to speak as robustly and firmly as one should and to allow too much weight to the wish to be accommodating and amiable to one's opposite numbers' (Sir Patrick Dean, UN); 'Until Lord Home became Foreign Secretary, we have tended, I think, to speak and sometimes to act, a little too softly.' (Sir Paul Gore-Booth, New Delhi); 'One of our diplomatic failings is a natural British tendency to wrap things up, not from weakness but from normal politeness' (Sir Roderick Parkes, Amman); 'We should be more forthright and try to arrange for wider publicity for our views' (Sir Douglas Busk, Caracas). Such forthrightness would doubtless be relative in any case, within the context of diplomatic courtesy and English good manners, while Mr Vaughan (Panama) provides a reminder as to the uses of judicious flattery. And from the Commonwealth Relations Office Sir Saville Garner draws a valuable distinction between the virtue of plain speaking within the old Commonwealth and the reverse with the emergent nations of the new.

9. Any stronger conduct of British diplomacy can only, however, be practised in relation to the character and aims of British foreign policy: it still comes back to that. Here it is scarcely to be supposed that Lord Strang was advocating any slavish adherence to French models and, as Sir Paul Grey observes: 'Success in diplomacy (as in life) depends on developing one's own talents and character rather than trying to imitate one's neighbour': especially when he is very differently situated. In the present case Sir Norman Brain (Montevideo) tellingly epitomizes this difference: 'France has a more self-sufficient economy; her franc is not a major world currency; she has adequate *lebensraum* within her own frontiers; she knows that she is the key to the defence of Europe. She can thus throw her weight about without the fear of bringing any very valuable objects crashing down. For ourselves the position is very different. Our power depends very largely on the confidence of a large part of the world that our policies *will* take account of the general interest. This is surely one of the intangible bonds which hold the Commonwealth together, and one of the reasons for world confidence in sterling.'

10. Much the same master-theme of British, unlike French, identification with the general interest is developed by others such as Sir John Ward (Rome) and Sir Con O'Neill (then at Helsinki), who points up critical differences in temper ('liberalism in France has never conspicuously attached itself to international idealism as it has in England') and in geography: 'France enjoys a geographical position which makes her cooperation virtually indispensable in any organisation for European defence or European economic integration. We, on the other hand, could at a pinch be left out of both; as is, to a large extent, Scandinavia.' Though, even so, Lord Hankey (OECD) expresses the suggestive opinion that General de Gaulle may be repeating the mistake of Napoleon III in 'basing a sort of French empire in Europe on a totally inadequate geopolitical and strategical foundation'. The similarities between the two regimes, though only partial, certainly add up rather strikingly, perhaps even starting from the fact that both French leaders arrived back in France as refugees from England.

11. It would certainly seem arguable that even now the strength of France is more economic, possessing a basic sufficiency at least for her own purposes, than it is political. The brilliant makeshift of the Gaullist regime reminds one that *tour-de-force* is a French expression; also, perhaps, that ever since the overdue yet too radical break with the past in 1789 France has been a nation in search of an adequate present. Hence often today in France, one suspects, even among her keen logicians and republicans, a submerged yearning and envy of the evolving continuities of British political society culminating, by no means least even for them, in our constitutional monarchy.

12. Any French tendency to envy Great Britain her insular and constitutional advantages was liable to be strongly reinforced by the simple circumstance that in the Second World War France was defeated and we were not. Furthermore the present Franco-German rapprochement was largely predictable since in 1945, for the first time since 1815, France and Germany had shared the intimate experience of defeat. Also, the Vichy regime had considerably deeper psychological roots than quisling governments elsewhere, while on the economic side Franco-German big-business integration with an eye to eventual European hegemony can be significantly traced back to the Stresemann Era and the International Steel Cartel of 1926 (cf. the chapter 'From Thoiry to Vichy' in Godfrey Scheele, *The Weimar Republic* pp 297-306).

13. One hears a story that M. Jean Monnet has described the Common Market as the '*club des battus*'. General de Gaulle himself has made it sufficiently evident that it is not only in economic respects that he holds that Great Britain does not fit comfortably into his new model for Western Europe. And although that model is at present mainly cast in the economic image of the Common Market yet, by a seeming paradox, one may perhaps sense, and not from France alone, a partial and obscure reaction on the continent and even throughout the world against the economic values of the Anglo-Saxon winners from the industrial revolution and the world wars which it nourished.

14. If Napoleon I tried to unite the continent against England, so did Hitler. Had it not been for his crass cruelty and oppression, the Nazi New Order with its technological and emotive drive might well have evoked some real response on the continent to the lasting discomfiture of the British offshore island whose livelihood especially hangs on trade. In the long run the attitude of General de Gaulle towards Britain might come to matter less for us than the extent to which leading Germans in the changed circumstances of today incline towards some civilized adaptation either of the continental New Order or of Hitler's earlier dream of an Anglo-German partnership to lead the world. Franco-German reconciliation is indeed to be welcomed as a long-sought key to a hopeful future for Europe. At the same time Germany with her indefatigable thrust looks like acquiring a strongly balancing position, if not as traditionally between east and west, or even now in regard to the United States, then perhaps between France and England. That may be the price of a rift in the Entente Cordiale.

15. Since the Second World War, British underestimation of the continental impulse towards something more than economic integration, our special relation with the United States and our justly hard bargaining regarding entry into the Common Market have perhaps combined to associate us in some continental eyes with an overweening materialism which is to them often scarcely more attractive in

its American than in its Russian guise. Nor is the American variety always so popular as gratitude would dictate to the former beneficiaries of its enlightened generosity, as when the Marshall Plan so largely rebuilt the shattered economy of Western Europe as a potential competitor to America herself. One challenging task for British foreign policy might prove to be to try to reconcile the retention of our most necessary friendship with America with some intimation to our friends on the continent and indeed elsewhere (cf. observations from Mexico by Sir Peter Garran) that, while economics must clearly remain the bedrock of association, we are truly of them as Europeans in something more besides, with a more than material contribution to make from our admired heritage and aspirations.

16. On the French side, however, one must for the present doubtless reckon with General de Gaulle as still interposing a rigid block, if a fragile one since it depends so heavily upon a single life. Meanwhile a high proportion of HM Representatives abroad are at one in nursing consoling doubts as to whether the general's selfish and overbearing diplomacy will pay off in the long run. There is certainly much to sustain such doubts. For all their great qualities the French, as Sir Paul Grey says, 'have a mean streak'; their diplomacy is apt to be somewhat flimsy (compare Napoleon III again) and to overreach itself in cleverness, not least perhaps in its insufficient attention to the fact that it is, after all, rather undiplomatic to be too conspicuously and too selfishly successful. All this and much more besides may quite likely, though by no means necessarily in the circumstances, add up to ultimate failure for French policy.

17. Meanwhile French policy is more or less successfully maintained against us in the great European community of the Common Market. More than that, there are at any rate grounds for arguing, as Sir Harold Beeley (Cairo) suggests, that latterly the French have been more successful than we have both in their economic planning and, at high cost, in much of their decolonization (compare also Sir John Ward and Sir John Coulson from Stockholm). More than that again, it would appear that, temporarily at least, sizeable sections of the French nation have been impelled by the government of General de Gaulle into fresh activity and resolution. While it is fair enough to stress the precarious foundation and unamiable shortcomings of his diplomacy, it is surely only accurate to recognize that, however one may judge his rather precious and unaccommodating aims, he is pursuing them with impressive clarity of purpose and strength of will. In these respects at least the present French example may not be wholly without meaning for British diplomacy.

III *Obstacles to a strong British foreign policy*

18. Last autumn the Secretary of State said: 'I believe that we hide our head in the sand if we do not recognize that when we deliberately shed an Empire we shed with it a lot of wealth, influence and power. I believe that the knowledge of this, which has been felt throughout the nation, has accounted very largely for the unsureness of the nation and the discontent which I have observed in recent years, because although people recognized the facts they did not see how to redress the balance.' Perhaps, too, this recognition, like many popular reactions, has rather operated by delayed action so that it is only comparatively recently that the discontenting truth has begun to sink in and correct the previous prevalence of the vaguely wishful notion that by becoming weaker Great Britain would somehow almost grow stronger: the happy belief, as Mr Peck (Dakar) tellingly puts it, 'that

moral influence and good example are somehow an alternative to building up positions of strength'.

19. Britain yet remains, if not a world power, then 'a world-wide power' (Sir Patrick Dean) with corresponding obligations towards others. Yet her loss of empire may at times constrain her, however reluctantly, to look more keenly to her own interests even within the Commonwealth, as the recent negotiations regarding the Common Market have demonstrated. It is noticeable that our Ambassador in Cape Town and High Commissioner in Salisbury, though generally writing in different veins, both suggest that we have tended to be over-considerate in past dealings with the Old Commonwealth. Lord Alport comments: 'This attitude is partly a hangover from the days when Great Britain was the "top nation" and felt a moral obligation to avoid riding rough-shod over the susceptibilities of smaller countries, and partly to our sensitiveness as a "colonialist power".' If *noblesse oblige* then a reduction in status may, however regrettably, diminish altruistic obligations upon a nation which, like ours, increasingly has to live on its wits and look sharp for tangible returns on benefits bestowed.

20. Nearly all HM Representatives are strikingly forward-looking in their substantial agreement with Sir Roderick Parkes (Amman) that there should be 'no harking back to the old spacious days'. This does not entirely prevent a good deal of 'wistful thinking' (Mr Aldington, Luxembourg) of a slightly different order. From their vantage-points abroad our ambassadors are only too conscious of the practical difficulties of our redressing the balance of national advantage indicated by Lord Home. In the main, though not invariably, they fully appreciate the attractions of a stronger British foreign policy, but—there is nearly always a but, or several. Three of the main ones recur with impressive regularity through many letters:

(i) *The British character*. 'On the whole', writes Sir Con O'Neill, 'my conclusion is that the principal limitation on the power of any British Government to pursue strong and openly selfish national policies lies in the kind of people we are and the kind of relationship we are prepared to tolerate between ourselves and our government.' Other correspondents steadily emphasize the diplomatic value of British steadiness, decency, compromise, fair play. In fully agreeing with this fundamental point, which can clearly be neglected only at our peril, it may yet be fair to recall that it was a great French diplomatist, M. Jules Cambon, who observed that 'moral influence is the most essential qualification of a diplomatist'.

Moral influence, however, does not necessarily, or perhaps even often, lie in mere niceness of passivity. If, as one writer suggests, 'both by temperament and institutionally we are . . . better adapted to reacting to situations than to creating them', that is far from fully true historically, for instance of Britain in the eighteenth century. Though in much of that century too prudent Englishmen might, and sometimes, did, think like another of the present writers that 'our ultimate objective cannot be to make Britain an important power because we have not got the physical resources, and history is not running that way'. It is only too natural that long years of diplomatic practice should occasionally, perhaps, blur the distinction between the maintenance of good relations with foreigners as a means to an end or as an end in itself. Though Mr Peck from Dakar, for instance, demonstrates how far from inevitable this is when he suggests that the long-term objectives of British foreign policy are really 'means of achieving an end which it is unfashionable to discuss or redefine, namely the greater material strength, intellectual and cultural development and general prestige and standing in the world of the United Kingdom'.

Sir Patrick Dean sums up: 'Some of us tend to forget that what we are paid to do and what must be our proper objective is to get the best we can for our government and country, and not merely to take the next step in a diplomatic or bureaucratic process. Having spent quite a part of my life outside the Foreign Service, I have noticed at times that some of us tend, however innocently and sub-consciously, to think and act as though the *raison d'être* of a Foreign Service is to avoid trouble and to remain popular with one's colleagues. Goodwill is worth a lot, specially, I may say, at the United Nations, but it is not everything.' Sir Patrick Dean goes on, in effect, to suggest some implementation of the Foreign Secretary's injunction that 'the British people must recognise who are their friends and who are not'—and who is favouring whom: Sir Patrick here instances Ghana, as also does Mr Parrott (Prague). If ruthlessness in action is most often both dangerous and happily alien from British traditions, yet the cultivation of ruthless clarity in thought (cf. paragraph 8) may be the necessary condition for pursuing a coherent and successful foreign policy.

'Anything for a quiet life' may be hardly the best maxim in international affairs at a time when life is anything but quiet. Meek and mild policies for Britain abroad might indeed match a considerable section of public opinion at home. Though here Sir Harold Caccia's circular letter of March 1, 1963, sounded a warning note, and it seems far from certain that the current keenness for growth and radical efficiency (e.g. the Beeching Plan) at home may not extend abroad. Even if that is at present not so, that in itself should not necessarily be decisive for the conduct of foreign policy, as a prewar precedent suggests. In regard to British policy towards Nazi Germany in the nineteen-thirties history is rather unlikely just to absolve the British government of weakness because contemporary British opinion was largely weak. As Sir Douglas Busk (Caracas) urges: 'Let leaders lead.' Only if one is going to lead it is of course helpful to get the direction right (cf. iii below).

(ii) *British economic weakness.* 'Diplomacy by itself . . . cannot make a great power out of an economic question mark' (Sir Geoffrey Wallinger, Rio de Janeiro). This, more or less, is a favourite theme in over two-thirds of the communications received. In Sir Roger Stevens' professionally reassuring version: 'Our urgent needs are not so much, I suggest, a new look to our diplomacy as a new look at ourselves: more hard work, better educational opportunities, compulsory military service, more imagination in business, a more constructive attitude on the part of the trade unions, a better equipped industry, more forward planning, a greater belief in our civic and civilised virtues and in the immense asset represented by our language.'

Lord Hankey notes the end of 150 years of British predominance primarily based upon the industrial revolution, while indicating his awareness that England was yet a robustly expansionist and imperial power long before that. In conclusion Lord Hankey writes of our present economic pass: 'Already the Germans have a larger international trade than we have; the French have more motor-cars per head of the population; our reserves of foreign exchange are even now at a remarkably low level, considering our wide responsibilities, compared with those of France, Germany and even Italy; our exports and current trade balance are almost incontestably running at the lowest possible rate at which it is possible to maintain real economic stability even in years when the terms of trade are very favourable, and even at our present soggy growth rate. It is partly the tremendous French economic expansion based on an effective series of National Plans which has made it possible for General de Gaulle to indulge in his present degree of hubris. I earnestly hope that NEDC and the government will be able to make our economy more buoyant and more expansionary even though we cannot now join the Common Market.'

General de Gaulle's exclusion of Great Britain from the Common Market may be one example of the way in which strictly economic considerations may often steer, but in the last resort more rarely control, a resolute foreign policy. Few, however, would minimize the economic drags on British foreign policy; but it might be at least equally wrong to minimize the commercial power, and the influence of London as an international centre of finance and insurance, which Great Britain still does retain in the world arena. Here, though, Sir Con O'Neill adduces one consideration which cuts deep: 'By far the greatest economic advantage we can in theory grant to or withhold from other countries is access to our market. But given the present system of multilateral trade, which we have done so much ourselves to create, this is an advantage which, with a few exceptions, we have deprived ourselves of the power to exploit. Bilateral trading can confer political power, as we can see from the efforts the Russians make to sell us oil . . . This . . . is not a plea that we should revert to bilateral trading; I am sure we should not. I want only to illustrate that we do, by our multilateral trading system, deprive ourselves of an opportunity to influence other countries.'

Another economic handicap is suggested by Sir Geoffrey Wallinger in relation to Latin America, an area which might perhaps be regarded as one of crucial opportunity for Britain today. Sir Geoffrey notes: 'This continent is looking for an alternative to the United States: had we the surplus investment capital that Germany and France are now adjudged to have, our diplomacy could have been much more aggressive.' Mr Vaughan from Panama questions the wisdom of our having held off from any campaign against France in Latin America after 'the Common Market debacle'. As things are, Sir Peter Garran writes: 'All in all, France is seen, from Mexico, as a more powerful force and therefore one that requires to be humoured and placated. There is plenty of goodwill towards us, but we tend to be discounted for our apparent weakness.'

References to the commercial promotion of our export-drive in South America are apt to strike a depressing, not to say disturbing, note. Mr Vaughan remarks that 'the indifference of the exporter is so discouraging', and Sir Peter Garran provides a glum reminder that the British trade exhibition, projected for 1962 in Mexico City, 'was cancelled for lack of interest at home'. From Caracas Sir Douglas Busk writes: 'In the last three posts, in three continents, that I have served in as Ambassador, any British [export] drive was conspicuous for its absence. Any successes we had were due to hard work by the Embassy using the 'old boy net' to persuade British firms to come out . . . and get down to the job.' (Sir Douglas Busk served previously at Addis Ababa and at Helsinki.)

The Foreign Secretary told the Institute of Directors last October: 'Britain's future really depends upon our interpretation of three words, "Britain must sell" if Britain is to live. A lot of us have been very slow, I think, to recognize what these three simple words imply in the modern market-place . . . I feel that there is a new atmosphere . . . which brings a will for efficiency as a means to expansion and as a means to enable Britain to play her full part in a developing world. I want to catch that mood on the tide.' Lord Home went on to suggest that 'we are finding a theme, the theme of national efficiency' wherewith to try to redress the balance from the loss of empire (cf. paragraph 18). Any possible improvement in diplomatic and consular support and stimulation of Britain's economic expansion overseas should surely receive high priority: cf. sections IV and V below. And, while one must clearly take full account of those weaknesses of Britain which many correspondents are careful to underline, perhaps one should be not less careful to weigh up also our undoubted advantages (cf. section IV below) in a resolute effort to wring success out of Britain's jumble of perplexities and opportunities. For if bluff can certainly be called yet confidence breeds confidence. 'I have myself noticed', writes Sir Roderick Parkes, 'ever since I entered the Foreign Service in 1948, a tendency to underestimate our own cards and concentrate excessively on the strength of our opponents' hands.' A more positive approach might to some extent help towards resolving the difficulty experienced by Lord Alport in judging 'how far results can be achieved by a new approach to diplomatic methods and how far it depends upon a revival of national self-confidence.'

(iii) *Failure at Suez.* Sir John Maud justly brackets our experience at Suez in 1956 with our earlier omission to give strong backing to European integration as the two main failures of British foreign policy since the Second World War. One suspects that for large sections of the British public Suez in 1956 was a traumatic humiliation comparable only perhaps to that other one, whose spirit it had been meant to contradict, at Munich in 1938. Only, within a year we began to wipe out Munich by war. Whereas the letters from HM Representatives abroad often underline the extent to which the long shadow from Suez, and from the loss of empire which it betokens, still lies heavy across our thinking. It is rather striking that whereas ten or more correspondents refer to the inhibiting lessons of Suez in one way or another, only one, Mr Vaughan from Panama, mentions our subsequent and notably successful armed intervention at Kuwait. In his speech to the Conservative Party Conference last autumn the Secretary of State associated this success with the fact that our having troops in the SEATO alliance and the Commonwealth Brigade in Malaya had in 1962 enabled our diplomacy 'to avert a war in Laos which could have turned into a world war'. Now Borneo would appear to be added to this rather impressive list, also including Jordan in 1958, of successful military reinforcement of our diplomacy.

A detailed examination of British policy and action over Suez in 1956 might possibly reveal that their failure was largely due to personal factors plus more or less technical military or diplomatic shortcomings. If so, and in the light of countervailing and subsequent examples of military validation of our diplomacy, though in admittedly different circumstances, it might be especially unfortunate if the error of Suez should become a defeatist bogey to be regularly trundled out, without fresh and keen appraisal, against proposed courses of vigour and resource in the conduct of British foreign policy. At the same time it may be comprehensible enough that recent small-scale successes with military backing should not have effaced the much larger failure at Suez with its large and lasting lessons. Two of these are that:

(*a*) The decline of Britain's strength in the world is not only imperial and economic but also directly military, as is underlined by Mr Parrott (Prague). Also from behind the Iron Curtain, in Moscow, comes Sir Humphrey Trevelyan's reminder of relative British weakness in nuclear weapons. Their abandonment, though, would spell little short of impotence in the main issues of the Cold War, would gravely prejudice the British aim of strengthening the Western Alliance, and would sharply emphasise:

(*b*) The decline of Britain, perhaps especially resented (and cf. section II above), into a large measure of dependence upon the United States in foreign affairs. This has been a long, slow process, only accelerated of late. The pregnant observations in Sir Patrick Dean's letter (paragraphs 4-6) regarding the conduct of our relations with the United States rather put one in mind of what one of our greatest ambassadors (with two American wives) wrote a generation ago. Sir Ronald Lindsay was writing from Washington in 1932: 'I know that the Americans are dreadful people to deal with—they cannot make firm promises, but they jolly you along with fair prospects and when you are committed they let you down. Taking the short view it is hard to remember a bargain with them that has been really satisfactory to us in itself; but on the long view there has never been a case when we were not right to have made the bargain.' Sir Patrick Dean's contention that we tend, however, 'to underrate the extent to which we already oblige the Americans to "appease" us' is reinforced by Sir John Coulson, who adds that for Britain, in this Anglo-American interdependence, 'the disadvantages take the form of having to toe on occasion the American line and are immediately apparent in public, while the advantages are of a much more subtle kind of which the public is ignorant.'

21. This suggestion of a rather feminine role for Great Britain in relation to the United States illustrates the fact that while diplomacy is necessarily based upon power, power can, so to speak, be exploited diplomatically upon three main levels: first upon the surface openly, as naked force, as in the policy of Hitler, the Russian try-on and American reaction over Cuba last year or General de Gaulle's prohibition of British entry into the Common Market. Secondly, power, if genuine, can be kept discreetly latent, breeding power merely by its own existence rather as capital accrues interest. Indeed, expenditure of power necessarily represents a diminution of its potential. Thus, as the Secretary of State recently pointed out, 'nuclear power can only be used to deter; and even by saying that I am making a misstatement because if nuclear power has to be used it will not have deterred'. It is latent power which can impart an underlying drive to diplomacy of a rather traditionally British kind, *suaviter in modo, fortiter in re*. Latent power can, however, be allowed to slip down to the third, bottom, level where it becomes so submerged as to suggest weakness. Sir Harold Caccia remarked in his circular letter of March 1 that in the United Nations 'there have been occasions when we have gone along with measures which we believed to be unwise or damaging to ourselves. This may sometimes be justified in the interests of our position in New York and with the uncommitted world. The question is whether in this and other such cases we should not in the sharper climate of today watch our instinct for the general good to see that it does not lead too readily to the weakening of other important and more strictly national interests.'

22. British diplomacy today surely needs to persevere in its traditional, almost instinctive, attempt to avoid both the bottom level of weakness and the superficial one of crude power, as lately illustrated by General de Gaulle, in favour of the middle, second level of latent power. Only for this a sufficient degree of power must indeed be potentially present, ready to surface occasionally as at Kuwait. In terms of power-politics this diplomatic doctrine of the second level should perhaps be

particularly suited both to the British temperament and to Britain's present standing, not indeed as a second-class power but perhaps as one of 'one-and-a-half rate importance' (Sir Paul Gore-Booth).

23. Diplomatic exploitation of latent power at the second level may suggest the important part played in diplomacy, as in life itself, by indirection: the achievement of aims, which may and often should be clear enough, by indirect means not always fully calculable in advance because of the free play of chance, contingency and human nature, still imperfectly predictable; but if one gets the broad lay of affairs roughly right then even an apparently tiresome detour may somehow approximate to a short cut so that sometimes, almost without realizing, one finds oneself nearly home by an unexpected path. Which is perhaps only another way of saying that successful diplomacy calls not only for cleverness but for wisdom.

24. Indirection can indeed degenerate into clever deviousness, recognised by nearly all authorities since Callières as a bad and self-defeating quality in diplomacy. Such deviousness, though, is scarcely the British way. Our indirection has traditionally approximated, rather, to muddling through. Britain can be credited with whatever exaggeration, with having acquired, if scarcely also lost, an empire in a fit of absence of mind. And 'we have a way—as foreigners have noticed—of sometimes being right for the wrong reasons' (Sir Paul Grey).

25. Sir William Hayter in *The Diplomacy of the Great Powers* has, while recently stressing the importance of planning for foreign policy, also emphasised its difficulty owing, in effect, to the incidence of indirection. In trying to beam a searchlight into the future one nearly always has to calculate angles of refraction as the light-ray of policy is bent in traversing the prism of affairs. In such calculations, though, perhaps it might be possible to try increasingly to exploit this refraction and give it deliberate twists to our advantage. Thus Sir Patrick Dean suggests that we should 'do better if we were sometimes a little less honest in our discussions and negotiations and were more willing to adopt positions which we do not intend to hold until the bitter end, but which can be given away in return for concessions by the other side. That tactic is employed against us by the majority of foreign governments, and I am rarely impressed by the arguments [against employing it] on our side . . . All my experience at the United Nations goes to confirm this.'

26. It is possible, too, that the mere collection of bargaining cards might sometimes stimulate perception of fresh possibilities and combinations. If I may instance one suggestion which I ventured to make some time ago, it might be just possible, in a negotiation with the Russians on the forbidding problem of Berlin, to loosen it forward a little at some future stage by introducing, in whatever form, the geographical coincidence that a line drawn parallel to the Iron Curtain one hundred miles east of it would, subject to checking on large-scale maps, run through the western sectors of Greater Berlin but would not, I rather think, include the eastern sector or, perhaps, the city-centre. The potential utility of this rather interesting coincidence is doubtless limited. Yet if one were reduced to extremities or if there were ever any signs of some variant revival of the Eden Plan of 1955 for military inspection in a control-zone of fixed depth on either side of the Iron Curtain, or of the Rapacki Plan, it might conceivably be possible to relate the problem of Berlin to this wider and perhaps more hopeful context, while giving the eastern boundaries of the western sectors a functionally fresh and positive significance as part of the eastern limit of a Safety Belt across Germany, possibly with some assimilation of

western garrisons to inspection-teams. This is only one example of a possible gambit for surprise-play and for rendering our diplomacy more efficiently flexible by increasing the number of its choices in negotiation. Other and better examples can doubtless be suggested.

27. In waging the Cold War British diplomacy, indicated by Sir Harold Nicolson as being of the mercantile variety, should doubtless remain true to itself in essentials while perhaps sharpening its technique, if only to take account of the fact that the Russians, in their creed of militant communism, approximate rather towards the 'warrior diplomacy' of the Germans with its incessant *Kraftprobe*. In planning negotiations special attention should perhaps be given to such factors as contingent options, bargaining and fall-back positions, breaking-points, maxima and minima. And, as Mr Vaughan says from the receiving end, 'all instructions should be scrutinised in the light of the best and the worst that can happen'.

28. Such, perhaps, is one way in which British diplomacy, in the context of the Cold War, can equip itself to play to win what Lord Strang calls 'the active game of diplomacy'. And the Secretary of State recently reminded us that the Russian national game is chess.

IV *Opportunities for a strong British foreign policy*

29. Passing from diplomatic technique to foreign policy, Sir Ian Scott (Khartoum) urges convincingly: 'Always we must keep outward-looking. That is our strength.' But such strength, if it is to be securely grounded upon the inward truth, must first rest upon a dispassionate appraisal of the blots on the horizon which today tend to depress many Englishmen when they do look outwards. They see America and Russia, but much less Britain, reaching towards the stars in space—a contrast of more lowering effect, perhaps, than is immediately apparent. On earth the red is fast fading from the map, colonies ending, bases packing up in an imperial aftermath not yet, at all events, fully redeemed by the imaginative venture of the new, multiracial Commonwealth. Britain in her reduced condition confronts a world of harsher economic competition amid the grinding tensions and dangers of the Cold War in the atomic age, an age morally darkened also by its inheritance, mainly from Nazi Germany, of the revival of torture, concentration-camps and the odious apparatus of a secret police.

30. In the long shadows of Hiroshima and of Auschwitz perhaps it is not wholly surprising, nor even wholly reprehensible, that a good many youthful and impressionable inheritors of the Welfare State tend today to echo the ancient lament: 'O Thou Adam, what has thou done? . . . For what profit is it unto us, if there be promised us an immortal time, whereas we have done the works that bring death? . . . And that there should be shewed a paradise, whose fruit endureth for ever, wherein is security and medicine, since we shall not enter into it? (For we have walked in unpleasant places.)'

31. Such is the sombre backcloth to the practical obstacles to a strong British foreign policy cogently represented by many of our ambassadors (cf. section III above). Their advice, however, is far from matching those prudently negative arguments from Whitehall which once caused Lord Morrison when Foreign Secretary to minute sardonically: 'What's the good of anythink? Why nothink!' In the circumstances it is natural that such suggestions as are made towards stronger policy tend to be practically circumscribed, if sometimes possessing extensive

implications.

32. The possibility of stronger action is envisaged for countering foreign discrimination against British shipping (Sir Malcolm Henderson, Vienna) and with regard to overflying (Sir Roger Stevens). From Africa both Mr Peck and Mr King urge steps to spread the English language in former French possessions, which for this would certainly seem to be lands of opportunity, liable to repay special attention. Sir Ian Scott proposes that a larger proportion of British aid to under-developed countries should be channelled bilaterally rather than through the United Nations, and comments: 'We should be tougher and more realistic about the spending of our money abroad.' Sir Con O'Neill substantially agrees, while noticing that 'our public opinion seems to have come to accept the nonsensical proposition that every people has the natural right to be equally rich.' Perhaps especially noteworthy, despite obvious difficulties from the American quarter, are suggestions towards a British expansion of east-west trade. Here Mr King tellingly recalls advice from Sir Frank Roberts when in Moscow in favour of such expansion 'in the long run for political even more than for economic reasons'. It is a suggestive line of thought even if there is no practical relevance in the fact that the Anglo-Soviet treaty of alliance was only terminated in 1955. If ever, for instance, it were to prove practicable for some or all of the EFTA powers to operate some joint machinery, even if only consultative, for trading behind the Iron Curtain, it might help to bring EFTA out in front of the Common Market in that important direction.

33. All these suggestions from HM Representatives seem worthy of purposeful consideration, perhaps as part of a concerted programme by a special committee at high level if a fully appropriate one does not already exist. Such a Positive Planning Committee might begin to approximate, at all events, towards the formation, advocated by Mr Peck, of 'a small militant planning group devoted exclusively to the direct furthering of immediate British interests'. The committee would probably need to plan in relation to the whole potential of the British economy, and this itself might fruitfully stimulate a two-way exchange of thought upon the problems of our domestic economy and of foreign affairs, while maintaining, as is essential, the political direction of the Foreign Office.

34. A Positive Planning Committee or its equivalent, while taking full account of the heavy drawbacks and drags on British foreign policy, would yet, one might hope, resolutely try to approach problems constructively even when it would be easy to be negative. For instance, reading a number of the letters from our ambassadors, it is sometimes difficult to resist the glum inference that somehow the size and weight of Britain in the modern world is just wrong for a vigorous foreign policy. For much more is obviously open to the greatest powers, America and Russia; while rather the same seems to apply at the other end to small, relatively irresponsible countries, whom it is almost bad form, and often indeed bad policy, to oppose—emergent, uncommitted nations cashing in on the Cold War, sometimes blackmailing the two power-blocs into economic aid which even liberal benevolence might otherwise scarcely grant. 'It is,' writes Sir Savile Garner, 'the weaker countries, with everything to gain and little to lose, who have the bargaining power.' All this might seem to leave Great Britain as a somewhat impotent middleweight and has-been in international affairs. As Sir Geoffrey Wallinger puts it: 'Our difficulties seem to have turned us into the rather muscle-bound policeman of the Western world, reliable and comforting to have around, but a little unenterprising and primarily engaged in the

somewhat negative task of trying to stop the fast-moving traffic all about us from getting out of hand.'

35. Perhaps the chief lesson for us from General de Gaulle's policy lies not in its precise methods or objectives, but in its challenging reassertion of efficient vigour by an old power of the middle rank by modern standards. Doubtless there is much here that we in our different circumstances could not and should not copy (cf. section II above). Though one might instance the Secretary of State's observation last year: 'If, and I believe it is true, the greatest powers are unable to use the nuclear weapon for national purposes, this is going to redress to a great extent—a marked extent— the discrepancy in the political influence between the biggest powers and the medium and the small. Therefore, alongside our resolution that we will keep the balance of strength I want to make it our purpose to turn the nuclear stalemate politically to good account . . . We must exploit to the full the stalemate of power.'

36. For diplomatic exploitation of the stalemate of power Great Britain still possesses splendid opportunities unmatched by any other country in the world. Though it is doubtless rather natural that the arguments of HM Representatives abroad should often stress Britain's weakness in strict terms of power rather than her strength in diplomatic potential. For Britain this unique strength in potential forms a diplomatic card-table standing upon four legs:

(i) Our great inheritance of the multiracial Commonwealth, the outstanding product of British liberal idealism, proved by over 500 million people in former British dependencies who have become completely self-governing since the Second World War. If this Commonwealth is inevitably rich in difficulties of adjustment, it is no less so in existing opportunities and still affords Britain intimate access to nearly every quarter of the world.

(ii) Great Britain enjoys a special, productive and unmatched relationship with the United States; our common language is on the way to becoming the *lingua franca* of the world.

(iii) Great Britain is a full participant, as the United States and the Soviet Union can never be, in the old European community which cradled western civilisation. British membership not only of NATO but also of the Western European Union, with its heavy military commitment in Germany, and our persisting aim to participate in a liberal Common Market are evidence enough of our real involvement in the continent of Europe.

(iv) Even within the context of the Cold War it is possible that Britain, as compared with America, France or West Germany, may at times, as in trade, be able to utilize her relative flexibility of approach towards Russia and her satellites. Any Sino-Soviet rift might evidently increase such opportunities. Last autumn the Secretary of State, in basing 'a modern edition of British foreign policy' upon the modern theme of interdependence, notably declared: 'I do not limit it to interdependence between the nations of the free world; I include cooperation with the Communists although that may be a long-term goal . . . We should oppose the Communist encroachment on the preserves of free men patiently and without illusion. We should try to accelerate the thaw in the cold war, because that thaw must come.'

37. No other power in the world possesses such a diplomatic potential as this. Doubtless the rich diversity of its opportunities presents special complications. The challenge to British diplomacy is to sort out such complications with positive intent,

as it notably did in applying to join the Common Market by surmounting the arguments, largely drawn from an insular and imperial past, which had long precluded such a bold and modern initiative (compare Sir John Maud's criticism of earlier planning in Whitehall). Though General de Gaulle has blocked British policy for a time, yet its new and vigorous direction shows how the complexities of the possible combinations open to British diplomacy can stimulate keen thinking from fresh angles, with the ingenuity and purpose necessary to push through difficult reconciliations of different interests, instead of allowing their tangled skeins to tie our hands. If Great Britain with her international assets of language, of sterling, of liberal traditions gets weaving on her modern theme of interdependence she might yet render herself almost as indispensable to the world as France, in her more restricted sphere and outlook, is to Western Europe. And we should thus be true to our traditions. The Secretary of State said last year: 'Some people are afraid that we cannot lead the Commonwealth and, at the same time, play a leading part in Europe. I must say, I think they are faint hearts. What have we been doing for the last 500 years if we have not been equipping ourselves for world leadership? . . . Leadership in a world of interdependence is right up our street.'

38. The most successful leadership may be by guidance and example. Even so it is rarely achieved without some will to lead or higher purpose to lead towards. To consider moral possibilities of rediscovering for Britain a sense of higher purpose, partly lost in the modern world, would exceed the competence of a paper on diplomacy. Except to stress their relevance nonetheless and, perhaps, to suggest that, behind temporary appearances, many English men and women retain their traditional aspiration to do excellent things in the world—the urge which has regularly given British foreign policy, and in wartime war-aims, an idealistic bent: and that some of the less attractive aspects of British society today may be part of a groping transition from old rigidities towards more complex but, one hopes, fuller ways of life, rather as in the international field the British Empire has been loosening and evolving, sometimes painfully and apparently unattractively, towards the greater equality and interdependence through independence that lies at the heart of our multiracial Commonwealth of Nations.

39. If moral issues cannot profitably be discussed here, nor can the particular policies which will need to be weighed and pursued in given areas and situation in order to exploit the opportunities afforded by our diplomatic potential. That can only be done by persons and organisms, possibly including a Positive Planning Committee among others, that, unlike the present writer, possess close experience and special information for the conduct of British foreign policy. But perhaps, despite the risk of overlapping with findings of the Plowden Committee, this study may suggest, more modestly and more functionally, one or two tentative ideas for a rather fresh approach on the organizational side towards asserting for Britain an outward-looking leadership in a world of interdependence.

V *The possible institution of British High Delegations*

40. 'The Foreign Service is confronted by a frustrating paradox. British self-sufficiency decreases annually. Our existence as an individual entity depends more and more upon our international relations; but the relative importance of the Department and Service responsible for our international relations diminishes, and that of other departments of state, notably the Board of Trade and the Treasury, increases' (Mr Peck, Dakar; cf. also Sir Peter Garran, Mexico City). Nor, perhaps,

is that the only frustrating paradox confronting the Foreign Service.

41. Trying to view the execution of British foreign policy as a whole, one is struck by a rather depressing contrast: at the centre Whitehall and the Foreign Office in particular tend to become more choked year by year by the ever-growing complexity and concentration of affairs in a divided yet interdependent world; ministers and officials are in constant danger of being swamped by remorselessly multiplying papers and committees, not least of an interdepartmental kind; whereas at the other end the execution of foreign policy in the aftermath of imperialism appears to be ravelling out in a patchwork of small diplomatic missions unmatched since the German and Italian principalities of the eighteenth century—some sixty new independent countries created since the inception of the United Nations, each with its own interests needing to be taken into fresh account. Small wonder if British foreign policy occasionally looks a trifle frayed around the edges. Small wonder too if, as letters from ambassadors rather suggest, those in more distant posts sometimes feel a little frustrated.

42. The sobering testimony of Sir Douglas Busk and of Mr Vaughan on trying to speed the export-drive abroad has already been cited. Sir Geoffrey Wallinger and Mr Parrott are critical in different ways of arrangements regarding service attachés. 'On a shoestring' is the impression of the financing of various aspects of our representation abroad which seems to emerge from a number of letters, notably that of Sir Peter Garran, who sees French culture lapping ahead in Mexico while Mr King deplores the stinted British effort in Guinea. Mr Peck lists ten government departments in Whitehall upon which British interests in tropical Africa depend and comments: 'An Ambassador on the spot with a constructive suggestion to make for furthering British interests . . . has to be prepared for weeks and months of . . . interdepartmental discussion, probably ending with a judicious compromise . . . liable to deposit us neatly between two stools.' Sir Ian Scott has questioned a seemingly striking disproportion in the allocation of British military assistance to the Sudan and to Ghana, with the comment: 'It would be good to feel sure that this kind of overall critical assessment [of British interests] is continuously being made.'

43. To contrast the ninety British ambassadors and ambassadorial delegates in the world today with the nine ambassadors of fifty years ago is a familiar exercise. Rather less remarked, perhaps, is that on the other hand the number of embassies of the very highest rank, where world-issues might centre for negotiation, has if anything been reduced from eight or nine in 1914 to something more like three or four today—after them, one begins to hesitate as to which others are quite on a par. This is partly a hangover from the historic concentration of diplomacy in Europe in the age of imperialism when, with such notable exceptions as the United States and Japan, territories overseas could for practical purposes mainly be dealt with in tidy terms of colonies and dominions. Whereas today they present a somewhat illogical jumble of new nations, often small and inexperienced, residual colonies sometimes left rather stranded, and somewhat precarious regional groupings, all subject to communist infiltration (Soviet Union) on the one hand and to well-intentioned if sometimes inept initiatives by the United Nations (United States) on the other. For the former imperial powers of Western Europe this spells greatly diminished influence with rather little diplomatic co-ordination on the spot on any broad basis to comprehend the newer continents in their critical emergence into world affairs. Even in North America and in Europe the traditional pattern of embassies is being

complicated and to some extent fragmented by functional delegations on a permanent basis, to the United Nations in New York and Geneva, to the North Atlantic Treaty Organization and to OECD at Paris, to the European Communities at Brussels, to the Council of Europe at Strasbourg, to the European Free Trade Area at Geneva.

44. The end of the western empires in the aftermath of the Second World War was due not only to the weakening of Western Europe but to the added circumstance that both the new super-powers of the Soviet Union and the United States were, for different reasons, hostile to such empires. If the Russo-American rapprochement at Tehran and Yalta proved ephemeral, yet the United States has in the past been a little slow to appreciate how considerably her natural anti-imperialism weakened her own side in the Cold War. That is mainly done now. But though Great Britain has surrendered her imperial heritage, she should perhaps yet remain true to her traditions by conducting her relations overseas in novel forms indeed but also within the spacious context befitting those who look outward. (On the other side, one suspects, the very scale of Russia may incline her towards the not negligible Nazi habit of thinking in terms of great areas, *Grossraüme*. Upon the one hand, it is a little ironic that some of the most imaginative British official thinking about economic enterprise overseas was in 1938-39, in fear of Germany; on the other, those who still denounce British colonialism in Africa might with advantage be reminded of what we saved her from, as illustrated by a Nazi blueprint of 1940 for that continent, printed in *Documents on German Foreign Policy 1918-1945*, Series D, vol. xi, pp 483-91.)

45. It might be worth considering whether Her Majesty's Government today might not partially emulate Canning, when confronted by the reactionary Europe of Metternich, and call in the new continents to redress the balance of the old, partly perhaps by thinking of them as continents or sub-continents and organizing accordingly. One possible form of such organization might be the institution overseas of central missions, diplomatic and administrative, at high level. These might be British High Delegations to, for example, Africa, Latin America, South-East Asia, perhaps also, eventually, to the Middle East once more and to the Pacific; even in Europe, which would of course remain a linchpin for British policy, some co-ordination of existing functional missions might prove possible, and our embassy to the European Communities seems suggestive. Overseas, partial, though only partial, models, apart from our largest embassies, might be the Middle East Development Division under the Department of Technical Cooperation at Beirut and, in a rather different way, the organization of the British Commissioner-General in South-East Asia. It might be preferable not to designate such co-ordinating missions for our diplomacy as embassies since that might both provoke invidious comparisons and complications with territorial embassies and also involve technical difficulties insofar as the new missions might or might not be accredited to particular governments or organizations. It would, however, be important that the title of such new missions should avoid both imperial or commonwealth overtones (e.g. High Commissioner or Commissioner-General) and also the more uninspiring forms of bureaucratic nomenclature. With this in mind, suggestions for such a title are General Delegation, or, perhaps preferably, High Delegation.

46. British High Delegations of continental scope would be directly subordinate to the Foreign Office and the Foreign Secretary. The political role of the High

Delegations might prove very considerable in certain circumstances—for instance in Africa if the African movement towards unity made headway—and one would hope that the High Delegate would usually be drawn from the Foreign Service. Though, initially at any rate, his political functions might be chiefly on the side of planning and coordination since it would, of course, be essential that the existing British embassies to all governments should be retained with full right of direct access to the Foreign Office, in the interests both of the proper functioning of our embassies and of the susceptibilities of foreign governments. In such increasingly important fields, however, as trade, aid, welfare, information and culture—the essential context of an efficient diplomacy in the modern world—a High Delegation might function with special effect, through a sizeable secretariat drawn from the Foreign Service and other interested services and ministries in Whitehall, and perhaps not only from them. Temporary secondments from business or industry to the Foreign Service might prove especially fruitful at the level of High Delegations, with important experts for a given continent directing technical cooperation or radiating our export-drive as really big business. While unobtrusive methods might well prove best in a number of instances, yet in others British High Delegations might visibly become our modern trading-posts, supermarkets and shop-windows upon the further continents. And each one would ideally have associated with it an English language-institute and other cultural amenities to reassert the British presence in a world, no longer of discarded imperialism, but of growing interdependence. The British Empire largely originated from trading-posts. Perhaps its termination through transformation could spell a fruitful return to trading-posts of a modern kind.

47. Much detailed consideration would clearly need to be given, perhaps initially by a Positive Planning Committee or similar body, to the form, status and location of High Delegations. Regional variations would doubtless prove desirable. Problems that can only be indicated here would include: whether or (perhaps preferably) not a High Delegate should also be an Ambassador accredited to a particular government; how unobtrusively or openly given functions should be performed; which foreign regime if any in a particular area would be so reliably friendly as to warrant and permit the institution of a High Delegation on its territory, or indeed whether in some cases a British territory might not even prove preferable—in some cases the establishment of a High Delegation in a small colony, if politically acceptable, might do much incidentally to improve its economy. Many pros and cons would need to be weighed.

48. The main arguments against High Delegations would appear to be:

(i) They would call for a good deal of fresh thinking and new organization, probably with some overall increase in staff. Though one would hope that that might be accepted as a challenge rather than an obstacle.

(ii) High Delegations would cost a considerable amount of money. Lord Strang has pointed out (*The Foreign Office*, p. 65) that in the financial year 1956/7 the total estimated cost of running the Foreign Service, at a little under £20 million, was roughly the same as the cost of building one large aircraft-carrier and was only two-thirds of the estimated governmental expenditure that year on general dental services in England and Wales alone. Such examples can doubtless be modernized and multiplied. It is difficult to resist an impression that governmental expenditure on the Foreign Service has been pegged down out of all proportion to that on the material benefits of the Welfare States upon the one hand and, upon the other, on military requirements. The very great and necessary expenditure on nuclear armaments is doubtless largely, in the last resort, in support of British foreign policy. But it would seem distinctly lopsided then to withhold the far smaller sum directly needed to equip that policy (including such ancillaries as technical cooperation and the British Council) for efficient functioning, more particularly in trying to prevent war with its terrible cost in men and money. Since we cannot compete with American expenditure on nuclear weapons and rockets perhaps we could at least, at much smaller cost but most fruitfully, attempt rather more on the diplomatic side. The Cold War is all one war, demanding both military and diplomatic effort, while the liquidation of the old British Empire and run-down of the Colonial Service has mainly left it, as never before, to the Foreign Service to uphold the place of Britain in the world.

(iii) Some of our ambassadors might object to High Delegations as diminishing their importance. But the direct relations between the embassies and the Foreign Office would naturally be maintained (cf. paragraph 46), while the additional resource of a Delegation in the area would on the contrary be strongly liable to facilitate the work and correspondence of our ambassadors. They would, one might hope, get quicker and more informed decisions in many cases, and be spared such wearisome toing-and-froing between departments in Whitehall by co-ordination within High Delegations. Those bodies might be able to supply backing to strengthen the hands of ambassadors, especially in smaller posts, in dealing with governments. Periodic meetings of ambassadors at the High Delegation might put them more fully in the broader picture, actually bring them closer to Whitehall and enable them to operate more vigorously as a single team upon their continent.

(iv) Our communist enemies would denounce High Delegations as fine specimens of neoimperialism and neocolonialism. But since we have already lost one battle by allowing those to become dirty words, perhaps we need not worry too much about such additional attacks provided that the High Delegations were carefully organized and presented to emphasize their diplomatic character as visible evidence, indeed, that we are turning over a new leaf from imperialism to interdependence, while fully intending to play a leading and beneficent role in evolving interdependence also. A more serious concern, perhaps, might be suspicions and possible dislike in the United States. The High Delegations would naturally need to cooperate with the Americans. It would be for decision how early the Americans should be told of any plans for High Delegations. Interdependence would certainly remain the theme but it might seem important that such a new initiative should get off with a good head-start as a truly British one.

49. The main arguments in favour of High Delegations would appear to be:

(i) They should permit some compensating economies in the staffing of smaller posts abroad and even, be it hoped, in Whitehall: also economies, for instance, in correspondence since one might expect that a fair proportion of that from embassies, as of a local consular or commercial nature, might be telegraphed or despatched to High Delegations, perhaps with copies as necessary to the Foreign Office by slower, cheaper means. This should be possible since:

(ii) The High Delegate would direct an integrated secretariat primarily drawn from the Foreign Service but with interdepartmental (e.g. commercial and colonial) staffing as necessary to facilitate the decision of as many regional issues as possible on the spot, with direct benefit to ambassadors (cf. paragraph 48. iii). The High Delegate would be pro-consular in the true sense as a plenipotentiary with large powers of decision. This would be most desirable in order to relieve the Foreign Office so that:

(iii) A High Delegation would represent a true delegation of authority from the Foreign Office and Whitehall, where the formidable proliferation of interdepartmental consultation might mercifully be reduced; since a good range of lesser issues might now be settled more quickly, and perhaps with less interdepartmental friction, within the smaller and more integrated High Delegation. Or at least it could present Whitehall with advice or proposals already co-ordinated between representatives of several departments. The Foreign Office should be less heavily oppressed by the conglomeration of local problems, economic, technical and cultural—all relevant indeed to foreign policy but to a considerable extent peripheral, in the last resort, to the central issues of diplomacy and high policy which must remain the true and overriding concern of the Foreign Office. This relief, perhaps even including a consequential reduction in staff, might possibly be reinforced by certain administrative reforms which I ventured to suggest as conclusions from my study of *British Policy in the relinquishment of Abadan*. Thus lightened and streamlined, the Foreign Office might be able to devote more and deeper attention to the overall planning and coordination of priorities, opportunities and policies for Britain in the modern world.

(iv) Such a streamlined Foreign Office would stand to regain a good proportion of its proper primacy in the conduct of foreign affairs. For recommendations from the interdepartmental secretariats of High Delegations would normally be made through or by the High Delegates, usually drawn from the Foreign Service. Though sometimes such appointments might go to political ministers or others.

(v) It would further seem desirable that each High Delegation should coordinate British policies in its area not only for all foreign countries but also for Commonwealth and British territories. If this could be established functionally, then the question of any formal merger between the Foreign and Colonial Services might become almost secondary for foreign policy. And our remaining colonies, sometimes inevitably left rather as bits and pieces, might benefit materially and even acquire new significance from being viewed, for some purposes at least, as an integral part of a continental framework for unified policies.

(vi) The posts of High Delegate would be splendid positions of responsibility and opportunity, encouraging to the Foreign Service as a whole. The institution of High Delegations might, one would hope, do something to stir imaginations at home and stimulate recruitment of young men and women keen to carry on the British purpose overseas, but refined now from imperial domination and territorial rule so as to broaden our remaining scope, our benevolent expertise, to include all nations.

(vii) High Delegations should speed our vital export-drive by cutting out wasteful dispersion and duplication of effort in our embassies, as reflected in correspondence and perhaps, for instance, in arrangements for translations (compare Mr Vaughan's pertinent complaint about translations for Latin America of Mr Heath's last speech at Brussels). The local frustrations here of our ambassadors might be appreciably reduced since the planning of economic operations with official backing on a continental scale should be considerably more attractive to really big business. Special teams and enquiries would as necessary radiate out from the High

Delegations. Such delegations might be an exemplification in our foreign policy of the Secretary of State's recent observations: 'I do not think it can be questioned that in modern life there is a premium on bigness—that is true of industry.' And, in the same speech, 'the basis of power and influence is wealth'.

(viii) The economic drive from each High Delegation could be backed by a cultural one, with a really good show at each centre (cf. paragraph 46). While one would certainly wish to maintain the flow of African students, for instance, to Great Britain, in a number of more elementary cases it might be more economical and practical to encourage attendance, at any rate as a first step, at English institutions associated with High Delegations in something much closer to the students' own climate and environment.

(ix) Where appropriate High Delegates might also fulfil important functions of liaison with such military organizations as CENTO or SEATO, if not NATO itself. Even in other cases High Delegations might fit in well with British military planning for foreign-based task-forces capable of quick deployment in support of political objectives. Opportunities for intelligence might also be increased.

(x) Great Britain has been a good deal concerned lately with the inevitably rather depressing business of packing up an empire. The institution of High Delegations might represent a small swing of the pendulum in the opposite, positive direction. It might even prove practicable to associate interested countries of the Commonwealth, to their material advantage, in some at any rate of the less highly political activities of High Delegations. To this extent they might become outposts of the Commonwealth in a new, fruitful sense, bringing its nations closer once more not by British rule and superiority but, on the contrary, by partnership and understanding in doing an important job of work together. It might even be worth considering whether at some stage such a development might be extended in certain measure to our partners in EFTA and ultimately, if we manage to join it, to a liberalized, outward-looking European Economic Community. If our High Delegations proved successful we might really have something to offer in terms of organization to people looking outwards. And other nations might realize, more than they have lately always done, that it is still good to be friends with Great Britain, less good to get across her.

50. The pros would appear to outweigh cons. By instituting High Delegations Her Majesty's Government would be taking a bold initiative, not least perhaps in the Cold War instead of the initiative coming so often from the other side. While the Americans and the Russians compete in potentials of nuclear rocketry and in the sterile reaches of outer space, at least Britain could perhaps be strengthening herself and her allies on the ground, for instance by helping to clinch the remarkable failure, relatively, of Russia to penetrate Africa or even, perhaps, fully to consolidate Eastern Europe under her domination.

VI. *Towards a revived diplomacy for Britain*

51. A triple consolidation and revision of the conduct of British diplomacy at each level might thus comprise:

(i) increased attention to public relations at home for mobilising support for British foreign policy, matched by sharper thinking and, sometimes, plainer speaking in its execution, in general accordance with the Permanent Under-Secretary's monthly letter of March 1, 1963 (cf. section II);

(ii) in Whitehall, or perhaps the Foreign Office alone, a Positive Planning Committee or similar existing body to review possibilities for imparting extra thrust.

This might be facilitated if it proved possible to lighten the burden of the Foreign Office and streamline its operation to some extent in order, especially, to strengthen control and execution of its essential responsibility for high policy (cf. paragraphs 33-4, 47, 49 iii-iv);

(iii) a corresponding strengthening and modernization of our representation abroad, more particularly, perhaps, by the institution of High Delegations.

52. Even were such a programme, or something like it, accepted as broadly desirable, it would certainly be far from easy to achieve. But if a start were made in that direction, and especially in the positive spirit which must inspire such effort, then the Foreign Service could truly feel that it was taking a lead in vindicating the position of a modern Britain in a modern world; and in supplying her sufficient answer to the poetic enquiry which still echoes from across the Atlantic:

'Have the elder races halted? Do they droop and end their lesson?'[1]

One lesson, still, might be that even the New World has no monopoly of new frontiers. Because the British blend of the possible and the perfectible has traditionally translated a fruitful continuity into ever new and imaginative enterprise not even for Britain alone but for all within the wider commonwealth of nations.

May 24, 1963   ROHAN BUTLER

---

[1] Lines taken from Walt Whitman's poem Pioneers! O Pioneers!.

Don't mention Suez:
the Butler report on the Abadan crisis, 1950-51
Gill Bennett

There are a number of singular aspects to the report, *British Policy in the Relinquishment of Abadan in 1951,* submitted to Foreign Office (FO) ministers and senior officials in March 1962 by Rohan Butler of the Foreign Office Historical Section,[1] and published for the first time in this volume of *Documents from the British Archives.* Firstly, the report documents the loss in 1951 of Britain's greatest single overseas investment, when the British government was forced to accept the nationalisation of the Iranian oil industry and to withdraw British staff entirely from the Anglo-Iranian Oil Company's key refinery at Abadan.[2] The impact of the relinquishment of Abadan was even greater in political than in commercial terms, as it was considered a humiliating blow to British prestige and influence in the Middle East, a major failure of both policy and process.

The Abadan report was also singular in that it was the lone response to a suggestion made in September 1957 by the Cabinet Secretary, Sir Norman Brook, that Whitehall departments should commission internal histories of 'particularly significant episodes of policy or administration' that would 'enable the administrator to see current problems in perspective'. It was, Brook observed, characteristic of the British administrative system to have 'many forecasts but few retrospects'.[3] Post-mortems of the kind he now proposed—what today would be called 'lessons learned' exercises—would be salutary for an analysis of how well initial judgements and forecasts had stood the test of time. But five years later, when the Butler report was finished, the Cabinet Office appeared to have forgotten about the whole exercise. Future royal biographer Philip Ziegler, then a Second Secretary in the FO, commented that while Butler's report should certainly be sent to Sir Norman Brook, he was 'sure it will come as a surprise to him'. Indeed it did: no other government department had produced anything at all.

The steering committee chaired by Permanent Under-Secretary of State Sir Frederick Hoyer Millar that had commissioned the report in 1959 chose the Abadan crisis as a case study since, they said, it represented 'a complex concentration and critical balance of factors, political economic, juridical and military'.[4] The resulting

---

[1] Dr Rohan D'Olier Butler (1917-1996), Fellow of All Souls College Oxford, joined Professor E.L. Woodward at the FO in 1945 as an editor, on a part-time basis, of the official documentary history of British foreign policy *Documents on British Foreign Policy 1919-1939 (DBFP).* Woodward retired in 1958. Butler was appointed Historical Adviser to the Secretary of State in 1963.

[2] The Anglo-Iranian Oil Company (AIOC) (formerly Anglo-Persian Oil Company and later British Petroleum (BP)) was formed in 1909, originally an offshoot of Burmah Oil. Under an agreement in 1914 the British government took a controlling share of the voting interest, with the Treasury appointing two directors to the board of directors. In 1935, the Shah, Reza Khan, requested that other countries use 'Iran', rather than 'Persia', but the names were used interchangeably at the period of the Abadan crisis (and after), including in the Butler report. Iran is used in this essay except in quotations.

[3] References to commentary on the Abadan Report, and its consideration in Whitehall, are taken unless otherwise noted from FO 370/2964, TNA.

[4] Further detail on the commissioning of the Butler report is given in its Preface. See also detail in the valuable forensic examination of the Butler report, and its use by the Foreign Office, in Peter J. Beck, *Using History,*

account, produced by Rohan Butler with the help of his colleague Margaret Lambert,[5] is a singular document that had a considerable impact on the FO. For one thing, it is monumental in scale: nearly a quarter of a million words in length. The Table of Contents alone is five thousand words long and provides a detailed synopsis of the whole. Butler's principal source was, in his words, 'thousands upon thousands' of FO and Cabinet records, although he complained formally in the report about being denied access to certain (presumably intelligence-related) material.[6] He did not use other departments' records, nor had access to the AIOC's archive. But as Butler himself argued, eschewing the use of interviews, widening his research scope would have made his task even more time-consuming and the result more unwieldy. The main report comprises sixteen chapters of which the last contains sixty-eight 'Political Conclusions', followed by the historian's recommendations for the improvement of FO working methods and of the future conduct of British foreign policy.

Beginning with an account of British oil enterprise in Iran from 1901, Butler sets out the background to the British government's acquisition of a controlling interest in the AIOC in 1914, as well as the growth of Russian influence and the ambitions of American business in oil production in the region. He describes the decline of British economic, political and military power after the Second World War and the effect of this decline on British influence in the Middle East, including the implications for policy of Indian independence in 1947. The report then recounts in sometimes painful detail the struggles of the Labour government, Whitehall officials and British diplomats to cope with the unfolding crisis during 1950-51, culminating in the enforced abandonment of Abadan and thereby British oil interests in Iran. The tail end of the crisis coincided with the access to power of Winston Churchill's Conservative government in October 1951, when Anthony Eden, the new foreign secretary, was left to salvage what he could from the wreckage. A short section on the aftermath of Abadan describes the road to a final settlement of the Iranian oil question in 1954.

Although the senior FO officials to whom the Butler report was submitted in the spring of 1962 appeared initially somewhat overfaced by its length and scope, there was general agreement that it was 'a most valuable document not only in substance but for the lessons it draws'. After a certain amount of discussion about the number of copies that should be printed (the Finance Officer was consulted, but it turned out that HMSO would pay), 100 were eventually produced and sent to a number of senior officials in the FO and selected Whitehall departments, as well as to selected ambassadors. Ministers might shrink from tackling such a magnum opus (Lord Home's Private Secretary insisted there was no question of the Foreign Secretary's

---

Making British Policy: The Treasury and the Foreign Office, 1950-76 (London: Palgrave Macmillan, 2006), Part III.

[5] Margaret Esterel Lambert, MA, later Pelly (1930-97) joined the Historical Section in 1953; later Editor of *DBFP*, Series Ia and *DBPO*, Series I, and Head of Historical Section from 1988-90. For further details of both Butler and Lambert see FCDO Historians, History Note No. 22, *History at the Heart of Diplomacy: Historians in the Foreign Office, 1918-2018*; FCO, 2018: www.issuu.com/fcohistorians.

[6] See Preface. As an official historian, Butler was scrupulous in expressing regret that he had not been permitted to see 'all relevant papers'. He did not mention intelligence, but it is likely that it was the files of the FO Permanent Under-Secretary's Department (PUSD), responsible for liaison with the UK's intelligence agencies, to which he was denied access. If there were others, for example, certain Private Office papers, the record does not specify this.

private office tackling even the Conclusions); but Home, prompted by Permanent Under-Secretary (PUS) Sir Harold Caccia, was interested enough to ask Lord Strang, who had been PUS at the time of Abadan, to read it over Christmas and prepare a response. (As Lord Dunglass, Home had been vocal on the shortcomings of British policy during the Abadan crisis, as the Butler report makes clear, so his interest is perhaps unsurprising.)

The resulting round of comment and synthesis, provoking radical suggestions for a 'new perspective' on British diplomacy, is a singular testament to the potential influence, on both policy and administration, of an historical case study. Strang's commentary was circulated in February 1963 to HM Representatives overseas, provoking such an avalanche of diplomatic responses that Butler was commissioned to collate them into a single document together with a critical analysis. His memorandum of 24 May 1963, 'A New Perspective for British Diplomacy,' was instrumental in the formation later that year of the new Foreign Office Planning Staff (today called the Strategy Unit).[7] In these respects the Abadan report did, perhaps, fulfil Brook's desire that officials should draw on the past to see current problems in perspective.

To the contemporary reader, however, one of the most singular aspects of the Abadan report and associated papers is the virtual absence of any mention of what was surely the elephant in the room: Suez. Brook's original request, in September 1957, cited as justification for writing departmental studies the fact that the series of Official Histories commissioned at the end of the Second World War was coming to an end. He did not mention the crisis, precipitated by Egyptian leader Gamal Abdel Nasser's nationalisation of the Suez Canal in July 1956, that had convulsed the British government and all of Whitehall less than a year earlier, ending with the humiliating withdrawal of Anglo-French forces from Egypt under American pressure and the resignation of prime minister Anthony Eden.[8] Nor was Suez on the Steering Committee's shortlist of topics. Yet the two episodes contain many of the same elements: nationalisation of commercial interests by a foreign power; a threat to oil supplies and a challenge to British influence in the Middle East; problems caused by an American administration that intervened constantly in pursuit of its own political and economic aims; a fear of the spread of communism, or even of Soviet intervention, in the region.

It is easy to understand why Butler was not asked to tackle Suez—it was still too much of a hot topic, as he himself acknowledged in 1963.[9] The crisis of 1956 was to touch a raw nerve for both politicians and officials for many years; indeed, some sensitivities remain today, partly because of the persistent tendency on the part of politicians to use Suez as a kind of shorthand for national humiliation.[10] Certainly, while the Abadan report was being prepared, only a few years after the searing events of 1956, those sensitivities were acute. Possibly, also, the fact that Harold

---

[7] Both the Strang commentary and Butler's resulting memorandum are reproduced. They are discussed in Beck, pp. 211-24.

[8] There are many published accounts of the crisis of 1956, of which that by Keith Kyle, *Suez* (London: Weidenfeld and Nicolson, 1991) remains one of the best. The FCDO Historians are currently preparing a volume in the official documentary history of British foreign policy, *Documents on British Policy Overseas (DBPO)*, on *The Geopolitics of Suez: British Foreign Policy in 1956*.

[9] Minute by Butler, 15 February 1963, FO 370/2694, TNA.

[10] See on this point Gill Bennett, *Six Moments of Crisis: Inside British Foreign Policy* (Oxford University Press, 2013), Chapter 2.

Macmillan, prime minister in 1962-3, had been a key figure in the Suez crisis and rose to the premiership as a result of it, made any more explicit linkage undesirable. Even in 1965, when foreign secretary Michael Stewart suggested that Butler might be asked to do a study of Suez as he had of Abadan, he was dissuaded by PUS Sir Paul Gore-Booth from opening what officials thought would be Pandora's Box. The lesson from Suez was, in Gore-Booth's mind, a clear one: it was perfectly proper for ministers to consult officials and reject their advice, but if they deliberately did not consult them or keep them informed, 'the result would in due course be disastrous'.[11]

It is true that when Strang's commentary on the Butler report was circulated to British diplomats early in 1963, many of them referred to Suez in their replies. As Butler noted in his summary memorandum, 'the long shadow from Suez, and from the loss of empire which it betokens, still lies heavy across our thinking'.[12] Sir John Maud, in particular, bracketed the British experience at Suez in 1956 with the refusal to back European integration as 'the two main failures of British foreign policy since the Second World War'.[13] Maud was not the only diplomat to note the confluence of de Gaulle's rejection in January 1963 of the first British application to join the EEC, and the circulation of a report detailing the decline of British influence in the Middle East. Yet the official synthesis of diplomatic comment on the Abadan report steered away from Suez (and Europe), and its principal outcome was to be the creation of a Foreign Office Planning Staff. The message was clear: don't mention Suez.

Nevertheless, Butler could not resist, in the Abadan report, a few gentle, if pointed warnings about the possible future implications of the Persian oil crisis of 1950-51 for the Suez Canal, including a section on 'repercussions in Egypt' in the chapter on the aftermath of Abadan that rang unmistakeably all the Suez alarm bells. He even went so far, in one of his Conclusions, to call the two crises 'contrasting yet largely complementary'. But Butler was careful to avoid emphasising the clear linear connection between Abadan and Suez, a line that ran straight through the 1953 coup, encouraged by Anglo-American covert action, in which the Iranian leader, Dr Musaddiq,[14] principal architect of the Abadan crisis, was deposed, clearing the way at last for a settlement of the Anglo-Iranian oil question.[15]

Even if he did not spell it out, Butler's very detailed—and at times extremely critical—narrative on the British relinquishment of Abadan shows that there were indeed instructive similarities between the crises in the Middle East faced by the British government in 1950-1 and in 1956. This essay seeks to join some of the dots that Butler could not, or at any rate did not, by considering some of those elements detailed in his report on the Abadan crisis, from a primarily British perspective, that were to be most relevant five years later. For the continuities are indeed striking:

[11] Minutes by Stewart and Gore-Booth, 5 and 13 July 1965 (FO 270/2807), quoted in Beck, p. 224.
[12] The individual comments by HMRR, synthesised by Butler, are preserved in file WP 30, FO 371/173334, TNA.
[13] See [para 20.iii of new Perspectives]. Sir John (later Lord) Redcliffe-Maud brought a wide Whitehall perspective to the issue, having served as Permanent Secretary to the Ministry of Fuel and Power from 1952-59 (and so during Suez) before serving as High Commissioner, later Ambassador to South Africa, 1959-63.
[14] Spelling of the Iranian leader's name varies in both the contemporary documentation and in subsequent narratives. For the sake of consistency, Butler's use of 'Musaddiq' is retained here.
[15] Butler's references to Musaddiq's fall are confined to political factors. A good account of the coup is given in Michael Smith, *The Real Special Relationship: The True Story of how the British and US Secret Services Work Together* (London: Simon & Schuster, 2022), Chapter 9.

politically, economically, internationally and even personally, since a number of the politicians concerned, and even more of the officials, were active during both crises.

The crisis in 1950-51 over the ownership—and profits—of oil production in Iran coincided with the final eighteen months of the Labour government headed by Clement Attlee since July 1945. The UK's economic situation was precarious, resources strained to the limit by global responsibilities as well as by the implementation of an ambitious domestic agenda. That agenda included the nationalisation of major British industries, which made some Labour ministers reluctant to criticise another government for doing the same thing, a vulnerability the Iranians exploited with their (not unfounded) complaints of profiteering by the AIOC. In February 1950, as both the Shah and the US State Department were urging concessions by the British to an increasingly nationalistic Iranian government, a general election reduced Labour's majority to 6. In the final stages of the crisis, leading to the relinquishment of the Abadan refinery in October 1951, the government was preparing for a general election in which it was voted out of office. The period covered by Butler's report coincided therefore with one of diminished authority for the Attlee government, as well as considerable financial insecurity that increased British dependence on the United States.

That dependence was one reason why Attlee, and his foreign secretary Ernest Bevin, considered close alignment with the United States an imperative, particularly on foreign policy issues. Yet while the Attlee government and the Truman administration shared the same overall views and aims, sometimes there were sharp conflicts of opinion. They did not always see eye to eye on the approach to be adopted, particularly when competing Anglo-American commercial interests were involved. This was certainly true during the Abadan crisis, when requests for political support from the US received a lukewarm response, and British ministers and diplomats felt on occasion that the Americans were working actively against them. Partly this perception arose from differing priorities; partly from the disparity in economic and military power, particularly after 1945, between Britain and the US, fostering in the latter an assumption of dominance; and partly from mutual suspicion. Britain suspected the US of seeking to supplant its global position economically, while the US suspected Britain of wishing to re-establish its empire. Neither suspicion was completely justified nor entirely unfounded, but the scope for mutual misunderstanding was considerable. The situation was not improved by a series of security scares, including the exposure in 1950 of atomic scientist Klaus Fuchs as a Soviet agent, and the disappearance in May 1951 of diplomats Guy Burgess and Donald Maclean, that undermined American trust in Britain as a partner.[16]

The Middle East, a region where Britain had long-established political and military ties as well as commercial interests, was a particularly fertile ground for such a clash of perceptions and priorities, as the Iranian oil crisis in 1950-51 demonstrated. For the US administration, preventing Iran from succumbing to communism was a key objective, and in 1950-51 the wily nationalist Dr Musaddiq, despite his links with the Tudeh party, seemed to Washington more likely than other candidate to stand out against Soviet influence. This was more important than securing an Iranian premier open to an oil agreement with the British. The British government, though also concerned about the spread of communism, was more

---

[16] These security concerns were not, of course, covered in Butler's report.

worried about the damage to its global influence and investment position if the Iranians were seen to 'get away with' nationalising the oil industry and expelling the AIOC. One assumption the Americans and British did share was that they were quite entitled to try and remove and replace Arab leaders, and even governments, of which they disapproved. It was unfortunate for the British that during Abadan, the US government was not ready to get rid of Musaddiq—that was to come in 1953—while the British were not strong enough to impose their preferences.

Of course, another US priority was to protect and promote the interests of American oil companies operating in the region, which meant taking a keen interest in any arrangements the British might make in Iran (with an eye to stepping into the breach if negotiations failed). The deal done between the Saudi government and Aramco in 1950 to split profits 50-50 was one of the factors that strengthened Iranian determination to ramp up the pressure on the British to get an equally good, or better deal for themselves. In fact, the US government and American oil interests did offer what proved to be good early advice, when the Iranians were first flexing their muscles, on how best to respond in order to avoid a full crisis. But the AIOC would not take it, and the British government failed to understand the need to take it, in time to rescue its position.

It would be wrong to exaggerate Anglo-American differences, although they certainly contributed to the way the Abadan episode unfolded. The relationship remained strong, and close. But it is also important to remember that the future control of British oil interests in Iran was only one of a wide range of difficult problems and challenges faced concurrently by the British government. Some of these, such as the outbreak in June 1950 of a war on the Korean peninsula that many believed could presage another global conflict, were of far greater immediate significance and required close coordination with the US and other Western powers. Other pressing problems included tensions with the USSR in Berlin and over Eastern Europe, West German rearmament, policy towards the new People's Republic of China, delicate Anglo-American negotiations on nuclear cooperation, and initiatives towards European integration. All these required urgent consideration and sometimes rapid decisions by the Attlee government. All required close policy coordination with the Americans, if possible. In this context, the future of the Iranian oil industry, though important, was only one portion on the ministerial plate.

It did not help matters that in 1950-51 the British governmental machine was creaking at the seams, as Butler makes clear in his report. Many ministers were exhausted by their efforts since 1945 in service of a government that, under constant threat of bankruptcy, had tackled both a major domestic legislative programme and concurrent set of unprecedented foreign policy challenges in the early years of what we now call the cold war. Chancellor of the Exchequer Sir Stafford Cripps was forced to resign from ill-health in October 1950; and crucially, Ernest Bevin, driving force of British foreign policy since 1945, worn down by his titanic efforts to construct a system of Western security (including playing a major role in the formation of NATO), spent most of 1950 overseas or in hospital, was forced by illness to leave office in March 1951 and died the following month.

Bevin had resisted successfully in 1946-7 Attlee's proposals for disengagement from the Middle East, a region where Britain struggled to maintain its influence over what the prime minister described as 'this congeries of weak, backward and reactionary States' in the face of a USSR 'organised under an iron discipline'. The foreign secretary argued that this constituted a reversal of his entire policy: a retreat from the region would mean an abdication of Britain's position as a world power and would 'lead the United States to write us off'.[17] He had also argued, in 1946, that the AIOC's methods and policies in Iran were not 'sufficiently progressive' in a country where living standards were low. During the Abadan crisis, however, while Bevin did at times make his views felt, stressing the need for close cooperation with the Americans and encouraging the AIOC to make concessions to the Iranians, he was not in a position to play an active part in determining policy.

Bevin's successor Herbert Morrison had a fractious relationship with a number of his ministerial colleagues and a distant one with Attlee, whose partnership with Bevin had been exceptionally close. Morrison took office in March 1951 with little experience of foreign affairs or feel for how diplomacy worked, just as the most acute phase of the Abadan crisis began, when Iranian premier General Razmara was assassinated and Anglo-American talks on oil were foundering. Nor did Morrison find it easy to deal with an American government determined to pursue its own policies in the Middle East and disinclined towards any open show of solidarity with the British. Like his predecessor, Morrison faced many difficulties simultaneously and was still struggling to come to terms with his task seven months later when the government fell.

Ministers are responsible for policy, but the condition of their official supporting apparatus is also important. In the Abadan crisis, barely five years after the end of the second world war, the FO was extremely short of good staff, as indeed was Whitehall overall. As the bloated wartime bureaucratic machine contracted, the supply of younger, able officials was inadequate to cope with rapidly expanding administrative demand. Financial constraints inhibited recruitment. Older staff who had not retired tended to be overworked and weary, and consequently not best placed to embark on the 'imaginative diplomacy' whose lack Butler so frequently laments in his report. On an issue such as oil in Iran, in which a number of government departments, including the Treasury and Ministry of Fuel and Power, had an interest—not to mention the AIOC itself—coordination was intermittent and handled at too low a level. Pressure of government business also affected the time taken to consider incoming communications, with a deleterious effect on coordination between the FO and overseas posts. During the Abadan crisis Butler notes many instances where suggestions from the embassy in Tehran, for example, were registered too late in London to be read in good time, let alone acted upon.

The British armed services faced similar challenges, with inadequate forces available to meet global obligations, including maintaining occupation forces in Germany and, under American pressure, sending a brigade to Korea.[18] Military difficulties were exacerbated by decolonisation and budget constraints, and the decrease in capacity after August 1947, when Indian armed forces could no longer be called upon, made it very difficult to contemplate the use of force in the Middle East, however reluctant the Chiefs of Staff might be to admit this. Attlee, having taken advice, set his face against military action to resist the Iranian nationalisation

[17] Butler report, p. 52. See also *DBPO*, Series I, Vol. XI, pp. 90-102, for documentation of the policy debate between Attlee and Bevin on this issue.
[18] On this decision, reversing a previous one by the Defence Committee, see Bennett, *Six Moments of Crisis*, Chapter 1.

of British oil interests, or indeed to protect property and personnel. He was prepared to resist the urgings of military or official advisers to take a tough line, particularly with the Americans, however humiliating the outcome. The capacity to accept uncomfortable realities was always one of Attlee's strengths, and while others (including Morrison) might protest that there 'must be *something* we can do', the prime minister understood that in this case, there was not.

Other foreign policy commitments, not least the Korean war, had to take precedence, and the UK's economic position remained precarious. The US administration had made it crystal clear—as they would in 1956, over Suez—that the use of force by Britain in Iran would not receive its support, and that many members of the United Nations would oppose it. That did not mean Attlee or his colleagues did not resent what they saw as outrageous Iranian behaviour (including the lynching of three British subjects in April 1951 during riots in which many were injured), or consistent American interference that included sending Averell Harriman on a mission to Tehran in the summer of 1951 against the express wishes of the British government. But if the answer to the question 'do we have the capacity to enforce our will in Iran, without the help of Indian forces, and without support either in Washington or in the UN?' was 'no', Attlee did not shirk it—in that it is true, he differed from Eden in 1956.

In his report on Abadan, Butler did not shy away from the political and economic difficulties encountered by the Labour government, nor indeed from criticising the policies adopted, though he clearly felt constrained, as a historian, in commenting on the way officials and politicians behaved, especially when their performance was less than optimal. Strang, in his commentary, had far less compunction in apportioning responsibility to individuals and was extremely critical of his former diplomatic colleagues. In particular, he made clear his views on Morrison's shortcomings as foreign secretary, and was open about his own relief, as PUS, when the experienced Eden took office in October 1951. Only then, commented Strang, did a minister 'take over our foreign policy with a strong hand'. He also praised the 'beneficent effect upon the conduct of public business' resulting from the 'vitally different' relationship between Eden and Churchill from that between Morrison and Attlee. Strang had to admit, however, that Eden's task was made easier by the fact that 'we now had little left to lose in Persia'.

In fact, the change of government in October 1951 brought little alteration in government policy. During the Abadan crisis many senior Conservative politicians, including Eden, Macmillan and Dunglass—all of whom would play a prominent role in 1956—had been vocal in their criticisms of the Labour government's handling of the issue, denouncing its inability to stand up for British interests in Iran and lack of decisive action, and condemning what they saw as a blow to British prestige in the Middle East. Many opposition MPs (and some on the government benches) called for the use of military force, or at least the threat of it, initially to deter the Iranians from pressing ahead with oil nationalisation, or, later, to protect British lives and property. By the time that Eden took office, it may have been too late to save Abadan, but there was still an agreement to be hammered out on oil. In principle, the Churchill government had a chance to take a firm lead, learning from Labour's mistakes. In reality, however, they proceeded on the same assumptions, and pursued the same policies, as their predecessors.

That was certainly the opinion, expressed with some bitterness, of US Secretary of State Dean Acheson. After discussions in Paris in early November 1951 with Eden, who presented him with a list of Britain's 'minimum requirements' for compensation and future international control of the Iranian oil industry, Acheson told his colleagues that the only difference between the new Conservative and the previous Labour government was the addition of what he called 'a certain truculent braggadocio'. Ministers were, he wrote, 'depressingly out of touch with the world of 1951, and they are being advised by the same officials who have allowed the gov[ernmen]t to follow the AIOC meekly into disaster. Of course, these officials continue the same arguments and the same analyses. The ministers admit that they know nothing about the facts and must rely on the officials. The circle is complete.'[19] Acheson's judgment was perhaps a little harsh, but his point about the continuity of both policy and personnel is relevant. There was a new government and new ministers, but the majority of Whitehall officials involved in Abadan remained in post, and there were few signs that any lessons had been learned from the crisis or new policies worked out.

Five years later, a Conservative government was still in power, and many of the same men were still in prominent positions, including Eden as prime minister, Macmillan as chancellor of the exchequer (after serving as foreign secretary) and Home at the Commonwealth Relations Office. As for the official machine, while a new postwar generation was rising through the ranks, senior posts still tended to be held by men with wartime (sometimes pre-war) experience, who were serving at the time of Abadan even if not involved directly in dealing with it, and many of whom were approaching retirement. Many of the FO officials serving during the Abadan crisis had also gone on to occupy senior positions in the region. To name only a few: Sir Michael Wright, assistant under-secretary supervising Eastern Department in 1950, was ambassador to Iraq in 1956; Sir Bernard Burrows, who had served as head of Eastern Department before dealing with the Abadan issue from Washington in 1950-51, ambassador in Bahrein; George Middleton, Counsellor and later Chargé d'Affaires in Tehran in 1951, ambassador to the Lebanon; even the hapless Geoffrey Furlonge, head of Eastern Department during Abadan and much castigated by Strang for his performance, was still dealing with Arab nationalism in 1956 in his post as ambassador at Addis Ababa.

Given these continuities, it is perhaps not surprising that when faced with a new crisis caused by the nationalisation of a foreign-controlled asset, in this case the Anglo-French controlled Suez Canal Company in Egypt, both ministers and officials appear to have operated on the same assumptions as in 1950-51: that an Arab country's decision to nationalise a foreign-controlled asset was unacceptable and must be reversed, by force if necessary; that it was legitimate to engineer the replacement of an Arab leader or government by one more amenable to British demands; and that US support could be relied on to support British policies. There is little sign, in documentation of the Suez crisis, that the weakness of these assumptions, as revealed by the Abadan crisis, was factored into decision-making by either ministers or officials. In Chapter XV of his report, Butler gives a summary account of events between the relinquishment of Abadan and the settlement of the

---

[19] Memorandum by Dean Acheson, 10 November 1951, *FRUS 1952-54, Iran 1951-54*, Vol. X, Nos. 127 and 129.

oil dispute in August 1954, including the rupture and resumption of Anglo-Iranian relations and the part played by the US in the forming of an oil consortium. He also notes that the eviction of the British from Abadan 'stimulated strong political currents in Egypt' that carried Colonel Nasser to power, leading to the signature in July 1954 of the Canal Base agreement providing for the complete withdrawal of British forces by June 1956 (an agreement that provoked a backbench revolt in the House of Commons). These events demonstrate clearly the continuous line that runs between Abadan and Suez. They also raise the question of whether, or to what extent the events of 1950-51 detailed in Butler's report provided any guidance for ministers and officials five years later.

In a memorandum prepared at Eden's request in 1957, his former private secretary Guy Millard, commented that during the Suez crisis, many people looked back to Abadan.[20] If they did, they rarely committed it to paper. One who did was Sir Roger Stevens, appointed ambassador in Tehran in 1954 (he had been in Stockholm in 1951). He wrote a thoughtful despatch on 7 August 1956 on the Iranian attitude to the nationalisation of the Suez Canal. One the one hand, he wrote, Nasser's actions reminded the Iranians of their own actions in 1951 so that their instinct was 'to cheer and beat the nationalist drum'; on the other, sour grapes meant that they rather wanted him to fail, since their attempts to run their own oil industry had failed and they had been forced to turn to an international consortium. In addition, Iran, like other countries, relied on the movement of oil through the Canal.[21]

In late August 1956, a series of minutes by FO officials reviewed the events of 1951 in respect of the legal position concerning a potential resort to force, and of referring the dispute to the United Nations. It was noted that although the International Court at first issued a ruling in favour of HMG in 1951, the Iranians paid no attention to it whatsoever. Sir I. Kirkpatrick noted gloomily on 29 August 1956 that it seemed to him 'that the rules of the game including the Charter are so framed as to ensure that everyone can commit every crime with impunity except the crimes of launching war or going to war to defend oneself'.[22] In general, however, a review of Suez documentation makes it impossible to avoid the conclusion that those conducting British policy in 1956, only five years after the Abadan disaster, not only failed to draw any lessons from the previous episode, but indeed proceeded as if they had forgotten it ever happened.

That seems unlikely, although in view of the general verdict that Suez was a 'disaster' it might seem uncontentious. But if we look through the lens of the detailed account given by Butler in his report on the Abadan crisis of 1950-51, a review of certain aspects of Suez might produce a rather more nuanced conclusion. At first glance, the political situation in 1956 might appear quite different. A Conservative government had been in power for five years, and was to remain in office for eight more. Yet in some respects it was an administration running out of steam; Suez was to constitute a turning point. By the time Eden became prime minister in April 1955, having waited far longer than he (or others) anticipated to take over from Churchill,

---

[20] Millard's memorandum, which focusses on international aspects of the crisis rather than operational matters, is in FO 800/278, TNA. See Beck, pp. 225-26.

[21] Tehran despatch 83, 7 August 1956, JE 14211/747, FO 371/119104, TNA.

[22] Minutes on JE 14214/85G, FO 371/119177, TNA.

exhaustion and poor health were taking their toll, and affected his response to the Egyptian crisis.[23] Suez proved to be Eden's downfall; for the ambitious Macmillan, who played a key role in the crisis, it was the road to power. Yet as Macmillan discovered when he was moved from the FO to the Treasury in December 1955, Britain faced many of the same economic difficulties it faced during the Attlee governments: insufficient resources to meet global obligations, dependence on the Americans, particularly in nuclear matters, slow growth and a pressing need for domestic investment, particularly in housing. Macmillan's successor at the FO, Selwyn Lloyd, was no match for a prime minister determined to dominate foreign policy, egged on by his chancellor. There was even a row over security, this time over the emergence in Moscow of Burgess and Maclean, and the activities of 'Buster' Crabb in Portsmouth harbour on an unauthorised mission to inspect visiting Soviet warships.

The Eden government in 1956 also faced a formidable array of foreign policy challenges, just as the Attlee government had in 1950-51. These included difficult negotiations with territories seeking self-government, including Malta, Cyprus and Singapore; the subversive effect of Arab nationalism, not just in the Middle East but across the globe; continuing concerns about divided Germany; and the spread of unrest in Soviet satellites, including East Germany and Poland, culminating in the savage suppression of the Hungarian uprising in November, just as the Suez crisis was at its height. It is true that to Eden and his colleagues, the nationalisation of the Suez Canal appeared a more potent economic threat than had the loss of the AIOC refinery in Iran. But they faced the same difficulties as the Attlee government in reaching agreement with the US government on priorities, and the best way of maintaining stability in the region. Again, resisting the spread of communism was more important to the Eisenhower administration than maintaining British and French 'imperial' interests in Egypt. Again, British requests for political support fell on stony ground.

This is not the place for a detailed comparison of Abadan and Suez, nor yet a study of British policy in the Middle East in the 1950s. Rather, the brief summary above is intended to underline two important conclusions that emerge from Rohan Butler's magisterial report on British policy in 1950-51. The first is that no matter how great the crisis, any government will always face a wide range of other challenges at the same time, and its response will always depend in part on the quality and ability of its ministers and their officials. Secondly, there is no doubt that a detailed study of a relevant historical episode, prepared from official documentation (even if access is not unlimited), can be an extremely useful source of precedent and information to policymakers at times of crisis. But ministers and senior officials not only have to be aware of these studies, they also have to be able to accept that, while history never repeats itself, there are always lessons to be learned. It is part of the job of official historians to help them to realise this.

---

[23] On this point see David Owen, *In Sickness and in Power: Illness in Heads of Government during the last 100 Years* (London: Methuen, 2011), Chapter 3.

Sir,

I observe that there is a good deal of loose talk in Britain just now about our eviction from the Middle East under United States pressure—a process which is supposed to have begun at Abadan. At the risk of recapitulating the obvious, it may be useful to examine these charges, in so far as they apply to Iran.

2. I am not sufficiently well versed in the background of the events of 1951 to know how much truth there may be in the accusation that the dispute between the Iranian Government and the Anglo-Iranian Oil Company was contrived by the United States. It is I know commonly believed that the nationalisation of the Iranian oil industry was stimulated and encouraged by Americans in the service of the Iranians who were not in any sense officials of the US Government (notably Mr Thornberg). What seems to me clear from a study of official and other documents relating to this period is:

(*a*) the nationalistic tendencies developing within Iran, confronted by the massive presence and rather unimaginative policy of AIOC, were quite enough of themselves to produce an explosion, without adventitious aid.

(*b*) there is no evidence that the US Government gave any official encouragement to the Iranians up to the time that Musaddiq came to power.

(*c*) US efforts to mediate during the second half of 1951, though frequently inept and not to our liking, had as their object not to get us out—that had already been largely accomplished—but to try to keep Iran, for all its manifestations of nationalism, within the Western orbit.

(*d*) the events of 1953, leading to the resumption of relations between the United Kingdom and Iran and eventually to the oil agreement were the fruit of long and patient US diplomatic and planning activity for which we have every reason to be deeply grateful.

If this analysis is in any way incorrect, I must plead ignorance—and ask for enlightenment.

3. My real object in this despatch is however not to analyse the causes of what is popularly known as 'Abadan', but to examine its consequences in terms of Anglo-American-Iranian relations. In the one Middle Eastern country from which, before November 1956, we *had* been evicted, what has happened since we came back?

4. I can testify from personal knowledge that, first and foremost, the path of our return was greatly smoothed by the Americans here, and above all by Mr Loy Henderson. We received unstinted help and impartial advice from American civilians at all levels. In the oil negotiations, except for occasional interventions by Mr Herbert Hoover which were often as embarrassing to his own team as to the rest of us, we worked harmoniously and confidently together. The Iranians though always polite, were at first reserved and suspicious. The Americans helped markedly to break this down. They assisted our efforts to make it known that we intended to establish our relations with Iran on a new basis, appropriate to relations between independent powers with common interests; that we did not seek a dominant position in the political or economic life of the country; that we had no 'imperialistic' designs; that we were determined not to intervene in Iranian domestic affairs or pull strings behind the scenes; that we wanted to deal directly and frankly with the officially-

constituted Iranian authorities, and were resolved to dispense with, and if need be to discredit, the host of intermediaries and intriguers who swarmed about Tehran and gave the impression, rightly or wrongly, that they were 'friends of the British'. On this new basis, and with consistent help from the Americans (who pursue the same policy) we have I think succeeded in establishing a fair degree of confidence, at least among the governing classes, in our honest intentions and good faith. Some, though not I fear all, of this will survive the events of the last month.

5. It would not I believe be vainglorious to claim that in psychological and political terms we are on firmer ground here now than in the past. Old suspicions, inevitably, remain. We are still regarded in many quarters as the power behind the throne. All this will take time, patience and tact to dissipate. But the best proof of progress is perhaps our satisfactory association with Iran in the Bagdad Pact. It is hard to imagine that this could have come about if the Iranian nationalist virus had not (for the moment at least) worked itself out of the system—in other words if there had been no 'Abadan', with (perhaps equally important) the long period of isolation and economic and administrative run-down which followed it.

6. In practical terms, we have not done too badly, either. Our investment in Iranian oil may be reduced from 100% to something under 50%, but it is on a healthier foundation, and the prospects of increased production—and revenue—with full Iranian cooperation are much more favourable than they were before the break. The 'consideration' (from the other oil companies) and 'compensation' (from the Iranians) obtained by the Anglo-Iranian Oil (now British Petroleum) Company cannot be regarded as unsatisfactory from a financial point of view. As a result of being seen in juxtaposition with American, Dutch and others, the British element in the management of the oil industry, instead of being a butt for nationalistic attack, are regarded by their Iranian associates, at worst as the devil they know, and at best as old and experienced friends. British companies, in common with others, have been given the opportunity of acquiring exclusively new exploitation rights on an agency basis, though admittedly so far on terms so stiff that they have not seen fit to conclude an agreement.

7. In the field of economic development, we have received our fair share of new contracts and consultancy agreements. The trials that have beset British firms in connexion with such contracts have been no greater than those experienced by firms of other nationalities. We certainly cannot complain that there has been any discrimination against us on account of the past; equally certainly, for reasons of price rather than of politics, we have done substantially better than the Americans. In trade with Iran we have largely recovered our pre-Abadan position, despite greatly increased German competition, and there is plenty of evidence of Iranian willingness to buy even more extensively from us, commercial conditions permitting. These results have been achieved without any abnormal activity on the part of Her Majesty's Government, save for the provision of a £10 million line of credit in early 1955. Meanwhile, the Americans have been making grants to the Iranian economy of some $50 million per year which has helped to maintain stability and purchasing power. Through their Point IV organisation, the largest of its kind in the world, they have helped to improve agricultural, industrial, administrative and other techniques, thereby making Iran a better trading partner primarily for themselves—Point IV purchases have been made increasingly and are now almost exclusively from the US—but also for the rest of the world. Somewhat similar work is being performed

by the United Nations Technical Assistance Board to which we contribute but from which we also benefit.

8. As regards military aid and training the attitude of the American armed forces is unquestionably more possessive than that of the civilians, and moreover the Americans have the military field almost entirely to themselves. But this is the result of the Irano-American Military Agreement of October 1947, and has nothing to do with 'Abadan'. Their programme was indeed suspended for political reasons during the last year of the Musaddiq régime to the general prejudice of Western defence interests. American supremacy in this field is due to two causes. Firstly they were in a better position to fill the vacuum than we, with our preoccupations and commitments in other parts of the Middle East. Secondly they were financially in a position to implement their plans to some extent—though not to the extent the Iranians—or we, for that matter—would like. It is difficult to imagine that, had the US Government not done something towards filling this vacuum, we should have had either the ability, or—given the oil dispute—the will, to do so. Having taken on the responsibility for providing military assistance to Iran, the Americans have no disposition to share it with us or others. This is particularly noticeable in the case of the Iranian navy, where we still have a foothold. But the Americans control the defence budget, and therefore have the whip hand; and there are signs that they would not be sorry to see us dislodged. This, I believe, reflects the 'forward' policy of the Pentagon in the Persian Gulf (on which I am reporting separately), rather than that of the State Department towards our position in Iran.

9. It is true that there are certain fields—Consular representation, education and civil aviation are examples which at once spring to mind—in which the British position before 1951 has not been fully restored. But the reason for this is to be sought, not in US rivalry or Iranian reluctance, but in our own policy, or financial exigencies.

10. It would be absurd not to recognise that the United States—despite her coyness in regard to the Bagdad Pact—is Iran's predominant Western partner. This was true in the late 40s, it was true before our intervention in Egypt, and it is likely to be even truer henceforth. But I do not think we have a grievance, or anything to be ashamed of. It is the result partly of America's policy of anticolonialism, partly of our own allegedly tainted past in this country; but primarily of American's superior resources. There is no real evidence that the US has used its influence consistently against us, or that it has taken undue advantage of its position. On the contrary, the Americans realise, not least as a result of our own experience, that it does not pay to occupy too dominant a position in this spasmodically xenophobic country, and they are therefore quite glad to have us around. This however is not to say that they would willingly or gracefully yield their priority to us in any sphere—as we have had occasion to discover from time to time in the course of commercial competition, the only field in which we have distinct advantages over them. The Iranians, for their part, like to maintain a reasonable balance between us.

11. I would not wish to suggest that Iran is a typical Middle Eastern country, or that our experiences here are likely to be paralleled elsewhere—least of all in Egypt. Musaddiq had no imperialist designs on his neighbours, no international asset to hold up to ransom; Iran is aloof on Palestine, but acutely aware of the Soviet danger. It may nevertheless be desirable to state certain conclusions, for what they are worth, drawn from events in the last six years here:

(i) 'Abadan', however painful, has enabled us to stage a comeback on a better foundation—better probably than if the 'eviction' had been less complete.

(ii) The Americans had little to do with our eviction; they welcomed and facilitated our return and rehabilitation.

(iii) Their predominant position in Iran is due primarily to their greater wealth and power in the world, not to local pressure or local rivalries.

(iv) We have recovered our position here because we have been enabled to make a fresh start, because there are now no serious Anglo-Iranian differences, because of the need to stand together in the face of the Soviet danger, and because the force of Iranian nationalism is for the moment spent.

(v) It is spent because it had to work itself out the hard way over a ten-year period, at the end of which the myth of nationalistic self-sufficiency was exploded, and economic disaster stared the country in the face.

12. I am copying this despatch to Her Majesty's Representatives at Amman, Ankara, Beirut, Bagdad, Karachi, Washington and to the Political Office with the Middle East Forces.

I have, etc,
ROGER STEVENS

British Documents from the Archives

Also available online: www.issuu.com/fcohistorians

Printed in Great Britain
by Amazon

12184076R00294